BOTTOM LINE YEAR BOOK 2010

BY THE EDITORS OF

Bottom Line
PERSONAL
www.BottomLineSecrets.com

Contents

PART TWO: YOUR MONEY

7 • MONEY MANAGER

8 • INSURANCE ANSWERS

9 • TAX TUNE-UP

13 • ESTATE PLANNING GUIDE

PART FOUR: YOUR LEISURE

14 • SAVVY TRAVEL

15 • HAVE SOME FUN

16 • CARS AND DRIVERS

PART FIVE: YOUR LIFE

17 • FAMILY AND HOME

18 • LIFE COACH

1

Health Watch

Epidemics Are on the Rise: How to Protect Yourself

More than one-quarter of all deaths around the world are caused by infectious diseases. In the US, more than 170,000 people die from these diseases each year—and the number is likely to get much higher. *In just the last few years...*

• **Reemerging diseases that were nearly eradicated in the US,** such as measles, malaria and tuberculosis, now are occurring in increasing numbers.

• **In the spring of 2009, the deadly swine flu broke out in Mexico and quickly spread** to the US and other countries.

• **Bird (avian) flu has killed more than half of those infected**—though none of these cases has occurred in the US to date and most cases have resulted from people having direct contact with infected birds or contaminated surfaces. Should the virus mutate to permit human-to-human transmission, the death rate could rise into the millions.

• **Methicillin-resistant Staphylococcus aureus (MRSA) now is the sixth-leading cause of death in the US.** It is a strain of bacteria that causes an infection—often called "staph"—that can be deadly even when patients are treated with state-of-the-art antibiotics.

Below, Georges Benjamin, MD, executive director of the American Public Health Association, answers questions about the risks for infectious diseases...

• **Are epidemics on the rise?** Yes. Every two or three years, there is a new epidemic somewhere in the world. The term epidemic means that a particular health-associated

Georges Benjamin, MD, a professional lecturer at George Washington University School of Public Health and executive director of the American Public Health Association (*www.apha.org*), both in Washington, DC. He is a former secretary of the Maryland Department of Health and Mental Hygiene and a leading expert in emergency preparedness.

problem—an infectious disease, obesity, even car accidents—is occurring more often than expected. The frequency of epidemics seems to be increasing.

One of the reasons for the increase is that global warming has extended the population and range of mosquitoes, leading to increases in malaria, dengue fever and other mosquito-borne diseases.

In addition, human and animal populations worldwide are living in closer proximity than in the past. More than half of all infectious diseases can infect species other than their original hosts. Many of the most dangerous pathogens, including the virus that causes AIDS, originated in animals and only later developed the ability to infect humans.

A century ago, a disease in a remote area might sicken or kill a few dozen people and then "burn out." Now more than two billion people fly on airplanes every year. A deadly pathogen, such as Ebola virus, could start to spread into more populated areas and infect thousands—or worse.

• **How dangerous is the next epidemic likely to be?** It depends on the organism. In the best-case scenario, something such as a cold virus could mutate and gain the ability to infect more people than it had in the past. But because this virus isn't lethal, it would be more of a nuisance than anything else.

The most serious epidemics involve organisms that are both *highly transmissible* and *lethal*. The Spanish flu of 1918–1919 had both of these traits. It was readily passed from person to person, and it was uncommonly virulent. Worldwide, it killed between 20 million and 40 million people within about two years and has been called the most devastating epidemic in recorded history.

A disease that can be transmitted via indirect contact—for example, from inhaling airborne organisms from sneezes—is more likely to emerge as an epidemic than a disease that can be transmitted only under specific circumstances, such as hepatitis C from infected blood.

• **If you had to guess, what epidemic is likely to be next?** There's no way to know. Any infectious organism could be involved.

Many bacterial infections (including tuberculosis) have reached epidemic proportions, but we often can control these illnesses with the use of antibiotics.

Viral infections are more worrisome. We have only a few antiviral drugs. Viruses replicate far more rapidly than bacteria, which means that they can develop drug resistance more quickly than bacteria. The same mechanism also allows them to mutate rapidly into more lethal forms.

• **Is it likely that an epidemic will be caused by bioterrorism?** It's a serious risk. People used to need specialized training and sophisticated equipment to produce or disseminate lethal agents. This is no longer the case. Knowledge in general is more widely available than it used to be, thanks to the Internet, and technology is more available and affordable.

It doesn't take much sophistication to launch a crude attack. In 1984, a religious cult in Oregon spiked area salad bars with a *Salmonella* culture. No one died, but more than 750 people were sickened. It was the largest bioterrorist attack in the US.

• **What emergency supplies should we have on hand?** We recommend stockpiling at least a three-day supply of nonperishable foods, including canned meats, fish, beans, fruits and vegetables. Check these expiration dates every six months. Also, have on hand one gallon of water per person per day. Be aware that your water supply also needs to be rotated because microbes may build up in it. Also, try to keep prescriptions filled and pain relievers/fever reducers on hand.

• **Should we stockpile antibiotics?** You don't want to stockpile an antibiotic, because you don't know which one you are going to need.

• **What will the authorities do?** State health departments and the Centers for Disease Control and Prevention have surveillance systems that look for unusual symptoms or disease clusters that could indicate an emerging epidemic. In the early years of the AIDS crisis, it was noted that there was an increase in requests for a drug used to treat a rare fungal infection. This, along with an increase in unusual diseases later known to be associated with AIDS, indicated that a new organism was spreading fast.

Once a new (or reemerging) infectious disease has been identified, the goal is to both treat it and limit its spread. In addition to educating the public, public health officials might resort to isolation (keeping sick patients away from the general population to avoid infecting others) or quarantine (isolating people who have been exposed to an organism but who may or may not actually have the disease). There also will be a push to develop vaccines and other medications to treat the disease, protect healthy people and limit the spread of the disease.

•**It almost sounds as if the government will have everything under control. What are your thoughts on that?** There is a need for people to be as self-reliant as they can. Local officials will help out as soon as they can, but the government can't do everything. The greater the number of people who are self-reliant, the more help that will be available for those who are unable to help themselves.

The Best Way to Protect Yourself from the Swine Flu and Other Viruses

William Schaffner, MD, professor and chair of the department of preventive medicine at Vanderbilt University School of Medicine in Nashville. An internationally recognized authority on vaccines, Dr. Schaffner has published more than 60 professional articles on the subject and is president-elect of the National Foundation for Infectious Diseases, *www.nfid.org.*

William Schaffner, MD, president-elect of the National Foundation for Infectious Diseases, answers some important questions on what you need to do to protect yourself from the swine flu…

•**What is the best way to avoid getting the swine flu?** *The measures are the same as against any virus…*

•Wash hands often. *Best soap-and-water technique:* Rub hands together for at least 20 seconds ("Happy Birthday" sung twice). Dry off hands with a paper towel or air dryer, not a shared towel. If possible, use a paper towel to turn off the faucet. *Best technique for sanitizer:* Apply a product such as Purell to the palm of one hand. Rub it all over your hands and fingers until dry.

•Avoid touching your eyes, nose or mouth.

•Avoid people who are coughing, sneezing or sniffling.

•Keep immunity high by eating healthfully, exercising regularly, getting enough sleep and minimizing stress.

•**Does getting a flu shot help?** The currently available flu vaccine does not protect against swine flu. As of press time, it was uncertain whether a swine flu vaccine would be available for the 2009–2010 flu season.

•**Can I get swine flu from such foods as bacon, ham or pork?** Swine flu viruses are *not* transmitted by eating or handling pork. The virus is now transmitted person-to-person, so being around pigs is not a viral hazard either.

•**What are all the symptoms?** Symptoms, which typically develop about two days after exposure, include a fever greater than 100°F, sore throat, cough, stuffy nose, chills, headaches/body aches and fatigue. Diarrhea and vomiting also have been reported.

•**What should I do if I have flulike symptoms?** Stay home to reduce the risk of spreading the virus. If the patient has an underlying illness, is a senior citizen or a young child, call the doctor. Do not go to the emergency room or the doctor's office (where you can spread the infection) unless your doctor advises you to. Your physician may prescribe a prescription drug—either *oseltamivir* (Tamiflu), which is sold as tablets, or *zanamivir* (Relenza), an inhaled drug—to shorten the severity and duration of the flu. But these medications need to be taken within 48 hours of experiencing symptoms to be effective.

•**How can I find out more?** The US Centers for Disease Control and Prevention (CDC) posts up-to-date information on the Web site *www.cdc.gov/swineflu.*

Self-Defense Against Deadly Listeriosis

Michael Doyle, PhD, the Regents Professor of Food Microbiology and director of the Center for Food Safety in the department of food science and technology at the University of Georgia in Griffin, Georgia.

The food-borne illness *listeriosis* can result from contamination that may occur at any point in the food-production and delivery cycle. *For protection...*

•**Separate raw meats from such foods as fruits,** salad greens or other ready-to-eat foods. Bacteria from a leaky package of raw meat can contaminate foods that are eaten raw.

•**Wash your hands after handling any raw animal product,** including meats or eggs. Use hot, soapy water to clean cutting boards and knives.

•**Use heat—and cold.** Heat foods, including ready-to-eat products like hot dogs, to 165°F to kill Listeria. Set your refrigerator to 40°F or colder to inhibit most harmful microbes.

•**Use caution when buying cheese.** Hard cheeses are generally safer—in part, because their low pH (acidity) inhibits Listeria.

•**Avoid cold cuts if you're in a high-risk group.** As few as 10 Listeria cells in a package of luncheon meat can multiply to millions within a few weeks on the shelf even when the meats are refrigerated. Meat spreads and smoked seafood also can become contaminated.

If you buy deli meats: Look for those that list diacetate and lactate on the label. These organic acids inhibit Listeria growth.

Caution: Listeriosis symptoms may not appear for 30 days. If you're over age 60 and/or have a weakened immune system due to cancer treatment, chronic illness, long-term steroid use or pregnancy, and experience flu-like symptoms such as persistent fever or muscle aches, call your doctor right away. Listeriosis is easily diagnosed with a blood test and can be cured with antibiotics when treated early.

Surprising Places Germs Lurk: The Yuckiest Room Is *Not* the Bathroom

Charles Peter Gerba, PhD, professor of environmental microbiology who specializes in virology, parasitology and risk assessment at the University of Arizona College of Agriculture and Life Sciences, Tucson. He is coauthor, with Allison Janse, of *The Germ Freak's Guide to Outwitting Colds and Flu* (HCI).

Bacteria and viruses are everywhere. The vast majority of germs don't make us sick—though some, of course, do. The average adult gets two to four colds or other respiratory infections annually...children may get up to 12 colds a year.

Surprisingly, the bathroom is not the main microbial hot spot. *Where the germs really are lurking...*

CLEAN LAUNDRY

We know that dirty laundry is germ-laden. In fact, it has been associated with outbreaks of *salmonellosis* and *hepatitis A*, along with *rotavirus*, the most common cause of severe diarrhea.

But seemingly clean laundry also can be loaded with bacteria and viruses.

Fact: The average pair of used underwear contains 0.1 gram of fecal matter, one of the main sources of infectious organisms. Up to 99% of the organisms are killed during an average wash cycle, but that still leaves about one million infectious agents.

Self-defense: Wash undergarments in hot water (140°F or hotter)—about 95% of American households use cooler water. Add bleach to the wash cycle for whites—three-quarter cup per washer load. It will kill an additional 90% of the organisms. A 45-minute dry cycle can kill the majority of any remaining pathogens.

Also important: Wash your hands immediately after transferring damp clothes to the dryer. Damp clothes are more likely to harbor germs than dry.

RESTAURANT TABLETOPS

Every year in the US, there are about 76 million cases of food-borne gastroenteritis, with

Health Watch

symptoms ranging from mild diarrhea to serious liver or kidney disease. Many of these cases originate in the home, but restaurants also can be bacterial hot spots.

When we swabbed restaurant tabletops, we found that 70% were contaminated with *coliform* (fecal) bacteria, such as *E. coli*, organisms that are commonly found on meats as well as on vegetables and in water and soil.

In the same study, we found that the bacterial load on tabletops was 45 times greater after the tables were wiped.

Reason: The damp cloths used in restaurants are supposed to be sanitized between uses, but this usually is not done. The cloths tend to remain damp for long periods, which encourages bacterial growth. More than 89% of restaurant dishcloths were contaminated—and the bacterial level on bar dishcloths was even higher.

Self-defense: When you go to a restaurant, carry disposable disinfectant wipes and clean the table yourself. If you're at a bar, wipe the area in front of you with a disinfectant wipe—or spread a paper napkin to rest your elbows on. Also, clean your hands with a disinfectant wipe after you handle restaurant menus and those gadgets that vibrate when your table is ready—both are very rarely cleaned.

KITCHEN SINKS

We tested 14 surfaces in each of 15 homes.

The result: A kitchen sink, including the faucet handles, had the highest bacterial load. There's more bacteria in the average kitchen sink than in the average toilet.

From a microbial perspective, the kitchen is the dirtiest room in the house. Many foods, particularly raw meats, transfer coliforms and other disease-causing organisms to sinks, counters and cutting boards. Some of these organisms can survive for up to 24 hours, providing ample opportunities to cause infection.

Self-defense: After preparing raw meats, clean the kitchen sink with a bleach solution (one-quarter cup of bleach per gallon of water) or a commercial cleaning solution with bleach. Use the same solution to sanitize countertops, refrigerator handles and other surfaces.

Also beneficial: Pour one-quarter cup of bleach into the garbage disposal at least once a month.

Because a cutting board often is used for meats, merely wiping the board isn't enough. Use a generous amount of a bleach or cleaning solution, let it sit for five to 10 minutes, then rinse off.

Also, sanitize sponges and dishcloths at least once a week. You can run them through the clothes washer and dryer. Or soak them in a bleach solution for about an hour. You also can sanitize sponges and dishcloths in the microwave—soak them with water, and microwave for 30 seconds.

TV REMOTE CONTROLS

Certain household gadgets are rarely cleaned, including TV remote controls. If someone in your house catches the flu, more than 50% of household gadgets, including remote controls and telephones, can harbor the virus.

Self-defense: Wipe off all remote controls, telephones, your keyboard, mouse and other often-used devices with an alcohol sanitizer every two to three days—more often if someone who is using these devices is infected.

LIQUID HAND SOAPS

The refillable soap containers in public restrooms often are contaminated with fecal bacteria.

Reason: The antimicrobial preservatives used in liquid soaps can break down, allowing harmful organisms to proliferate. One "pull" can dispense millions of bacteria.

Self-defense: Use only the soap from dispensers that contain bagged soap. This soap doesn't get contaminated. To play it safe, wipe your hands with a disposable wipe or alcohol gel.

If you have refillable dispensers at home, wash them carefully using hot water prior to refilling.

GROCERY CARTS

About two-thirds of grocery store shopping-cart handles are contaminated with *coliform* bacteria. Many carts had a higher concentration of bacteria than public restrooms.

Self-defense: Some supermarkets offer sanitary wipes for cart handles or have installed systems to disinfect entire carts. Look for these supermarkets, or bring your own wipes. Place fresh produce (including melons), meat and poultry in plastic bags.

Copper Combats Germs

Copper has been shown to reduce the spread of germs. On a busy medical ward, copper door push plates and toilet seats had 90% to 100% fewer bacteria than similar items made of aluminum and plastic. Research has shown that the flu virus, *E. coli* and the *MRSA* and *C. difficile* superbugs do not survive on copper surfaces. Copper fixtures are available at home-improvement stores.

Tom Elliott, MD, consultant microbiologist and deputy medical director, University Hospitals Birmingham NHS Foundation Trust, Birmingham, England, and lead researcher of a study presented at the Interscience Conference on Antimicrobial Agents and Chemotherapy.

Why Bottled Water May Be Worse Than Tap And Much More

David O. Carpenter, MD, director of the Institute for Health and the Environment and a professor in the department of environmental health sciences at the University of Albany, both in Rensselaer, New York. He is a member of the editorial board of the *International Journal of Occupational Medicine and Environmental Health*, and an editorial adviser of *Cellular and Molecular Neurobiology*.

The average American drinks nearly 28 gallons of bottled water each year. Much of this consumer demand is fueled by the belief that bottled water is safer than tap water. But is this really true?

There's little evidence that most bottled water is purer than what comes out of the tap in the majority of American cities. In fact, about 25% of bottled water is tap water (sometimes further treated, sometimes not) that's been repackaged and branded with a wholesome-looking label. This means that these bottled waters may be just as likely as the tap water that comes out of the faucets to contain contaminants, such as infectious organisms, pesticide residues and heavy metals.

A **warning:** Bottled water could be even worse than tap water in some cases. *Potential problems...*

•**Lax oversight.** The Environmental Protection Agency (EPA) sets and enforces purity standards for municipal water. Bottled water, however, is regulated by the Food and Drug Administration (FDA)—but it is subject to inspection only when it's shipped out of state. About 60% of bottled waters are sold in the same state in which they're packaged. Therefore, they're exempt from FDA oversight and may not meet EPA standards.

•**Lack of chlorine.** Most bottled water, including that labeled "spring water," doesn't contain the disinfectant chlorine. Water without chlorine is far more likely to contain bacteria and viruses.

Bottled water companies typically use ozone gas (as an antimicrobial agent), but this process provides disinfection for a limited time, depending on storage and other factors, according to the FDA.

COMMON DANGERS

The safest water in the US typically comes from municipal systems. Yet even "clean" tap water may contain trace levels of contaminants that can be harmful to anyone—but especially to those with chronic illnesses or impaired immunity, as well as older adults, very young children and pregnant women. *For example...*

•**Infectious organisms.** The chlorine that's added to municipal water is very effective at killing bacteria and viruses, but it has little effect on parasites, such as *Cryptosporidium*, which can lead to severe diarrhea, abdominal pain and weight loss.

The vast majority of US water systems have procedures in place that prevent Cryptosporidium and other parasites from reaching the tap. Water utilities are required by law to test out supplies frequently and give consumers up-to-date information on the safety of tap water in their local areas.

To review water-quality reports for many American cities, consult the EPA at *www.epa. gov/safewater*...for more general information, call the EPA's Safe Drinking Water Hotline at 800-426-4791.

Self-defense: If there's a water-quality alert in your area (based on testing that identifies the presence of microorganisms), use bottled water—preferably water that is either distilled or filtered through reverse osmosis, a process by which water is forced through membranes, separating it from any potentially harmful substances. Boiling your water also will kill all infectious organisms, including parasites.

Also helpful: An activated carbon filter will trap Cryptosporidium, Giardia and other parasites. These filters are available at home-goods stores and online for about $50* for a faucet type...and up to $150 for the under-the-sink version.

● **Pharmaceuticals.** Whenever people take drugs, certain amounts pass through the body and are then flushed down the toilet. Wastewater treatment plants, which treat water that comes from community sewer systems, do remove some—but not all—of the residues from drinking water. It is not known if these residues affect human health, but there's strong evidence that they're harming wildlife—and may be dangerous for people.

Of particular concern are residues from such medications as chemotherapy agents, psychiatric drugs and antibiotics (which could contribute to the development of antibiotic resistance). Bottled water that is repackaged tap water is just as likely to contain drug residues as tap water itself.

Self-defense: Under-the-sink or whole-house reverse osmosis filtration systems. Available at home-goods stores and online. Under-the-sink models cost $150 to $450...whole-house systems cost up to $3,000. Systems with particularly small-pore membranes may remove pharmaceutical contaminants.

*Prices subject to change.

● **Lead.** Until the 1980s, water pipes—both in homes and city systems—were often made of lead or joined with lead-based solders. Even small amounts of lead can impair intellectual development and behavior in young children. Lead also can cross the placenta in pregnant women and impair fetal health. In adults, lead has been shown to reduce memory function and raise blood pressure.

Self-defense: If you live in an older home (built prior to 1986), let the water run for a minute in the morning before taking a drink. Standing water in lead pipes contains trace amounts of lead.

Caution 1: Do not use the hot-water tap for drinking water. Older hot-water tanks often used lead solder—and there's always standing water in the tank. The solder used in newer hot-water tanks does not contain lead, but it may contain other harmful metals. Brass faucets and fittings, which may contain lead, also can leach this metal, as can copper pipes with lead solder.

Caution 2: Let the water run before drinking from a public water fountain, particularly after periods when lead may accumulate due to infrequent use.

● **Plastics.** It's not yet known if people who drink out of plastic water bottles have more health risks—but research has shown that the phthalates and other chemicals that are in plastics have estrogen-like effects and may cause birth defects.

Self-defense: Avoid disposable plastic bottles. People who want the convenience of bottled water should use a stainless steel bottle or a reusable, firm plastic bottle—that is not polycarbonate—and fill it from the tap. Polycarbonate bottles can usually be identified by the recycling number "7" on the bottom. Firm plastics are less likely to contain phthalates than "squishy" plastic bottles.

A New Key to Longevity: Take Good Care of Your Teeth

Robert J. Genco, DDS, PhD, distinguished professor in the department of oral biology, School of Dental Medicine, and in the department of microbiology, School of Medicine and Biomedical Sciences at the State University of New York at Buffalo. He is also a professor in the department of immunology at the Roswell Park Cancer Institute and a recipient of the American Dental Association's Gold Medal for Excellence in Research.

Until recently, most people who took good care of their teeth and gums did so to ensure appealing smiles and to perhaps prevent dentures. Now, a significant body of research shows that oral health may play a key role in preventing a wide variety of serious health conditions, including heart disease, diabetes, some types of cancer and perhaps even dementia.

Healthy teeth and gums also may improve longevity. Swedish scientists recently tracked 3,273 adults for 16 years and found that those with chronic gum infections were significantly more likely to die before age 50, on average, than were people without gum disease.

What's the connection? Periodontal disease (called gingivitis in mild stages…and periodontitis when it becomes more severe) is caused mainly by bacteria that accumulate on the teeth and gums. As the body attempts to battle the bacteria, inflammatory molecules are released (as demonstrated by redness and swelling of the gums). Over time, this complex biological response affects the entire body, causing systemic inflammation which promotes the development of many serious diseases. *Scientific evidence links poor oral health to…*

• **Heart disease.** At least 20 new scientific studies have now found links between chronic periodontal disease and an increased risk for heart disease. Most recently, Boston University researchers found that periodontal disease in men younger than age 60 was associated with a twofold increase in angina (chest pain), or nonfatal or fatal heart attack, when compared with men whose teeth and gums are healthy.

• **Diabetes.** State University of New York at Buffalo studies and other research show that people with diabetes have an associated risk for periodontitis that is two to three times greater than that of people without diabetes. Conversely, diabetics with periodontal disease generally have poorer control of their blood sugar than diabetics without periodontal disease—a factor that contributes to their having twice the risk of dying of a heart attack and three times the risk of dying of kidney failure.

• **Cancer.** Chronic gum disease may raise your risk for tongue cancer. State University of New York at Buffalo researchers recently compared males with and without tongue cancer and found that those with cancer had a 65% greater loss of alveolar bone (which supports the teeth)—a common measure of periodontitis. Meanwhile, a Harvard School of Public Health study shows that periodontal disease is associated with a 63% higher risk for pancreatic cancer.

• **Rheumatoid arthritis.** In patients with rheumatoid arthritis, the condition is linked to an 82% increased risk for periodontal disease, compared with people who do not have rheumatoid arthritis.

Good news: Treating the periodontitis appears to ease rheumatoid arthritis symptoms. In one recent study, almost 59% of patients with rheumatoid arthritis and chronic periodontal disease who had their gums treated experienced less severe arthritis symptoms—possibly because eliminating the periodontitis reduced their systemic inflammation.

• **Dementia.** When Swedish researchers recently reviewed dental and cognitive records for 638 women, they found that tooth loss (a sign of severe gum disease) was linked to a 30% to 40% increased risk for dementia over a 32-year period, with the highest dementia rates suffered by women who had the fewest teeth at middle age. More research is needed to confirm and explain this link.

STEPS TO IMPROVE YOUR ORAL HEALTH

Even though the rate of gum disease significantly increases with age, it's not inevitable.

To promote oral health, brush (twice daily with a soft-bristled brush, using gentle, short strokes starting at a 45-degree angle to the gums) and floss (once daily, using gentle rubbing motions—do not snap against the gums). *In addition…*

•**See your dentist at least twice yearly.** Ask at every exam, "Do I have gum disease?" This will serve as a gentle reminder to dentists that you want to be carefully screened for the condition. Most mild-to-moderate infections can be treated with a nonsurgical procedure that removes plaque and tartar in the tooth pockets and smooths the root surfaces. For more severe periodontal disease, your dentist may refer you to a periodontist (a dentist who specializes in the treatment of gum disease).

Note: Patients with gum disease often need to see a dentist three to four times a year to prevent recurrence of gum disease after the initial treatment.

Good news: Modern techniques to regenerate bone and soft tissue can reverse much of the damage and halt progression of periodontitis, particularly in patients who have lost no more than 30% of the bone to which the teeth are attached.

•**Boost your intake of calcium.** Research conducted at the State University of New York at Buffalo has indicated that postmenopausal women with osteoporosis typically have more alveolar bone loss and weaker attachments between their teeth and bone, putting them at substantially higher risk for periodontal disease. Other studies have linked low dietary calcium with heightened periodontal risk in both men and women.

Self-defense: Postmenopausal women, and men over age 65, should consume 1,000 mg to 1,200 mg of calcium daily to preserve teeth and bones. Aim for two to three daily servings of dairy products (providing a total of 600 mg of calcium), plus a 600-mg calcium supplement with added vitamin D for maximum absorption.

Helpful: Yogurt may offer an edge over other calcium sources. In a recent Japanese study involving 942 adults, ages 40 to 79, those who ate at least 55 grams (about two ounces) of yogurt daily were 40% less likely to suffer from severe periodontal disease—perhaps because the "friendly" bacteria and calcium in yogurt make a powerful combination against the infection-causing bacteria of dental disease.

•**Control your weight.** Obesity is also associated with periodontitis, probably because fat cells release chemicals that may contribute to inflammatory conditions anywhere in the body, including the gums.

•**Don't ignore dry mouth.** Aging and many medications, including some antidepressants, antihistamines, high blood pressure drugs and steroids, can decrease flow of saliva, allowing plaque to build up on teeth and gums. If you're taking a drug that leaves your mouth dry, talk to your doctor about possible alternatives. Prescription artificial saliva products—for example, Caphosol or Numoisyn—also can provide some temporary moistening, as can chewing on sugarless gum.

•**Relax.** Recent studies reveal a strong link between periodontal disease and stress, depression, anxiety and loneliness. Researchers are focusing on the stress hormone cortisol as a possible culprit—high levels of cortisol may exacerbate the gum and jawbone destruction caused by oral infections.

•**Sleep.** Japanese researchers recently studied 219 factory workers for four years and found that those who slept seven to eight hours nightly suffered significantly less periodontal disease progression than those who slept six hours or less. The scientists speculated that lack of sleep lowers the body's ability to fend off infections. However, more research is needed to confirm the results of this small study.

More from Dr. Robert Genco…

Do You Have Gum Disease?

At least half of adults over age 55 have gum (periodontal) disease, an inflammation of the soft tissues (gums) surrounding the teeth. It results primarily from the accumulation of plaque (a sticky substance comprised mainly of bacteria) around the teeth and along the gum line. *What to watch for…*

- **Red, swollen gums that bleed easily** during brushing or flossing.
- **A change in your teeth's appearance.**
- **Chronic bad breath.**
- **Gum recession** (loss of gum tissue at the base of a tooth).

Important: With advanced gum disease, the gums rarely bleed because they become firmer due to the disease.

How to Live A Long Life

Laurel B. Yates, MD, MPH, Brigham and Women's Hospital, Boston, lead study researcher.

Studies indicate that about 25% of the difference in longevity between people results from heredity.

But most of the rest of the difference results from controllable factors—smoking, diabetes, obesity and high blood pressure, which reduce life span, and regular vigorous exercise, which increases it.

Study: Starting in 1981, more than 2,300 men with an average age of 72 were followed until 2006.

Findings: On average, a 70-year-old male had a 54% chance of living to age 90 if he did not smoke, did not have diabetes and had normal blood pressure, normal body weight and exercised two to four times per week.

However, if he had adverse factors, his probability of living to age 90 was reduced to the following...

- **Sedentary lifestyle,** to 44%.
- **High blood pressure,** to 36%.
- **Obesity,** to 26%.
- **Smoking,** to 22%.
- **Three factors,** such as sedentary lifestyle, obesity and diabetes, to 14%.
- **Five factors,** to only 4%.

Poor Air Quality Can Be Bad for the Heart

Steffen Loft, MD, head, department of occupational and environmental health, Institute of Public Health, University of Copenhagen, Denmark.

Recent research has shown that air quality does affect heart health. In a study of 21 nonsmoking couples ages 60 to 75 who lived within about two miles of a road traveled by more than 10,000 vehicles per day, participants ran an air purifier equipped with a high-efficiency particulate air (HEPA) filter for 48 hours, then operated the purifier for another 48 hours without a HEPA filter.

Result: After use of the HEPA filter, there was an 8.1% improvement, on average, in participants' small blood vessel function (measured with finger sensors)—an indication of overall improvement in the function of small blood vessels, including those supplying the heart.

More study is needed. In the meantime, if you live in an urban or a densely populated suburban community, consider using an air purifier equipped with a HEPA filter, available at home-improvement stores.

Popular Drug Linked to Heart Problem

In a recent finding, women who used *alendronate* (Fosamax) at any time in their lives had an 86% greater risk of atrial fibrillation (AF) than women who never used the drug.

AF is a rapid, irregular heartbeat that can lead to blood clots and strokes. Women who have heart disease or diabetes should discuss the risks of Fosamax with their physicians.

Susan Heckbert, MD, PhD, professor of epidemiology and adjunct professor of pharmacy, Cardiovascular Health Research Unit, University of Washington School of Public Health and Community Medicine, Seattle. She is the lead author of a study of 1,685 women, published in *Archives of Internal Medicine*.

What You're *Not* Being Told About Hypertension

Samuel J. Mann, MD, a hypertension specialist at New York–Presbyterian Hospital and professor of clinical medicine at Weill-Cornell Medical College, both in New York City. He is the author of *Healing Hypertension: A Revolutionary New Approach* (Wiley).

Getting your blood pressure checked is a routine part of most physical exams. But how your measurement is taken and the treatment your doctor recommends if you have high blood pressure (hypertension)* can have a profound effect on your health.

It's well-known that hypertension is often "silent" (causing no symptoms) and that it can lead to death or disability due to heart attack …stroke…and kidney damage.

What you may not know: One-third to one-half of all patients who take medication for hypertension lower their blood pressure insufficiently…take the wrong drugs…or suffer unnecessary side effects.

Samuel J. Mann, MD, a renowned hypertension specialist at New York–Presbyterian Hospital in New York City, discusses all these and other dangerous traps…

Trap: **Getting inaccurate blood pressure readings.** The equipment in doctors' offices and home arm-cuff blood pressure monitors are usually accurate, but how they are used can greatly affect readings. *Some common mistakes that are made…*

Mistake 1: Rushing the test. It takes five to 10 minutes of sitting quietly for blood pressure to stabilize. Testing too quickly can produce a reading that's considerably higher than your usual resting blood pressure.

Mistake 2: Using a cuff that's too small. Doctors often use the same blood pressure cuff on all patients—but if you have a large arm, the reading can be artificially high. Ask your doctor whether the blood pressure cuff size is right for you.

Mistake 3: Talking while blood pressure is being measured. It can add 10 millimeters

*Hypertension typically is defined as 140/90 mmHg or above, although readings 120/80 mmHg or above are considered higher than optimal.

or even more to the systolic (or top number) reading.

Trap: **Ignoring "white-coat hypertension."** Up to 20% of people exhibit elevations in blood pressure in the doctor's office even though their pressure at home is normal. This phenomenon, known as white-coat hypertension, sometimes is due to the anxiety many people experience when they go to the doctor.

We used to think that white-coat hypertension was insignificant. Now, a study published in the *Journal of Human Hypertension* shows that people who exhibit this trait do face higher risks—for both heart attack and true hypertension at some point in their lives—than those whose office blood pressure is normal.

It's not yet clear why these patients have higher risks. Studies of patients who perform home monitoring suggest that their pressure tends to be slightly higher than what is considered optimal even if it's not high enough to be classified as hypertension.

Warning: Some patients who have white-coat hypertension are undertreated because their doctors tend to overlook elevated office readings while not paying attention to a gradual rise in readings at home. Others are overtreated based on the elevated office readings, even though home readings are normal.

Helpful: People who have hypertension—or those at risk of getting it (due to such factors as family history and being overweight)—should use a home monitor to check their blood pressure two or three times per week. Take three readings each time, waiting about one to two minutes between each measurement.

Trap: **Overtreating hypertension because of high readings obtained at times of stress.** It's clear that blood pressure rises sharply at moments when people are angry, anxious or stressed. Many people have their blood pressure checked out—or check it themselves—at such times, and their doctors increase medication based on these readings.

Helpful: Blood pressure elevation during emotional moments is normal. If your blood pressure is otherwise normal, an increase in medication usually is not necessary.

11

Trap: **Taking the wrong drug.** Up to 25% of patients with hypertension take a beta-blocker to lower blood pressure. This type of drug inhibits the kidneys' secretion of the enzyme renin, which results in lower levels of angiotensin II, a peptide that constricts blood vessels.

Beta-blockers also reduce the rate and force of heart contractions. However, most of these medications, including the widely prescribed *metoprolol* (Lopressor) and *atenolol* (Tenormin), have the undesirable effect of reducing blood flow.

These effects often result in fatigue. Many patients don't even realize how fatigued they are until they stop taking the beta-blocker and experience a sudden boost in energy.

Fact: The majority of patients with hypertension who suffer from fatigue due to a beta-blocker don't even need to take this drug.

For most patients, it's best to start with other drugs or drug combinations, such as a diuretic (sodium-excreting pill) and/or an angiotensin-converting enzyme (ACE) inhibitor or an angiotensin receptor blocker (ARB).

Exception: Beta-blockers are usually a good choice for patients with hypertension who also have underlying coronary artery disease or who have had a heart attack.

If you need a beta-blocker: Ask your doctor about newer versions, such as *nebivolol* (Bystolic), that dilate arteries. Nebivolol is less likely to cause fatigue.

Trap: **Switching to a newer drug—without good reason.** Even if people are getting good results with the blood pressure medication they are taking, there is often the temptation to switch to a newer drug. Some newer drugs may have features that are an improvement over older medications, but others may offer little advantage and are not worth the extra cost.

Example: Aliskiren (Tekturna) is the first FDA-approved medication in a newer class of blood pressure drugs known as renin inhibitors. Aliskiren decreases the blood pressure–raising effects of the renin-angiotensin system. However, it is no more effective at lowering blood pressure than older treatments, such as ACE inhibitors or ARBs.

Switching drugs does make sense if you're not achieving optimal control—or if your current treatment is causing side effects. But for most patients, the older drugs are both effective and well-tolerated—and they tend to be much less expensive.

Trap: **Taking medication unnecessarily.** It's estimated that only about 40% of patients with hypertension achieve optimal control by taking a single drug (monotherapy). Most patients will eventually need multiple drugs—but monotherapy is effective for some patients, particularly those with mild (stage 1) hypertension (defined as systolic pressure of 140 mmHg to 159 mmHg and/or diastolic pressure of 90 mmHg to 99 mmHg).

Adding drugs invariably increases both the cost of treatment and the risk for side effects. If a drug does not work within a few weeks, then switching drugs is an alternative to simply adding drugs. Or if a second drug is added and it normalizes your blood pressure, your doctor may consider reducing the dose of—or stopping—the first drug.

Better Blood Pressure Screening

A diagnosis of high blood pressure (hypertension) routinely is based on both systolic (top number) and diastolic (bottom number) blood pressure readings.

New thinking: For people older than age 50, only systolic blood pressure needs to be used to diagnose hypertension and determine treatment.

Reason: Diastolic pressure increases until age 50, on average, and falls thereafter.

If you are age 51 or older: Ask your doctor whether focusing on your systolic pressure is appropriate for you.

Bryan Williams, MD, professor of medicine, University of Leicester School of Medicine, United Kingdom.

Why You Should Monitor Blood Pressure at Home

In a one-year study of 430 people with high blood pressure, those who monitored their blood pressure at home with arm-cuff devices (several times daily for one week every two months) were able to reduce their blood pressure drug dosages without any loss in blood pressure control, while dosages remained the same in people whose blood pressure was monitored only in their doctors' offices (once every two months).

If you suffer high blood pressure: Ask your doctor whether at-home blood pressure monitoring is appropriate for you. Devices are available at drugstores for about $50.*

Abraham A. Kroon, MD, vascular medicine specialist, Maastricht University Medical Center, The Netherlands.

*Price subject to change.

Keep It Quiet at Night

Night noise raises blood pressure even if it doesn't wake you. So-called "noise events" —such as an airplane flying overhead or a partner's snoring—can raise systolic pressure (top number) by an average of up to 6.2 points and diastolic (bottom number) pressure by 7.4 points.

Imperial College London, *www3.imperial.ac.uk.*

Nighttime Aspirin Lowers Blood Pressure

In a recent three-month study of 240 men and women with prehypertension (120/80 mmHg to 139/89 mmHg), those who took 100 mg of aspirin at bedtime lowered their systolic (top number) and diastolic (bottom number) blood pressures by an average of 5.4 and 3.4 points, respectively. Participants who took aspirin in the morning saw no change.

Theory: The production of hormones and other chemicals that raise blood pressure is inhibited by aspirin and occurs mainly when the body is at rest.

If you take aspirin for heart health: Ask your doctor if you should take your daily dose at bedtime.

Ramón C. Hermida, MD, director, department of bioengineering and chronobiology, University of Vigo, Spain.

Statins Provide a Double Whammy

Statins may help lower blood pressure as well as lowering cholesterol. Study participants who took a statin drug for six months had a decrease of two to three points in both their systolic (top number) and diastolic (bottom number) pressure.

Possible reason: Statins may activate compounds that widen blood vessels, improving their functioning.

If your doctor is already prescribing a statin drug for high cholesterol, but your blood pressure is currently just slightly elevated, discuss waiting to see if you also require blood pressure medication.

Beatrice Golomb, MD, PhD, associate professor of medicine, lead author of study, San Diego School of Medicine, University of California, San Diego.

A Vaccine for High Blood Pressure?

An experimental vaccine immunizes against *angiotensin II,* a protein that constricts blood vessels. The vaccine, given a few times per year, could potentially replace traditional blood pressure medications.

The Lancet, www.thelancet.com.

Better Heart Disease Screening

In recent research, 3,601 women received computed tomography (CT) chest scans to detect calcium deposits in the coronary arteries, a heart disease risk factor not included in the Framingham score, the well-known heart disease risk assessment that relies on such factors as cholesterol and blood pressure levels.

Result: 30% of all the women rated as "low risk" by the Framingham risk score had detectable coronary calcification.

If you are at risk for cardiovascular disease: Ask your doctor if you should have a CT scan to screen for coronary calcification.

Susan G. Lakoski, MD, assistant professor of cardiology, Wake Forest University Baptist Medical Center, Winston-Salem, North Carolina.

New Way to Determine Heart Disease Risk

A new way to gauge heart disease risk is to compare blood pressure measured at the ankle against pressure taken at the upper arm. The ankle pressure needs to be at least as high as upper-arm pressure. If ankle pressure is less than 90% of arm pressure, the patient may have peripheral arterial disease—a major cause of heart attack and stroke. The comparison is most useful in people over age 70 and those over age 50 with diabetes and/or a history of smoking.

Jonathan L. Halperin, MD, Robert and Harriet Heilbrunn Professor of Medicine (Cardiology) at Mount Sinai School of Medicine, New York City.

It's All in the Eyes

Major health problems can often show up in the eyes first.

Research: People with damage to the blood vessels of the retina—the light-sensitive tissue at the back of the eye—have a 33% increase in risk of dying from heart disease in the next 12 years. They also have increased risk for high blood pressure and stroke. In a person with diabetes, the retinal damage called diabetic retinopathy more than doubles the risk for heart disease.

Self-defense: Have regular eye exams even if your vision seems fine.

Jie Jin Wang, PhD, senior research fellow and associate professor of ophthalmology, University of Sydney, Australia, and senior author of a study of 2,967 people, published in *Heart*.

Psoriasis Tied to Heart Disease

In recent research, patients with severe psoriasis at age 30 had more than three times the risk for a heart attack compared with those of the same age without psoriasis.

Theory: Inflammation plays a role in the development of both psoriasis and cardiovascular disease.

If you have psoriasis: Ask your doctor to screen you at least every two years for high blood pressure and obesity…and at least every two to five years for elevated cholesterol and triglyceride (blood fat) levels and diabetes—all are cardiovascular disease risk factors.

Lyn C. Guenther, MD, professor and chair, division of dermatology, University of Western Ontario, London, Ontario, Canada.

Respiratory Infection Linked to Heart Attack And Stroke

In the week following a severe respiratory infection, such as influenza, patients have at least two times the risk for heart attack or stroke as people who did not have respiratory infections.

Self-defense: Wash hands often…get a flu shot yearly.

Tom Meade, DM, epidemiology professor, London School of Hygiene and Tropical Medicine, and coresearcher of a study of 20,363 people, published in the *European Heart Journal.*

Little-Known Heart Attack Risk Factor

In a recent study of nearly 15,000 people, researchers found that kidney stone disease (buildup of crystals in the kidneys from substances in urine) was up to three times more probable in those with metabolic syndrome—heart attack and stroke risk factors, such as diabetes and high blood pressure.

Theory: People with metabolic syndrome have the propensity to develop highly acidic urine, which raises kidney stone risk.

If you have kidney stones: Ask your doctor whether you need to be tested for metabolic syndrome.

Bradford West, MD, fellow, department of nephrology, University of Chicago.

Calcium Supplements May Increase Heart Attack Risk in Women

In a recent study, women ages 55 and older who took 1,000 mg of calcium daily were 50% to 70% more likely to have heart attacks over five years than women taking placebos. Men were not studied.

Self-defense: Heart disease is most prevalent over age 70. Women in this age group should consult their physicians about stopping calcium and starting osteoporosis drugs,

if needed. Younger women with heart disease also should consider stopping.

Ian Reid, MD, professor of medicine and endocrinology, University of Auckland, New Zealand, and author of a study of 1,471 postmenopausal women, published in *British Medical Journal.*

Getting Drunk Raises Heart Attack Risk

Women who drank alcohol to the point of intoxication at least once a month were six times as likely to suffer a heart attack (not necessarily while drinking) as women who drank at least monthly but not enough to be intoxicated.

Best: Never drink alcohol to the point of intoxication.

Joan M. Dorn, PhD, associate professor, department of social and preventive medicine, University of Buffalo, and leader of a study of 1,885 women, published in the journal *Addiction.*

A Real Lifesaver

Taking a statin after a heart attack can save your life.

Recent study: Patients who stopped taking statin drugs after their heart attacks were 88% more likely to die within the next year than those who never took statins. Those who started taking statins after a heart attack were 28% less likely to die.

Statins are cholesterol-lowering drugs. They include *rosuvastatin* (Crestor), *atorvastatin* (Lipitor), *pravastatin* (Pravachol) and *simvastatin* (Zocor).

Stella Daskalopoulou, MD, PhD, assistant professor of medicine, McGill University, Montreal, Quebec, and lead author of a study of 9,939 heart attack patients, published in *European Heart Journal.*

Women Don't Get Quick Care for Heart Attacks: What to Do

Women with heart attack symptoms are not treated as promptly as men. Response time for ambulances is the same for women and men, but when the patient is a woman, there are more delays after ambulances arrive.

Among the reasons: Women don't always have classic heart attack symptoms and often minimize symptoms that they do have.

Self-defense: Know the warning signs of a heart attack, such as chest pain. Women often experience symptoms as indigestion, shortness of breath, extreme fatigue and/or a feeling of throat tightness. Tell emergency workers if you have a family history of heart attacks. Explain symptoms in detail. Do not self-diagnose, and do not minimize your pain.

Nieca Goldberg, MD, a cardiologist and medical director, NYU Women's Heart Program, New York University School of Medicine, New York City, and author of *The Women's Healthy Heart Program* (Ballantine).

Be Prepared

Put together a heart-attack/health "emergency kit."

What it should contain: A bottle of uncoated aspirin…a contact list with your physicians and key family members and friends as well as the hospital to go to in an emergency… a list of medications you are currently taking …notes on any allergies or adverse reactions to medications…medical insurance plan information and the procedures to follow for using your hospital of choice.

Make sure your family members know where you keep the "kit" in the event that they need it in an emergency when you are disabled.

Jennifer Mieres, MD, associate professor, New York University Department of Medicine, New York City.

Why Headphones and Pacemakers Don't Mix

Headphones for digital music players can interfere with pacemakers and defibrillators. The players (including iPods) themselves are not a problem, and the headphones are not a problem while they are in the ears.

But: When placed within an inch or so of an implanted pacemaker or defibrillator, the powerful magnets in the headphones can cause the medical devices to malfunction temporarily.

Self-defense: Keep headphones away from pacemakers and defibrillators. Do not drape headphones around your neck so that they dangle over your chest, and do not carry them in a pocket near the chest.

Kevin Fu, PhD, assistant professor, computer science department, University of Massachusetts at Amherst, and a member of a team that studied the effects of headphones on implanted medical devices, presented at the American Heart Association's Scientific Sessions 2008.

Think You're Having a Stroke? One Word Can Save Your Life

Lori Mosca, MD, PhD, MPH, director of the New York–Presbyterian Hospital Preventive Cardiology Program in New York City, *www.hearthealthtimes.com.* She is professor of medicine at Columbia University Medical Center, past-chair of the American Heart Association Council on Epidemiology, and author of *Heart to Heart: A Personal Plan for Creating a Heart-Healthy Family* (HCI).

Stroke is a medical emergency requiring immediate care. Brain cells starved of oxygen die off and do not regenerate. *To remember the sudden symptoms of stroke, think of the word "FAST"*…

• **Face.** Sudden numbness or weakness of the face, especially on one side…severe headache …dizziness…vision trouble.

• **Arm and leg.** Sudden numbness or weakness of the arm and/or leg, especially on one side…trouble walking…loss of coordination.

•**Speech.** Sudden confusion and difficulty speaking or understanding speech.

•**Time.** Time is critical—if you think you or someone else is having a stroke, call 911 right away.

RLS Linked to Stroke

In a study of 3,433 adults, those with restless legs syndrome (RLS)—the neurological disorder that causes restlessness in legs while awake and involuntary leg movements during sleep—were twice as likely to have a stroke or heart disease as those without RLS.

A theory: The frequent leg movements in RLS patients may cause spikes in blood pressure and heart rate that, over time, may lead to cardiovascular disease.

If you have RLS: Ask your doctor whether you need iron supplements to fix an iron deficiency (one trigger of RLS) or an RLS drug.

John W. Winkelman, MD, PhD, assistant professor of psychiatry, Harvard Medical School, Boston.

Too Much Sleep And Stroke Risk

Too much sleep increases stroke risk among older women.

Recent findings: Postmenopausal women who habitually sleep for nine hours or more a night have a 70% higher risk for ischemic stroke—the most common type of stroke—than women who regularly sleep seven hours per night. However, postmenopausal women who sleep less than six hours a night have a 14% elevated stroke risk.

Self-defense: Take steps to lower risk factors for stroke, especially high blood pressure.

Sylvia Wassertheil-Smoller, PhD, a professor, department of epidemiology and population health, Albert Einstein College of Medicine of Yeshiva University, Bronx, New York, and coauthor of a study of 93,175 women, ages 50 to 79, published in *Stroke*.

Aspirin Alert

When researchers tracked 653 stroke patients who took aspirin to prevent a second stroke, they found that 20% of them were "aspirin resistant"—that is, taking a daily low-dose aspirin did not help prevent the patients' blood platelets from sticking together.

Theory: In some individuals, genetic factors may reduce aspirin's anticlotting effects.

If your doctor recommends daily aspirin: Ask him/her if you should receive a blood test for aspirin resistance.

Francis M. Gengo, PharmD, associate professor of pharmacy and neurology, University at Buffalo School of Pharmacy and Pharmaceutical Sciences and neuropharmacologist, DENT Neurologic Institute, Amherst, New York.

Latest Breakthroughs in Stroke Recovery

Joel Stein, MD, chief medical officer at the Spaulding Rehabilitation Hospital and an associate professor in the department of physical medicine and rehabilitation at Harvard Medical School, both in Boston. Dr. Stein is coauthor of *Life After Stroke* (Johns Hopkins University) as well as the author of *Stroke and the Family* (Harvard University).

Until recently, if you lost the use of an arm or leg due to a stroke, doctors assumed that the disability was permanent.

Latest: Sophisticated imaging tests have shown that the brain can "rewire" itself and compensate for some brain damage caused by a stroke (often resulting in paralysis or problems controlling movement of a limb).

This exciting, new understanding of brain physiology means that the estimated 700,000 Americans who suffer a stroke each year will now have a much better chance of regaining their independence.

Joel Stein, MD, a renowned expert in the field and chief medical officer at one of the country's leading rehabilitation centers, discusses the latest advances in stroke rehabilitation…

A "BRAIN ATTACK"

All body movements are controlled by brain cells called *neurons*. During a stroke, a blood clot blocks blood supply to an area of the brain (*ischemic* stroke) or a broken or leaking blood vessel causes bleeding into or around the brain (*hemorrhagic* stroke). In both cases, neurons die, and areas of the brain that are responsible for movement or other functions do not send and receive information correctly as a result.

Dead brain cells can't be revived, but the ability of the brain to "rewire" itself—a trait that is known as *plasticity*—means it is possible for new brain connections (also known as pathways) to take over and do the job of the nonfunctioning neurons.

Even though some stroke-produced brain damage is too great to repair, state-of-the-art stroke rehabilitation helps maximize the brain's power to create new connections and improve control over body movement.

EXERCISE THE BRAIN AND BODY

Supervised physical therapy should begin, if possible, within a week of suffering a stroke. Movement can reinforce brain communication pathways—the more you "work" these pathways, the stronger they become and the easier it is to move the body. The goal of exercise after stroke is to practice movements and to help the brain regain as much function as possible.

The best type of physical therapy depends on the stroke survivor's abilities and on the resources of the rehabilitation facility. Therapies described in this article are usually used for weeks to months (at least three times per week for one-hour sessions) as one part of an overall rehabilitation program that includes occupational therapy and, in some cases, speech therapy.

If you or a loved one is recovering from a stroke, discuss with your stroke rehabilitation physician—generally a physiatrist (a physician who specializes in rehabilitation medicine) or a neurologist—how these breakthrough techniques might fit into your program...*

• **Constraint-Induced Movement Therapy (CIMT).**

*To locate a stroke rehabilitation center near you, contact the Commission on Accreditation of Rehabilitation Facilities (888-281-6531, *www.carf.org*).

Recommended for: People who have limited use of an arm due to a stroke.

After recovery, stroke survivors often depend on the more functional, "good" arm to perform daily functions. That causes the affected arm to regress and lose even more function. CIMT forces use of the affected arm.

In a typical two-week course of CIMT, the good arm is restrained in a sling or mitt for nearly all waking hours, including during six hours of daily intensive physical therapy. Research shows that CIMT gives lasting improvement in movement and usage and enhances emotional well-being and quality of life.

• **Robotics.**

Recommended for: People with partial use of an affected arm or leg who may need help completing movements, such as using eating utensils. Rehabilitation robotics are sophisticated, programmable mechanical exercise devices. *For example...*

• InMotion2 shoulder-elbow robot. With an arm in a brace attached to the arm of a robot, you "play" adaptive video games that require arm movements. The games get progressively more difficult as your abilities improve. They work by encouraging intense repetition of movements, which strengthens brain connections.

• Myomo e100 NeuroRobotic System. This assistive elbow brace straps onto the stroke patient's affected arm. It works by "reading" your muscle signals and then completing the motion —for example, bending your elbow to lift an object—even if you don't have complete control yet.

Because you perform the full movement (albeit with help), fresh brain communication pathways are formed, and eventually you may be able to complete the movement without the mechanical brace.

• Hocoma Lokomat. This robot helps with walking. You are strapped into a large machine that supports your body and legs. The robot guides your legs as you walk on the treadmill. It works by helping brain cells re-establish a communication pathway that governs walking.

ELECTRICAL STIMULATION

Just as electrical impulses allow cells in your brain and other parts of your body to communicate with one another, the use of electrical stimulation devices may help the brain restore connections.

Limb systems strap onto the affected arm or leg and deliver mild electrical stimulation to the skin to improve motor abilities. Arm stimulation allows you to grab a glass or write with a pencil. Leg stimulation prevents "foot drop" to make walking easier.

Brain systems work by electrically encouraging the brain to rewire itself. The two main techniques are *transcranial magnetic stimulation* (TMS), which uses a powerful magnetic pulse to stimulate the part of the brain affected by the stroke…and *direct electrical current*, a noninvasive technique in which the current passes through the skull and into the brain. These brain systems are still being researched, but scientists hope that electrical stimulation might be enough to help connect the circuits that were damaged during a stroke.

Stroke Patients: Don't Give Up!

Stroke patients can improve *years* after their strokes.

Recent finding: Even two to three years after their strokes, patients still can learn to use undamaged areas of the brain to perform tasks, especially if their physical therapy incorporates long-term, supervised walking on a treadmill.

Physical therapy typically is prescribed for merely 30 to 60 days following a stroke because, until recently, it was believed that patients could make significant improvements only within that time frame.

Daniel F. Hanley, MD, department of neurology, Johns Hopkins University, Baltimore, and leader of a study published in *Stroke*.

The Cancer Danger No One Is Talking About

Devra Davis, PhD, MPH, director of the Center for Environmental Oncology at the University of Pittsburgh Cancer Institute and professor in the department of epidemiology at the University of Pittsburgh. She has authored more than 170 papers that have appeared in books and journals ranging from *Scientific American* to the *Journal of the American Medical Association*. She is the author of *The Secret History of the War on Cancer* (Basic).

When the US government announced its "war on cancer" in 1971, the goal was to find the cure for this deadly disease. Nearly 40 years later, some victories have been declared. There are an estimated 11 million cancer survivors in the US—a sign that people with some types of cancer are living longer than ever—and far fewer people are smoking.

But there also is a startling reality that is not being openly discussed. If the war on cancer had been conducted differently—by focusing not only on *treating* cancer, but also on its many *causes*—more than 1.5 million cancer deaths worldwide could have been prevented. These untimely deaths could have been avoided had we discouraged the use of tobacco, asbestos and other known cancer causes which were documented as early as the 1930s in dozens of scientific studies throughout the world.

That is the provocative assertion of Devra Davis, PhD, MPH, a leading authority on environmental and industrial causes of cancer and director of the Center for Environmental Oncology at the University of Pittsburgh Cancer Institute. *Here, she discusses the war on cancer and what it means for your health…*

•**Why do you believe that the public is not being told all the facts about the war on cancer?** The cancer-causing potential of many commonly used industrial and environmental chemicals is *known*, but this knowledge has not always been brought to the public's attention by industry and government.

The result is that humans have been treated, in my opinion, like experimental animals in a vast and largely uncontrolled scientific study. For example, the link between smoking and cancer was reported by a number of scientists in the US and England in the 1950s, and even earlier—but government efforts to discourage tobacco use in the US did not occur until much later.

In the interim, the tobacco industry actively supported medical research but was not forthcoming with evidence showing that its own products triggered cancer. Meanwhile, the industry widely publicized research that raised doubts—I refer to this as the "science of doubt promotion"—about the harmful effects of tobacco in an effort to foment uncertainty about tobacco hazards.

I am not anti-industry. There are many honest scientists working in industry, but their results about dangerous substances have often been manipulated or suppressed.

• **Has the so-called "science of doubt promotion" endangered Americans?** Certainly, and one of the main reasons is that legal safeguards against carcinogens have been loosened, largely because the federal budget does not provide adequate funding for regulatory agencies to monitor environmental and workplace contamination or to investigate chemical accidents.

In the 1970s, when many major environmental laws were passed in the US, the intent was to decrease our exposure to potential hazards and prevent harm. Under a law that guided many of the early consumer health protection efforts, if a substance caused cancer in animals, it was deemed hazardous and could be controlled or banned by the federal government. Now, it is no longer enough to prove that a substance is likely to do harm based on animal studies. Proof is required that harm has *already happened* to humans. Whenever proof of such harm is lacking—and it typically is—nothing can be done legally to prevent the potentially harmful exposure.

• **How can we tell whether scientific evidence is objective and factual?** The most effective public relations work often appears as scientific advice rather than what it actually is—advertising. Consider who signs the paycheck of the person giving you the information —be it a drug company, trade group or other organization with a stake in the product or technology being promoted. There often is a hidden agenda that supports the interests of the financial backer.

• **What can we do to minimize our exposure to carcinogens?** There are so many risk factors in the environment that we cannot minimize exposure to all of them. But we can start with simple preventive actions. *My recommendations, based on my analysis of the data…*

• Do not consume food or beverages that contain the sugar substitute aspartame (also sold as NutraSweet and Equal). It did receive FDA approval in 1981, but it remains controversial among some scientists who are concerned about its potential to cause cancer.

• Do not use mothballs and room deodorizers. Many contain *naphthalene*, a carcinogen in animals.

• Don't microwave food or liquids in plastic containers regardless of the directions. Some plastic chemicals—possible carcinogens—may leach into the food.

• Use a cell phone earpiece and/or a speakerphone so the phone isn't held against your head. Cell phones emit radiation that can penetrate the brains of rats, damaging brain cells critical to memory, learning and movement, according to a 2003 Swedish study.

• Discuss the risks and benefits of any X-ray procedure with your doctor and ask about nonradiation diagnostic alternatives, including ultrasound. Although X-rays generally are not dangerous and are appropriate when medically indicated, overexposure to X-rays—especially computed tomography (CT) scans—can cause cancer. (Children face the greatest risk, which accumulates over time.)

• Hire a certified contractor to check for asbestos, which has been linked to *mesothelioma*, a rare form of cancer, before doing home renovations or repairs of attics, roofing, and ceiling and flooring tiles. America has banned asbestos in many products, but it still can be found in certain construction materials, such as some roofing and siding shingles, and in older products, such as attic insulation that was sold under the brand name Zonolite and old stocks of drywall tape. Half of all people with mesothelioma have no known workplace contact with asbestos.

Cell Phone/Cancer Link

When researchers compared the lifetime cell phone use of 1,300 healthy adults with 500 adults newly diagnosed with benign or malignant tumors in their salivary glands, they found a 50% greater risk for such a tumor in heavy cell phone users who usually held the phone on the side of the head where the tumor developed.

Theory: Excessive radio-frequency radiation emitted by cell phones may lead to cell changes that promote cancer.

Siegal Sadetzki, MD, MPH, head of cancer and radiation, epidemiology unit, Gertner Institute, Chaim Sheba Medical Center, Israel.

How Cell Phone Users Can Minimize Cancer Risk

Ronald B. Herberman, MD, the director of the University of Pittsburgh Cancer Institute, a National Cancer Institute–designated Comprehensive Cancer Center, *www.upci.upmc.edu.* He is also associate vice chancellor for cancer research, Health Sciences, Hillman Professor of Oncology and professor of medicine at the University of Pittsburgh School of Medicine.

The director of the University of Pittsburgh Cancer Institute (UPCI) recently issued a memo warning faculty members and staff about possible dangers associated with long-term cell phone use. The memo is based on the UPCI's analysis of the existing data. *Key points…*

• **Use the speakerphone mode,** whenever possible, or the wireless Bluetooth headset, which produces significantly less electromagnetic emission than a normal cell phone. Use of an earpiece attachment (with a wire) also may reduce radiation exposure. (More research is needed on such earpieces.)

• **Avoid carrying your cell phone on your body.** If you must do so, make sure that the cell phone's keypad is positioned toward your body so that the transmitted electromagnetic fields move away from you. (Even when not in use, cell phones continue to connect to relay antennas, exposing the owner to electromagnetic radiation.)

• **Use text messaging** rather than making a call, whenever possible. This limits the duration of exposure and the proximity to the body.

• **Do not keep your cell phone near your body at night**—for example, under the pillow or on a bedside table—particularly if you're pregnant. Keep the phone at least three feet away.

• **Avoid using your cell phone when the signal is weak or when moving at a high speed,** such as in a car or train—this automatically increases the phone's power as it repeatedly attempts to establish a connection to a new relay antenna.

• **Choose a cell phone with the lowest possible Specific Absorption Rate (SAR),** which is a measure of the strength of the magnetic field absorbed by the body. (Check the phone manual or Web sites, such as *www.cnet.com,* that review technology products. In the US, the SAR value limit is 1.6 watts per kilogram.)

• **Limit the number and duration of cell phone calls.**

Cordless Phone Warning

Cordless phones may carry as many health risks as cell phones. One Swedish study found that both cordless and cell phones increase the risk for brain tumors in people who use them frequently for more than 10 years. The risk is higher when people start using the phones as children…and higher with newer, high-frequency cordless phones than with older ones operating at 900 MHz. More research is needed to confirm or counter these findings.

Self-defense: Replace cordless phones with corded models.

David O. Carpenter, MD, director, Institute for Health and the Environment, University at Albany–SUNY, Rensselaer, New York.

Cancer Linked to Changes in the Hands

Palmar fasciitis and polyarthritis syndrome (PFPAS), a thickening or curling of the palm and swelling of the fingers that gives the palms a wooden appearance, has been linked to cancers of the prostate, blood, lung, breast, pancreas and ovaries. This rare condition primarily affects older people.

Theory: Connective tissue growth factor, a chemical signal in the body, may trigger both the growth of malignancies and overgrowth of connective tissues in the palm.

If your palms suddenly become thickened: Consult a physician who specializes in internal medicine.

Richard Stratton, MD, consultant physician, Royal Free Hospital, London.

Why Antibiotics Can Prevent Stomach Cancer

The *Helicobacter pylori bacterium* causes chronic stomach inflammation and peptic ulcers, which can progress to gastric cancer.

New finding: The sooner antibiotics are given, the more effectively they reverse cell damage that leads to cancer, animal studies show.

Best: See your doctor without delay if you have H. pylori symptoms—persistent abdominal pain, bloating, tarry stool—especially if you have a family history of peptic ulcers or gastric cancer.

James G. Fox, DVM, director, division of comparative medicine, Massachusetts Institute of Technology, Boston, and coauthor of a study published in *Cancer Research.*

A Sunscreen You Can Swallow

Albert M. Lefkovits, MD, an associate clinical professor of dermatology at Mount Sinai School of Medicine and codirector of the Mount Sinai Dermatological Cosmetic Surgery Program, both in New York City. He is a member of the Medical Advisory Council of the Skin Cancer Foundation (SCF), *www.skincancer.org*, and presented "New Strategies for Melanoma Prevention" at an international gathering of the SCF.

The dietary supplement Heliocare (available online or by special order at your pharmacy) contains an extract of *Polypodium leucotomos*, a tropical plant, which can improve the skin's resistance to UV radiation. Studies published in the *Journal of the American Academy of Dermatology* found that the extract significantly decreased sunburn as well as cell damage—both can increase cancer risk.

How to use: Take one 240-mg capsule in the morning on a day when you're planning to spend time in the sun. Take a second capsule at noon if you will be exposed to intense sunlight (such as that in a tropical climate). The extract has no known side effects.

Caution: Heliocare should be used in conjunction with—and not as a substitute for—sunscreen.

More from Dr. Albert Lefkovits...

New Rule for Skin Cancer Detection

Melanoma deaths could be curbed by 60% if everyone performed monthly self-exams. Patients have traditionally been advised to see a doctor if a mole or other growth can be described by the "A, B, C, D" guidelines—that is, it is *Asymmetric*, in which the two halves are different...has an irregular *Border*...has variations in *Color*...and/or has a *Diameter* that is greater than the size of a pencil eraser.

What you may not know: "E" for *Evolving* has been added to the guidelines. If a mole or other growth *changes* in appearance, sensation (itching and tenderness) or size, see a dermatologist. Lesions that change, particularly over a period of a few months, are far more likely to be melanoma than areas that stay the same over a period of years.

Warning: It's unusual for patients to develop new moles after age 40. To be safe, if you develop a new mole after age 40, see a doctor right away, particularly if you have melanoma risk factors—a personal or family history of melanoma, a large number of moles (more than 20) or fair skin that burns easily.

Where Skin Cancer Is The Deadliest

Skin cancer on the scalp or neck is more deadly than skin cancer on other parts of the body.

Recent finding: For people with scalp or neck melanoma, the probability of surviving after 10 years was 76%, compared with 89% for people with melanoma elsewhere.

Possible reason: Scalp and neck melanomas often are thicker when detected, suggesting that they either are found later or are more aggressive.

Self-defense: Have an annual skin check by a dermatologist…wear a wide-brimmed hat and sunscreen when outside.

Anne Lachiewicz, MD, University of North Carolina at Chapel Hill School of Medicine and lead author of a study of 51,704 melanoma patients, published in *Archives of Dermatology*.

Men Get Skin Cancer More Than Women

Squamous cell carcinoma occurs three times more often in men than in women.

Theory: Women have more antioxidants in their skin, which protects them from getting skin cancer.

Tatiana Oberyszyn, PhD, associate professor of pathology, The Ohio State University Medical Center, Columbus, and leader of a study of UVB rays, published in *Cancer Research*.

Skin Cancer Increases Risk for Other Cancers

People who have had basal or squamous cell skin cancer are twice as likely to get another type of cancer—such as breast, lung, colorectal or melanoma skin cancer—as people with no cancer history.

Best: Alert your doctor if you have had skin cancer…and ask about cancer warning signs to watch for.

Anthony J. Alberg, PhD, associate director for cancer prevention and control, Hollings Cancer Center, Medical University of South Carolina, Charleston, and senior author of a study of 19,000 people, published in *Journal of the National Cancer Institute*.

Hair-Dye Danger

Women who color their hair have a 50% to 70% higher risk of developing certain forms of non-Hodgkin's lymphoma, compared with women who never color their hair. The study found no increased risk for men. The cancer may be linked to a chemical that's in dye called *paraphenylenediamine* (PPD).

PPD-free alternative: Shiseido Re:nual Serum. To find a distributor in your area, go to *www.joico.com*.

Yawei Zhang, MD, PhD, assistant professor, division of environmental health sciences, Yale School of Public Health, New Haven, Connecticut, and author of a study of personal use of hair dye, published in *American Journal of Epidemiology*.

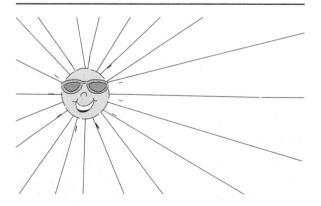

Weight-Loss Surgery Can "Cure" Diabetes

John Dixon, MD, PhD, Baker-IDI Heart and Diabetes Research Institute, Melbourne, Australia.

Weight-loss surgery works much better than standard treatments for type 2 diabetes when the patient is obese. It often puts diabetes into remission. Type 2 diabetes most often is caused by excess weight and can be remedied by losing more than 10% of body weight, but few people can lose that much weight and keep it off without surgery. It is important to note that surgery only assists the weight loss. Best results still come from surgery with diet and physical activity.

Recent four-year study: Obese patients who had been diagnosed as having diabetes within the prior two years were randomly assigned to one of two groups. One group underwent weight-loss surgery that reduced the amount of food the stomach can hold. The other group underwent standard treatment for diabetes (diet, exercise, drugs and insulin).

Among the group that had surgery, the average weight loss was 20.7% of body weight, and 73% experienced "complete remission" of their diabetes, experiencing no more symptoms.

Among the group that received standard treatment, average weight loss was only 1.7% of body weight, and 13% experienced remission.

Caution: Weight-loss surgery might not have the same benefits for people who have not just recently become diabetic, because the condition becomes harder to reverse over time.

Why Fat on the Hips Can Be a Good Thing

Abdominal fat increases a person's risk for type 2 diabetes, but fat on the hips may *protect* against diabetes.

How: Fat just beneath the skin on hips and thighs actually may improve insulin sensitivity (the ability of the body's cells to recognize and properly respond to insulin).

Theory: Subcutaneous fat produces *adipokines*, hormones that have beneficial effects on glucose metabolism.

C. Ronald Kahn, MD, vice-chairman, Joslin Diabetes Center, Mary K. Iacocca professor of medicine, Harvard Medical School, Boston, and leader of an animal study published in *Cell Metabolism*.

A Risky Breakfast

Eggs may be linked to increased death risk. Men who ate at least seven eggs per week over an average of 20 years were 23% more likely to die during the study period than those who ate less than one egg per week. Among men with diabetes, the mortality rate doubled. However, the health of men without diabetes who ate up to six eggs was not affected. More research is needed.

Luc Djoussé, MD, MPH, DSc, assistant professor of medicine, Harvard Medical School, and associate epidemiologist, Brigham & Women's Hospital, both in Boston, and lead author of a study of 21,327 men, published in *The American Journal of Clinical Nutrition*.

Better Dialysis

In a one-year study of 224 kidney disease patients, those who received eight hours of dialysis overnight (while sleeping) had a 78% lower death rate than patients who received conventional dialysis (four hours, three days weekly).

Theory: Overnight dialysis patients are less likely to experience drops in blood pressure, which can lead to complications.

Ercan Ok, MD, professor of internal medicine and nephrology, Ege University Hospital, Izmir, Turkey.

Aspirin: The Great Protector

Aspirin may protect the liver against damage from *acetaminophen* and other drugs. This potent anti-inflammatory also may protect against liver disease resulting from alcohol, obesity and other causes. Clinical trials are needed to confirm aspirin's liver-protecting benefits.

Future possibility: Medications could be formulated containing both acetaminophen and enough aspirin to ward off possible liver damage.

Wajahat Z. Mehal, MD, associate professor, section of digestive diseases, Yale School of Medicine in New Haven, Connecticut, and leader of a study of aspirin's effect on liver damage, published in *Journal of Clinical Investigation*.

Can Alzheimer's Be Prevented?

A recent study finds that one type of blood pressure medication—*angiotensin receptor blocker* (ARB)—decreases risk for dementia in seniors and slows its progress in cases where it is already diagnosed.

A study of the medical records of five million people found that patients taking ARBs had a 35% to 40% lower chance of getting Alzheimer's disease or other forms of dementia, while patients taking ARBs who were already suffering from Alzheimer's or other forms of dementia had up to a 45% lower chance of developing delirium, being admitted to nursing homes or dying. How ARBs produce this benefit is not certain. Consult your doctor.

Benjamin Wolozin, MD, PhD, professor of pharmacology and neurology, Boston University School of Medicine, Boston.

Early Indicator of Alzheimer's

One of the first signs of early-stage Alzheimer's disease is difficulty handling financial affairs. For that reason, people who have even mild symptoms should immediately get help managing their affairs before the disease progresses. They also should speak to their doctors about treatment options.

Symptoms to watch out for: Forgetting to pay bills or paying them more than once... difficulty balancing the checkbook or doing simple calculations...increased susceptibility to scam artists.

If you or a loved one is showing any of these signs: A relative or close friend can be given "financial power of attorney" to handle financial duties if it becomes necessary.

Stephen McConnell, PhD, vice president for advocacy and public policy, Alzheimer's Association, Chicago.

BP Drug Reduces Parkinson's Risk

Parkinson's risk can be cut by blood pressure drug.

Recent study: In an analysis of the health data for 7,374 men and women (half of whom had Parkinson's disease), those who had been taking *calcium channel blockers* (CCBs), such as *nifedipine* (Procardia) or *amlodipine* (Norvasc), were 23% less likely to develop Parkinson's than those who didn't take the drugs. No such effect was found for other blood pressure drugs.

Theory: CCBs may protect nerve cells in the central nervous system.

If you take blood pressure medication: Ask your doctor if a CCB is right for you.

Christoph R. Meier, PhD, associate professor, pharmacoepidemiology unit, University Hospital Basel, Basel, Switzerland.

Painkillers May Prevent Parkinson's

Painkillers may reduce Parkinson's risk. A study of 579 men and women found that patients who regularly took two or more pills of non-aspirin nonsteroidal anti-inflammatory drugs (or NSAIDs), such as *ibuprofen* (Advil), weekly for at least one month during their lifetimes had up to a 60% lower risk for Parkinson's than those who took NSAIDs less often or never.

Theory: NSAIDs' anti-inflammatory effect may halt or slow brain-cell death, a process that often occurs in the brains of Parkinson's patients.

More research is needed before NSAIDs can be recommended to prevent Parkinson's.

Angelika D. Wahner, PhD, assistant research faculty, department of epidemiology, University of California, Los Angeles.

Research Reveals Better Osteoarthritis Treatment

When 178 individuals with moderate-to-severe osteoarthritis of the knee were treated with physical therapy and medical therapy, including anti-inflammatory drugs... or with arthroscopic surgery (in which lens-equipped instruments are used to repair knee joint problems), the surgery provided no additional benefit (related to joint pain, stiffness and function) over medical treatment in the next two years.

If you have osteoarthritis in a knee: Ask your doctor whether physical therapy, along with medications (such as nonsteroidal anti-inflammatory drugs), if necessary, would be helpful for you.

Brian Feagan, MD, professor of medicine, epidemiology and biostatistics, Robarts Research Institute, University of Western Ontario, London, Ontario.

Best Shoes for Arthritis

In one study of 16 adults who have knee osteoarthritis, clogs and foot-stabilizing shoes (athletic shoes) put significantly more stress on the knees than flat walking shoes, flip-flops and walking barefoot.

Theory: Shoes that promote a natural foot motion may allow for a better transfer of the body's weight as the foot hits the ground.

If you have knee arthritis: Speak to your doctor about appropriate footwear.

Najia Shakoor, MD, associate professor of internal medicine, section of rheumatology, Rush Medical College, Chicago.

New Lyme Prevention?

There isn't a vaccine against Lyme disease, but in a recent study, a single injection of a sustained-release antibiotic was 100% effective at preventing Lyme disease in mice. More research is needed.

Journal of Medical Microbiology, on the Internet at *http://jmm.sgmjournals.org*.

A New Bone-Builder

Aspirin can help build bone. Low doses of aspirin—81 milligrams per day—increase production of bone-forming cells. More study is needed before aspirin can be recommended as an osteoporosis preventive.

Songtao Shi, DDS, PhD, associate professor, University of Southern California School of Dentistry, Los Angeles, and leader of an animal study reported in *PLoS One 2008*.

Take the Frailty Test

Frailty—weight loss, weakness, exhaustion and a slowed walking speed—increases your risk for a fall, a leading cause of death among adults over age 65. We all lose muscle mass as we age, but frailty is not normal.

What to do: Test the strength of your thighs. Thigh strength is a predictor of frailty.

To test your thighs: Sit down and fold your arms across your chest. While having someone time you, stand up and sit down five times, as rapidly as possible. If five chair-squats take 14 seconds or more, your thighs are weak. Ask your doctor for advice on thigh-strengthening exercises.

Robert N. Butler, MD, president and CEO of the New York City–located International Longevity Center and a former medical editor-in-chief of the journal *Geriatrics*. He's also the author of many books, including the Pulitzer Prize–winning *Why Survive? Being Old in America* (Johns Hopkins University Press).

You Can Have Cataracts And Not Even Know It: Check Out the Signs

David F. Chang, MD, clinical professor of ophthalmology at the University of California in San Francisco. Dr. Chang codiscovered intraoperative floppy iris syndrome (IFIS), an iris problem that can complicate cataract surgery. He serves as chair of the Cataract Clinical Committee of the American Society of Cataract and Refractive Surgery and is coauthor of *Cataracts: A Patient's Guide to Treatment* (Addicus).

Cataracts can develop so slowly in some people that they do not even realize they have an eye problem. In the early stages, just a small portion of the eye's lens may become cloudy. Only when the cloudiness of the eye's lens increases over time—sometimes over a period of years—does the person's vision worsen.

Even though cataracts are quite common—about half of people over age 65 have some signs of the condition—few people are aware that many common vision problems actually can be the result of cataracts.

Here, an internationally recognized cataract surgeon and researcher, David F. Chang, MD, discusses diagnosis and the latest in treatment options…

SYMPTOMS THAT CAN BE MISSED

If your eyesight starts to appear cloudy or blurred, you might suspect a cataract—these are among the most widely recognized symptoms. But there are many other symptoms that are not nearly as well-known and that could prevent people from getting proper eye care. Symptoms can vary greatly, depending on the location, severity and type of cataract. Cataracts may be age-related, due to an eye injury or congenital (present at birth or appearing in childhood). *Questions to ask yourself…*

•**Do colors appear faded or washed out?**

•**Do I have trouble seeing distant objects,** such as highway signs, while wearing eyeglasses?

•**Do I need more light than I used to for close work,** such as reading small print and sewing? Do my eyes tire more easily when I'm engaged in these activities?

•**Does glare make it much harder for me to drive at night** or see well in bright sunlight?

•**Do I ever experience "ghost images,"** such as seeing multiple moons at night?

If you answered "yes" to several of these questions, consult an ophthalmologist (a physician who specializes in medical and surgical eye care) or an optometrist (a nonphysician who can test for common eye problems, such as nearsightedness and cataracts, but does not perform surgery).

A doctor can identify a cataract by dilating a patient's pupil and examining the eye with a table-mounted microscope called a slit lamp.

Important: Even if you do not experience any of the symptoms described just above, get your eyes checked regularly after age 40 to help identify any treatable eye problems, such as glaucoma, a vision-robbing eye disease marked by increased pressure inside of the eyeball.

ARE YOU AT INCREASED RISK?

Age is a primary risk factor for cataracts. After age 50, cataracts are the most common cause of decreased vision. *Other risk factors...*

• **Family history.** In some families, cataracts tend to occur at an earlier age. If a family member, such as a parent or a sibling, developed cataracts before age 60, you also may be at increased risk of developing cataracts at around the same age.

• **Medical conditions.** Diabetes increases the risk for cataracts three- to fourfold. This is because elevated blood sugar levels can cause changes in the lens that, in turn, can lead to cataracts.

Self-defense: Work with your doctor to manage your blood sugar levels.

• **Nearsightedness.** For reasons that are not yet understood, severely nearsighted people often develop cataracts at an earlier age.

• **Steroid use.** Long-term (one year or more) oral steroid use can increase risk for cataracts. Long-term use of inhaled steroids, taken at high doses, also may increase risk.

• **Eye diseases.** Some eye diseases, such as chronic eye inflammation (*uveitis*), increase risk for cataracts. Prior eye surgery—for retinal problems, for example—also raises risk.

• **Eye injuries.** Cataracts may develop, sometimes years later, as a result of eye injuries, such as those that can occur when being struck by a blunt object (like a ball).

Self-defense: Don polycarbonate safety goggles (available at sporting-goods stores) when playing sports such as squash and racketball.

• **Sun exposure.** The sun's ultraviolet rays also can increase cataract risk. Wear a broad-brimmed hat and UV-blocking sunglasses.

DO YOU NEED SURGERY?

If cataracts interfere with the ability to read, drive, work or enjoy a hobby, you may need surgery.

Most ophthalmologists in the US perform "small-incision" surgery, a 20- to 30-minute outpatient procedure in which the surgeon uses an ultrathin blade to make an incision of about one-eighth inch in the cornea. The cataract is removed with ultrasound wave technology, vibrating at 40,000 times per second, to break up the cloudy lens into smaller fragments.

After these pieces of the lens are gently suctioned out, an artificial lens, called an intraocular lens, is permanently implanted in place of the natural lens. Once removed, cataracts will never recur, and the artificial lens will last for the patient's lifetime.

Small-incision surgery can be performed using topical anesthesia (eyedrops) and usually requires no sutures. (A tiny flap is created that closes on its own.) The success rate of cataract surgery in otherwise healthy eyes approaches 98%. Severe complications, such as infection or bleeding in the eye, are rare.

Latest development: New artificial lens implants that can reduce a patient's dependence on eyeglasses are now available. These multifocal lenses may provide focus for both near and far distances, allowing many patients to read without eyeglasses.

Because multifocal lenses are considered a convenience—rather than a medical necessity—patients must pay an additional out-of-pocket cost ($2,000 to $3,000 per lens*) under Medicare and private insurance plans.

Important new finding: Recent research has indicated that use of drugs called alpha-blockers, such as *tamsulosin* (Flomax) taken for an enlarged prostate, can interfere with the necessary dilation of the pupil during surgery. Known as *intraoperative floppy iris syndrome*, this condition can make the cataract surgery more difficult for your surgeon.

If you are planning to have cataract surgery, tell your doctor if you are taking an alpha-blocker, such as tamsulosin. Patients who have cataracts or symptoms of poor vision should have an eye exam before starting to take an alpha-blocker.

*Prices subject to change.

Quiet the Ringing in Your Ears

Aaron G. Benson, MD, clinical adjunct professor, division of otology/neurotology (ear health), department of otolaryngology–head and neck surgery, at the University of Michigan Health System in Ann Arbor. Also in private practice in Maumee, Ohio, he specializes in hearing disorders, *www.toledoent.com.*

Perhaps you hear a high-pitched ringing ...perhaps a buzzing, chirping, whistling or whirring. Nobody else can hear it—but the quieter it gets around you, the worse the noise in your head.

Tinnitus most often develops when a person has hearing loss caused by nerve damage from prolonged or extreme exposure to loud noise. It also can be a side effect of antibiotics, aspirin, diuretics and some cancer drugs. Tinnitus usually appears after age 50 but is now increasingly common in younger people due to high-volume use of personal music players (iPod, Walkman). It can occur in pregnancy—and may or may not go away after delivery.

Tinnitus usually is not a serious health problem, but it should be evaluated—so consult an otolaryngologist.

Referrals: American Tinnitus Association, (800-634-8978, *www.ata.org*).

There is no cure, but various strategies can ease symptoms and help you cope...

•**Cut caffeine and salt.** Caffeine (in coffee, tea, cola and chocolate) constricts blood flow to the ear...and salt can raise blood pressure, aggravating tinnitus.

•**Keep ears clean.** Excessive earwax can muffle outside noises and amplify ringing.

Home remedy: Mix in hydrogen peroxide with an equal amount of water, and place two drops in each ear weekly. Or see your doctor to have your ears irrigated.

•**Reduce stress.** Muscle relaxation, meditation, biofeedback, exercise and other stress-reducing techniques may alleviate symptoms.

•**Fill the room with white noise.** A constant low-level background sound masks the inner ringing. In a quiet room and at bedtime, turn on a fan or tabletop fountain, or use a white-noise machine (about $30 to $60* at home-products stores).

•**Wear a tinnitus masker.** This miniature white-noise device resembles a hearing aid and fits behind or in the ear.

Cost: About $2,000.

To obtain one, ask your doctor for a referral to an audiologist.

•**Try a hearing aid.** This relieves tinnitus for about half of people with significant hearing loss. It amplifies outside sounds, which obscures inner sounds.

•**Retrain your brain.** A new treatment provided by trained audiologists, tinnitus retraining therapy (TRT) may help up to 80% of patients. Sometimes improvement is noticed after just a few sessions. Typically, you attend weekly or monthly hour-long sessions during which you wear a special hearing aid programmed with a facsimile of your particular tinnitus sound. You are shown how to train your brain to be less sensitive to the ringing.

Rarely, tinnitus may be caused by a tumor. Call your doctor without delay if your tinnitus sounds like a pulsing or whooshing...is heard on only one side of your head...or is accompanied by dizziness or a sudden decrease in ability to discriminate between similar words, such as cat and hat.

*Prices subject to change.

No-Surgery Nose Job— In Just Minutes

Nelson Lee Novick, MD, clinical professor of dermatology at Mount Sinai School of Medicine and a cosmetic dermatologist in private practice, both in New York City. He is author of *Super Skin* (iUniverse). A pioneer in nonsurgical cosmetic procedures, he has gotten numerous awards, including the American Academy of Dermatology's Leadership Circle Award. His online site is *www. youngerlookingwithoutsurgery.com.*

Using new, safe and practically painless nonsurgical techniques, a dermatologist now can reshape the nose in less than 10 minutes, giving an immediate result that lasts about a year or longer.

Average cost: $750 to $1,500.*

Options…

•**Smooth a bump or straighten a bend.** Radiesse, a synthetic gel with tiny bone-like calcium-based spheres, is injected beneath the skin where desired—for instance, above or below a bump on the bridge or along the side of the nose. Then it is quickly molded like clay to the desired shape and fully retains its shape within about a day. For more precise shaping, the doctor also might inject Juvéderm or Restylane, fillers made of synthetic hyaluronic acid. (In the body, one function of *natural hyaluronic* acid is to provide volume to the skin.)

•**Lift up a long, drooping tip.** Botox (a purified form of a protein produced by the *Clostridium botulinum* bacterium) is injected into the crevices on each side and at the base of the nose, weakening the muscles that pull the nose tip downward and permitting muscles higher up on the nose to draw the tip upward. Next, Radiesse is injected at the base of the nose to buttress the tip, providing longer-lasting effects than from Botox alone.

With either procedure: Prior to treatment, the area is injected with a local anesthetic plus *epinephrine* (a blood vessel constrictor).

Recovery: There are no restrictions on activities. You may have minor swelling and bruising for a few days. Risk for infection is very slight. Generally, results last for 12 to 18 months with Radiesse…eight to 12 months with Juvéderm and Restylane…and three to six months with Botox. After that, touch-ups may be desirable.

*Prices subject to change.

Depression Treatment Boosts Longevity

In a study of 1,226 people, those with clinical depression whose treatment involved a depression care manager (a nurse, social worker or psychologist who oversees psychotherapy and/or antidepressant use) were 45% less likely to die over a five-year period than those who received primary-care treatment without this additional resource.

If you've been diagnosed with clinical depression: Ask your doctor about all your treatment options.

Joseph J. Gallo, MD, MPH, an associate professor of family medicine and community health, University of Pennsylvania, Philadelphia.

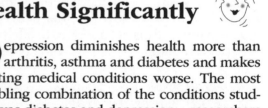

Depression Hurts Health Significantly

Depression diminishes health more than arthritis, asthma and diabetes and makes existing medical conditions worse. The most disabling combination of the conditions studied was diabetes and depression—researchers estimate that people living with both these conditions are at only 60% of full health.

Self-defense: Treat your depression as you would any other chronic illness.

Somnath Chatterji, MD, team leader, multi-country studies, measurement and health information systems, World Health Organization, Geneva, Switzerland, and leader of a study of 245,000 people in 60 countries, published in *The Lancet.*

2

The Best Medical Care

Surprising Ways You Can Hurt Your Health

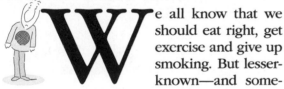e all know that we should eat right, get exercise and give up smoking. But lesser-known—and sometimes seemingly insignificant—decisions also can affect our health and longevity. *Some of the most important—and often overlooked—health issues include...*

NOT HAVING A PRIMARY DOCTOR

Millions of Americans don't have a primary-care physician, the gatekeeper to their overall care. Get one now. A primary-care doctor reviews all your records at every visit...recommends screening tests...and coordinates care when you're seeing more than one doctor.

Studies have consistently shown that adults who have a primary-care physician have lower health-care costs and are less likely to die than those who use a specialist. The primary-care

doctor can help you navigate the confusing health-care system. One health plan found that 41% of all referrals to specialists were made by the patients themselves, and 60% of those self-referrals were to the wrong specialists.

POOR CHECKUP PREPARATION

The average office visit is about 17 minutes, and one study found that doctors usually interrupt patients within the first 23 seconds.

Much of what doctors learn about a patient's health comes from listening to the patient, so you must take responsibility. Before walking into a doctor's office, decide what you want to talk about. Restrict your topics to no more than four items—that's about all that can be adequately covered in the time period—and start with the most important one. *For each item, tell the doctor about the Four Ws...*

Davis Liu, MD, a board-certified family physician with the Permanente Medical Group in northern California. He has a degree from Wharton School of Business at University of Pennsylvania, Philadelphia, and is an expert in evaluating health-care policy. He is author of *Stay Healthy, Live Longer, Spend Wisely* (Stetho).

• **When the problem began, when it occurs and when it last occurred.**

• **What activities, treatments or behaviors seem to make the problem better or worse…** what the problem feels like (sharp pain, comes and goes, etc.)…and what other problems and symptoms seem to be associated with it.

• **Where in the body the problem began** and whether it moves to different locations in the body.

• **Why you're seeing the doctor.** You probably want to know if the problem is serious or if you need to change your behavior or medications. Maybe the problem is interfering with your lifestyle or family members are worried about you. This is important information.

INATTENTION

A study at the Mayo Clinic found that patients remember less than half of what physicians tell them.

The solution: Take notes during office visits, or ask a friend or family member to come along and write notes for you. To remember the most important details, use the acronym DATE. Be sure that you fully understand the Diagnosis…whether you need any Additional tests or procedures…what the Treatment plan is…and when you need to return for further Evaluation.

UNNECESSARY DRUGS

Doctors are just as influenced by drug-company marketing as anyone. They are likely to prescribe a newer—and higher-priced—drug when an older medication would work just as well. They also tend to prescribe drugs when no medication is required.

Example: In 2000, Merck, the big pharmaceutical company, spent millions promoting Vioxx, a new anti-inflammatory drug that was less likely to cause stomach bleeding and ulcers than older drugs. It was good for a select group of patients, but millions of Americans without gastrointestinal risk factors also were given Vioxx—which was found to increase the risk for heart attack.

Before accepting any prescription, ask your doctor if the medication is really necessary…if the medication has been proved effective for your condition…and if there are less expensive alternatives that work just as well.

NOT GETTING VACCINATIONS

Few adults receive all of the recommended immunizations. For example, barely two-thirds of Americans 65 years and beyond are vaccinated for the flu, even though 36,000 people (90% of whom are 65 and older) in the US die annually from flu-related complications. *In addition to an annual flu shot, ask your doctor about the following vaccines…*

• **Tetanus** protects against a bacterium found in soil and animal feces that is fatal in more than 10% of cases. A booster dosage is given once every 10 years (assuming adequate childhood immunization).

• **Meningococcal,** given once by injection, prevents meningitis, a serious brain inflammation. The vaccine is recommended for those living in group settings, such as dormitories and nursing homes, as well as for international travelers.

• **Pneumococcal,** a one-time vaccine usually given at age 65, protects against a bacterium that causes pneumonia, blood infections and many other diseases.

For more information about vaccines, go to *www.cdc.gov/vaccines* or call 800-232-4636.

The Perfect Doctor's Appointment

Jessie Gruman, PhD, founder and president of the Center for Advancing Health, *www.cfah.org*, an independent, nonpartisan Washington, DC–located policy institute dedicated to improving the quality of health care. She is the author of *AfterShock: What to Do When the Doctor Gives You—or Someone You Love—a Devastating Diagnosis* (Walker).

W e all know that our overall health is greatly affected by how well we take care of ourselves and the effectiveness of any medical treatments we receive. What comes as a big surprise to most people is the degree to which our doctor's appointments impact our health.

Little-known fact: Research indicates that people who achieve the best results for common medical problems—such as high blood pressure, diabetes or asthma—report having good communication with their doctors during appointments.

To get the best possible care…

Step 1: **Schedule according to the urgency of your problem.** If you think you have a life-threatening emergency, call 911. If you think you have an urgent problem (for example, a sudden severe rash or fever of 102°F or above), call your doctor and express this urgency to the receptionist. Don't hint—be direct. Say, "I have had these symptoms with this severity and this frequency over this amount of time, and I am quite concerned."

If you feel that the receptionist doesn't understand your urgency, ask to speak with a nurse, who is much better trained to evaluate symptoms.

Your goal: To get the right care from the right professional at the right time.

Self-defense: If it is not an emergency, try to schedule one of the first appointments of the day—as the day gets later, your doctor's schedule may fall behind. Ask the receptionist which days are the busiest—usually it is best to avoid Fridays and Mondays, when many people try to get in just before or after the weekend. You also can ask whether another doctor or a nurse practitioner in the practice could see you sooner.

Step 2: **Practice your "elevator speech."** Research shows that only 2% of patients get to finish their opening comments at an appointment before the doctor interrupts.

Self-defense: Imagine that you are on an elevator and must give all your relevant information in the 20 to 30 seconds it takes to arrive at your destination. A good summary of your current health situation can help the doctor focus in more quickly. *Your elevator speech should include…*

• **What your symptoms are,** when they began and their frequency and severity.

• **What happened near the time the symptoms began.**

Examples: "I was shoveling snow all morning" or "I just started taking this new dietary supplement."

• **What you have done so far to manage the symptoms** on your own.

Step 3: **Know what to bring.** Review what you don't understand regarding your condition, and assemble information that will help your doctor to assess your health and recommend treatment.

Self-defense: Bring a list of all the questions you want to ask, including any questions about your fears—for example, worries that a symptom might mean cancer. In addition, bring a list of all the medications, vitamins and supplements that you take.

Also helpful: A great deal of information could be communicated during a doctor appointment—in both directions—so it's a good idea to take notes or even to tape-record your discussion with a handheld recorder (be sure to ask the doctor first).

Also recommended: Bring someone with you who can take notes and help you reflect on the visit, even if it's only a routine visit.

Step 4: **Have something to occupy your time in the waiting room.** Delays are sometimes unavoidable—your doctor may be called away for an emergency or may need to spend more time than expected with another patient. If a delay in the waiting room leaves you feeling stressed or annoyed, these emotions could make your interaction with the doctor tense and unpleasant once you are called into the examining room.

Self-defense: Bring a book, a pen and paper to catch up on correspondence or even a laptop computer to read your e-mail.

Step 5: **Obtain the "missing" information on medication.** When prescribing medication, many doctors don't go into detail about drug side effects. That's often because they suspect that if patients worry about possible adverse effects, they may be more likely to experience them. But many patients cope better when they know what to expect.

Self-defense: Tell your doctor that you don't expect any side effects, but you want to be prepared just in case. Ask him/her to explain the common side effects and what to do if you experience any of them.

Step 6: Set general expectations. When seeing your doctor, your goal is to establish expectations that will help you to manage your treatment regimen.

Self-defense: Ask "when" questions to get the details you require. For example, "When should I start to feel better?…When can I get back to my normal routine?…When will it be safe to stop taking the medication?…When should I expect to get results of this blood work?…When should I return for a follow-up visit?"

Step 7: Confirm what you have learned. To ensure that you understand everything that occurred during your visit, restate to your doctor what you have learned.

Self-defense: Say something like, "Just to make sure I understand, you are saying that what is wrong with me is probably this…the expected course is this…I'm supposed to do this…and I should call or come back if this happens."

Step 8: Obtain contact information for any follow-up questions. You may have questions after-hours or need an efficient way to communicate later with your doctor about symptoms or drug side effects.

Self-defense: Before leaving the office, confirm all contact information with the receptionist—the emergency contact number, office hours, e-mail protocol (if there is one) and fax number.

Beware: Faxes are rarely confidential.

Step 9: Get copies of your test results. The best way to ensure that the results of diagnostic and screening tests get to your primary care provider or a specialist is to hand-deliver them.

Self-defense: Ask your doctor's office for a copy of your test reports. (You may have to pay for photocopying.) Keep these records in a file at home, and bring the most recent, relevant results whenever you have a medical appointment.

Appointment Secret

To get in to see your doctor quickly, phone the office as soon as it opens to try to get the appointment of someone who canceled—people often leave cancellation messages late at night or very early in the morning.

Lorraine Lorenc, executive director for her husband, Z. Paul Lorenc, MD, a plastic surgeon based in New York City.

Is Your Doctor "Ageist"?

No matter what your age, your physician should take seriously any condition that would be considered abnormal in a younger person. To do otherwise is "ageist." A careful history and physical exam can diagnose 90% of all diseases without costly medical tests. For a person age 65 or over, a good history takes about an hour.

Problem: Doctors rarely spend that much time with a patient because of reimbursement issues—one 60-minute session pays no more than one 30-minute session.

Solution: Ask your doctor to do a thorough history over two sessions rather than one. The second can usually be billed to insurance as a follow-up visit.

Robert N. Butler, MD, president and CEO of the New York City–located International Longevity Center and a former medical editor-in-chief of the journal Geriatrics. Dr. Butler introduced the concept of "Ageism" in 1968. He's also the author of many books, including the Pulitzer Prize–winning Why Survive? Being Old in America (Johns Hopkins University Press).

If You're Having Blood Taken…

Don't clench your fist while having blood drawn. Clenching might trigger excess release of potassium from skeletal muscles, which may prompt your doctor to prescribe unnecessary tests or treatments. High serum potassium is a sign of kidney disease and of heart problems. Also, high potassium may be a side effect of medication—so a doctor may stop a medicine or reduce the dosage.

Better: Close your hand lightly when the needle is being inserted—then open up your hand as blood is being drawn.

Vanessa R. Thurlow and Ian R. Bailey, Fellows of the Royal College of Pathologists, department of chemical pathology, Princess Royal University Hospital, Farnborough, Kent, United Kingdom, and coauthors of a study published in *Annals of Clinical Biochemistry*.

If You Dread Going To the Dentist...

Robert J. Genco, DDS, PhD, a distinguished professor in the department of oral biology, School of Dental Medicine, and in the department of microbiology, School of Medicine and Biomedical Sciences at the State University of New York at Buffalo. He is also a professor in the department of immunology at the Roswell Park Cancer Institute and a recipient of the American Dental Association's Gold Medal for Excellence in Research.

S tudies show that up to 20% of Americans have "dental anxiety"—many to the point of avoidance.

To overcome this problem, find a dentist who makes you feel comfortable. *Then...*

•**Don't delay seeing your dentist for tooth or gum problems.** Generally, earlier diagnosis means less troublesome and more successful treatment.

•**Schedule appointments for times when you won't be harried or rushed.**

•**Admit that you are anxious.** In a study conducted by researchers at the University of Liverpool School of Dentistry, highly anxious patients who told their dentists about their fears at the beginning of the appointment experienced significantly less anxiety while getting treated than patients who kept mum.

•**If you have sensitive teeth, request a topical numbing agent,** such as Oraqix, before cleanings or other procedures.

•**Ask about using a throat-numbing spray** if a strong gag reflex makes getting dental impressions or X-rays difficult.

•**Agree on a hand signal** that you can use to alert the dentist when you need to take a break.

•**Consider conscious sedation.** If you are extremely anxious or require extensive work, consult with a dentist specializing in "relaxation" dentistry. He/she might prescribe a tranquilizer, such as *diazepam* (Valium), and/or a sedative, such as *triazolam* (Halcion), to be taken prior to (and/or during) your visit.

Important: Many states require dentists to meet certain requirements, including at least 18 hours of training, before using conscious sedation in their practices.

Follow Prescription Drug Instructions...or Else!

Ruth Murphey Parker, MD, professor of medicine, Emory University School of Medicine in Atlanta, lead study author.

M illions of people fail to follow the instructions for their prescription medications, either taking their medicine incorrectly or not taking it at all.

Study findings...

•**Only 51% of patients take their blood pressure medication properly,** even though high blood pressure triples heart attack risk.

•**Among people blind in one eye because of glaucoma,** only 58% were properly taking their medication to protect their other eye.

•**Among all kidney transplant recipients,** 18% weren't following medication instructions to prevent rejection of the kidney.

In addition to the human cost of the maladies that are unnecessarily incurred...

•**Financial cost for an individual can be $2,000 per year** in doctor visits alone.

•**Up to 40% of nursing home admissions** may result from failing to follow medication instructions.

• **The nation may lose $177 billion per year** in avoidable medical expenses and lost productivity.

Reasons for errors in taking medicines…

• **Instructions often are provided in confusing places** in complex packaging.

• **The wording of instructions frequently is ambiguous.**

Example: "Take two tablets twice a day" may be read to mean to take either two or four tablets daily.

• **Poor eyesight** prevents many people from clearly reading small-type instructions.

Self-defense: When prescribed a new drug, ask your doctor and pharmacist questions until you fully understand what it is supposed to do and how and when you are supposed to take it. Follow those instructions until your doctor changes them.

Stop Drug Errors

To avoid prescription drug errors, have your doctor give you a copy of your prescription so you can check what the pharmacist gives to you…go to only one pharmacist, who will then know your history and be familiar with your needs…double-check all instructions with your pharmacist…check each refill to be sure it is the correct drug at the right dosage… and ask your doctor to list generic equivalent medicines, so if one isn't available or covered by your medical plan, you know that you can take another.

Ken Farbstein, medication safety consultant, Patient AdvoCare, Needham, Massachusetts, *www.patientsafety blog.com.*

Generic Drug Caution

Do not assume a generic drug works just like a brand name. The Food and Drug Administration (FDA) requires that all generic drugs provide labels identical to the labels of their corresponding brand-name drugs—but this can lead to errors.

Example: There is evidence that the generic version of the antidepressant Wellbutrin XL is more quickly absorbed than the original.

Self-defense: If you switch to any generic from any brand-name drug and you notice a difference, let your doctor know immediately.

Tod Cooperman, MD, president, ConsumerLab.com, White Plains, New York.

Why the Latest Drugs Can Be Dangerous

Jan Garavaglia, MD, chief medical examiner for the District Nine Medical Examiner's Office in Orlando, Florida. Dr. Garavaglia is host of Discovery Health channel's top-rated series *Dr. G: Medical Examiner* and is author of *How Not to Die: Surprising Lessons on Living Longer, Safer, and Healthier from America's Favorite Medical Examiner* (Crown, *www.hownottodie.com*).

The FDA has taken about a dozen drugs off the market in just the last 10 years. Medications that appear to be safe during the approval process can later turn out to have dangerous effects.

Example: The antibiotic *gatifloxacin* (Tequin), originally approved for respiratory infections, was later found to trigger dangerous changes in blood sugar levels, resulting in the deaths of some patients. The deaths were especially tragic because most patients would've done as well with older—and safer—drugs.

Most new drugs are tested on only a few thousand patients at most. If a drug causes a deadly reaction in, say, one in 20,000 patients, it might be years before the dangers become apparent.

Avoid any drug until it has been on the market for at least two years. That's long enough for serious problems to be revealed. (Of course, some patients benefit greatly from new, breakthrough drugs, but for most conditions, older drugs with proven safety profiles are equally effective.)

The Wrong Antibiotic Can Be Deadly: Be Sure You Get the Right One

B. Joseph Guglielmo, PharmD, professor and chair of the department of clinical pharmacy at the University of California, San Francisco (UCSF), and founder of the Antimicrobial Management Program at UCSF Medical Center. He is a coauthor of *Applied Therapeutics: The Clinical Use of Drugs* (Lippincott Williams & Wilkins).

Antibiotic medications are among the most frequently prescribed drugs in the US today.

What most people don't realize: Because drug companies generally do not make much profit from developing oral antibiotics, there are few new options available. That's why it's especially important that the available drugs be used correctly. Taking the wrong antibiotic can allow infections to linger—and sometimes even become life-threatening. *What you need to know...*

WHEN TO TAKE AN ANTIBIOTIC

The immune system in healthy adults is very effective at eliminating the minor infections—even ones caused by bacteria. Antibiotics are needed only when an infection overwhelms the immune system's ability to stop it or when an infection is too dangerous (or too painful) to be allowed to clear up on its own.

Examples: A bacterial infection of the lungs can be fatal, so it is almost always treated with antibiotics. Bacterial ear infections in general will go away without medical treatment, but antibiotics may decrease the duration of symptoms.

A good rule of thumb: Most infections of the ears, sinuses and respiratory tract are viral and don't require antibiotics.

How to tell: Viral infections of the respiratory tract typically start to improve in five to seven days. If you get worse after that time, there's a good chance that the infection is bacterial and may require antibiotics.

SHOULD YOU GET A CULTURE?

Doctors usually can guess which organism is causing an infection—and choose the right antibiotic—just by reviewing a patient's description of his/her symptoms.

However, cultures (taken from the throat, for example) should be performed when it's unclear what's causing an infection—or when previous antibiotics weren't effective. In otherwise healthy adults, antibiotics start to ease symptoms of an infection within 24 hours. Symptoms that don't improve within two days may indicate that the initial diagnosis or antibiotic choice was incorrect.

BEWARE OF SIDE EFFECTS

Nearly every antibiotic may cause diarrhea, intestinal cramps or yeast infections in the mouth or vagina. That's because the drugs not only kill harmful microbes, but also reduce the numbers of "good" bacteria which keep harmful bacteria and fungi in check.

Besides the general side effects, each antibiotic also has other risks. *For example...*

•*Amoxicillin* plus *clavulanate* (Augmentin), commonly used for certain respiratory tract infections, may cause skin rashes and hives.

•*Doxycycline* (Doryx), for chronic eye infections and Lyme disease, increases sensitivity to sunlight.

•*Ciprofloxacin* (Cipro), for urinary tract infections, can trigger headache, abdominal pain and vomiting.

WHAT TO TAKE FOR COMMON INFECTIONS

Most effective antibiotics for common medical conditions...

•**Bacterial pneumonia.** Most times this is caused by the organism called *Streptococcus pneumoniae*, but some patients are infected with multiple and/or "resistant" organisms.

Main treatment: Hospitalized patients who have community-acquired pneumonia usually are prescribed an intravenous antibiotic, such as *ceftriaxone* (Rocephin) with *azithromycin* (Zithromax), or a "respiratory" *fluoroquinolone*, such as *levofloxacin* (Levaquin).

•**Ear infections.** Even doctors have difficulty differentiating viral from bacterial ear infections. Antibiotics often are used "just in case." If the infection is bacterial, the symptoms will start to abate within 24 hours of starting an antibiotic.

Main treatment: Amoxicillin for seven to 10 days. Patients who have a history of antibiotic use for ear infections may have resistant organisms and will probably be given a broad-spectrum *cephalosporin* medication, such as *cefdinir* (Omnicef). Similarly, patients who are allergic to amoxicillin may be given a cephalosporin antibiotic if the allergy is mild—or a fluoroquinolone, such as levofloxacin, if the allergy is severe.

•**Sinus infections.** Recent research done at the Cochrane Collaboration, which analyzes health-care practices and research evidence, found that about 80% of patients with sinus infections recover within two weeks *without* antibiotics.

However, a viral sinus infection can sometimes progress into a more serious, secondary bacterial infection. Patients having sinus pain that lasts for more than a week to 10 days—or who have a period of recovery followed by a painful relapse—probably need antibiotics.

Main treatment: The same as that used for ear infections.

•**Skin infections** are usually from *Staphylococcus aureus* or *Streptococcus pyogenes*, both common bacteria that can get into your skin through a cut or scrape.

Recent danger: A virulent, drug-resistant form of staph, known as *methicillin-resistant Staphylococcus aureus* (MRSA), could trigger cellulitis, a life-threatening infection even in healthy adults.

What to look for: Although most localized skin infections will clear up on their own, an area of skin that is red and feels warm and tender and might spread rapidly could be cellulitis. In severe cases, the center area will turn black as the tissue degenerates. Treatment of MRSA usually requires consultation with an infectious-disease specialist.

•**Urinary tract infections** (or UTIs) usually occur when fecal bacteria enter the urethra. Women have UTIs more often than men because of the close proximity of the urethra to the anus.

Mild UTIs often will clear up on their own. In studies, about two-thirds of women who take a placebo will recover within seven to 10 days, compared with 80% to 85% of those taking antibiotics. However, antibiotics are usually recommended both for symptom relief and to prevent a UTI from progressing to *pyelonephritis*, a dangerous kidney infection.

Main treatment: *Trimethoprim* plus *sulfamethoxazole* (Septra or Bactrim), a combination treatment usually taken for three days.

Important: If you get two or more UTIs a year, you may have resistant organisms. Your doctor may perform a urine culture to identify the organism, which will determine the appropriate antibiotic.

Caution: Don't combine ciprofloxacin with antacids or iron supplements—both can interfere with the absorption of this antibiotic.

Do You Really Need Antibiotics?

David H. Newman, MD, emergency physician and clinical professor of medicine at St. Luke's-Roosevelt Hospital and director of a clinical research program at Columbia University, both in New York City. He is author of *Hippocrates' Shadow: Secrets from the House of Medicine* (Scribner).

M ost infections clear up without treatment. It's estimated that at least 80% of all outpatient antibiotic prescriptions don't help.

Reason: Most infections are caused by viruses, not by bacteria—and antibiotics have no effect on viruses. The vast majority of upper respiratory infections, for example, are viral. Yet half of patients who see a doctor with one of these infections are given antibiotics.

Even when patients do have a bacterial infection, such as bronchitis, antibiotics may not be necessary. Infections will often clear up on their own.

Antibiotics are not harmless. They kill beneficial organisms in the body that help curtail harmful microbes. Also, the unnecessary use of antibiotics may be responsible for an estimated 24,000 life-threatening allergic reactions annually.

Self-defense: If you have an infection, ask your doctor if it has to be treated. Take antibiotics only if an untreated infection—something such as bacterial pneumonia or a wound with spreading redness—is likely to cause serious complications.

What to Do If You Miss a Dose Of Antibiotics

Stuart Levy, MD, professor of medicine, molecular biology and microbiology, Tufts University School of Medicine, Boston, and the founder/director, Center for Adaptive Genetics and Drug Resistance at Tufts. He is president of the Alliance for the Prudent Use of Antibiotics, *www.tufts.edu/med/apua.*

Missing one dose of an antibiotic is unlikely to be harmful. However, antibiotics work best when the amount in the body is consistent. If you miss a dose, try to make it up—but never take two doses at once. When in doubt, consult your physician or pharmacist.

One-a-day antibiotics: Take your missed dose as soon as possible. If you are less than 12 hours away from the next regularly scheduled dose, skip the one you missed. You can take the missed dose if it will be at least 12 hours before the next dose.

Two-a-day/three-a-day antibiotics: Take the missed dose as soon as you can, and then take other doses scheduled for that day at a slightly later time. Resume your regular dosing schedule the next day.

Alert! Don't Take Your Meds with These Popular Drinks

Beverly J. McCabe-Sellers, PhD, RD, who was a professor of dietetics and nutrition at the University of Arkansas for Medical Sciences in Little Rock for more than 20 years. She continues as an adjunct professor of nutrition at the university's School of Public Health and is a coeditor of the *Handbook of Food-Drug Interactions* (CRC).

If you take any variety of prescription or an over-the-counter (OTC) medication, you may be unwittingly reducing its benefits and/or increasing its risks by drinking certain beverages when you swallow the drug. The potentially harmful interactions also may occur if you drink the beverage hours before or after taking the medication.

For example…

DANGERS OF GRAPEFRUIT JUICE

Grapefruit juice has long been known to interfere with the effectiveness of certain medications, but not all doctors warn their patients about these potential dangers.*

Grapefruit juice contains compounds that inhibit an important enzyme called *CYP3A4,* which is found in the liver and intestines. CYP3A4 is one of several enzymes that help metabolize up to 70% of all medications.

Grapefruit juice that is made from concentrate generally contains the entire fruit, including the rind—this is the primary source of the compound that affects medicine metabolism. Grapefruit juice that is not made from concentrate contains less of this compound. However, to stay safe, it's better to avoid grapefruit juice (and grapefruit itself) altogether if you take certain medications.

Among the medicines that can interact with grapefruit juice…

• **The anti-arrhythmic medications,** such as *amiodarone* (Cordarone), *quinidine* (Quinidex) and *disopyramide* (Norpace), which are taken for abnormal heart rhythms.

*As a general guideline, it is best not to drink any juice at the same time that you take medication. Use water to swallow pills.

Risks: Heart arrhythmias as well as thyroid, pulmonary or liver damage.

•**Blood pressure–lowering calcium channel blockers,** such as *felodipine* (Plendil), *nifedipine* (Procardia) and *verapamil* (Calan).

Risks: A precipitous drop in blood pressure, as well as flushing, swelling of the extremities, headaches, irregular heartbeat and, in rare cases, heart attack.

•**Cholesterol-lowering medications,** such as *atorvastatin* (Lipitor), *lovastatin* (Mevacor) and *simvastatin* (Zocor).

Risks: Headache, stomach upset, liver inflammation and muscle pain or weakness.

•**Sedatives** such as *diazepam* (Valium) and *triazolam* (Halcion).

Risks: Dizziness, confusion and drowsiness.

DANGERS OF APPLE JUICE AND ORANGE JUICE

New research shows that apple juice and orange juice can decrease the absorption of several drugs if the juice is swallowed at the same time as the pill. Grapefruit juice is also believed to have this effect.

Specifically, researchers found that apple, orange and grapefruit juice decrease the absorption of...

•**The common allergy medication** *fexofenadine* (Allegra).

•**Antibiotics,** such as *ciprofloxacin* (Cipro) and *levofloxacin* (Levaquin).

•**Antifungal drug** *itraconazole* (Sporanox).

•**Blood pressure–lowering beta-blockers,** such as *atenolol* (Tenormin).

•**Chemotherapy drug** *etoposide* (Toposar).

If you are taking any of these drugs, it is probably safe to drink apple or orange juice (and eat whole fruits) at least two hours before or three hours after taking the medications. Check with your doctor first. Avoid grapefruit juice (and grapefruit itself) altogether.

DANGERS OF COFFEE

Coffee can interact with certain medications in a variety of ways. Do not drink coffee at the same time that you take any medication. *Limit daily consumption of coffee to one to two cups if you take...*

•**Antacids.** Because coffee contains acid, it counteracts the effectiveness of OTC antacids such as *calcium carbonate* (or TUMS) and Maalox.

•**Aspirin** or other nonsteroidal anti-inflammatory (NSAID) medications, including *ibuprofen* (Advil) or *naproxen* (Aleve). Because coffee increases stomach acidity, combining it with these drugs may increase risk for gastrointestinal side effects, including stomach irritation and bleeding.

•**Bronchodilator** *theophylline* (Elixophyllin), used to treat asthma or emphysema. Consuming coffee with the bronchodilator could slow the breakdown of the drug, leading to higher blood levels and an increased risk for nausea, vomiting, palpitations and seizures.

•**Monoamine oxidase inhibitor (MAOI)** antidepressants, including *phenelzine* (Nardil) and *selegiline* (Eldepryl). The combination may increase anxiety.

•**Osteoporosis drug** *alendronate* (Fosamax). Studies show that coffee (and orange juice) can inhibit absorption of Fosamax by 60%. If you take Fosamax or any other osteoporosis medication, ask your pharmacist about foods or other beverages that may interact with the drug.

DANGERS OF CRANBERRY JUICE

In the United Kingdom, there have been at least eight recent reports of bleeding in patients (one of whom died) after they drank cranberry juice with the blood-thinning medication *warfarin* (Coumadin).

Health officials were unable to definitively link the bleeding to the combination of cranberry juice and warfarin, but it's probably safest to avoid cranberry juice altogether if you are taking this medication. Cranberry juice has been shown to inhibit a key enzyme that is responsible for warfarin metabolism, but more research on this interaction is needed.

If you take another drug with blood-thinning effects, such as aspirin, you can probably drink cranberry juice occasionally (no more than four ounces—at least two hours before or three hours after taking the medication). Consult your doctor.

DANGERS OF MILK

The calcium in milk can interact with certain medications. *Drink milk at least two hours before or three hours after taking…*

•**Antacids,** such as the *calcium carbonate* products (Rolaids) or the *sodium bicarbonate* products (Alka-Seltzer and Brioschi). Drinking milk with these antacids can cause milk-alkali syndrome, a condition characterized by high blood calcium levels which can lead to kidney stones or even kidney failure.

•**Antibiotics,** such as tetracyclines and *ciprofloxacin* (Cipro). Calcium blocks absorption of these drugs, decreasing their effectiveness. Calcium-fortified juices are believed to have the same effect.

BETTER MEDICATION METABOLISM

Our bodies need nutrients to properly metabolize most medications. Chief among these nutrients is protein. Though we tend to consume less protein as we age—due to a variety of reasons, such as dental problems that make it harder to chew meat—we actually require *more* of this nutrient, since our bodies become less efficient at digesting and utilizing it.

Because the lining of the small and large intestines—where medicine is absorbed—regenerates every three to seven days, you need a continual supply of protein to maintain adequate amounts of the enzymes that promote metabolism of medications.

To facilitate drug metabolism: Aim to eat about half a gram of protein daily for every pound of body weight.

Good sources: Fish, meats, eggs, peanut butter and soybeans.

B vitamins also play a crucial role in drug metabolism. Food sources rich in B vitamins include meats, fortified cereals, bananas and oatmeal.

Helpful: If you skip breakfast and are not much of a meat eater, consider taking a multivitamin containing the recommended daily intake of B vitamins.

To learn more about drug-beverage interactions, go to the FDA Web site (*www.fda.gov/cder/consumerinfo/druginteractions.htm*).

Drugs That Can Cause Or Worsen High Blood Pressure

Joe Graedon, MS, pharmacologist, and Teresa Graedon, PhD. The Durham, North Carolina–based consumer advocates specialize in drugs and supplements. Their syndicated newspaper column, "The People's Pharmacy," appears in newspapers nationwide and abroad. The couple are coauthors of 12 books, including *Best Choices from The People's Pharmacy* (Rodale, *www.peoplespharmacy.com*).

I n many cases, a side effect of a drug you are taking may be causing—or worsening—high blood pressure…

•**Pain relievers.** Researchers from Boston's Brigham and Women's Hospital found that older men who used nonsteroidal anti-inflammatory drugs (NSAIDs), such as *ibuprofen* (Advil) or *naproxen* (Aleve), six to seven times weekly had a 38% higher risk of developing high blood pressure (hypertension) than men who did not use an NSAID. *Acetaminophen* (Tylenol) users had a 34% increased risk.

Theory: Pain relievers may raise blood pressure because of their effect on *prostaglandins*, hormone-like chemicals that affect the dilation and constriction of blood vessels and blood flow.

Our advice: You may be able to decrease your NSAID use—and the potential for increased hypertension risk—by trying topical pain relievers, such as over-the-counter (OTC) BenGay arthritis ointment or the prescription topical NSAID *diclofenac* (Voltaren). Or ask your doctor about anti-inflammatory fish oil supplements. In a recent nine-month Scottish study, 39% of rheumatoid arthritis sufferers who consumed 2.2 g of omega-3 fatty acids from fish oils daily reduced their NSAID use by 30% or more.

•**Estrogen drugs** that are used as hormone replacement therapy (HRT) in postmenopausal women may raise blood pressure and increase the risk for blood clots, which elevates stroke risk.

Our advice: If you use HRT, take the lowest possible dose for the shortest possible time. If you are bothered by hot flashes, consider taking the herbal supplement *pine bark extract* (Pycnogenol), which may provide some relief.

•**Pseudoephedrine,** the decongestant in Sudafed and many other cold remedies, works by constricting blood vessels to reduce nasal stuffiness, but the drug's effect can increase blood pressure.

Our advice: If you have high blood pressure, never take pseudoephedrine unless it is recommended by your doctor. For congestion, use a saline nasal wash or spray for its soothing effects.

Important: If you're using any of the above drugs, it is crucial to regularly monitor your blood pressure. (Ask your physician to recommend a reliable home monitor.) When starting the medication, check your blood pressure two to three times a day, gradually tapering off to once or twice a week (unless your doctor advises otherwise).

Caution: Never stop taking a prescription medication without your doctor's consent. If you're concerned about side effects, call your physician.

Popular Drugs That Can Lead to Decreased Physical Abilities

Many drugs produce *anticholinergic* side effects, which means that they block an important nervous system chemical known as *acetylcholine.*

New finding: Older adults who took anticholinergic medications—including common drugs for high blood pressure, incontinence and allergies—were more likely to walk slowly and require help with tasks of daily living. In a separate study, nursing home residents who took medications for dementia as well as an anticholinergic for incontinence had a 50% faster decline in physical function than those who took only dementia drugs.

Wise: If you take any anticholinergics, discuss safer alternatives with your doctor.

Kaycee M. Sink, MD, assistant professor of internal medicine and gerontology, Wake Forest University School of Medicine in Winston-Salem, North Carolina, and the lead author of both studies involving a total of 6,500 people age 65 and over.

Beware These Three Drugs

Most drug-associated emergency room visits among older adults are due to one of three drugs. The blood thinner *warfarin*, the diabetes drug *insulin* and the heart drug *digoxin* each can cause adverse reactions. They are commonly used by people age 65 and older, and it can be hard to determine correct doses.

Problem: For many patients, there are no good alternative drugs. Patients should talk with their doctors about how to maximize benefits while minimizing risks of these drugs.

Daniel Budnitz, MD, medical officer, US Centers for Disease Control and Prevention, Atlanta, and leader of an analysis of emergency room visits in 2004 and 2005, published in *Annals of Internal Medicine.*

Common Drugs That Are Dangerous to Stop Quickly

Larry D. Sasich, PharmD, MPH, chair of the department of pharmacy practice at Lake Erie College of Osteopathic Medicine (LECOM) School of Pharmacy, Erie, Pennsylvania. He's also the consumer representative on the Science Board of the Food and Drug Administration (FDA). Dr. Sasich is coauthor of *Worst Pills, Best Pills* (Pocket), which has sold more than 2.3 million copies, *www.worstpills.org.*

Have you ever wanted to cease taking a medication because of an annoying side effect or due to some other reason? About 60% of people taking a prescription medication decide on their own, without talking with their doctors, to stop a medication, sometimes suddenly.

Warning: The consequences of suddenly stopping a medication can be deadly.

Some of the medications that you should never stop quickly…

BETA-BLOCKERS

Beta-blockers, which decrease the heartbeat, are prescribed for high blood pressure, angina (chest pain) and even for stage fright.

Drowsiness is a common side effect. If you take the medication for high blood pressure, which has no symptoms, you may decide that you feel a whole lot better when you are not taking the drug than when you are taking it—and so you suddenly stop.

What can happen: Quickly stopping your beta-blocker can trigger *arrhythmias* (or heart rhythm disturbances), even in people without heart disease, and/or worsen angina, possibly even triggering a heart attack.

What to do: Stopping safely requires tapering the dosage—lowering the intake slowly and progressively over a period of one to two weeks. Do so only under the supervision of a physician or other health-care professional.

If you have any withdrawal reactions—for example, if angina worsens—talk to your doctor. You may need to stop tapering and return to the full dosage, at least temporarily.

Beta-blockers include: *Acebutolol* (Sectral)… *atenolol* (Tenormin)…*atenolol* with *chlorthalidone* (Tenoretic)…*betaxolol* (Kerlone)…*bisoprolol* (Zebeta)…*bisoprolol* with *hydrochlorothiazide* (Ziac)…*carvedilol* (Coreg)…*labetalol* (Normodyne, Trandate)…*metoprolol* (Lopressor, Toprol-XL)…*metoprolol* with *hydrochlorothiazide* (Lopressor HCT)…*nadolol* (Corgard)… *penbutolol* (Levatol)…*pindolol* (Visken)…*propranolol* (Inderal, Inderal LA)…*propranolol* with *hydrochlorothiazide* (Inderide LA)…*timolol* (Blocadren)…*timolol* with *hydrochlorothiazide* (Timolide).

DRUGS FOR DEPRESSION OR ANXIETY

The Selective Serotonin Reuptake Inhibitors (SSRIs) and Serotonin-Norepinephrine Reuptake Inhibitors (SNRIs) work by increasing the amount of neurotransmitters, brain chemicals that speed messages from neuron to neuron and play an important role in mood. SSRIs increase the neurotransmitter *serotonin*, while SNRIs increase both serotonin and the neurotransmitter *norepinephrine*.

SSRIs are prescribed for depression, anxiety disorders (including panic attacks, general anxiety disorder, social anxiety disorder and posttraumatic stress disorder) and other types of intense and/or ongoing emotional distress. SNRIs also are prescribed for depression.

What can happen: If you suddenly stop taking an SSRI or SNRI, you may go through intense physical withdrawal. It usually starts one to three days after the drug is stopped, and symptoms can include dizziness, vertigo (a spinning or whirling sensation), poor coordination, nausea and diarrhea, and flulike symptoms, such as fatigue, headache, muscle pain and chills. You also may experience some disturbing emotional symptoms, such as depression, irritability, agitation, anxiety, confusion and mood swings, along with insomnia. Withdrawal symptoms generally go away after one or two weeks.

What to do: If you and your doctor have decided that you should no longer take an SSRI or an SNRI—because of side effects (such as sexual dysfunction or weight gain) or cost, or because you feel that you are ready to go off the drug—create a plan to stop the drug gradually, by tapering the dosage.

If you begin to experience intolerable withdrawal symptoms while stopping the drug, return to your previous dose and decrease at a more gradual rate.

SSRIs include: *Citalopram* (Celexa)…*escitalopram* (Lexapro)…*fluoxetine* (Prozac, Sarafem)… *fluoxetine* with *olanzapine* (Symbyax)…*fluvoxamine* (Luvox)…*paroxetine* (Paxil)…*sertraline* (Zoloft).

SNRIs include: *Duloxetine* (Cymbalta)…*venlafaxine* (Effexor).

SLEEPING PILLS

The new generation of *nonbenzodiazepine* sleeping pills was formulated to replace *benzodiazepines*, such as Valium and Xanax (which also are prescribed for anxiety).

That is because benzodiazepines are highly addictive and work by sedating the body, which in turn adapts to the drug. As a result, higher and higher doses are needed to produce an effect. When a benzodiazepine drug is suddenly halted, you can experience symptoms similar to those experienced by an alcoholic who abruptly stops drinking—tremors, cramps, convulsions, sweating and vomiting. If you have been taking a benzodiazepine for insomnia and stop suddenly, you also may experience rebound insomnia, in which you have an even harder time falling asleep and more nighttime awakenings than before you started the drug.

What can happen: Many patients, even some doctors, don't realize that the nonbenzodiazepines—*eszopiclone* (Lunesta), *zaleplon* (Sonata) and *zolpidem* (Ambien), which are used mainly to help you fall asleep—work in almost the same way as benzodiazepines and, it turns out, also are addictive. The nonbenzodiazepines have a different chemical structure than the benzodiazepines, but they act on the same area of the brain.

Sudden withdrawal from these sleeping pills can produce exactly the same type of physical withdrawal symptoms—such as nausea, sweating and shaking—and rebound insomnia as sudden withdrawal from a benzodiazepine. And those problems can develop after taking a nonbenzodiazepine every night for just a week or two.

What to do: As with all sleep medications, after a week or two of nightly use, work with your doctor to stop the drug gradually, tapering the dosage.

HOW TO WORK WITH YOUR PHYSICIAN

Some physicians might not know about all the withdrawal reactions discussed here, particularly the reactions for nonbenzodiazepine sleeping pills. When you discuss stopping a drug with your doctor, bring a copy of the "professional product label" for your medication—the comprehensive printed descriptions and warnings that accompany each drug when you fill a prescription. With this information in hand, you can emphasize that

caution is warranted and that the drug needs to be stopped gradually.

Resources: If you have access to the Internet, you can locate and print professional product labels for almost 4,000 prescription drugs at *http://dailymed.nlm.nih.gov/dailymed/about.cfm*.

You also can find detailed drug information in the *Physician's Desk Reference*, or PDR (Thomson Healthcare), which is available in libraries and bookstores. Or go online to *www.pdrhealth.com* or the drug manufacturer's official Web site.

How to Harness the Power of the Placebo

Richard L. Kradin, MD, a pulmonologist, internist, anatomic pathologist and researcher at Massachusetts General Hospital and associate professor of pathology at Harvard Medical School, both are in Boston. He has written more than 150 medical articles and also serves as codirector of Harvard Medical School's postgraduate study on Mind/Body Science. Dr. Kradin is the author of *The Placebo Response and the Power of Unconscious Healing* (Routledge).

Researchers at several American institutions recently reported that half of 679 American doctors who had been surveyed said they regularly prescribed placebos to their patients. This news came as a shock to many people—and it raised serious ethical questions.

Everyone knows what placebos are—"sugar pills" or "dummy pills" that masquerade as medication. But is it that simple?

There is a lot more to the question than meets the eye, according to Richard L. Kradin, MD, one of the country's foremost experts on the use of placebo treatments. *He answers important questions below...*

• **What exactly is a placebo?** It's any type of therapeutic intervention—for example, a fake or unproven medication, a sham surgical procedure or a talk with the doctor—that, in and of itself, is judged to have no therapeutic capacity. When it works, the success is attributed to an activation of what's called the "placebo response."

• **How is the placebo response believed to work?** Before there were any scientific medical treatments, people got sick and got well. In species such as ours, some of these responses involve the body's ability to soothe itself and to restore states of physical and mental well-being. This self-soothing process is key to the placebo response.

Particular memories are probably involved. For example, children are usually soothed by their parents. Their mothers kiss minor hurts to make them better. They are given pills and told the medicine will make them well. When adults are sick and receive care from someone who's supposed to help them, the situation can reawaken this capacity to be soothed. After a visit to the doctor, some people report that they feel better right away.

• **Can a person who has a serious illness be healed by the placebo response?** There are people who appear to have been cured of cancer by what might be termed the placebo response. In one case, an experimental chemotherapy drug—later shown to be inactive —was highly effective in a patient as long as he truly believed it was capable of curing his cancer. But that scenario is quite rare.

The placebo seems best able to restore well-being when the problem is simple, such as a headache or stomachache. It's important to remember that the placebo response isn't necessarily separate from real therapeutic responses brought about by effective treatment, but part of them. If you take medicine that works, the placebo response may help it to work better. Many of the factors involved in the placebo response have been scientifically confirmed in a number of studies on the topic.

• **Do placebos do more for some people than for others?** In most clinical trials, one-third of patients who receive a sugar pill feel better. But it's hard to predict which people will respond positively to placebo treatment.

Trust and expectation increase the chance of a positive response. If you believe that a drug or treatment is likely to help you, the odds are that it will work as a placebo.

If the doctor or other caregiver conveys a sense of competence and authority, and the visit to the doctor's office promotes relaxation and trust, these factors also seem to elicit the placebo response. The doctor's ability to listen and make patients feel that they're understood is important. If the doctor doesn't convey his/her own belief that the intervention will work, the chances are good that it won't work.

• **Could a placebo have harmful effects?** Negative, or so-called nocebo, responses are quite common. For example, about 25% of the participants in clinical trials indicate side effects after receiving a harmless pill. Similarly, a certain proportion of adverse reactions to prescribed medications are no doubt due to the nocebo response.

Here, too, expectation plays a role. Nocebo effects commonly occur after a patient reads the drug package insert which lists, often in alarming detail, a medication's potential side effects. The health-care provider can bring on the nocebo response, too. People sometimes leave the office of a brusque, uncaring doctor feeling much worse, and getting little benefit from the medication the doctor prescribed. If a caregiver expresses too many doubts about the treatment, patients detect that as well.

• **Is it ethical for a doctor to prescribe a drug as a placebo without the patient's consent?** In many situations, with many types of people, conveying the entire truth, including doubts surrounding the treatment, may not be in the patient's best interest in terms of therapeutic outcome. On the other hand, if a doctor is caught prescribing a placebo, he risks losing his credibility. Most placebos are prescribed unwittingly by doctors who prescribe a medication "off-label"—for an unapproved use—in the belief that it will help.

By the same token, when I speak in detail with a patient about a particular drug's potential side effects, as mandated by law, I can see fear well up in his face. Is that the role of a healer? I'm not so sure.

• **How can medical consumers harness the power of their own placebo responses?** In choosing a health professional, you should try to find someone you can trust and have confidence in. Do not go to anyone who doesn't evoke this trust. It's possible for a doctor to be brusque and still convey the confidence that a patient needs. Some people respond well to that kind of personality.

Know yourself. If you leave any treatment situation feeling doubtful and not reassured, you're probably in the wrong place.

• **How can you minimize nocebo effects?** I suggest to my patients that they read the medication package insert only if they experience a side effect, to check whether it is a common one. I believe it's better to stay modestly informed—and to recognize and respect the expertise of your physician or other health professional.

Important: Any side effect that is not short-lived should be reported to your physician so that potentially serious adverse reactions are not missed.

You should be a working partner in your treatment and have some idea of what's going on. But when people start involving themselves in the fine details, it tends to have a disturbing effect on mind-body processes—either resulting in a nocebo response or limiting the advantages of the placebo response.

How Does Your Hospital Measure Up?

Michael T. Rapp, MD, JD, director of the Quality Measurement and Health Assessment Group in the Office of Clinical Standards and Quality at the US Department of Health and Human Services Centers for Medicare and Medicaid Services in Baltimore. The group evaluates measurement systems to assess health-care quality in a range of settings. Dr. Rapp, an emergency physician, served on the board of directors and as president of the American College of Emergency Physicians.

If you or a family member is hospitalized for a serious medical condition, you are likely to count on your doctor and/or other medical personnel to know the best way to treat the problem.

Latest resource: By consulting a Web site known as Hospital Compare (*www.hospital compare.hhs.gov*), you can learn how conditions that often land people in the hospital should be treated—and how more than 4,000 US hospitals (about 95% of the nation's total) measure up in administering this care.*

Developed by the US Department of Health and Human Services in partnership with the Hospital Quality Alliance (a public-private collaboration to improve hospital care), the Web site details the performance of US hospitals in handling four key areas of hospital care—heart attack, heart failure, pneumonia and prevention of surgical infections.

Important: In some cases, there may be valid reasons for an exception to the recommended treatment (for example, an allergy to a particular drug).

HEART ATTACK

Until recently, there was a considerable gap in the care that hospitals across the US provided for heart patients. Now there is much more consistency in the treatment standards and the hospitals' performance. *Among the recommended measures…*

• **Aspirin on arrival.** Most heart attacks occur when a blood clot is blocking a coronary artery. Patients who are given an aspirin to chew (not swallow) upon arrival at a hospital at the onset of heart attack symptoms are more likely to survive.

National average performance: 93%.

• **Clot-removing treatment within 90 minutes.** A percutaneous coronary intervention (PCI), in which a catheter is inserted in a coronary artery and used to remove blockages, is the fastest way to restore circulation to the heart. If the procedure is performed within 90 minutes of a patient's arrival, it can significantly improve patient outcomes.

National average performance: 60%.

Additional heart-attack measures: Aspirin given at discharge, 90%…the use of *angiotensin-converting enzyme* (ACE) inhibitors or *angiotensin receptor blockers* for heart attack prevention, 85%.

*Click the "Find and Compare Hospitals" button on the home page. By following the prompts, you can look up specific hospitals in your area or across the nation and review up to three hospitals' ratings side-by-side.

HEART FAILURE

Also known as congestive heart failure, this condition occurs when the heart's pumping action is inadequate. It is often caused by high blood pressure, coronary artery disease or cardiomyopathy (a condition in which the heart muscle is severely damaged by infection, drug and/or alcohol use or other causes). *Among the recommended measures...*

•**An evaluation of left ventricular systolic (LVS) function.** This is an important test that tells whether the left side of the heart is pumping properly.

National average performance: 85%.

•**Discharge instructions.** Heart failure is a chronic condition that requires lifelong management. Patients should be given instructions on diet, exercise, medication use and monitoring their weight (even a small gain can signal potentially dangerous fluid retention) and instructions to make follow-up appointments.

National average performance: 66%.

Other heart-failure measures: Use of ACE inhibitors or angiotensin receptor blockers for treatment of heart-failure symptoms, 84%.

PNEUMONIA

•**Pneumonia is one of the most common and potentially serious lung diseases,** killing about 60,000 Americans annually. *Among the recommended measures...*

•**Identify bacteria prior to giving antibiotics.** Patients who arrive at the emergency room having symptoms of pneumonia (such as shortness of breath, chills, fever and chest pain) always should be given a blood-culture test to identify the type of bacterium causing the infection—and to ascertain the most effective antibiotic.

National average performance: 90%.

•**Antibiotics within six hours.** Research has shown that pneumonia patients who are given antibiotics within six hours of arrival at the hospital have better outcomes than those who are given antibiotics later.

National average performance: 93%.

•**Pneumococcal vaccine.** Even when a patient already has bacterial pneumonia, giving a pneumococcal vaccine can help to prevent future bacterial pneumonia infections. Every hospital patient who has pneumonia should be given the vaccine.

National average performance: 75%.

Other pneumonia measures: The use of oxygenation assessment (to gauge the amount of oxygen in the patient's bloodstream and to determine if he/she needs oxygen therapy), 99%...smoking-cessation advice, 84%...the use of the most appropriate antibiotic, 86%.

SURGICAL CARE

Surgery is among the most routine hospital procedures but is associated with some of the highest risks. *Among the recommended measures to reduce problems...*

•**Stopping antibiotics within 24 hours.** Taking antibiotics prior to surgery can greatly reduce the risk for infection—but continuing the drugs longer than 24 hours after the operation increases the risk for stomach pain, serious diarrhea and other side effects.

National average performance: 78%.

•**Measures to prevent blood clots.** Certain types of surgery, particularly orthopedic procedures such as hip replacement surgery, can result in venous thrombosis (a condition in which a blood clot forms, usually in a leg, and can travel to the lungs, triggering pulmonary embolism—an often-fatal condition). Venous thrombosis is most likely to occur after procedures that make it difficult for patients to move for extended periods.

Blood clots can be prevented with the use of blood-thinning medications, elastic stockings or mechanical air stockings that foster blood circulation in the legs.

National average performance: 79%.

Other surgical measures: Administering preventive antibiotics one hour before incision, 82%...the use of the appropriate preventive antibiotic, 90%.

Medication Mistakes Are a Common Cause of Repeat Hospitalizations: How to Protect Yourself

Mary D. Naylor, PhD, RN, the Marian S. Ware Professor in Gerontology and director of the New Courtland Center for Transitions and Health at the University of Pennsylvania School of Nursing in Philadelphia. She is cofounder of Living Independently for Elders (*www. lifeupenn.org*), which provides health, day care and other services designed to help older adults remain in their homes and communities.

M edication errors (such as being given the wrong medication or no dosage instructions) are a main cause of repeat hospital admissions. Potentially dangerous drugs, such as *warfarin* (Coumadin) or other types of blood-thinning medication, are among the drugs most commonly involved in repeat hospitalizations.

When researchers at the University of Pennsylvania tracked patients after their discharge from the hospital, they found a 70% error rate in medication use.

For example, some patients were given inaccurate information about medication types or dosages…or necessary drugs that were discontinued when patients entered the hospital were not always restarted when the patients left the hospital.

Self-defense: Keep an up-to-date list of all your medications (including over-the-counter drugs) and supplements where family members can find it if you go to the hospital unexpectedly. In the hospital, post a list of your medications beside your bed in the hospital. Every time you see a new doctor, ask him/her to review the list.

Helpful: Don't throw away your older lists. Compare older medication lists with the newest one. If there's been a change in a drug or dose, ask your doctor about it to ensure that it's not a mistake.

The Pros and Cons Of "Off-Shore" Medicine

Charles B. Inlander, a consumer advocate and healthcare consultant located in Fogelsville, Pennsylvania. He was the founding president of the nonprofit People's Medical Society, a consumer advocacy organization credited with key improvements in the quality of US health care in the 1980s and 1990s, and is the author of 20 books, including *Take This Book to the Hospital with You: A Consumer Guide to Surviving Your Hospital Stay* (St. Martin's).

I n years past, "medical tourism" referred mainly to the practice of bringing people from foreign countries to the US for high-quality medical care. In recent years, the term has assumed a new definition, as US citizens leave the country for more affordable surgery and other treatments. Hundreds of thousands of Americans are seeking foreign medical care each year, and this trend is expected to grow as US insurance companies consider covering "off-shore" medicine. *But before you jump on an airplane, here are some important points to consider…*

•**Is it safe?** Americans have long assumed that foreign medical care is more dangerous than that provided here in the US. But high-quality medical care can be located in many places throughout the world. The Joint Commission on the Accreditation of Healthcare Organizations, the private group that accredits hospitals in the US, offers an international office (*www.jointcommissioninternational.org*) that accredits foreign hospitals.

If you are thinking about going abroad for medical care, make sure that the facility you are considering has been accredited by the joint commission. Also, check on the training of the doctors who would be caring for you. Look for physicians who were educated at US medical schools and completed a residency in their area of concentration at a US hospital. This is not a guarantee that you will receive high-quality care, but it does give you some reassurance because it is easier to check the reputation of medical schools and residency programs in the US.

• **Will I really save money?** MedSolution (*www.medsolution.com*), a Canadian medical-tourism firm, recently released some expense comparisons: Hip replacement—$40,000 in North America, $15,000 in France and $5,800 in India…coronary angioplasty—$35,000 in North America, $18,400 in France and $3,700 in India.* Many people going abroad for face-lifts and other cosmetic procedures are paying 30% to 50% of US prices.

• **Do I have all the facts?** It's usually best to use a medical-tourism firm. To locate one, search the term "medical tourism" on the Internet and/or consult the informational Web site *www.medicaltourismguide.org*. The firm you select will ask for your medical records to review, and you will then be matched with a doctor and hospital. These firms handle all the details, including travel and hotel arrangements. But make sure you get references for the firm (check for complaints with the Better Business Bureau or the attorney general's office in the firm's home state) as well as the hospital and doctors they recommend to you (ask the firm for contact information for patients treated at these medical facilities).

Buyer beware: If something goes wrong with your overseas medical care, emergency treatment will be provided (health insurance probably won't cover the cost, though). Also, you have no legal recourse in the US against the overseas provider. Every country has its own malpractice laws. Most are not as protective as those in the US. Very few foreign hospitals or doctors will be of much help to you once you return to the US. Make sure that you have a doctor here who is ready to provide follow-up care.

*Prices and figures subject to change.

More from Charles Inlander…

Surviving Your Hospital Stay

I recently had to put all my years of experience as a medical-consumer advocate to the test when I found myself in the hospital recuperating from surgery to fix an enlarged prostate gland. My surgery was a success—in part because I chose a surgeon who had performed the procedure, a transurethral resection

of the prostate (TURP), more than 1,000 times. But my hospital stay went without major incident also because I knew what to do to avoid problems. *Here's what you—or a loved one—can do to have a successful hospital stay…*

• **Bring a list of your medications.** I always advise people to bring a list of all their medications—and the dosages—when they go to the doctor, but the same applies if you are headed to the hospital. Coming prepared with your medication list is one of the best steps you can take to protect yourself against medication errors. I brought my medication list and kept it on the adjustable table by my bedside. One nurse thanked me and used it to be sure that her records were correct.

• **Hang signs.** The 84-year-old man in the bed next to mine was nearly deaf and couldn't understand the questions that the doctors and nurses asked him. He would simply nod and say "yes" to everything. When I realized this was happening, I made a sign with bold print that read, "You have to speak directly into my ear!" and hung it on the wall above his head. This worked. Once my roommate was able to hear the staff, they got real answers. You can make a sign for a variety of messages, such as "Contact my son/daughter (and give a phone number) for any medical permissions."

• **Use the phone.** One night, I needed the nurse but was not getting a response when I pushed the call button. I waited for 20 minutes and finally picked up the phone, dialed "0" and asked for the nurses' station on my unit. A nurse answered on the initial ring. I asked her to come to my room, and she showed up about 10 seconds later. I never had a problem again when I pushed the call button.

• **Bring earplugs.** Hospitals are noisy places. Knowing this, I brought earplugs with me and slept peacefully. A portable music player with earphones or noise-canceling earplugs can provide the same escape.

• **Phone home.** Twice during my three-day hospitalization, my physician checked in when no one from my family was around. So when my doctor entered the room, I picked up the phone, called my spouse and had the doctor talk to her at the same time he was talking to me. This is the best way to keep your family informed, and it is especially helpful if you are not feeling well or need someone to ask questions for you.

• **Check the bill.** I received a bill from the hospital that said I owed $2,600. I knew this was wrong. By going over the itemized bill (which I had requested at my discharge), I discovered that I had been inadvertently charged for services received by another patient. Because I was diligent and made a lot of calls, the insurer found the error. Since an estimated 85% of all hospital bills have errors in them, it's buyer beware!

Also from Charles Inlander...

New Hospital Danger

Hospitals are recycling some single-use medical devices to save money and limit medical waste. Recycling scissors, surgical blades and other medical equipment is legal as long as certain FDA guidelines are followed—but manufacturers maintain that single-use medical devices are not designed to hold up to the intense chemicals used to sterilize them...and even when they are sterilized properly, tissue and/or bodily fluids on porous surfaces and in crevices could allow transmission of viral and bacterial infections. The FDA is working on a new strategy for monitoring and communicating information about reprocessed devices and conducting research on "acceptable" single-use device-cleaning criteria.

Self-defense: When you or a loved one are in the hospital, ask nurses and doctors to use only new medical equipment when treating you. You are paying the price for new equipment, even though they may be reusing some.

Bacteria in the Hospital

Hospital patients are at risk for dangerous bacteria.

A recent study indicates a 200% increase in the number of patients infected with *C. difficile*. Most patients have few or no symptoms, but C. difficile can trigger difficult problems, such as diarrhea and colitis, in some people within a few days of a hospital stay or within two months of taking antibiotics, which may kill the helpful bacteria that keep asymptomatic C. difficile in check.

Self-defense: Always wash hands with soap and water before eating.

Note: Alcohol hand sanitizers are not effective for this bacteria. All surfaces suspected of being contaminated with C. difficile should be cleaned with a disinfectant, such as bleach.

Edward K. Chapnick, MD, director, division of infectious diseases, Maimonides Medical Center, Brooklyn, New York, and associate professor of medicine, Mount Sinai School of Medicine, New York City.

Preventing Dangerous Medical Errors

Peter J. Pronovost, MD, PhD, professor in the departments of anesthesiology and critical care medicine and surgery at Johns Hopkins University School of Medicine and medical director for the Center for Innovations in Quality Patient Care, which promotes patient safety at the Johns Hopkins Hospital, both in Baltimore. In 2003, he founded the Quality and Safety Research Group at Johns Hopkins University to advance the science and safety of health-care delivery (*www.safetyresearch.jhu.edu/qsr*).

Misdiagnoses...prescription mistakes ...hospital-acquired infections...and messed up surgeries are among the most common causes of preventable deaths due to medical errors. These sort of mistakes are the fifth-leading cause of death in the nation, killing up to 98,000 Americans annually.

What can you do now to protect yourself? Dr. Peter J. Pronovost, gives answers below.

Dr. Pronovost's strong commitment to patient safety began when his father was mistakenly diagnosed, at age 50, with leukemia instead of lymphoma—an error that prevented him from getting potentially lifesaving treatment.

His biggest breakthrough: A checklist to eliminate deadly hospital-acquired infections. The checklist (see page 52) reminds health-care providers of five simple steps proven to decrease infection due to a central line catheter (inserted in a vein in the neck, groin or chest to administer medication or fluids). In

Michigan, where the checklist has been adopted, catheter-caused bloodstream infections have dropped by 66%. New Jersey and Rhode Island also have adopted the checklist, and 30 other states plan to do so.

For his efforts, Dr. Pronovost was recently awarded a prestigious MacArthur Foundation Fellowship "Genius Grant."

•**Your father's misdiagnosis was tragic. How common are these diagnostic errors?** Misdiagnosis is an enormous problem. Most of the evidence we have comes from autopsies, which show that up to 40% to 50% of the time the diagnosis was wrong. It could be that misdiagnoses are disproportionately high among autopsied patients. We just don't know, because we still don't have a good way of measuring misdiagnoses in patients before it's too late.

•**What can patients do to help ensure a correct diagnosis?** Take the time to articulate not only your symptoms, but also your perception of what may be wrong. Patients have wisdom. You're living with the disease.

When you are diagnosed, ask your doctor: "How confident are you in this diagnosis?" If there's any uncertainty—and especially if there are treatments with varying degrees of risk—get a second opinion. If your doctor's prescribed treatment is not working, ask him/her to re-evaluate the therapy.

•**Your checklist to prevent catheter infections is said to be saving more lives than perhaps any laboratory advance of the last decade. What explains the checklist's huge impact?** The information—from the Centers for Disease Control and Prevention (CDC)—was out there, but it was inefficiently packaged. No one is going to look at 200 pages of guidelines. We simplified it into the five most important actions that health-care providers can take to prevent infections.

If we create similar checklists for diagnosing common medical conditions, it is going to make it easier for patients to communicate with their doctors so that they always get the care they're supposed to.

•**Is there evidence that patients are not always getting the care they should be receiving?** A large study published in *The New England Journal of Medicine* indicated that,

on average, for a wide variety of conditions at most hospitals in this country, patients will get only half of the available interventions or therapies that might benefit them.

•**What can patients do about it?** If you know your diagnosis, you can look up clinical practice guidelines through the National Guideline Clearinghouse (*www.guideline.gov*), sponsored by the US Department of Health and Human Services' Agency for Healthcare Research and Quality. I also hope to have checklists for common diseases and conditions available to the public soon.

•**What can patients do in an emergency to make sure that they are offered the best medicine?**

Help the doctor create his own checklist by asking: "What are the three most important things you can do to help me, and are you doing them?" If you are too ill to ask, a family member should do so.

•**What other questions should patients ask?** When your doctor recommends a therapy, ask about the risks, benefits and alternatives so you can make an informed decision. For example, if you're taking a blood thinner and require any type of operation, the blood thinner should be stopped prior to your surgery to prevent excessive bleeding. However, discontinuing this medication raises your risk for a blood clot that could lead to a stroke. (Certain patients, such as those with a history of blood clots or a stent should ask their doctors whether their blood thinner should not be stopped.)

In deciding when to resume the blood thinner, we are trading off your risk for a stroke against your risk for bleeding. Most of the time, we do not even mention those risks, but you need to know what they are because you may weigh them differently than your physician.

•**Are there other factors that can affect a patient's safety?** Staffing—especially in the intensive care unit (ICU)—is important. Studies show that your risk for dying is 30% higher in the ICU if you don't have an intensive care physician (who has received specialized training in treating ICU patients) looking after you.

51

Even so, 80% of ICU patients do not have intensive care specialists.

My advice: If you or a loved one is in an ICU for more than a day without a specialist, transfer to a hospital that will provide one.

More from Dr. Peter Pronovost...

Infection-Fighting Checklist

Before a patient receives a central line catheter (to administer fluids or medication), health-care providers should...

•**Assess whether the catheter is necessary for the patient.**

If yes...

•**Wash their hands with soap.**

•**Clean the patient's skin with *chlorhexidine*** (an antiseptic).

•**Place sterile drapes over the entire patient and wear a sterile mask,** hat, gown and gloves.

•**Avoid the femoral (thigh area) site** (because of higher infection risk).

Hypnosis Helps

Hypnosis can ease cancer surgery pain. Breast cancer patients who were hypnotized within one hour before surgery required less anesthesia and reported less postsurgical pain, nausea, fatigue and emotional upset than women who spoke with a psychologist before surgery.

Guy Montgomery, PhD, associate professor, department of oncological sciences, Mount Sinai School of Medicine, New York City, and lead author of a study of 200 women, published in *Journal of the National Cancer Institute*.

Statins and Surgery

Statins may help curb surgical complication risk.

Recent study: Researchers analyzed data for 1,059 patients who had cardiac surgery.

Finding: Those who had been taking cholesterol-lowering statin drugs—such as *atorvastatin* (Lipitor) or *rosuvastatin* (Crestor)—before their hospital stays were 46% less likely to suffer delirium, a common surgical complication in which patients experience changes in levels of consciousness and an inability to maintain attention.

Theory: Protection against delirium may be due to statins' cholesterol-lowering and anti-inflammatory effects.

Rita Katznelson, MD, assistant professor of anesthesia, Toronto General Hospital, University of Toronto, Canada.

Beware of Medical Blogs

In a recent study, 42% of blogs (online journals) written by medical professionals contained descriptions of individual patients—17% included enough information for patients to identify themselves or their doctors. Patients were depicted negatively more often than positively...some blogs even had patients' photos.

Wise: Ask your doctors if they have blogs and how they protect patients' privacy.

Tara Lagu, MD, MPH, clinical scholar, University of Pennsylvania, Philadelphia, and lead author of a study of 271 blogs, published in *Journal of General Internal Medicine*.

Medical Research Misconduct

In a survey of scientists, 9% said they had evidence of falsification or plagiarism—but more than one-third did not report it.

Reasons: Scientists are reluctant to turn in colleagues, and they don't want to risk losing research funding.

James A. Wells, PhD, director, Office of Research Policy, University of Wisconsin, Madison, who helped conduct a survey of 2,212 scientists, published in *Nature*.

3

Everyday Health

Wonderful Scents That Heal Common Health Ailments

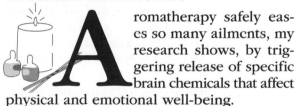romatherapy safely eases so many ailments, my research shows, by triggering release of specific brain chemicals that affect physical and emotional well-being.

Best: Hold a food, flower, essential oil or naturally scented toiletry one-half inch away from your face and level with your lips. Inhale for three minutes…take a five-minute break… repeat up to two dozen times.

ANXIETY

Try: Lavender.

It may work by: Increasing the alpha brain waves that promote a relaxed, meditative state.

To use: Inhale lavender essential oil…light a lavender-scented candle…or place a lavender eye pillow over your eyes.

FATIGUE

Try: Jasmine.

It may work by: Boosting the beta brain waves that improve alertness.

To use: Close one nostril with a finger and deeply inhale a jasmine oil or jasmine-scented toiletry…repeat with other nostril. Continue alternating for five minutes. This single-nostril technique prolongs the effects.

HEADACHE

Try: Green apple (sliced).

It may work by: Triggering the release of brain chemicals, such as endorphins and serotonin, that inhibit pain sensations and alleviate tension.

To use: To reduce migraine or tension-headache pain and duration, inhale the apple scent

Alan Hirsch, MD, founder and neurological director of the Smell & Taste Treatment and Research Foundation in Chicago, *www.smellandtaste.org*. A neurologist and psychiatrist, he has published more than 300 articles on smell and taste disorders and is author of eight books, including *Life's a Smelling Success* (Authors of Unity).

53

as soon as you feel a headache coming on. This seems to work best for people who like the smell of green apple.

LOW LIBIDO

Try: Good & Plenty candies plus cucumber or banana.

It may work by: Stimulating the arousal centers of the female brain, reducing inhibitions and promoting alertness.

To use: Best results are achieved by simultaneously smelling the candy and either of the other foods—so hold both up together.

MENOPAUSE-RELATED MEMORY PROBLEMS

Try: Flowers.

It may work by: Acting on the connection between the olfactory nerve and the parts of the brain involved in memory.

To use: Whenever you want to retain new information, smell mixed scents to increase learning speed. Smell a bouquet of fragrant mixed flowers or a floral-scented perfume.

MENSTRUAL CRAMPS

Try: Green apple (sliced) plus any personal favorite scent.

It may work by: Easing muscle contractions (the apple)…and lifting mood.

To use: Select an aroma you particularly enjoy—a favorite scent helps to eradicate the blues by distracting you from pain.

OVEREATING

Try: Banana or slices of green apple or peppermint.

It may work by: Stimulating the satiety center of the brain that registers when your stomach is full.

To use: To decrease food cravings, deeply inhale three times in each nostril, alternating sides. Alternate among fragrances monthly to help prevent weight-loss plateaus.

SADNESS

Try: Baked goods.

It may work by: Evoking happy memories of childhood.

To use: Bake or buy a favorite pie, cake or other fragrant treat—the aroma alone will help you feel better. If your diet permits, take a few bites for an extra boost in mood.

How a Chiropractor Can Relieve Your Health Problems

Karen Erickson, DC, a chiropractor in private practice, New York City, and a spokesperson for the American Chiropractic Association. She is the author of several academic texts on the role of chiropractic in integrative health care and is on the board of trustees at New York Chiropractic College, New York City.

W

ell-designed studies have now proven that chiropractic care (often just called "chiropractic") is at least as effective—and sometimes more effective—than conventional medicine for the treatment of certain types of physical complaints.

Emerging research now indicates that chiropractic affects more than just the spine and its surrounding muscles. It has been used to successfully treat a variety of conditions, including digestive complaints and ear infections.

Ways chiropractic can help…

DIGESTIVE DISORDERS

A survey of 1,494 patients found that 22% reported digestive relief following chiropractic treatments, even though the majority had never mentioned digestive problems to their chiropractors.

Many of the spinal nerves that are affected by chiropractic manipulation control digestive functions. Patients who undergo routine manipulations may experience changes in their levels of digestive fluids, the speed at which food moves through the intestinal tract or the strength and/or frequency of their intestinal contractions.

We're often told by patients that manipulations for, say, neck or low-back pain not only helped their musculoskeletal complaints but also resulted in improvement in constipation, irritable bowel syndrome and other digestive issues.

Digestive problems need to be medically diagnosed initially, but the most effective treatments involve an integrative approach, which can include chiropractic. I often get referrals from medical doctors of patients with constipation, colitis or irritable bowel syndrome.

Help for colic: A study published in *Journal of Manipulative and Physiological Therapeutics* found that colicky babies treated with chiropractic cried about three hours less daily than they did before, compared to a one-hour reduction in those given the drug *dimethicone*, a standard treatment. The manipulations given to children are very gentle. Many have a reduction in colic after just one or two treatments. Look for a chiropractor who specializes in children's problems.

TENSION HEADACHE

The headaches that we all get from time to time often are related to the cervical spine in the neck. Known as *cervicogenic* headaches, they occur whenever vertebral misalignments cause muscle tightness or spasms. The tension begins in the neck but can radiate through the occipital nerves that rise upward from the base of the skull.

One study that compared patients receiving chiropractic care for tension headaches with those who were treated with the antidepressant *amitriptyline* showed reduction in both the frequency and pain intensity of these types of headaches. Most important, the chiropractic patients sustained these improvements after the treatment period, unlike patients treated with medication.

In a typical treatment, the chiropractor attempts to realign the cervical joints by manipulating the neck and head. The main goals of the treatment, apart from adjusting the vertebrae, are to increase the range of motion, relax the surrounding muscles and decrease pain and inflammation.

People who have only recently started getting headaches often will improve after one or two sessions with a chiropractor. Patients who have suffered from headaches for years probably will require multiple treatments before they start to see significant improvement.

Also important: The chiropractor will take a detailed history to learn why there is excess misalignment in the neck. This usually is due to lifestyle situations. For example, many of us look down at our computer monitors, which puts excessive tension on the neck. Raising the monitor to eye level can correct this. Women may be advised to carry a handbag rather than a heavy shoulder bag. Cradling a telephone between your neck and shoulder also can cause problems. If you often notice yourself doing this, get a headset.

It's not clear if chiropractic is as effective for migraines, but preliminary research suggests that chiropractic manipulations may affect nerves that control vascular expansion and contraction, a key component of migraines.

EAR INFECTIONS

Some adults and virtually all children accumulate fluids in the eustachian tube, the passage between the throat and middle ear. The fluid is a perfect medium for viruses and bacteria, which can cause otitis media, an infection or inflammation of the middle ear.

Many studies have shown that chiropractic can relieve and prevent ear infections without antibiotics. The treatments, which include chiropractic adjustment and massage of the lymph nodes along the neck and around the ear, help drain excess fluid. The adjustment helps regulate the nervous system, which in turn drains the eustachian tube and promotes long-term drainage.

SINUSITIS

People with chronic sinusitis (an inflammation of the mucous membranes in the sinuses) rarely get long-term relief from antibiotics or other types of conventional medicine, such as antihistamines and decongestants. Chiropractic can sometimes relieve all or most of the typical symptoms, such as facial pain and nasal congestion.

People with chronic sinusitis often have a misalignment in their cervical vertebrae. Chiropractic adjustments may help sinuses drain more efficiently. The treatment for sinusitis also includes applying pressure to the sinuses near the eyebrows and on either side of the nose.

REPETITIVE STRESS DISORDERS

Most repetitive stress disorders, including tennis elbow, are caused by tendonitis, an inflammation of the fibrous tissue that connects muscles to bones. Carpal tunnel syndrome, another repetitive stress injury, is caused from nerve inflammation in the wrist.

Doctors usually treat these conditions with anti-inflammatory drugs, including steroid injections in severe cases. For carpal tunnel syndrome, surgery to "release" pressure on the nerve is sometimes recommended.

Chiropractic, a more conservative approach, is effective for practically all types of repetitive stress disorders. Manipulations to realign joints and improve range of motion can decrease pressure on tendons and nerves. The movements also improve lymphatic drainage, which reduces inflammation, improves circulation and accelerates healing.

To find a chiropractor: Go to the American Chiropractic Association Web site, *www. amerchiro.org*, and click on the "Find a Doc" icon.

Aches and Pains? Stomach Upset? Relief Is At Your Fingertips

Paula Koepke, CMT, a massage therapist at the University of California, San Francisco Osher Center for Integrative Medicine, and an instructor at the McKinnon Institute of Massage, Oakland, California, *www.paula koepke.massagetherapy.com.*

Massage is far more than a mere luxury. It may reduce the stress that contributes to heart disease and digestive disorders...relieve pain by manipulating pressure points that relax muscles...and raise levels of mood-boosting brain chemicals.

Good news: You can take your health into your own hands—literally—with simple self-massage techniques.

What to do: Always apply firm but comfortable pressure, repeating each sequence of motions for three to five minutes. Unless noted, techniques can be done while sitting or lying down. Use scented lotion or oil if desired—lavender and rose are calming...peppermint and rosemary are stimulating.

SINUS OR TENSION HEADACHE

• **Lying on your back,** place the fingertips of both hands in the center of your forehead...stroke outward toward the temples...make 10 small slow circles over the temples. Move fingertips to the cheeks, where the jaw hinges...make 10 small slow circles there.

• **Place the pads of your thumbs** just below each upper eye ridge (near the brow), where the ridge meets the bridge of the nose, and press up toward your forehead for 10 seconds. In small increments, move thumbs along the eye ridges toward the outside edges of eyes, pressing for several seconds at each stopping point.

Caution: Always press upward on the bony ridge, not into the eye socket.

• **With the fingertips,** make small circles all over the scalp for 30 seconds as if washing hair. Then place fingertips at the back of the neck and make 10 small slow circles at the base of the skull.

STOMACH UPSET OR CONSTIPATION

• **Lying on your back,** place one hand flat on your abdomen (either over or under clothing) right above your navel. Pressing gently, but firmly, slowly move your hand clockwise to circle the navel.

NECK AND/OR SHOULDER PAIN

• **Sitting,** reach your left hand over your right shoulder until it touches above the shoulder blade. With fingertips, firmly knead muscles, focusing on any sore spots. Repeat on other side.

• **Sitting,** place fingertips of both hands on the back of the neck at the base of the skull. Pressing in firmly, move fingers up and down along the sides of the vertebrae. To protect major blood vessels, do not massage front or sides of the neck.

FOOT SORENESS

• **Sitting,** place your left ankle on your right knee. Grasp the left foot with your right hand and slowly rotate the foot at the ankle three times in each direction. Then use your fingers to gently rotate toes, one at a time, three times in each direction. Repeat on the other side.

• **Sitting,** place your left ankle on your right knee and cradle the left foot in both hands. With thumbs, make five small slow circles— first on the instep…then the ball of the foot…the heel…and the pad of each toe. Repeat on other foot.

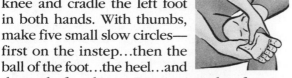

Bonus: Performing a foot massage for 10 minutes nightly may promote health overall.

Theory of reflexology: "Reflex points" on the feet are linked to various body systems and organs, which benefit from tactile stimulation.

Massage illustrations by Shawn Banner.

Back Hurt? Get More of This Healing Vitamin

Back pain has been linked to deficiency of vitamin D.

Recent study: Women with low blood levels of vitamin D were more than twice as likely to have low-back pain, perhaps due to bone softening.

Best: Ask your doctor about taking vitamin D supplements.

Gregory E. Hicks, PT, PhD, assistant professor, department of physical therapy, University of Delaware, Newark, and leader of a study of 958 people, published in *Journal of the American Geriatrics Society.*

Omega-3s to the Rescue

Neck and back pain could be relieved by omega-3 fatty acids. Omega-3s, found in fish and fish oil supplements, block inflammation and accompanying pain.

Study: 60% of participants with neck or back pain who were given 1,200 milligrams (mg) of fish oil per day reported relief after

two to four weeks, and almost all of that group were able to discontinue their use of nonsteroidal anti-inflammatory drugs (NSAIDs), such as Celebrex and Motrin. The study also found that most patients taking fish oil had no significant side effects.

Joseph C. Maroon, MD, professor, and vice-chair, department of neurological surgery, University of Pittsburgh School of Medicine, and lead author of a study of 250 people, published in *Surgical Neurology.*

Real Help for Chronic Low Back Pain

In a study of 1,162 people with chronic low back pain, one group received acupuncture and another group received conventional therapy using painkillers, physical therapy and exercise. Individuals who had 10 half-hour acupuncture sessions over six weeks were nearly twice as likely to report improvements in pain and functional ability as patients given conventional therapy.

Theory: Acupuncture triggers a pain-dulling response by the central nervous system.

If you have chronic low back pain: Ask your doctor if you should try acupuncture.

Heinz G. Endres, MD, a clinical epidemiology specialist, Ruhr-University Bochum, Germany.

The Best Mattress for Back Pain

Better than a hard mattress for people who suffer chronic back pain—a softer, body-conforming mattress or a waterbed.

Recent finding: Back-pain sufferers who tried those alternatives for one month slept better and had slightly less pain than those who slept on hard mattresses.

Possible reason: Hard mattresses increase pressure on certain body parts, causing more turning at night.

Study by Kim Bergholdt, DC, Back Research Center Funen, Ringe, Denmark, published in *Spine*.

Meds That Make Migraines Worse

Medications that can relieve migraines may make headaches more frequent over time. Prescription pain medication containing barbiturates, such as Fiorinal, or narcotics, such as codeine, are associated with increasing headache frequency, perhaps because they make the brain more sensitive to pain.

Self-defense for migraine sufferers: Talk with your physician about other ways to treat migraine episodes, such as nonsteroidal anti-inflammatory drugs, including Motrin and Advil (although these drugs can cause rebound headaches), and triptans, such as Imitrex. Also ask about preventives, including beta-blockers, epilepsy drugs and certain antidepressants, as well as natural products, such as vitamin B-2. Do not take barbiturate or narcotic painkillers more than two days per week.

Richard Lipton, MD, vice-chair, professor of neurology, Albert Einstein College of Medicine, and director, Montefiore Headache Center, both in the Bronx, New York, and leader of a study of 8,200 migraine sufferers, published in *Headache*.

Drug-Free Ways to Fight Colds: No Nasty Side Effects

Effie Poy Yew Chow, PhD, RN, founder and president of East West Academy of Healing Arts in San Francisco, *www.eastwestqi.com*. A licensed acupuncturist, qigong grandmaster and registered psychiatric and public health nurse, she was appointed by President Clinton to the original 15-member White House Commission on Complementary and Alternative Medicine Policy. Dr. Chow is a coauthor of *Miracle Healing from China: Qigong* (Medipress) and is on the *Bottom Line/Women's Health* advisory board.

When a cold makes you feel terrible, you want to get relief fast. But drugs designed to relieve cold symptoms can produce side effects, like increased blood pressure and heart rate, gastric upset, blurred vision, trouble concentrating, insomnia.

Instead, I recommend the practices of traditional Chinese medicine, which have been used for thousands of years. These practices may ease inflammation...fight infection...boost the immune system...and promote the healthful flow of qi (energy) through the body.

YIN OR YANG?

According to traditional Chinese medicine, two seemingly opposing yet interdependent natural forces called yin and yang must be in balance for a person to maintain good health. When one force predominates, illness results.

Colds can be characterized as either yin or yang. With a yin cold, you get the chills...feel exhausted...and want to crawl into bed. With a yang cold, you have a fever...perspire...and feel agitated. *To reestablish the body's natural balance...*

• **Feed a yin cold**—primarily with yang foods. Yang foods are warming. Generally, they include meat, chicken and fish...and vegetables that grow in the earth, such as carrots, beets, jicama, turnips and yams. Eat as much as you comfortably can. Drink three six-ounce cups of ginger tea daily—ginger has anti-inflammatory and antiseptic effects.

Also soothing: Submerge yourself up to your earlobes in a bathtub of comfortably hot water mixed with Epsom salts.

• **For a yang cold, eat lightly.** Avoid yang foods, and instead focus on cooling yin foods —especially green vegetables, sprouts, fruits and other foods that grow in the open air. Drink eight to 10 cups of water per day. Also drink two or three cups of garlic tea daily— garlic is an antibacterial, antiviral and anti-inflammatory agent.

To make garlic tea: Boil a cup of water… add a clove of garlic cut in half…steep five to 10 minutes…remove garlic…add in honey and lemon juice to taste.

Also helpful: Use garlic liberally in cooking.

TIME-HONORED REMEDIES

Many traditional treatments may be helpful no matter what type of cold you have. Products mentioned below are sold at health-food stores, Asian markets and/or online. Check with your health-care provider before taking any supplement, especially if you have a chronic health condition or take any medication. *Consider…*

• **Loquat syrup.** Made from the yellow pear-shaped loquat fruit, this syrup quiets coughs and soothes sore throats. Try a brand called Nin Jiom Pei Pa Koa cough syrup or a natural loquat extract. See product labels for specific dosage guidelines.

• **White Flower Analgesic Balm.** A product that combines essential oils of wintergreen, menthol, camphor, eucalyptus, peppermint and lavender.

To relieve nasal congestion: Put a drop of White Flower onto your palm, rub palms together, then bring your hands up to your nose (avoiding the eyes) and inhale for four to eight breaths. Repeat up to four times daily as needed.

To ease headache or body aches: Massage a few drops into achy areas up to four times daily.

• **Acupressure.** This practice stimulates certain points along the body's meridians (energy channels) to eliminate qi blockages. To open sinuses, squeeze the acupressure point on the fleshy area between your thumb and index finger, near the thumb joint. The more blocked your qi is, the more tender this spot may feel. Apply just enough pressure to trigger mild discomfort. Hold for several minutes, then switch sides. Repeat as needed.

• **Acupuncture.** This can clear even serious sinus congestion, sometimes in a single session. The acupuncturist inserts one or more very fine needles at particular points on the body, depending on the individual's needs, to restore qi flow.

Referrals: The American Association of Acupuncture and Oriental Medicine (866-455-7999, *www.aaaomonline.org*).

• **Cupping.** Some acupuncturists and massage therapists will provide this treatment. A small glass or bamboo cup is heated and then placed on the person's back for about five minutes. The heat creates a vacuum that pulls on the skin and underlying muscle, improving qi flow and blood circulation to bring healing nutrients to the body's tissues. Cupping sometimes leaves a red mark on the skin—it's not a burn, just a result of the suction—which fades within a few days. If the practitioner opts to leave the cup on the back for a longer period of time, slight bruising may result—but again, this soon fades.

• **Diaphragmatic breath work.** This technique uses the diaphragm as a piston to improve oxygen flow and blood circulation and relieve congestion. Sit or stand up straight to allow lungs to fill…gently draw in air through your nose (if you're not too congested), letting your abdomen expand outward…then pull in your abdomen so that it pushes the air out through your mouth. Continue for one minute. Consciously repeat several times daily, aiming for this to become the way you automatically breathe throughout the day.

• **Tui na massage.** This Chinese system of massage vigorously stimulates the acupressure points and manipulates muscles and joints to promote qi flow. To find a practitioner, contact the National Certification Commission for Acupuncture and Oriental Medicine (904-598-1005, *www.nccaom.org*), and check for practitioners certified in "Asian bodywork." Other types of massage also can be helpful.

More from Dr. Effie Poy Yew Chow...

How to *Not* Catch a Cold

The best defense against colds is to avoid catching them in the first place. That requires a strong immune system—and certain nutrients can help.

Advised: In addition to a daily multivitamin, take any or all of the following supplements. For maximum effect, use year-round.

• **Coenzyme Q10 (CoQ10).** This vitamin-like substance boosts cellular energy.

Recommended dosage: 100 mg to 200 mg twice daily.

• **Fish oil.** This is rich in the omega-3 fatty acids *eicosapentaenoic acid* (EPA) and *docosahexaenoic acid* (DHA), which reduce disease-promoting inflammation. Take fish oil liquid or capsules at a dosage that provides 3,000 mg daily of combined EPA and DHA.

• **Vitamin D.** This is a fat-soluble vitamin that benefits the body in many ways, including by strengthening the immune system. I recommend taking 2,000 international units (IU) daily of vitamin D3 (*cholecalciferol*).

Alternative: Take one teaspoon of cod-liver oil daily for each 50 pounds of body weight.

Free or Low-Cost Flu Shots

Free or low-cost flu shots are available at an increasing number of locations, including county health departments and pharmacies. At most of these locations, however, the shots are offered for a very limited time. The American Lung Association's online Flu Clinic Locator (*www.flucliniclocator.org*) can search for upcoming flu shot clinics in your area so you don't miss your chance.

Virtually everyone should get an annual flu shot, particularly people over age 50...between ages two and 18...suffering from a chronic lung or heart problem...or in regular contact with someone who falls under any of these

increased-risk categories. The flu shot usually becomes available in late September. Flu and flu complications kill about 36,000 Americans each year.

Norman Edelman, MD, chief medical officer, American Lung Association, and professor of medicine, State University of New York at Stony Brook.

Dental Plaque Danger

Dental plaque can cause pneumonia. Dental plaque, which is composed mostly of germs, and gum disease have been found to be connected to heart disease and other maladies as a result of germs entering the bloodstream from the mouth. Studies now indicate plaque may contribute to pneumonia as well, due to germs moving from mouth to lungs. At greatest risk are patients on ventilators—as a ventilator pushes air into the lungs, it can push germs from the mouth with it. Between 10% and 25% of patients on ventilators come-down with pneumonia.

Self-defense: Brush and floss regularly to prevent plaque buildup and gum disease, and see your dentist if they do develop.

Harvard Health Letter, 10 Shattuck St., Boston, www.health.harvard.edu.

Germ-Fighting Tactics Most People Overlook

Philip M. Tierno, Jr., PhD, director of clinical microbiology and immunology at New York University Medical Center and a member of the faculty at New York University School of Medicine, both in New York City. He is the author of The Secret Lives of Germs (Atria).

You eat right, get enough sleep and wash your hands several times a day—but you still catch a cold. Even worse, you follow all of this standard advice—and get a flu vaccination—but still develop the flu.

Each year, the average American adult contracts two to four colds, while up to one of every five Americans contracts the flu, a debilitating illness that can lead to life-threatening pneumonia.

Why do so many people get sick when the preventive strategies are relatively simple?

Everyone knows the hand-washing drill. For example, if you shake hands with someone who is congested and has just blown his/her nose, you know to wash your own hands afterward. (See page 62 for proper hand-washing instructions.)

But the key to staying healthy during cold and flu season is to recognize the less obvious routes of transmission. *For example…*

• **Handshakes with people who do not look sick.** People often get colds through direct contact with an infected person, as well as from touching something that an infected person has touched within hours—or even days. That makes hand-shaking optimal for the transmission of cold viruses.

Stay-well strategy: If you need to shake hands with someone who shows cold or flu symptoms, such as a runny nose, sneezing or coughing, don't touch your face—especially your eyes, nose or mouth, the main "portals of entry"—until you've washed your hands.

Also important: Don't assume that a person without symptoms is safe. Even though colds are the most contagious once symptoms start, someone who harbors the virus can be contagious 24 hours beforehand. People with the flu are contagious one to three days before they develop symptoms. To be safe, assume that all people with whom you shake hands are infected, and wash your own hands afterward.

• **Contaminated air.** The flu can be spread through touch, but it is primarily transmitted through airborne droplets projected by coughs and/or sneezes. If you're around someone with obvious flu or cold symptoms, moving farther away will minimize your exposure to the "aerosol dispersal" of infectious organisms.

Stay-well strategy: Avoid touching (or kissing) any part of the face of anyone who is sick—it is a repository of infectious particles.

• **Countertops and money.** It's well-known that doorknobs often are contaminated with viruses and/or bacteria. If a person who has a cold covers his mouth while coughing and then opens a door, he will deposit viral particles on the doorknob.

However, few people recognize that other public surfaces, such as buttons in elevators, countertops and handrails—as well as paper money—are commonly contaminated. (Coins contain trace metal elements that help inhibit viruses and bacteria.)

Stay-well strategy: Wash your hands after touching any public surface and after all cash transactions. When hand-washing isn't practical, carry alcohol-based wipes (such as Wash 'n' Dri or Wet Ones) or liquid hand sanitizer (such as Purell or Germ-X). The wipes and liquid sanitizers should contain at least 62% alcohol.

Also important: If someone in your household is sick, disinfect doorknobs, light switches, remote controls and any other commonly used items in your home daily with alcohol wipes or an antiseptic spray, such as Lysol.

OTHER STAY-WELL STRATEGIES

Even if you are vigilant about avoiding the transmission routes described above, other actions can give you added protection…

• **Humidify.** Up to 50% of Americans catch respiratory infections (colds and flu) during the winter months, compared with only about 10% in midsummer. One reason may be indoor heating. It dries the mucous membranes and may increase the risk for infection. (The body's immune cells need moisture to function at their best.) The optimal indoor humidity is 30% to 60%.

Helpful: Open up a window or door for at least a few minutes during the day, or use a humidifier.

• **Get enough vitamin D.** Some evidence suggests that people who get enough vitamin D suffer fewer bouts of colds and flu. Vitamin D (which is synthesized in the body following sun exposure) stimulates the body's production of cathelicidin, a substance that appears to inhibit the production of viruses.

Helpful: Take a daily supplement that provides 1,000 international units (IU) to 2,000 IU of vitamin D. You also can get vitamin D from fortified milk and juices.

•**Combine echinacea with vitamin C.** The herb echinacea and vitamin C have traditionally been used for cold prevention and treatment because they both help increase immune activity.

In a recent report in *The Lancet Infectious Diseases,* researchers who combined the results of 14 studies found that taking echinacea alone reduced the incidence of colds by 65%. When echinacea was combined with vitamin C, colds were reduced by 86%.

To try the combination approach, take 300 mg of standardized echinacea three times per day, along with 500 mg to 1,000 mg of vitamin C daily. If you take 1,000 mg of vitamin C daily, take half in the morning and the other half in the late afternoon. Some forms, such as ester-C, are less apt to cause diarrhea, which can occur in some people at these dosages.

More from Dr. Philip Tierno...

Hand-Washing 101

Use plenty of soap and lukewarm water (primarily for comfort), and wash for 20 to 30 seconds. Be sure to wash your wrists, fingertips and between your fingers.

Remember: Antibacterial soaps kill most bacteria but provide only limited protection against viruses that cause colds and the flu. Alcohol-based cleansers do get rid of most of these viruses.

Important: To reduce your risk for contaminating your clean hands in a public restroom, use a motion-activated paper towel dispenser if one is available (if not, it's okay to use other types of paper towel dispensers). After drying your hands, use the towel to open the door and exit. Carry a paper towel or tissue in your pocket or handbag to open restroom doors at times when only a blower-type hand dryer is available.

Little-Known Asthma Trigger

Thunderstorms can be the cause of an asthma attack.

A recent finding: When researchers analyzed about 10 million emergency room visits, those due to asthma attacks were 3% higher on days following a thunderstorm versus days when a storm had not occurred.

Theory: During thunderstorms, rain, possibly combined with the electrical fields produced by lightning, breaks up pollen grains that are spread by gusty winds.

If you have asthma: Try to stay indoors during and immediately after thunderstorms.

Andrew Grundstein, PhD, associate professor, climatology research laboratory, University of Georgia, Athens.

Got Gas? Fast Help

To get rid of uncomfortable (and embarrassing) gas, go somewhere private, and let it out. Don't be embarrassed—the average person passes gas 14 times a day. Holding it in can be painful. Gassiness may increase after ingesting carbohydrates—such as *lactose* (in milk), *fructose* (in fruit), *raffinose* (in vegetables and grains) and *sorbitol* (in sugar-free gum). If you are bloated, nonprescription *simethicone* (Gas-X) or activated charcoal tablets (Charcocaps) may help you release gas. To ease discomfort, try peppermint tea—it contains menthol, which may ease cramping.

Samuel Meyers, MD, gastroenterologist and clinical professor of medicine at Mount Sinai School of Medicine, New York City.

Quick Fix for Pinkeye

If you have pinkeye, try the following before calling your doctor.

Place your thumb and index finger just below the bridge of the nose, where the pads of eyeglasses would rest. Gently massage the area. Then soak a clean washcloth in warm water, wring it out and place it over one eye for 10 minutes. Repeat with the other eye. Do this three or four times a day. These steps can unblock tear ducts so that the body clears up a minor infection itself. Results should be noticeable within a few hours. If the condition does not improve by then, call your doctor.

Ken Haller, MD, assistant professor of pediatrics, Saint Louis University School of Medicine, St. Louis.

No More Raccoon Eyes

Nooshin Darvish, ND, medical director and founder of the Holistique Medical Center, Bellevue, Washington. She is a former faculty member of Bastyr University and doctor-on-call for *The Dr. Pat Show,* an internationally broadcast talk radio program.

D ark under-eye circles are not just a cosmetic concern or genetic legacy— they can signal an underlying health problem.

How: When veins are overtaxed, they swell and dilate. Veins beneath the eyes become visible because the area has many blood vessels and the overlying skin is thin.

Veins can be affected by sleep deprivation, dehydration, smoking and excessive alcohol or caffeine—so under-eye circles often disappear with improvements in lifestyle. *However, if dark circles persist, the culprit could be…*

●**Allergies.** Sensitivities to foods (wheat, dairy), environmental triggers (pollen, dust) or chemicals (gasoline, paint) can provoke an inflammatory response from the immune system. This makes veins swell.

●**Digestive problems.** Conditions such as intestinal infections or irritable bowel syndrome can impair the digestive system's ability to completely process food. This triggers an inflammatory immune reaction that makes veins swell.

●**Hormonal imbalance.** An underperforming thyroid or adrenal gland can affect blood circulation.

See your doctor for a checkup and follow any prescribed treatment. *Also…*

To ease inflammation: Take vitamin C at 1,000 milligrams (mg) twice daily…and drink three to six cups of green tea every day.

To improve digestion: Supplement with L-glutamine (an amino acid) at 500 mg three times daily, between meals. Also take probiotics (beneficial digestive bacteria)—ask your doctor about the best type and dosage for you.

To balance hormones: Take selenium at 100 micrograms daily…and vitamin B-6 at 50 mg per day (with food). Drink one cup of Panax ginseng tea each morning—but get your doctor's approval first if you use any medication.

*A **quick temporary fix:*** Chilled cucumber slices placed over the eye area for 10 minutes can reduce inflammation.

A Younger-Looking Neck—Without Surgery

Nelson Lee Novick, MD, clinical professor of dermatology at Mount Sinai School of Medicine and a cosmetic dermatologist in private practice, both in New York City. He is author of *Super Skin* (iUniverse). A pioneer in nonsurgical cosmetic procedures, he has gotten numerous awards, including the American Academy of Dermatology's Leadership Circle Award. His online site is *www.youngerlookingwithoutsurgery.com.*

N ew nonsurgical techniques improve the appearance of "necklace lines" (bands of wrinkles encircling the neck) and "turkey wattle" (saggy chin skin and ropey vertical cords at the front of the neck)—without the pain, risks, recuperation or expense of cosmetic surgery. *Fixes for…*

●**Necklace lines.** Microdroplets of muscle-relaxing Botox (a purified form of a protein produced by the *Clostridium botulinum* bacterium) are injected at half-inch intervals along, above and/or below each band (except where covered by hair at the back of the neck). Within about 14 days, as the sheetlike platysma muscle relaxes in the treated areas, the muscle in the nontreated areas pulls the skin tight so wrinkles smooth out.

Cost: About $500 to $750 per treatment.*

• **Turkey wattle.** Botox injections down the full length of each ropey cord will make the platysma muscle drape more smoothly. Botox beneath the jawline allows the muscles above to pull the neck skin upward. Then injections of Radiesse (a synthetic gel of tiny calcium-based spheres) along the jawline and under the chin give added volume where needed to make the neck skin more taut. Radiesse also helps stimulate the body's own production of skin-firming collagen.

Cost: About $1,500 per treatment.

With either procedure: There is minor discomfort as local anesthesia is injected. Only tiny amounts of Botox are given at each site, so swallowing and breathing muscles are not affected. No recovery time or activity restrictions are needed. Minor redness, swelling and bruising all disappear within two days. Botox lasts about six months…Radiesse lasts nine to 18 months.

*Prices subject to change.

Natural Wrinkle Reducer

In a recent finding, people who consumed the most vitamin C had 11% fewer wrinkles than those who consumed the least vitamin C.

Theory: The antioxidants in vitamin C are an important component in the production of collagen, a protein that helps keep skin firm and smooth.

Good sources of vitamin C: Oranges, tomatoes, strawberries and broccoli.

Maeve Cosgrove, PhD, nutritional epidemiologist, Unilever Food and Health Research Institute, The Netherlands, and lead author of a study of 4,025 women, reported in *The American Journal of Clinical Nutrition*.

Wake Up and Smell The Coffee

Just the smell of coffee can make you much more alert.

Recent study: Participants typed significantly faster and more accurately when exposed to the scent of coffee.

Study by researchers at Wheeling Jesuit University, Wheeling, West Virginia, reported in *North American Journal of Psychology*.

Tired All the Time? Try a Juice Cleanse

Woodson C. Merrell, MD, chairman of the department of integrative medicine at Beth Israel Medical Center and assistant clinical professor of medicine at Columbia University College of Physicians and Surgeons, both in New York City. He is author, with Kathleen Merrell, of *The Source: Unleash Your Natural Energy, Power Up Your Health, and Feel 10 Years Younger* (Free Press). Dr. Merrell's Web site is *www.woodsonmerrell.com*.

Juice fasts allow the digestive tract to rest while promoting detoxification, reducing inflammation and dramatically increasing energy. One study even found that individuals who fasted once a month were 39% more likely to have healthy hearts than nonfasters.

Once a month, consume nothing but juice for an entire day. Use a juicer to combine a variety of organic vegetables, such as spinach, carrots and broccoli. Add a small amount of apples, cherries or other fruits as a natural sweetener.

It's normal to feel a little worse during the day of the fast. That's when the body is shedding the most toxins. Most people feel much more energized and clear-headed on the day after the fast.

Caution: If you have a severe chronic disease, diabetes or are pregnant, consult your physician before fasting.

A Simple Way to Sleep Better

Avoid cell phone use just before sleeping. Cell phones seem to interfere with deep sleep—possibly because their electromagnetic fields excite the brain or interrupt hormone production.

Better: Use a land line when making calls close to bedtime.

Bengt B. Arnetz, MD, professor, Wayne State University, Detroit.

Stop Nighttime Calf Cramps Tonight

An imbalance of electrolytes (the minerals needed for normal body fluid function) may bring on nighttime calf cramps, so eat more foods rich in potassium (sweet potatoes, bananas)…magnesium (nuts, spinach)…and calcium (dairy foods, sardines). Consume enough clear fluids (water, broth, light tea) to keep urine pale yellow.

Also, stretch your calves before bed.

How: Stand up with toes pointed straight ahead. With your left foot, step forward about 18 inches. Keeping both heels on the ground and your right leg straight, bend your left knee until you feel a stretch in your right calf. Hold for 30 seconds. Repeat on the other side.

Timothy W. Flynn, PT, PhD, president, American Academy of Orthopaedic Manual Physical Therapists and associate professor of physical therapy, Regis University, Denver.

The Three Best Stress-Busters for Women

Alice Domar, PhD, assistant professor of obstetrics, gynecology and reproductive biology at Harvard Medical School, Boston, and executive director of the Domar Center for Mind/Body Health, Waltham, Massachusetts, *www.domarcenter.com.* She is the author of four books, including *Be Happy Without Being Perfect* (Crown).

On any given day, research suggests, a woman is likely to become stressed more often and more intensely than a man—and to do so in reaction to a wider variety of concerns. She even may stress out in more vivid detail, often with accompanying headaches or insomnia. One reason for these differences is hormones.

Smart: Use biology to advantage by honing three stress-relieving techniques that work especially well for women.

•**Deep breathing.** Research suggests that, during stress, the hormone *adrenaline* may activate neurons in the part of the brain that controls emotions. This triggers strong visceral responses (racing heart, roiling stomach). Men may metabolize adrenaline more quickly, so their visceral response abates sooner. Deep breathing can interrupt the visceral response, which in turn calms the mind.

What to do: Breathe in through your nose and then out through the mouth, slowly and deeply, clearing your mind by focusing in on your breath.

•**Challenging negative thoughts.** In times of stress, a woman's level of the stress hormone *cortisol* might remain elevated longer than a man's, according to a recent study. Cortisol affects memory formation—so a woman remembers stressful events more vividly. By challenging the validity of a habitual negative thought, you defuse the power of the stressful memory.

What to do: Identify the situation—for instance, your cousin made a crack about your cluttered house and now you keep thinking that you're a slob.

Next, ask and answer these questions: *Where did this thought come from?* (It made me remember how embarrassed I always felt when my mother criticized my messy room.) *Is it logical?* (Not necessarily—a house can be cluttered but clean.) *Is it true?* (No, I'm not a slob—I dress impeccably.)

•**Reaching out.** When women are stressed, they release the bonding hormone *oxytocin*, which encourages them to seek solace from other people. However, the male hormone *testosterone* may reduce the effects of oxytocin, so men often withdraw when stressed. Another woman may best provide comfort because she understands how you feel.

What to do: Phone or e-mail a girlfriend, and talk through all your troubles. Better yet, take a walk together while you talk—exercising is also a stress antidote.

Reach Out and Touch Someone

Touch helps to reduce stress. In a recent finding, married couples who gave each other back rubs or touched each other affectionately in other ways for at least 30 minutes three times a week had 34% lower levels of stress. Researchers found that being affectionate releases the hormone *oxytocin*, which may protect against stress-related illnesses.

Julianne Holt-Lunstad, PhD, assistant professor, department of psychology at Brigham Young University, Provo, Utah, and leader of a study published in *Psychosomatic Medicine*.

Nosebleed Know-How

Don't tilt your head back during a nosebleed. It can let blood run into the esophagus, which can cause choking, or run into the stomach, which can lead to irritation and vomiting.

Instead: Sit down, lean forward and keep your head above your heart. Use your thumb and index finger to squeeze the soft tissue below the bridge of your nose for five to 20 minutes. Also, a small wad of cotton or gauze sprayed with a topical decongestant can be placed in the bleeding nostril for 10 to 15 minutes.

American Academy of Family Physicians, Leawood, Kansas, *www.aafp.org*.

Natural Remedies for Bruises

After you've been bumped and know a bruise is on the way, reduce swelling by applying an ice pack to the area—about 30 seconds on and 30 seconds off three times—twice daily. Rub one teaspoon of arnica lotion or oil into the area three times daily for five days to alleviate swelling and stimulate the healing action of white blood cells. Also, take 500 mg of the herb gotu kola three times daily for two days to help skin cells knit together. (Products are sold in health-food stores.)

To minimize future bruising, strengthen the blood vessel walls by taking 1,000 mg of vitamin C daily, continuing indefinitely. Several times a week, eat blueberries or other berries —these are rich in flavonoids, which improve circulation.

Laurie Steelsmith, ND, a naturopathic doctor and acupuncturist in private practice in Honolulu and the author of *Natural Choices for Women's Health* (Three Rivers, *www.naturalchoicesforwomen.com*).

Rubbing Alcohol Or Hydrogen Peroxide to Clean a Cut?

For minor cuts (such as those from paper, a kitchen knife or other sharp objects), I recommend using rubbing alcohol that contains 70% alcohol. It is very effective at killing germs. However, if the wound contains dirt or other debris, which can occur if you have fallen on the ground or been scraped or cut on a tree branch, I recommend using hydrogen peroxide to clean the wound. Hydrogen peroxide "bubbles" on contact with skin—an action that helps remove debris and other impurities. However, keep in mind that various studies have found that while hydrogen peroxide kills germs, it also may damage normal skin cells and even delay healing. That's why its use should be limited to wounds that contain dirt and other particles.

Neal Schultz, MD, assistant clinical professor of dermatology, Mount Sinai School of Medicine, New York City.

4

Easy Fitness

10 Ways to Keep Lost Weight Off for Good— Strategies That Work

Too often, the triumph of dropping unwanted weight is followed within months by utter frustration as the lost pounds creep back on. Disappointed dieters wind up as heavy as ever —and then in despair, give up all attempts at weight control.

It doesn't have to be this way. Weight regain, though common, is not inevitable.

What studies show: Among overweight individuals who lose 10% or more of their body weight, one in five succeeds in keeping the pounds off for at least one year. You can be that one.

If you are overweight: A 10% weight loss provides significant health benefits, including lowering diabetes risk, blood pressure and cholesterol levels. And, this is the case even if a 10% weight loss still leaves you somewhat overweight.

What are the secrets to success for people who keep weight off? Answers are found in studies of the members of the National Weight Control Registry—a group of more than 6,000 women and men who have lost 30 pounds or more (their average weight loss is 70 pounds) and kept it off for at least one year. Women account for 78% of Registry members. *Based on members' experiences, here are 10 practical, proven strategies that can work for you…*

1. Try, try again. Almost everyone in the Registry had tried to lose weight and failed many times before shedding the pounds for good. This is very similar to the experience of

---

Rena R. Wing, PhD, professor of psychiatry and human behavior at Brown Medical School and director of the Weight Control and Diabetes Research Center at The Miriam Hospital, both in Providence. Along with James O. Hill, PhD, of the University of Colorado, she founded the National Weight Control Registry in 1994 to study the behaviors and attitudes of successful dieters, *www. nwcr.ws*. It is the largest study ever conducted of long-term, successful weight-loss maintenance.

smokers, who typically make a number of attempts before they finally manage to quit smoking.

2. Do not believe that a history of weight problems means that you are destined to fail. Half of Registry members were overweight as children…for two-thirds, one or both parents were obese. These factors make it more difficult to control weight—but it definitely is possible for you to overcome a genetic predisposition to obesity.

3. Stick with a relatively small variety of foods. Registry members use all different types of diets—commercial weight-loss programs, guidelines in best-selling books and plans they devise themselves. What almost all of them have in common, however, is a habit of eating their favorite low-fat, low-calorie foods over and over again. Research shows that people who have a lot of variety in their diets tend to eat more and have a harder time maintaining weight loss.

4. Make a permanent commitment to a new lifestyle. For many Registry members, changes in eating and exercise habits were initially sparked by a medical problem (such as diabetes) that they developed or witnessed in a family member…an emotional trigger, such as being criticized about their size…or an upcoming event (such as a high school reunion or a hallmark birthday) for which they wanted to look their best. The key to success was that afterward, Registry members continued to watch their diets and to be more physically active than they had been in the past.

5. Watch less TV. The average American watches about 30 hours of TV per week—but most Registry members watch less than 10 hours per week.

Likely explanation: Members replace at least some of their former couch potato time with exercise, which is proven to help prevent weight regain.

6. Do not take diet breaks. Registry members say no when asked if they allow themselves extra eating flexibility on weekends or vacations. One study showed that those who ate about the same amount of food day after day were more likely to keep their weight

within a five-pound range than those who gave themselves more freedom on weekends and holidays.

7. Always have breakfast. Among Registry members, 78% report that they never skip the morning meal. Most eat three meals plus one or two snacks per day. In contrast, typical dieters skip breakfast and have a light lunch—then by mid-afternoon or evening, they are so ravenous that they overeat.

8. Devote one hour a day to exercise. A full 90% of Registry members exercise for at least 60 minutes daily. They favor walking, but any physical activity will do—biking, dancing or whatever else you enjoy. You don't have to do your entire workout at once. It is just as effective to accumulate exercise over the course of the day—for instance, by taking a 15-minute walk after breakfast and lunch, then walking for 30 minutes or more after dinner.

9. Continue to monitor weight even after the goal is reached. Careful attention to how you are doing is critical not only to taking off weight, but also to keeping it off.

What works: Weigh yourself daily or weekly, and plot the numbers on a graph…keep a food diary for one week per month…make a habit of counting calories in your head…and/or keep a chart of all your exercise goals and achievements.

10. Try like crazy to break the two-year mark. The riskiest time for weight regain is in the first two years after weight loss. Once Registry members pass that mark, their new healthier habits have become thoroughly ingrained in their lives. They generally feel so positive about the changes they've made that it seems to require less effort to maintain their new weight.

Inspiring thought: The longer you keep the weight off, the easier it will get—and the better you will feel.

Why Pine Nuts Help You Lose Weight...and Other Tricks to Drop Pounds

Jodi Citrin Greebel, RD, CDN, a registered dietitian and president of Citrition, LLC, a nutrition consulting company in New York City. She is also coauthor, with Melissa Gibson and Katie Nuanes, of *The Little Black Apron: A Single Girl's Guide to Cooking with Style & Grace* (Polka Dot).

Most weight-loss diets are hard to stick to. That's because you have to eliminate 3,500 calories to lose *just one pound* a week and that comes to 500 calories a day. This degree of calorie restriction can make people feel hungry all the time—and reluctant to stick with any diet for very long. That's also why it is hard for people to maintain the weight that they do take off. Roughly 95% of those who lose weight are unable to maintain the weight loss longer than a year or two.

Better: Eat foods that curtail appetite and increase feelings of fullness. People who do this naturally take in fewer calories overall and are more likely to maintain their weight loss.

What to eat...

•**Protein at every meal.** Protein is a natural appetite suppressant. People who often feel hungry probably are not getting enough protein.

Self-test: Have a regular meal or snack. If you are hungry again within two hours, the meal probably didn't include enough protein.

Protein should make up about 25% of every meal—three ounces to six ounces of protein is ideal. Good protein sources include chicken, seafood, lean red meats, egg whites, beans and low- or nonfat dairy.

Trap: Many conventional breakfast foods, such as a bagel or a Danish, are high in calories but low in protein. People who start the day with these foods invariably want to eat more within a few hours, adding unnecessary calories.

Always include protein with your morning meal—by spreading peanut butter on whole-wheat toast, for example.

Also helpful: High-protein snacks, such as string cheese or yogurt. They're more satisfying than carbohydrate snacks, such as pretzels or chips.

•**More fat.** Until recently, weight-loss experts advised people to eat less fat. This made intuitive sense because fat has about twice the calories as an equal amount of protein or carbohydrate. But today, after about 15 years of low-fat dieting, Americans are heavier than ever.

Reason: People who don't feel satisfied on a low-fat diet often eat excessive carbohydrates to make up the difference.

Fat is a satisfying nutrient. You may feel full after eating a lot of carbohydrates, including pasta or bread, but you'll still want more. Fat, on the other hand, makes you crave less food, so you'll be less likely to fill up on calories from other sources.

Have a little fat with every meal. If you're having a salad, for example, use full-fat dressing in moderation rather than fat-free. Add in a tablespoon of olive oil when making pasta sauce. A slice of cheese or a serving of cottage cheese also provides satisfying amounts of fat.

Easy does it: Use fats only in small amounts to avoid excess calories. One tablespoon of olive oil, for example, has about 120 calories. Small amounts curtail your appetite without adding too many calories.

•**A handful of pine nuts.** A hormone called *cholecystokinin* (CCK) has been found to increase feelings of fullness. About one ounce or a small handful of pine nuts (which actually are seeds, not nuts) stimulates the body to release CCK. This reduces appetite and helps you feel fuller even when you take in fewer calories overall.

•**Fiber,** especially earlier in the day. High-fiber diets increase sensations of fullness and aid in weight loss. High-fiber foods also may stimulate the release of appetite-suppressing hormones.

Virtually all foods that are high in fiber, such as fruits, vegetables, legumes and whole grains, are relatively low in calories. People who eat a lot of these foods tend to feel full even when they take in fewer calories during the day.

Try to get 25 to 30 grams of fiber per day. Beans are high in fiber, with about six grams in one-half cup. Blackberries are another excellent source, with about eight grams of fiber per cup.

•**Spicy foods as often as possible.** Cayenne, jalapeños, curries and other spicy foods contain *capsaicin* and other compounds that may increase metabolism and cause the body to burn slightly more calories. More important, these foods appear to affect the "satiety center" in the brain, causing people to feel more satisfied and consume fewer calories.

•**Water before a meal.** Drink a full glass of water before you start eating, and keep on sipping water throughout the meal. Water will take up space in the stomach. Or you could start your meal with a broth-based soup (not a cream soup, which is higher in calories). People who consume liquids before and during meals consume fewer calories than those who go straight to the main course.

Caution: Avoid high-calorie liquids. Americans consume about 20% more calories now than they did 20 years ago. Many of these calories come from soft drinks, sports drinks and coffee beverages that include sugar and cream. Some of these drinks contain 400 calories or more, which could result in almost one extra pound of weight a week if consumed daily.

Curb Your Appetite Naturally

Jane Guiltinan, ND, a clinical professor at Bastyr Center for Natural Health in Seattle. She is also a past president of the American Association of Naturopathic Physicians and a member of the *Bottom Line/Women's Health* advisory board.

Unscrupulous marketers claim that various supplements can depress appetite. Should you try them? No. *What doesn't work—and what does...*

•**Never take ephedra (or ma huang).** This stimulant does suppress appetite—but at the price of increased heart rate, nervousness and agitation. In moderate-to-large doses, ephedra has killed people. The FDA banned ephedra from dietary supplements in the US in 2004—yet it still is marketed illegally.

•**Skip garcinia cambogia.** This fruit from India contains a compound called hydroxycitrate. In animal studies, rats given hydroxycitrate ate less and lost weight—but there is no evidence that garcinia has the same effect on humans. Short-term studies (12 weeks) have not yet revealed safety problems, but no long-term studies have been done.

•**Don't waste money on hoodia.** A plant found in Africa, hoodia is said to trick your brain into thinking that you're full. It is not a stimulant, so it's probably safe—but no published long-term studies on humans show that it's effective.

•**Do drink plenty of water.** People often mistake thirst for hunger and eat when they should be hydrating.

•**Opt for hot tea or coffee.** In my experience, hot beverages curb hunger better than cold beverages do. Also, caffeine is a stimulant that has a mild appetite-suppressing effect. To avoid insomnia, limit caffeinated beverages to a few per day.

•**Eat "volume" foods that fill you up—** such as high-fiber, low-calorie carrots, broccoli, salad greens, apples and brown rice.

•**Eat more often.** Go no more than three hours without a regular meal or a healthful snack, such as peanut butter on whole-grain crackers. Otherwise, you end up so ravenous that when you do eat, you are more likely to consume too many calories and make poor food choices.

•**Block sugar cravings.** Supplement with 100 micrograms twice per day of the mineral *chromium*—it may lessen sugar cravings by stabilizing blood sugar levels. Or consider the herb *gymnema sylvestre,* which may temporarily block sweet taste receptors on the tongue and also help stabilize blood sugar. Speak to a health-care professional who is knowledgeable about botanical medicine to determine the proper dosage. If you take medication to control blood sugar, do not use either supplement without your doctor's approval.

A French Lesson—Why They Don't Gain Weight

Americans rely on external cues to determine when to stop eating, such as at the end of a TV program or getting to the bottom of a glass of soda. This can mean that they ignore the body's own cues and eat more than the body needs to feel full.

Healthier: Use internal cues, such as when you no longer feel hungry, to decide when to stop eating. This is what the French usually do, which could be one reason why they do not gain as much weight as Americans, even though they eat many high-fat foods.

Study of 133 Paris residents and 145 Chicago residents by researchers at Cornell University, Ithaca, New York, published in *Obesity*.

How to Lose Three Times More Weight

Dieters who write down what they eat lose three times as much weight as those who don't, previous research suggests.

Recent study: For one week, volunteers kept written food logs and also photographed their meals and snacks. Participants reported that their photo logs were less time-consuming… more accurate…and far more effective at influencing their choices at the critical moments —before the food was eaten.

Convenient: Use your cell phone or a pocket-sized digital camera to snap food photos.

Lydia Zepeda, PhD, professor of consumer science, University of Wisconsin, Madison, and the leader of a study of 43 people, published in *International Journal of Consumer Studies*.

Why You Should Wear Jeans to Work

People took about 8% more steps during the workday when they dressed casually in jeans than when they wore business attire. The additional steps—491 per day, on average, as measured by pedometers—burned an extra 25 calories daily, or the equivalent of about 1.8 pounds of body weight per year.

Bottom line: The average American adult gains 0.4 to 1.8 pounds yearly. Dressing casually encourages increased physical activity that could more than offset this weight gain.

John Porcari, PhD, director, clinical exercise physiology program at University of Wisconsin, La Crosse, and leader of a study of 53 people, sponsored by the American Council on Exercise.

To Lose Weight, Slow Down

When researchers recently surveyed the eating habits of 3,000 men and women, those who ate meals and snacks quickly were three times more likely to be overweight than those who did not eat quickly.

Theory: Quick ingestion of food does not allow sufficient time for the body's signals of satiety (feeling of fullness) to register, leading to overeating.

To maintain a healthy weight: Dine in a relaxed setting (such as at a dining room or kitchen table), and avoid fast food and eating while watching television.

Hiroyasu Iso, MD, professor, department of social and environmental health, Osaka University Graduate School of Medicine, Osaka, Japan.

Satisfy Your Sweet Tooth with Gum

In a study of 60 people, some participants chewed on gum (sugar-sweetened or sugar-free) for at least 15 minutes every hour, three hours before eating a snack. One time, the snack was sweet (such as a chocolate-coated biscuit), while another time, it was salty (such as potato chips).

Result: Those who chewed gum consumed 39 fewer calories from sweets than those who did not chew gum.

Theory: Chewing gum may be satisfying in itself, diminishing the desire to eat a similarly sweet food.

Self-defense: The next time you have the urge to snack, try chewing a piece of sugar-free gum, which contains about five calories.

Marion Hetherington, DPhil, professor of biopsychology, Glasgow Caledonian University, Scotland.

Minty Weight Loss

In a recent finding, people who sniffed peppermint oil every two hours ate almost 350 fewer calories a day than those who did not.

Possible reason: Peppermint boosts alertness, so people who smell it may be less likely to snack because of fatigue or boredom.

Bryan Raudenbush, PhD/L Pharm, associate professor of psychology and director of undergraduate research, Wheeling Jesuit University, Wheeling, West Virginia, and coauthor of a study published in *Appetite*.

Lose 10 Pounds Just by Eating This Breakfast Food

In a recent study, people who added half a grapefruit to each meal dropped up to 10 pounds in 12 weeks and lowered their insulin levels significantly.

Best: Eat up to one-half grapefruit every day or drink eight ounces of grapefruit juice.

Caution: Grapefruit and grapefruit juice can interfere with some medications—check with your doctor.

Ken Fujioka, MD, director of nutrition and metabolic research at the San Diego Scripps Clinic, and lead author of a study of 91 obese people over 12 weeks, published in *Journal of Medicinal Food.*

Skip MSG to Stay Slim

People who used the flavor enhancer *monosodium glutamate* (MSG) the most were nearly three times as likely to be overweight or obese as people who did not use MSG, a recent study found—even though calorie consumption and physical activity levels were the same in both groups. MSG may affect the part of the brain that helps regulate appetite and fat metabolism. Check food labels—many processed and Asian foods contain MSG...as do the flavor-enhancing ingredients yeast extract, *hydrolyzed protein* and *calcium caseinate.*

Ka He, MD, assistant professor of nutrition and epidemiology, University of North Carolina at Chapel Hill School of Public Health, and author of a study of 752 people, published in *Obesity.*

What to Do When Fast Food Is Your Only Option

When fast food is the only food available, look over the nutritional information, including calories and fat, on the charts posted in the restaurant. And, don't be afraid to customize the order. For example, ask for fries to be replaced with vegetables or a baked potato. Also, stay away from combo meals—they often have larger portions and more calories, and remove the top half of the bun from the sandwich or burger. Finally, skip regular soft drinks—one nondiet soft drink can have 400 calories or more. Ask for water or diet soda instead.

Consumer Reports on Health, 101 Truman Ave., Yonkers, New York 10703, *www.consumerreports.org/health.*

Low-Fat Diet Not So Healthy After All

Paul Marantz, MD, PhD, MPH, associate dean for clinical research education, Albert Einstein College of Medicine, Yeshiva University, Bronx, New York.

Doctors warn that previous guidelines' emphasis on encouraging low-fat diets may have been harmful. They claim that a surge in obesity and the incidence of diabetes have occurred since low-fat diets have been heavily encouraged.

The mistake: Obesity is triggered by consumption of calories, not fat. Heavily emphasizing a low-fat intake may have encouraged many individuals who did decrease their fat intake to believe that their diets were much healthier—and they could then eat more. So they increased their calorie intake by eating too much, especially too many carbohydrates. High-carbohydrate diets can adversely affect the body's metabolism—and the increase in obesity and carbohydrate consumption have occurred together, after the "low-fat diet" recommendations were heavily publicized.

Best: Control weight by restricting calorie consumption in a balanced diet…and exercise regularly.

Healthier Holidays

How to have a delicious holiday feast without all the fat…

Mashed potatoes: Use fat-free sour cream and skim milk, and sneak in some steamed and puréed cauliflower.

Gravy: Skim the fat off the top before you serve it.

Stuffing: Make it outside the bird so that it does not absorb chicken or turkey fat, and use chicken broth and a little olive oil to moisten the stuffing instead of butter.

Turkey: Stick to white meat, and avoid eating any skin.

Dessert: Go with an apple crisp or a crustless pumpkin custard, instead of pie, to avoid the butter-rich pastry.

Sarah Krieger, licensed dietitian/nutritionist, American Dietetic Association, Chicago.

Portion Sizes Are Expanding

Newer recipes provide larger portion sizes and more calories.

Example: One brownie recipe from the 1960s *Joy of Cooking* yielded 30 brownies, but the same recipe made only 15 in the 1990s edition.

Self-defense: Stay conscious of portion size when eating.

Study of seven editions of *The Joy of Cooking,* from the 1936 edition to the 2006 edition, by researchers at Cornell University, Ithaca, New York, and New Mexico State University, Las Cruces, published in *Annals of Internal Medicine.*

Why Belly Fat Is the Worst Fat to Have

JoAnn E. Manson, MD, DrPH, a professor of medicine and women's health at Harvard Medical School and chief of the division of preventive medicine at Brigham and Women's Hospital, both in Boston. She is one of the lead investigators for two highly influential studies on women's health—the Harvard Nurses' Health Study and the Women's Health Initiative. Dr. Manson is the author, with Shari Bassuk, ScD, of *Hot Flashes, Hormones & Your Health* (McGraw-Hill).

To determine whether they are a healthy size, many people rely on a scale, height-and-weight chart or mathematical formula that calculates body mass index (BMI). Yet new research reveals that a tape measure more accurately predicts a person's risk for many major health problems. That's because waist measurement indicates the amount of belly fat—the fat that accumulates deep in the abdomen, around the intestines, liver and other internal organs. Belly fat is linked to a strongly elevated risk for diabetes, heart disease, stroke, high blood pressure and abnormal cholesterol levels...some types of cancer, including breast and colorectal cancers...and dementia.

Surprising: Having a large belly is more dangerous than simply being overweight or even obese. In a 16-year study of 45,000 female nurses, women whose waists measured 35 inches or more were much more likely to die prematurely than women with waists of less than 28 inches—even when their weight was within the normal range for their height. Women in the middle range had a small-to-moderate increase in risk. *Reasons...*

• **Belly fat may be more metabolically active than other fat,** releasing free fatty acids (fat cell products that circulate in the bloodstream) directly to the liver. This can lead to insulin resistance (inability of the body's cells to use insulin properly) and widespread inflammation, both of which will significantly increase diabetes and heart disease risk.

• **Belly fat may be a sign of fat deposits in the liver and around the heart,** which can impair organ function.

• **After menopause, the tendency to accumulate belly fat increases** as women produce less estrogen relative to androgens (male hormones). Androgens promote abdominal fat.

To measure: Wrap a tape measure around your torso at the level of your navel—usually slightly below the narrowest part of the abdomen. The tape should be snug but not cut into your flesh. For women of any height, a waist of less than 30 inches is optimal...30 inches to 35 inches indicates moderately elevated health risk...and more than 35 inches indicates high risk. *To reduce belly fat...*

• Lose weight. Often the first fat to go is abdominal fat. Even a modest loss of 10% of your starting weight confers great health benefits.

• Reduce stress. Stress causes the adrenal glands to release the hormone cortisol, which promotes belly fat.

• Get the right kinds of exercise. You cannot melt away belly fat with targeted abdominal exercises, such as sit-ups. Instead, engage in aerobic activity, such as brisk walking and racket sports. Doing three hours of aerobic exercise weekly can eliminate about 50% of the excess risk for heart disease associated with belly fat and up to 25% of the excess risk for diabetes. *Also healthful:* Resistance exercises (such as using arm and leg weights).

Fitness Trumps Weight Loss

Normal-weight people do not outlive the moderately overweight, more than a dozen research studies now report. Being physically fit and active compensates for problems that result from excess weight.

Recent survey of 170,000 people: Those who were happy with their weight (even if overweight) reported better mental and physical health.

Caution: Being obese or very overweight does pose serious health risks.

Katherine M. Flegal, PhD, National Center for Health Statistics, Centers for Disease Control and Prevention, Hyattsville, Maryland.

Feel-Good Exercises You Can Do in Bed

Genie Tartell, DC, RN, a New York City–based chiropractor and registered nurse who focuses on physical rehabilitation. She is a coauthor of *Get Fit in Bed* (New Harbinger).

Think back to the last time you really stretched your body. Didn't you feel so good afterward?

Unfortunately, most individuals—including many who are physically active—just don't do enough to improve their muscle tone, flexibility and strength. To help people incorporate a simple workout regimen into their daily routines, I have devised a program that can be performed in a comfortable setting you are bound to visit each day—your bed.

These bed exercises not only increase your strength, flexibility and endurance, but also stimulate production of the mood-enhancing brain chemical serotonin, leaving you feeling serene and relaxed. As a result, most people find that they sleep better when they do these exercises at night, and feel invigorated if they do the routine in the morning.

The following exercises are designed for anyone but are particularly helpful for people who are confined to a bed (while recovering from an illness or injury) and for those unable to find time during the day to exercise. They can be completed in just 10 minutes a day.

Important: When performing each movement, breathe in slowly for a count of four... hold for a count of one...then exhale through pursed lips for a count of four.

ALTERNATE LEG LENGTHENER

Purpose: Tones and stretches the spine and pelvis, which bears much of the upper body's weight.

What to do: While lying on your back with your body centered on the bed and your hips and legs flat on the bed, stretch your right leg forward by pushing with the heel of your right foot. Return your leg to the starting position. Do the same stretch with your left leg. Repeat five times with each leg.

HIP SIDE TO SIDE

Purpose: Tones and stretches the hips and low back.

What to do: While lying on your back with your hips flat on the bed, rock your hips gently —as far as comfortable—to the right and then to the left. Keep your upper body stable. Repeat five times in each direction.

ARMS-SHOULDER SEESAW

Purpose: Tones and stretches the shoulders and upper back.

What to do: While lying on your back, place your arms at your sides. Slide your right arm and shoulder toward your right foot. Next, raise your right shoulder toward your head, while at the same time sliding your left arm and shoulder toward your left foot. Then raise your left shoulder toward your head, while lowering your right arm and shoulder toward your right foot. Repeat five times on each side, moving your shoulders up and down like a seesaw.

ARMS TOWARD THE HEADBOARD

Purpose: Stretches the shoulders and rib cage, allowing for deeper, much more relaxed breathing.

What to do: While lying on your back, extend your arms behind your head. Stretch your right arm toward the headboard of your bed or the wall behind you. Return your right arm to your side and then extend your left arm behind you. Repeat five times on each side.

ELBOW-KNEE PISTON

Purpose: Strengthens your abdominal muscles while increasing your heart rate (improves heart muscle strength and endurance).

What to do: While lying on your back, raise your knees and, using your stomach muscles, lift your upper body toward them. Bend your arms so that your elbows are pointing at your knees. Bring your left elbow toward your right knee, then return to the starting position. Then bring your right elbow toward your left knee, maintaining a continuous pumping motion. Repeat six times.

COBRA

Purpose: Builds upper body strength (important for daily activities such as bathing and cooking).

What to do: Lie on your stomach with your elbows bent and palms flat on the bed next to your shoulders. Fully straighten your arms to lift your upper body so that it curves into a cobra-like position. Hold for a few seconds, then return to the starting position. Repeat three times.

MODIFIED BOW

Purpose: Tones and strengthens the back and improves muscular coordination.

What to do: Lie on your stomach with your arms at your sides. Raise your legs and upper body simultaneously (only to a level that is comfortable), then reach back with your arms as if you are trying to touch your raised feet. Hold for a few seconds, then return to the starting position. Repeat three times.

SWIMMING IN BED

Purpose: Strengthens the arms and legs, while increasing heart rate and stimulating blood flow throughout the body.

What to do: While lying on your stomach, move one arm forward, then move it back while moving your other arm forward, simultaneously kicking your legs. Repeat 20 times, counting each arm movement as one repetition.

BRIDGE

Purpose: Cools down the body and directs blood flow away from the legs to the heart, reducing risk for blood clots in the legs.

What to do: Lie on your back with your knees bent, feet flat on the bed and your arms at your sides. Tighten up your buttock muscles as you lift your pelvis up toward the ceiling —until your pelvis is in line with your thighs. Then gently lower your body back to the bed. Repeat five times.

Important: If you think any of these exercises may be too strenuous for you, check with your doctor before trying them.

Exercise illustrations by Shawn Banner.

A Jolt of Caffeine May Help Aches and Pains

Drinking coffee may reduce postworkout achiness. Moderate doses of caffeine—the amount in approximately two cups of coffee—can reduce muscle pain that often accompanies exercise. Caffeine may work by blocking the body's receptors for a chemical released in response to inflammation.

Caution: The study was small, and research was done only on women who were not regular coffee drinkers.

Patrick O'Connor, PhD, codirector of the Exercise Psychology Laboratory, University of Georgia, Athens, and leader of a study of female college students, published in The Journal of Pain.

How to Get the Most Out of Your Workouts

Heidi Skolnik, CDN, a certified dietitian nutritionist and director of sports nutrition for the Women's Sports Medical Center at the Hospital for Special Surgery in New York City. A regular contributor to NBC's Today *show, she also is a sports nutrition consultant to the New York Giants football team and the School of American Ballet.*

You already know that a regular exercise routine—ideally, at least 30 minutes of vigorous activity daily—is among the smartest moves you can take to protect your health.

What you may not know: Consuming the right foods and fluids is one of the best ways to improve your exercise performance.

If your body is not sufficiently fueled—regardless of the type, frequency and intensity of physical activity—your levels of energy are more likely to decrease, all your muscles will be more susceptible to fatigue and soreness, and you will find it harder to maintain your desired weight. *My secrets…*

1. Remember to drink enough fluids before exercise. Research shows that about half of people who work out in the morning are dehydrated when they begin to exercise.

Why is fluid consumption so important? When you're dehydrated, your heart needs to pump harder to get blood to your muscles. Being dehydrated also impairs your ability to perspire and cool yourself.

Advice: Drink one cup of water or a sports drink, such as Gatorade, before your workout and another during your workout. If your workout is vigorous or lasts more than 60 minutes, you may need to consume more fluids.

Also remember to drink fluids throughout the day. You do not have to limit yourself to water. Milk, tea, coffee, fruit juice and carbonated beverages also count toward your daily fluid intake.

Caution: Your risk for dehydration is increased if you take a diuretic drug, have diabetes or are an older adult—the body's thirst center functions less efficiently with age.

2. Don't exercise on an empty stomach. If you do not eat for several hours—including the time when you are sleeping—your blood sugar levels decline. This can leave you with less energy for physical activity and at risk for injury.

The quickest solution is to consume carbohydrates, which are your body's primary energy source. Carbohydrates are found mainly in starchy foods, such as grains, breads and vegetables, as well as in fruit, milk and yogurt.

Advice: If you're exercising before breakfast, first have half a banana or a slice of toast. If you are exercising just before lunch, eat a healthful mid-morning snack—and a mid- to late-afternoon snack if your workout is before dinner. It's okay to eat the snack right before your workout.

3. Eat a balanced breakfast. Eating a good breakfast helps get your metabolism going—and may help you consume fewer calories during the rest of the day.

Advice: Choose whole-grain foods (such as oatmeal or whole-grain cereal or toast) to fuel your muscles...a serving of dairy (yogurt, low-fat milk or cheese) or another protein (such as eggs or Canadian bacon) to promote muscle repair...and fruit (such as a mango, berries or melon) for vitamins and disease-fighting phytonutrients.

4. Fill in your nutritional "gaps" with lunch. Like breakfast, your midday meal should include healthful carbohydrates and protein.

Advice: At lunch, get some of the nutrients you may not have included in your breakfast. For example, if you ate fruit in the morning, eat vegetables at lunch. If your breakfast included a dairy product as your protein source, eat lean meat or fish at lunch.

Example of a healthful lunch: A salad with grilled chicken, legumes, peppers, broccoli and an olive oil–based dressing.

5. Eat an evening meal. If you exercise late in the afternoon or after work, don't skip your evening meal. You may wake up the following morning with a "deficit" that can lead you to overeat.

Advice: Strive for a balance of unprocessed carbohydrates (such as brown rice or vegetables), lean protein (such as fish or poultry) and a little healthful fat (such as nuts or olive oil).

Example: A shrimp and vegetable stir-fry served over one-quarter cup of brown rice.

"Fore!" a Longer Life

In a recent study of 300,000 Swedish golfers, researchers found that the death rate among people who regularly play the sport is 40% lower than for the rest of the population—a statistic that equates to an increased life expectancy of five years.

Theory: The low-intensity exercise associated with golfing is responsible for the health benefits.

Karolinska Institutet, Stockholm, Sweden.

Walk Your Way to Vibrant Health

Jamison Starbuck, ND, a naturopathic physician in family practice and lecturer at the University of Montana, both in Missoula. She is past president of the American Association of Naturopathic Physicians and a contributing editor to *The Alternative Advisor: The Complete Guide to Natural Therapies and Alternative Treatments* (Time Life).

Not too long ago, I saw a patient who had started walking regularly to lose weight. "Walking is now the best part of my day!" he proudly announced. He did lose weight—and a significant body of scientific research shows that walking also reduces the risk for cardiovascular disease (including heart attack and stroke) as well as diabetes, breast cancer and colon cancer. Walking also helps fight osteoporosis, anxiety, depression and memory problems. It even improves immune health, reducing the frequency and duration of colds and flu.

For thousands of years, walking—at a speed of about three miles per hour, on average—was our primary mode of transportation. Now, nearly 40% of Americans don't walk beyond the bare minimum needed to get through the day. If this describes you, you are not letting your body do what it was designed to do. *My advice...*

•**Make walking a priority.** Set aside specific times to walk five days per week. If you keep a daily calendar, write down when you plan to walk. Also, invest in a good pair of walking shoes. Depending on where you live, you also may need rain gear as well as warm, but not restrictive, clothing and a head covering for cold weather. In hot weather, try to avoid the hottest part of the day—and wear a hat to avoid excessive sun exposure. In harsh weather, you can walk in a shopping mall.

•**Start slowly.** Many people are far too ambitious when they first start walking. In the beginning, walk only five minutes up to five days a week. Then increase your time by five minutes per session every week. If possible, work up to 30 minutes per day, five days per week within six weeks.

•**Walk outside whenever possible.** Walking is most enjoyable when it exposes you to fresh air, sunlight and views of nature—even urban greenery and flower boxes. The varied terrain of outdoor walking, including uneven sidewalks or the slope of a trail, improve proprioception—the brain's awareness of body position and balance—and will help you be more agile and less vulnerable to falls. To prevent injury, pay attention to the terrain, your surroundings and to how your body feels as you walk. If your balance is poor, invest in a walking stick, available at most outdoor-sports stores for $20 and up.*

•**Get the right amount of fluid and take supplements.** Drink about one-half ounce of water per pound of body weight throughout the day—and at least 12 ounces of water just before walking. In addition, ask your doctor about taking daily mineral supplements containing 300 mg of magnesium and 99 mg of potassium. Following all these steps will help you avoid muscle cramps, which are usually caused by dehydration, a deficiency of magnesium and/or potassium or lack of strength.

Caution: If you are taking blood pressure medication or have kidney disease, be sure to discuss potassium supplementation with your doctor before trying it.

Even if you don't need to lose weight, as my patient did, I'm betting that walking will make you feel healthier and stronger.

*Price subject to change.

Improve Your Fitness Without Extra Exercise

B*eta-alanine*, a sports nutrition supplement favored by Olympic athletes, can improve muscle endurance in older people. Beta-alanine is an amino acid that helps form *carnosine,* important to muscle function during exercise.

Recent study: Participants (about age 73 on average) who did not increase their normal levels of exercise and took 800 mg of this supplement three times a day for 90 days had a 67% improvement in their fitness levels...and did not experience any ill effects while taking the supplement.

Jeffrey Stout, PhD, assistant professor, exercise physiology, University of Oklahoma, Norman, Oklahoma.

5

Natural Solutions

Stay Healthy to 100+

f you were told that it's entirely possible to live in good health to age 100 and beyond, you'd probably think that the claim sounds far-fetched.

But health and longevity researcher John Robbins has found people who do just that. The son of the cofounder of Baskin-Robbins (the world's largest chain of ice cream shops), Robbins walked away from the family business in 1968 and has since dedicated himself to studying healthful lifestyle habits, including practices of the world's longest-living and healthiest people. *Robbins answers questions below…*

●**Where do people live the longest healthy lives?** The communities I studied are found in the valley of Vilcabamba in Ecuador…in the Hunza region of Pakistan…on the Japanese island of Okinawa…and in the republic of Abkhazia, which was in the news due to a conflict between Georgia and Russia. I chose to write about centenarians in these regions because they have all been exhaustively observed and researched.

●**What is special about the centenarians in these areas?** In these communities, large numbers of people not only live to be 100, but they're also remarkably healthy at this age. In the US, most of us hit our peak of physical fitness, strength and overall health between the ages of 20 and 30 and gradually decline after that. Research shows that by the age of 70, most Americans have lost 30% to 40% of their maximum breathing capacity…40% of their kidney and liver functions…15% to 30% of their bone mass…and 30% of their strength.

In the communities I researched and wrote about, residents live extraordinarily long lives

---

John Robbins, author of *Healthy at 100: The Scientifically Proven Secrets of the World's Healthiest and Longest-Lived Peoples* (Random House, *www.healthyat100.org*). A recipient of the Albert Schweitzer Humanitarian Award, Robbins lives in Northern California. His book *Diet for a New America* (Stillpoint) was nominated for the Pulitzer Prize and was the basis for a PBS special.

and have extremely low rates of heart disease, cancer, arthritis, osteoporosis, asthma, dementia and other degenerative diseases that plague so many older people in the West. Many of the centenarians remain vigorous until weeks or months before their deaths.

•**What are the eating habits of people living in these locations?** They derive their protein primarily from plant sources that include beans, peas, whole grains, seeds and nuts. This method of eating is supported by a recent major international study, which found that a diet based on plant foods—with only a minimal amount of foods derived from animals—results in lower total cholesterol levels. As most people know, lower total cholesterol has been closely linked to lower rates of heart disease, some types of cancer and other so-called "Western diseases," such as diabetes.

•**What else is unique about their diets?** The centenarians I studied eat diets that are low in calories. For example, even with their active lifestyles, the men in these locations consume an average of about 1,900 calories a day compared with an average daily consumption of 2,650 calories by men in the US, where the lifestyles tend to be more sedentary. Also, the fats that the centenarians eat are derived from food sources, including seeds (such as flaxseeds, sesame and sunflower seeds) and many kinds of nuts, and in some cases wild fish, rather than from bottled oils, margarines or saturated animal fats.

•**Is there any obesity among the centenarians?** No. Interestingly, all the longest-lived people eat very slowly. They savor their food and simply enjoy each other's company—their evening meal can last for hours. This leisurely pace gives their digestive systems time to register when they have eaten enough—and it allows them to stop eating when they feel nearly full. As a result, there is not a single instance of obesity among the centenarians in these communities. In contrast, a recent study predicted that nearly 90% of Americans will be overweight or obese by 2030.

•**Does it help to transform one's eating patterns later in life?** Beginning to eat well can make an extraordinary difference in your health and longevity even if you've eaten poorly for decades. That is because most of your body's cells and tissues are in a constant state of renewal. Almost all the cells of your body—including those lining the stomach—are being continually regenerated, so that what you eat today will have a direct impact on your body tomorrow.

•**What about exercise?** In all the cultures I studied, daily life involves plenty of vigorous walking and, in most cases, mountain climbing. *The Journal of Epidemiology and Community Health* published a study that found mountain dwellers live longer than their lowland counterparts because their hearts get a better daily workout.

Numerous studies have found that physical exercise plays an essential role in preventing a variety of serious illnesses, including Alzheimer's disease. For example, one study published in *Archives of Neurology* found that those people who engaged in moderate physical exercise (activity three or more times per week at an intensity equal to walking) had a significant reduction in Alzheimer's risk.

Obviously, few Americans regularly walk up and down mountains, but we still could walk much more than we do, climb stairs instead of taking elevators and, when we do drive, park our cars at the far end of parking lots.

•**What other habits contribute to the centenarians' longevity?** There is a deep sense of human connection in all four of the communities. People continually help one another, believe in one another and enjoy spending time with each other.

For example, when an Abkhazian host invites someone over for dinner, the invitation always says, "Come and be our guest." It never says, "Come for dinner." Of course, dinner is served, but the emphasis is on the pleasure of being together rather than on the meal.

In Vilcabamba, a popular saying covers social connections: The left leg and the right leg help keep people healthy, since they carry individuals to their friends' homes.

•**Were any of the lifestyle practices surprising to you?** In all these societies, people actually look forward to growing older. They expect to be healthy and vital and know that they will be respected, since age is equated with wisdom.

The power of our attitudes toward aging is demonstrated in recent research conducted at the Yale School of Public Health. One landmark study concluded that negative thoughts about aging can undermine a person's health. In fact, one's perceptions about aging proved to be a more accurate indicator of life span than blood pressure, level of cholesterol or if the person smoked or exercised.

Drink Coffee…Eat Chocolate…and Other Surprising Ways to Live Longer

Michael F. Roizen, MD, chair of the division of anesthesiology, critical care medicine and pain management at Cleveland Clinic in Cleveland, Ohio. Dr. Roizen is coauthor, with Mehmet C. Oz, MD, of several books, including *You: Staying Young* (Free Press).

Many of the proven strategies for living longer—including restricting calories and exercising on a regular basis—can feel like punishment for some people. Fortunately, there are many enjoyable ways to stay healthy—but doctors do not recommend these strategies as often as they should. Research has shown that activities nearly everyone likes can literally add years to a person's life.

Fun-filled ways to live longer…

1. Get the right kind of sleep. Studies have found that people who get deep, restorative sleep typically live for three years longer than those who don't. During deep sleep, the body normally produces higher levels of melatonin, a hormone that improves immunity and reduces the risk for infections as well as cancer. Deep sleep also increases levels of growth hormone, which improves energy level and helps to promote a healthy weight.

Good news: You don't have to sleep uninterrupted through the night to get the benefits of deep sleep, as long as you complete a series of at least 90-minute sleep cycles—each one beginning with light sleep (stages 1 and 2)…progressing through deeper sleep (stages 3 and 4)…and then into the deepest stage, known as rapid eye movement (REM) sleep. As long as you complete this 90-minute cycle several times a night, it doesn't matter if you wake up a time or two.

2. Enjoy your coffee. Many people assume that coffee—unlike green tea, for example—isn't a healthful beverage. But that's not true. Studies have found that caffeinated and decaffeinated coffee are a main source of antioxidants in the average American's diet.

Research has now shown that caffeinated coffee decreases the risk for Parkinson's and Alzheimer's diseases by 30% to 40%—health benefits that are largely attributed to the beverage's caffeine. (Decaffeinated coffee doesn't provide these same benefits.) The caffeine in coffee also is good for cognitive health.

Important: Caffeinated coffee may cause several side effects, such as spikes in blood pressure, an abnormal heartbeat, anxiety and gastric upset.

My recommendation: If you do not experience any of these side effects, and you enjoy drinking coffee, have as many cups of caffeinated coffee as you like. If you do experience side effects, you may prefer to drink decaffeinated coffee. Even though it does not have the health benefits previously described, studies show that decaffeinated coffee may help fight type 2 diabetes.

3. Go dancing. Men and women who have optimal amounts of physical activity—about 30 minutes a day, seven days a week—can make their "RealAges" (the "biological ages" of their bodies, based on lifestyle and behaviors) 6.4 years younger.

Many types of dancing give a superb physical workout. Ballroom and square dancing are particularly good for cognitive health. They involve both physical and mental stimulation (in order to execute the appropriate dance steps) and may help reduce the risk for dementia. Aim to dance at least 30 minutes a day.

4. Do some singing. Whether you lend your voice to a choir or merely sing for pleasure in the shower, singing improves immunity and elevates levels of hormones known as *endorphins* and *dopamine*—both of which reduce stress and activate the brain's pleasure centers. Studies have shown that singing helps people with asthma…reduces stress hormones…and may temporarily help improve memory in patients with Alzheimer's disease.

5. Continue learning. People who take pleasure in expanding their minds—for example, by learning to paint, attending lectures or doing puzzles—can make their RealAges about 2.5 years younger.

Studies have shown that people with higher levels of education, and those who continue learning throughout life, form more connections between brain cells, making them less likely to experience later-life memory loss.

6. Eat some chocolate. The powerful antioxidants known as flavonoids in dark chocolate increase levels of the body's *nitric oxide* (NO), a gas that dilates arteries (to help prevent blockages) and can help reduce blood pressure in people with hypertension.

This is particularly helpful for people over age 50, because age-related buildup of fatty deposits in the arteries (*atherosclerosis*) lowers natural levels of NO.

My recommendation: Eat one-half ounce of dark chocolate (at least 70% cocoa) twice daily. But don't overindulge in chocolate—it is high in calories.

Other good sources of flavonoids include brewed black or green tea…red wine…dark grape juice…strawberries, cranberries and apples…and brussels sprouts and onions.

7. Find opportunities to laugh. People who laugh—and who make others laugh—tend to have better immunity than people who are humor-impaired. Telling a joke is also a good way to improve your memory. It requires the teller—as well as the listener—to pay attention, and we laugh when we expect one outcome but are surprised with a different one. Psychologists call this "conceptual blending."

Benefit: Jokes and riddles challenge your brain, improve memory and can help delay the onset of cognitive decline. In addition, laughter is a well-known stress reducer. People who are calmer and more relaxed have lower levels of heart disease and cancer.

8. Have more sex. Men and women who have sex (that results in orgasm) an average of twice a week have arteries with greater elasticity (which helps prevent hardening of the arteries). Overall, those who have sex twice a week have lower rates of mortality and a RealAge that's about two years younger than their calendar age. Men and women who have sex daily, on average, are biologically eight years younger than those who have it just once per week.

9. Rest more often. Everyone enjoys taking a break from life's stresses. Research shows that people who give themselves time to relax (thus minimizing the effects of stress) can live up to eight years longer.

Stress decreasers—such as meditating, taking long walks, watching the sunset—can add years to your life. Yoga is particularly good. It lowers blood pressure, heart rate and stress hormones, and increases levels of dopamine and the "feel good" hormone serotonin. Aim for about 10 minutes daily of a stress-reduction activity.

10. Get a pet. People who are pet owners can make themselves an average of one year younger. Studies show that taking care of and bonding with a pet decreases depression and blood pressure.

After a heart attack, people with pets have a one-year survival rate of 94%, compared with 72% for people who don't have pets. Studies show that dog owners, who live about three years longer, tend to be a little healthier than those with other pets—in part because they get regular exercise when they take their dogs out for a walk.

The Real Scoop on Coffee and Caffeine

JoAnn E. Manson, MD, DrPH, a professor of medicine and women's health at Harvard Medical School and chief of the division of preventive medicine at Brigham and Women's Hospital, both in Boston. She is one of the lead investigators for two highly influential studies on women's health—the Harvard Nurses' Health Study and the Women's Health Initiative. Dr. Manson is the author, with Shari Bassuk, ScD, of *Hot Flashes, Hormones & Your Health* (McGraw-Hill).

D o you worry that coffee could harm your health? Relax. The studies suggest that, when it is consumed in moderation—meaning two to four eight-ounce servings daily—coffee may in fact be good for you. It is not clear whether the benefits come from coffee itself or it's caffeine. Even decaffeinated coffee may contain some caffeine, and there is limited research on the other caffeinated beverages. Per cup, coffee has about 100 milligrams (mg) of caffeine…black tea has about half as much. *Studies show that coffee may…*

• **Reduce risk for some cancers.** An analysis of nine studies found that drinking two cups of coffee daily was associated with a 43% lower risk of liver cancer. Coffee also may protect against colorectal cancer.

• **Help prevent diabetes.** Among 200,000 study participants, those who drank four to six cups of regular or decaffeinated coffee a day were 28% less likely to develop type 2 diabetes than people who drank two cups or less daily.

Possible reason: Chlorogenic acid, an antioxidant in coffee, slows sugar's release into the bloodstream.

• **Protect memory.** In one study with 7,000 seniors, women who drank more than three cups of caffeinated coffee or six cups of caffeinated tea daily had less memory loss than women who drank two cups or less.

• **Prevent gallstones.** In a study of 80,000 female nurses, drinking two or more cups of caffeinated coffee daily cut their gallstone risk by about 20%.

Why: Caffeine may aid the digestive fluid bile, reducing formation of cholesterol crystals that become stones…and stimulate gallbladder contractions, flushing away crystals.

• **Lower Parkinson's disease risk.** In the nurses' study, women who drank one to three cups of caffeinated coffee daily were 40% less likely than the nondrinkers to develop Parkinson's, a movement disorder caused by loss of brain cells.

• **Improve physical performance.** The caffeine in two to five cups of coffee boosts endurance…helps the body burn fat instead of carbohydrates…and eases muscle soreness.

Reassuring: Coffee drinkers are no more likely to suffer heart attacks or chronic high blood pressure than nondrinkers. Coffee oils can raise cholesterol, but paper filters remove these oils. Coffee does not appear to increase risk for ovarian or breast cancer. Some women say coffee worsens premenstrual syndrome and fibrocystic breast disease (benign breast lumps), but research does not support this.

Cautions: Both regular and decaf coffee can cause digestive upset. Caffeine can trigger migraine or cause insomnia. Animal studies suggest that at high doses, caffeine may weaken bones by blocking absorption of calcium. Moderate amounts of caffeine do not impair fertility or cause birth defects, but consuming more than 200 mg daily may double miscarriage risk—so limit caffeine to 100 mg per day while pregnant.

Beer and Hard Liquor Just as Healthful as Wine?

Charles Bamforth, PhD, chair of the department of food science and technology and Anheuser-Busch Endowed Professor of Malting and Brewing Science at University of California, Davis. He is editor in chief of *Journal of the American Society of Brewing Chemists* and author of *Grape versus Grain* (Cambridge University), a comparison of wine and beer.

M aybe you drink a glass or two of red wine every day because you've heard about its high levels of heart-protecting antioxidants, such as *resveratrol*.

What you may not know: The main heart-helping ingredient in alcoholic drinks is *ethanol*—alcohol itself.

Landmark study: An international team of scientists led by researchers in the department of nutrition at Harvard School of Public Health analyzed 10 studies that linked moderate intake of alcohol with a lower risk of heart disease. Four studies showed that wine lowered risk…four indicated beer decreased risk…and four showed spirits lowered risk. All alcoholic drinks are linked with lower risk of heart disease, concluded the authors, in *BJM* (formerly *British Medical Journal*).

That study and others caused the American Heart Association to declare, "There is no clear evidence wine is more beneficial than other forms of alcoholic drink."

Why it works: Scientists do not yet know the exact mechanism by which ethanol helps the heart, but it's probably by boosting HDL (good) cholesterol…decreasing levels of the clotting protein *fibrinogen*, thereby reducing the risk of artery-clogging blood clots…and normalizing blood sugar levels (diabetes is a risk factor for heart disease).

LIFESTYLE FACTORS

But, you might ask, isn't it true that many studies have found that drinkers of wine are healthier than beer drinkers? *Yes, but it might not be the wine…*

Recent finding: Researchers in Denmark analyzed more than 3.5 million checkout receipts from 98 branches of two large supermarket chains. They found that wine buyers bought more fruits, vegetables, olives, poultry, milk and low-fat cheese than beer buyers. On the other hand, beer buyers bought more chips, soft drinks, cold cuts, sausages and sugar. Other studies show that, compared with beer drinkers, wine drinkers consume less saturated fat, exercise more and smoke less.

New thinking: It might not be wine but the overall lifestyle of wine drinkers that accounts for their better health.

There is no reason why you cannot drink moderate amounts of beer and/or spirits as part of a healthy lifestyle.

BENEFITS OF BEER

In fact, beer may be a healthier choice than wine because beer has…

• **B vitamins,** particularly folate, which may help protect against heart disease, stroke, Alzheimer's and various cancers.

• **Silicone.** Beer is one of the richest dietary sources of silicone, a mineral that helps counter the bone-eroding disease of osteoporosis.

• **Effective antioxidants.** Red wine provides more antioxidants than beer—in the test tube, but studies indicate that antioxidants in beer may be more effective in raising blood levels of antioxidants. In fact, beer is better than a tomato at raising blood levels of *ferulic acid*, a potent antioxidant that scientists say may help fight heart disease, diabetes, cancer and Alzheimer's.

• **Fiber.** Beer contains healthful amounts of soluble fiber.

• **No sulfites.** Beer does not contain added sulfites (a preservative), a cause of headaches in some drinkers of red wine.

"Beer Belly" myth: Studies show that moderate drinking does not contribute to a beer belly—it is the calories in alcohol that are fattening, not in any particular component of the beer, such as the carbohydrate *maltose*. In fact, many wines contain more carbohydrates and more calories than beer per serving.

MODERATION IS KEY

The health benefits from drinking alcoholic beverages depend on moderation—on average, no more than one drink a day for women and two drinks a day for men.

Example: A drink is five ounces of wine, 12 ounces of beer, or 1½ ounces of distilled spirits or liquor, such as vodka or whiskey.

Health benefits also depend on frequency. Studies show that it is healthier to have one or two daily drinks than one or two on just a few days a week. Binge drinking, of course, is not healthful—and alcoholics and those with a family history of alcoholism need to avoid drinking alcohol.

Also, alcohol and a lot of medications, including sedatives, don't mix. If you're taking a medication, ask your physician if moderate drinking is okay.

Red flag: There are fewer large-scale studies on the health benefits of spirits, because in nations where spirits are the drink of choice (such as Russia), people tend to drink heavily. Heavy drinking is associated with a range of health problems from cirrhosis to cancer.

DRINK TO YOUR HEALTH

Preventing heart disease might be the primary benefit of moderate alcohol intake, but studies show alcohol can benefit your health in many other ways…

•**Aging and longevity.** Italian researchers analyzed data from 34 scientific investigations into alcohol and health conducted in the US, Europe, Australia, Japan and China, and involving more than one million people. They found that moderate drinking of any kind—wine, beer or spirits—was associated with an 18% lower death rate for women and a 17% lower death rate in men. However, death rates were higher among men drinking more than four drinks a day and women drinking more than two.

•**Dementia.** The scientists who study memory loss and dementia divide the process into three stages of advancing severity. The stages are age-related memory loss, mild cognitive impairment and finally dementia.

Recent studies: Italian researchers studied 121 people ages 65 to 84 with mild cognitive impairment. Those who had at least one alcoholic drink a day developed dementia at an 85% slower rate than those who didn't drink. And Harvard researchers, in a study published in *The Journal of the American Medical Association*, found that moderate drinking was associated with a 54% lower risk for Alzheimer's compared with not drinking.

•**Diabetes.** Researchers working at the Albert Einstein Medical Center in New York City analyzed 32 studies on alcohol intake and diabetes and found that moderate consumption of alcohol (one to three drinks per day) lowered the risk for diabetes by 33% to 56% and the risk of developing diabetes-related heart disease by 34% to 55%.

•**Kidney stones.** Finnish researchers found that drinking a bottle of beer a day was associated with a 40% lower risk for kidney stones.

•**Gallstone disease.** Harvard researchers found that both wine and beer was associated with a reduced risk of gallstone disease (by speeding up the emptying of the gallbladder after a meal).

•**Osteoporosis.** Researchers from the California Pacific Medical Center in San Francisco found that social drinking in older men was associated with higher bone mineral density.

•**Prostate cancer.** Men ages 40 to 64 who drank four or more glasses of red wine a week halved their risk of prostate cancer, say scientists from Fred Hutchinson Cancer Research Center in Seattle. And researchers in Australia and New Zealand found that beer intake decreases *prostate specific antigen* (PSA), a biomarker for prostate cancer.

Caution: The National Cancer Institute says that immoderate drinking can cause cancer of the mouth, esophagus, pharynx and larynx, and the National Institute on Alcohol Abuse and Alcoholism says that chronic alcohol intake may increase the risk of breast cancer by about 10%.

•**Rheumatoid arthritis.** People who drank alcohol regularly were 50% less likely to develop rheumatoid arthritis than nondrinkers in a Scandinavian study published in the June 5, 2008, issue of *Annals of Rheumatic Diseases*.

Possible reason: Alcohol helps decrease inflammation.

•**Stress.** A clinical psychologist at the University of Pennsylvania reviewed the scientific literature on the psychological benefits of moderate drinking and found that it increased happiness, euphoria, conviviality and pleasant and carefree feelings, and decreased tension, depression and self-consciousness. The heavy drinkers, however, had higher rates of clinical depression.

The Amazing Healing Vitamin

Reinhold Vieth, PhD, a professor in the department of nutritional sciences and the department of laboratory medicine and pathobiology at Mount Sinai Hospital, University of Toronto, Canada. He is also director of the bone and mineral laboratory. Dr. Vieth has studied vitamin D for 30 years and has written more than 70 related professional articles.

Until recently, physicians seldom diagnosed deficiencies of vitamin D except in occasional cases of childhood rickets (a disease in which the bones do not harden).

Now: One in three Americans is considered to be deficient in vitamin D—and most of them don't even know it, according to the US National Center for Health Statistics.

How did vitamin D deficiency become such a widespread problem so quickly—and what should be done about it? *Reinhold Vieth, PhD, a leading expert on vitamin D, provides the answers below...*

NEW DISCOVERIES

To produce adequate levels of vitamin D naturally, you must expose your skin (without sunscreen) to ultraviolet B (UVB) rays from sunshine for about 15 minutes, as a general guideline, twice a week. If you use sunscreen, your body makes little or no vitamin D. And, UVB rays don't pass through glass, so sitting in a sunny window will not produce vitamin D. Generations ago, when large numbers of Americans began working indoors—thus reducing their exposure to sunlight—their average vitamin D blood levels declined.

More recently, average blood levels of vitamin D in the US have remained fairly constant. What has changed is the amount of scientific research pointing to the importance of the vitamin for good health.

An overwhelming body of evidence shows that vitamin D not only affects bone health (by facilitating the absorption of calcium), but also may play a main role in fighting a wide variety of ailments that include cardiovascular disease...autoimmune diseases (such as rheumatoid arthritis, lupus and multiple sclerosis)...chronic bone or muscle pain (including back pain)...macular degeneration...and an increased susceptibility to colds and flu.

A number of studies also have shown a link between adequate blood levels of vitamin D and lower risk for some types of cancer, including colon, lung, breast and prostate cancers as well as Hodgkin's lymphoma (cancer of the lymphatic system).

Important new finding: In one study of 13,000 initially healthy men and women, researchers at Johns Hopkins found that vitamin D deficiency was associated with a 26% increase in death from *any* cause during a median period of nine years.

HOW VITAMIN D HELPS

Recent scientific discoveries have demonstrated that vitamin D is critical for the health of every organ in the body. By acting as a signaling molecule, vitamin D helps cells "talk" to each other, which in turn helps control how they behave. Cellular communication is essential for healthy biology.

To understand the function of vitamin D, think of paper in an office—you need paper to send memos and create reports. With enough paper, communication occurs easily. Without adequate paper supplies, the office may continue to function, but some important messages will not be communicated and mistakes will be made. Similarly, without enough vitamin D, your body is more likely to experience a breakdown of cellular communication that can lead to the conditions described above.

ARE YOU AT RISK?

Vitamin D deficiency is considered a "silent disease" because it can occur without any obvious signs. When symptoms do occur, muscle weakness and musculoskeletal pain are common symptoms.

Frightening recent study: People with a severe vitamin D deficiency were more than *twice* as likely to die of heart disease and other causes than people with normal levels of vitamin D.

Among those at greatest risk for a vitamin D deficiency...

•**People over age 50.** Beginning at about age 50, our skin progressively loses some of its ability to convert sunlight to the active form of vitamin D.

• **People with dark skin** (anyone who is of non-European ancestry). Dark skin pigmentation offers some protection from skin cancer because it naturally reduces the sun's cancer-causing UVB rays. But, these are the same rays that we need to produce vitamin D.

• **People who have limited sun exposure.** Those who live in most parts of the US, except the extreme South, do not produce sufficient vitamin D from sun exposure in the winter months. Elderly people who may spend less time outdoors also are at increased risk for vitamin D deficiency.

AVOIDING A DEFICIENCY

Many doctors now advise their patients to receive a blood test that measures levels of *25-hydroxy*—a form of vitamin D that acts as a marker for vitamin D deficiency. If you are concerned about your vitamin D levels, ask your primary care physician for the test—it typically costs $75* or more and is covered by some health insurers.

My recommendation: Get the test in the winter. If done in the summer, when you are likely to get more sun exposure, the test may reflect higher vitamin D levels than is typical for you at other times of the year.

As research confirming vitamin D's health benefits continues to mount, medical experts have increased the recommended blood levels for the vitamin—currently, levels of 30 nanograms per milliliter (ng/mL) are considered adequate—but a more desirable range for most people is 31 ng/mL to 90 ng/mL.

The US adequate intake level for vitamin D (from food and/or supplements) is 400 international units (IU) per day for adults under age 70 and 600 IU for adults age 70 and older.

However, the consensus among vitamin D researchers is that most adults should be taking vitamin D supplements totaling 1,000 IU daily…and 2,000 IU daily might be even better for meeting the body's needs. Ask your doctor what the right dosage is for you. Either dosage can be taken along with a multivitamin.

*Price subject to change.

It is nearly impossible to get enough vitamin D from diet alone. In the US, milk and other dairy products and some breakfast cereals are fortified with vitamin D. Other food sources such as salmon, sardines, egg yolks and beef liver also provide small amounts.

How difficult is it to get 1,000 IU of vitamin D per day from food? You would need to drink about 10 cups of vitamin D–fortified milk or orange juice…eat 30 sardines…or eat 55 egg yolks.

Helpful: When looking to buy a vitamin D supplement, check for vitamin D3 (*cholecalciferol*). This is twice as potent as vitamin D2 (*ergocalciferol*).

Caution: Because vitamin D is fat-soluble (stored in the body), consuming more than 10,000 IU daily (or 70,000 IU weekly) can lead to toxic reactions, such as weakness, nausea and vomiting.

Five Popular Herbs With Unexpected Health Benefits

Holly Phaneuf, PhD, an expert in medicinal chemistry and the author of *Herbs Demystified* (Avalon). She is a member of the American Chemical Society and is currently conducting research on exercise and herb use.

You may know that the tiny, fiber-rich seeds of the flax plant can be used as a laxative and that ginger helps ease nausea. But can you name any of the other health benefits provided by these two plant-derived remedies?

Few people can. However, credible scientific evidence shows that many herbs that are well-known for treating a particular ailment have other important—but little-known—uses.* *For example…*

*If you use prescription drugs and/or suffer a chronic medical condition, such as diabetes, cancer or heart disease, speak to your doctor before trying herbal remedies. In some cases, herbs may interfere with medication or cause an undesired effect on a chronic medical problem. Women who are pregnant or breast-feeding also should consult a doctor before taking herbs.

ARTICHOKE LEAF

Extract of artichoke leaf is used by some people with mildly elevated cholesterol levels as an alternative to prescription statin drugs. Exactly how the herb works is unknown, but animal studies suggest that it inhibits *HMG CoA-reductase*, an enzyme that plays a main role in the liver's production of cholesterol.

In a placebo-controlled, randomized study conducted at the University of Reading in England, adults who took 1,280 milligrams (mg) of artichoke leaf extract daily for three months decreased their cholesterol levels by 4.2%, on average, while levels increased by 1.9%, on average, in those taking a placebo.

What else artichoke leaf can do: Calm indigestion. In a placebo-controlled, randomized study, patients rated their chronic indigestion as significantly improved after taking artichoke leaf extract twice daily for six weeks. Tests on rats suggest that the herb stimulates the gallbladder's bile production, which helps facilitate the digestion of dietary fat.

Typical dose: About 320 mg daily of artichoke leaf soothes digestive complaints. This dosage can be taken until the indigestion is no longer a problem.

Caution: Avoid artichoke if you are allergic to plants in the daisy family or if you have gallstones (artichoke appears to make the gallbladder contract).

FLAX

Often used for a gentle laxative, the seeds of the flax plant (flaxseeds) contain fiber and phytonutrients known as *lignans*, a combination that can help draw water into the gut to speed digestion. For laxative effects, eat one tablespoon of whole or ground seeds (sprinkled on cereal, for example) daily. Be sure to drink at least eight ounces of water when eating flaxseeds to prevent them from forming a temporary blockage in the intestines.

What else flaxseed can do: Help prevent breast and prostate cancers. Lignans form estrogen-like compounds that inhibit the body's production of the hormone in women and in men. This effect is believed to reduce risk for estrogen-dependent malignancies, including some breast and prostate cancers.

Typical initial dose: One to two tablespoons of ground flaxseed daily, which can be increased gradually to as many as five tablespoons daily.

Grinding flaxseed (in a coffee grinder, for example) rather than eating it whole releases more of its cancer-fighting compounds. Also, ground flaxseed is better than flaxseed oil, which lacks the plant's beneficial lignans unless they are replaced during the manufacturing process.

Helpful: Be sure to refrigerate flaxseed to prolong freshness and preserve potency.

Caution: Do not consume flaxseed within two hours of taking an oral medication—flaxseed may interfere with absorption of some drugs.

GARLIC

Due to its powerful blood-thinning effects, garlic is widely used to help prevent artery-blocking blood clots that can lead to a heart attack or stroke. The typical recommendation for this purpose is one clove of fresh garlic or one-half to three-quarters of a teaspoon of garlic powder daily.

What else garlic can do: Help to prevent stomach and colorectal cancers. The National Cancer Institute funded an analysis of 23 clinical studies that linked garlic consumption (raw, cooked or from garlic supplements) to a 10% to 50% decrease in risk for these types of cancers. This cancer-fighting effect is believed to result from the antioxidant activity of garlic's sulfur-containing molecules. Garlic also is a popular remedy to stave off the common cold, but research on its virus-fighting properties has shown mixed results.

Recommended: One fresh crushed garlic clove four to seven times a week.

GINGER

Ginger is widely used to treat nausea, including that due to motion sickness (one-quarter to one-half teaspoon of ginger powder)...and chemotherapy (one to two teaspoons daily of ginger powder). Ginger is believed to reduce queasiness by stopping intense stomach motions that can interfere with digestion.

What else ginger can do: Relieve arthritis pain. With its aspirin-like effects, ginger inhibits both *COX-1* and *COX-2* enzymes, two substances involved in production of inflammatory hormones known as *prostaglandins*.

Typical dose: One-quarter to one-half teaspoon daily of ginger powder.

TURMERIC

In India, turmeric is a popular remedy for indigestion. It contains *curcumin*, an oily, yellow pigment that appears to prevent gut muscles from contracting and cramping.

What else turmeric can do: Relieve arthritis, morning stiffness and minor sprains. Turmeric reduces levels of an inflammatory, hormone-like substance known as *PGE2*. In lab studies, researchers also are finding that turmeric helps stave off colorectal and skin cancers, but its specific cancer-fighting mechanism has not yet been identified.

In addition, turmeric is being studied for its possible role in decreasing risk for Alzheimer's disease. Test tube and animal studies suggest that turmeric interferes with the formation of *amyloid plaque*, a hallmark of this neurodegenerative disease.

Recommended: Consume turmeric powder regularly by adding it to food, such as Asian dishes.

Caution: Because turmeric can cause gallbladder contractions, people with gallbladder problems should avoid the herb.

Spices That Lower Cholesterol, Boost The Brain and More

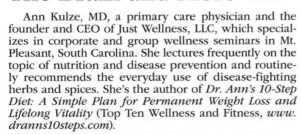

Ann Kulze, MD, a primary care physician and the founder and CEO of Just Wellness, LLC, which specializes in corporate and group wellness seminars in Mt. Pleasant, South Carolina. She lectures frequently on the topic of nutrition and disease prevention and routinely recommends the everyday use of disease-fighting herbs and spices. She's the author of *Dr. Ann's 10-Step Diet: A Simple Plan for Permanent Weight Loss and Lifelong Vitality* (Top Ten Wellness and Fitness, *www.dranns10steps.com*).

Spices and herbs not only boost the flavor of your food, they also boost your health. Powerful compounds in plants known as *phytochemicals* are found in high concentrations in many spices and herbs. Phytochemicals help fight heart disease, cancer, Alzheimer's, type 2 diabetes, arthritis and other diseases.

Here are the seasonings to add liberally to your food as often as possible. Unless otherwise noted, fresh herbs and spices provide a higher concentration of phytochemicals, but dried still are powerful.

SUPER SPICES

The following spices have been shown to be particularly beneficial to our health...

• **Cinnamon.** Cinnamon has an almost medicinal power. Recent studies have shown that cinnamon enhances the metabolism of glucose and cholesterol and thus might provide protection from type 2 diabetes and cardiovascular disease.

A study reported in *Diabetes Care* highlighted cinnamon's favorable impact on the blood fat levels of people with type 2 diabetes. After eating one to six grams (about one-quarter to one-and-one-quarter teaspoons) of cinnamon daily for 40 days, overall levels of unhealthy blood fats dropped significantly—up to 26% for total cholesterol and 30% for triglycerides (a type of blood fat).

Even healthy people can benefit from cinnamon's impact on blood sugar, according to a study in *The American Journal of Clinical Nutrition*. Adding cinnamon to rice pudding significantly decreased the test subjects' normal, post-dessert elevations of blood sugar.

Interestingly, at least a part of this benefit was related to the spice's ability to delay how quickly food departs the stomach and enters the intestines. In this regard, cinnamon also may be helpful in reducing appetite and hastening weight loss by enhancing satiety (the feeling of fullness).

Suggested uses: Cinnamon can be mixed into oatmeal, cereal and yogurt...coffee and tea...pumpkin and apple dishes...and rice and beans for an Indian touch.

• **Turmeric.** *Curcumin* (turmeric's active ingredient) is one of the most potent of naturally occurring anti-inflammatory agents ever identified and thus may be one of the best all-round spices for disease protection and antiaging. Inflammation plays a central role in most chronic diseases.

Turmeric also can be considered a "brain health food." Research studies on mice demonstrate turmeric's ability to reduce the build-up of plaque in the brain that is associated with Alzheimer's and cognitive decline. Laboratory research has shown that turmeric also has potent anticancer properties.

Suggested uses: Add turmeric to your favorite bean, poultry, seafood, tofu and rice dishes, as well as to soups and stews. Turmeric often is used in classic Indian dishes, such as curries.

MORE HEALTH HELPERS

• **Cilantro.** Cilantro is high in the vitamins A and K and beta-carotene, and like any dark, leafy green, it is full of beneficial phytochemicals, including a natural antibiotic called *dodecenal*. In a University of California, Berkeley, laboratory study, dodecenal killed the bacteria *Salmonella* more effectively than a powerful prescription antibiotic.

Suggested uses: Add fresh, chopped cilantro to salsa, guacamole, omelets, salads, soups and stews.

• **Ginger.** Ginger is the anti-inflammatory superstar because it suppresses the action of inflammatory *cytokines* and *chemokines*. And for people plagued with motion sickness or morning sickness or experiencing postoperative nausea and vomiting, ginger—fresh and dried—has proved to be an effective and safe option. The phytochemicals in ginger also are valuable for boosting immunity, especially to combat viral infections.

Suggested uses: Dried powdered ginger is even more effective than fresh. Add it into sauces and salad dressings, or sprinkle it on salad, poultry or seafood. You also could add a thumbnail-sized piece of raw ginger to hot tea. Ginger is delicious in its candied form, and pickled ginger is perfect with sushi.

• **Parsley.** One tablespoon of fresh parsley provides more than half of the daily recommended value of vitamin K. It is also rich in vitamin A, lutein and zeaxanthin (which promote eye health) and provides nature's most

concentrated source of *flavonoids*, plant pigments that provide health benefits. Parsley is among those plants that may be particularly effective for combatting cancer, allergies and heart disease.

Suggested uses: Add fresh chopped parsley to salads, pasta and rice dishes, soups and stews. Parsley is a main ingredient in the Mediterranean cracked-wheat dish tabouli.

• **Rosemary.** This savory herb contains phytochemicals that can reduce the formation of cancer-causing compounds known as *heterocyclic amines* (HCAs). HCAs can form when the proteins in meat are heated to very high temperatures.

The preliminary research also indicates that rosemary may enhance insulin sensitivity, improving the action and efficiency of insulin in the body, aiding in a healthy metabolism and slowing the aging process. And it turns out that Shakespeare's Ophelia wasn't all that far off when she said that rosemary is for remembrance. According to one study in *Journal of Neurochemistry*, rosemary contains the compound *carnosic acid* (CA), which helps protect the brain.

Suggested uses: I always add one teaspoon of dried rosemary or a tablespoon or two of fresh to a pound of ground meat before grilling burgers. Rosemary also is good in lamb and potato dishes, soups and stews.

Healthier Grilling

In a recent study, researchers grilled steaks that had been marinated for one hour in mixtures containing several herbs and spices, such as rosemary, thyme, basil, oregano and/or allspice.

Result: The steaks were 87% lower in *heterocyclic amines* (HCAs), compounds linked to increased risk for colorectal, prostate and pancreatic cancers, than un-marinated meat.

Theory: Antioxidants in herbs and spices curb formation of HCAs.

Before grilling red meat or poultry: Marinate it for 30 to 60 minutes in a mixture of herbs and spices blended with olive oil or citrus juice.

J. Scott Smith, PhD, professor of food chemistry, Kansas State University, Manhattan.

Seven Foods Proven To Fight Off Cancer

David Grotto, RD, LDN, a registered dietitian and former spokesperson for the American Dietetic Association. He is also founder and president of Nutrition Housecall, LLC, a Chicago-area consulting firm specializing in family nutrition programs. Grotto is also on the advisory board of *Fitness* magazine and is author of *101 Foods That Could Save Your Life* (Bantam). To read his nutrition blog, go to *www.101foodsthatcould saveyourlife.blogspot.com.*

Up to one-third of all cancers could be prevented if people embraced healthier lifestyles, including eating healthier foods. *For even better odds, choose these seven specific foods that have been proven to prevent cancer...*

CABBAGE

It is high in anticarcinogenic compounds called *glucosinolates*. Raw cabbage, particularly when it is fermented as sauerkraut, also is a good source for *indole-3-carbinol* (I3C), a substance that promotes the elimination of carcinogens from the body.

The Polish Women's Health Study, which looked at hundreds of Polish women in the US, found that those who had eaten four or more servings per week of raw, lightly cooked or fermented cabbage throughout adolescence were 72% less likely to develop breast cancer than women who had eaten only one-and-a-half servings per week. High consumption of cabbage during adulthood also provided significant protection even if little cabbage was eaten at a young age.

Recommended: Three or more one-half-cup servings per week of cabbage, cooked or raw.

Alternatives: Any cruciferous vegetable, including brussels sprouts, cauliflower, kale and broccoli. A recent study found that men who ate at least three servings per week of broccoli or other cruciferous vegetables were 41% less likely to get prostate cancer than men who ate less than one serving per week. Kimchi, a Korean pickled dish that is similar to sauerkraut, also is a good choice.

FLAXSEEDS

Little seeds with a nutty flavor, flaxseeds contain *lignans*, compounds that act like a weak form of estrogen. One study found that women who had high levels of *enterolactone* (linked to a high intake of lignans) had a 58% lower risk for breast cancer. Flaxseeds also contain omega-3 fatty acids, which appear to inhibit colon cancer in both men and women.

Recommended: One to two tablespoons of ground flaxseed daily. You can sprinkle it on cereal or yogurt or add it to soups or stews.

Alternatives: Two or more servings every week of cold-water fish, such as mackerel or salmon, provide cancer-fighting amounts of omega-3s.

For more lignans: Eat walnuts, and cook with canola oil.

MUSHROOMS

Common white button mushrooms found in supermarkets contains anticancer compounds. Scientists who compared vegetable extracts in the lab noticed that the extract made out of white button mushrooms was the most effective at blocking *aromatase*, one enzyme that can promote breast cancer. Button mushrooms also appear to suppress the growth of prostate cancer cells.

Recommended: Eat one-half cup of button mushrooms, three or four times per week.

Alternatives: Porcinis or chanterelles, wild mushrooms with a nuttier taste.

OLIVES

A Spanish laboratory study found that two compounds in olives—*maslinic acid* and *oleanolic acid*—inhibit the proliferation of cancer cells and promote *apoptosis*, the death of these cells. Other studies suggest that people who have olives as part of a classic Mediterranean diet have lower rates of a variety of cancers, including colon cancer.

Recommended: Eight olives a day, green or black.

An alternative: One to two tablespoons of extra-virgin olive oil daily. Drizzle it on salad or vegetables to enhance absorption of their healthy nutrients.

ONIONS

When researchers compared the 10 vegetables most frequently consumed in the US, onions had the third-highest level of *phenolic* compounds, which are thought to be among the most potent anticancer substances found in foods.

In a Finnish study, men who frequently ate onions, apples and other foods high in *quercetin* (a phenolic compound) were 60% less likely to develop lung cancer than men who ate smaller amounts. Quercetin also appears to reduce the risk for liver and colon cancers.

Recommended: One-half cup of onions, cooked or raw, three times each week. Yellow and red onions contain the most cancer-preventing substances.

Alternatives: Apples, capers and green and black tea, all of which are high in quercetin. Garlic, a botanical relative of onions, provides many of the same active ingredients.

PUMPKIN

Pumpkin, similar to winter squash, is extremely high in *carotenoids*, including beta-carotene. A long-running Japanese study that looked at more than 57,000 participants found that people who ate the most pumpkin had lower rates of gastric, breast, lung and colorectal cancers. There also is some evidence that pumpkin seeds can help reduce the risk for prostate cancer.

Recommended: Three or more one-half-cup servings a week. Pumpkin can be baked like any winter squash.

Alternatives: Carrots, broccoli and all of the winter squashes, including acorn, butternut and spaghetti squash.

RASPBERRIES

All of the foods that end in "erry"—including cherry, blueberry and strawberry—contain anti-inflammatory compounds which decrease cell damage that can lead to cancer. Raspberries are higher in fiber than most berries and are an excellent source of *ellagic acid* and *selenium*, both of which protect against a variety of cancers.

Recent studies have shown that raspberries (or raspberry extract) inhibit both oral and liver cancer cells. The responses in these studies were dose-dependent—the more raspberry extract used, the greater the effect.

Recommended: Have one-and-a-half cups of raspberries, two or three times per week.

An alternative: Cherries (and cherry juice) contain about as much ellagic acid as raspberries. Frozen berries and cherries, which contain less water, provide a higher concentration of protective compounds than fresh ones.

Smaller Fruit Is More Nutritious

As fruits and vegetables grow larger, their vitamin and mineral content decreases—as does their taste and aroma. Organic fruits and vegetables tend to be smaller in general, so the average organic product may contain more nutrients than a comparable one that is traditionally grown.

Charles Benbrook, PhD, chief scientist, The Organic Center, which gathers science on the health benefits of organic foods, Enterprise, Oregon.

Broccoli Sprouts Take On Cancer

Broccoli sprouts have 30 times more *isothiocyanates*—natural anticancer chemicals—than mature broccoli.

Recent study: Animals fed a concentrated broccoli sprout extract developed fewer than half as many bladder tumors as animals not given the extract.

Good idea: Add broccoli sprouts to salads and sandwiches.

Yuesheng Zhang, MD, PhD, professor of oncology, Roswell Park Cancer Institute, Buffalo, and leader of a study published in *Cancer Research*.

A Spot of Tea Reduces Skin Cancer Risk

Tea may help to reduce the risk of getting skin cancer.

Recent study: Dermatological researchers found that people who drank two or more cups of either black or green tea daily were 30% less likely than people who did not drink tea to suffer squamous cell carcinoma. Moreover, the effect grew over time—those who drank tea for 47 years had a 51% reduced risk. Researchers think that the *polyphenols* in tea serve as antioxidants that counter free radicals triggered by the sun, helping protect skin from moderate sun exposure.

Judy Rees, MD, PhD, research assistant professor, Dartmouth Medical School, lead author of study.

Boost Green Tea's Power with OJ

Increase green tea's cancer-fighting power by adding three tablespoons of orange, lemon or lime juice to one cup of the hot tea.

Reason: These juices improve the stability of the cancer-fighting antioxidants and make them more available for absorption.

Mario Ferruzzi, PhD, an associate professor of food science at Purdue University, West Lafayette, Indiana, and lead researcher of a laboratory study published in *Journal of Molecular Nutrition and Food Research*.

A Tea That Lowers BP

Reduce blood pressure with hibiscus, commonly found in blended herbal teas.

Recent finding: After drinking eight ounces of hibiscus tea three times a day for six weeks, participants' systolic (the top number) blood pressure dropped by an average of seven points—about as much as with standard hypertension drugs. People with higher blood pressure had an even larger drop.

Pure (unblended) hibiscus tea can be found on the Internet.

Diane L. McKay, PhD, a scientist in the Antioxidants Research Laboratory at the Jean Mayer USDA Human Nutrition Research Center on Aging at Tufts University, Boston. She led a study presented at a meeting of the American Heart Association.

Doctor's Orders: Enjoy a Bit of Chocolate Every Day

Antioxidants known as *polyphenols* in dark chocolate may lower blood pressure by improving blood vessel functioning. In a recent German trial, adults with prehypertension or stage 1 hypertension who consumed 6.3 g of dark chocolate (less than two chocolate kisses) daily for 18 weeks decreased systolic pressure by an average of 2.9 mmHg and diastolic pressure by 1.9 mmHg, without increasing weight, cholesterol or insulin levels. For a modest blood pressure–lowering effect, enjoy a bite or two of dark chocolate daily. Skip milk chocolate, which contains too few polyphenols to curb blood pressure.

Mark Houston, MD, associate clinical professor of medicine, Vanderbilt University School of Medicine, and director, Hypertension Institute, both in Nashville.

More Chocolate News

Eating three 100-calorie servings of dark chocolate every week can lower chronic inflammation by 17% and cut heart disease risk by 26%.

Caution: Eating more chocolate than this may increase risk.

Licia Iacoviello, MD, PhD, chair, Laboratory of Genetic and Environmental Epidemiology, Catholic University in Campobasso, Italy, and leader of a study of 10,994 people, published in *The Journal of Nutrition.*

Magnesium Miracle

In a recent study, women with normal blood pressure who got a daily average of 434 mg of magnesium from their diets lowered their risk for high blood pressure by 7%.

Best: Consume foods that are rich in magnesium, such as whole grains, nuts, legumes, leafy green vegetables, fish and yogurt.

Yiqing Song, MD, associate epidemiologist, division of preventive medicine, Brigham and Women's Hospital instructor in medicine, and Harvard Medical School, both in Boston, and leader of a study of 28,349 women, published in *The American Journal of Cardiology.*

Supplements vs. Drugs

Supplements beat drugs for high cholesterol. In a 12-week study of 74 adults who did not have heart disease but did have high LDL "bad" cholesterol levels (155 mg/dL, on average), one group took 40 mg daily of the statin drug *simvastatin* (Zocor). The other group took fish oil (three capsules daily) and red yeast rice supplements (2,400 mg to 3,600 mg daily) and made lifestyle changes, such as limiting fat intake and exercising five to six times weekly.

Result: LDL levels dropped by 42%, on average, in the supplement/lifestyle change group and 39%, on average, in the statin group.

Talk to your doctor before trying such supplement/lifestyle therapy.

David J. Becker, MD, cardiologist at Chestnut Hill Hospital and the University of Pennsylvania Health System, both in Philadelphia.

Lower Cholesterol More Than 10% with Tasty Tomato Products

When 21 healthy people ate a tomato-free diet for three weeks, followed by a three-week diet that included about two tablespoons of ketchup and nearly two cups of tomato juice daily, participants' LDL "bad" cholesterol levels decreased, on average, by 12.9%.

Theory: The antioxidants in tomatoes help inhibit oxidation of fats.

For heart health: Add some tomato products (such as low-sodium tomato juice) to your daily diet.

Sohvi Hörkko, MD, PhD, research fellow, department of pharmacology and toxicology, University of Oulu, Finland.

White Wine Protects The Heart, Too

In a study of 35 healthy women, participants drank 6.8 ounces daily of red wine (widely recognized for its heart-protective effects) for four weeks…no wine for one month…followed up by 6.8 ounces of white wine daily for four weeks.

Result: After the two wine intake periods, the participants' HDL (good) cholesterol levels rose and their blood levels of two substances linked to chronic inflammation and heart disease dropped. Previous studies in men produced similar results.

Caution: Long-term consumption of more than five ounces of alcohol per day in women may increase breast cancer risk.

Ramon Estruch, MD, PhD, senior consultant, department of internal medicine, Hospital Clinic, Barcelona, Spain.

Red Wine Scores Again

Animals given red wine (known to reduce heart disease risk in humans) along with turkey meat had lower levels of the chemicals that have been linked to cancer and heart disease.

Theory: Wine (and berries and grape juice) contain substances that help block the harmful effects of a meat-rich diet.

Journal of Agricultural and Food Chemistry, www. pubs.acs.org/journal/jafcau.

If You Don't Drink, Should You Start?

Dana E. King, MD, professor of family medicine, Medical University of South Carolina, Charleston.

The most recent research indicates that it's worth considering. In a recent 10-year study of 7,697 healthy men and women (ages 45 to 64), 442 nondrinkers had become moderate drinkers—up to one drink daily for women and up to two drinks daily for men—by the six-year point.

Result: The new moderate drinkers were 38% less likely to suffer from cardiovascular events, such as heart attacks, during the next four years than those who did not drink at all. Wine drinkers had 68% fewer cardiovascular events.

Theory: Alcohol helps prevent formation of blood clots, raises HDL "good" cholesterol and has other heart-protective effects.

If you are a middle-aged nondrinker: Ask your doctor whether you should start to drink in moderation.

Caution: People with liver disease, a history of alcoholism (themselves or in their family) or people taking certain medications, such as sedatives or cardiovascular drugs, should avoid alcohol.

Cleanse Your System

Fasting once each month may lower heart disease risk. Having nothing but water for 24 hours allows the body to reset its metabolism and adjust its glucose and insulin sensitivities. A monthly fast for decades can have substantial benefits, including 40% lower risk for clogged arteries. Short-term fasting has not been studied but also may be helpful.

Caution: People with chronic health conditions, such as diabetes, should not fast.

Benjamin D. Horne, PhD, MPH, director of cardiovascular and genetic epidemiology, Intermountain Medical Center in Murray, Utah. His analysis of more than 4,600 patients was presented at a recent American Heart Association conference.

The Healthiest Seafood

Sardines might be the healthiest seafood. They are nearly the richest in heart-healthy omega-3 fat—richer than tuna and many fish-oil supplements. And, sardines contain fewer contaminants than tuna, swordfish and most other fatty fish. They are also a good source of calcium if you eat the bones.

Caution: Canned sardines may be high in salt, so if you are on a sodium-restricted diet, check the can label.

UC Berkeley Wellness Letter, www.wellnessletter.com.

Being Argumentative Harms the Heart

When 300 married couples without heart disease were asked to rate their spouses on an "antagonism" scale, those who got high scores—indicating an argumentative, competitive or suspicious nature—were more likely to have significant calcium buildup in their arteries than those who were rated lower.

Theory: Negative emotions raise blood pressure and stimulate stress hormones, which adversely affect the heart.

Timothy W. Smith, PhD, professor of psychology, University of Utah, Salt Lake City.

Eating Fish May Lower Hostility

In a recent study, young adults who ate fish rich in omega-3 fatty acids, such as salmon or tuna, were less likely to be hostile. Hostility is a risk factor for heart disease.

Best: Eat between seven and 10 ounces of a variety of fish per week unless you are pregnant or are a nursing mother. Small children should not be exposed to the mercury often found in fish and other seafood.

More research is needed to fully understand the relationship between omega-3 fatty acids and hostility.

Carlos Iribarren, MD, PhD, research scientist, Kaiser Permanente, Oakland, California, and leader of a study of 3,581 young adults, published in *European Journal of Clinical Nutrition.*

"Runner's High" May Reduce Heart Attack Damage

In a recent study on rats, *opioids*—the body chemicals created when you do strenuous aerobic exercise that cause the euphoria called "runner's high"—appear to protect the heart from damage if a heart attack occurs.

Eric Dickson, MD, head, department of emergency medicine, University of Iowa, Iowa City, and leader of a study published in *American Journal of Physiology: Heart and Circulatory Physiology.*

Drink This Tea to Cut Stroke Risk by 42%!

In a recent finding, drinking three cups per day of green or black tea—not herbal teas—reduced stroke risk by 21%. Drinking six cups daily reduced risk by 42%.

Lenore Arab, PhD, MSc, professor of medicine, David Geffen School of Medicine at UCLA, and leader of an analysis of nine studies involving 195,000 people.

Music Speeds Stroke Recovery

In a recent finding, stroke victims who listened to their favorite music daily during the first months after a stroke showed faster and more significant improvements in memory and attention than stroke victims who did not listen to music or who listened to audio books. Three months after a stroke, verbal memory improved by 60% among music listeners, compared with 18% for audio book listeners and 29% for nonlisteners. Similar differences were found six months after a stroke.

Teppo Sarkamo, PhD student, cognitive brain research unit, department of psychology, Helsinki University of Finland, and leader of a study of 54 stroke patients, published in *Brain.*

What to Eat to Beat Diabetes Risk

JoAnn E. Manson, MD, DrPH, a professor of medicine and women's health at Harvard Medical School and chief of the division of preventive medicine at Brigham and Women's Hospital, both in Boston. She is one of the lead investigators for two highly influential studies on women's health—the Harvard Nurses' Health Study and the Women's Health Initiative.

The statistics are quite shocking—23% of all Americans age 60 and up now have diabetes, a deadly disease that can lead to heart disease, stroke, blindness, amputation, kidney failure and coma. Yet the Nurses' Health Study (NHS), which followed 84,941 women for 16 years, suggests that about 90% of cases could be prevented.

With type 2 diabetes (it's the most common form), either the pancreas does not produce enough *insulin* (the hormone needed to convert glucose into energy) or the body's cells ignore insulin. Certain risk factors cannot be helped—a family history of diabetes…a personal history of polycystic ovary syndrome or diabetes during pregnancy…delivering a baby with a birth weight of nine pounds or more… or being non-Caucasian. However, the majority of risk factors are within your control.

•**Avoid "diabesity."** Researchers developed this term to emphasize the interconnection between obesity and diabetes. In the NHS, obese women were *10 times* more likely to get diabetes than women of normal weight.

Theory: Fat cells—particularly those deep inside the abdomen—produce hormones and chemical messengers that trigger inflammation and interfere with cells' insulin receptors. Even modest weight loss can cut diabetes risk in half.

•**Stand, don't sit.** Just getting off the couch can help. The NHS participants had a 14% *increased* risk for diabetes for every two hours per day spent watching TV—and a 12% *decreased* risk for every two hours per day spent standing or walking around at home.

Even better: A brisk one-hour walk daily can reduce diabetes risk by 34%.

•**Skip soda and fruit punch.** Sugar-sweetened soft drinks are the largest single source of calories in the US diet. Daily soda drinkers tend to consume more calories, gain more weight and develop diabetes more often than people who seldom drink soda.

Smart: Drink only water or unsweetened beverages.

•**Choose the right fats.** Polyunsaturated fats—found in corn oil, soybean oil, nuts and fish—may affect cell membranes in a way that improves insulin use. Avoid trans fats—found in various deep-fried fast foods, stick marga-

rines and packaged snack foods—which may have the opposite effect.

•**Limit red meat.** In the NHS, a one-serving-per-day increase in red meat (beef, pork, lamb) or processed meat (cold cuts, hot dogs) increased the risk for diabetes by 26% and 38%, respectively.

Theory: Excessive *heme iron* (the type of iron in meat) and/or *sodium nitrate* (a preservative) may damage the pancreas.

•**Go for whole grains.** Compared with refined grains (white flour, white rice), whole grains minimize blood sugar fluctuations, easing demands on the pancreas…and provide more magnesium, which makes insulin more effective.

•**Drink coffee.** In studies involving about 200,000 people, drinking four to six cups of coffee daily was associated with a 28% reduction in diabetes risk compared with drinking two or fewer cups daily. *Chlorogenic acid*, an antioxidant in regular and decaf coffee, may make cells more responsive to insulin.

Legumes Fight Off Diabetes

Eating legumes may lower diabetes risk. In a recent finding, women who consumed the most peanuts, soybeans and other legumes had significantly lower risk for type 2 diabetes. Legumes are good sources of magnesium, *isoflavones* and fiber, and they have a low glycemic index, which may explain why they help lower diabetes risk. Of all legumes, soybeans (though not most processed soy products) appear to be the most beneficial. Women who consumed the most soybeans were 47% less likely to develop diabetes than women who consumed the least.

Raquel Villegas, PhD, research assistant professor of medicine, School of Medicine at Vanderbilt University in Nashville, and lead author of a study of 64,227 women, published in *The American Journal of Clinical Nutrition.*

Add Some Spice

In a recent study, 24 herbs and spices were analyzed and found to contain high levels of *polyphenols*—antioxidant compounds that block the formation of inflammation-promoting substances that raise diabetes risk. Levels were highest in ground cloves...followed by cinnamon (shown in earlier research to help fight diabetes)...sage...marjoram...tarragon... and rosemary.

Instead of seasoning with salt: Consider trying these herbs and spices.

James L. Hargrove, PhD, associate professor in the department of foods and nutrition at the University of Georgia, Athens.

Cheers! How Wine Can Increase Life Span

A new study suggests that a glass of red or white wine a day reduces the risk of developing nonalcoholic fatty liver disease, which can progress to irreversible scarring and liver cancer. Drinking beer or liquor doesn't protect the liver. It's possible that wine's nonalcoholic components may be responsible for the findings. The data do not support the use of larger amounts of alcohol.

Jeffrey B. Schwimmer, MD, an associate professor of pediatrics, division of gastroenterology, hepatology and nutrition, University of California School of Medicine, San Diego.

A Supplement That Protects the Liver

The antioxidant *N-acetylcysteine* (NAC) is so effective at protecting the liver that hospitals use it to treat overdoses of *acetaminophen* (Tylenol), which can cause liver failure.

New finding: NAC may help the body excrete mercury, often found in fish.

Dosage: 500 mg daily.

Shari Lieberman, PhD, CNS, FACN, a nutrition scientist in Hillsboro Beach, Florida, who has been in private practice for more than 25 years, *www.drshari.net*. She is a board member of the Certification Board for Nutrition Specialists, fellow of the American College of Nutrition and coauthor of *User's Guide to Detoxification* (Basic Health).

Keep Joints Feeling Young! The Diet That Fights Arthritis

Harris McIlwain, MD, a board-certified specialist in rheumatology and geriatric medicine who is the founder of the Tampa Medical Group in Florida, *www.tampa medicalgroup.com*. He is also an adjunct professor at the University of South Florida College of Public Health and coauthor of *Pain-Free Arthritis: A 7-Step Program for Feeling Better Again* (Owl).

In my rheumatology practice I often treat patients suffering from painfully arthritic joints who have been unable to get relief, despite seeing many doctors. I tell them that one of the most important things they can do for their arthritis is to change their diets. After just a few weeks on my pain-free eating plan, I've had many patients cut back on their anti-inflammatory medications and even put off joint-replacement surgery. The diet helps alleviate pain and stiffness in most types of arthritis, including both rheumatoid arthritis and osteoarthritis.

How this works: The pain-free diet guides you toward healing foods that are known to reduce inflammation and boost the immune system. It helps you to eliminate those foods that promote inflammation and might trigger symptoms. The diet also includes recommendations on nutritional supplements.

A bonus: This nutritional approach makes it simpler to maintain a healthy body weight, which is essential for those patients who need to take pressure off their joints. Maintaining a healthy body weight also produces metabolic changes that lessen the body's inflammatory response.

Helpful: It is easier to maintain a healthy weight when you eat frequent, smaller meals. Instead of three large meals, have about six mini-meals throughout the day. In addition to a breakfast, lunch and dinner of about 300 calories each, eat three snacks between meals of about 150 to 200 calories each.

FOODS THAT HEAL

Foods that are high in antioxidants and other inflammation-fighting nutrients can noticeably reduce arthritis pain and stiffness when consumed daily. *The following are especially effective...*

•**High-antioxidant fruits and vegetables.** Antioxidants help reduce inflammation. Several years ago, the US Department of Agriculture ranked the following foods according to their antioxidant activity. Among the top 10 fruits and vegetables from highest to lowest were blueberries, kale, strawberries, spinach, Brussels sprouts, plums, broccoli, beets, oranges and red grapes. Eat a variety of these foods, raw and cooked, to obtain the greatest benefit.

Also beneficial: Asparagus, cabbage, cauliflower, tomatoes, sweet potatoes, avocados, grapefruit, peaches and watermelon.

•**Oil-rich fish.** Research has shown that the omega-3 fatty acids contained in anchovies, mackerel, salmon, sardines, shad, tuna, whitefish and herring help reduce inflammation—particularly levels of *leukotriene B4*, a chemical that contributes to various types of arthritis. Researchers have found that women who ate at least three servings of baked or broiled fish weekly had about half the risk of getting rheumatoid arthritis as those who ate only one serving.

•**Soy.** Studies have found that a diet rich in soy may help reduce inflammation-related pain and swelling. Try tofu, soy milk, soy yogurt, soybeans or miso, a traditional Japanese food consisting of fermented soybeans and made into a thick paste.

•**Green and black tea.** Green tea contains a *polyphenol* (a chemical found in plants that acts as an antioxidant) called *EGCG*, which can inhibit a key gene involved in the arthritis inflammation response. Research suggests that the more you drink, the more benefit you will get. Black tea, while it's processed differently than green, also provides benefits. It contains anti-inflammatory chemicals of its own called *theaflavins.* The Iowa Women's Health Study found that women who drank three or more cups of tea (not including herbal tea) reduced their risk of rheumatoid arthritis by 60%.

•**Pineapple.** This tasty fruit contains *bromelain*, an enzyme that reduces inflammation associated with arthritis. Fresh pineapple is the most beneficial, but canned is also good.

•**Onions and apples.** Both of these foods are especially high in flavonoids, which are also inflammation-fighting compounds. Eat a variety of these foods, both raw and cooked.

FOODS TO AVOID

The only way to know which of the foods below affect your joint pain is to eliminate each one for at least two weeks and assess your symptoms. That way, you'll know which type of food increases your inflammation and pain.

•**Avoid foods that increase inflammation.** There are a variety of foods that trigger the body to produce *cytokines*—naturally occurring proteins that can promote inflammation, leading to pain and deterioration of cartilage in the joints. These include beef and other red meat...foods cooked using high temperatures, particularly fried foods...and any foods containing man-made trans fats (often called partially hydrogenated fats or oils on food labels), including junk food and commercial baked goods. Eat these types of foods sparingly.

•**Decrease intake of foods from animal products.** I tell my patients to eat turkey and chicken in moderation. But the reality is that all animal products—including poultry, some farm-raised fish, egg yolks and dairy products—contain *arachidonic acid*, a fatty acid that is converted by the body into *prostaglandins* and *leukotrienes*, two other types of inflammation-causing chemicals. I've had many patients tell me that they have reduced arthritis symptoms by adopting a "modified vegetarian" diet.

Key: Decrease your intake of animal protein and increase the amount of protein you get from fish and plant sources, such as beans, nuts, soy, portobello mushrooms (a common meat substitute) and whole grains.

Start by substituting one-fourth of the animal protein you normally eat with plant-based foods, cold-water fish and low-fat dairy. After about two or three months, increase the substitution to half—adding more vegetables, fruits, lentils, beans, fish, whole grains and low-fat dairy. After doing this, many of my patients choose to give up all animal protein because they enjoy the benefit of decreased pain and inflammation.

Note: A small percentage of patients find that particular vegetables—including tomatoes, white potatoes, peppers and eggplant—make their arthritis worse. These nightshade family plants contain *solanine,* a substance that can be toxic if not sufficiently digested in the intestines. Eliminate all of these foods, then add them back one at a time—as long as you do not have pain or inflammation.

• **Stay away from foods with a high glycemic index.** While high-glycemic foods (foods that quickly raise your blood sugar) should be avoided by people with diabetes or prediabetes, they pose problems for people with arthritis as well.

Reason: They increase insulin production, which promotes accumulation of body fat and causes a rebound sensation of hunger a few hours after eating—making it harder to maintain a healthy weight, which is important for reducing arthritis symptoms.

The high-glycemic foods include table sugar, baked white potatoes, French fries, pretzels, white bread and rolls, white and brown rice, potato and corn chips, pancakes, waffles, doughnuts and corn flakes.

More from Dr. Harris McIlwain...

Supplements That Can Ease Arthritis

The following supplements may also help reduce arthritis inflammation. Remember to check with your doctor before taking any dietary supplement—even a "natural" one.

• **Glucosamine** (1,500 mg/daily). While the data on this nutritional supplement are mixed, it's perfectly safe. Some studies suggest that it may slow arthritis progression. It's often combined with chondroitin (1,200 mg), another nutritional supplement that may help to relieve arthritis symptoms for some people.

• **Vitamin C** (500 mg to 1,000 mg/per day) plays a key role in building and protecting collagen, an important component of cartilage. Among other things, it contains antioxidants that combat inflammation and help regenerate damaged joint tissue.

• **Bromelain.** This top anti-inflammatory enzyme is found in pineapple, but it's also available in a tablet or capsule form. Include fresh pineapple (two servings daily) in your diet or take capsules (follow directions on label for amounts)—or do both.

• **Fish oil capsules.** For people who aren't eating two or more servings of fish per week, this is a good option. Your dose should provide 600 mg of combined DHA and EPA in a 2:1 ratio—the ratio that occurs naturally in wild salmon. Read your product's label for its DHA/EPA content.

• **Ginger.** Clinical studies have found that this herb decreases arthritis symptoms and inflammation. It can be taken in the form of tincture, capsules, as a spice added to foods or as a tea made from boiling ginger root. You may benefit by drinking ginger juice or extract. Since ginger inhibits blood clotting, do not consume more than four grams a day.

Little-Known Knee Arthritis Predictor

Women whose index fingers are shorter than their ring fingers may be three times more likely to develop knee osteoarthritis.

Reason: Unknown.

Self-defense: If your index finger is shorter than your ring finger, decrease other arthritis risk factors by controlling your weight and exercising regularly.

Michael Doherty, MD, rheumatology professor, academic rheumatology department, University of Nottingham, England, and coauthor of a study of more than 3,000 people, published in *Arthritis & Rheumatism*.

Delicious Pain Relief

Eating pineapple may relieve arthritic pain. It may also help other inflammation, such as sunburn and joint pain.

Why: Pineapple contains *bromelain*, an enzyme that recent research shows has anti-inflammatory benefits.

Bromelain can also be purchased in supplement form, with a recommended dose of about 100 milligrams per day for sore joints. Check with your own doctor to be sure it is OK for you.

Michael Roizen, MD, chair, division of anesthesiology, critical care medicine and pain management for Cleveland Clinic, and Mehmet Oz, MD, vice-chair of surgery and professor of cardiac surgery at Columbia University, coauthors of *You: On a Diet* (Free Press).

Try Cod Liver Oil Instead of NSAIDs

Cod liver oil can benefit rheumatoid arthritis sufferers.

Study: People taking 10 grams of cod liver oil a day can cut their reliance on nonsteroidal anti-inflammatory drugs (or NSAIDs), such as *ibuprofen*, by more than 30%. The reduction in drug use wasn't associated with any worsening of pain or the disease.

Caution: Avoid oil with added vitamin A—it may lead to consuming unsafe amounts of that vitamin.

Jill Belch, MD, head of the Cardiovascular and Lung Biology Centre, Ninewells Hospital, University of Dundee Medical School, Dundee, Scotland.

Want Knee Arthritis to Wane? Try a Cane

Cane use could slow osteoarthritis progression. In a recent study of 40 patients with knee osteoarthritis (OA), subjects who used a cane had a 10% average decrease in the load on the inside of the knee while walking.

Theory: Cane-aided walking reduces load on the knee and possibly prevents worsening of OA damage.

Kay Crossley, PhD, research fellow, School of Physiotherapy, University of Melbourne, Victoria, Australia.

A Vitamin That Reduces Your Risk of Falls

Each year, one-third of women over the age of 65 fall.

Recent study: Older women who supplemented daily with 1,000 international units (IU) of vitamin D plus 1,000 mg of calcium had about a 20% lower risk of falling than women who took calcium alone.

Theory: Vitamin D promotes both muscle strength and nervous system function, which improves balance.

Richard L. Prince, MD, associate professor, department of endocrinology and diabetes at University of Western Australia, Perth, and leader of a study of 302 women, published in *Archives of Internal Medicine*.

Soothing Supplement For Fibromyalgia Pain

Chlorella, a type of green algae, decreased fibromyalgia pain by 22% in one study.

Possible reasons: It may boost the immune system and/or increase absorption of essential nutrients.

Dosage: 5 g to 10 g daily.

Alan C. Logan, ND, nutrition editor of the *International Journal of Naturopathic Medicine* and coauthor of *Hope and Help for Chronic Fatigue Syndrome and Fibromyalgia* (Cumberland House). His online site is *www.drlogan.com.*

Cut Your Risk for Alzheimer's with "Brain Fitness"

Pierce J. Howard, PhD, a leading cognitive researcher and cofounder and director of research at the Center for Applied Cognitive Studies in Charlotte, North Carolina. He is the author of *The Owner's Manual for the Brain: Everyday Applications from Mind-Brain Research* (Bard).

It's easy to blame fading memory and waning cognitive skills on advancing age. But in reality, age does not hurt the brain as much as unhealthful habits, such as a sedentary lifestyle…poor food choices…excessive alcohol use…and chronic health problems, such as heart disease, high blood pressure, diabetes, obesity and depression.

A recent development: Although the evidence is not yet definitive, a growing body of scientific research suggests that people who incorporate a steady dose of mental challenges into their daily activities are less likely to suffer cognitive decline—including that associated with Alzheimer's disease.

For example, a landmark study of 678 nuns found that although autopsies revealed some of them had late-stage Alzheimer's disease upon death, those who were mentally active did not develop behavioral symptoms of the disease while they were alive—perhaps because they had reserves of brain cells.

While some neurologists recommend crossword puzzles and the popular number-placement game Sudoku to help promote brain fitness, there are a variety of other activities that are less well-known but perhaps just as effective—if not more so. By varying your brain-fitness workout, you will maximize the benefits.

My five favorites…

1. Develop a "back-to-school" attitude. Until recently, the scientists believed that we had a finite number of brain cells. Now, research shows that we are able to generate new brain cells (*neurons*) and connections (*synapses*) between them. Acquiring new knowledge and skills—no matter what your age—is one of the best ways to stimulate brain activity.

Even if you do develop all the classic brain changes associated with Alzheimer's disease, having a ready supply of additional brain cells may help protect you from the signs and symptoms of dementia. The key is to learn something *brand new* and *mentally challenging.*

What to try: If you enjoy books, read about an unfamiliar topic and grapple with it until you understand it. If you play music, learn a new piece—or better yet, a new instrument—and practice until you master it. Learning a foreign language (CDs are available at most public libraries) also promotes brain health.

Helpful: Devote the first part of the day to learning. At that time of day, you are less likely to be fatigued, and your attention will be better. During the day, review the material and other information you learned on previous days.

Smart idea: You can study a wide variety of subjects, ranging from pure science and the humanities to architecture and engineering, by enrolling in one of the 1,800 free college-level online classes offered by the Massachusetts Institute of Technology. To learn more, go to MIT OpenCourseWare at *http://ocw.mit.edu.* To learn a new vocabulary word every day, sign up for A.Word.A.Day at *www.wordsmith.org.*

2. Involve others in your brain workouts. Research shows that people who interact socially on a regular basis are less likely to suffer cognitive decline—perhaps due to the soothing effects of the brain chemicals called *serotonin* and *endorphins,* which are secreted during positive interactions with others. This, in turn, reduces levels of the hormone cortisol, which contributes to deterioration of the hippocampus, the brain's memory storage center. By involving other people in your brain activities, you not only challenge your cognitive abilities but also increase your social connections, thus further protecting your brain.

What to try: Chess, bridge, backgammon or board games, such as Stratego or Risk, that test your ability to strategize.

Also helpful: Increase your social interactions by joining a book club, a civic organization or a religious group. Or get involved in volunteer work.

3. Do brain-building exercises on the Web. For times when you are alone, online brain-training games are a good option. Researchers at the University of Michigan in Ann Arbor recently found that individuals who performed computer-based brain-training exercises for about 30 minutes daily boosted their ability to reason and solve new problems.

What to try: Play different games on different days. This helps to thicken the *myelin sheath* (fatty tissue surrounding nerve fibers) on existing neural pathways and fosters the emergence of new synapses. For a wide variety of free online games and brain teasers, go to *www.gamesforthebrain.com* or *www.sharp brains.com*.

4. Surprise your brain with new habits. Experts call these exercises "neurobics," activities that jar the brain into forming new synapses by creating new associations. The idea is to do something familiar—but in an unfamiliar way. A good plan for doing this is to tweak one old habit every week. Find a pattern that works for you. Later, disrupt the pattern—to keep yourself on your toes!

What to try: Drive a different route to your work…eat a type of ethnic food you've never experienced…if you wear your watch on your left wrist, try putting it on your right…switch the part in your hair to the other side…and brush your teeth or hold eating utensils with your nondominant hand.

5. Preserve your brain's equilibrium. As we age, changes occur in our sense of balance, which is controlled by signals that the brain receives from certain sensory systems. To adapt gradually to this change, we need to force ourselves to experiment with unaccustomed postures, which helps us become familiar with our new "internal gyroscope."

What to try: Whenever you're waiting in line, lift one foot off of the ground and balance your weight on the other foot for as long as possible. Then, switch feet and rest your weight on the other foot. A good sense of balance helps to prevent falls and preserves the brain's equilibrium.

Caution: If you feel unsteady on your feet, do not attempt this activity unless you can support yourself by holding on to a counter.

B-12 Power

In a recent finding, older people with the highest blood levels of vitamin B-12 showed six times less brain shrinkage over a five-year period than those with the lowest levels. A new study is under way to determine whether B vitamins can slow brain loss.

To boost B-12 levels: Eat meat, fish, shellfish, eggs, dairy products and fortified cereals. Liver, oysters and clams have the highest B-12 content.

Anna Vogiatzoglou, MSc, RD, a doctoral candidate in the department of physiology, anatomy and genetics, University of Oxford, England, and lead author of a study of 107 people, published in *Neurology*.

Black Tea Reduces Parkinson's Risk by 71%!

When researchers analyzed health data for 63,257 adults, they found that those who drank at least 23 cups of black tea monthly (caffeinated or decaffeinated) had a 71% lower risk for Parkinson's disease over a 12-year period than those who drank less black tea. Intake of green tea had no effect on Parkinson's risk.

Theory: Black tea contains complex antioxidants that may help protect against Parkinson's disease.

Louis C. Tan, MD, senior consultant, department of neurology, National Neuroscience Institute, Singapore.

Parkinson's Patients: Tango Your Way To Better Mobility

The tango can help Parkinson's patients in a variety of areas.

Recent study: People with Parkinson's disease who took tango lessons improved their mobility compared with study subjects who attended traditional exercise classes instead. The dancers also had better balance and were at lower risk for falling.

Gammon M. Earhart, PhD, assistant professor of physical therapy, anatomy and neurobiology and neurology, Washington University School of Medicine, St. Louis, and coauthor of a study reported in *Scientific American*.

Eat Your Veggies to Prevent Cataracts

Women who consumed the most *carotenoids* (pigments in plants) called *lutein* and *zeaxanthin* were 18% less likely to develop cataracts than women who consumed the least. These carotenoids may protect against cataracts by filtering harmful blue light.

Best food sources: Kale, spinach, collard greens, peppers.

William Christen, ScD, associate professor, Harvard Medical School, Boston, and leader of a study of 35,551 women, published in *Archives of Ophthalmology*.

Depressed? Give New Eyeglasses a Try

New eyeglasses can help relieve depression among the elderly.

Recent finding: After two months, seniors who received properly prescribed eyeglasses had higher scores for activities, hobbies and social interaction—and fewer indications for depression—than seniors with similar visual acuity who were not given new eyeglasses.

Cynthia Owsley, PhD, professor, department of ophthalmology, University of Alabama at Birmingham, and leader of a study of 78 nursing home residents, published in *Archives of Ophthalmology*.

Perk Up Your Taste Buds

The loss of taste can be age-related and/or linked to the use of certain drugs—such as the blood pressure–lowering drug *captopril* (Capoten) and some antibiotics, including *metronidazole* (Flagyl)—as well as chronic sinus infections, which inhibit taste by interfering with a person's sense of smell.

If your sense of taste is declining: Get more zinc—from wheat germ, brown rice and kidney beans…or ask your doctor about taking a 25 mg to 50 mg zinc supplement daily (in addition to your multivitamin).

Henri Roca, MD, medical director of the Greenwich Hospital Center for Integrative Medicine, Greenwich, Connecticut.

Do Expiration Dates on Supplements Matter?

Supplements, just like medications and food, have a particular life on the shelf. Deteriorated products do not work as well—and could even be dangerous. Fish oil, for example, can become rancid and turn into a tissue-damaging pro-oxidant.

But most manufacturers label products with a conservative expiration date that's well before the time the product is likely to deteriorate. I believe that nutritional supplements, if stored as recommended by manufacturers, generally can be used safely for up to three months beyond the stated expiration date.

Best: Buy supplements in quantities you expect to use before the expiration date.

Jane Guiltinan, ND, clinical professor, Bastyr Center for Natural Health, Seattle.

6

Strictly Personal

A Couple's Guide to Boosting Desire

One out of five marriages is virtually without sex. These couples have sex 10 or even fewer times per year. And, in about one in three marriages, one spouse has a considerably larger sexual appetite than the other. If you see yourself in these statistics, do not despair—there's a great deal that can be done to boost your marriage's libido.

WHO'S SEX-STARVED?

A sex-starved marriage happens when one spouse is desperately longing for more physical affection. Sex-starved marriages cannot be defined by the number of times per week or month that a couple has sex, because there are no daily or weekly minimum requirements to ensure a healthy sex life. What works for one couple is grounds for divorce for another.

Most people believe that it is principally women who struggle with low sexual desire. While it's true that more men than women complain about the frequency of sex, the difference between genders isn't great. In fact, low desire in men is one of America's best-kept secrets. Too many men are simply unwilling to discuss their low desire with doctors, therapists or even their wives.

In a sex-starved marriage, the less interested spouse, whether male or female, typically will think, *Why are you making such a big deal out of this? It's just sex.* But to the spouse who desires more physical closeness, sex is extremely important because it's not just a physical act. It's about feeling wanted, attractive, appreciated and emotionally connected. When the low-desire spouse doesn't

Michele Weiner-Davis, MSW, a social worker and relationship expert who is founder and director of The Divorce Busting Center in Boulder, Colorado, *www.divorce busting.com.* A regular guest on *Oprah, 48 Hours* and the *Today* show, she is author of seven books, including *The Sex-Starved Wife: What to Do When He's Lost Desire* (Simon & Schuster).

understand sex's significance and continues to reject sexual advances, intimacy on many different levels tends to fall off. The couple stops cuddling up on the couch, laughing at each other's jokes, going on dates together. In short, they stop being friends. This places their marriage in jeopardy.

CATCH-22

Frequently, the lower-desire spouse needs to feel close and connected on an emotional level before he/she is interested in being sexual. This usually entails spending quality time together and talking about intimate issues.

The catch-22 is that typically the higher-desire spouse needs to feel connected physically in order to open up with conversation or feel that spending time together is a priority.

One spouse may wait for time together and heart-to-heart talks before committing to the physical relationship, while the other spouse waits to be touched before initiating time together or intimate conversation.

Each waits for the other to change.

THE NOs HAVE VETO POWER

The spouse who has the lower sexual drive usually controls the frequency of sex—if he does not want it, it generally doesn't happen. This is not due to maliciousness or a desire for power—it just seems unimaginable to be sexual if one partner is not in the mood.

Furthermore, there is an unspoken and often unconscious expectation that the higher-desire spouse must accept the no-sex verdict, not complain about it—and, of course, remain monogamous. After decades of working with couples, I can attest that this is an unfair and unworkable arrangement. This is not to say that infidelity is a solution, but as with all relationship conflicts, being willing to find middle ground is the best way to ensure love's longevity.

If you're in a sex-starved marriage, you and your spouse need to work on some changes. Don't worry about who takes the lead. Relationships are such that if one person changes, the relationship changes.

ADVICE FOR HIGH-DESIRE SPOUSES

Tune in to your spouse's needs outside the bedroom. High-desire people will usually try to boost their spouses' desire by doing things that would turn themselves on, such as buying sexy lingerie and renting X-rated videos. However, these actions often don't work for their spouses, who are more likely to be responsive to loving behaviors outside the bedroom, such as helping more with housework and offering more compliments and fewer criticisms.

Speak from the heart. Some people talk to their spouses about their sexual unhappiness, but instead of speaking from their hearts—which might prompt their spouses' empathy—harsh words are exchanged and tempers flare. Although it is understandable that unending rejection might lead to anger and resentment, these emotions are not aphrodisiacs. Instead of complaining, say, "I miss being close to you physically. We seem to get along so much better after we make love. I'm hoping that we can be more affectionate this week."

ADVICE FOR LOW-DESIRE SPOUSES

Don't ignore the problem. If you and your spouse have been arguing about sex, don't stick your head in the sand. Your differences won't disappear—the only thing that will disappear is your emotional connection and friendship. There are so many excellent resources to help you feel more sexual. Good books include *Hot Monogamy* by Patricia Love, MD, and Jo Robinson...*Rekindling Desire: A Step-by-Step Program to Help Low-Sex and No-Sex Marriages* by Barry and Emily McCarthy...and my book, *The Sex-Starved Marriage*. Also, licensed sex therapists can be found through the American Association of Sexuality Educators, Counselors and Therapists (*www.aasect.org*).

Just do it. Perhaps you've had the experience of not feeling in the mood when your spouse approached you, but you gave it a try, and once you got into it, you enjoyed it. You're not alone. There are millions of people who simply don't experience out-of-the-blue sexy thoughts—which is unlike their more highly sexed spouses who may have lusty thoughts many times every day.

Try this: During the next two weeks, initiate sex twice each week. Also, flirt, call your spouse pet names, dress more provocatively and be more physically affectionate. Do this whether you feel like it or not. Then carefully watch your spouse for any changes in his behavior. An irritable, withdrawn, uncooperative spouse most likely will become much more fun to be around.

led to significant improvement in sexual satisfaction. The spray is in clinical trials.

Susan Davis, PhD, professor of medicine, Monash University, Victoria, Australia, and leader of a study of 261 women ages 35 to 46, published in *Annals of Internal Medicine*.

Attraction Is Purely Chemical

A woman is attracted to a man's scent based on a single gene. The OR7D4 gene reacts strongly with the chemical androstenone, formed when a man's body breaks down the hormone testosterone. Depending on a woman's variation of OR7D4, a man's androstenone may smell like vanilla, urine or nothing.

Bottom line: Some aspects of attraction really are chemical.

Leslie B. Vosshall, PhD, associate professor, laboratory of neurogenetics and behavior, Rockefeller University, New York City, and coauthor of a study of 400 people, published online in *Nature*.

The Color of Love

M en who looked at photographs of women wearing (or surrounded by) red rated them as more sexually desirable than when the same women wore other colors.

University of Rochester, Rochester, New York, *www. rochester.edu*.

One Spritz Boosts Sexual Satisfaction

A daily spritz of hormones may boost sexual satisfaction in some women.

Recent finding: Among premenopausal women who lacked interest in sex, a daily dose of a testosterone spray to the abdomen

The Little Blue Pill For Women?

V iagra may help women who experience sexual dysfunction caused by the antidepressants they take.

Recent finding: 72% of women who took Viagra because of antidepressant-related sexual dysfunction experienced improvement, compared with 27% of women who took the placebo. There were no serious side effects among the women using Viagra.

H. George Nurnberg, MD, executive vice chair of the department of psychiatry, University of New Mexico School of Medicine, Albuquerque, and leader of a study published in *The Journal of the American Medical Association*.

 ## A Delicious Aphrodisiac

W atermelon has ingredients that may deliver Viagra-like effects to blood vessels and may increase libido.

Included: Watermelon has *lycopene, beta carotene* and *citrulline*, whose beneficial functions—one of which is relaxing blood vessels, similar to what Viagra offers—are still being researched.

Bonus: There are no drug side effects.

Bhimanagouda S. Patil, PhD, director, Vegetable and Fruit Development Center, Texas A&M University, College Station.

Daily ED Drug Now Available

A daily low-dose erectile dysfunction (ED) drug is now available. The new, low-dose Cialis (*tadalafil*)—which should be taken at about the same time every day—is best for men with ED who are sexually active at least twice a week. Less sexually active men may benefit more from the higher-dose form, which is taken 30 to 60 minutes before sexual activity and lasts for 36 hours.

Caution: Taking nitroglycerin or other nitrate drugs with even a low dose of Cialis can cause dangerously low blood pressure.

Irwin Goldstein, MD, director of sexual medicine at Alvarado Hospital, *www.sandiegosexualmedicine. com,* and clinical professor of surgery at University of California, both in San Diego.

ED Drugs and Short-Term Memory Loss

Erectile dysfunction (ED) drugs may cause short-duration amnesia. *Transient global amnesia* (TGA) is a brief spell of amnesia, lasting no longer than a day. It does not affect long-term memory or other aspects of health. Any ED medicines that are *phosphodiesterase type 5* (PDE-5) inhibitors, such as Levitra, Cialis and Viagra, could cause TGA. TGA appears to be more common among individuals who have migraine headaches and also use ED medication.

Louis R. Caplan, MD, professor of neurology at Harvard Medical School and a physician in the stroke center at Beth Israel Deaconess Medical Center, both in Boston.

Holistic Cures for Impotence

Geovanni Espinosa, ND, LAc, director of naturopathic medicine, clinician and coinvestigator at the Center for Holistic Urology at Columbia University Medical Center in New York City, *www.holisticurology.columbia.edu.* Dr. Espinosa is the author of the naturopathy section in *1,000 Cures for 200 Ailments* (HarperCollins).

For stronger and more reliable erections, conventional medicine gives you several medications, such as *sildenafil* (Viagra) and *vardenafil* (Levitra). But these drugs can have side effects, including painful, prolonged erections and sudden vision loss. *My holistic approach...*

• **Maca** is a root vegetable from South America. In supplement form, it has been shown to increase libido in healthy men.

Recommended dosage: 500 mg to 1,000 mg three times daily.

• **Asian ginseng,** a well-studied herb from China and Korea, can improve erections. Take 900 mg three times daily.

• **Ginkgo biloba,** derived from a tree native to China, may improve erections by boosting circulation. Take 120 milligrams (mg) to 240 mg daily. Maca, Asian ginseng and ginkgo biloba can all be combined.

Caution: Ginkgo biloba can inhibit blood clotting and may increase the risk of internal bleeding in people on blood thinners. It may also slow down the metabolism of cardiovascular drugs.

• **Niacin,** a B vitamin, widens blood vessels when taken in higher doses (500 mg to 1,000 mg daily) and may help promote erections in some men who do not improve with the three impotence remedies described above.

• **Vigorous exercise** (such as weight lifting, jogging or cycling) promotes healthy circulation and boosts testosterone.

Important: Erectile dysfunction may be an early warning of heart problems, so consult a doctor before starting an exercise program. Erectile dysfunction also may be a symptom of diabetes or other systemic illness—or stress and relationship issues. For this reason, men who experience erectile dysfunction should see a doctor for a full evaluation before trying holistic therapies.

Viagra Worsens Sleep Apnea

Sleep apnea sufferers who take Viagra or other erectile dysfunction (ED) drugs increase their risk for oxygen deprivation during sleep.

Theory: The drugs may promote upper-airway congestion, making breathing difficult.

Self-defense: If you have any symptoms of sleep apnea, including snoring or excessive daytime sleepiness, get tested for sleep apnea before taking an erectile dysfunction drug. If you do have sleep apnea, ask your health-care provider about alternative treatments for erectile dysfunction.

Study by researchers in the department of psychobiology, Federal University of São Paulo, Brazil, and Stanford University Medical Center, Stanford, California, published in *Archives of Internal Medicine*.

Sugar Dampens Sex Drive

A high-sugar diet may decrease a man's sex drive. Foods that are high in the simple sugars, such as candy and soda pop, reduce blood levels of the protein that transports testosterone—an effect that occurs rapidly after high sugar consumption and may continue as long as the high-sugar diet does. Men whose sex drive has dropped should consider eating fewer sweets—that may be enough to increase testosterone levels and restore sex drive.

Geoffrey Hammond, PhD, scientific director, Child and Family Research Institute, and professor, department of obstetrics and gynecology, University of British Columbia, both in Vancouver, Canada, and leader of a study on the effect of a high-sugar diet on mice and human liver cells, published in *Journal of Clinical Investigation*.

Study Shows Alcohol *Improves* Men's Sex Lives

The belief that moderate drinking makes it more difficult for men to maintain erections is false. Men who drink alcohol within safe guidelines—no more than 20 drinks per week—indicate 30% fewer erection problems than men who do not drink.

Kew-Kim Chew, MD, clinical specialist, Keogh Institute for Medical Research, Perth, Australia, and leader of a study of 1,580 men, published in *The Journal of Sexual Medicine*.

How Cell Phones Can Hamper Fertility

In a recent finding, among men who visited an infertility clinic, those who reported using cell phones at least four hours a day generally had the lowest sperm counts and the greatest percentage of abnormal sperm. Because the study involved self-reporting of cell phone use by men already seeking infertility treatment, it is not certain whether cell phones affect most men's sperm. Further research is planned.

Ashok Agarwal, PhD, director of the andrology laboratory, Cleveland Clinic, Cleveland, Ohio, and leader of a study of 361 men, published in *Fertility and Sterility*.

Mom's Diet May Affect Baby's Sex

In one study, women who ate high-calorie diets with a wide range of nutrients around the time of conception were more likely to deliver boys. Women who ate breakfast cereal daily had more boys...those who seldom ate cereal had more girls.

Caution: Even if you hope for a girl, do not restrict calories—your baby needs nutrients. Do not avoid cereal—it often has folic acid, which combats birth defects.

Fiona Mathews, PhD, lecturer, University of Exeter, England, and head of a study of 740 women that was published in *Proceedings of the Royal Society B: Biological Sciences.*

Hot Flash Help

Omega-3s may fight hot flashes. In a study with 120 menopausal women, one group took an omega-3 fatty acid supplement three times per day for eight weeks, while the other group took placebos.

Result: Among women who had hot flashes before the study began, those who took omega-3 supplements had an average of 1.6 fewer hot flashes daily, compared with a decrease of 0.50 in the placebo group.

Theory: Omega-3s may play a role in regulating the interaction of brain chemicals that have been linked to hot flashes.

If you have hot flashes: Ask your doctor about trying an omega-3 supplement.

Michel Lucas, PhD, epidemiologist and nutritionist, Laval University, Quebec City, Canada.

Earwax and Antiperspirants Linked To Breast Cancer?

Nancy L. Snyderman, MD, who is on staff in the department of otolaryngology–head and neck surgery at University of Pennsylvania, Philadelphia. She's the chief medical editor for NBC News and also reports for *NBC Nightly News, Today* and MSNBC. She is author of *Medical Myths That Can Kill You: And the 101 Truths That Will Save, Extend, and Improve Your Life* (Crown).

There's a lot we don't know about cancer, so we can be swayed by misinformation. *Below, a truth and common myth about breast cancer...*

Truth: **Earwax predicts breast cancer.** Most people have a dry form of earwax, but some

produce a wax that's unusually moist. There appears to be an association between this wet earwax and the development of breast cancer.

According to the National Cancer Institute, women with excessive wet earwax are twice as likely to develop breast cancer as those with the dry form. Wet earwax is more common in Caucasians and African-Americans. It's less common in Asians and Native Americans.

If your ears frequently get plugged up with wax or if you notice large amounts of sticky wax in the ear canal or outer ear, see a doctor. He/she can tell if it's the dry or wet form—and whether you'll need more frequent screening tests for cancer.

Myth: **Antiperspirants cause breast cancer.** Many people believe that antiperspirants increase the risk for breast cancer. Not true.

How the myth started: Women who shave under their arms invariably take off skin cells at the same time. The chemicals in antiperspirants can penetrate the broken skin and irritate a nearby lymph gland. The swollen gland can feel like a tumor, but it's not. (Of course, a lump that doesn't disappear within a few days should be checked by your doctor.)

Popular Supplement May Cause Breast Cancer to Spread

Black cohosh does not increase a woman's breast cancer risk, but in women who already have breast tumors, it could make the cancer more likely to spread to the lungs and to other organs. Products with black cohosh, including Remifemin, often are used to ease the symptoms of menopause, but they're not FDA regulated. To be safe, women with breast cancer or at high risk for it should avoid any products containing black cohosh.

Vicki L. Davis, PhD, assistant professor of pharmacology-toxicology at Duquesne University, Pittsburgh, and leader of a study of the effects of black cohosh on female mice, published in *Cancer Research.*

Trans Fats Linked to Breast Cancer

In a study of 19,934 women, those who had the highest blood levels of trans fatty acids (a harmful fat found in processed and fried foods) were nearly twice as likely to develop breast cancer during a seven-year period as those with the lowest levels.

To decrease your risk for breast cancer: Limit consumption of foods high in trans fats —the ingredient may be listed as "trans fat" or "partially hydrogenated oil" on the product's label.

Françoise Clavel-Chapelon, PhD, research director at the National Institute of Health and Medical Research, Villejuif, France.

Should You Have a Digital Mammography?

In a study of 42,760 women, digital mammographies (which take electronic images of the breast and store them in a computer) yielded more accurate results than standard film mammography for women younger than 50 who were either premenopausal or perimenopausal (when the ovaries begin producing less estrogen) and had dense breast tissue (characterized by more glands and less fat). For other women, there was no significant difference in accuracy between the two screening methods.

Theory: Digital mammography images can be magnified or otherwise manipulated to get more accurate readings.

Self-defense: If you are a premenopausal or perimenopausal woman under age 50 with dense breasts, ask your doctor about receiving digital mammography.

Etta D. Pisano, MD, professor of radiology and biomedical engineering at University of North Carolina, Chapel Hill.

Better Breast Cancer Detection

When 2,637 women—about half with a personal history of breast cancer—were screened with both mammography and ultrasound, the combined techniques detected 91% of the 40 tumors diagnosed in the women… ultrasound alone found 80%…and mammography alone found 78%.

Theory: Certain types of breast cancer are detected only by mammography, while others are found only via ultrasound.

W. Phil Evans, MD, professor of radiology, University of Texas Southwestern Center for Breast Care, located in Dallas.

Why You Need an HPV Test with Your Pap Smear

The American College of Obstetricians and Gynecologists recommends routine testing for *human papillomavirus* (HPV)—a virus that causes genital warts and cervical cancer—in addition to a Pap for women age 30 and older.

Concern: While HPV infections are common, the specific types associated with cancer are not—so the HPV test often gives positive results in women whose cervices do not have cancerous or precancerous cells. This can lead to unnecessary alarm.

If a Pap shows a nonspecific abnormality in the cells and HPV results are negative, it is highly unlikely that significant precancerous lesions or cervical cancer will develop within the next three years. If both the Pap and HPV are positive, further testing is warranted.

Sondra Summers, MD, associate professor and associate residency program director for general gynecology, Loyola University Health System in Maywood, Illinois.

More Accurate Ovarian Cancer Testing

In a study of 496 pre- and postmenopausal women who had undergone surgery for diagnosis and treatment of their pelvic masses, researchers measured preoperative levels of the proteins HE4 and CA 125 in the women's blood. The presence of the two proteins accurately identified 94% of postmenopausal women and 75% of premenopausal women with ovarian cancer as high risk for malignancy.

Important note: CA 125 testing is currently available, but it is not as sensitive as the combination of blood tests in predicting ovarian cancer. A blood test for HE4 is under FDA review. If approved, it should be widely available soon.

Robert C. Bast, Jr., MD, professor, department of experimental therapeutics, M.D. Anderson Cancer Center, Houston.

Prostate Cancer Breakthroughs: New Research Is Saving Lives

Peter T. Scardino, MD, chairman of the department of surgery at Memorial Sloan-Kettering Cancer Center in New York City and head of the center's prostate cancer program. He is also a professor in the department of urology at Weill Medical College of Cornell University and at the State University of New York Downstate Medical Center. He is coauthor of *Dr. Peter Scardino's Prostate Book: The Complete Guide to Overcoming Prostate Cancer, Prostatitis, and BPH* (Avery).

One man out of six in the US will be diagnosed with prostate cancer during his lifetime—more than 230,000 American men a year—and 30,000 men die every year from the disease. *Recent scientific findings could dramatically change this situation, preventing tens of thousands of cases of prostate cancer and saving thousands of lives...*

FINASTERIDE UPDATE

Finasteride (Proscar) is utilized to treat *benign prostatic hyperplasia* (BPH), a noncancerous form of prostate enlargement. It limits the production of an enzyme that transforms testosterone to *dihydrotestosterone,* a male hormone that stimulates the growth of prostate cells. (The baldness drug Propecia is also finasteride, but it contains one-fifth the amount used to treat BPH.)

Landmark study: In 2003, an article in *The New England Journal of Medicine* announced the results of the seven-year Prostate Cancer Prevention Trial (PCPT), which involved nearly 19,000 men ages 55 and older. Those taking five milligrams (mg) a day of finasteride were 25% less likely to develop prostate cancer than those taking a placebo.

However, biopsies showed that those taking finasteride who did develop prostate cancer (18% of the finasteride test group) were slightly more likely to develop "high-grade" cancer, an aggressive form that can spread quickly. Because of this, the medical community did not endorse the drug for cancer prevention.

Latest development: In a study published in the August 2008 issue of *Cancer Prevention Research,* scientists from the Fred Hutchinson Cancer Research Center in Seattle revisited the trial results, conducting three new and careful analyses of the data. *They found...*

• **Men taking finasteride did not have a significantly higher incidence of aggressive prostate cancer.** In fact, one analysis showed that men on the drug had 27% less high-grade prostate cancer than men on the placebo.

• **The original finding that finasteride increased the risk for high-grade cancer was due to what scientists call a "sampling error."** Finasteride shrinks the size of the prostate about 20% to 30%, making it much more likely that a six-needle biopsy (the type used in the original study) will find a "nest" of high-grade cancer cells.

• **Finasteride can provide greater cancer-preventing power than previously estimated.** It reduces the risk for prostate cancer by 30%. In other words, it could prevent three out of every 10 cases of prostate cancer—nearly 70,000 cases a year.

The bottom line: "Men undergoing regular prostate cancer screening or who express an interest in cancer prevention need to be informed of the opportunity to take finasteride for preventing prostate cancer," concluded the researchers.

That conclusion is particularly important for males with a higher-than-normal risk for this disease. These include men with a family history of prostate cancer (two or more first-degree relatives diagnosed with the disease, such as a grandfather, father or brother)…African-American men (who, compared with Caucasians, have more than twice the risk for dying from prostate cancer)…and men with a level of prostate specific antigen (PSA) that is 2.5 nanograms per milliliter (ng/mL) or higher. (PSA is the primary biomarker for prostate cancer.)

EARLIER PSA TESTING

In a major study reported in 2007, researchers in Sweden analyzed data from more than 21,000 men who had their PSA measured for the first time (a baseline measurement) in the 1970s and 1980s, when they were 44 to 50 years old.

Twenty-five years later, higher baseline PSA levels were the best predictor of whether or not a man would subsequently develop prostate cancer. In fact, PSA was the only accurate predictor among the 90 different factors, including family history and various lifestyle, biochemical and medical parameters.

Latest development: In 2008, the researchers showed that an early baseline PSA also is the most accurate predictor of who will develop high-grade prostate cancer.

Bottom line: Earlier PSA tests can identify men at a higher risk for developing prostate cancer. Those males can have more intensive screening (such as biopsies), to improve the odds of finding and treating the disease at an early stage when a cure is more likely.

Every man should have his first PSA test at the age of 40, which is typically covered by insurance. (The American Cancer Society recommends annual PSA screening starting at age 50 for most men.) Men should be tested again at the age of 45. If the result at age 45 is 0.9 or higher, have a PSA test annually.

PSA TEST AFTER 75?

Approximately half of all American men 75 and older have had a PSA test in the past two years.

Latest development: Back in August 2008, the government's US Preventive Services Task Force recommended that men age 75 and over should not receive routine PSA screening for prostate cancer.

Reason: Most prostate cancers found with PSA are slow-growing. They take 10 years or more to cause death—and most 75-year-old men have a life expectancy of about 10 years. That means the potential harm from treating the cancer with surgery, radiation or another type of therapy—including erectile dysfunction, incontinence and bowel difficulties—is likely to be greater than the harm done from the cancer itself.

Bottom line: Routine PSA tests for men over 75 are not necessary. However, it's reasonable for your doctor to order a test if you're healthy and active, free of a life-shortening disease, such as heart failure or type 2 diabetes…and you have a concern about prostate cancer or an interest in receiving a PSA test.

COMPUTER PREDICTION

Once prostate cancer is diagnosed, a treatment decision is difficult. *That is because it's hard to determine whether the cancer is…*

- **Slow-growing** and unlikely to invade areas outside the prostate, a situation that may call for avoiding or delaying treatment or…

- **Fast-growing** and potentially invasive, a situation that may necessitate immediate treatment, such as surgery, radiation and/or hormonal therapy. These treatments can result in side effects that diminish the quality of life, such as erectile dysfunction, urinary incontinence and bowel difficulties.

Physicians use various factors to determine whether prostate cancer is slow- or fast-growing. These include PSA…digital rectal exam… the amount of cancer in a biopsy…the Gleason grade (the microscopic appearance, including size and shape of the cells, with high-grade cells being more aggressive)…and the size of the prostate (the larger the prostate, the less likely that cancer will spread beyond it).

Problem: Physicians tend to recommend immediate treatment based on one worrisome factor, such as high-grade cancer cells.

The solution: The nomogram—a sophisticated computer-based prostate cancer prediction tool that takes into account all the factors that determine the likely outcome of a case of prostate cancer.

Latest development: Utilizing data from nearly 2,000 men (average age 70) diagnosed with local (confined to the prostate) cancer, researchers at the Cleveland Clinic evaluated a nomogram that predicts whether a man will survive for at least five years when he doesn't immediately receive aggressive treatment. The nomogram was determined to be an accurate tool (73% accurate). The findings were published in the January 2008 issue of *Cancer,* the journal of the American Cancer Society.

Bottom line: If you're ever diagnosed with prostate cancer, ask your doctor about a nomogram. There are prostate cancer nomograms to analyze many different scenarios, such as the likely effectiveness of using radiation after a recurrence or using hormonal therapy after surgery and radiation.

You and/or your doctor can download free prostate cancer nomograms developed by the Memorial Sloan-Kettering Cancer Center from *www.mskcc.org/mskcc/html/10088.cfm.*

THE SURGEON MATTERS

Researchers from Memorial Sloan-Kettering Cancer Center analyzed results from 72 surgeons at four major medical centers who performed 7,765 radical prostatectomies (removal of the prostate) over 16 years.

The patients of surgeons who had performed 10 or fewer radical prostatectomies over their professional lifetimes had a 17.9% prostate cancer recurrence rate within five years. The patients of surgeons who had performed 250 or more radical prostatectomies had a recurrence rate of 10.7%. The study appeared in the August 2007 issue of *Journal of the National Cancer Institute.*

Latest development: During a subsequent analysis of the same results, published in the September 2008 issue of *Journal of Urology,* the researchers found that patients with low-grade cancer had nearly 100% freedom from recurrence when they were operated on by the most experienced surgeons.

Bottom line: If you're having a radical prostatectomy, seek out the most experienced surgeon available.

RADIATION AFTER RECURRENCE

If you had a radical prostatectomy for prostate cancer, but your cancer returned and your PSA is rising rapidly, what should you do? *To save your life, consider radiation...*

Latest development: Men who got radiation therapy within two years of surgery had an 86% chance of surviving for 10 years, compared with 62% among patients who did not have radiation, reported researchers from The Johns Hopkins School of Medicine in the June 18, 2008, issue of *The Journal of the American Medical Association.*

Bottom line: In the past, radiation therapy was not always recommended for men with a fast-growing recurrence and a high PSA. After this study, it should be.

WARNING: NEWER ISN'T ALWAYS BETTER

Many American men with prostate cancer are traveling to Canada, Mexico and other foreign locales to receive high-intensity focused ultrasound (HIFU).

This treatment—available in other countries for the past several years but not yet approved in the US—destroys prostate cancer cells by heating them to between 176°F and 212°F via a probe inserted into the rectum.

Red flag: There is not enough clinical data to show that HIFU is an effective way to treat prostate cancer. In fact, doctors in the US are beginning to see recurrences in men treated with HIFU—men who might have been cured with standard therapy.

Bottom line: New treatments for prostate cancer may be popular, but that doesn't mean they work. Only clinical data from large and rigorous studies can provide us with proof of effectiveness.

Aspirin Use May Affect PSA Testing

Men who take aspirin "regularly" have significantly lower PSA levels than those who do not, according to a new study. (A PSA test is used to screen men for prostate cancer.)

Impact: Aspirin use makes PSA testing less reliable. Tell your doctor about your aspirin use when scheduling a test.

Jay H. Fowke, PhD, MPH, assistant professor, Vanderbilt-Ingram Cancer Center, Nashville.

Statins May Stave Off Prostate Cancer

Patrick C. Walsh, MD, distinguished service professor of urology, Brady Urological Institute of the Johns Hopkins Medical Institutions, Baltimore.

Cholesterol-lowering statin drugs, such as *atorvastatin* (Lipitor), *simvastatin* (Zocor) or *lovastatin* (Mevacor), are often prescribed to help curb heart disease risk, but new research has examined the medication's effect on prostate cancer risk.

A 10-year study of nearly 35,000 men found that those who took a statin were up to 60% less likely to experience advanced metastatic prostate cancer (a prostate malignancy that's spread to other locations of the body, such as the bones) than men who did not take the medication. Researchers theorize that lowering cholesterol may inhibit the activity of proteins involved in prostate cancer development. It's also possible that the drugs have cancer-fighting effects (such as reducing inflammation) that are independent of cholesterol control.

It's too early to recommend statins for prostate cancer prevention—but men with high cholesterol or other cardiovascular risk factors who take statins may get this added protection.

How to Get a Better Colonoscopy

Rebecca Shannonhouse, editor, *Bottom Line/Health,* Boardroom Inc., 281 Tresser Blvd., Stamford, Connecticut 06901.

Most Americans have now gotten the message that colonoscopy can save lives, but a new study sheds light on a potential shortcoming of the test.

Colonoscopy—in which the large intestine is examined using a flexible viewing tube—has been mainly used to look for raised growths (polyps) that can turn into cancer.

New finding: A report in the *Journal of the American Medical Association* found that close to 10% of 1,819 patients who received colonoscopies had flat or depressed areas of abnormal tissue (lesions) that are harder to detect than polyps—and more likely to turn into cancer.

These lesions—which, like polyps, should be removed—can be missed if a doctor rushes through the colonoscopy…or, more commonly, if the colon isn't entirely cleared of waste (this occurs in about 25% of all colonoscopies), says Samuel Meyers, MD, a gastroenterologist at Mount Sinai School of Medicine in New York City.

His advice…

•**Follow "bowel prep" instructions exactly.** The prep usually involves following a liquid diet for one day and taking a "bowel-cleansing" laxative.

•**Ask your doctor whether he/she looks for lesions—not just polyps.** Prior to receiving a colonoscopy, it's wise to talk to your doctor about the types of abnormalities that may be discovered during the procedure.

No matter how recently you had a colonoscopy, be sure to see a doctor if you have persistent rectal bleeding or a change in bowel habits.

Less Invasive Surgery Effective for Colon Cancer

Surgeons typically perform open surgery—making big incisions in the abdominal wall—to view and remove cancerous colon tissue.

New finding: An analysis of 12 studies found no differences in rates of surgical complications, cancer recurrence or survival between open surgery and laparoscopic surgery, which involves much smaller incisions and the use of tiny cameras.

Bottom line: Consider a surgeon trained in laparoscopic surgery, as it involves less pain and quicker recovery.

Esther Kuhry, MD, PhD, Namsos Hospital, Namsos, Norway, and leader of a review involving 3,346 patients, published in *The Cochrane Library*.

Nuts and Popcorn Ward Off Diverticulitis? New Study Says Yes!

Nuts and popcorn can help *prevent* diverticulitis. Most people with this disease, in which small pouches form in the walls of the intestine, were told to avoid nuts and popcorn because the residue of these foods was thought to cause complications, such as internal bleeding. However, in a recent study, men who ate popcorn twice a week had a 28% lower risk of developing diverticulitis, and those who ate nuts twice a week had a 20% lower risk, compared with men who ate these foods less than once a month.

A study of 47,228 men, ages 40 to 75, by Lisa L. Strate, MD, MPH, acting assistant professor, division of gastroenterology, University of Washington in Seattle, published in *The Journal of the American Medical Association*.

IBS Treatment Without Drugs

For many people, a change in diet reduces irritable bowel syndrome (IBS) symptoms such as abdominal pain, cramping, constipation and/or diarrhea. IBS often is a result of sensitivity to gluten, a protein in wheat, rye and barley. Many IBS patients also are sensitive to dairy foods.

As a first step, eliminate gluten from your diet (gluten-containing products include many breads, cereals, crackers, cookies, cakes, pies, gravies and sauces) for two to three weeks to see if symptoms improve. In addition, keep a daily journal noting all the foods that seem to cause a flare-up of IBS. If your symptoms don't improve, try eliminating dairy products for two to three weeks. If these elimination diets don't help, consult your doctor or a certified nutrition specialist, who can recommend dietary changes that are appropriate for you.

Shari Lieberman, PhD, CNS, FACN, a nutrition scientist and author of *The Gluten Connection* (Rodale). Her Web site is *www.drshari.net*.

More Help for IBS

Researchers analyzed 38 studies on treatments for irritable bowel syndrome (IBS), a disorder that causes such symptoms as abdominal pain, constipation and/or diarrhea.

Result: Soluble fiber treatments, including *psyllium* (such as Metamucil)...peppermint oil capsules (about 200 mg, two to three times daily)...and some antispasmodic drugs—especially *scopolamine* (Transderm Scop)—significantly reduced IBS symptoms.

If you suffer from IBS: Ask your doctor if one or more of these treatments—which often have been overlooked since the introduction of IBS drugs—would be appropriate for you.

Alexander C. Ford, MD, clinical fellow, gastroenterology division, McMaster University Health Sciences Center, Ontario, Canada.

7

Money Manager

The New Road to Financial Security: A Survival Guide for Troubled Times

ou can restore your financial health in spite of the past year's setbacks. But to do this, you will likely have to change the ways that you save, invest and spend.

Below, five top financial advisers explain the best ways to improve your financial outlook now...

TO PROTECT YOUR RETIREMENT
STEVEN SASS

Increase your annual savings and investment rate by 16 percentage points if you plan to retire in 10 years. For the typical investor, that means if you were putting aside 6% of your annual income, you need to raise that to 22% to make up for the 2008 market meltdown—

not an easy task. If you have 18 years until retirement, you would have to increase your rate by six percentage points, meaning that if you were putting aside 6%, you need to raise that to 12%.

This assumes that you are depending on financial assets to fund about 75% of your expected expenses in retirement, with income sources such as Social Security and a pension providing the rest, and that you have about two-thirds of your portfolio in stocks and the rest in bonds.

Steven Sass, PhD, associate director, research, Center for Retirement Research, Boston College, Chestnut Hill, Massachusetts, *http://crr.bc.edu*.

Curtis Arnold, consumer advocate and founder of US Citizens for Fair Credit Card Terms, Inc., Little Rock, Arkansas, *www.cardratings.com*.

Daniel R. Solin, senior vice president, Index Funds Advisors, Bonita Springs, Florida, *www.ifa.com*.

Sheryl Garrett, CFP, founder of Garrett Planning Network, Shawnee Mission, Kansas, *www.garrettplanning network.com*.

Harold Evensky, Esq., CFP, president of Evensky & Katz Wealth Management, Coral Gables, Florida, *www.evensky.com*.

If you can't increase your savings drastically and/or you are even closer to retirement, consider postponing retirement. Working an extra two to 2.5 years will give you a good chance of recovering what you lost if you were planning to retire in 15 years or less.

TO PROTECT YOUR CREDIT
Curtis Arnold

Avoid spending more than 10% of your credit limit on any of your credit cards. Historically, many experts have suggested that you could spend up to 30% without hurting your credit score, but now many lenders require greater spending restraint for consumers to maintain their creditworthiness.

Self-defense: Ask for a higher credit limit, spread your spending among more cards and/or spend less.

Maintain FICO credit score of approximately 730 to qualify for the best interest rates on credit cards. For the best rates on mortgages, it is even higher—at least 760. The old standard to join the credit elite was 700.

What to do: For advice on how to improve your credit score, check the forum on my site, *www.cardratings.com*—click on "Credit Information"—or *www.creditbloggers.com,* a credit blog moderated by a former TransUnion consumer credit expert.

TO PROTECT YOUR PORTFOLIO
Daniel R. Solin

Check your investment portfolio four times a year to see if it needs to be rebalanced to match your original asset-allocation plan. The old rule of thumb was to rebalance once per year in December. But now, the stock market's nerve-racking volatility is throwing off allocation plans more quickly.

Important tip: Rebalance only if your asset allocation deviates more than five percentage points or 25% from your targeted allocations. (That means if your target for a particular type of investment is 20% of your portfolio and it strays to 15% or 25%, reallocate because it has shifted five points. Or, if the target is 10% and it shifts to 7.5% or 12.5%, reallocate because it has shifted by 25% of the target percentage.) If you shift more often than that, transaction and tax costs may become too high.

Do not own shares of your employer's stock in your 401(k). After the demise of Enron several years ago wiped out the savings of many employees, it seemed wise to reduce employer stock in one's 401(k) to no more than 10%. Following the collapse of companies such as Lehman Brothers and Circuit City, consider reducing that to 0%. Even companies that seem stable can run into trouble very quickly. Your paycheck depends on the economic health of your employer, so why should you rely on the same source for your retirement money?

Sheryl Garrett

Expect to get a 7% to 8% annual return on stocks when doing financial and retirement planning. Expect 4% on bonds—so a portfolio that is half stocks, half bonds can be expected to give you a long-term return of 6%. The old notion was that stocks average a return of 10% a year and bonds 6%. With markets likely to struggle over the coming years, it's more prudent to use the lower figures.

Harold Evensky

Try to keep 36 months' of anticipated expenses liquid (readily available in cashlike accounts) if you're retired or within five years of retirement. For example, if you spend $40,000 each year in addition to what you get from Social Security and other sources of income, you should try to have $120,000 in money-market funds, bank accounts, certificates of deposit (CDs) and/or short-term Treasury securities. In the past, many retirees kept only one year's worth of expenses in cash and put the rest in investments, such as stocks and bonds, so that they could earn higher rates of return. But that's too risky now, when the market may remain weak, forcing investors to sell securities at low prices to pay expenses.

If you're much younger and still working, you need to keep at least three to 12 months' of income in a cashlike emergency fund. You may need a larger cash reserve if you are at risk of losing your job, are the sole wage earner in the family, own your own company or rely on unpredictable commissions or bonuses.

Better Expense Tracking

Housing should take no more than 20% to 35% of your after-tax income…food, 15% to 30%…transportation, 6% to 20%…medical costs, 2% to 6%…insurance, 4% to 6%…utilities, 4% to 7%…clothing, 3% to 10%…personal care, 2% to 4%…miscellaneous expenses, 1% to 4%. Percentages apply after you've set aside at least 10% of what you earn as savings.

Guidelines from Money Management International's Consumer Credit Counseling Services, Houston.

Breaking Bad Habits

Sheryl Garrett, CFP, founder of Garrett Planning Network, an international network of fee-only planners, Shawnee Mission, Kansas, *www.garrettplanningnetwork. com.* She is author of *Just Give Me the Answer$: Expert Advisors Address Your Most Pressing Financial Questions* (Kaplan Business) and *Investing in an Uncertain Economy for Dummies* (Wiley). Garrett was recognized by *Investment Advisor* as one of the 25 most influential people in financial planning.

Bad financial practices are enough of a problem in the best of times, but in the middle of a recession and bear market they can be especially destructive. *Bad habits that I help my clients break…*

•**Casual spending.** You buy things using your credit card that you do not really need and $20 bills seem to just disappear from your wallet or pocketbook.

Solutions: Enlist technology to make you more mindful of your spending habits. Sign up for Web access to your credit card transactions. Check them once a week to make sure that you're not going over what you budgeted for the month. If you hit the ATM for small purchases, write down on the back of the receipts what you use the money for in order to track where your pocket cash is going.

•**Organizing but not executing.** You sort and file all of the bills that you have to pay. You remove investment statements from their envelopes and stack them for review. You do list each checking transaction so that you can balance your checkbook monthly. But you repeatedly delay completing all these financial tasks and end up paying bills late, putting off investment decisions and/or bouncing checks occasionally.

Solution: Divide your financial duties into bite-sized assignments rather than trying to take on your entire financial package at once. Pay bills every week rather than saving them up. File financial papers that require action according to deadlines for when you will deal with each one rather than alphabetically. Get through as much of your financial to-do list as you can in 15 minutes. Mark specific dates on your calendar to balance the checkbook. Once you overcome your initial resistance and gain some momentum, you will usually want to keep going.

•**Putting off planning for the future.** You postpone all tasks that are important for the long term, such as estate planning or drafting your will, because they produce anxiety in the short term.

Solution: Stop pretending that you will live forever, but also stop fearing that if you draft a will or an estate plan, you will die soon. Realize that tackling the task now will reduce ongoing anxiety over leaving your loved ones in the lurch. Make an appointment to see an estate-planning attorney—and don't cancel!

How to Bounce Back From Money Misfortunes

Stephen M. Pollan, a New York City–based attorney, financial adviser and career counselor. He is a former CNBC on-air personal finance expert, and coauthor of several books, including *Die Broke: A Radical Four-Part Financial Plan* (Collins) and *Lifelines for Money Misfortunes: How to Overcome Life's Greatest Challenges* (Wiley). His Web site is *www.stephenpollan.com.*

You can better cope with financial misfortunes if you know in advance the major steps to take. *How to handle six common financial challenges…*

•**You can't pay monthly bills because of unexpected expenses.** Take action as soon as the problem becomes apparent. Waiting until payments are past due and collection agencies are involved will only make things worse.

Separate your expenses into three different categories...

•Expenses that cannot be delayed. *Example:* Insurance premiums.

•Expenses that might be deferrable if the lender agrees. *Some examples:* Mortgage and car loans.

•Expenses that are discretionary. *Examples:* Eating out and new clothes.

First, eliminate all discretionary spending. Second, contact mortgage and auto loan providers. Explain that you had an unexpected expense and request "forbearance." Propose a specific payment plan that would make your debt manageable. The mortgage and car loan companies do not want to get stuck with your house or car, so they often will be flexible.

Example: A 32-year-old man faced $3,200 in travel and burial expenses after the death of his uncle. His mortgage lender agreed to accept interest-only payments for three months.

•**You can't pay a large, uncovered medical bill.** Explain your financial situation to the hospital's or doctor's billing department, and ask to set up a payment plan that fits your budget. Next, speak to hospital social workers and local family service charities to see if any grants or loans are available to people in your situation. Ask family members and employers for financial assistance—big companies sometimes have emergency loan or hardship grant money available to help employees.

If you have health insurance but your insurer will not cover the bill, get a specific explanation of why. If the insurance company claims the treatment was not necessary, ask your doctor to write a letter stating why it was necessary. There are multiple levels of appeal possible if your first request is denied.

Example: A 58-year-old widow was hit with a five-figure charge when her insurance company claimed her colon cancer treatment was not necessary. She negotiated a $200-per-month payment plan with the hospital. Then she asked her doctor to write a letter explaining why the procedure was necessary. Her insurer eventually agreed to pay a large portion of the bill. She paid off the remaining debt in less than 18 months.

•**You are dropped by your homeowner's insurance company.** Unfortunately, insurers discontinue various policies—especially homeowner's policies—all the time for all sorts of reasons. Do not bother trying to get the decision reversed—that almost never works—but do make sure you are given the grace period guaranteed by your contract before it is terminated. Then ask your accountant, attorney or real estate agent to recommend an insurance broker. Unlike an insurance agent, insurance brokers work with many different insurance companies and can help you find the lowest rates. They often have access to better policy information than you can find quickly online.

The policies available to you might be considerably more expensive than your old coverage. Ask your broker for cost-cutting strategies. Increasing the size of copayments and deductibles often can dramatically reduce premiums. Increase the size of your emergency fund as well, in case you need to pay a large deductible later.

•**A parent dies with bills outstanding.** Carefully go through your deceased parent's papers, and construct a list of assets and liabilities. Keep an eye peeled for any life insurance policies or evidence of safe-deposit boxes. (For example, the check register in your parent's checkbook might list ongoing payments to an insurance company or a bank.) Destroy credit cards, and cancel the accounts.

When bills arrive, write "deceased" on them and send them back, with a copy of the death certificate. If bill collectors call, explain that the estate will deal with the deceased's debts once the funds are in the executor's control. Repeat this as often as is necessary. Surviving family members are not responsible for a deceased parent's debts (unless the debt stems from a joint account with a surviving spouse or family member). Some debts will have to be paid out of the parent's estate, but waiting until that stage will at least allow you to sort out financial obligations first. All secured debts, such as auto loans signed by only the deceased, that are not paid off by the estate will result in repossession.

• **Your adult child needs financial help.** First consider your own finances. Would solving your child's financial problem then create a financial problem for you? Would it significantly affect your retirement plans? If you are considering making a loan, rather than a gift, calculate how your finances would be affected if this loan were not repaid. Many loans to relatives never are repaid.

• If you cannot afford to make the loan, explain to your child that you love him or her but cannot give money that you do not have to spare.

• If you decide to help, first insist on having a conversation with your adult child about budgets, spending and saving. Explain what he needs to do differently financially. Next, determine exactly how large a gift or loan he needs to make ends meet and how much you can afford to give. Make it clear that this is a onetime loan or gift, not an ongoing line of credit. If the gift is sizable, inform your other children that the gift will be taken into consideration when you divide your assets in your will. This will prevent concerns about inequity.

Important: Deciding whether to assist your adult child financially could drive a wedge between you and your spouse. Agree in advance to make this decision as a team.

• **You lose your job.** If your employer insists that you sign a release form in order to receive your severance package, do not do it right away. It often is possible to obtain better severance terms through negotiation. These negotiations could be very simple—whatever the company offers, ask for more.

• If you have a good relationship with someone high up in your company, ask that person to put in a good word for you with the human resources department regarding your severance package.

• Insist on credit for unused vacation days and a prorated portion of any annual bonus. Ask if you can keep your company car and/or laptop until you find a new job. Request continuation of health insurance benefits. If continued benefits are not available, see if you are eligible to continue coverage under the *Consolidated Omnibus Budget Reconciliation Act* (COBRA), the program that allows former employees to pay out of pocket to continue their benefits for up to 18 months. COBRA coverage may be expensive, but it can be a vital bridge until you arrange other coverage. COBRA coverage can be expensive, but many who use it can get a temporary break in 2009. The *American Recovery and Reinvestment Act of 2009* reduces premiums by 65% for up to nine months for workers who become eligible for COBRA coverage between September 1, 2008 and December 3, 2009.

• Determine how long you can continue to pay all your bills out of your savings and severance pay, and decide what resources you will tap next if you have not found another job by the time this money runs out. Will you liquidate investments? Borrow from family members?

• If need be, consider taking a job that you normally would not to keep money coming in, even if it has no connection to your previous experience. Sometimes these "emergency jobs" lead people into other career directions. Don't worry that your emergency job means you will have to schedule future job interviews around your work schedule—most interviewers consider it a good thing when applicants are working.

What Debt Collectors Don't Want You to Know

Gerri Detweiler, a credit adviser for the consumer education and financial services company Credit.com. An expert on consumer money matters, she has written or coauthored four books, including *Stop Debt Collectors: How to Protect Your Rights and Resolve Your Debts* (Credit.com).

More and more Americans are getting calls from debt collectors—for unpaid medical bills, mortgages, auto loans, credit card bills, etc. In fact, one out of seven American families has a debt in collection. The Federal Trade Commission (FTC) notes that it received more consumer complaints about the debt-collection industry in 2008 than about any other industry. *What you must know now...*

ASK FOR VERIFICATION

When you first get a phone call from a debt collector, don't give out any information about yourself or your financial situation. Instead, politely ask for written verification of the debt, which the collector must send you within five days. Written verification includes the name of the creditor, the balance due, original due date, your account number and what action you should take if you believe that you don't owe the money.

It's critical not to acknowledge the debt in that initial call. If you acknowledge a debt on which the statute of limitations has run out, the clock may start all over again. The statute of limitations is the period of time a debt collector has to sue you to collect a debt. It varies by state and type of debt, generally running between three and 15 years. Check with your state attorney general's office to see which period applies to your situation. (To locate your state attorney general, go to the Web site for the National Association of Attorneys General, *www.naag.org.*)

After you get the written verification, you have 30 days to dispute the debt. If you don't believe that you owe the debt or you are sure that the statute of limitations has run out, send the collection company a letter explaining concisely why you don't owe the debt and requesting that the collector stop calling or writing to you. By law, a debt collector needs to stop contacting you when he/she receives your letter, although he is allowed to contact you one time to notify you of his intent or to say that there will be no further contact. This doesn't mean that the collector must stop pursuing payment. If he/she thinks you owe the debt, he must notify you of any legal action that he intends to take.

Warning: In certain cases, collectors can sue to collect a debt that's outside the statute of limitations, and you must respond to a legal notice or risk a judgment by default.

NEGOTIATE

If you do owe the debt but can't pay it in full, phone the debt-collection agency and say that you can't afford to pay in full but would like to resolve the debt within your means. Decide what you could afford, then offer an amount 20% to 25% lower than that as a starting point.

Example: If you owe $1,200 and feel that you can pay $400, you might say, "I can pay $300 in a lump sum to settle the debt." Debt collectors prefer single payments over installments. Politely hold your ground if the collector tries to insist on an amount that you can't afford. If he keeps insisting, tell him that you will contact him when you have more money.

If you're being contacted by several debt collectors, prioritize your debts by working to pay off secured loans first. These are debts, such as mortgages and car loans, that are "secured" by collateral—namely, your house or car—which the lender could repossess.

Once you have agreed on payment, ask the debt collector to agree to remove the collection from your credit report after you have paid the debt. Collectors are not obligated to comply, but they may honor your request as a courtesy if the debt is settled to their satisfaction. Do not pay anything until you receive written confirmation of the amount and the terms to which you and the collector have settled on.

Never send the debt collector your personal check or provide a credit card number. Use a bank-certified check or Western Union money transfer, which allows you to prove payment without revealing any personal financial information.

Keep copies and written records of all communications, and send any letters by certified mail, return receipt requested. These records can help you negotiate and will be useful if you wind up in court. You can download the free worksheet from *www.credit.com/stopdebt collectors* to help you keep track of all your interactions.

COLLECTION NO-NOs

Be aware that under the *Fair Debt Collection Practices Act*, collection agencies...

•**Cannot threaten to use violence or use violence.**

● **Cannot use obscene, profane or abusive language,** including racial slurs.

● **Cannot call repeatedly with the intent of harassing you.** (There is no set number of allowed calls—it has been left up to the courts to decide this in specific cases.) Debt collectors also may not call at "unreasonable" times, which usually means before 8 am and after 9 pm.

● **Cannot send a letter that appears to come from a lawyer when it does not,** or otherwise falsely claim to be initiating legal action.

● **Cannot send a letter that shows on the envelope that it's from a debt collector.**

● **Cannot threaten to ruin your credit rating forever.**

● **Cannot tell your employer about your debt or threaten to do so.**

● **Cannot imply any affiliation with the government** or with law-enforcement.

If you believe that a debt collector is in violation of the law, file a complaint with the FTC (877-382-4357, *www.ftc.gov*) or with your state attorney general's office. Numerous consumer complaints about the same debt-collection company could prompt an investigation. You also may wish to retain a consumer-law attorney to see if suing the debt collector for actual and/or punitive damages is an alternative. It may make sense if the collector has broken the law or is suing you. A lawyer may be willing to take your case on a contingency basis (no fee unless you win). The first consultation usually is free of charge, but be sure to ask in advance.

More from Gerri Detweiler...

Free Credit Scores For You

You can check your credit scores for free at Web sites such as CreditKarma.com and Quizzle.com. The scores, which are prepared by the major credit bureaus, are indicative of, but not identical to, the widely utilized FICO score from Fair Isaac.

How Debt Can Hurt Your Health

Marjory Abrams, publisher, *Bottom Line* newsletters, Boardroom Inc., 281 Tresser Blvd., Stamford, Connecticut 06901.

Today's epidemic financial problems are bad enough. But Gerri Detweiler, credit adviser for Credit.com and the author of *Stop Debt Collectors: How to Protect Your Rights and Resolve Your Debts,* reminded me recently that debt-related stress also can hurt our physical and emotional health. She says that the most common complaints are lack of sleep, difficulty concentrating, headaches, nausea and depression.

The good news: Research shows that credit-counseling programs actually can promote health. According to a study done by Rutgers professor Barbara O'Neill, PhD, 48% of consumers who joined a debt-management plan reported fewer headaches, less insomnia and other improvements in health—changes that they attributed to their debt-management program. *Detweiler's prescription to render debt less stressful...*

● **Work with your creditors.** If you have problems repaying a debt, contact the creditor and explain the situation. You may be able to arrange a more doable payment plan.

● **Consult a credit counselor if you have long-term difficulty making payments.** Putting together all the necessary documents and acknowledging your financial situation are major steps in resolving debt problems.

Detweiler says that it is important to use counselors who are recommended by a reputable organization, such as the Association of Independent Consumer Credit Counseling Agencies (866-703-8787, *www.aiccca.org*) or the National Foundation for Credit Counseling (800-388-2227, *www.nfcc.org*). Usually, the initial consultation is free, and a budgeting session may be all that you need to get back on track. Credit-counseling agencies may waive charges in hardship cases, but generally, consumers should count on some kind of fee, even if it's nominal.

Some people might require a more formal debt-management plan, which would involve paying down debt through regular deposits to the credit-counseling agency. Debtors benefit from reduced or waived finance charges and fewer collection calls. Although sometimes all services are free, the typical monthly cost is from $10 to $50.*

Finally, don't forget about other tried-and-true strategies that reduce stress, financial or otherwise. These include having a healthful diet…exercising…reducing caffeine and sugar intake…avoiding excessive alcohol…and setting aside time for meditating, journaling, gardening and other restorative activities.

*Prices subject to change.

Where to Get Help

Get debt-management help if you are falling behind in payments. The US Trustee Program of the Department of Justice (202-514-4100, *www.usdoj.gov/ust*) provides a list of approved credit-counseling and money-management programs. If possible, consolidate all of your debts or ask lenders to agree to lower payments or reduce interest rates. If nothing works and you need to consider bankruptcy, first contact the Institute for Financial Literacy (866-662-4932, *www.financiallit.org,* click on "Resources") for a state-by-state list of free and low-cost lawyers who can help.

AARP Bulletin, 601 E St. NW, Washington, DC, on the Web at *www.aarp.org.*

Beat Credit Card Tricks

Curtis Arnold, consumer advocate and the founder of US Citizens for Fair Credit Card Terms, Inc., which educates consumers about credit cards, based in Little Rock, Arkansas. Its Web site, CardRatings.com, features consumer reviews of credit cards. Arnold is author of *How You Can Profit from Credit Cards* (FT Press).

Credit card fees continue to climb at an appalling rate. Balance transfer charges have gone up by 300% industrywide…

and late-payment fees now average more than $30,* up from around $10 in the late 1990s. But the most infuriating credit card fees are those that most cardholders do not even know about until they are imposed—this industry is notorious for burying important details in the fine print.

Below are some of the credit card industry's most egregious tricks, traps and fees…

•**Fees for going over your credit limit.** You use your card more than usual during a particular month, but it is not declined by a merchant, so you assume that you have stayed under your credit limit.

The trick: Most credit card issuers no longer decline purchases when cardholders exceed their credit limits. Instead, they allow the transactions to go through, then they charge the cardholder an over-the-limit penalty of up to $39. The credit card issuer also might use this as an excuse to increase the cardholder's interest rate to a "default rate," potentially 30% or higher.

Self-defense: Phone your credit card issuer (the toll-free number is on the back of your credit card) and request that any charges exceeding your credit limit be declined. Credit card companies do not legally have to agree to decline purchases above your credit limit, although most will do so if asked.

Also ask if the card issuer can provide balance alerts via e-mail or cell phone text message if your balance nears your limit. Most credit card issuers now offer this service.

•**Fishing for late fees.** You pay your credit card bill on the first of the month, the same as always. Perhaps you even use an automatic bill-paying service so that the payment is withdrawn directly from your bank account each month like clockwork—yet you are still charged a late fee of $30 or more.

The trick: Credit card companies have been quietly shortening their "grace periods" (the time between the end of the billing cycle and the date that the payment is due) from 25 or 30 days down to only 20 in some cases. Even though you paid your bill on the same day as always, this now counts as late.

*Rates and figures subject to change.

124

Self-defense: Pay bills as soon as they arrive, preferably online to avoid the risk that your payment will be lost or delayed in the mail.

● **Phantom interest charges.** You are about to leave on an extended vacation and do not want to worry about making credit card payments during the trip, so before departing you pay the full amount that your credit card statement says you owe. When you get back from your trip more than a month later, you discover that your payment did not bring the account balance to $0—and you have been charged a late payment fee of as much as $39.

The trick: Credit card accounts accrue interest between the day a statement is mailed and the day the cardholder pays the bill (unless the account balance was paid in full the previous month). Those few days of interest charges might amount to only a couple of dollars or less, but credit card companies consider the tiny balance enough to trigger late-payment penalties.

Self-defense: If you wish to pay off a credit card account completely, do not just pay the amount on the bill if the account is accruing interest charges. Call the card company and ask how much you need to pay as of five days down the road in order to bring the account down to zero. (The five-day lead time should give your check time to reach the payment center.) If you pay the bill online, check how much you need to pay today or tomorrow.

● **Overseas usage fees.** You use your Visa or MasterCard extensively during a vacation to a foreign country because it is simpler than converting your dollars to the local currency. When you receive your next account statement, you discover that you have been charged extra fees amounting to more than $100.

The trick: In addition to the 1% fee that Visa and MasterCard charge for foreign purchases, the bank that issued your card is likely to add an additional fee, typically 2%, for a total 3% fee for foreign purchases. With the high cost of foreign travel, this could easily become a big chunk of money.

Self-defense: Call your card issuers before your trip and ask about their fees for foreign use. If all your credit cards charge hefty fees,

consider applying for the Capital One Visa or Capital One MasterCard. Capital One does not impose a "foreign exchange fee"—and it absorbs the 1% Visa/MasterCard fee rather than passing it along to customers (800-695-5500, *www.capitalone.com*).

● **"Convenience" checks.** Your credit card issuer sends you blank checks and suggests that you write yourself a loan.

The trick: These checks probably do not make it clear that this loan will be treated as a cash advance, possibly with ultra-steep interest rates in excess of 20% plus a cash-advance fee of 3% to 5% and no grace period.

Self-defense: Call the credit card issuer that sent the checks, and ask about the details of loan terms before taking them up on the offer. If you determine that the checks are treated as a cash advance, steer clear.

How Does Your Bank Rate?

Nancy Dunnan, a New York City–based financial and travel adviser and author or coauthor of 25 books, including *How to Invest $50–$5,000* (HarperCollins).

The Federal Deposit Insurance Corporation (FDIC) says that it never reveals its "Bank Watch List" (a list of banks in trouble) to the public.

But there are companies that rate financial institutions, including AM Best Company Inc., Bankrate, Inc., BauerFinancial, Inc. and Veribanc Inc. Most charge for their information.

Examples: AM Best will charge $75 per report*…BauerFinancial charges $10 for the first telephone report and $4 for each additional bank…Veribanc charges $10 for the first "short" report via telephone, $5 per short telephone report thereafter and $25 and up for longer written reports.

One reliable company, fortunately, offers its ratings and comments at no cost—Bankrate. com. Its "Safe & Sound Service" (*www.bankrate. com/brm/safesound/ss_home.asp*) evaluates the

*Prices subject to change.

financial strength of 17,000 banks, thrifts and credit unions, rating each from one to five, five being the top rating. You can search by name of the institution, state, zip code, asset size and rating. I recommend starting there to find out more about your bank. While a high rating is not a guarantee of financial strength, it (along with other available information, such as annual and quarterly reports) at least gives you facts to use when forming your own opinion.

How Safe Is Your Money In the Bank? What You Need to Know About FDIC Insurance

Greg McBride, CFA, a senior financial analyst with Bankrate.com, a personal finance Internet site based in North Palm Beach, Florida. McBride often is called on by cable and network television to be a broadcast commentator providing financial analysis and advice.

California-based IndyMac Bank failed in July 2008, leading many bank customers to wonder how safe their money really was. For most, the answer is extremely safe. Prior to 1934, bank failures often meant major disaster for depositors, but the Federal Deposit Insurance Corp. (FDIC) now guarantees most bank deposits.

As crucial as FDIC insurance is for our financial security, so few Americans know very much about it—and what they do not know could cost them a bundle. *Top financial analyst Greg McBride answers questions on the topic below...*

• **Do bank customers need to worry about money they have in banks?** The vast majority do not. The only people who should worry at all are those whose accounts at any single bank exceed the limits of FDIC insurance—$250,000 until 2013. Stay below this limit, and 100% of your deposits are completely protected even if the bank fails.

• **What should people do if they want to keep more in a bank?** The easiest way around the rules is to divide up your money among

several banks—that means among different bank companies, not just several branches of the same bank. FDIC insurance covers up to $250,000 at each bank with which you conduct business.

If you prefer to keep more than $250,000 in a single bank, you still can be 100% covered by FDIC insurance as long as you divide your money among several "ownership categories." Ownership categories could include personal accounts in your name...personal accounts in your spouse's name...joint accounts that are co-owned by you and someone else (such as your spouse)...and trust accounts naming someone other than yourself as trust beneficiary.

Example: With proper planning, a married couple can deposit $2 million in a single bank with all of their money insured by the FDIC. Each spouse can put $250,000 in an account in his or her own name...each can have $250,000 in a retirement account...the couple can co-own a joint account up to $500,000... and each can have a trust containing $250,000 that names the other spouse as the beneficiary. *Total:* $2 million.

• **Which types of bank accounts are protected by the FDIC, and which types are not protected?** Checking accounts, savings accounts, CDs, Christmas accounts and money-market savings accounts are all covered by the FDIC.

Investment products, such as stocks, bonds and mutual fund shares (including the money-market mutual fund shares) are not covered even if they were purchased through an FDIC bank.

The Securities Investor Protection Corporation (SIPC), an organization not related to the FDIC, does protect investors when brokerages, including bank brokerages, fail. Look for the phrase "Member SIPC" on bank signage...ask your bank's brokerage department whether the bank (or the subsidiary that holds investments) is a member of the SIPC...or contact the SIPC to check membership (202-371-8300, *www.sipc.org*).

Note: SIPC coverage does not protect investors from losses from market fluctuations.

●**Aside from not knowing all the rules, what are other ways that customers wind up with uncovered deposits?** People sometimes will purchase "brokered CDs", CDs sold through investment brokers, without realizing that these CDs could be placed in a bank at which they already have accounts. If the CD and all these other accounts total more than $250,000, they might not be completely covered. Ask where a brokered CD will be placed before buying.

Others put money into interest-bearing accounts right up to the FDIC limit. Then the interest earned by these accounts pushes them over the limit and leaves them less than fully covered.

●**Is money in a credit union or a savings and loan as safe as in the bank?** Yes. Most savings-and-loan deposits are FDIC insured. Most credit union deposits are covered by the National Credit Union Share Insurance Fund, which is essentially identical to FDIC insurance (go to *www.ncua.gov,* and click on "Share Insurance").

●**How long after a bank fails do depositors have to wait to receive their money from the FDIC?** You might be hearing the myth that it requires months for the FDIC to pay up, but in truth, depositors usually have full access to their money by the next business day after a bank is closed by regulators. Typically, failed banks are closed on Fridays, and funds are fully available by the following Monday. Even during that weekend, bank customers generally can use their ATM cards and write checks, though they might not be able to use online banking services. (Deposited funds held through brokered accounts or trusts might take slightly longer to become fully available.)

●**Do bank customers who exceed FDIC limits lose all of their uncovered deposits when their banks fail?** They are likely to recover a portion of their uncovered money after the bank's assets are sold, but probably not everything. Historically, they can expect to receive around 70 cents on the dollar, though this varies.

●**Do you expect many more bank failures?** I do anticipate more failures as banks deal with the bad mortgages and other failed loans, but keep this in context. For this year, as of early May 2009, only 33 out of 8,300 US banks have failed. The vast majority remain financially sound.

For more information: Call 877-ASK-FDIC, or go to *www.fdic.gov.*

More from Greg McBride, CFA...

Banking from Home

You can make bank deposits from home by scanning checks into your computer. Businesses have been using this process for some time. The service, Remote Deposit Capture for Consumers by CheckFree, requires a scanner, a computer and an Internet connection. Depositors enter information and scan checks—with image transfer encrypted to protect data. An increasing number of banks are offering this technology to online banking customers. Check with your bank.

Beat the Wily Banks on Overdraft Fees

Jean Ann Fox, director of financial services for the Consumer Federation of America, a not-for-profit consumer organization located in Washington, DC, *www. consumerfed.org.*

The penalties have soared for overdrawing money from your checking account. The average fee charged by the 10 largest US banks for withdrawing more money than is in an account is now $34.65. And such fees are per withdrawal.

Example: One large bank allows up to five overdraft fees per day, which could total $175 each day. Most banks also add "sustained overdraft fees" of as much as $8 per day if the overdrawn funds are not repaid within three to seven days.

What can happen: Your bank takes longer than you expect to clear a check you deposited, and your account is overdrawn before the money becomes available. When the check finally clears, the bank claims the money for itself to pay the overdraft fees you unknowingly incurred. So you wind up overdrawing even more money.

To avoid overdraft fees…

• **Have your paycheck directly deposited into your checking account,** because direct deposits clear right away.

• **Sign up for true overdraft protection,** which links your checking to your savings account, credit card or line of credit to cover overages. There may be a fee each time, but it should be $5, and not $30 or $35. Better yet, choose a bank that does not charge any fees at all.

• **Ask whether your bank can provide e-mail or text-message warnings** when your checking account balance falls below a certain level.

• **If you do incur overdraft fees,** ask your bank to waive them.

Get Banks to Bid for Your Cash

Have banks bid for your cash at Money-Aisle (*www.moneyaisle.com*). There are 108 banks participating in the site to offer the best rate on FDIC-insured certificates of deposit (CDs). You enter the amount you want to invest and for how long, and the banks then make interest rate offers in an auction operated by automated software. There is no charge for consumers to use the site—and you are not required to accept any offer.

Helpful: Before trying the auction site, log on to *www.bankrate.com* to find out the best rates currently available for CDs. Then find out if MoneyAisle can do better.

The New York Times, www.nytimes.com.

Alternative to Traditional CDs

An alternative to traditional CDs if you have more than $250,000 to invest and want to keep Federal Deposit Insurance Corporation (FDIC) protection is the Certificate of Deposit Account Registry Service (CDARS).

This banking network service splits large deposits into amounts just below the $250,000 limit (to ensure that both principal and interest are eligible for full FDIC insurance) and spreads the money among CDs at a network of more than 2,700 financial institutions. Maturities from four weeks to five years are available. CD purchasers do not pay for the service, but each customer needs to choose a specific bank from the CDARS list as his or her home bank—and if that bank fails, access to others might be difficult. Interest rates obtained through CDARS may be lower than rates available directly from banks.

More information: *www.cdars.com.*

BusinessWeek, 1221 Avenue of the Americas, New York City 10020, *www.businessweek.com.*

Turn Real Estate Lemons into Super-Bargains

Barbara Corcoran, founder of The Corcoran Group, the largest residential real estate brokerage firm in the New York metropolitan region. She is a frequent commentator on television and author of *Nextville: Amazing Places to Live the Rest of Your Life* (Springboard). Her Web site is *www.barbaracorcoran.com.*

Real estate professionals love the lemon. That's what many brokers call a less-than-perfect house whose flaws would be inexpensive to fix or relatively easy to live with, giving the lucky buyer the opportunity to snag a super-bargain.

Drawbacks, such as an awkward layout, and even purely cosmetic issues, such as peeling paint, can get you a price reduction of 20% to

30% off what a comparable home would fetch. If the discount is not already reflected in the asking price, point out the problem and negotiate. Especially in today's market, the power lies in the buyer's hands. *When you see any of the following defects, you're probably looking at big savings and only a small headache...*

• **Flawed paint.** Paint is the cheapest and simplest way to give a house a total makeover, inside and out. Yet an unsightly exterior reduces curb appeal so dramatically that most buyers will drive by. That gives you leverage to bargain—plus you can then choose the color you want.

• **Ugly ceilings.** Next to repainting, putting up a new ceiling is the cheapest big improvement you can make to a room. Out-of-date "popcorn" (pebbly) ceilings or "drop" ceilings made of panels can be a huge turnoff, but they can be demolished and replaced at reasonable cost in two to three days. Cracked plaster ceilings are also neither difficult nor expensive to fix—and new paint will hide the repair.

• **No air-conditioning.** Especially in warm climates, this may look like a deal breaker. Before you walk away, consider that a 10,000-BTU window unit is sufficient to cool 400 to 450 square feet—and it sells for less than $500.* Central air for a home that already has a forced-air heating system starts at around $4,000 and can be installed in a couple of days, usually with little or no change to the existing ducts in the house.

• **Old fuse boxes.** Houses of a certain age often come with outdated fuse boxes. Do not let visions of blackouts or smoking wires discourage you—a licensed electrician can make the conversion easily. An old box with eight fuses costs less than $400 to convert, and it can be done without ripping up your walls. Most older homes have 100 amps of electricity. That's usually adequate for today's usage, but a house inspector will be able to tell you if your intended electrical demands will require more amperage.

• **A dated kitchen.** You can brighten up a dingy kitchen for well under $5,000. Instead

*Prices subject to change.

of tearing down cabinets, simply replace their fronts (glass is a good way to update). Countertops are simple to change or to refinish and seal. Even a backsplash you dislike won't cost much to redo, because it covers such a small area. It will make a big difference in the look of your kitchen, however.

• **A formal dining room.** Most of today's house hunters do not want a separate dining room next to a tiny kitchen.

Solution: Knock down the wall (it's usually not structural) and combine the spaces. A favorite tactic of house flippers, this is a simple change that fulfills many needs.

Good news: It doesn't always require a soup-to-nuts kitchen renovation to be successful.

• **An inaccessible basement.** Houses whose basements can be reached only from outside may put off lots of buyers, but it takes very little floor space to break through and create internal access. The front-hall coat closet is often a good place to put the stairs.

• **Awkward laundry space.** Basement laundry rooms are antiquated—most people want to wash their clothes on the main level or upstairs close to the master bedroom. As long as there's space to accommodate a stacked washer/dryer unit—in the pantry or in a linen closet, for example—plumbing is close enough for a hookup and you can vent the dryer, this is an easy and smart fix to make.

• **Spiral staircases.** Usually found in small houses because they provide access to another floor in just a three-by-three-foot area, spiral staircases terrify parents of small children. A traditional staircase requires double or triple the space. So take out your measuring tape. If there's enough room to replace it, a spiral staircase shouldn't rule out an otherwise desirable home.

• **An overwhelming deck.** Unless it's concrete, the deck can be easily decreased or removed to give a house more yard. Cutting a deck back, including moving the supports and railings, is a fairly simple project for a professional and will get you more than your money back when it comes time to sell.

Who Is Eligible for the Mortgage Rescue Plan?

The president's $75 billion plan to stem the tide of foreclosures is designed to provide more affordable mortgage terms for up to nine million US home owners.

It is meant to help families that are facing foreclosures, as well as those who are struggling to keep up with their payments even though they "played by the rules," in President Obama's words.

If you owe up to 105% of what your home is worth, you may qualify for low-cost refinancing. If you spend more than 31% of your gross monthly income on mortgage payments, you may qualify for loan modification.

Prepare for possible refinancing or a loan modification by calculating how much equity you have in your home and what your gross monthly income is.

Keith T. Gumbinger, senior vice president at the financial publisher HSH Associates and a frequent commentator on mortgage trends. HSH, based in Pompton Plains, New Jersey, is the nation's largest publisher of independent mortgage and consumer loan information and statistics. For more information, go to *www.hsh.com.*

Pay Your Mortgage Early?

Janice M. Johnson, CPA, JD, consultant, A.B. Watley Group, a financial services company, New York City.

In this troubled economy, you might think you should make extra payments on your home mortgage early to get rid of debt.

This is probably not a good idea. You get the most financial benefit from prepaying your highest-interest-rate debt first, starting with credit cards. Assuming that your home mortgage carries a fixed interest rate, it is probably your lowest-rate debt, especially after the tax deduction for the interest on it, so it would be the last one you should pay.

Possible exception: A 0% vehicle loan of the type often offered by carmakers.

Even if your mortgage is your only debt, you probably shouldn't pay it down more quickly than you have to.

Two reasons: First off, if a later emergency need for funds arises, it may not be easy to get a new home-equity loan quickly and the rate may be higher than your current mortgage rate. Second, if you have to borrow from a source other than your home, not only will your interest rate likely be higher than it is on your mortgage loan, but you will lose the tax deduction you get for the mortgage interest.

Better: Take the funds that you would use to prepay your mortgage, and save them in a separate interest-bearing account. You will increase your wealth and maintain your liquidity.

If Your Mortgage Company Is Asking for Extra Escrow...

You might not have to add extra escrow money, even if your mortgage company tells you to. A mortgage company establishes an escrow account to pay property tax and insurance. Federal law lets mortgage companies increase escrow reserves in case of future tax hikes, but it does not require the increases and suggests that they be made purely voluntary. If your escrow holder says an increase is mandatory, look for an opt-out clause in your statement. Even if you do not find one, contact the company and insist on opting out of the increase. Follow up with a letter, and insist on getting a revised statement within 14 days. If you do not receive one, write again—and, if necessary, file a complaint with your state's attorney general (*www.naag.org*).

Money, Time-Life Bldg., Rockefeller Center, New York City 10020, *http://money.cnn.com.*

To Avoid Foreclosure...

Worried about a foreclosure? *Follow these helpful tips to prevent it...*

• **If you fall behind in payments,** contact your lender's payment resolutions department immediately.

• **Don't try to hide from the lender**—answer the phone and open all mail. Lenders are highly motivated to work out solutions to avoid foreclosure.

• **Tell your lender about your situation and listen to its proposal,** but do not agree to anything until you speak with an attorney or credit counselor.

• **Figure out if your problem is short term or long term**—this will help the lender come up with options.

• **Check with your lender to see whether you can make partial payments** if you cannot currently afford full ones.

• **Keep notes of all your phone calls and correspondence,** including mailed envelopes with postmarks.

Edward Mrkvicka, Jr., president, Reliance Enterprises, Inc., Marengo, Illinois.

In Danger of Foreclosure?

Request loan modification from your lender if you are ever in danger of foreclosure. If you meet certain financial criteria, you may be able to have your interest rate decreased temporarily or permanently...stretch out your payments for a longer term, such as 40 years ...or have principal repayment deferred, usually at zero interest. Call the number on your monthly mortgage statement, and then ask to speak to someone about a loan modification. Be prepared to discuss your entire financial situation, including any recent hardships, and to hand over copies of recent paycheck stubs and bank statements.

Chris Spagnuolo, spokesperson based in New York City, Bankrate.com.

Five Ways to Sell Your House in Today's Market

Robert Irwin, who has been a real estate investor and licensed real estate broker in California for more than 35 years, *www.robertirwin.com*. He's also author of *Fix It, Stage It, Sell It QUICK! A Do-It-Yourselfer's Guide for Rapid-Turnover of Any Home in Any Market* (Kaplan).

The real estate market is likely to remain sluggish for at least another year in most regions. The usual selling strategy—hire a broker and set an asking price comparable to that of similar homes—might not lead to a sale under these conditions. Some sellers even have resorted to raffling off their houses—a strategy that rarely works and violates gambling laws in many states. *Five sales strategies that offer a better chance of success...*

• **Offer a "for sale by owner"** (FSBO) discount if you have the time and savvy to price, market and present your home to buyers without the help of an agent.

Price your home 6% below the comparable homes on the market. This lets your buyer in effect receive the commission that you would have paid a real estate agent had you hired one. Explain this in your FSBO classified ads.

Note: If a buyer has his/her own real estate agent, this agent will still expect a 2.5% to 3% commission. FSBO sellers are not required to pay this commission, but the buyer's contract with the agent might hinder him from purchasing the home if you won't. See if his broker will accept a reduced "finder's fee" rather than the full commission, and explain to the buyer that paying this money to his broker means you cannot come down far from your asking price. Explain to all buyers who arrive with agents that your asking price was based on an agent-less transaction.

Use an Internet FSBO service, such as Owners.com (888-645-6305), to list your home on the Multiple Listing Service (MLS) for $395.* FSBO Web sites, such as Owners.com or ForSaleByOwner.com, offer tips on these topics, or consult a book on do-it-yourself home selling, such as my *For Sale By Owner* (Kaplan).

*Price and rates subject to change.

•**"Future price" your home.** Rather than setting your asking price based on what you think your home is worth today, set it based on what your home is likely to be worth in four to six months based on regional price trends during the previous year.

Example: If real estate prices fell 15% in your region during the prior 12 months, extend that trend forward four to six months and subtract 5% to 7.5% from your home's current value. Make this lower figure your asking price.

"Future pricing" a home makes it look like a bargain, which draws potential buyers. It also decreases buyers' fears that the property will soon be worth less than they paid. Brokers will identify the bargain and steer clients to you.

You can even explain what you've done in your ads: "Priced 7% below the market to protect you from any future real estate declines."

In a falling market, most sellers refuse to future price because it means accepting less than current market value—but if houses in your area are sitting on the market for months without selling, then this "current market value" is an illusion. Home owners who demand current market value are likely to discover that their homes are still languishing on the market months later, at which point they will have to slash their asking prices to become competitive. It is better to get ahead of the curve, cut your price from the beginning and find a buyer now.

•**Auction your home.** A heavily advertised auction might attract more potential buyers to your home than a traditional sale because many home buyers believe that there are bargains to be had at auctions. Several of these buyers could get caught up in the excitement of the auction, bid aggressively against each other and drive up the price.

A "minimum bid" (the minimum amount to start the bidding) or a "reserve" (price below which you are not required to sell your home) auction can eliminate the risk that your home sells for much less than it is worth, but these safety nets also deter the bidders in search of bargains.

If you do decide to auction your home, work with an auction company that specializes in real estate. The National Auctioneers Association (*www.auctioneers.org*) can help you find one in your region.

Auction fees and commissions can be just as high as or higher than broker commissions (average is 7% to 10%). Make sure you know how much the auction company will take if your home sells…and how much you will owe if it doesn't.

An auction is not a good idea if there are many similar homes on the market, because there is no reason for auction bidders to drive up the price.

An auction is a good idea when the home is custom built—or in an area where similar homes are for sale, if you are willing to have a reserve significantly below the prices asked for those other homes.

•**Offer financing.** If you offer private financing, your home will be appealing to buyers who cannot obtain mortgages in this tight credit market.

Bonus: You could earn an attractive 6% to 8% interest rate on the amount you loan.

Downside: If your buyer defaults, you can foreclose, but this is a time-consuming and expensive process. If home values fall by more than the size of the buyer's down payment, the buyer may walk away and dump the less-valuable property back in your lap.

Finding the right buyer is crucial. The buyer's down payment must be substantial (15% to 20%), his income must be stable, other debts must be limited and the credit history must be sound. It is worth accepting a slightly lower sales price if that's what's necessary to get an appealing buyer.

Hire an experienced real estate attorney to draft the loan documents. Make sure the contract includes a late-payment penalty of at least $50 to $100 to encourage on-time mortgage payment. Don't hire a loan servicing company to handle the money—you're better off knowing as soon as possible if payments are arriving late so that you can take prompt action.

Offer financing only if you are willing to accept some financial risk…your mortgage is mostly or completely paid off, so you do not need a huge amount of cash to pay off a lender…you possess the financial resources to live without the big cash influx that you would receive if you sold the home outright…you have the financial skills to evaluate potential buyers' finances…and you would like to turn your home into a steady source of income without the hassle of renting.

• **Rent out your home until the real estate market rebounds.** Rental prices are climbing in many regions even as real estate prices fall. You might be able to rent out your home for enough money to pay the mortgage and taxes, then sell in a few years when buyers are more plentiful.

Ask would-be tenants for the contact information for their three most recent landlords. Don't bother calling the current landlord—he might say glowing things about terrible tenants just to be rid of them—but do phone the prior landlords and ask for an opinion. Favor tenants who have credit scores of at least 620 to 640 (have the tenant obtain his credit score from *www.myfico.com* and show it to you)… steady jobs…and no pets, to avoid damage to the home.

Contact your insurance agent to make sure that you're covered if the tenant damages your home or sues you.

More information: The Landlord Protection Agency (877-984-3572, *www.thelpa.com*)… National Apartment Association (703-518-6141, *www.naahq.org*).

Renting out your home is one good option if you don't need to raise cash by selling the home right away and local rents are higher than your mortgage payments.

How to Sell a House *Faster*

Sell a house more quickly by filling it with attractive rental furniture. A house that is nicely furnished can have more appeal to buyers than an empty one. If you've moved your furnishings out of a home that you are trying to sell, consider renting furnishings to fill it.

Sources: Churchill Furniture Rental, *www.furniturerent.com,* operates in the East in 11 states from New Hampshire to Virginia. Fashion Furniture, *www.fashionfurniture.com,* operates in California. Check for rental sources in your area.

Good Housekeeping, 300 W. 57 St., New York City 10019, *www.goodhousekeeping.com.*

Secrets to Selling Your Time-Share

If you are looking to sell a time-share, you will likely get less than half of what you paid for it from the developer. Time-shares are more like prepaid hotel stays than real estate investments. See if your resort-management company will buy the time-share or help to sell it. Or try the Timeshare User's Group (*www.tug2.net*), which charges $15 for a one-year membership,* during which you can post as many ads as you like to sell your unit…or RedWeek.com, which charges a $49.99 fee for 12 months.

Bill Rogers, founder of Timeshare User's Group in Orange Park, Florida.

*Prices subject to change.

How to Pay Much Less For College

Lynn O'Shaughnessy, a financial journalist and the author of four books, including her latest, *The College Solution: A Guide for Everyone Looking for the Right School at the Right Price* (Financial Times). Based in La Mesa, California, she has two children, one attending a liberal arts college in Pennsylvania. For more information, go to *www.thecollegesolution.com.*

The average tuition for one year of private college in the US has increased to $25,143*…the average state school tuition to $6,585. And tuitions at some schools significantly exceed these figures. But they are sticker prices. A lot of colleges are discounting

*Prices and rates subject to change.

tuition. The average private tuition discount is 33.5%, and the average public school discount is nearly 15%. *Here's how to increase the odds that you'll get a discount…*

•**Look for no-loan schools.** If your family qualifies for need-based aid, check out schools that give out more need-based grants—which don't have to be repaid—than loans. A growing number of the nation's most selective schools no longer include loans in their financial-aid packages. Instead, they award grants to families who need them.

Examples of no-loan schools: Amherst, Bowdoin, Colby, Davidson, Harvard, Haverford, Pomona, Princeton, Swarthmore, Williams and Yale.

Find a list of schools with favorable financial-aid policies at the Web site of the Project on Student Debt (*www.projectonstudentdebt. org,* type "Financial Aid Pledges to Reduce Student Debt" into its search engine).

To determine if you qualify for financial aid, use the online calculator at *www.fafsa4caster. ed.gov.* You will find more college-funding calculators at *www.finaid.org,* including an "Expected Family Contribution and Financial Aid Calculator."

•**Look for merit dispensers.** If your family is too affluent to qualify for need-based cash, look for schools that hand out lots of merit aid, which is given to promising students without regard to whether they require the money. A sampling of the schools in this category, along with their average annual renewable merit aid awards, includes Tulane University ($20,541), Rice University ($15,912), Pepperdine University ($19,673), Boston College ($17,224) and Case Western Reserve University ($19,497).

Lots of public institutions also are offering merit-based discounts. These include the University of Virginia, University of Florida, University of South Carolina and Miami University in Ohio.

•**Check online to find generous schools.** To discover how much money an institution gives out, check the school's profile on *www. collegeboard.com* by entering the name of the school in the search box. That will take you to the "College Quick Finder." Under the college information, click on "Cost and Financial Aid." There you'll find statistics on financial aid and merit aid (aid that's not based on need).

Another resource: Each school's "Common Data Set" is a gold mine of statistics that includes information on need-based financial aid, merit aid, student retention, majors, freshman class profiles, gender breakdown and much more. Most schools post their Common Data Sets on their Web sites. To find the information, try a Google search for the name of the school and the phrase "Common Data Set."

•**Skip the very selective schools.** Students are more apt to receive financial help if they are among the top 25% to 30% of applicants to a particular school. You can compare SAT and grade-point averages by looking at college snapshots at *www.collegeboard.com.*

•**Play the gender card.** At schools where females are in abundance, male applicants do not always have to be as qualified to be accepted and/or may receive more financial aid —and vice versa.

Example: The technical and engineering schools may be more inclined to offer aid to women.

College Tuition Cost-Savers

To cut tuition costs, sign up for classes during break periods—many universities offer courses that can give you full credit for one to two weeks of study, at a lower price per credit than is charged for regular courses. Or, take extra classes during regular semesters—many colleges charge a single price for tuition no matter how many courses you take. If most students take four courses per semester and you can take five for no extra cost, each course costs you less money and you may be able to graduate early—saving even more.

Marc Scheer, PhD, career counselor and educational consultant, New York City, and author of *No Sucker Left Behind: Avoiding the Great College Rip-Off* (Common Courage).

Looking for a Better Deal Than A 529 Plan? Try This...

State-run prepaid tuition plans might be a better deal than 529 plans, which have suffered severely in the market downturn. With a prepaid plan, you pay the cost of tuition today, in a lump sum or monthly installments, and you are guaranteed that your child's tuition will be covered at your state college or university. Prepaid plans protect against tuition increases—but they require that your child go to a state school.

Fortune, Time-Life Bldg., Rockefeller Center, New York City 10020, *http://money.cnn.com.*

How to Unfreeze Your 529 Plan

You can unfreeze your 529 college-savings plan. Investors in 529s typically are permitted to change investments within the account only once per year, which means that many people couldn't make shifts when stocks plunged.*

To get around this restriction: Transfer the account to another 529 plan in a different state...or switch the beneficiaries if you have more than one child...or cash out your 529 if it is worth less than you put in and then, if you wish, invest in a new 529. You will owe no federal taxes if you cash out now, because only earnings are assessed.

Joseph F. Hurley, CPA, founder of Savingforcollege. com, which analyzes 529 savings plans across the US, Pittsford, New York.

*A rule change for 2009 only will allow 529 investors to make two investing changes instead of one during the calendar year.

Veterans Benefits You May Not Know About

Christopher Michel, former naval flight officer and the founder of Military.com, America's largest military membership organization, located in San Francisco. He is author of *The Military Advantage: A Comprehensive Guide to Your Military & Veterans Benefits* (Simon & Schuster).

No country in the world provides more benefits to those who have served in its armed forces than the United States. Some of the benefits are available only to active service members or military retirees (those who have retired after at least 20 years of service), but many are offered to all of America's 24 million veterans and their families.

HOME LOANS

Under the GI Bill, veterans can buy homes worth up to $417,000 with no money down and without a monthly mortgage insurance premium. The Veterans Administration (or VA) doesn't actually lend money—it simply guarantees a portion of the loan with your lender. (You do have to meet the lender's credit standards.)

More information: Call 800-827-1000 or go to *www.homeloans.va.gov,* where you can download VA Form 26-1880.

EDUCATION

Under the GI Bill, if you have served in the military in the past 10 years, you are probably eligible for up to $1,321 per month in education expenses (for almost any type of course) for up to 36 academic months (a total of four years). This money is tax free.

More information: Log on to *www.gibillex press.com,* where you can download VA Form 22-1990. Or call 888-442-4551.

The post-9/11 GI Bill, signed into law in 2008, will cover from 40% to 100% of higher-education tuition, plus related expenses, for service members with at least 90 days of active duty after September 11, 2001.

More information: *www.gibill.va.gov.*

Other educational benefits for vets include...

•**Scholarships.** More than $300 million in scholarships from colleges and universities are available to vets and their dependents. Many of these scholarships are poorly publicized, improving your odds of winning one.

More information: Visit my organization, Military.com (*www.military.com*), the country's largest military and veteran organization and a business unit of Monster Worldwide. Type "scholarships" into the search box…or select "Scholarships" from the left-hand menu to use the Scholarship Finder.

• **College credits.** Colleges often award vets credits for their military training and experience, meaning less time (and expense) until graduation.

More information: Visit *http://education. military.com/timesaving-programs/college-credit-for-military-experience* or contact individual schools for information regarding the benefits they offer.

• **State education benefit programs.** Some states offer veterans tuition discounts at their public colleges.

More information: Visit *www.military.com/ education/statebenefits*.

CAREERS

Thousands of jobs are listed on Military.com (*www.military.com/careers*) by organizations that are eager to hire vets. Or head to the Veteran Career Network (*http://benefits.military. com/vcn/search.do*) to find a helpful vet in the company, industry or city where you would like to work. There are more than 600,000 veterans willing to provide fellow vets with career assistance.

TRAVEL

• **Air travel.** Veterans who are retired from the military and family members who fly with them can fly for free or close to free on certain military flights, space permitting. This is standby travel, so it's only appropriate when your schedule is flexible. Military flights aren't always comfortable, be sure to bring a jacket and snacks.

More information: Visit Military Living's SpaceA.info (*www.spacea.info*) or Military.com (*www.military.com/spacea*).

• **Lodging.** Military retirees and their families have access to inexpensive lodging—either at on-base lodging or the Armed Forces Recreation Centers—on a space-available basis.

Examples: Shades of Green resort within Walt Disney World and Hale Koa Hotel on the beach at Waikiki.

More information: Air Force retirees, visit Air Force Services Agency (*www.afsv.af.mil*)… Army retirees, US Army MWR (*www.armymwr. com*)…Coast Guard retirees, see the US Coast Guard site (*www.uscg.mil/mwr*)…Marine Corp retirees, the MCCS site (*www.usmc-mccs.org/ lodging/index.cfm*)…and Navy retirees, Navy Lodge (*www.navy-lodge.com*).

MEDICAL BENEFITS

The Department of Veteran's Affairs is required by law to provide eligible veterans with "needed" hospital care and outpatient care. VA defines "needed" as care or service that will promote, preserve and restore health. This includes treatment, supplies and services, such as physical exams and immunizations. The decision of "need" will be based on the judgment of the vet's health-care provider at the VA and in accordance with generally accepted standards of clinical practice. There are also VA clinical health programs that vets may be eligible for, including treatment for blindness, Agent Orange exposure and HIV/AIDS.

Veterans' dependents are also eligible for these VA health-care programs in many cases. Final eligibility depends on several factors for each program. These factors include the nature of a veteran's discharge from military service (e.g., honorable, other than honorable, dishonorable), duration of service, service-connected disabilities, income level and available VA resources, among others. In general, the vet must be enrolled in the VA health-care system—there are 1,326 VA facilities throughout the country—to receive benefits.

More information: Visit the United States Department of Veterans Affairs site at *www. va.gov/healtheligibility*.

CORPORATE DISCOUNTS

Many companies offer discounts to all active military personnel, and some also extend the discounts to vets. Military.com lists more than 700 discount programs, including some for airfare, computers and electronics and dining and entertainment.

8

Insurance Answers

How to Get Your Health Insurer to Pay Up

You may pay the health insurance policy premiums without fail, but doing so doesn't mean your insurance company will be as reliable when you send in a claim. It is very possible that your claim will be improperly denied.

Very few people bother to fight these denials. That's unfortunate, because policyholders who intelligently contest health insurance claims denials often get them reversed.

If a seemingly valid health insurance claim you make is denied in whole or in part, ask the insurance company to send you a full explanation of why it was denied (or accepted for only a lesser amount). *Then follow these steps to get your claim covered...*

Step 1: **Request support.** If you have a group health policy, ask the group benefits administrator to help you with contesting the denial. If you purchased an individual policy through an independent insurance agent, ask this agent to help. Not only do benefits administrators and insurance agents have experience with these matters, they have clout with the insurance companies. The insurer might relent to an administrator's or agent's request to pay a claim simply to avoid losing future business.

Step 2: **Write a letter to the insurer** requesting a formal review of the denial and explaining why you believe it is incorrect. Get the name of the person to write to from your benefits administrator or agent. Send this letter via certified mail, return receipt requested.

William M. Shernoff, JD, senior and managing partner of the law firm Shernoff Bidart Darras & Echeverria LLP, Claremont, California, www.sbd-law.com. The firm represents policyholders who have been treated unfairly by insurers and HMOs. Shernoff also established the consumer law program at the University of Wisconsin, Madison, and is author of several books, including Fight Back and Win: How to Get HMOs and Health Insurance to Pay Up (Capital).

Cite the insurance company's own literature if it seems to contradict the argument made in the denial. If the policy literature is vague or confusing—it often is—do not accept the insurance company's position that it means what it says it means. In most states, the courts interpret insurance policy provisions as a layperson would understand them, not as a corporate lawyer would interpret them.

Example: Your insurance company refuses to pay for your home care following a serious accident, arguing that the care you received was "custodial" care, which is not covered, rather than "skilled" care, which is. If you received what the average person would consider skilled care and your policy does not specifically define these terms in a way that defends the insurer's position, the law is likely on your side.

Some common reasons for claims denials and possible responses...

• **The procedure was not medically necessary.** Ask your doctor to write a letter to the insurer explaining why the procedure was necessary in your case.

• **The procedure was experimental.** Ask your doctor to write a letter to the insurer noting that Medicare or other insurers cover the procedure or citing statistics showing that it is widely used.

• **There was a filing error, such as a missed deadline.** In most states, the insurer cannot legally deny your claim because of a technical filing mistake unless it can show that it was harmed by this mistake.

• **The bill exceeds "reasonable and customary" charges.** Ask your physician if there were special circumstances in your case that would justify higher costs. If there were, have him/her write a letter to the insurer describing them. Another option is to call other medical facilities in the region and ask what they charge for the procedure. Insurers often rely on old data or data from other parts of the country when they set these "reasonable and customary" estimates. If you can establish that your doctor did not charge more than others in your region do, the insurer might back down.

Step 3: **If your letter doesn't work, repeat your argument in a letter to the manager** or supervisor of the insurance company's claims department. Obtain the name of the individual from your claims representative. Work your way up the corporate ladder. You may need to convince only one person to agree with you for your denial to be reversed.

Remain calm and polite. Contesting an insurance claim denial is frustrating, but insurance company employees are more likely to take your side if they like you. Write down the name of any person you speak to, as well as the date and time and what you were told.

Step 4: **Contact your state's department of insurance, and ask what it can do to help you.** The quality and power of state insurance departments vary significantly. Some do help policyholders stand up to unfair insurance company practices or conduct independent reviews of denied claims.

Example: California's Department of Insurance and Department of Managed Health Care offer "independent medical reviews" of denied health insurance claims. Approximately 40% of those reviewed are decided in the patient's favor.

Simply involving your state's department of insurance may be enough to convince an insurer that it is easier to pay your claim than fight it.

Step 5: **Phone the media.** Local TV news programs and newspapers love stories about people being treated unfairly by big health insurance companies. Insurers don't want this bad press and sometimes relent when reporters call. Determine which local reporters cover human-interest stories of this sort, contact them and ask if they would be interested in your story.

Step 6: **Go to court.** If your claim is in the low four figures or less, it might qualify for small-claims court. If it is larger, you will need to hire an attorney. If your case appears strong, there will be plenty of attorneys willing to take it on a contingency basis (they get paid only if they win or settle).

Hiring an attorney makes the most sense when the insurance company's unfair claim denial has interfered with your medical treatment and endangered your health. Juries often award substantial damages when this occurs.

More from William Shernoff, JD...

If Your Insurance Company Tries to Drop You...

If you have an individual health insurance policy, *not a group health plan*, having a claim unjustly denied is not the only risk. If you develop an expensive health condition, your insurance company might attempt to retroactively terminate your coverage, a process known as "rescission."

When you file a major claim, your insurer could have an investigator examine your original policy application. If the investigator finds even the smallest error, the insurer may use this as an excuse to rescind your policy even if the application mistake has nothing to do with the current claim.

Example: Blue Cross of California canceled the policy of a woman who needed surgery to remove her gallbladder and refused to pay her $60,000 medical bills. The insurer argued that the woman's husband had failed to note on the couple's original policy application that he once had an elevated cholesterol reading.

States are beginning to enact rules to protect policyholders from this tactic, but for now, the danger remains. *To minimize your risk...*

• **Take your time doing health insurance applications.** If it's possible, obtain a copy of your health records from your doctor and use these to fill out the form, rather than rely on your memory.

• **Contact the insurance company for clarification if a question on the application is confusing.** Don't provide an answer until you truly understand the question.

• **Include your medical providers' contact information on the application form.** If the insurer later attempts to rescind your policy, you can argue in court that you didn't intentionally hide anything and that the insurer should have contacted your doctors.

Should You Fill Out a Health Questionnaire?

Health questionnaires could impact what you pay out for insurance. The questionnaires, which are used by more than 80% of employers, can help connect employees with appropriate wellness programs and possible discounts—but they also can result in higher fees for workers who admit to risk factors such as smoking. If your company requires that you fill out the questionnaire, you must do so. If it is optional, ask who will see it and how it will be used—and consider not filling it out if you have costly health issues that you do not want to reveal.

Money, Time-Life Bldg., Rockefeller Center, New York City 10020, *http://money.cnn.com*.

Hidden Perks in Health Insurance

Robert Hurley and Samuel Gibbs, senior vice presidents for eHealthInsurance Services, Inc., a Web site where consumers can compare health insurance plans and apply for and purchase health insurance online. Hurley is an insurance industry expert formerly with Health Net, Inc., a managed health-care company. Gibbs specializes in helping companies understand health care. eHealth Insurance is not affiliated with any particular health insurance provider, *http://ehealthinsurance.com*.

Your health insurance might offer some unexpected savings. Some group and individual health insurers have negotiated discounts on behalf of their members on products and services. These discounts are not always well-publicized, and many plan members don't even realize they exist. Read your health insurance company's mailings, or visit its Web site to see if there are any special discounts through your plan.

These discounts typically are categorized as "perks" rather than plan benefits, which means insurance companies can alter or discontinue them without first notifying plan members.

Contact your insurance provider or the company featured in the offer to confirm that a discount still is in effect. Also, ask if any special rules or limitations apply.

COMMON DISCOUNTS

Among the benefits found in many health insurance plans...

• **Fitness club memberships.** Many health plans offer a discount of 10% to 20% or more off the cost of gym membership.* This discount usually is available only at select national fitness chains, and you may have to prove that you use the gym regularly. Some plans also include discounts at yoga studios...or discounts on the purchase of fitness equipment from participating retailers.

• **Naturopathic treatments.** Some insurance companies cover these treatments. Those that don't may offer discounts of 20% or more on acupuncture, chiropractic services, massage therapy and hypnotherapy.

• **Weight-loss programs.** Savings of 20% or more off membership in national weight-loss chains, such as Jenny Craig and Weight Watchers, are common. Even the special low-calorie meals required by some weight-loss programs may be discounted.

• **Quit-smoking programs.** Insurance plans often cover quit-smoking programs in part or in whole. Discounts might be available on nicotine patches, gum and related products.

OTHER PERKS

These discounts show up only occasionally in health insurance plans, but they are worth watching for...

• **Cosmetic surgery and dentistry.** Cosmetic procedures will not typically be covered by health insurance, but some plans do offer special negotiated prices for elective surgery at participating providers. Covered procedures could include Botox injections, face-lifts and tooth whitening. The savings often are 20% or more off standard rates.

• **Vision correction.** Some insurance companies offer discounts on eyeglasses, contact lenses, even laser surgery.

*Offers subject to change.

• **Prescription and nonprescription drug coverage without a drug plan.** Even if your health plan does not include drug coverage, there might be a discount of 10% or more if you purchase your medications at a "featured" or "partner" drugstore.

• **Vitamins and supplements.** Discounts of as much as 40% to 50% sometimes are available. You will need to buy your vitamins from a designated provider to receive these savings.

• **Discounts on books.** Some insurance plans have partnered with online book sellers to offer discounts of 5% or 10% on "featured" books. These books typically focus on health and/or wellness topics.

• **Travel discounts.** Some major health insurers have negotiated discount rates for their members at hotel chains, car-rental chains and amusement parks. Savings of 10% to 20% are typical. Read the discount terms carefully—in some cases, members need to provide special discount codes or reserve their discount rates in advance...in other cases, members simply show their insurance plan membership cards upon arrival.

Do You Need Disability Insurance?

Tamara Eberlein, editor, *Bottom Line/Women's Health*, Boardroom Inc., 281 Tresser Blvd., Stamford, Connecticut, 06901.

A 50-something friend who suffered a stroke has mounting medical bills and will probably never be able to go back to work again.

Fortunate: She had an individual disability insurance policy.

Three in 10 Americans from age 35 to 65 will, at some point, become too disabled to work for three months or longer. Women are at higher risk than men, so they generally pay more for disability insurance.

Disability litigator Frank Darras, managing partner at the law firm Shernoff, Bidart, Darras Echeverria in Claremont, California, told us that anyone who works and needs her income to get by should have individual coverage. Do not depend on a policy from your employer— group coverage generally provides only 50% of income, payout periods are quite limited and benefits often are taxable. *Look for...*

• **A policy that covers at least 60% of your income to age 65.**

• **Individual "own occupation" coverage,** which pays if you are unable to carry out the important duties of your occupation due to an accident or illness. Without this type of coverage, benefits could be denied if, for instance, a former dentist could work as a waitress.

• **A guaranteed renewable, noncancelable policy.** Even if you are laid off or quit, your policy stays in force at the same price if you pay premiums.

Individual disability insurance is not cheap. But it is money well spent.

Profit from Selling Your Life Insurance

Lee Slavutin, MD, CLU, principal of Stern Slavutin-2 Inc., an insurance and estate-planning firm at 530 Fifth Ave., New York City 10036, *www.sternslavutin.com.* Dr. Slavutin is author of *Guide to Life Insurance Strategies* (Practitioners).

D o you have a life insurance policy you no longer need? Do you have a parent with an old policy who requires more income? In such situations, selling the policy to a third party who will keep it in force is a possibility. Even after you pay the tax on the sale, there might be more money remaining than would be the case if the policy were surrendered to the insurance company. *What you need to know...*

LIFE SETTLEMENTS

Today, there is an active market in "life settlements," purchases of insurance policies from individuals.

Seller: Typically, the seller will be age 65 or older with a health condition, such as cancer, heart disease or diabetes. The illness need not be terminal, but there must be a shortened life expectancy.

Buyer: Several life insurance policies will be bought by companies known as life settlement providers, packaged as securities and sold to investors. As the insured individuals die, investors will receive shares of the death benefits.

TAX TREATMENT

For most life settlements, the taxation consequences will depend on the amount paid and the seller's cost basis in the policy.

Determining cost basis: This usually will be the total amount of premiums paid for the coverage. If any withdrawals or cash dividends have been received, they will be subtracted from the basis.

Situation: John Jones, age 67, is covered by a $1 million permanent life insurance policy (one that has an investment account known as the cash value—explained below). Over the years, he has paid $150,000 in premiums and has taken a $10,000 withdrawal.

John is widowed, and his children are financially very comfortable, so this policy is no longer necessary.

An investor group evaluates John's medical history and estimates his life expectancy. Based on this estimate, it offers John $140,000 for the policy.

Result: John's basis in the policy is $140,000 —$150,000 paid in premiums minus a $10,000 withdrawal. With the $140,000 basis and a $140,000 selling price, no taxes will be due. If John had paid only $100,000 in premiums and had taken a $10,000 withdrawal, giving him a $90,000 basis, there would be tax due on $50,000 of income, assuming it was sold for $140,000.

Settling up: The tax rate that applies to that $50,000 of income will depend on the type of life insurance policy...

• **Permanent life insurance,** which includes whole life, universal life and variable life insurance policies. They have an investment account known as the cash value.

When a policy is sold, the buyers become the owners. The owners name a new beneficiary. An insurance company has no say in this. Premiums are paid by the new owners on the existing schedule. When such a policy is sold by the original owner at a gain, the difference between the basis and the cash value will be ordinary income, taxed at a rate as high as 35%. Any excess received in the sale should qualify for the bargain 15% rate on capital gains.

Example: Suppose the policy's basis is $90,000, the cash value is $110,000, and the purchase price is $140,000. Of the $50,000 in gain, the first $20,000 ($110,000 of cash value minus the $90,000 basis) will be taxed as ordinary income while the remaining $30,000 will probably be a long-term capital gain.

• **Term life insurance.** When a term life policy is sold, the taxable income is most likely a long-term capital gain. The gain is the sales price over basis.

Loophole: Purchases of life insurance policies from terminally ill individuals are known as "viatical" settlements. There is no federal income tax on these transactions.

Required: To get the tax exclusion, the seller must have a physician's certification that the insured individual's death is reasonably expected within 24 months. The payment needs to come from a "viatical settlement provider," who will report the amounts received by the insured individual to the IRS on Form 1099-LTC, *Long-Term Care and Accelerated Death Benefits*. Viatical settlement providers generally need licenses in the states where they do business.

WHAT BUYERS WANT

A life insurance policy will have the most appeal to buyers if it was bought back when you were considerably younger, and healthier, than you are now. If so, it will have premiums that are low in relation to the death benefit.

If the insured individual's health has deteriorated, those low premiums will be a good deal for the buyer—who will pay premiums based on the insured individual's previous excellent health and who will stand to benefit from the insured individual's shortened life expectancy. Thus, as your health declines, the resale value of your life insurance policy rises.

Price points: The shorter the seller's life expectancy, the greater the purchase price as a percentage of the policy's face value.

Situation: Wendy Brown has a life expectancy between three and four years. An investor group might offer 40% of her policy's face value.

Say Wendy owns a $300,000 life insurance policy. She might get $120,000 (40%) because the investors hope to collect $300,000 in a relatively short time.

On the other hand, suppose Victor Green has a 12-year life expectancy. He might be offered only $45,000 (15%) for a $300,000 policy.

The type of policy you hold also may affect the price you receive. Universal life (permanent life insurance that provides the owner flexibility in paying premiums) and convertible term life (term life insurance that can be switched to permanent life, at the owner's request, without a medical exam) are the most attractive policies to potential buyers. Buyers like these types of policies because they generally require relatively low premiums, compared with the death benefit.

Safety first: If you want to put your insurance policy up for sale, work with an experienced life settlement broker, one who will offer the policy to at least 20 potential institutional buyers. Your own life insurance agent, your attorney, or your accountant may provide a referral.

To protect yourself, request that an unrelated third party, such as an attorney or bank, hold the buyer's funds in escrow. Then your insurance policy can be placed in escrow and the sale can be concluded.

This process can make sure that the money really is available and, since you are not dealing directly with the buyer, that your privacy is not unduly compromised.

Insurance Claims That Can Kill Your Coverage: What to Do...

J.D. Howard, executive director of the Insurance Consumer Advocate Network, which provides information for consumers on insurance, Branson West, Missouri, *www. ican2000.com*. Howard has worked in the insurance industry since 1965, mainly as an insurance adjuster.

Prepare to be punished when you submit an automobile or homeowner's insurance claim. Insurance companies often raise rates or even decline to renew policies when customers dare to use their coverage. *Claims that are likely to backfire...*

RISKY AUTO INSURANCE CLAIMS

In many states, auto insurance companies can cancel a driver's policy simply because he/she makes too many claims—sometimes as few as three. The companies also can substantially increase policy premiums.

Helpful: A few insurers, including Allstate (800-255-7828, *www.allstate.com*) and AARP and The Hartford (888-808-5254, *www.aarp. thehartford.com*), do not raise their rates after a driver's first accident claim.*

Claims particularly likely to lead to substantially higher auto insurance rates...

•**Accidents caused by poorly maintained vehicles.** Do expect your insurance company's claims adjuster to take a close look at your vehicle if you report that a mechanical problem caused your accident. Your rates are likely to increase substantially if the adjuster discovers that there was indeed a mechanical problem and it was the result of poor vehicle maintenance. Drivers who do not take care of their vehicles are at greater risk for future accidents.

Example: You tell the insurer that your accident was the result of brake failure. The insurance inspector discovers that the brake pads should have been replaced long ago.

•**Suspicious vandalism claims.** Insurance companies are very suspicious when vehicles

*Offers subject to change.

with fading paint are "keyed" (scratched by a vandal)...when worn-out tires are slashed...or when poor engine performance is claimed to have been from someone putting sugar into the gas tank. Such acts of vandalism are often the work of dishonest car owners who want their insurance companies to pay for otherwise uncovered repairs.

If the police are willing to write the incident up as an act of vandalism, the insurance company is likely to accept the decision and not increase the policyholder's rates very much. But if the police are not notified of the incident or the police report suggests that insurance fraud is possible, the policyholder's rates will increase dramatically.

RISKY HOMEOWNER'S CLAIMS

Rule of thumb: To avoid unnecessary rate increases, it typically makes sense to pay home repair bills out of your own pocket if the cost is less than three times the size of the insurance policy's deductible. Generally, choose a deductible equal to about two weeks' salary or as much as your budget will allow.

If you must make a homeowner's insurance claim that you think will put you at risk for cancellation, apply for a new policy through an independent agent *before* the current policy approaches its renewal date. By acting preemptively, you can honestly answer "no" to the application question, "Have you ever had your policy canceled?"

Certain types of homeowner's claims are particularly likely to result in policy cancellations or big rate increases...

•**Maintenance claims.** Home owners sometimes submit insurance claims for repair bills stemming from poor home maintenance. Such bills are not covered by homeowner's insurance, and filing these claims could increase your rates. Home owners who do not keep up with necessary home maintenance are viewed as increased risks by their insurers.

Example: Expect a visit from an insurance company inspector when you submit a claim for water damage. If the inspector finds old, corroding pipes, a decrepit roof or other problems that suggest additional water damage claims might be in your home's future, your policy might not get renewed. Or, the company might send a letter listing specific improvements that must be made to maintain your policy.

• **"Slip and fall" claims.** You and your insurance company might be liable if someone is injured while on your property, assuming that the injury was caused from a dangerous condition. If an insurance company inspector discovers that your property is poorly maintained, your policy might not be renewed at an attractive rate, if at all.

• **Dog bites.** Your insurance company will very likely not renew your coverage if you file any claim related to your dog biting someone —even the first time you put in such a claim. The insurer might not cancel your policy outright midterm unless you lied about owning a dog—but in some cases, it might. Also, insurance companies keep lists of "do not insure" breeds based on what breeds are most often implicated in that company's claims.

More from J.D. Howard…

How to Find the Best Auto Insurer

Some insurance companies make an honest effort to look out for their customers' interests while others mostly look out for their own bottom lines. *Shrewd ways to tell which are which…*

• **Check the level of customer complaints.** Call your state's department of insurance and ask which insurers have the lowest rates of customer complaints.

In many states, Amica (800-242-6422, *www. amica.com*) has the most-satisfied customers. Other auto insurance companies with generally low rates of customer complaints are Erie (800-458-0811, option 1, ext. 3040, *www.erie insurance.com*) and State Farm (contact a local agent for a quote, *www.statefarm.com*).

• **Check the customer satisfaction ratings.** Business research firm JD Power and Associates produces its own annual survey of auto insurance customer satisfaction. Its most recent ratings are available at *www.jdpower.com/ autos/ratings/autos-insurance*. Amica, State

Farm, Erie, Auto-Owners and American National Property and Casualty ranked highest in the most recent survey.

• **Get recommendations from body shop managers or owners.** Ask which insurers treat their customers well and which try to cut corners on repairs.

Drive Less, Pay Less

Nancy Dunnan, a New York City–based financial and travel adviser and author or coauthor of 25 books, including *How to Invest $50–$5,000* (HarperCollins).

There is a "drive less, pay less" benefit available at various companies. Pay-as-you-drive (PAYD) insurance is logical in that the more you drive, the more likely it is that you will have an accident. *Here are two plans* (check with your insurance company to see if it offers a similar one)…*

• **Progressive Insurance Corp.** provides a MyRate plan in Alabama, Kentucky, Louisiana, Maryland, Michigan, Minnesota, New Jersey and Oregon. To participate, you must install a device (sent to you free by the company) in your car that tracks mileage, how aggressively you drive (such as how often you slam on the brakes) and when you drive (commuting hours are most expensive). If your car was made after 1996, it probably has an OnBoard Diagnostic port to which the MyRate device can be connected.

The company then reviews all the collected information and lets you know how much of a discount you're entitled to. To get the best discount, keep your mileage down and avoid excessive acceleration, hard braking, driving during peak hours and driving after midnight.

Details: 800-776-4737, *www.progressive.com/ myrate*.

• **GMAC** offers a similar program available in 34 states. You must own a GM car that is equipped with the OnStar navigation system, which verifies your mileage. GMAC says that

*Offers subject to change.

you can save up to 54% on premiums if you drive less than 15,000 miles annually. And you receive a 26% initial discount for enrolling in the low mileage program. Unlike Progressive, GMAC tracks only mileage.

Details: 877-469-5619, *www.lowmileage discount.com.*

Note: For both programs, you receive an initial discount just for enrolling. After six months of having your driving habits monitored, the discount will either increase or decrease.

How to Save on Car Insurance If You're Out of Work

Driving less could save you an average of 5% to 15% on auto insurance rates,* which are based in part on how much you drive. If you've lost your job, call your insurance company and explain how many fewer miles you're driving because you no longer drive to work. Ask for a lower rate to reflect your new circumstances.

J. Robert Hunter, director of insurance, Consumer Federation of America, Washington, DC.

*Rates subject to change.

New Danger on The Roads

The number of uninsured motorists on the roads is rising as the recession worsens. About one in seven drivers is without coverage.

Self-defense: Carry uninsured-motorist coverage. The insurance is mandated in about 20 states and adds about 7% to your premium.*

Robert Hartwig, PhD, CPCU, president of Insurance Information Institute, which serves as a communications arm for the industry, *www.iii.org.* Dr. Hartwig is based in New York City.

*Rates subject to change.

If You Have Teenagers...

Car insurance for teenagers can add 50% to 100% to a family auto insurance bill.*

To keep rates down: Have the teen take a safety course (less than $100)—his/her insurance rates may be discounted by 5% to 15%. Let your insurer know if your child has good grades in school—insurers provide "good student" discounts for teens who maintain grade-point averages of B or better. Allow your child to drive only the car that is the least expensive to insure. Put the teen's insurance on hold when he is away at college. If your child is involved in a car accident, ask about "accident forgiveness" programs to prevent your premiums from rising.

The Wall Street Journal, 200 Liberty St., New York City, *http://online.wsj.com.*

*Rates subject to change.

Do You Need Umbrella Coverage?

Home owners probably need "umbrella" insurance protection. This is low-cost protection that can provide millions of dollars of liability coverage on top of your regular homeowner's and auto insurance.

Example: A visitor to your home is injured and suffers $250,000 of harm for which you are held liable. If your homeowner's insurance offers only $100,000 of coverage for such claims, you will be liable for the rest. But if you have an umbrella policy, it will cover the liability.

Cost: Only a few hundred dollars per year* can buy a million dollars or more of umbrella coverage—cheap enough to be well worth the cost to anyone with valuable assets to protect.

See your insurance adviser for details.

Ken and Daria Dolan, Florida-based hosts of a nationally syndicated weekly radio call-in show, *The Dolans, www.dolans.com.*

*Price subject to change.

Five Ways to Cut Home Insurance Costs

To reduce home insurance premiums, don't insure the land under your house…insure the full cost of rebuilding your home, and not its market value…increase your deductible—increasing it from $500 to $1,000 may reduce premiums by as much as 20%*…get discounts—some insurers provide premium reductions when home security systems and smoke detectors are installed, when homes are "disaster-proofed" with storm shutters, etc. or when a central monitoring system is installed that can shut off water if there is a leak or raise the house temperature if it drops too low… and buy home insurance from the same firm that provides your auto and other insurance (e.g., an umbrella liability policy) for additional discounts.

Insurance Information Institute, *www.iii.org*.

*Rates subject to change.

Should You Get Cell Phone Insurance?

Cell phone insurance makes sense only if you are hard on phones and tend to lose or break them once or twice a year. In addition to the typical $5 monthly charge, you pay a deductible for the replacement phone—$25 or $50.* The replacements often are refurbished phones. If your model is no longer made, the insurer will provide a comparable newer model or an upgrade.

Helpful: Take advantage of your carrier's online backup service. It allows you to store your phone data on the Web so that you can recover your information and quickly program a new phone if yours breaks or is lost. Some

*Rates subject to change.

carriers offer this for free, but others charge about $2 a month.

Joni Blecher, the editorial director for LetsTalk.com, a San Francisco–based independent online retailer of wireless products and services.

Insurance Safety

David F. Babbel, PhD, a professor emeritus of insurance and risk management at Wharton School of Business, University of Pennsylvania, Philadelphia. He is also a senior adviser at CRA International, New York City.

All the trouble with AIG, the huge insurer, may have people worried about their own insurance companies. If they fail, what will happen to your policies and annuities?

As long as you use an insurer registered in the state where you live and your premium payments are up-to-date, your policies will remain in force, and payouts on annuities and other claims will continue without interruption. That's because states require insurance companies to set aside enough reserves even in bankruptcy to guarantee they can meet obligations to policyholders.

If the reserves of the insurance company aren't enough to cover claims and payouts due to fraud or mismanagement of investments, you have an additional layer of protection. Guaranty associations, funded by other insurers in your state, exist to cover shortfalls, either within policy limits or limits set by state laws.

Typical: Life insurance policy death benefits are generally guaranteed up to $300,000, and cash surrender or withdrawal value of life insurance up to $100,000…$100,000 for withdrawal and cash value of annuities (20 states provide annuity coverage limits of $300,000 to $500,000)…$100,000 for health insurance benefits…$300,000 for homeowner's and auto policies.

To find out the guaranteed coverage in your state, go to *www.nolhga.com*, 703-481-5206 (life/health/annuities) or *www.ncigf.org*, 317-464-8199 (property/casualty).

9

Tax Tune-Up

Greatest Tax Loopholes Of All Time

The Tax Code is full of loopholes—they just need to be sought out. *Here are some of the greatest tax loopholes I have come across in my practice of advising clients...*

Loophole: **When taking a lump sum distribution, instead of rolling over company stock you have in your 401(k) plan to an IRA, have the company give you the shares, and hold them in a taxable account.**

When you do this, you pay ordinary income tax at the time of the distribution only on the tax basis of the stock when it was put into the 401(k) account (plus an early withdrawal penalty if you're under age 59½). You *don't* pay tax at that time on the built-up appreciation.

That built-up appreciation isn't taxed until you sell the stock—and then it is taxed at favorable long-term capital gains rates. If you've had the stock for at least one year and a day, any additional appreciation will be similarly tax favored.

Example: You receive a distribution of 1,000 shares of your employer's stock from your 401(k) plan with a tax basis of $20,000 and a $100,000 current value. You will immediately owe ordinary income tax on $20,000, and may also owe a 10% early withdrawal penalty on that amount. The $80,000 appreciation is not recognized. When the shares are sold, proceeds over the $20,000 will be taxed as described above. If the shares are retained until death, your heirs will receive a stepped-up basis.

Note: If these shares are transferred to an IRA rollover account, any capital gains tax benefit is lost and there will be no basis step up

Edward Mendlowitz, CPA, partner in the CPA firm WithumSmith+Brown in New Brunswick, New Jersey, ranked among the top 35 accounting firms in the US by the industry's leading publications, *www.withum.com*. He has more than 40 years of public accounting experience and is author of numerous books, including *The Adviser's Guide to Family Business Succession Planning* (American Institute of Certified Public Accountants).

at death, causing the beneficiaries to pay full income tax on any distributions from the IRA.

***Loophole:* Donate appreciated long-term stock, not cash, to your favorite charities.**

When you do this, you can deduct the full fair market value of the shares and owe no capital gains tax on the stock's buildup in value since you bought it.

Example: You own 100 shares of stock purchased 10 years prior for $20 per share. When you donate the shares, now worth $50 each, to charity, you deduct the full $5,000 fair market value—not your $2,000 cost. You also avoid paying capital gains tax on the $3,000 of appreciation in the shares.

***Loophole:* Sell real estate at a gain, but defer paying taxes, by executing a Section 1031 exchange.**

When you exchange real property for "like-kind" property, all taxes are deferred until the second property is sold.

Example: You pay no tax when you swap a motel or warehouse for an apartment or office building because this is considered a "like-kind" exchange.

Caution: You cannot swap tax-free property that is not held for business or investment purposes, such as a vacation home.

Strategy: Property qualifies for a tax-free transfer even if it is sold before the exchange can be completed, as long as the exchange transaction is identified at the closing…the proceeds are held in trust…the exchanged property is identified within 45 days…and the exchange is completed in 180 days.

Note: Consult your tax adviser for details.

***Loophole:* Beneficiaries inheriting partnership or LLC shares can "step up" the basis of a deceased's interest by a Section 754 election.**

Stepped-up basis refers to increasing the basis of the underlying property to reflect the price paid or value when inherited. This should be done when the value of the underlying assets, such as real estate, is higher than the deceased partner's or member's basis in the entity. The election, made by the partnership on behalf of the new partner or member (beneficiary), permits the business to take bigger depreciation deductions that are then passed through to the beneficiary.

***Loophole:* Plan your asset allocation to maximize tax benefits.**

Invest your tax-deferred accounts, such as a 401(k) and a regular IRA, in higher-yielding fixed-income securities and in certificates of deposit, and invest non–tax-deferred accounts in assets that are lower-yielding but capital-gains–producing.

Reason: Realized long-term capital gains and dividends are taxed at favorable tax rates—a maximum of 15% federal tax—when held in taxable accounts. Unrealized capital gains are not taxed at all until the asset is sold.

Contrast: Capital gains in a tax-deferred account will be taxed at much higher ordinary income tax rates when distributed from those accounts.

***Loophole:* Make a Section 83(b) election to minimize tax when you receive restricted stock or stock options from your employer or exercise incentive stock options.**

This election will permit you to use tax-favored capital gains rates when you eventually dispose of the stock (or pay lower alternative minimum tax with respect to incentive stock options). On the sale of the shares, the election means that you pay tax at capital gains rates on the difference between the sales proceeds from the shares and your basis, which includes the amount taken when you made the 83(b) election.

Note: The election has to be made within 30 days of the receipt of the option or restricted stock.

More from Edward Mendlowitz, CPA…

The IRA Loophole That Lets You Make Back What You Lost And Other Shrewd Moves

This has been a year of losses for so many taxpayers…stocks have fallen to multiyear lows…values of homes have plunged. But there are ways to use losses to capture valuable tax benefits. *While you wait for the stock market to turn around, take these steps before filing your tax return…*

BENEFIT FROM LOSSES

If you hold stocks, bonds or fund shares in a taxable account, those securities now may trade at lower prices than the amounts you paid for them.

What to do: Sell some of them now to realize a "capital loss" for tax purposes.

Here is how this can help you. When you prepare your 2009 tax return, you'll tabulate your realized capital gains (from assets you sold at a profit) and losses for the year. If you have more losses than gains, you'll have a net loss, meaning that no capital gains tax will be due. What's more, up to $3,000 of your net capital losses can be deducted to offset your salary and other ordinary income each year, further reducing your tax.

Excess losses can be carried forward to future years. These losses can offset gains that you take, as well as up to $3,000 of other income each year.

Strategy: After taking a capital loss, immediately buy a similar but not identical security or fund. (If you buy something "identical" within 30 days, the capital loss won't count, because of the *wash sale rule*, but if you buy something similar, the loss will count.)

Example: You sell three health-care stocks and take capital losses. Then you reinvest in an exchange-traded fund (ETF) that tracks a health-care index, such as Vanguard Health Care ETF (VHT). You'll have your capital losses —and the tax benefits they provide—yet you'll still be in a position to gain if health-care stocks rebound.

Also, when you reinvest in a similar security, the makeup of your portfolio won't substantially change and you'll have the same exposure to market risk.

BEWARE OF DISTRIBUTIONS

Mutual fund investors may receive capital gains distributions from their funds in late 2009. Those distributions will be taxable even if your fund shares lost value in 2009.

Why this happens: Many investors bailed out of stock mutual funds when the stock market tanked. To pay these investors, funds had to sell their holdings. If a mutual fund winds up its year with a net profit on those sales, that profit has to be passed through to its investors. These investors, in turn, owe tax on the distributions (assuming that the fund shares are held in a taxable account).

Strategy: If you plan to sell mutual fund shares for a capital loss, complete the sale before the "record date" of the fund's distribution. That date will be posted on the fund's Web site. Selling before the distribution allows you to avoid the taxable gains.

After selling a mutual fund at a loss, you can invest in a similar mutual fund without jeopardizing your taxable loss, as explained above. You might sell one large-cap growth fund and buy another large-cap growth fund.

However, if you reinvest too soon, you might pick up the taxable distribution from the new mutual fund. Instead, hold the money in an interest-bearing account until after the new mutual fund makes its capital gains distribution.

CHEAPER IRA CONVERSIONS

If your modified adjusted gross income (MAGI) is lower than $100,000 for 2009 (not counting the conversion), you can convert all or part of a traditional IRA to a Roth IRA.

Advantage: After five years and after age 59½, all withdrawals from a Roth IRA become tax free.

The sagging stock market helps with conversions. You pay tax when you convert a traditional IRA to a Roth IRA. The less valuable your traditional IRA at the time you convert it, the less you'll owe in tax.

Situation: Paul had $100,000 in his traditional IRA in early 2009. All of the money in the account came from various tax-deductible contributions.

If Paul had converted his entire IRA at that time, it would have counted as $100,000 of additional taxable income for 2009. In his 28% tax bracket, Paul would have owed $28,000 in tax on the conversion.

Better deal: Suppose that Paul didn't convert his IRA and that it now is worth only $60,000 because the market has dropped. A Roth IRA conversion now would cost him only $16,800 in tax (28% of $60,000).

Added advantage: All Roth IRA conversions in 2009 have a January 1, 2009, starting date for purposes of the five-year requirement mentioned above. Thus, Paul will meet the five-year test for tax-free income on January 1, 2014, just a little more than four years from now.

Loophole: What if Paul's IRA continues to lose value after he converts it to a Roth IRA? He can "recharacterize" (undo) a 2009 conversion at any time up to October 15, 2010, and retrieve any tax already paid on the conversion.

After waiting more than 30 days, he can re-convert the account to a Roth IRA and pay less tax if the account's value is still depressed. That will be a 2010 transaction if the reconversion occurs before December 31, 2010.

BEAT ESTATE TAX

Real estate has lost value, too.

Strategy: Lock in today's low value for estate tax purposes.

How: Sell your principal residence or vacation home to your children.

If housing values rebound in the future, the growth (and future income taxes, if any) will belong to your children, the new owners—and it will be out of your estate.

One approach is to use a self-canceling installment note (SCIN) to sell property to your children. A SCIN is an installment sale that is stretched out over more than one year. If you die before all of the payments have been made, the outstanding payments will be canceled. The value of unpaid installments won't be included in your taxable estate.

Requirements: The children, who will benefit if any of the outstanding payments are canceled, must pay more with an SCIN than they would with a regular installment sale, one that is not self-canceling. They might pay a higher purchase price or a higher interest rate than the current market would dictate. This is determined by the judgment of the sellers.

Advantage: You can live in or use the house after the sale as long as a fair rent is paid to the new owners—your children. These payments will remove still more wealth from your taxable estate.

It is true that any debt forgiveness resulting from the SCIN will result in a taxable gain. However, that gain might be taxed at the favorable long-term capital gains rate, 15%. Talk

with a knowledgeable tax adviser about your specific situation.

Also from Edward Mendlowitz...

Just Say "No" to the IRS

It amazes me to hear people brag about the size of their tax refunds. If you'll get a big refund this year, you made the IRS an interest-free loan. Why subsidize the IRS? You're better off with the use of your own money throughout the year, money that you might invest or use to pay down debt.

If you are an employee, get IRS Form W-4, *Employee's Withholding Allowance Certificate*, from your employer or at the IRS's Web site, *www.irs.gov*. Page through the worksheets to see how many personal exemptions you can claim. The more tax exemptions you take, the less money will be withheld from each paycheck and the more you'll take home month to month.

Say you just bought a house. Considering all your deductions for mortgage interest and property tax, you might owe very little income tax.

You could wind up claiming 10 personal exemptions even if you don't have a large family. Don't let anyone at your company talk you out of claiming those exemptions on a W-4. By claiming the number of exemptions these worksheets point you toward, you'll enjoy the tax savings to which you're entitled in every paycheck.

Caution: Don't claim excess exemptions—you could end up owing a lot of tax when you file your return, and you might owe an underpayment penalty.

Pitfall for the self-employed: Doing the wrong thing with your quarterly estimated tax payments. One year, you pay too little and have to pay an underpayment penalty. The next year, you pay much more in estimated taxes to avoid a penalty and effectively make an interest-free loan to the IRS, just like an employee with paycheck overwithholding.

To avoid this trap, project your annual self-employment income throughout the year. If your income is going to be less than last year's income, adjust your estimated tax payments so you pay only enough estimated tax to total 90% of your tax liability for the year.

On the other hand, if your income for the current year will be higher than last year's, pay enough estimated tax to match 100% of the total tax you paid last year. If your adjusted gross income last year was more than $150,000, pay 110% of last year's tax bill via estimated tax.

Note: A new special rule on estimated taxes applies to some small-business owners. Talk to your tax adviser.

Bigger Tax Breaks From the IRS

Barbara Weltman, Esq., an attorney based in Millwood, New York, and author of *J.K. Lasser's 1001 Deductions and Tax Breaks* (Wiley). She is also publisher of the free online newsletter, *Big Ideas for Small Business*, at *www. barbaraweltman.com.*

Good news for taxpayers—the IRS provides cost-of-living adjustments to tax provisions for 2009. *Key changes...*

• **Bigger 401(k) contributions.** The maximum employee contribution to 401(k) plans goes up in 2009 to $16,500 (from $15,500 in 2008). Those age 50 or beyond by the end of 2009 can make an additional $5,500 of contributions (up from $5,000 in 2008), for a total of $22,000.

• **Higher standard deductions.** The amount taxpayers can write off on their returns in lieu of itemizing their tax deductions—the standard deduction—increases in 2009 to $11,400 for married couples filing jointly and $5,700 for singles (up from $10,900 and $5,450 respectively). Taxpayers age 65 or older and/or who are blind can take an additional standard deduction amount of $1,100 for joint filers and $1,400 for singles, up from $1,050 and $1,350, respectively, in 2008.

Additional write-off: Home owners who do not itemize their personal deductions can add another $500 ($1,000 for joint filers) to their standard deduction amount for real estate taxes that they pay in 2009.

• **Increased earnings limit for Social Security recipients who work.** While those who have attained full retirement age (for example, 66 years for those born in 1943 to 1954) can earn any amount from a job or self-employment without losing Social Security benefits, younger recipients lose $1 of benefit for each $2 of earnings over a limit. For 2009, this limit increases to $14,160 a year of earnings (up from $13,560 a year in 2008).

• **More freedom from the "kiddie tax."** Children under 18 and dependents under 24 who are full-time students pay income taxes at their parents' highest tax rate on investment income over a threshold amount. This amount increases in 2009 to $1,900 (up from $1,800 in 2008).

Example: With a 5% rate of investment return, a child would need $38,000 in investments to become subject to the kiddie tax in 2009.

• **Larger tax-free gifts.** You can give up to a fixed amount annually (called an exclusion) to as many recipients as you want free from gift tax each year. This annual gift-tax exclusion is $13,000 in 2009 (up from $12,000 in 2008). In addition to the annual exclusion, you can use a lifetime exemption to make tax-free gifts— the lifetime exemption remains at $1 million and is not adjusted for inflation.

More from Barbara Weltman, Esq....

Charitable Deduction for License Plates

If your state lets you obtain a plate supporting a cause—autism, breast cancer, wildlife, the arts—and it gives part of your fee to that cause, you can claim that part as a charitable contribution deduction if you itemize deductions on Schedule A of Form 1040.

To learn custom plate options and the portion of the fees that goes to charity, check with your state's department of motor vehicles.

Stimulus Tax Breaks: The Fine Print

Clint Stretch, JD, managing principal, tax policy, at the tax advisory firm Deloitte Tax LLP, Washington, DC, *www.deloitte.com.*

You've read about the tax breaks in the Obama administration's $787 billion economic stimulus plan, and you have probably tried to add up what's in it for you. But be careful doing the math—almost all the new breaks have limitations and catches. *Details you need to know…*

• **Work credit.** Taxpayers who work are entitled to a tax credit of up to $400 (single) or $800 (married filing jointly) in both 2009 and 2010.

Catch: To get the full credit, your adjusted gross income (AGI) must be less than $75,000 (single) or $150,000 (joint). To get any credit, these limits are $95,000 (single) and $190,000 (joint). Employees will receive their credits by reductions in withholding starting April 1, but self-employed taxpayers will have to adjust their quarterly estimated taxes themselves.

• **Social Security payment.** Social Security recipients, disabled veterans and recipients of Supplemental Security Income will get a one-time payment of $250. The payment will come from the Social Security Administration or the Department of Veterans Affairs, not the IRS.

Catch: If you're eligible for the work credit while collecting Social Security, you can't get both that credit and the $250.

• **First-time home buyer credit.** Depending on their income, first-time home buyers—which actually means those people who haven't owned a principal residence for three years—who purchase their homes between January 1 and November 30, 2009, are eligible for an $8,000 tax credit ($4,000 for single filers or married filing separately).

Catch: The credit phases out at AGIs between $75,000 and $95,000 (single), $150,000 and $170,000 (joint). Unlike last year's $7,500 credit, this one doesn't have to be repaid, unless you sell the house for a gain within three years or stop using it as your principal residence.

• **Home owners.** The tax break every home owner can get regardless of their income is a tax credit (up to $1,500) for energy-saving improvements, such as an energy-efficient furnace, insulation and storm windows, made to a home in 2009 and 2010.

Catch: You can't claim more than $1,500 of credit over the *two* years. And watch out for the heightened standards for qualified energy-efficient property.

• **Higher-education credit.** Parents of college-age students are eligible for up to $2,500 per year, per student in tax credit for education expenses.

Catch: This credit is phased out for taxpayers with AGIs between $80,000 and $90,000 (single), $160,000 and $180,000 (joint)…and you cannot take the credit for anything other than a list of specific "qualifying expenses." See IRS Publication 970, *Tax Benefits for Education*, the section on the Hope credit.

• **New-car buyers.** State and local sales and excise taxes paid on new cars and light trucks bought after February 17, 2009, through the end of the year are federally deductible, even for taxpayers who don't itemize.

Catch: Used cars don't qualify for the deduction, the deduction is limited to tax on a maximum of $49,500 per vehicle and the deduction phases out for taxpayers with AGIs between $125,000 and $135,000 (single filers), $250,000 and $260,000 (joint filers).

Hidden Traps in Buying a Hybrid Car

James Glass, Esq., a tax attorney based in New York City and a contributing writer to *Bottom Line/Wealth.*

Due to recent high gas prices, vehicles with fuel-saving "hybrid" gas-electric power have become popular—especially since a federal tax credit of up to $3,400 is available for hybrids. But there are *traps* in this credit—and even with high gas prices, a hybrid may not save all the money you would think.

TAX SURPRISES

In most cases, the size of the federal hybrid-vehicle tax credit is much lower than $3,400 because it varies with each vehicle's fuel efficiency. Also, you may not be able to claim the credit at all. *Possible problems...*

•**The tax credit for the hybrid you want doesn't exist.** The law limits the number of vehicles each hybrid car manufacturer sells that are eligible for the credit—and reduces the credit as that number is approached. For the most popular hybrids, the credit has already been eliminated. *Examples...*

•The Toyota Prius (about 47 mpg combined city/highway driving) and other Toyota hybrids are no longer eligible for any credit.

•The credit for the Honda Civic hybrid (about 42 mpg) and other Honda hybrids has also been eliminated.

The tax-credit status of all hybrids is available online at *www.fueleconomy.gov* (click on "Hybrid Vehicles/Tax Incentives").

•**You are subject to the alternative minimum tax (AMT).** The hybrid tax credit isn't allowed at all under AMT rules.

COST SURPRISES

Hybrids are expensive compared with non-hybrid vehicles of similar size and features—and their higher purchase cost can eat up their gas savings.

The vehicle information Web site Edmunds.com calculates vehicles' total cost of ownership, including gasoline (at different prices), depreciation, financing, taxes, fees, insurance premiums, maintenance and repairs. Hybrids rated according to these criteria rank below other popular nonhybrid cars. The best-ranked hybrid, the Honda Civic Hybrid, places only 14th, followed by the Prius at 34th and the Nissan Altima Hybrid (about 34 mpg) at 66th, all in the gasoline-at-$4-per-gallon category. (Rankings include the effect of the federal hybrid credit.)

In contrast, the conventional Honda Civic ranked fifth in total cost of ownership, meaning that it will likely be a better financial deal than its hybrid sibling. Even if gasoline rises to $6 a gallon, the conventional Civic will still cost less to own than the hybrid version.

Wisest move: You may have environmental, social or political reasons for buying a hybrid vehicle, but when comparing costs, look at total ownership costs, not just gas mileage—and don't count on a tax credit for it.

Note: Some states offer tax breaks to hybrid buyers—Connecticut is one example. For tax breaks in your state, visit the "State & Federal Incentives & Laws" Web page on the US Department of Energy site at *www.eere.energy.gov/afdc/incentives_laws.html*.

More from James Glass, Esq....

Overseas Accounts Targeted by IRS

Assets held in overseas accounts are an increasing target for the IRS. Any US taxpayer with an overseas account that exceeds $10,000 at any time during the year must disclose the account to the IRS by both checking the appropriate box on Schedule B of Form 1040, *US Individual Income Tax Return*, and by filing form TDF 90-22.1, *Report of Foreign Bank and Financial Accounts*, by June 30 of the following year. Failure to do so can lead to penalties of up to $500,000 plus prison terms of up to five years. This rule applies even to US citizens who are living overseas and doing their banking locally.

Vacation Home and Travel Tax Breaks

Laurence I. Foster, CPA/PFS, tax consultant based in New York City and former partner at KPMG LLP. Foster was chairman of the Personal Financial Specialist Credential Committee of the American Institute of Certified Public Accountants.

Summertime is the prime time for many people to enjoy vacation homes and travel. And vacation time is even more enjoyable if you can finance it with tax-free income and take tax deductions for your expenses. *Opportunities...*

HOME AND VACATION HOME

• **Tax-free income from your home or vacation home.** If you rent out your home and/or a second home that you own (such as a vacation home) to others for fewer than 15 days during the year, the rental income you receive is totally tax free—you don't even have to report it on your tax return. This is one of the simplest and best tax breaks in the Tax Code.

Vacation planning: If any special event (sports competition, concert, etc.) draws tourists to the area where you live, or there is a "high season" during which rentals are highest where your vacation home is located, rent your home/vacation home out at that time for up to two weeks. Use the tax-free income you receive to finance your own vacation.

• **Mortgage deduction for buying a boat, recreational vehicle (RV) or vacation home.** You can deduct interest on a total of up to $1 million of mortgage borrowing used to acquire your primary personal residence and a second residence.

Opportunity: The second residence may be a boat or RV, not just a conventional vacation home. To qualify as a residence, a boat or RV must have "living accommodations," including a sleeping space and kitchen and bathroom facilities, and you must use it *more* than 14 days a year. Property taxes, if any, are deductible on your second residence, including a boat or an RV, too.

• **Vacation home tax shelter.** If you rent out your vacation home for more than 14 days during the year, all of the income that you receive is taxable, but you also become entitled to deduct expenses related to your rental activity.

Examples: Depreciation, maintenance expenses, utilities, insurance, advertising.

To get full deductions, you must limit your own use of the home to no more than the greater of 14 days or 10% of the number of days it is rented to others. If your deductions exceed the rental income you receive, up to $25,000 of this excess can be deducted against your income from other sources, such as salary. (This loss deduction phases out as adjusted gross income increases from $100,000 to $150,000.)

This tax loss deduction can turn your vacation home into a legal tax shelter. You can claim it even as the home appreciates in value and even if it provides you with positive cash flow. (Depreciation is a deduction having no cash cost, so it can result in a tax loss even if rent is giving you net cash income.)

Deduction rules can be complex, so check them in IRS Publication 527, *Residential Rental Property.*

TRAVEL TACTICS

Combining business with pleasure can provide generous business expense deductions for a business trip that has a substantial pleasure element—even if you bring along a personal companion.

Basic rule: If the primary reason for a trip made within the US is for business, you can deduct the full cost of travel to and from your destination and also hotel costs at your destination, even if the trip contains a significant pleasure element.

You can even have days on which you do no business if they are between business days, such as a weekend between a Friday and Monday on which you do business, or a holiday weekday, such as July 4 or Labor Day.

Note: You cannot deduct the extra cost of nonbusiness side trips or purely recreational expenses (such as sports event tickets). If you extend your stay for personal reasons, you can't deduct hotel costs incurred for the extra days.

• **Foreign travel.** Different rules apply when you travel outside the US. You can deduct the full cost of travel to and from your destination if travel is viewed as entirely for business.

Some ways to qualify: Travel lasts no more than seven days...travel is more than a week but you spend no more than 25% of the time on nonbusiness activities.

Business days are those during which you actually perform business. They include days spent traveling to and from your destination, provided the day after you arrive and the day before you leave are days of business. Therefore, plan vacation days in the middle of a trip rather than next to travel days.

If you fail both of these tests, then the tax deduction for travel expense is limited to the proportion of travel expenses that matches the percentage of trip days that were business days, plus actual business day expenses.

Example: You spend 30 days in Paris, 20 of which are business days. You can deduct two-thirds of the cost of traveling there and back, along with the expenses of the 20 business days.

• **Companion's expenses.** If you travel with a companion, you can still deduct the full cost you would have incurred if you had traveled alone—and the extra cost of bringing a spouse along may be slight.

Examples: You can deduct the full cost of a single hotel room, even if a double room costs only a little more…the full cost of a rental car you would incur traveling alone, even if having a companion adds no cost…the full cost of a single airfare, even if the cost of two tickets is little more than one due to a family fare discount.

You can also sometimes claim business meal and entertainment deductions for a spouse (or other personal companion) who travels with you.

Example: Your spouse accompanies you on a business trip and to a business meal and entertainment (M&E) activity (such as a theater performance after the meal) that you attend with a business associate and the associate's spouse. Since the associate's spouse is there, your spouse can be considered to be there on a business basis (to help entertain). Even if the associate does not bring a companion, your spouse's attendance for business purposes— perhaps he or she is a native of the associate's country—might still be allowed. The expense for all four people is deductible under normal M&E rules (with 50% of the cost deductible).

Net result: If you travel with a companion, you may be able to deduct much more than half your total trip cost.

• **Conventions.** If your trip is not to a business meeting but for a business convention held within the "North American area," normal business travel deduction rules apply. This is true even if the convention or seminar is held at a location noted for its entertainment, such as Las Vegas.

The North American area includes Canada, Mexico, several Caribbean nations and certain Pacific Island locations.

Requirement: The business convention or seminar must specifically relate to your business or profession.

If you attend a business convention held outside the North American area, no deduction is allowed unless you show that it is "reasonable for the convention to be held outside of North America"—you must show a justification for its location.

You cannot deduct trips for personal investment purposes (such as conventions, seminars, or shareholder meetings).

For detailed rules about deducting business travel, and exceptions that apply in special circumstances, see IRS Publication 463, *Travel, Entertainment, Gift, and Car Expenses.*

Get a Bigger Tax Deduction for Donated Clothing

William R. Lewis, CPA, CFP, an accountant in Lincoln, Nebraska, with more than 30 years of experience. He is author of *Money for Your Used Clothing*, a booklet published annually since 1990 with up-to-date used-clothing valuations for tax purposes (Certified Used Clothing Values, Inc.). His Web site is *www.mfyuc.com.*

That clothing packed away in your attic could be worth hundreds or even thousands of dollars in tax deductions, much more than it would bring at a garage sale. Simply donate those clothes to a charity, such as Goodwill Industries or the Salvation Army.

According to IRS rules, you are allowed to deduct the "fair market value" of clothing— the amount that it would sell for in a thrift or consignment store. Trouble is, most taxpayers assign lower values to their donated clothing —and pay higher taxes as a result.

Below is a sampling of fair-market values of common used clothes based on nationwide thrift and consignment store prices. You also can locate fair-market values at charity Web sites, including *www.goodwill.org* and *www. salvationarmyusa.org*. When donating your clothes, write up a list of all the items, with fair-market value assigned to each one. Get your list signed and dated by the charity.

Important rules: You must file Form 8283, *Noncash Charitable Contributions*, with your taxes if you claim property donations of more than $500 in a year. An independent appraisal is required if total noncash donations come to more than $5,000. Your charitable contribution tax deductions cannot exceed 50% of your Adjusted Gross Income in any year. If they do, the excess contributions could be applied to future tax years.

MEN'S CLOTHING

	Condition	
	Like New	Good
Two-piece suit	$51	$41
Sport coat	$20	$18
Long-sleeve dress shirt	$16	$11
Blue jeans	$15	$10
Silk tie	$10	$8

WOMEN'S CLOTHING

	Condition	
	Like New	Good
Two-piece suit	$40	$26
Long-sleeve dress shirt	$14.50	$10.50
Casual dress	$22	$13.50
Blue jeans	$16	$10
Leather dress shoes	$20	$11

CHILDREN'S CLOTHING

	Condition			
	Like New		Good	
	Boys	Girls	Boys	Girls
Long-sleeve pullover sweater	$7	$9.50	$5	$7.50
Long-sleeve casual shirt	$6	$8.50	$4	$6.50
T-shirt	$4	$2.50	$2	$1.50
Blue jeans	$8	$11.50	$5	$9.50
Dress shoes	$8	$10	$5.50	$7.50

Gambling Winnings Must Be Reported

Gambling winnings are taxable and must be reported as *Other Income* on the first page of your tax return. The amount won is the net gain—how much you took home, including fair-market value of noncash prizes, minus the cost of making your wagers. Casinos, racetracks and other gambling facilities are required to report winnings beyond certain thresholds directly to the IRS—their requirements vary by type of gambling activity. Gambling losses are deductible (as an itemized tax deduction) up to the amount of gambling winnings in any given tax year. Save all the records associated with wagers made for gambling activities in case of an audit.

Bob D. Scharin, JD, senior tax analyst, RIA, business unit of Thomson Corporation, provider of tax information and software to tax professionals, New York City.

Tax-Free Damages For Physical Injury

Robert W. Wood, Esq., partner, Wood & Porter, 333 Sacramento St., San Francisco 94111. The firm's Web site is *www.woodporter.com*.

Damages received for personal injury are tax free only when the injury is "physical." In 1996, Congress adopted this rule in the Tax Code to end excessive claims of tax-free damages for emotional distress and other forms of mental harm. In enforcing this rule, the IRS has strictly insisted that an injury be "visible" to be deemed physical.

Situation: A woman was given damages for being sexually abused by an employer, the abuse consisting of lewd remarks and improper physical contact. The physical contacts resulted in no injury or visible marks. Then, one day, an assault *did* result in a visible physical injury.

IRS ruling: The damages the woman received allocable to the period before the date of the visible injury were taxable, and those allocable to that date and later were tax free. (*Letter Ruling* 200041022)

Problem: Damages may be received for a physical injury that is no longer visible at the time a case is pursued. Thus, it might be impossible to then verify the visible nature of the harm.

New case: An individual recovered damages for sexual abuse. A substantial period of time had elapsed since the wrong occurred. The plaintiff continues to struggle with the trauma resulting from the wrongful act.

The IRS said in such a case "it is reasonable …to presume that the settlement compensated [the plaintiff] for personal physical injuries, and that all damages for emotional distress were attributable to the physical injuries."

Thus, all the damages are free of tax, even though no visible physical injury was ever proven to exist, but was only reasonably presumed. (*IRS Legal Memorandum* 200809001)

Tax Break for Widowed Home Owners

A home can now be sold anytime within two years of a spouse's death for the surviving spouse to shelter profits up to $500,000 from taxes. Home owners used to be required to sell in the same year as the spouse's death to be eligible for the $500,000 exclusion. Ask your tax adviser for details.

Sidney Kess, attorney and CPA, New York City. Over the years, he has taught tax law to more than 700,000 tax professionals.

More from Sidney Kess, Esq., CPA…

Tax Cheats Beware

More than 900 cases of taxpayer wrongdoing were reported to the IRS Whistleblower Office in 2008, up from 80 cases the previous year. In 2006, Congress created a new set of "whistleblower" rules which gives those who report tax wrongdoing the right to a reward of 15% to 30% of tax collected as a result,

when wrongdoing exceeds $2 million. If the wrongdoer is an individual, he/she must have income exceeding $200,000. (In smaller cases, the IRS decides whether to pay a reward.) To report wrongdoing and seek a reward, file IRS Form 211, *Application for Award for Original Information*.

Should You Hire a Tax Preparer or Do Your Return Yourself?

Ian M. Weinberg, CFP, chief executive officer of Family Wealth & Pension Management LLC, Woodbury, New York. He advises privately held companies on investing and advanced wealth planning and lectures in the Certified Financial Planning Program at Long Island University, C.W. Post Campus.

When April 15 nears, taxpayers face a decision. Is it worth the expense to hire a tax preparer to do your tax return? Or should you use tax software and do it yourself?

HOW TO DECIDE

Any knowledgeable tax professional might charge $500 or more to prepare your return, depending on its complexity. Big companies, such as H&R Block, might charge somewhat less.

Software, including *TurboTax*, *TaxACT* and *TaxCut*, have various versions ranging in price from $12.95 to $79.95 or more* depending on your tax needs. (*TurboTax* and *TaxACT* also have free versions available.) Thus, a program seems to save you money.

Caution: Such programs are fine for typical taxpayers having straightforward returns. For example, you might have nothing other than W-2 income from your employer, bank account interest income and some basic itemized deductions, such as state income taxes and mortgage interest.

However, taxpayers who have more complex financial situations probably will save more in

*Prices subject to change.

taxes by using a tax preparer than it costs to hire one.

Situation: Jim kept some stock in a brokerage account, but he also held some shares personally, in certificate form. One year, he prepared his own tax return using computer software.

Trap: Although all of Jim's dividend income qualified for the bargain 15% tax rate, his software program applied that lower rate only to the dividends from his certificate shares. On those dividends reported by his broker, Jim's software calculated tax payments at his 35% ordinary tax rate.

Result: Jim overpaid tax on that dividend income by thousands of dollars.

TRICKY TAXES

Complex issues that might be better handled by a tax preparer include...

- **Capital gains.**
- **Sale of a residence.**
- **Rental property losses.**
- **Casualty losses.**
- **Employee business expenses.**
- **Medical costs incurred for a dependent parent.**
- **Margin loan interest.**
- **Investment advisory and other professional fees.**

For these and other complex tax issues, you might want to work with an experienced professional, such as a partner in a certified public accounting (CPA) firm or someone recognized by the IRS as an enrolled agent (EA). To find a good tax preparer, ask trusted professionals you already work with.

THE BEST OF BOTH WORLDS

If you have been in the habit of preparing your own tax return, one strategy to consider is to use a software program, enter the data and prepare a tax return but don't file it. Bring this preliminary return to a tax preparer, on paper or on disk. This approach might save you money if it saves the tax pro time.

For the Quickest Refund...

Martin S. Kaplan, a CPA in private practice in New York City. He is a frequent guest speaker at insurance, banking and financial-planning seminars and author of *What the IRS Doesn't Want You to Know* (Wiley).

I f the IRS owes you a refund, you'll want to get it as quickly as possible. *Most effective ways to do it...*

FILING STRATEGIES

- **File electronically.** This greatly speeds the receipt and processing of your tax return. It also prevents many common filing errors that delay the processing of paper returns—and the receipt of refunds due on them.

Examples of common errors: Omitted forms, math mistakes, missing Social Security numbers for dependents, missing signatures.

Electronically filed tax returns are computer-checked in the filing process, catching these errors before filing. You can file electronically from your home computer using commercial tax preparation software or have your return prepared by a professional who will then file it electronically for you.

File for free: This year, all taxpayers can file electronically for free through the IRS's Free File program. For details, visit the IRS site (*www.irs.gov*) and click on "1040 Central."

- **Receive your refund by direct deposit.** Have the IRS send your tax refund electronically to the bank or investment account you specify, including an IRA, if you wish. You can split a direct-deposit refund among up to three different accounts. This speeds refund delivery and eliminates risk that your refund check will get lost in the mail, misplaced or misappropriated. To request a direct-deposit refund, simply follow the directions in your tax return's instructions.

Payoff: You can get your refund in as little as three weeks by using both electronic filing and direct deposit—compared with six weeks if filing a paper return to get a mailed refund check.

BUSINESS TAXES

Many self-employed people and business owners have been hit hard by the recession.

But there is good news—businesses may have special "fast refund" opportunities.

A regular corporation that overpaid its estimated taxes can get a "quick refund" of them by filing IRS Form 4466, *Corporation Application for Quick Refund of Overpayment of Estimated Tax*, before it files its regular tax return, as soon as its tax year is over. The IRS will act on the request within 45 days.

A business that suffered a loss may be able to claim a refund of taxes paid for the prior two years through a "net operating loss carryback" deduction. *If the business is a...*

•**Regular corporation**—have it file an IRS Form 1139, *Corporation Application for Tentative Refund*. The IRS will act on this request within 90 days. Form 1139 needs to be filed on or after the filing date of the regular tax return, so file the corporation's return as soon as possible.

•**Proprietorship or pass-through entity** (such as a partnership or S corporation) taxed on your personal return—claim a carryback refund by filing IRS Form 1045, *Application for Tentative Refund*, when you file your personal tax return.

Inside the IRS

In the following articles, Ms. X, Esq., a former IRS agent who is still well connected, reveals insider secrets from the IRS.

LOST YOUR JOB AND OWE THE IRS MONEY?

When you owe the IRS money and you have lost your job, the IRS does have the authority to place your tax debt in a currently noncollectible status. This essentially means that it will not pursue collection activity (a levy on your bank account, for instance) because doing so would cause you to suffer a financial hardship—for example, you would not be able to pay your rent. If the IRS collection person does not agree to halt collection efforts, then request a collection due process (CDP) hearing. You will then be given an opportunity to

deal with a settlement officer in the appeals division who will reconsider the facts. While the CDP request is pending, the IRS will not take enforced collection action.

Important: Be sure that you properly document your current financial position so that the settlement officer can justify a decision not to pursue collection.

IF YOUR TAX RETURN WAS FRAUDULENTLY PREPARED

The accountant who prepared a fraudulent tax return may be susceptible to pressure from an IRS agent who discovers that he/she helped the taxpayer coordinate a transaction that resulted in tax evasion.

Example: The accountant advised a taxpayer that the business deposits made into a checking account should be classified as loan payments to avoid reflecting them as income on the tax return. When faced with going to jail, the accountant will likely tell the IRS agent everything he wants to hear.

Self-defense: When a tax return was fraudulently prepared, the accountant who prepared it should never represent the taxpayer before the IRS. The taxpayer should hire an experienced tax attorney who will be able to rely on attorney-client privilege to avoid providing incriminating information to the IRS.

STATUTE OF LIMITATIONS TO THE RESCUE

Consider the statute of limitations when the IRS proposes to assess additional tax. The general rule is that the IRS must assess additional income tax within three years from the date your personal income tax return was filed.

Two important exceptions: If you understated your gross income by more than 25%, then the IRS has six years to assess tax. And if your original tax return claimed false deductions or you intentionally failed to report income, then there is no statute of limitations—which means that the IRS can make you pay the extra tax, interest, and penalties whenever it catches up with you.

Fight back: If the IRS claims that your tax return is false or fraudulent, it is the IRS's burden to prove so. Make the IRS meet its burden by insisting, for example, that each item of income it claims you did not report was really income (gifts, loans, and return of capital are not income), and make the IRS prove that you failed to report the income fraudulently rather than because of an honest mistake on your part or an error on the part of your tax preparer.

DEDUCTING MEDICAL EXPENSES EVEN IF YOU ARE NOT SICK

Under IRS rules, a tax deduction will be allowed for an expense paid for the "diagnosis, cure, mitigation, treatment or prevention of disease, for the purpose of affecting any structure or function of the body." What about a pregnancy test? The IRS ruled in *Revenue Ruling 2007-72* that the amount paid for a pregnancy test qualifies as an expense for medical care, since it affects the function of the body.

Also deductible: Although not part of the revenue ruling, whirlpool baths prescribed by a physician and a mattress bought specifically to alleviate an arthritic condition are also deductible.

WINNING THE LOTTERY AND PAYING INCOME TAX

It seems that any number of lucky individuals who have won millions of dollars in state-run lotteries acted recklessly when it came to paying tax on their winnings. Some lottery recipients have taken the tax position that they realized a tax-favored long-term capital gain when they sold their right to receive future annual installments in return for a discounted lump sum payment. Different courts have ruled against these lottery winners by adopting the "substitute for ordinary income" doctrine, which says that capital gains treatment is not available for what would otherwise be received at a future time as ordinary income.

Scams "From the Government"

Increasingly brazen scam artists pose as being from the government (IRS, Social Security Administration, local police or courthouse) to cheat victims out of money and confidential information.

How: They offer to assist with a problem (such as with one's taxes, or an "outstanding violation") or to provide something (a refund, extra benefit payment) if the victim pays a fee and/or provides confidential information (perhaps to "confirm identity").

Self-defense: Unsolicited contacts from government agencies are almost always scams. To find out for sure, call the agency at its publicly published phone number and ask.

Marc Huffman, contributing editor, ConsumerAffairs. com, a free consumer news publication, Washington, DC.

10

Investment Forecast

How to Stay Safe—and Even Profit—in Today's Treacherous Markets

Investors have dramatically altered their views of how to reduce investment risk since the 2008 stock market meltdowns. To help you find better ways to manage risk, reinvigorate your portfolio and take advantage of opportunities, we interviewed one of the most successful and respected risk managers currently in the world, Mohamed El-Erian, chief executive officer and co-chief investment officer of the giant investment management company Pimco. *What he sees ahead...*

RADICAL SHIFTS

We are witnessing huge shifts in the global economy that require *every* investor to adjust his/her portfolio. Over the past 10 years, the world was driven by a huge engine called the US consumer. But as our economic expansion began to slow, Americans were spending far in excess of their incomes. We took on much more financial risk to support our lifestyles. That included no-money-down loans on increasingly expensive homes...high-interest credit card balances...and investments that turned out to be much more vulnerable than we were led to believe. Meanwhile, much of the rest of the world was growing stronger and wealthier. Annual percentage gains in growth in both China and India were greater than in the US in 2007. That will continue even though the US recession is causing a slowdown in such countries.

With the bursting of the housing and credit bubbles, and the continuing transformation of the global economy, the old formulas for risk

---

Mohamed El-Erian, the chief executive officer and co-chief investment officer of Pimco, based in Newport Beach, California. Pimco oversees more than $800 billion in assets. Formerly, El-Erian was president and CEO of Harvard Management Company, which oversees the university's $29.2 billion endowment portfolio. He's also author of the best seller *When Markets Collide: Investment Strategies for the Age of Global Economic Change* (McGraw-Hill). It won the Financial Times and Goldman Sachs Business Book of the Year Award for 2008.

161

management that investors relied on failed in 2008. Take the classic balanced portfolio of 60% stocks (mostly US stocks) and 40% US bonds. So many financial advisers have advocated this allocation for so long because it produced good returns with only moderate risk. That portfolio was down 25% near the end of 2008—the worst performance in more than 30 years. In fact, that portfolio has returned an average of only 2.6% a year over the past decade. Even worse, it's unlikely to protect you any better in the future because it focuses on the way the world used to be, not the way it *will* be.

WHAT TO DO NOW

• **Concentrate on financial safety.** For conservative investors, this means staying in cash until opportunities are more compelling. It is not an exciting strategy, but this is one of those times when return *of* your capital is of much greater concern than return *on* your capital. *What to do…*

• If you currently own investments that you consider to be high quality, even if they are worth far less than you paid for them, hold on to them and wait for an eventual economic recovery.

• If you are in investments that you consider very risky, wait for them to rebound somewhat in a bear-market rally and then sell them, even if you do so at a loss.

• **Resist being seduced by "cheap" stocks.** Based on historical market performance, stocks are bargains right now. So why not buy? Because they could get a lot cheaper. Wall Street's earnings expectations for 2009 are too optimistic as corporate America braces for a nasty recession and more job losses.

Don't worry about missing out on the beginning of a new bull market. The financial system has been too severely damaged to bounce back in a sustained fashion anytime soon.

LONG TERM

I don't know when the current crisis will pass. But I do know that the handoff of wealth among all the nations continues to transform the global financial landscape. To manage your risk most effectively, you need to tap into this transformation. Be willing to introduce new asset classes into your portfolio and practice much, much broader diversification over time.

Concentrate on making the following changes to your portfolio over the next few years…

• **Limit your US stock holdings.** My general recommendation now is to have no more than 15% of an overall financial portfolio in US stocks. This shocks many US investors, but when you look at where the world is heading, it's risky to hold any more than that. Seventy percent of the world's growth will come from the emerging markets in the future. The US economy will provide less than 10% a decade from now.

• **Increase your emerging-market stock holdings.** I recommend investing 15% of your portfolio in stocks of other developed economies and up to 18% in emerging-market stocks. You should no longer consider foreign stocks to be a supplement to your core investments. They should be the core. After several years in which foreign stocks soared, those stocks have pulled back sharply—use this as a gradual buying opportunity. Why invest in emerging economies if they are still volatile and suffered *greater* losses than US stocks in 2008? Because many developing nations are in some ways much stronger financially than the US. The US is more than $10 trillion in debt. China had very little debt and a $534 billion surplus in 2008.

• **Add inflation protection.** Investors can gain inflation protection through a 5% allocation to Treasury Inflation-Protected Securities (TIPS), as well as a 22% exposure to alternative assets, such as real estate and commodities that tend to do well in inflationary environments.

Reason: The massive amount of money that the US is pouring into the financial system will eventually result in inflation. More important, the forces that have kept consumer prices low are now conspiring to push them higher.

PORTFOLIO FOR THE NEW ECONOMY

This model portfolio is geared toward the long-term investor who is looking to generate an annual return of 8% to 10% over the next several years and has the risk tolerance to accept a one-year loss as high as 12%.

Stocks **48%**
US 15%
Foreign stocks in…
    Developed markets 15%
    Emerging markets 18%

Bonds **20%**
US 6%
Foreign 9%
TIPS 5%
Real assets **22%**
Real estate investment trusts 6%
Commodities funds 11%
Infrastructure 5%*
Other **10%**

Conservative investors may keep this 10% in cash and cash equivalents. Aggressive investors may prefer to divide it evenly among the nine asset classes above.

*Infrastructure investments include stocks of utilities ...bonds of water companies, road authorities and airport operations firms...and other infrastructure companies that produce reliable cash flows that tend to rise with inflation.

How to Profit from the Next Big Thing: Invest In Infrastructure

Jason Schwarz, chief investment analyst for Review Services, Inc., a financial-planning and investment management firm located in Brookfield, Wisconsin, *www. reviewservicesinc.com*. He was previously investment strategist for Lone Peak Asset Management in Westlake Village, California.

Back in August 2008, after oil prices hit a record $147 per barrel, investment strategist Jason Schwarz publicly made what seemed to be a ridiculous prediction. He said that oil would plunge to between $30 and $50 a barrel within one year. This forecast turned out to be right on the mark, and Schwarz more than doubled the value of commodities investments at his firm by betting against oil.

Now Schwarz claims that oil is yesterday's news, meaning that there is not much money to be made in betting that it will either soar or plummet. Instead, he has high expectations for infrastructure—the industry that President Barack Obama has stated will be a centerpiece of his multibillion-dollar plan to jump-start the economy. Attractive infrastructure investments include construction and engineering firms

that specialize in building and running public works projects, such as roads, bridges, airports, public school buildings and utility and water systems.

Why Schwarz says his investment focus is shifting and how you can profit...

OIL DEMAND SLACKENS

Even professional investors will be hard-pressed to make money in energy stocks this year. *Oil prices will remain in a trading range between $30 and $50 per barrel for several reasons...*

• **The world is not about to run out of oil.** In fact, new discoveries are plentiful. A find offshore of Brazil may be the world's biggest discovery in 30 years. A trio of oil companies, led by Chevron, has tapped a petroleum pool deep beneath the Gulf of Mexico that could hold up to 15 billion barrels and boost US reserves by more than 50%.

• **New transportation technology has become mainstream.** Not long ago Toyota hit the one million mark in sales of its hybrids. If there is a next generation of cars coming out of Detroit, I guarantee that they won't be gas-guzzling SUVs.

• **The $787 billion economic stimulus plan signed into law in 2009 by President Obama** will provide a tax credit of up to $7,500 for purchasers of plug-in hybrid electric cars.

INVESTORS SHIFT FOCUS

As an indicator of how drastically investor focus has shifted, record amounts of cash have been pulled from investments centered on oil and other commodities. That money needs a place to go. Infrastructure stocks have everything going for them.

The economic stimulus plan, known officially as the *American Recovery and Reinvestment Act of 2009*, authorizes $126 billion in spending and tax breaks for infrastructure and science. The National Governors Association has presented to President Obama's aides a list of planned infrastructure projects that would cost an estimated $136 billion. Some of the projects have been suspended because the states are running short of funds, but they could be reignited by new federal funds. The projects include transportation-related construction, expansion of ports and renewable energy.

• **Infrastructure stocks aren't glamorous.** No one is bragging at the cocktail party that he/she has gotten into a hot Mexican cement company. That's what I like about them. These stocks will increase by double-digit percentages before most people notice. *Reasons...*

• Developing nations. While rich countries such as the US are upgrading decades-old infrastructure, developing nations need to create infrastructure to make their economies competitive. China has responded to its own economic maladies by targeting $600 billion to construct new railways, bridges, highways, subways and airports. Persian Gulf countries, such as Dubai and Qatar, say that they will lay out $1 trillion over the next decade to build up their public systems.

• Understandable investment. After years of chicanery by financial institutions that has crippled the US economy, infrastructure stocks offer simple, long-term investments that investors can understand.

• Barriers to competition. There are barriers that make it very difficult for new competitors to challenge incumbents. For example, environmental regulations make it very costly and difficult to build new cement plants but rather easy to expand existing ones.

• Predictable revenue. Many infrastructure companies provide predictable revenue streams from massive, multiyear projects. Their stocks can provide reasonably low volatility and income from attractive dividend yields.

PICKING THE BEST

Many infrastructure companies are greatly undervalued now because business has been hurt by the recession and panicky investors have dumped even the most financially stable stocks in a rush to safety. *What to do...*

• **Locate beaten-down stocks backed by healthy balance sheets.** This recession has pounded many infrastructure firms because cash-strapped municipalities have postponed large public projects. The collapse and panic surrounding the real estate market have further reduced many stocks to five-year lows. For example, the demand for steel, essential to construction projects, has dried up, sending

the stock of the giant producer US Steel down nearly 80% from its 2008 peak.

• **Concentrate on the two biggest challenges that the Obama administration has indicated it will tackle**—repairing roadways and bridges...and improving the technology infrastructure in schools, hospitals and public buildings.

Most likely to benefit: Companies that provide basic construction materials, such as cement and asphalt, as well as tech firms that provide hardware for Internet and computer networks.

• **Find infrastructure stocks that are also a good hedge against inflation.** I do expect that massive government spending around the world and huge deficits in the US will cause significant inflation over years to come. So it makes sense to find investments that not only will benefit from economic stimulus spending but also will shine in periods of rising inflation. These include commodity producers and overseers of vital assets, such as toll roads and airports, which can raise their fees.

Here are the investments I believe will be the biggest beneficiaries of government infrastructure spending...

BEST STOCKS NOW

• **Astec Industries, Inc. (ASTE).** Located in Chattanooga, Astec is the nation's leading manufacturer of equipment used to pave asphalt roads and dig trenches for pipelines and utilities. The company's debt-free balance sheet gives it exceptional potential for expansion.

Recent share price: $23.84.*

• **Caterpillar Inc. (CAT)** makes a diversified line of construction, mining and forestry machinery, including tractors, dump trucks, gas engines and turbines. Although the recession has caused growth to stall and sent the stock down more than 40% in 2008, the company, based in Peoria, Illinois, has responded aggressively to maintain its profitability by announcing layoffs and executive pay cuts. It remains a cash cow with 2008 revenues of $5.1 billion.

Recent share price: $30.58.

*Prices as of July 8, 2009.

164

• **Cemex, SAB de CV (CX).** Based in Monterrey, Mexico, this is the third-largest cement and ready-to-mix concrete organization in the world, growing an average of 30% annually over the past five years. Outside of the US, Cemex operates in many countries that have pledged to spend heavily on infrastructure, such as Mexico, which plans to pour $200 billion into upgrading crumbling roads. This is a good buy, considering that the stock is about 65% below its 52-week high.

Recent share price: $7.86.

• **Cisco Systems, Inc. (CSCO),** based in San Jose, California, is the world's leading supplier of data-networking equipment and software to transmit video and data. Investors still don't understand how much the company stands to benefit from the federal government's massive spending on technology infrastructure.

Recent share price: $18.13.

• **Fluor Corp. (FLR),** based in Irving, Texas, is a global provider of engineering and maintenance services. It offers a multibillion-dollar backlog of contracts with the US government and large corporations. The stock fell by nearly 40% last year, but the firm is well-positioned to bid for new federal projects. Current work includes the $1.4 billion reconstruction of the San Francisco Bay Bridge, the largest public infrastructure project in California's history, and a $1.8 billion contract to build the world's largest offshore wind farm, near the coast of England.

Recent share price: $46.16.

• **United States Steel Corp. (X).** Steel industry output plunged 50% in the final few months of 2008, but Pittsburgh-based US Steel, the world's fifth-largest producer of steel, will benefit as spending on infrastructure increases and the economy recovers, inflation rises and global commodities prices rebound.

Recent share price: $30.50.

BEST FUND NOW

If you don't have the time or ability to pick individual stocks, you still can gain exposure from funds that specialize in infrastructure. *My favorite…*

• **iShares Global Infrastructure Index Fund (IGF).** A newer exchange-traded fund (ETF), IGF provides cost-effective diversification among 77 stocks from 22 countries. The fund's portfolio, down 40% in the past year, is filled with bargains.

Recent annual yield: 3.16%.
Recent share price: $27.66.

Stocks That Go Up When Consumers "Trade Down"

Brian Lazorishak, CFA, quantitative analyst and vice president, and Peter Tuz, CFA, senior analyst and vice president at Chase Investment Counsel Corporation in Charlottesville, Virginia, which is investment adviser for the Chase Midcap Growth Fund (CHAMX). The company's Web site is *www.chaseinv.com*.

Not every stock loses money in a bear market and recession. While the Standard & Poor's 500 stock index lost 37% in 2008, Walmart stock was up by 20% and McDonald's rose 7.5%.

These stocks have bucked the economy's big downward slide and flourished because many consumers are "trading down," swapping premium purchases for cheaper alternatives. Times have grown so difficult and the economic outlook is so uncertain that Americans are drastically changing not only how much they buy but also what they buy.

While obvious winners from this "trading-down" effect—stocks including Walmart and McDonald's—have already become expensive, there still are plenty of other businesses that offer investors opportunities to profit.

Examples of attractive stocks that capitalize on the trading-down trend…

DOWNSCALE EATING

Many consumers are forgoing moderate and expensive restaurants in favor of fast food.

Example: Brinker International, which owns casual dining chains, including Chili's Grill & Bar, had a 7.8% drop in sales for the second quarter of fiscal year 2009 and a $22 million loss.

While fast-food joints are offering burgers for 99 cents, most midrange and upscale restaurants can't engage in deep discounting and still maintain quality and profitability.

Consumers also are abandoning premium brands that they were loyal to at the supermarket.

Downscale-eating stocks include...

•**Burger King Holdings, Inc. (BKC).** Burger King is the world's second-biggest hamburger chain. The company has delivered 20 consecutive quarters of sales growth in the US and Canada. While still maintaining its "value menu" items, Burger King is drawing in higher-spending consumers with new products, such as the "Steakhouse XT" burger, typically priced at $3.50.

Recent share price: $16.71.*

•**Ralcorp Holdings, Inc. (RAH).** In addition to owning the Post cereal brand, Ralcorp is the largest US producer of store-brand and generic food products, including breakfast cereal, snacks, sweets and condiments. In the past year, the stock price fell by 4%.

Recent share price: $62.34.

THE AUTO AFTERMARKET

Auto manufacturers are on life support these days, but amid this gloom, businesses involved in used cars and auto parts are bucking that trend.

Reason: Cash-strapped consumers can't afford new cars—and even flush consumers are hesitant to buy them—so they're buying used vehicles or trying to get every last mile out of their old clunkers. The average age of cars on the road is 10 years and rising, so the need for maintenance is growing. Also, cheaper gas prices have boosted driver miles in the past six months, and an unusually cold winter has increased wear and tear, creating even more demand for used cars and replacement parts.

Examples of auto-related stocks benefiting from this trend...

•**Copart, Inc. (CPRT).** The leading online auctioneer of salvaged and repossessed automobiles, Copart sells one million used cars a

*Prices as of July 8, 2009.

year, mostly from insurance companies, charities and car dealerships. Buyers typically are dismantlers, used-vehicle dealers and exporters. Copart was on Forbes's list of "The 200 Best Small Companies" nine years in a row.

Recent share price: $32.80.

•**O'Reilly Automotive, Inc. (ORLY)** is one of the larger specialty retailers of automotive aftermarket parts, tools and do-it-yourself accessories, with more than 3,200 stores in 38 states. Rather than just relying on sales to car owners, it is now signing up commercial buyers at service stations and repair shops.

Recent share price: $39.94.

DISCOUNT SHOPPING

In bad times, members of the middle class slash their spending on luxury items. They avoid department stores in favor of discount shopping at clearance stores or smaller chains.

Accordingly, stocks such as Coach and The Limited (owner of both Victoria's Secret and Bath & Body Works) have fallen by nearly half in the past year. Even Target, which sells more product lines from trendy designers than other discount stores, has been hard hit.

Examples of discount-shopping stocks that are doing well include...

•**Dollar Tree, Inc. (DLTR).** This general-merchandise retailer offers more than 3,500 stores in 48 states. It offers everything from health and beauty items to holiday goods at rock-bottom prices. The company is able to attract more middle-class consumers and higher average sales per customer than its competitors because of its mostly suburban locations.

Recent share price: $43.82.

•**GameStop Corp. (GME)** is the world's largest retailer of new video game products, with more than 6,000 stores, primarily in shopping malls and shopping centers in the US and Europe. GameStop also has built a lucrative business in secondhand merchandise, buying and selling used video games and hardware, which are more affordable than new merchandise.

Recent share price: $20.94.

•**The TJX Companies, Inc. (TJX).** This is the nation's largest off-price retailer of brand-name apparel and home fashions, with prices

20% to 60% lower than department stores. It operates 2,600 stores under the names TJ Maxx, Marshalls, HomeGoods and others. In the 2001 recession, TJX stock returned 44%.

Recent share price: $31.10.

ADULT EDUCATION

The employment picture appears to grow bleaker every day as more and more companies lay off workers. But some companies actually profit from unemployment, which the Federal Reserve expects to rise to nearly 9% by the end of 2009.

When people are unemployed or are dissatisfied with their jobs, they want to improve their skills and résumés so that they can keep their jobs or get better ones. That's a boon to for-profit adult education companies that train students in specific vocations, such as law enforcement, health care and computer science.

Example of a beneficiary of this trend...

• **Apollo Group, Inc. (APOL)** is the nation's largest for-profit education company and parent of the University of Phoenix chain, with more than 380,000 students. It offers classes online and through learning centers in 39 states. Apollo has increased its enrollment in this weak economy and is in good financial health, with no debt and more than $800 million in cash. Most of Apollo's revenue comes from Title IV funding, which includes loans guaranteed by the government.

Recent share price: $66.13.

How Many Stocks Should You Own?

Janice M. Johnson, CPA, JD, consultant, A.B. Watley Group, a financial services company, New York City.

We all know the importance of having a diversified stock portfolio, but how many stocks does it take to be "diversified"?

To fully diversify against risk of loss in the stock market requires owning hundreds of stocks. That is simple to do through a broad market index mutual fund—but that restricts you to earning the market rate of return.

If you try to "beat the market" by buying individual stocks, you must assume some risk of lack of diversification. Owning 12 to 16 varied stocks will get you about 60% of the maximum benefit of diversification. Every stock beyond this number may add safety—but only a little.

Important: To diversify, you *must* buy dissimilar stocks—you can't diversify by buying four oil industry stocks or even four energy stocks.

Best: Buy stocks that move in opposite directions on the same news.

Example: Airline and oil company stocks tend to move in opposite directions on news of the price of oil. You can invest in both to get their average long-run return with small risk that both of them are likely to be down at the same time due to the price of oil.

Better: Use exchange traded funds (ETFs) to invest in *sectors* such as oil and airlines. You'll be diversified within each sector to avoid single-company risk.

The Strongest Months For the S&P

The performance of the S&P 500 is traditionally strongest from November through April. Since World War II, the S&P 500 has gained an average of 6.8% during this period versus only 1.1% from May through October.

Reasons why: Large pension fund cash infusions early in the year...the investment of year-end employee bonuses...IRA and 401(k) contributions...and tax refund investing.

At the same time, market sector leadership has, since 1990, switched from consumer staples and health care in the summer months to financials, industrials and materials in the November to April time frame.

Sam Stovall, CFP chief investment strategist, Standard & Poor's Equity Research, New York City.

What's a Delayed Opening?

A "delayed opening" takes place when there's a large imbalance in buy and sell orders for a particular stock. You will not be able to buy a stock during a delayed opening.

Most common reasons: Discussion about a takeover of a company…a pending announcement—bad earnings, the death of a CEO, a strike, etc.

When such news is about to be made public, officials at the exchange want to give investors time to absorb the information. A delayed opening helps avoid panic buying or selling.

When you next encounter a delayed opening, check radio or TV news or online business news for more information.

Nancy Dunnan, a New York City–based financial and travel adviser and author or coauthor of 25 books, including How to Invest $50–$5,000 *(HarperCollins).*

Shorting the Market

Steve Cohen, managing director at mutual fund and exchange-traded fund manager ProShare Advisors in Bethesda, Maryland, www.proshares.com.

There is one way to bet that stocks will continue to go down that's easier (and frankly, less risky) than "short-selling" stocks through a broker.

Buy a "short" exchange-traded fund (ETF). These ETFs, also called inverse ETFs, track a given stock market index, such as the Standard & Poor's 500 stock index or the NASDAQ 100. Unlike most index funds, they are designed to go up when the index goes down. If the S&P 500 loses 5% on a given day, for example, a short ETF tracking that index should gain 5%, less fees and expenses.

In addition, there are short *leveraged* ETFs. With these, you get about twice as much movement as the underlying index generates on a given day. If the S&P 500 drops 5% in a day, a short leveraged S&P 500 ETF would gain 10%, again before fees and expenses.

Caution: Taking the inverse of an index cuts both ways. If the S&P 500 *gains* 5% in a day, a short leveraged S&P 500 ETF would lose about 10%.

You can buy and sell an inverse ETF as you would any stock, through a full-service or discount broker. There is no need to set up a margin account, as there is for short sales, and no chance of getting a margin call for more cash or securities. And you may be able to use these ETFs in accounts where you can't use margin, such as retirement accounts.

There are dozens of short ETFs available. They track broad as well as narrow stock market indexes. Locate them by going to ETFConnect.com and clicking on "Find a Fund." Short ETFs are those with the word "short" or "ultrashort" in their names.

Brokerage Accounts Are Still Safe

Peter G. Crane, president and CEO of Crane Data LLC, which tracks money-market and mutual fund information and publishes Money Fund Intelligence, *Westboro, Massachusetts, www.cranedata.com.*

With all the strife at brokerage firms of late, some investors are worried about keeping accounts at brokerages that have run into trouble. But keeping your account at a wounded brokerage firm is generally safe.

Concerns about account safety at firms that serve individual investors have grown since Bear Stearns—which primarily serves institutional investors—began crumbling. It was rescued by JPMorgan Chase & Co., with federal government backing.

Providing a safety cushion, the Federal Reserve recently made it easier for firms to borrow money, using even non-Treasury securities as collateral.

Other reasons that your money is generally safe…

• **The Securities & Exchange Commission (SEC)** requires US brokerage firms to meet specific capital requirements to repay all obligations to customers. In addition, client assets need to be segregated from a firm's assets so that the firm cannot dip into them to shore up its finances.

• **The Securities Investor Protection Corporation (SIPC)** covers missing securities up to $500,000 per customer (including up to $100,000 in cash), and most firms have insurance covering securities over that amount.

• **The Federal Deposit Insurance Corporation (FDIC)** protects bank deposits held at a brokerage up to $250,000 through 2013.

Of course, if the upheaval means you have lost your favorite broker or it will take longer to get hold of a broker, you might consider switching firms.

How to Pick a Financial Adviser: Get the Help You Need at a Fair Price

David Richman, national director, Eaton Vance Advisor Institute, a training program for wealth managers located in West Hartford, Connecticut. He is coauthor of *Questions Great Financial Advisors Ask...and Investors Need to Know* (Kaplan Business).

The recent investment and home-price losses have endangered the retirement goals of millions of Americans. If this describes you, or even if you just feel nervous, hiring a financial adviser could help you get back on track. While most financial advisers are skilled, trustworthy professionals, others may lack the necessary experience, skills or motivation to help you.

Best first move: Ask trusted friends whether they would recommend their own financial advisers. If so, listen to how they describe these advisers—they should paint a picture of a trusted partner who is dedicated to understanding them and how they make financial decisions.

If your friends do not strongly recommend their financial advisers, ask your lawyer or accountant for referrals. If this doesn't pan out either, ask other members of your community whom you respect.

QUESTIONS TO ASK

When you meet with a candidate, be sure to ask...

• **What professional certifications have you earned?** Make sure that he/she is a Certified Financial Planner (CFP), a Certified Investment Management Analyst (CIMA) or a Chartered Financial Analyst (CFA). These designations ensure that the adviser receives ongoing financial training and has passed a difficult exam. Titles such as "investment adviser" or "financial adviser" do not have the same guarantee.

• **If I had been your client last year and lost a lot of money, what would you be advising me now?** The answer should include some basics—such as how to rebalance your portfolio following stock losses and how to sell securities that have declined in value to offset taxes—as well as suggest a long-term perspective.

The adviser also should understand that his job is about managing a client's emotions as well. The amount of risk that a client is predisposed to take does not often correspond with the amount of risk that makes sense for his situation, and the adviser must be able to steer clients into an appropriate portfolio in a way that still allows them to sleep at night.

• **I'm retired, and my portfolio has lost a lot of money. What can I do to get my savings back on track?** It's an excellent sign if the adviser's suggestions include spending less and saving more and/or taking a part-time job during retirement. A financial adviser must be willing to provide painful advice when necessary just as a doctor must be willing to tell a patient to "lose weight" or "stop smoking." You should be extremely wary if an adviser suggests some aggressive strategy to "make it back."

• **What should I be doing to manage my financial risk?** Many financial advisers will talk about asset selection and diversification.

That is fine, but it's a bad sign if the adviser doesn't also discuss insurance.

Insurance is crucial for risk management—if you don't have enough, one mishap or lawsuit could cost you everything you own. Types of insurance to discuss could include homeowners', umbrella, business, auto, life, health, disability and long-term-care insurance.

•**I'm worried about the bleak economic forecasts on the news. What should I do?** The adviser should encourage you to ignore all the news and spend your free time thinking about more enjoyable matters. Becoming wrapped up in the endless recession coverage won't help you make informed decisions—it will cause you to make knee-jerk emotional decisions that are likely to be detrimental to your mental and financial health.

•**What financial decisions will you make for me?** This is a trick question. The adviser should answer that he will provide guidance on a wide range of financial decisions but will not make your decisions for you.

The adviser might take the lead in making decisions about specific investments *if* this is what the client wants—but he still should discuss these decisions and what they mean with the client before proceeding. The best financial advisers have a collaborative approach but are also likely to have strong opinions.

•**What words would your clients use to describe you?** Most advisers will cite words such as intelligent, experienced, trustworthy and prudent. Make sure the list also includes "accessible"—it shows that the adviser understands that being available when needed is part of his job. The list also should include a word like "confidant" to show that the adviser stresses a personal connection with clients.

•**How many clients do you have?** If it is more than 250 (for a solo practice), it's unlikely that he can give each client the time and attention that each deserves. If you're investing millions of dollars, anything more than 100 clients is probably too many, unless there is a strong support team. Large portfolios tend to be more complex and time-consuming for advisers, and if you have this much money,

it is worth it to pay a little more for one who can give you extra attention.

•**How often will we meet?** You need to have at least two face-to-face meetings per year. If your assets are well into the millions, you should probably arrange four meetings. Phone conversations can be useful, but most people feel more comfortable when they have in-person contact with the adviser who is handling their money…and this gives the adviser a better chance to learn his client's goals and fears.

•**How do you charge?** Choose an adviser who charges a fee for his services, not one who charges commissions. Don't make a decision based on price. Base it on your sense of an adviser's competence, perspective and "fit." Chemistry is vital. (Fees often are based on the amount of assets under management even though the adviser should provide guidance beyond investment advice.)

•**What is your typical client's net worth?** This adviser might not have much experience with the financial issues most important to you if his other clients have significantly more or less money.

More from David Richman…

Questions a Financial Adviser Should Ask *You*

During an initial interview, a financial adviser should seem like a doctor trying to diagnose the source of a patient's problems—not a salesperson trying to make a sale. *Questions an adviser should ask…*

•**Have you lost sleep over the markets recently?** This helps the adviser understand your risk tolerance, which will help him design your portfolio.

•**Which of your financial goals is most important to you?** Most clients have a long list of goals. They want to buy a second home, retire at a certain time, travel, help pay the grandkids' college bills, leave an estate, etc. These days, few can afford to achieve them all.

•**What is your history with money?** Did you grow up wealthy or poor? How did your portfolio fare in the latest bull market? The current bear market? Good financial advisers understand that the way money has affected your life in the past will have an effect on how you react to financial issues in the future.

•**What do you want from a financial adviser?** The adviser should understand that financial planning is not one size fits all. It is his/her job to adjust the services provided to fit your needs and desires.

Four Reasons to Fire Your Financial Adviser

Jack Waymire, cofounder of Paladin Registry, an Internet company that matches investors with financial advisers, *www.paladinregistry.com*. He was president of the money management firm Lexington Capital Management for 21 years and is author of *Who's Watching Your Money? The 17 Paladin Principles for Selecting a Financial Adviser* (Wiley).

It is not your financial adviser's fault that the economy hit the skids in 2008, but he/she may deserve the boot if any one of the following is true…

•**An adviser disappeared.** Telephone calls weren't returned or your meetings were repeatedly canceled. Some advisers will dodge difficult conversations with clients who have lost big bucks—but that's when clients need their help most.

•**Your portfolio underperformed appropriate benchmarks over several years.** If the stock portion of your portfolio performed roughly as well as the Standard & Poor's 500 Index during the five-year bull market, it should not have lost much more than the S&P 500 during the bear market. Use the Nasdaq Composite Index as your measuring stick if you have an aggressive portfolio of small-caps. And use an appropriate bond index, perhaps one of the Barclays Capital bond indices, to judge the fixed-income portion of your portfolio (visit *http://ecommerce.barcap.com/indices*).

•**Your portfolio was riskier than was appropriate for you.** If you are retired or near retirement, or you told your adviser that you wanted a conservative portfolio, a significant portion of your money—30% or more—should have been invested in bonds or cash. And no more than a few percent should have been in any one stock.

•**Your adviser offered no constructive advice as the market declined.** If your adviser's only guidance during the rout was "just hang in there—the market will turn the corner soon," there is no need to hang on to him. The financial world changed last year, and your adviser should have been suggesting ways in which your portfolio and financial plan should have changed in response.

Examples of good advice: Sell off some weak securities that lost money to reduce 2008 taxes…select stocks and sectors well-positioned for a rebound.

Check Out Your Stockbroker Now

Stockbrokers can't have complaints expunged from their records even if customers agree to it. An appeals court reversed a ruling allowing a complaint to be removed from a broker's record, saying that customers must be able to find out about all actions against brokers. To check out a broker, access the free database of the Financial Industry Regulatory Authority at *http://brokercheck.finra.org*. Also check with your state's securities regulator by going to *www.nasaa.org*.

The Washington Post, 1150 15th St. NW, Washington, DC 20071, *www.washingtonpost.com*.

How to Spot a Ponzi Scheme: Lessons from The Madoff Scandal

Dan Brecher, JD, a securities attorney in New York City who specializes in claims against brokerage firms.

In December 2008, Bernard Madoff, a widely respected money manager and former chair of the Nasdaq Stock Market, was arrested for securities fraud.

Operating a classic Ponzi scheme,* Madoff fleeced $50 billion from banks, charities, 401(k) plans, a US senator and many individual investors by using funds from new clients to pay off older ones. Faced with mounting losses, he confessed to perhaps the biggest scam in Wall Street history, prompting investors everywhere to wonder just whom they can trust.

Red flags that Madoff's clients should have noticed—and that no one should ignore...

• **Profits that sound too good to be true.** Even Warren Buffett loses money sometimes. Madoff's fund returned about 1% to 2% every month. A steady performance like this should have raised eyebrows—but it opened wallets instead.

• **Fuzzy investment strategy.** Madoff reportedly would say, "It's a proprietary strategy. I can't go into it in great detail." Investors who cannot decipher a fund's methodology on their own should ask a fee-based adviser whether it makes sense. If the adviser can't make sense of it, stay away. While the independent review may cost $500 or more, it can save you a fortune.

• **An obscure accountant.** The accounting practice that Madoff used was a little-known company that reportedly operated from a tiny office staffed with only three employees.

Trap: A big-name accounting firm is not a guarantee either. In fact, it can lull investors into a false feeling of security. Feeder funds, which market investments from other companies, may retain a major accounting firm to audit their own books—but not necessarily the books of the investment managers they "feed" into. Investors should find out who is auditing the company where the money ends up.

• **Promise of exclusivity.** Madoff's clients were invited to join an exclusive circle. Not just anyone could invest. The marketing approach was, "It is a privilege to invest with us." It is not unusual for exclusivity to be based upon a minimum required investment of a substantial amount, but in Madoff's case, you typically had to know someone to get in.

*Ponzi schemes are named for Charles Ponzi, who swindled thousands of New Englanders in a postage stamp speculation scheme in the 1920s.

• **Unwillingness to answer questions.** Investors who asked too many questions were actually kicked out of Madoff's fund. At the least, you should be given sufficient detail to allow you or your adviser to understand the investment strategy being used and how results are calculated, reported and audited.

Other self-defense strategies...

• **Allocate wisely.** Don't put all your money in just one or two investments. Anything can go bust. But also beware of too diversified a portfolio. Tracking more than 15 or 20 investments is difficult.

• **Don't invest solely on the say-so of a friend or colleague.** Their recommendation may be well-intentioned but naïve. It is your money. Do your own due diligence.

• **Review all monthly or quarterly statements.** In some cases, the statements from Madoff's firm did not even contain the names of any securities—which should have raised eyebrows, at least.

More from Dan Brecher, JD...

Ask Your Broker for This Important Statement

To defend yourself against today's financial industry turmoil, ask your brokerage firm for a written statement affirming that it is creditworthy and not in danger of failing. This helps your case if your assets go missing and you sue to recover uninsured amounts. Up to $500,000 of your brokerage assets are protected by the Securities Investor Protection Corporation (SIPC), including up to $100,000 in cash, per brokerage account.

If You Lost Money in a Ponzi Scheme...

There's tax help for victims of Ponzi schemes, such as the one run by Bernard Madoff. Victims can deduct up to 95% of their losses as theft losses on their 2008 tax returns and "carry back" unused losses to be used on prior years' returns for up to five years, according to new rules just released by the IRS. The deduction includes the amount invested (and lost), plus fictitious investment income "earned," less any amounts recovered under the government's insurance program, the Securities Investor Protection Corporation (SIPC). A special limitation that usually reduces casualty and theft-loss deductions by 10% of adjusted gross income will not apply for these cases. For details, see IRS Revenue Procedure 2009-20 (go to *www.irs.gov* and type "Ponzi" into the search box.)

Thomas P. Ochsenschlager, Esq., CPA, vice president, taxation, American Institute of Certified Public Accountants, Washington, DC, *www.aicpa.org.*

The Sleaziest Investment Scams Today

Chuck Whitlock, founder of Crimeline, a company that offers online fraud identification and prevention training to police departments, West Linn, Oregon. He is also a journalist whose work exposing scams has been featured on TV programs including *Inside Edition* and *Extra*. A member of the *Bottom Line/Wealth* panel of experts, Whitlock is author of several books about scams, including *Age Without Rage* (R-W International). His Web site is *www.chuckwhitlock.com.*

The unstable markets are bringing con artists out of the woodwork—and they are promoting investment scams that promise huge returns but deliver only misery. *Watch out for...*

•**Gold in the vault.** You are told that an investment broker will buy gold for you for a small fee and store it in a bank vault.

The scam: The supposed broker never buys the gold and disappears with your money.

What to do: Invest in precious metals only through a broker at a well-known investment company, or buy mining company stocks or shares of a mutual fund focused on precious metals.

•**High-yield bank paper.** You are told that you have a rare opportunity to invest in safe, high-yield financial instruments, such as debt or letters of credit, that are from established European banks and that usually are available only to governments or other banks.

The scam: These bank securities, that are touted as "prime bank" instruments, do not exist. The con artist will disappear with your money.

What to do: Be wary of anyone who promises huge returns for low risk...or who suggests that you invest in anything that you have never heard of.

•**Old bonds.** You are told that you have a chance to buy—for a very low price—a bond that was issued from a well-known company decades ago when interest rates were much higher.

The scam: The matured bond has been cashed in and no longer has any investment value. Scammers buy older bond certificates traded as collectibles and sell them to investors looking for high yields.

What to do: Be skeptical of any corporate bond that is offered by anyone other than a well-known brokerage firm. Call investor relations at the company that issued the bond. And be aware that any bond with a rate higher than current market rates would normally have a premium price that erases all or much of the advantage.

How to Locate Lost Savings Bonds

To find lost savings bonds, go to Treasury-Direct.gov and then look up Form 1048, *Claim for Lost, Stolen or Destroyed US Savings Bonds*. Fill in the following information—the bond owner's name, address and Social Security number...approximate date of issue...and serial number if available. Once this form is certified at a bank, mail it to the Department of Treasury (the address can be found on the form). With the serial number, the process will take three to four weeks...without it, you may be waiting months to get a duplicate bond.

Kiplinger.com.

How Tax-Exempt Bonds May Be Taxable

Even though interest paid on tax-exempt bonds generally is free of tax, such bonds are subject to the same capital gain and loss tax rules as other investments. Capital gains on tax-exempt bonds are taxable, and capital losses may be deductible.

Also: Interest paid on tax-exempt bonds that are issued for nongovernmental purposes (such as financing sports stadiums), called "private activity bonds," are subject to income tax under the rules of the alternative minimum tax (AMT), which affects more taxpayers every year.

If these facts may affect you, consult your tax adviser.

William G. Brennan, CPA/PFS, CFP, principal, Capital Management Group, LLC, Washington, DC, *www.cmg-llc.net*.

A Nasty Tax Surprise for Fund Investors

Tom Roseen, senior analyst for Lipper, a division of Thomson Reuters Inc., Denver, *www.lipperweb.com*. He is author of *Taxes in the Mutual Fund Industry* (Lipper).

A tax shock could surprise many mutual fund investors this year. Even if your fund's value has plunged 40% or more with the stock market, it may deliver a capital gains tax bill to you at year-end.

This year's big fall in the stock market has led many investors to cash out of their stock fund shares, forcing some funds to sell appreciated investments to redeem these shares.

Trap: When a fund sells its appreciated investments, it realizes taxable capital gains on those investments that are passed through to its shareholders. This is true even if the overall value of the fund's own shares has fallen.

These taxable gains are distributed to the shareholders when the fund makes taxable distributions.

This is especially a problem if the fund is cashing in stocks that soared during the five-year bull market.

Even worse: Fund distributions can include short-term gains and nonqualified dividends taxed at the ordinary income tax rates up to 35%.

Biggest mistake: Buying shares in a fund just before it pays a taxable distribution. If you wait until after the fund distributes gains and dividends ("goes ex-dividend"), you avoid the immediate tax bill.

TO HELP MINIMIZE THE TAX HIT

Not all mutual funds are in this tax-trap–creating situation. For example, if your fund's managers sold investments that declined in value, the fund may have realized enough losses to offset its gains and keep its shareholders from receiving a taxable distribution.

Planning advice…

• **Learn the expected distribution of any mutual fund you own and in which you might invest.** Many funds make distributions in December but provide estimates in mid- to late November. Funds typically post estimated distributions on their Web sites—if not, call the fund management to inquire.

• **Learn the fund's ex-dividend date.** If it will distribute significant taxable gains, consider buying shares after that date. Or, if you own shares in such a fund and will continue to do so, sell shares in other funds (or stocks) that have lost value in order to "lock in" those losses.

Reason: Losses can be used to offset gains or up to $3,000 of other income. Unused losses can be carried forward to offset gains and up to $3,000 a year of other income in future tax years.

Caution: Do not make investment moves solely for tax purposes. That's one of the easiest ways for you to make a bad investment mistake.

Why Gold Will Shine In Your Portfolio

Allan S. Roth, CPA, CFP, president of Wealth Logic, LLC, a financial advisory firm in Colorado Springs that serves clients with investments ranging from $10,000 to $2 million. He is author of *How a Second Grader Beats Wall Street: Golden Rules Any Investor Can Learn* (Wiley). His Web site is *www.daretobedull.com*.

Are you ever tempted to invest in gold but frightened by its intense ups and downs? Some gold investing gurus will tell you that gold is the one safe place left to invest your money…and that it will hit $5,000 per ounce within a few years. Skeptics claim that gold is much too volatile. For instance, it soared by nearly 50% to $1,000 an ounce between October 2008 and February 2009 and then pulled back to $907 by early July 2009.

There are good reasons to put a portion of your assets in gold—if you do it the right way. *Here's why and how…*

GOLD PROVIDES DIVERSIFICATION

Stocks, bonds and real estate are all very dangerous for investors now. Historically, gold has done well when the economy is shaky… investors panic…and stocks and bonds seem too risky.

Example: In the economically troubled seven-year period from 1973 to 1980, the price of gold rose by 2,300%, from $35 to $850 per ounce.

Right now, the federal government is making unprecedented moves to shore up the economy and ward off deflation by lowering interest rates to nearly zero and pumping trillions of dollars into bailouts and stimulus plans. This raises the real possibility of soaring inflation in the coming years. Inflation typically leads to higher gold prices because investors realize that their paper money is losing value.

That doesn't mean you should buy gold because you think you can make a killing. Gold prices are notoriously hard to predict. Investors can't analyze gold like they can a company, which has quarterly earnings and may pay a dividend.

The truth is that, as an investment, gold's average annualized returns have only barely kept up with inflation. For example, back in 1979, I used my college graduation money to invest in 10 ounces of gold coins at $664 per ounce. I was sure gold prices would quickly soar to $2,000 per ounce because of high inflation. But after three decades, the value of my gold coins has risen to less than half that, a gain of less than 50%.

Where gold does shine, however, is as a terrific way to diversify your portfolio. Its price has so little correlation with stock and bond returns that adding just a little gold can lower your overall volatility and protect you in bad times. Gold held its value in the credit crisis of 2008, rising 4% when almost every other major asset class plunged in value. In the past decade, gold has increased by about 13% annually, on average, compared with a 3% annualized drop for the Standard & Poor's 500 stock index.

INVEST FOR THE LONG-TERM

I recommend gold only for clients who can stay invested for 10 years or more and are willing to accept wild, short-term swings in gold prices. *Consider the following guidelines…*

• **Devote a maximum of 3% of your overall portfolio to gold.**

• **Invest fixed amounts at regular intervals,** say once a month over the next year, because gold prices bounce around. That way you are likely to buy during periods when gold pulls back, which happens often.

• **Rebalance gold holdings at least once a year.** If gold rises during 2009, you will want to take some profits at the end of the year and trim back to your original 3% target.

FOR CONSERVATIVE INVESTORS

Avoid buying into gold mines or gold futures contracts. Just invest directly in the mineral. That gives you the most control over your investment. *Best ways to invest directly…*

• **Gold bullion coins.** This is pure gold metal cast as coins. Buy only from a dealer found through the Professional Coin Grading Service (800-447-8848, *www.pcgs.com*) or the Numismatic Guaranty Corporation (800-642-2646, *www.ngccoin.com*), whose members have to abide by stringent standards and procedures. Both organizations offer a money-back guarantee for grading accuracy and authenticity.

Ask for one-ounce coins, either South African Krugerrands, Canadian Maple Leafs or American Eagles. These are the most widely traded coins and the easiest to sell if you want or need to. Prices are based on the market price of gold (which you can find at *www.kitco.com*) plus a 3%-to-5% premium charged by dealers.

Drawbacks: The IRS classifies gold coins as a "collectible," which means that capital gains on the sale of this type of gold are taxed at a flat 28% rate—not at the usual 15% rate for most other capital gains. Also, you may have to pay to store your coins in a bank safe-deposit box. Another option is to keep your coins in a home safe. Check to see what your homeowner's insurance policy will cover, or consider becoming a member of the American Numismatic Association (800-367-9723 or *www.money.org*) and getting coverage from its insurance plan.

● **SPDR Gold Shares (GLD),** a gold exchange-traded fund (ETF), may be a better option if you don't want the drawbacks of actual physical possession of your gold. Each share represents one-tenth of one ounce of actual gold. With a total market value of more than $31 billion, the fund now is the second-largest ETF on the market. The gold backing the shares is kept in vaults in Europe and audited regularly. Keep in mind that the 0.4% annual expense ratio will take a bite out of your account every year.

Recent share price: $89.27.*

FOR MORE AGGRESSIVE INVESTORS

If you are willing to take more risk, consider investing in stocks of precious-metal firms and gold-mining companies. When the price of gold rises, these stocks tend to gain even more because the cost of producing gold doesn't necessarily increase, which means much higher profits for the company. This is especially true if a company finds new reserves or develops more cost-effective mining technology. *How to invest now...*

● **To mute volatility, use a mutual fund focused largely on gold.** Gold-related stocks can plunge a lot faster than gold itself because a company's profitability can disappear quickly—and the stocks carry the additional risks that come with an investment in any

*Prices and rates as of July 8, 2009.

176

company, including the danger that management will make bad decisions.

I like Vanguard Precious Metals and Mining Fund (VGPMX) because of its low volatility and low fees. The fund invests in stocks of companies that mine for gold and other precious metals (800-523-7731, *www.vanguard.com*).

10-year annualized performance: 14.99%.

● **If you prefer a passively managed fund** that tracks an index and whose expenses likely are lower than a fund whose managers choose the investments, consider Market Vectors Gold Miners (GDX), an ETF that owns shares in the world's leading gold-mining companies.

Recent share price: $35.19.

Can You Still Make Money In Real Estate? This Expert Says "Yes!"

Dean Graziosi, a real estate investor for more than 20 years. Based in Phoenix, he is author of two books on real estate, including *Be a Real Estate Millionaire* (Vanguard). His Web site is *www.deangraziosi.com*.

Millions of Americans have lost their jobs in the past year, and finding new employment in this economy is very difficult. Some of the newly unemployed are searching for ways to make money on their own until the economy improves and employers are hiring again.

Creative real estate investor Dean Graziosi says that despite the bursting of the real estate bubble, there still is money to be made. You don't even need a lot of money. All you need is a smart strategy and the patience to wait for great deals. *He answers questions below...*

● **Home prices have fallen by more than 20% from their 2006 peak. Where are they headed from here?** I believe real estate prices finally are bottoming out in most regions—but I don't anticipate a quick rebound. Lenders are now making it very difficult to get mortgages, and many Americans lack confidence in the economy. Real estate will not rebound substantially from its current levels until both of these things change, and that is not likely to happen before late 2010 at the earliest. Real estate prices are not likely to overtake their 2006 peak until perhaps 2015.

• **Given this gloomy outlook for home prices, why do you believe people should invest in real estate?** Because home buyers are scarce these days, and some home owners are so desperate to sell that they are willing to accept very low offers. The only way to make money in this market is to buy property when it can be had for considerably less than its market value.

This typically means offering 30% to 50% less than the asking price. Most sellers will turn you down, but a small percentage—perhaps one in 25—will accept your lowball offer.

• **How can people who have lost their jobs take advantage of their free time to make money in real estate?** Mortgage lenders are being very cautious these days, so people who are out of work are likely to have trouble obtaining mortgages. But there is a low-risk real estate investment strategy that does not require big financial risks, mortgage loans or long time horizons.

First, put together a list of local real estate investors. To find them, check area real estate investment clubs. You can find real estate clubs through the Web site of the National Real Estate Investor Association (*www.nation alreia.com*) or REIClub.com.

Next, make lowball offers on dozens of local properties. Most of your offers will be turned down, but in this market, some desperate sellers are likely to accept your offer. When someone does, execute a contract that gives you the exclusive right to buy the property at the agreed-upon price within a certain period of time, usually seven to 30 days. Make sure this contract includes an "assignment clause" that allows you to transfer the contract to another real estate investor. If you find a great deal on a house, other investors likely will be more than willing to pay you to take over the deal themselves. I know real estate investors who have made $2,000 to $20,000 per house by selling contracts—it all depends on how good the deal is that you have found.

Speak with a real estate attorney before attempting this. Your bid must be made properly in order for you to back out of the deal if you cannot find a buyer for the contract…and contracts you sign must be written properly in order to be transferable. An attorney typically charges an hourly rate of $200 to $500.* Most contracts can be written up in an hour or less.

• **How can real estate investors find sellers willing to accept low offers?** Start by finding a helpful real estate agent. Explain to him/her that you intend to make many lowball offers, and confirm that he is willing to help you do this—some agents consider this strategy too time-consuming even in this economy.

Your agent can use the Multiple Listing Service (MLS) to search for homes that are likely to have motivated sellers. *These include…*

• Homes that have been on the market for at least 90 days. The longer any home sits, the more desperate its owner.

• Homes in preforeclosure. Owners might lose their homes to their lenders if they do not sell quickly.

• Foreclosed homes being sold by lenders (also referred to as "Real Estate Owned," or REO, properties). Banks and other mortgage lenders sometimes sell such homes at steep discounts.

If a home has been on the market or owned by a lender for more than six months—or a preforeclosure is very close to its foreclosure date—offer about 40% to 50% below the asking price rather than 30% below.

• **Which locations are the best?** Stick with neighborhoods in your region where prices have dropped the least. It is tempting to buy in neighborhoods where prices have dropped furthest and the bargains seem greatest, but when a real estate bear market ends, prices rebound fastest and most dependably in the most desirable neighborhoods.

Within these relatively stronger neighborhoods, favor homes in the price bracket that has best held on to value. In some neighborhoods, high-end properties have held up best —in others, it is the moderately priced homes. Your real estate agent can utilize the MLS to identify homes that meet these criteria.

*Rates subject to change.

•**How can home owners afford to sell way below market value?** Many sellers cannot afford to, but some can. Those who have lived in their homes for a decade or longer may have enough equity to do so.

•**Is selling the contract to another investor always the best strategy?** If you do not need to turn a quick profit and you can qualify for a mortgage on the property (or buy it outright), consider buying the home and renting it out until the real estate market recovers. Demand for rental homes is quite strong in most regions because people who are unable to obtain mortgages or unwilling to buy property in this declining market are renting instead.

Mortgages are available for borrowers with great credit scores. If your credit score is above 700, you should be able to obtain a mortgage without a problem. If it is between 650 and 700, it might take some shopping around, but you probably can find a lender.

To gauge your local rental market, review the "homes for rent" section of the local newspaper to see how much properties are renting for in the neighborhoods that you are considering. If the rents are more than high enough to cover your anticipated tax, insurance and mortgage payments as well as maintenance costs, odds are good that your property will at least break even until the real estate market rebounds and you can sell for a decent profit.

You also can run a home-for-rent ad in the local paper and on Craigslist.org before you buy a property. The ad should imply that you already have a home for rent in the neighborhood where you intend to buy. It should describe a typical home for that region and list a rent high enough to cover your expenses. If you get a lot of calls in response to the ad, it's an excellent sign that you would be able to rent out an investment property in that area. (Tell would-be renters who call that you might have something opening up in the area soon, and take their names and numbers.)

More from Dean Graziosi…

Great Real Estate Bargains

Some of the better real estate bargains are in homes facing foreclosure. These owners must sell fast or lose their homes to lenders. In many cases, you are helping the owners out of a very stressful situation. If you stop the foreclosure process while the home is in "preforeclosure," you could help save the owner from a black mark on his/her credit record.

Notices of pending foreclosures are available at county courthouses. Contact the owner of a home facing foreclosure in person or by mail, and politely say that you might be interested in buying his home if he decides to sell. Search for properties where the home owner has some equity in his home, not those with mortgages and liens in excess of the property's value. (Hire a title company to research whether there are liens on the property before you buy it. Expect to pay the title company $100 to $150* for this service.)

However, if a home is overleveraged (more is owed than it is worth) in today's market, you have a good chance of doing a "short sale," which involves offering the bank less money than is owed on the home. For information on short sales, go to *www.credit.com*.

•**Auctions.** You can bid on homes at foreclosure auctions, but be aware that you will have to make a large cash down payment on the same day of the auction if you win…and that you might have to bid on properties "as is" without getting a chance to see the interior. For more information about foreclosure auctions, go to *www.foreclosurelistings.com*.

•**Bank sales.** Another alternative is to make offers on "real estate-owned" (REO) properties —those that have been repossessed and now are owned by the bank. With real estate prices falling, many banks are so anxious to be rid of these properties that they will accept offers 10% to 20% below market value. Visit the REO Network's Web site (*www.reonetwork.com*) to find brokers in your region that specialize in REO properties.

Helpful: Buying foreclosures makes the most sense if you have some handyman skills. Foreclosed homes often require significant repairs because owners who expect to lose their houses rarely bother to maintain them.

*Prices subject to change.

11

Dollars and Sense

Six Money-Saving Rules For the New Economy

This new economy requires some savvier approaches for managing our finances and our lives. *Below are six of my favorite cash-saving strategies right now...*

1. Join the "$4-a-Gallon Savings Club." When gas hit $4 a gallon, we all complained about it, but for the most part, we adjusted our household budgets to accommodate this and—most important—we actually started to drive less for the first time in decades. As a result, demand decreased and Mother Earth breathed a little easier.

Now that gas prices are back down, let's not go back to our old driving habits. Instead, join the $4-a-Gallon Savings Club. Every time you fill up, calculate the difference between what you pay at the pump and what it would have cost if you had paid $4 a gallon. Then "deposit" that amount in your savings club envelope. It will encourage you to continue to go light on the gas pedal, help keep down demand for gasoline and (maybe) prices and allow you to save some money. Ever since gas prices fell below $4 a gallon, I have squirreled away more than $700 in my savings club envelope.

2. Conduct a financial fire drill. Don't wait to be blindsided by an unpleasant financial event. Spend one Sunday afternoon conducting a financial fire drill. Brainstorm various worst-case scenarios—job loss, continued declines in the stock market, loss of health-care insurance—and how you would handle each of them. For scenarios that seem to be most thorny, you can decide to research solutions either online, at the library or by talking with a financial professional.

Jeff Yeager, dubbed "The Ultimate Cheapskate" by NBC's *Today* program. Yeager honed his cheapskating skills during 25 years working with underfunded nonprofit agencies. He lives in Accokeek, Maryland, and is author of *The Ultimate Cheapskate's Road Map to True Riches* (Broadway). His online site is *www.theultimate cheapskate.com*.

179

Be sure to involve your family in your discussions. I have always found that when you get things out in the open, they generally are not as scary as they seemed before—and you tend to sleep a lot better because of it.

3. Barter. Bartering is the ancient practice of swapping goods and services rather than paying for them. Check out the swapping going on at Web sites, such as Craigslist.org, or join one of the increasing number of online bartering groups, such as BarterBart.com or uSwapit.com. Recent online swaps included a used laptop computer traded for a carton of home-brewing supplies...a Web site designer trading her services for a week's stay at a vacation cottage on the Gulf Coast...and two radial tires for a pair of concert tickets.

Many online bartering clubs permit you to trade goods and services for club credits. You can trade the credits—instead of specific goods or services—with club members who are offering something you want.

Caution: Consult IRS Publication 525, *Taxable and Nontaxable Income,* to determine the taxation consequences of your bartering. (Go to *www.irs.gov* to download the publication for free or call 800-TAX-FORM.)

4. Always put off until tomorrow what you could buy today. Here is where procrastination pays off. Studies have shown that most of us eventually regret more than half of all the discretionary purchases we make. Wait at least one week between the time you are first tempted to buy an item and when you go back to buy it. Odds are good that you'll never go back to buy it.

Also, make a list of things that you bought recently that you could have done without. Take a look at the list before you go shopping—it might curb your impulse buying.

5. Grow your own. It is time to bring back victory gardens, those small vegetable gardens that helped families through the two World Wars. Even a 4' x 4' raised-bed garden in the backyard can produce lots of fresh produce in a season. A few dollars' worth of seeds easily can quadruple your investment. If you do not have space for a garden, consider growing a pot or two of herbs on the kitchen windowsill

and patio-variety tomatoes and cucumbers in containers out on the deck.

More and more cities and towns have community gardens, where you get your own little plot for the season for a nominal fee. To find a garden, go to *www.communitygarden.org.*

Community Supported Agriculture (or CSA) programs allow you to buy shares of the harvest from local farms. CSA shares sometimes can be pricey—and vegetable quantities overwhelming—so research all of the options and consider splitting a share with your neighbors. Many CSA farms also offer volunteer opportunities to help with the gardening. For farms near you, go to *www.localharvest.org.*

6. Ask and you might receive. In difficult times such as these, customers gain bargaining muscle when it comes to negotiating better prices on goods and services. A study by the Consumer Reports National Research Center found that more than 90% of those who got up the nerve to ask for a discount on purchases (including electronics, appliances, furniture and even medical expenses) reported receiving a price concession at least once—and the average saving was $50 or more.

The key is always to be friendly and polite when asking for a better price or other concession. Even if you're unhappy with the service that you have received or the condition of the merchandise, ask nicely.

Also, go into the store knowing the price that you are willing to pay. Don't be afraid to say "No, thanks" and look elsewhere if need be.

Sneaky New Fees Coming at You from Stores...Banks ...Hotels...Web Sites

Bob Sullivan, a senior columnist for MSNBC.com in New York City and author of *Gotcha Capitalism: How Hidden Fees Rip You Off Every Day and What You Can Do About It* (Ballantine).

With the economy suffering, companies are relying more on extra fees and charges to stay profitable. For example, a company will offer low prices on consumer goods, then bury a $5.99 surcharge in the fine print of the contract or just neglect to tell you about additional costs until your bill arrives. These nickel-and-dime charges do add up. According to a survey conducted by independent business-research firm Ponemon Institute, the average consumer can expect to pay $946 this year in sneaky fees. *Be on the lookout for…*

STORES

• **Debt forgiveness insurance.** Electronics and furniture stores offer tempting deals that let you charge your purchase to a store credit card and delay payment for up to 18 months. As long as you pay the full amount on time, you are getting the equivalent of an interest-free loan.

Sneaky twist: Some stores now tack on a monthly $5 fee to ensure that your debt will be paid if you suffer "grave circumstances" (such as death). Sometimes, it's listed as "insurance fee" on your bill, other times it's just added to the amount you owe. Miss even one of these debt-forgiveness payments and you trigger all the back interest for 18 months—even if you pay off the original purchase amount on time.

Self-defense: Never ignore small monthly charges on a store credit card…never pay an amount less than you owe even if it looks like the store is mistaken.

BANKS

• **ATM denial charges.** You can sometimes be charged for using an ATM even when you don't withdraw money.

Example: Recently, I needed money but wasn't near a branch of my own bank. So I withdrew money from a different bank's ATM. I tried to get $400, but their machine let me have only $300, which they informed me was my daily limit. Later in that month, I received my bank statement. I was charged a fee from the competing bank for using its ATM and an additional $1.50 fee from my own bank for "ATM denial," supposedly to cover the cost of processing the request that exceeded my daily ATM withdrawal limit.

Self-defense: Find out from your bank the maximum you can withdraw in a day from an ATM. It can vary depending on your financial institution, the city you live in and what kind of accounts you have. Or consider banking at a credit union. They have fewer sneaky charges and typically refund your fees when you use ATMs other than their own. To find one, contact a credit union league representative in your state. (Access the Credit Union National Association Web site at *www.creditunion.coop/ statej_o.html* to find a representative.)

• **Cash withdrawal overdraft fees.** You can check your account balances using an ATM— but these machines don't always tell you the truth. Some automatically add the amount of your overdraft protection to the balance shown for your checking account. So, if there's $80 in your checking account and overdraft protection of $200, the ATM indicates that you have a checking account balance of $280.

Trap: If you believe this number and withdraw more than $80, you're hit with an overdraft fee ($35 to $40) and a daily fee ($2 to $10) until you pay off the overdraft. If you write a check for more than $80, you are charged a bounced-check fee ($25) from your bank and perhaps one from the merchant to whom you wrote the check.

Self-defense: Sign up for the type of overdraft protection that authorizes the bank to take a cash advance from your credit card to cover checks or withdrawals that exceed your account balance. That way, an ATM machine will not inflate your balance. Of course, you will have to pay interest on any cash advance you do take, but it's less punitive than "courtesy" overdraft fees.

HOTELS

• **Hidden in-room charges.** Most of us do know to avoid the jacked-up prices for mini-bars and long-distance telephone calls in hotel rooms. But you can be charged fees even if you don't actually use the minibar or telephone. At some hotels now, a special sensor in the minibar is activated if you remove an item. Fail to replace it within 60 seconds, and the "purchase" will show up on your bill. At other hotels, you can be charged a dollar a day for the ability to make room-to-room calls regardless of whether you actually make them.

Self-defense: When you check in, ask the management if the price is all-inclusive. Upon checkout, give yourself enough time to study the bill and complain, if necessary, before you leave. Most hotels don't want to lose the goodwill of a customer over a small, unfair charge. Unfortunately, many travelers are in such a rush that they do not look at their bills until they get home. Then they can't be bothered to write a complaint letter to get back a few dollars.

WEB SITES

• **Rush-order upgrade charges.** The Internet merchandise that comes with free shipping seems like a great deal. But some Web sites manage to charge you a fee anyway. The fine print in your bill of sale often says that it could take your package two weeks or more to arrive. That's because your item is "throttled"—purposely held back in the mailroom for 10 days—before it is shipped.

Trap: The only way to avoid this frustration and get your package sooner is to pay an additional $4.99. These rush orders do not mean the actual shipping is faster. It means the company won't process your order in their warehouse in slow motion.

Self-defense: Make sure that you are using the total price, including shipping and additional fees, when you compare deals on different Web sites.

FIGHTING BACK

If you've already been charged a sneaky fee, choose your battles efficiently. There are enormous disparities among the industries when it comes to who best accommodates complaining consumers. For example, it's always worth challenging credit card companies, as they're the most likely to issue an unhappy customer a refund on a fee or surcharge.

In one nationwide survey I commissioned, consumers had a 65% success rate in getting a fee refunded from the credit card company. That was followed up closely by airlines (60%) and supermarkets/grocery stores (57%). It's a bit trickier to get justice from hotels (37%) and banks (33%). And it's very difficult to prevail with cell phone providers (27%) and cable- and satellite-television providers (20%).

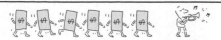

10 Easy Ways to Save $5,000 EACH Year

Gregory Karp, whose "Spending Smart" column appears in numerous newspapers, including the *Chicago Tribune* and *Baltimore Sun*. Based in Philadelphia, he is author of *Living Rich by Spending Smart: How to Get More of What You Really Want* (Financial Times).

With the economy sputtering and values of homes falling, many Americans are looking for ways to slash their bills. *The following strategies can add up to savings of more than $5,000 each year without significantly diminishing your quality of life...*

FOOD AND DRINK

• **Shop for groceries on your supermarket's 12-week sale cycle.** Most products in the typical grocery store—except milk, eggs and bread—are put on sale at least once every 12 weeks, often for 20% to 30% below their usual prices.* Rather than buy what you need once per week, buy three-month supplies of the items you use that are currently on sale. Of course, don't stock up on foods that spoil quickly unless they can be frozen.

Savings: $1,700. An average American family of four can spend about $8,500 on groceries each year. Trimming that bill by 20% saves $1,700.

• **Eat in restaurants when you really want to, not when you just feel like it.** There is nothing wrong with eating out when you are in the mood for a restaurant meal, but people often eat out simply because they are too tired or too rushed to cook.

Instead, cook about two or three times the amount of food you need when you do have the time and energy to cook, and freeze the excess. When time is precious, a home-cooked meal is just a few microwave minutes away.

Savings: $360. A restaurant meal for two costs $30 even at inexpensive chain restaurants. Home-cooked meals typically cost half as much, if not less. Convert two restaurant trips into two frozen homemade dinners each month, and you will save $360 per year.

*Figures, prices, rates and offers subject to change.

• **Don't buy bottled water.** Bottled water is no safer or better-tasting than most tap water. ABC News tested bottled and New York City tap water for bacteria and found that there was no difference in purity. Some people worry about traces of chemicals and minerals in tap water, but the trace amounts usually aren't harmful.

Savings: $311 per person per year. One person might drink one $6 case of bottled water a week. That's $312 a year. Tap water costs five cents per gallon, or less than two cents per equivalent case—about $1 for the year.

INSURANCE

• **Refinance term-life insurance.** Term-life rates have fallen dramatically during the past decade. If you bought your policy more than a few years ago and are still in good health, shop around for a better deal. The Web sites AccuQuote.com, Term4Sale.com and Insure.com can help you find the best rates.

Savings: $700 or above every year for a $500,000 policy.

• **Increase the deductibles on your home and auto insurance.** Higher deductibles mean lower premiums. They also mean more out of your own pocket if you need to make a claim, but making smaller claims is a bad idea anyway, because your insurance company could respond by rescinding your policy or raising your rates. Increase your auto insurance deductible to between $500 and $1,000 and your homeowner's insurance deductible to between $1,500 and $2,500.

Auto insurance savings: $280 per year. Increasing your deductible from $200 up to $1,000 could reduce premiums by as much as 40%—that's a $280 savings for someone paying $700 per year.

Home insurance savings: $210. Increasing your homeowner's insurance deductible from $250 to $2,500 could save you as much as 30%—that's $210 for someone paying $700 per year.

PHONE

• **Find telecom bargains.** If you have a computer and broadband Internet service, switch to Internet-based "VoIP" long-distance phone service. The service magicJack (800-897-8700,

www.magicjack.com) will provide you with a phone number and unlimited calls through a standard phone for just $40 the first year and $20 in subsequent years (calls to countries other than the US and Canada cost extra).

Downsides: Your computer and modem or high-speed service, such as DSL, must remain on…your phone will not work during power failures (unless your service has backup power)…and call quality will be only as good as your broadband connection.

If you do not have broadband Internet service, online sites such as ABTolls.com, TRAC.org, MyRatePlan.com, PhoneRateFinder.com, CheapTelephoneBills.com and SaveOnPhone.com can help you find long-distance rates as low as three cents per minute.

magicJack savings: $560. The typical family spends $600 per year on a phone line and long-distance bill. Switching to magicJack will save you $560 in the first year and $580 in following years.

Switching carrier savings: $100. A less expensive long-distance carrier might save you more than $100 per year, depending on your calling habits.

• **Switch to prepaid cellular service if you average less than 200 minutes of cellular talk-time per month.** Most cell phone users pay a hefty monthly fee for minutes that expire. Those who use their cell phones infrequently or irregularly should instead pay a flat up-front fee for "prepaid plan" minutes that do not expire for up to one year.

Savings: $520. The average cell phone user pays about $720 a year for 1,000 minutes per month. T-Mobile's Prepaid Plan charges $100 for 1,000 minutes which do not expire for 12 months, with no monthly fee. If you purchase 2,000 minutes per year, your total annual cell phone bill will be $200—a $520 savings.

OTHER SAVINGS

• **Cut ink-jet printer cartridge costs.** Replacement printer cartridges can cost as much as $30 to $40 apiece.

Store-brand cartridges are cheaper than the name brands and nearly as good. Cartridge-refill stores, such as Cartridge World (888-997-3345, *www.cartridgeworldusa.com*), put new ink in old cartridges for less than the cost of new cartridges.

Savings: $40 or more per year. Using store-brand cartridges or professional refill shops could cut your ink costs in half. Annual savings could be $40 or $50 if you use two printer cartridges per year.

• **Use your local library.** Borrow books for free. Most libraries have extensive DVD collections as well, although they may lack the newest releases.

Book savings: $300. Checking one hard-cover book out of your library every month rather than buying it for $25 saves you $300 per year.

Movie savings: $200. Checking out library movies once a week rather than subscribing to the Netflix movie delivery service (the most popular plan is $16.99 a month) saves almost $200.

• **Buy contact lenses online.** Get your prescription from your eye doctor, then order contact lenses online. Reliable Internet contact lens retailers include 1800Contacts and VisionDirect.

Savings: $50 a year based on average disposable contact lens use.

Money-Saving Web Sites

PriceProtectr.com helps you get money back if the price of an item you bought falls—you register purchases and get e-mails when prices drop. Claim the cash with an e-mail, a phone call or a store visit. GasBuddy.com and GasPriceWatch.com track the least expensive gas stations by area—just enter the appropriate zip code. RetailMeNot.com offers coupons for 20,000 online merchants. Honesty.com tells you how much things usually sell for on eBay so that you do not overpay. Bookingbuddy.com consolidates multiple travel sites at a single place so that you can search them all at once.

Good Housekeeping, 300 W. 57 St., New York City 10019, *www.goodhousekeeping.com.*

20 Ways to Cut Your Grocery Bills

Judy Walker, the food editor of *The Times-Picayune,* New Orleans, *www.timespicayune.com.* She is a member of the Association of Food Journalists, Southern Foodways Alliance and the Arizona Culinary Hall of Fame.

Sticker shock! That's what you face every time you go to your supermarket these days.

So, what's a consumer to do? *Here's how to keep your grocery bills as low as possible...*

PLAN YOUR TRIPS

1. Take a shopping list. To keep the list to a minimum, plan your meals for the week and then list the ingredients you need to buy. Stick to your list—but be flexible. Take advantage of store specials you come across.

2. Pay attention to what you have on hand—especially perishables. That way, you won't have to throw away unused food.

3. Learn the layout of your grocery store.

Sneaky secret: Stores put dairy products and meat in the back of the store to force you to walk down their aisles of temptation—processed foods sold at higher markups—to get there. If you're making a quick trip for milk, keep this in mind and be resolute—buy only milk.

4. Eat first. This tried-and-true tactic bears repeating. Going to the grocery store hungry is the reason we buy on impulse.

SKIP NONESSENTIALS

5. Drink the tap water. Nearly all municipal water in America is so good that nobody ever needs to drink water from Italy or France (or Maine, for that matter). Drinking the recommended eight glasses a day from bottled water costs as much as $1,400 annually. If you don't like the taste of your local water, buy a faucet filter or filtering pitcher.

6. Do not buy processed foods. They cost more than meals you put together yourself from basic ingredients and generally are not as nutritious.

7. Grate your own. Like processed foods, pre-grated carrots, cheese, etc., cost more—and often don't taste as fresh.

8. Skip the precuts. Cut meat and produce yourself, rather than buying individual servings or pieces.

9. Clean your own fish. It is cheaper per pound of edible fish to buy whole fish (the smaller varieties, of course) at the market and then remove the head, tail, etc., at home.

10. Don't buy toiletries at the grocery store. Write a separate list of toiletries and paper products for the discount stores, such as Costco, BJ's and Sam's Club, where they'll cost 20% to 40% less.

SHOPPING STRATEGIES

11. Don't be fooled by phony sales.

Sneaky secret: Items displayed on the ends of aisles aren't necessarily on sale. Manufacturers of those items pay for those prime display locations.

Better: Compare prices in the main aisles, where products compete against each other.

12. Know when to buy in bulk. Only buy groceries you know that you'll use before they go bad. Nonperishables are the safest to buy in bulk.

Also: Just because an item is available in a larger size doesn't mean it is cheaper. Take a calculator to the supermarket to check "unit prices" by dividing price by quantity.

13. Choose generic. You can almost always save money by choosing a store label or little-known brand instead of a well-known brand. In some cases, particularly with items such as orange juice and condiments, the savings can be tremendous.

14. Stoop and reach.

A sneaky secret: Food manufacturers pay for valuable, eye-level shelf space at grocery stores—and their prices reflect it. So, search high and low, literally, for comparable items on other shelves.

15. Buy "must go" foods. Bypass the more expensive fresh-baked bread and reach for the day-old selection. Keep it in the freezer for toasting. Also, most bakery departments will discount fresh items drastically as the end of the day nears—you may just have to ask.

Markets frequently discount dairy, baked goods, produce and meat as these items approach their "sell-by" dates or become less attractive (think very slightly bruised apples or crushed bread). These items are tasty and perfectly safe to eat, even several days after purchase. Ask the staff at your supermarket when they mark items down. Time your shopping accordingly.

16. Shop less often. Shoppers who make "quick trips" to the market usually purchase more than they planned. If you go to the store three times a week and spend $10 on impulse buys each trip, that adds up to $120 extra per month. But if you go only once a week and spend this same $10 on impulse buys every time, you'll spend $40 per month on impulse buys. That saves you $80 per month, or $960 per year.

17. Use the buddy system. Save money by sharing costs with someone else.

Examples: Split two-for-one offers...the contents of large, well-priced packages, such as a bag of potatoes...share the price of gas to the supermarket.

MAXIMIZE COUPONS

18. Check all sources for coupons. Americans saved an estimated $30 billion with manufacturers' coupons last year. Most of the 278 billion coupons redeemed came from Sunday papers. But it can really pay to check manufacturers' Web sites, as well as specialty Internet coupon sites, such as DealCatcher (*www.dealcatcher.com*) and CoolSavings (*www.coolsavings.com*).

Also: Take advantage of double- and triple-coupon policies at local supermarkets.

BE CHECKOUT SAVVY

You've come to the finish line—don't blow it now...

19. Fight checkout temptation. The candy, gadgets and magazines right around the cash registers are high-profit items for the store—and the least useful to you. Resist!

20. Keep a close eye on the scanner. Americans lose from $1 billion to $3 billion a year on scanning discrepancies. Scanners are not always reset with current sale prices, so your chance of being charged the full price on a sale item is high.

How to Cash In Big with Coupons

Susan Samtur, editor of *Refundle Bundle,* a newsletter covering coupon and rebate opportunities, *www. refundlebundle.com,* and operator of the online grocery coupon Web site SelectCouponProgram.com.

Coupon use has surged in recent months as consumers trim their budgets in this recession. During the fourth quarter of 2008, coupon redemptions rose by 15%, versus a year earlier.

Coupons easily can trim 10% to 20% from your grocery bill—and it is possible to save much more if you're willing to put in a little time and effort. I recently used coupons and rebates to purchase $211 in groceries for a total of 42 cents.

Supermarkets are no longer the only places to save. Pharmacies, hardware stores, home stores and online retailers are offering big savings, too. *Some of the best offers…*

ONLINE COUPONS

The most attractive of coupons often are available only on the Internet, not in Sunday newspaper circulars. Some Web sites—including Coupons.com…RetailMeNot.com…and my site, SelectCouponProgram.com—offer you a wide range of coupons.*

Also visit the Web sites of the companies that make the food products, over-the-counter pharmaceuticals, health and beauty products, household products and other consumer products that you buy. Many of these companies are likely to provide printable coupons on their Web sites, or they will mail or e-mail coupons to consumers who sign up for their e-letters.

---

*The companies and Web sites listed in this article offer attractive coupons and rebates continually, but the specific offers mentioned are subject to change.

Most consumer product companies list their Web addresses on the packaging. If not, try using the company's name followed by ".com," or search for the company's name on Google. com.

Once on a company's Web site, look for a link along the lines of "sign up," "newsletter," "promotions," "special offers" or "coupons." If a company's Web site is very complex, it might be easier to search for the product name on Google rather than the company name.

Example: At Bayer.com, it is not easy to locate coupons…but at Aleve.com—the Web site for Bayer's painkiller—it is easy to find a coupon for $1 off any Aleve product.

You likely will have to register on the company's Web site and provide an e-mail address to access the coupons. Some Web sites let you print coupons as soon as you register…while others e-mail the coupons to you periodically. You might want to create one e-mail account specifically for this purpose.

You may need to download a coupon-printing program. Download these programs only from the Internet sites of well-known companies. Downloading programs from disreputable Internet sites can upload viruses onto your computer.

Among the companies that frequently feature appealing Internet coupons…

• **Betty Crocker/General Mills** (*www.betty crocker.com,* select "Coupons" at the top of the screen). Brands include Betty Crocker…Bisquick…Cheerios…Chex…Häagen-Dazs…Pillsbury…Progresso…Green Giant…and Yoplait.

Examples: 60 cents off Bisquick…$1 off two Yoplait yogurts.

• **Colgate-Palmolive** (*www.colgate.com,* click "Special Offers"). Brands include Ajax…Colgate…Murphy Oil Soap…Palmolive…Softsoap …and Speed Stick.

Examples: $1 off Colgate Sensitive toothpaste…$1 off Palmolive Pure & Clear.

• **Del Monte** (go to *www.fruitundressed.com/ offers*).

Examples: $1 off of Del Monte Citrus Bowl…Orchard Select…or SunFresh refrigerated glass jar products.

• **Gorton's seafood** (go to *www.gortons.com,* click "Coupons & Promotions" at the bottom of the screen). Request a free wall calendar featuring $15 worth of coupons.

• **Iams pet foods** (at *www.iams.com,* click "Join Iams").

Example: $5 off Iams pet foods.

• **Procter & Gamble** (at *www.pgesaver.com,* register for the P&G Everyday Solutions free monthly newsletter). Brands include Cascade …Charmin…Clairol…Crest…Duracell…Fixodent…Gillette…Ivory…Metamucil…Mr. Clean…Old Spice…Pampers…Secret…Swiffer …Tide…and Vicks.

Examples: $7 for Crest Whitening Strips… $5 for Swiffer WetJet Starter Kit.

• **Quaker Oats** (*www.quakeroats.com,* select "Offers & Promotions" under the "Products" tab).

Example: $1 off Quaker True Delights snack bars.

PHARMACY REBATE PROGRAMS

The major pharmacy chains frequently offer products at below cost to draw shoppers into their stores. The savings usually are provided through rebates, not coupons, however. Shoppers must sign up for the chain's rebate program, then log onto its Web site to enter code numbers from their receipts and request rebate checks to obtain their savings. (If you do not have Internet access, you usually can pick up rebate booklets in the stores, then mail in your receipts and rebate requests.)

These rebate programs are worth the trouble if you take advantage of numerous rebates each month. Pharmacy chain Web sites sometimes offer printable coupons as well.

• **CVS** (*www.cvs.com*). Sign up for the CVS "ExtraCare" rewards card, and get 2% back on most purchases and an extra $1 back for every two prescriptions filled. CVS also offers printable online coupons on its Web site.

Examples: $3 off Huggies Pure & Natural diapers…$1 off Bausch & Lomb ReNu Multi-Plus Solution.

• **Rite Aid** (*http://riteaid.rebateplus.com*). The Rite Aid Rebate Plus program offers hundreds of dollars in savings each month.

Examples: $3 rebate on one box of Depends underwear…$3 rebate on 24-count or larger Claritin allergy relief pills…$1 rebate on any Mentholatum product.

• **Walgreens** (*www.walgreens.com,* click on "EasySaver Rebates"). Walgreens EasySaver rebate program offers dozens of rebates on health and beauty products each month. Walgreens' Web site also features printable coupons.

Examples: Free Axe shampoo or conditioner rebate, up to $6.99 value…a $10 rebate when you purchase two packages of Energizer batteries.

MORE SAVINGS

Some retailers offer attractive rebates and coupons so frequently that it's worth checking out their Web sites…signing up for their newsletters…or enrolling in their loyalty programs before buying anything.

Also, you can pick up at your post office a "Mover's Guide" address-forwarding packet, which often contains store coupons.

• **Ace Hardware** (at *www.acehardware.com,* click on "Ace Rewards" at the bottom of the screen). The Ace Rewards program offers 10 points for each $1 you spend, with $5 off your next purchase for each 2,500 points and 1,000 free bonus points for signing up.

• **Bed Bath & Beyond** (*www.bedbathandbeyond.com,* click "Email Signup"). Sign up for the company's mailing list online, and receive a continual stream of coupons.

Example: 20% off any item.

• **Gap** (or Gap Inc. sister stores Old Navy and Banana Republic). Visit the Web site listed on your receipt. Fill out the quick online survey to earn a 20% discount off one regularly priced item.

• **The Home Depot** (*www.homedepotmoving.com/moving*). Register a recent or upcoming move on the home center's Web site, and earn 10% off your next purchase, up to $200 in savings.

• **Lowe's** (*www.lowes.com,* click "Lowe's Moving Center" at the bottom of the screen under "Partner Websites," then "Request Your Coupon"). Get a 10% coupon on Lowe's purchases up to $5,000.

187

- **Staples** (*www.staples.com*). Staples often features office supplies priced below cost in its weekly circular or on its Web site.

    Example: Purchase one ream of paper, get one free.

- **True Value Hardware** (at *www.truevalue.com,* click on "True Value Rewards"). The True Value Rewards program provides one point per dollar spent, with $10 off for each 250 points. Program members receive other special offers as well.

    Example: True Value recently offered its members 20% off everything they could cram into a free canvas tote bag. To increase my savings, I filled my bag with items for which I also had newspaper coupons.

Delicious Coffee for Less

Great coffee doesn't have to cost a lot. In a recent taste test of 19 ground, caffeinated coffees, Eight O'Clock 100% Colombian, at $6.28/pound,* ranked highest—above more expensive Folgers, Maxwell House, Starbucks and other brands. Decaf coffees, in general, did not taste as good as caffeinated coffees. The best decaf coffees were Dunkin' Donuts Dunkin' Decaf, Millstone Decaf 100% Colombian and Folgers Gourmet Selections.

Bob Markovich, home and yard editor, *Consumer Reports,* 101 Truman Ave., Yonkers, New York 10703, *www.consumerreports.org.*

*Price subject to change.

The Incredible Shrinking Package

Companies are shrinking packaging as a way to increase prices. Ice cream makers, which downsized from the traditional half gallon to 1.75 quarts five years ago, are selling containers of 1.5 quarts—without reducing the price per container.

Result: A price hike on a per-serving basis.

Also: Mayonnaise jars that used to hold 32 ounces now hold 30 and cereals have shrunk from 11 ounces to 8.7 ounces.

Edgar Dworsky, founder of Consumerworld.org, and former Massachusetts assistant attorney general, Somerville, Massachusetts.

Cleaning Supplies for Less...All-Natural, Too

Cheaper cleaning products often are just as effective as brand-name ones. Baking soda removes baked-on food and gets stains off tile, glass and china. Cream of tartar gets stains off of sinks and tubs and removes spots from aluminum cookware. Lemon juice removes tarnish from brass, bronze, copper and aluminum. White vinegar cleans coffeemakers and chrome, removes some carpet stains and cleans wood floors (use one cup per pail of hot water).

Consumer Reports, 101 Truman Ave., Yonkers, New York 10703, *www.consumerreports.org.*

 # Dollar-Store Deals And Rip-Offs

Beth Pinsker-Gladstone, editor of AOL's WalletPop.com, a personal finance site, and Marlene Alexander, the dollar-store expert for WalletPop who also writes about dollar-store decorating ideas on her online site, *www.dollarstorestyle.com.*

Dollar stores—the discount retailers that charge about a dollar for each item—are popular in this unstable economic climate. But not everything they provide is a good bargain. Some dollar-store products are poorly made, and others could be purchased elsewhere for a better price.

Steep inflation in recent years has made it difficult for dollar stores to provide as much as they once did for $1. These retailers really can't raise their prices—they wouldn't be dollar stores if their merchandise cost more than $1—so they need to resort to subtler ways to charge more, such as reducing the quality or quantity of their goods.

Example: A dollar-store package of paper napkins that once provided 100 napkins for $1 now might provide just 50 or 75...or it might include 100 napkins made from lower-quality paper.

GREAT BUYS

A dozen products that tend to be excellent deals at dollar stores...

•**Cleaning products.** Cleaning solutions, clothing detergents, furniture polish and other common household products often cost less at dollar stores than anywhere else.

Exception: Dishwashing liquid. The dollar stores typically sell name-brand dishwashing liquid in 11-ounce bottles. You can find 32-ounce bottles at supermarkets for as little as $2,* a lower per-ounce price.

•**Dishes and glassware.** To find these at $1 per piece at other discount retailers, you would have to purchase prepackaged sets of 16 to 30 dishes or glasses. At a dollar store, you can buy only what you need. Quality and styling are comparable to what you'd find at Walmart.

•**Gift wrap.** A roll of gift wrap might cost just $5 at a stationery store or $3 at a standard discount store. A dollar-store roll is a deal if it contains at least the standard 12.5 square feet of paper. Dollar stores also sell colorful gift bags that can be used instead of wrapping paper. The $1-per-bag price is a fraction of the $2 to $5 you would pay elsewhere.

•**Greeting cards.** Most dollar stores offer nice greeting cards at two for $1. Comparable cards can cost $3.50 each at other retailers.

•**Grooming tools.** Dollar stores often stock basic manicure sets that include nail clippers, tweezers and cuticle scissors, all for $1. These items are likely to cost at least $1 apiece anywhere else. Emery boards, hairbrushes and hand mirrors also are good dollar-store buys.

•**Kitchen accessories.** Dollar stores offer a wide range of kitchen implements, such as

*Prices subject to change.

ladles, spatulas, dish racks and can openers, that typically cost several dollars or more elsewhere. Dollar-store kitchen tools generally are reasonably well-made, but don't expect fancy extras, such as ergonomic grips.

Exception: Avoid kitchen knives at a dollar store. The low-quality blades dull quickly.

•**Mops, brooms and scrub brushes.** Don't expect to find a large push broom for $1, but if all you need is a simple broom or mop, you won't beat the dollar-store price.

•**Picture frames.** Most dollar stores stock a wide variety of picture frames up to 8 x 12–inch and occasionally even larger. The quality is comparable to frames costing several dollars or more at other stores.

•**Plastic storage bins.** Many dollar stores feature a selection of stackable plastic storage bins and small plastic garbage pails, bargains at $1 each. Don't expect to find large storage bins or garbage pails, however.

•**Holiday decorations and party favors.** Most retailers offer great deals on seasonal merchandise only during end-of-season clearance sales. At the dollar store, you will find holiday decorations and other seasonal goods at $1 apiece when you need them.

Example: Christmas tree ornaments for just $1.

•**Simple tools.** Tools are much cheaper at the dollar store than in your hardware store. With most tools, it makes sense to pay extra for higher quality, but with certain basic tools, dollar-store quality is good enough.

Examples: All-metal 10-inch claw hammers...16-foot measuring tapes...pliers...and putty knives.

•**Socks.** Dollar-store socks often are just as good as department store socks that can cost $2.50 per pair or more.

DOLLAR STORE DON'TS

A dozen product categories best avoided at the dollar store...

•**Baby food.** Most baby food sold in dollar stores is perfectly fine, but some has been found to contain trace amounts of dangerous chemicals. The savings are not worth the risk.

• **Bagged candy.** You'll get more for your money if you purchase economy-sized packages of candy at one of the discount stores, such as Walmart.

• **Batteries.** Target and Walmart usually offer better deals on batteries, assuming that you are willing to buy in quantity. If you need four or fewer batteries of a certain size, dollar-store deals could be competitive. Buy only name-brand batteries.

• **Bottled water.** Dollar stores typically sell water in packs of four 16.9-ounce bottles for $1, which is 25 cents per bottle. Similarly sized bottles of water can be purchased at Walmart, Costco and other discounters for less than 15 cents per bottle if you buy in cases of 24 or 35.

• **Children's toys.** Dollar-store toys often break easily. They even can be hazardous (if the broken pieces are small enough for a child to swallow). Some dollar-store toys, including toy jewelry, contain lead.

Better bets: It is safe to buy coloring books, name-brand toys and toys for kids old enough to know not to put them in their mouths.

• **Disposable plates, cups and napkins.** You are likely to find better deals on paper, plastic and Styrofoam kitchen items at Walmart or other discounters, assuming that you buy them in large quantities.

Better bet: Dollar-store cloth napkins are a good deal, though perhaps not high enough quality for when guests visit.

• **Extension cords.** The low-quality extension cords like those typically sold at dollar stores can short out or even cause fires.

• **Off-brand food.** Food packaged by obscure food companies could be of poor quality, or it might be sold in smaller-than-standard quantities, meaning that it is not actually the bargain it seems. Food from well-known companies might be a good deal, but make sure it isn't past its expiration date.

• **Pet food and toys.** Pet food from obscure manufacturers might lack nutritional value or even contain unsafe ingredients. Off-brand pet toys might be made with chemicals dangerous to animals.

Better bet: Pet collars and other pet items that will not go into the pet's mouth can be good deals.

• **Resealable sandwich bags.** A dollar store might offer a box of 13 resealable sandwich bags for $1, a per-bag price of almost eight cents. You could find these bags for less than five cents apiece if you bought them in larger quantities at Walmart, Target or similar retailers…or as little as two cents apiece at a discount club, such as Costco or Sam's Club.

• **Toothpaste.** Dollar stores will typically sell 2.5-ounce tubes of name-brand toothpastes for $1. The discount stores offer lower per-ounce prices on the larger tubes. Supermarkets and pharmacies might offer better deals, too, if you wait for sales. Dollar stores sell larger tubes of off-brand toothpaste for $1, but dangerous ingredients have been found in some off-brand toothpastes. They are not worth the risk.

• **Vitamins.** Studies of off-brand vitamins, such as those sold in dollar stores, have found that they don't always deliver the vitamin content that they claim.

Going-Out-of-Business Sales: How to Get the Best Deals

Sue Goldstein, founder, The Underground Shopper, a 37-year-old company focused on bargain-shopping. Goldstein has written more than 70 books on the topic over the past four decades. She hosts a morning call-in radio program at radio station KVCE-AM in Dallas. Her Web site is *www.undergroundshopper.com*.

Retail bankruptcies and cutbacks are creating a flood of going-out-of-business sales.

What most people do not know: To get real bargains at liquidation sales, you need to be especially careful. That's because most of these sales are run by outside liquidation specialists that have zero incentive to retain you as a customer. They use merchandising tricks that could leave you with the illusion of a great deal that doesn't save you much money at all.

My favorite strategies for getting the most from going-out-of-business sales…

•**Skip the first few weeks of the sale.** Liquidators typically start with a 10% storewide discount.

But there's a catch: All the prices are first raised up to the full manufacturer's suggested retail prices (MSRPs) before the markdown is applied. That means many items start out at prices higher than what the store sold them for before bankruptcy.

Liquidators are hoping to attract a flood of customers and prey on consumer excitement and naïveté.

Better: Wait until week four. A liquidation sale usually runs six to 12 weeks, with prices dropping by about 10% each week. For shoppers, it's a cat-and-mouse game because as the discounts get deeper, the selection of products becomes more limited. I have found that week four is the sweet spot. That's when discounts are starting to get substantial, but there's still decent merchandise available.

•**Expect little help from salespeople or managers.** The liquidation sales staff is just a skeleton crew that cannot lower prices (if, say, you want to buy the floor model). They have little or no knowledge to answer your technical questions. They may not even know what merchandise will arrive at the store that week.

•**Confirm that a bargain really is a bargain.** This works best with brand-name items (especially electronics, toys and china), whose prices can be easily compared among various retailers. If you own an Internet-enabled phone, use it right in the store as a price checker. Key the product name and model number into a search engine, such as Google, or a retail or price-comparison site to see what it is selling for elsewhere. If you cannot use your cell phone, write down the model number of the item you want, then go on the Internet at home.

Examples of sites where you can compare prices: www.amazon.com…www.ebay. *com…www.consumersearch.com…www.price grabber.com.*

Smart: Call the store's nearest competitors. They're sometimes willing to match the liquidator's sale price. If you can get the same deal, go with the healthy store.

•**Check the price tag on an item to make sure that it looks like the others throughout the store.** Many liquidators supplement a store's existing stock with their own inferior merchandise or leftovers from previous liquidations. If the price tag has a different typeface, format or color, be wary.

Example: Electronics that may be brought in as part of excess inventory are sometimes reconditioned but sold as brand-new.

•**Inspect your merchandise thoroughly before purchasing.** Never buy a product if you're not allowed to open the box first in the store. When you open the box, make sure that the product comes with the appropriate accessories, instruction booklet and manufacturer warranty and that the item is in good condition. Plug in all electronics to make sure they work. Most liquidators impose a "no-return, no-exchange" policy. If you get home and realize that there is a problem, you're out of luck.

Help from the "Budget Fashionista"

Kathryn "The Budget Fashionista" Finney, a Jersey City, New Jersey, author of *How to Be a Budget Fashionista: The Ultimate Guide to Looking Fabulous for Less* (Ballantine). She has served as fashion and shopping expert for CNN, NBC's *Today* show, Fox Television Network, *Reader's Digest, USA Today* and *InStyle* magazine. Her Web site is *www.thebudgetfashionista.com.*

You can pick up top designers' clothing at bargain prices. JCPenney carries a "career bridge" collection called Nicole by designer Nicole Miller (known mostly for her beautiful dresses). Spiegel (800-345-4500, *www.spiegel.com*) features designs by Norma Kamali, who popularized the use of stretchy jersey knits in women's fashion in the 1980s. The jersey sportswear collection features more than 20 attractive convertible pieces, including dresses, pants and tank tops, priced at $99 or less.* Target sells Isaac Mizrahi's line of hip women's fashions, with most pieces retailing for less than $50. Sears carries budget lines by top fashion designers, such as Alvin Valley (known as "Lord of the Pants" to the fashion community, pants retail for $30 and below) and Anne Klein, whose AK2 line includes several career-oriented styles that are very similar to her higher-priced "red label" line.

*Prices subject to change.

To Get the Best Price for Your Jewelry...

Joe Brandt, consultant to retail jewelers, and president of J.L. Brandt Company Inc. in Ridgefield, Connecticut, *www.jlbrandtcompany.com*. He is author of *Protecting the Family Jewels* (J.L. Brandt).

Thinking of selling some of your jewelry pieces? *Be sure to keep the following advice in mind...*

• **Appraisals or bills of sale have little bearing on the price you'll get when selling.** Generally, you won't get more than the "scrap" value.

• **Take each piece to several places that buy jewelry and get competing offers.** Try the pawnshops, especially when selling gold. Most jewelers do not buy used jewelry.

• **To get more money, sell to an individual (such as to a friend or relative) through a private sale**—you might get as much as 50% of retail.

• **Sell through eBay.** This is reasonably safe if done carefully and if you use a third party, such as PayPal, for the financial transaction.

Note: Protect valuable jewelry from being stolen before you can sell it by storing it in a hard-to-find place, such as a hollowed-out book. Never use a jewelry box on your dresser. That should be reserved for costume jewelry only—if anything is stolen, it will probably be that box.

It Pays to Shop Around

Shop around for eyeglasses. The same pair of glasses was priced recently at $178 to $390* depending on where it was bought. There is price variation in lenses and in frames. Doctors and independent optical shops tend to charge more but provide more personal service. Chain stores often make glasses in about an hour and may provide discounts for members of AARP, AAA and other groups. Warehouse clubs offer low prices and, in some cases, do not require membership for eyeglass purchases. Internet merchants may offer the lowest prices of all. One, Zenni Optical, offers eyeglasses (frames and lenses) starting as low as $8.

Robert Krughoff, president of Consumers' Checkbook, a nonprofit consumer information guide, Washington, DC, *www.checkbook.org*.

*Prices subject to change.

The Best Stores

The National Quality Research Center has announced stores with the highest customer satisfaction. Nordstrom got the highest score from retail customers. Lowe's fared best in the home-improvement category. The highest-scoring supermarket was Publix, and among online retailers, Amazon.com and electronics retailer Newegg scored best. Walmart was lowest-rated among discount department stores, followed by home-improvement retailer The Home Depot. Among supermarkets, Whole Foods got good marks for quality but low scores for customer loyalty.

Claes G. Fornell, PhD, professor of business administration and marketing, and director, National Quality Research Center, which produces the American Customer Satisfaction Index (ACSI) based on more than 65,000 interviews annually, Stephen M. Ross School of Business, University of Michigan, Ann Arbor.

Beware Retail Therapy

For many people, shopping stimulates the brain's production of *dopamine*, which is associated with feelings of pleasure and satisfaction. This may be why some people shop too much.

Self-defense: Buy only items on a list you make before leaving the house…pay with cash or a debit card—not a credit card—to remain within your financial limits…window shop after stores have closed…don't shop when visiting friends or relatives—the added novelty can lead to even higher dopamine production, putting you at greater risk of buying things you don't need.

Gregory Berns, MD, PhD, neuroscientist at Emory University, Atlanta, and author of *Satisfaction: The Science of Finding True Fulfillment* (Holt).

Lost Your Receipt?

Here's how to improve your chances of getting a refund from a store when you don't have a receipt…

First, find out about the store's return policy, and conform to as much of it as possible. Emphasize what you do have, such as all the tags and the original packaging. Request store credit or an exchange if you cannot get cash back. If you are a regular customer, mention that. Talk to a supervisor if a lower-level person is not helpful, and see if the store will make a onetime exception for you. Continue speaking to higher-level people, up to the store manager if necessary. Finally, be sure to express gratitude for any help you receive.

Mary Hunt, editor, *Debt-Proof Living*, Box 2076, Paramount, California 90723, *www.debtproofliving.com.*

More from Mary Hunt…

Low-Cost Gift Giving

You don't have to spend a lot of money to give great gifts. *Here are some inexpensive—and fun—gifts to create for your friends and family…*

- **Have a family photo taken and framed.**
- **Create a book of your favorite recipes.**
- **Learn a craft,** such as knitting, and make gifts by hand.
- **Create gift baskets containing various small items** that each recipient especially values or enjoys.
- **Give an heirloom or family treasure** to someone in the next generation.
- **Put together an album with old family photos.**
- **Give everybody an experience,** such as dinner together, a movie or a night of reading for grandchildren.

A Wonderful Wedding for Less

For an elegant but less costly wedding, have a cocktail reception instead of a sit-down dinner. Schedule it for a Thursday or Friday night or a Sunday afternoon. Set up cocktail tables—enough for about half the guests so that people can sit whenever they wish and mingle the rest of the time. Set up finger-food buffets around the room, and have servers circulate with plenty of hors d'oeuvres. Have the cake-cutting ceremony toward the end, and serve cake, coffee, petits fours and chocolate-covered strawberries. Be sure to have music and dancing from start to finish.

Harriette Rose Katz, wedding specialist and event planner, New York City, and coeditor of *Where to Seat Aunt Edna and 500 Other Great Wedding Tips* (Hundreds of Heads).

The Best Cell Phone Plan for Your Family

Family cell phone plans aren't always the cheapest for the family. If different family members have very different usage patterns, separate plans may be cheaper.

Example: If one member uses the phone heavily for work, he or she may benefit from an unlimited calling plan. The other members could share minutes on a family plan.

Important: Even if family members have different plans, they should use the same carrier so that they can make unlimited calls to one another.

Joni Blecher, editorial director, LetsTalk.com, a San Francisco–based independent online retailer of wireless products and services.

Use Your Camera Phone To Save Time and Money

Bruce Pechman, who's known as the "Muscleman of Technology," *www.mrbicep.com.* He is a popular TV personality specializing in consumer technology and also appears regularly on major news programs.

Most cell phones now come with built-in digital cameras, which can aid you in a variety of ways…

SHOPPING

• **Take pictures of items you might want to purchase.** Make sure the full names and prices of the products are legible in your photos. Refer to the pictures when you see the item in other stores or when you shop for it online, to confirm that you are looking at exactly the same one…and to track which retailer offers the best price.

• **Record decorating ideas.** Take pictures of furniture, appliances and fabrics that you like when you see them in stores or other people's homes. Show these pictures to your spouse or your interior designer to confirm that everyone is on the same page. Or show them to clerks in stores to see if they have anything that is similar—perhaps at a lower price than that charged by the high-end store where you took the picture.

• **Remember a great wine.** Enjoy a bottle of wine at a restaurant? Taking a picture of its label will make it easier to find the same bottle in a wine store.

DRIVING AND PARKING

• **Find your parked vehicle quickly.** When you park in a large lot, take a picture of the nearest identifiable landmark or nearest lot section sign. When you park on a city street, take a picture of the street sign at the nearest intersection.

• **Document your traffic accident.** Photograph the damage to each vehicle, and get a picture of the other driver's license plate. Take a few pictures that show the entire accident scene as well. Later, if there's a dispute over what happened or how much damage was sustained, your pictures could settle it.

HEALTH HELP

• **Send a photo to your physician.** Are those harmless bug bites on your arm or a rash that requires medical attention? Your doctor might be willing to take a quick look at a digital picture and provide an opinion, saving you the expense and inconvenience of an office visit.

What to Do If Your Cell Phone Gets Wet

If your cell phone gets wet, immediately remove the battery. Turning it on can cause a short. Also, if your phone has a SIM card (a chip that stores information such as phone numbers), remove it, if possible. Use a can of compressed air or a vacuum cleaner to blow out as much water as possible. Never use a hair dryer, as the heat can warp components and melt internal adhesives. Finally, leave the phone and battery submerged in a bowl of uncooked rice overnight. This should help to wick away any leftover moisture.

Popular Mechanics, 300 W. 57 St., New York City 10019, *www.popularmechanics.com.*

Upgrade Your Computer or Buy New?

In general, upgrading a single component, such as the graphics card or hard drive, is quicker and cheaper than buying a new PC, setting it up on your network, removing and reinstalling all of your data and reconfiguring your programs. But if you are really looking for a complete overhaul—a new processor, more memory and a new graphics card and hard drive—then buying a new PC may be your better choice.

Rule of thumb: If you are thinking of replacing three parts that have a combined cost of $400 or more, instead put the money toward a new system.

PC World, 501 Second St., San Francisco 94107, on the Web at *www.pcworld.com.*

For Better Service, Turn It Off Once in Awhile

Periodically turn off and restart your computer, cell phone and any other software-driven devices to avoid problems. Turning off the device shuts down applications that you are not using and clears out the memory in the device. If you use a Web browser, shutting off the device frees up bits of memory left from previously closed windows, which gives your computer access to more memory for other programs.

Dana Blankenhorn, writer and blogger for the technology information site ZDNet, *www.zdnet.com.*

Simple Energy Saver

Most of today's electronic equipment and appliances consume electricity even if they are turned off. In fact, about 75% of the power consumed by home electronics is consumed when they aren't in use. Worst offenders tend to be televisions, DVD players, VCRs, cell phone chargers, computers and computing peripherals, and anything with a remote "on/off" control or continually lit LED light.

Simple energy saver: Plug such items into a surge-protector power strip, then turn the strip off when the plugged-in items are not in use.

Safety bonus: The surge protector lowers the risk for power overloads, reducing risk for fire—as does turning items truly "off" when not in use.

Meri-K Appy, president of the Home Safety Council, Washington, DC, *www.homesafetycouncil.org.*

Good Deals at Federal Auctions

To find a federal auction in your area, visit *www.usa.gov/shopping/shopping.shtml,* which lists federal auctions and state contacts for local auctions for boats, cars, real estate, books, jewelry, etc. IRS auctions (see *www.us treas.gov/auctions/irs*) sell off goods and real estate seized from delinquent taxpayers. Some companies hold no-fee auctions for federal, state and local governments.

Useful sites to visit: Bid4Assets (301-650-0003 or *www.bid4assets.com*), CWS Marketing Group (888-343-1313 or *www.cwsmarketing group.com*) and Government Liquidation (480-367-1300 or *www.govliquidation.com*).

Consumer Reports, 101 Truman Ave., Yonkers, New York 10703, *www.consumerreports.org.*

How to Get a Free Car

Get a free car in return for becoming a rolling advertisement. Some companies provide a vehicle with advertising on it to people who do a lot of driving in heavily populated areas. Other companies wrap your personal auto in vinyl film that promotes their products—and pay you for becoming a moving billboard. You may be asked to drive specific routes or park in specific places to maximize advertising exposure. To find legitimate companies offering free-car or vehicle-advertising deals, sign up with a specialized information directory, such as Free Car Index (*www.free carindex.com*) or The Free Car (*www.thefree car.com*).

Cost to sign up: Usually about $30.*

Used-Car-Advisor.com, an Internet site that provides a complete guide to buying, trading and selling used cars online.

*Price subject to change.

How to Pay Much Less for Health Care

Charles B. Inlander, a consumer advocate and health-care consultant located in Fogelsville, Pennsylvania. He was the founding president of the nonprofit People's Medical Society, a consumer advocacy organization credited with key improvements in the quality of US health care in the 1980s and 1990s, and is the author of 20 books, including *Take This Book to the Hospital with You: A Consumer Guide to Surviving Your Hospital Stay* (St. Martin's).

Most people never think about negotiating fees with a doctor or any other health-care provider. Negotiating is something we do with a car dealer or at a flea market. But the truth is, doctors and hospitals negotiate fees with insurance companies and the government all the time. So why not with you? If you have health insurance, you could save by negotiating such health-care fees as copayments. If you are uninsured or need a medical treatment that is not covered by your insurance, you could save even more. *How to negotiate charges for health care and medical products...*

• **Don't be afraid to ask.** Most doctors are willing to lower their fees for people with limited budgets who may not have health insurance

(or only very basic coverage). But you must initiate the negotiation.

My advice: If the quoted fee is more than you can pay, ask if some other payment arrangement, such as paying in monthly installments, can be made or if the quoted fee can be lowered.

What you might say: "What is the fee for this treatment/service? Unfortunately, I can't afford that. Can we negotiate?" If you've been treated by the health-care provider for many years, mention your loyal patronage.

• **Talk to the right person.** In a recent report published in *U.S. News & World Report*, a hospital's chief financial officer (CFO) noted that it is common for hospitals to decrease charges by 30% for needy or uninsured patients who contact the CFO directly. He noted that most hospitals give large health insurers discounts of 60% or more, so deals with individual patients are still profitable to the facility.

My advice: Always negotiate with a decision-maker. For fee reductions at a hospital, before you receive surgery or any other treatment, call the hospital and ask the operator to connect you to the office of the CFO or to the assistant CFO—one of them must sign off on all of the hospital's financial negotiations. At a doctor's office, talk directly to the doctor about lower fees—not the nurse, office manager or receptionist.

What you might say to a doctor or hospital CFO: "What does Medicare pay you for the service or treatment I am going to get? Will you accept the same payment from me?"

• **Request a discount on medical products.** Several years ago, I took a friend to a hearing-aid shop, and we negotiated 40% off the lowest quoted price. Since most stores that sell hearing aids, wheelchairs and other types of durable medical equipment are privately owned, and typically mark up products by 50% to 100%, you usually can strike a good bargain with the owner.

My advice: Shop around before negotiating and don't forget to check prices on the Internet. Then start by offering 20% less than the best price you found elsewhere. Offer to pay in cash rather than by credit card or check—this saves the merchant a processing fee.

The worst that can happen if you try to negotiate a medical fee is that your request will be turned down. But chances are you'll save a tidy sum with little effort on your part.

Get Your Drugs At 50% Off— Or Even Free

Edward Jardini, MD, a family physician at Twin Cities Community Hospital, Templeton, California, where he has served as chair of the pharmacy and therapeutics committee. He's also the author of *How to Save on Prescription Drugs: 20 Cost-Saving Methods* (Celestial Arts). His Web site is *www.howtosaveondrugs.com*.

Anyone who regularly uses prescription medication knows how pricey drugs can be.

Fortunately, there are places where you can buy your drugs for less—or even get them for free. The key is knowing where to look.

Important: Although most low-cost drug programs have income eligibility requirements, do not assume that you won't be accepted into a program just because your income is officially too high. Many programs will consider applications on a case-by-case basis.

Best resources for finding low-cost or free medications…

DRUG DISCOUNT NETWORKS

Some groups connect patients with public and private assistance programs that provide discounted or free drugs to eligible patients. *These include…*

• **Partnership for Prescription Assistance** (888-477-2669 or *www.pparx.org*). This large collaborative network of professional medical organizations, including the American Academy of Family Physicians, and private groups links patients with more than 475 public and private patient assistance programs that offer more than 2,500 drugs at reduced cost or no charge.* Income qualifications vary by state.

• **Together Rx Program** (800-444-4106 or *www.togetherrxaccess.com*). Backed by a consortium of big pharmaceutical companies, this

*Offers and rates subject to change.

program provides a 15% to 40% discount on more than 300 brand-name and generic prescription drugs. The program targets patients who do not have prescription drug coverage with annual incomes of $45,000 or less for individuals…$60,000 for a family of two…and up to $105,000 for a family of five.

PHARMACEUTICAL PATIENT-ASSISTANCE PROGRAMS

Major pharmaceutical companies have their own patient-assistance programs that provide many—though not all—drugs for a discount, or even for free, to people who cannot afford them. Eligibility requirements vary—even families earning up to $70,000 a year can qualify. Some companies evaluate the applications on a case-by-case basis.

To obtain a free copy of *Directory of Prescription Drug Patient Assistance Programs,* call the Partnership for Prescription Assistance at 800-762-4636. To determine the manufacturer of a particular drug, ask your pharmacist or go to *www.PDRhealth.com/drugs/drugs-index.aspx. Among the pharmaceutical companies with programs…*

• **Abbott Patient Assistance Program** (800-222-6885, *www.abbott.com*). Click on "Global Citizenship."

• **AstraZeneca's AZ & Me Prescription Savings Program** (800-292-6363, *www.astrazeneca-us.com*).

• **GlaxoSmithKline** (888-825-5249, *www.gskforyou.com*).

• **Lilly Cares Patient Assistance Program** (Eli Lilly) (800-545-6962, *www.lillycares.com*).

• **Merck Patient Assistance Program** (800-727-5400, *www.merck.com/merckhelps/patient assistance/home.html*).

• **Novartis Patient Assistance Foundation** (800-277-2254, *www.pharma.us.novartis.com*).

• **Pfizer Connection to Care** (866-776-3700, *www.pfizerhelpfulanswers.com*).

• **Roche Labs Patient Assistant Foundation** (877-757-6243, *www.rocheusa.com/programs/patientassist.asp*).

• **Schering-Plough Cares** (800-656-9485, *www.schering-plough.com*). First click "Consumer Health Care," then "Patient Assistance and Support Programs."

•**Wyeth Pharmaceutical Patient Assistance Program** (800-568-9938, *www.wyeth.com*).

Some pharmaceutical companies also offer coupons that can be printed from their Web sites, as well as discount card programs offering savings on some products. Check the drug manufacturer's Web site for details.

More from Dr. Edward Jardini...

Split Tablets to Save a Lot

Maybe you know that splitting tablets can save you money. But most people, including doctors, do not realize just how much you can save. Most prescription drugs are sold in a range of dosages. There might be a 20-milligram (mg) pill, a 40-mg pill and an 80-mg pill.

The higher-dose pills usually are a relative bargain, per milligram of medication, compared with the lower-dose pills. In other words, an 80-mg pill will almost always cost substantially less than twice the price of a 40-mg pill and less than four times the price of a 20-mg pill. In some cases, pills of different dosages are priced exactly the same.

Example: The 20-mg, 40-mg and 80-mg versions of the cholesterol medication Lipitor cost the same per pill.

Whenever you are prescribed an expensive medication, ask your doctor if it would be possible for him/her to prescribe half-tablet doses of pills twice as strong as you need—half of an 80-mg tablet rather than one 40-mg tablet, for example. Most doctors aren't very familiar with medication prices, so you might have to explain that this could save you a lot of money. Pill-splitting devices, sold at pharmacies, can help you divide pills accurately.

Caution: Certain types of pills, including capsules, gelcaps and extended-release tablets, cannot be split safely. Discuss any plans you have to split pills with your doctor and pharmacist.

Not-So-"Free" Drug Samples?

Rebecca Shannonhouse, editor of *Bottom Line/Health*, Boardroom Inc., 281 Tresser Blvd., Stamford, Connecticut 06901.

The free drug samples that many people get from their physicians can save them money and trips to the pharmacy. But there's a catch—your drug bill might wind up being higher in the long run.

New finding: Patients who never received free drug samples had estimated out-of-pocket prescription expenses of $178 over six months, while those who had received free samples for six months paid $212 for the six-month period following receipt of the freebies.

The study was not designed to identify the cause of the disparity, says Anirban Basu, PhD, a University of Chicago researcher and coauthor of the study. However, a likely explanation is that once patients receive free samples of a new, expensive medication, they're apt to keep taking it.

Free drug samples can be a bonus if you don't have health insurance. *Samples also can work well for...*

•**Short-term prescriptions,** such as those for some antibiotics or pain relievers.

•**Drugs that require a "test drive."** For some conditions—depression, for example—patients may need to try a number of drugs before finding the right one. Similarly, a patient may need to find out if a therapeutic approach—say, the use of a particular class of blood pressure drug—is effective.

Smart idea: If you need to continue a drug after trying a free sample, ask your doctor if you can switch to a similar, but older and less-expensive, medication.

Another option: Ask for a 60- to 90-day prescription (rather than 30 days) to save out-of-pocket costs.

12

Retirement Report

How to Keep a Recession From Ruining Your Retirement

These are tough times for investors, especially those who plan on retiring within 10 years or who have just retired within the past 10 years. Because they have already accumulated the bulk of their wealth and still have to draw on it for a long time, these people have the most to lose from an extended period of depressed stock prices. But if they don't stay invested for the long-term, they risk outliving their money.

Popular financial adviser William P. Bengen stresses that the current economic slowdown—including the mortgage and housing industry meltdown that has turned into a wider credit crunch—is potentially more dangerous to investors than many of the downturns of the past several decades. *He's cautioning his clients to do the following...*

• **Cut back annual spending by at least 3% to 5%.** Most people can spend a bit less without affecting their lifestyles. Scale back unnecessary expenses—go out to dinner one time less every month...put off a major purchase, such as an automobile or a luxury vacation...make do without the most expensive "premium" cable-TV channels...and buy only the clothing that you need for the time being.

• **Build financial cushions now,** before you really need them. Shore up your emergency cash reserve. I urge clients to have up to two years' worth of living expenses in a reserve account, such as a money-market mutual fund, that they can easily draw on. That should be enough to get past most market storms.

William P. Bengen, CFP, president, Bengen Financial Services, Inc., a fee-only financial advisory firm based in El Cajon, California. *The Wall Street Journal* named Bengen one of the 12 most important individuals shaping the retirement of Americans today. He is also the author of *Conserving Client Portfolios During Retirement* (FPA). His Web site is *www.billbengen.com*.

For those who are still working, I point out that recessions dramatically raise the risk for job loss. If you are working and lose your job, having cash means that you won't have to tap into your IRA or 401(k) account. If you are retired, you will not have to increase your withdrawals from your portfolio.

If you are still working, you should continue to make regular retirement plan contributions.

Another cushion: Set up a home equity line of credit (HELOC) if you have substantial equity remaining in your home and your credit rating is strong enough to get one. A HELOC is a second line of defense should your cash reserve run dry. If the economy worsens or you don't have a job, you may not be able to get a line of credit later.

• **Build up or maintain the cash portion of your investment portfolio** by selling stocks. My typical client allocation, which normally would be 65% stocks/35% bonds, is now 50% stocks/20% bonds/30% cash.

Now is not the time to buy much in stocks, even when the market declines, despite what many investors are doing. I think that there's more trouble ahead.

Place cash in safe, short-term investments. Use money-market mutual funds and/or three-month Treasury bills. For clients who do not need an investment that could be liquidated very easily, look for higher rates with FDIC-insured certificates of deposit (CDs).

• **Don't take risks for extra bond yields.** Bonds are typically a safe haven in economically troubled times. In general, bond portfolios will typically gain value as interest rates fall because the higher interest rates of older bonds make them more attractive than new ones. But this time, capital markets have destabilized enough that today's higher-yielding bonds are not worth the risk. I would prefer to take a 3% return and barely keep up with inflation right now, rather than worry about some credit crisis with my bonds in which I could actually lose money.

What to do: Consider building a "ladder" of short- and intermediate-term government bonds that have different maturities, no longer

than five years, so that part of your portfolio is maturing every year.

• **Don't count on your home's current value.** Many of my clients are planning to pump up their retirement nest eggs by selling their homes over the next decade and downsizing. That is fine as long as you factor in another 10% to 15% decline in home prices in the next few years. After that, the recovery in home values will be slow. Don't expect more than a 5% annual increase in residential real estate prices long-term.

How to Safely Tap Your Retirement Portfolio in a Down Market

Christopher J. Cordaro, CFP, CFA, chief investment officer, RegentAtlantic Capital, LLC, Morristown, New Jersey. He has been named one of the nation's top financial advisers by *Worth* magazine. Cordaro is also a past president of the New Jersey Chapter of the Financial Planning Association and serves on the advisory board of financial advisors for TD Ameritrade.

If you rely heavily on your investments as a source of spending money, you're probably feeling the squeeze from the stock market collapse. Are you now taking too much from your portfolio? Will you run short of money in later years?

How much you withdraw from your investment accounts is only part of the problem. *You also need to know…*

• **Which assets to sell.**

• **Which accounts to tap first.**

• **How to handle minimum required withdrawals from IRAs.**

• **How to rebalance your portfolio.**

If you're careful, you can navigate through troubling times in a way that leaves you better prepared for the recovery and that does not threaten your financial security.

THE 4% SOLUTION

If you've been following the popular "4% plan" for retirement withdrawals, stay with it. If you haven't, start now. Set your withdrawal schedule at 4% of your current portfolio balance. *Also...*

• **Defer large purchases if at all possible.**

• **Generate cash from your portfolio** by rebalancing to restore your asset allocation. This means selling from the asset classes that are now above their target allocations in your portfolio.

Many financial planners say that those retirees who need to live off of their investments should start by withdrawing no more than 4% of their portfolios' value, then increase withdrawals by the rate of inflation in subsequent years to maintain their standard of living.

Situation: Sally Martin retired at age 65 with $1 million in investments. She withdrew $40,000 (4%) in Year One of her retirement. Inflation during Year One was 5%. So, when Sally plans out her Year Two withdrawals, she ups her scheduled withdrawals by 5%, from $40,000 to $42,000.

Sally's strategy generates a high probability that her investment portfolio will last 30 years or longer. What would happen if Sally starts with, say, a 5% distribution at age 65? There is a high probability that her investment portfolio will be depleted in 20 to 25 years.

Suppose Sally's investment portfolio has fallen from $1 million to $750,000 as a result of the stock market slide. If she withdraws $42,000 this year, that would be a 5.6% withdrawal, far above the 4% rate considered "safe."

Cut expenses: If possible, Sally can trim her expenses and withdraw less from her portfolio. That will increase the chance that her money will last for the rest of her life. But Sally may need all of the money that she withdraws to pay for food, housing, medical care and other necessities. In that case, she can withdraw the full $42,000.

Reason: The 4% plan builds in market ups and downs. Even if an ongoing bear market reduces Sally's portfolio down to $700,000 or lower, a rebound may bring it up to $800,000 or more and put her back on target.

If you find that you need more than 4% to live on, increase the amount in your portfolio. You might sell your house when the housing market improves, then invest some of the money from the sale and move into a smaller place.

SELLING STRATEGIES

The bear market need not affect the size of your withdrawals if you've been prudent enough to start out at 4%. Nevertheless, you should reevaluate the way that you tap your portfolio. Because of the recent turmoil in the financial markets, it makes sense to sell your bonds to raise cash while holding onto depressed stocks.

In today's low-yield market, many retirees won't meet their withdrawal goals from interest and dividends. Some assets must be sold to raise money. To determine which assets to sell, look for asset classes that are above their target allocations in your portfolio.

Situation: Sally Martin's desired asset allocation is 60% in stocks and 40% in bonds. Her portfolio at the start of Year One held $600,000 in stocks and $400,000 in bonds. Now, after a steep decline, the stocks in her portfolio are worth only $370,000. Her bonds have held most of their value so they are now worth $380,000.

This year, Sally expects her investments to provide $20,000 in interest and dividend income. That money can go into her checking account for current spending.

Result: Sally needs another $22,000 from her portfolio this year to meet her withdrawal goal of $42,000. She'll have to sell some holdings to raise cash.

Strategy: Sally can sell off $22,000 worth of her bonds. With $380,000 of her $750,000 portfolio now in bonds (more than 50%), Sally is above her target allocation of 40%.

Every month or every quarter, Sally can revisit this decision when she transfers money to her checking account. She can keep selling bonds until they're back down to 40% of her assets.

The situation above is based on a simple stocks/bonds allocation. But Sally's asset allocation might be, say, 40% domestic stocks, 10% foreign stocks, 10% real estate investment trusts (REITs), 20% taxable bond funds and 20% municipal bond funds. No matter how many asset classes are in your portfolio, the withdrawal rebalancing strategy calls for you to sell those that are over their targets when liquidating securities to tap your portfolio.

WHICH ACCOUNTS?

Many retirees have tax-deferred accounts, such as IRAs, in addition to their regular taxable accounts.

Strategy: Take money from the taxable accounts first, whenever possible. If you leave money in tax-deferred accounts, you may benefit from more years of untaxed earnings. You might be able to sell assets in taxable accounts for a loss or for no gain, so you would owe little or no tax on the sale.

Trap: After age 70½, you must generally take required minimum distributions (RMDs) from IRAs (although no RMDs are required for 2009). At that point, you can take the RMD from your IRA and continue to sell taxable holdings for the rest of the money you need.

What if your rebalancing plan calls for you to sell bonds now, but all of the bonds that you own are in your tax-deferred IRA? *Take two steps…*

•**Sell stocks or shares of stock funds in your taxable account to generate the cash you need.**

•**Inside your IRA, sell bonds to match the amount of stocks you sold in your taxable account** and reinvest the proceeds in stocks to push your asset allocation back toward your targets.

Another View on Retirement Withdrawals

Christine Fahlund, senior financial planner, T. Rowe Price, 100 E. Pratt St., Baltimore 21202.

Don't depend on 4% annual withdrawals to get you through retirement. This common approach says to withdraw up to 4% of your portfolio in the first year of retirement and then increase the amount for inflation annually. But if you do this, you could run out of money.

Example: If you have only a 2%-to-3% annual return for the first five years of retirement, this plan means that you have a 64% chance of running out of money in less than three decades.

Self-defense: If you are considering retiring at a time of market turmoil, wait a year or two or take a part-time job. Check online tools to help you decide how much you can safely take out in any year based on how much you have left. Try the T. Rowe Price Retirement Income Calculator at *www.troweprice.com/ric* or Fidelity's Retirement Income Planner at *www.fidelity.com* (click on "Retirement & Guidance," then on "Retirement").

Better Ways to Build Your Nest Egg

Laurence J. Kotlikoff, PhD, professor of economics at Boston University and the president of Economic Security Planning, Inc., which produces personal financial planning software programs, Lexington, Massachusetts, *www.esplanner.com*. As a leading expert on saving, insurance and public policy, he has served on the Council of Economic Advisers and consulted for The World Bank, Merrill Lynch, Fidelity Investments and many others. He is author or coauthor of 13 books, including his latest, coauthored with Scott Burns, *Spend 'Til the End: The Revolutionary Guide to Raising Your Living Standard —Today and When You Retire* (Simon & Schuster).

A great deal of financial planning is based on myths. Especially common are myths about the best ways to save, spend, invest and draw on various sources of income. Here, one of the country's leading experts on personal finance and retirement planning, economics professor Laurence J. Kotlikoff, PhD, of Boston University, gives his myth-busting strategies for all stages of your adult life…

LOWER YOUR LIFE INSURANCE

Myth: Buy life insurance that's equal to seven times your annual wages if you are the big earner in the household.

Fact: Many people do not need that much. Remember, the goal of insurance is to equalize your living standard across good and bad times, not to pay high premiums and deprive yourself and your family of spending money so that they can have a better lifestyle when you die. In fact, if your spouse is several years younger than you or expects to retire much later than you, he/she may have more remaining lifetime earnings to protect than you do— even if you earn more in a given year. In this case, you may want greater life insurance coverage for your spouse. After all, your family's living standard is being financed not just by current earnings, but by all future earnings.

RIDE A STOCK ROLLER COASTER

Myth: The older you get, the more you need to increase your investment portfolio's allocation to relatively safe bonds and decrease the allocation to relatively risky stocks.

Fact: You might be better off putting your stock holdings on a "roller coaster."

Reason: To reduce risk and maintain a more consistent lifestyle from year to year. Instead of diversifying just your investment portfolio, to balance safety and risk you need to focus more on how that portfolio fits in with your total resources. That includes earnings at jobs and other income or benefits, such as inheritances, Social Security and Medicare.

HOW TO ADJUST YOUR ALLOCATIONS

• **When you're young, start with a relatively small stock allocation, perhaps under 20%,** and put the bulk of your money in safer investments that you can more easily draw on, such as bonds, bank certificates of deposit and money market funds.

Reason: You may have relatively little in assets and earnings to draw on, weak borrowing capacity and high expenses for such things as a mortgage and kids' educations.

• **Through middle age, increase your stock allocation dramatically, perhaps to 80%,** because rising job earnings help to support your lifestyle and to diversify your overall resources. This is especially wise if you are approaching a time when the last tuition bill will be paid.

• **As you approach retirement, decrease your stock allocation, perhaps to under 40%.** That's because at this point, a sharp, prolonged slide in the stock market or the unexpected loss of your job could have a bigger impact if you have not started getting a Social Security check yet or begun drawing on other sources of retirement income, such as pensions.

• **In early retirement, increase your stock allocation to at least 50%** as you start drawing on such reliable income sources as Social Security.

• **Finally, in late retirement (after age 75), reduce stocks to 20%** of your investment portfolio when the risk for rising health expenses mounts.

POSTPONE SOCIAL SECURITY

Myth: If you retire early, you would be wise to start collecting Social Security benefits as soon as you reach age 62.

Fact: Retirees are often better off postponing the start of these benefits, possibly to age 70, in particular as life spans grow longer on average.

Say that 66 is the age that the government calls your "full," or "normal," retirement age, and that you could start collecting $1,000 per month at that age. If, instead, you retire early at age 62 and start taking payments, your monthly check would be $750, or 25% lower (excluding cost-of-living adjustments).

If you wait until age 70, when the benefit you are eligible for would "top out" (except for cost-of-living increases), your monthly check would be $1,320. That means you would collect a total of $30,600 extra if you live to age 85, compared with the total you would receive if you started collecting at age 62.

Waiting until age 70 to start collecting is the right choice for most people, even when that means drawing more from your retirement accounts before age 70. This, of course, assumes that you have good reason to believe that you will live beyond your mid-70s, such as a history of parents and/or grandparents living long lives, and being in good health yourself.

For an estimate of your life expectancy, go to the "Living to 100 Life Expectancy Calculator" (*www.calculator.livingto100.com*).

An even better way: In many instances, you can choose to start collecting benefits at your full retirement age—which allows your spouse to start collecting benefits of up to 50% of yours—and then you can immediately "suspend" your benefits while your spouse keeps collecting his/hers. That way, you allow the size of your future checks to grow as you wait until age 70 to start collecting again.

Caution: If you are more concerned with leaving a bequest to your children and you have concerns regarding whether you will live much past 70, you may want to start collecting benefits earlier so that the money can help build up your assets sooner.

THE BOTTOM LINE

1. Base your life insurance coverage on expected lifetime earnings, not annual earnings.

2. Cut back on stocks a few years before retirement...then buy more when you retire.

3. Expect a long life? Don't take Social Security until age 70.

More from Dr. Laurence Kotlikoff...

When You Might Want to Repay Social Security

Consider repaying Social Security to boost your monthly income in the future. If you retired at age 62 and now are 70, you can give the government back the money you have received so far and then reapply for Social Security benefits at a new rate—which will be higher because you are older. You are not required to pay interest on benefits already received, and there are no repayment fees. Also, you can deduct the repayment. Repayment requires Form SSA-521, *Request for Withdrawal of Application*. This strategy generally makes most sense for people ages 68 to 72. For information, go to *www.esplanner.com/learn* (click on "Case Studies" at left).

People Are Losing Thousands of Dollars in Social Security: How *Not* To Be One of Them

Joseph L. Matthews, a San Francisco–based attorney specializing in concerns related to seniors, such as Social Security. He taught at the law school of University of California, Berkeley, and is author of *Social Security, Medicare & Government Pensions: Get the Most Out of Your Retirement & Medical Benefits, 13th edition* (Nolo).

Deciding when you should start collecting Social Security retirement benefits can be difficult. The decision could alter how much you and your survivors collect by tens of thousands of dollars.

WHEN YOU ARE ELIGIBLE

Although anyone eligible for Social Security retirement benefits can begin collecting their "reduced" amount as early as age 62, what the government terms "full" benefits are not available until the so-called "full" (or "normal") retirement age, which ranges from 65 to 67 years old, depending on the year you were born. And even beyond that full retirement age, the amount of the checks you receive will keep rising by 8% for each additional year that you wait—until you reach age 70, after which waiting will not increase your benefits. (The rate is lower than 8% for those born before 1943.)

Example: If your full retirement age is 66, starting benefits at age 62 will permanently reduce your monthly checks by 25% from what you would get at age 66. That means if your full monthly benefit is $1,000, you will receive $750 per month if you start collecting at age 62. If you live to age 85, that translates to $21,000 less in total payments, even with those four extra years of checks (not including cost-of-living adjustments). So it might be better to wait. (*Exception:* If you start taking benefits before full retirement age and save or invest the money wisely rather than spend it, you might close the gap.) If you wait until age 70, rather than age 66, to start collecting, that $1,000 "full retirement" monthly payment becomes a $1,320 monthly check. That is an additional $9,600 you collect from the Social Security Administration if you live to age 85.

Of course, the best time to start taking benefits varies depending on your situation, including how much you have saved, how much you need to spend each year, how long you expect that you and/or your spouse will live and how much, if any, income you expect to earn each year from age 62 until you reach full retirement age.

To get an estimate of your life expectancy, go to *http://moneycentral.msn.com/personal-finance,* and click "Retirement," then "View all tools," then "Life Expectancy Calculator."

Rule of thumb: The longer you expect to live, the more likely that delaying the start of Social Security benefits will pay off.

The Social Security Administration's calculator can help you decide the best time to start collecting benefits, based on how long you're expected to live. However, it does not take into account many other variables, including the possibility of earning interest or investment returns on any benefits you take early and don't spend immediately. You can find the calculator at *www.ssa.gov* (click on "Retirement").

OTHER REASONS TO WAIT

In most cases, it is best to wait until full retirement age, and in some cases, until age 70, to start collecting Social Security retirement benefits…

You still are working or expect to return to work. Until you reach full retirement age, Social Security benefits are reduced by $1 for every $2 in earned income over a specified amount that increases with the inflation rate. That amount is $14,160 in 2009.

Important note: This penalty applies only to earned income, not to investment income or rental income. When this penalty is figured into the equation, you almost certainly will be better off delaying benefits at least until your full retirement age and receiving larger benefits later.

You are married and are eligible for higher benefits than your spouse, based on your earnings history. After you die, your spouse can claim survivor's benefits equal to your full retirement benefit—but only if you wait until

full retirement age to start collecting benefits. If you start collecting early, the reduced benefits carry over to your spouse after you die. However, if you postpone the start of benefits past full retirement age, your spouse's benefits do not increase further.

An alternative strategy: If you are healthy and expect to live well into your 80s, consider filing for benefits at your full retirement age but then immediately suspending those benefits. Your spouse can't file for spousal benefits until you file for your own benefits.

To suspend your benefits, you must notify the Social Security Administration by phone or in writing.

Under this scenario, your spouse can start collecting benefits as a dependent as soon as you file, based on your salary history. A person age 62 or older is entitled to receive benefits of up to 50% of his/her spouse's benefits as a "dependent" of the spouse, as long as the person is not collecting benefits based on his own salary history.

At the same time, by immediately suspending your benefits, you allow the size of your future checks to further increase for each year you wait to resume collecting benefits until you reach age 70.

REASONS NOT TO WAIT

There are certain scenarios under which you are better off starting to collect your benefits before you reach full retirement age…

You have good reason to believe that you might not live beyond your mid-70s. This may apply if you are in poor health, have an unhealthy lifestyle and/or your parents, grandparents or other close relatives have a history of dying young.

Alternative: If you are forced to retire early because of poor health, consider applying for Social Security disability benefits (which are higher than early retirement benefits), rather than starting retirement benefits early.

Note: Disability benefits run only until full retirement age, at which time full Social Security benefits begin.

You have dependent children. If you have a child younger than 18 years of age (19 if he/she is still in high school) and you receive Social

Security benefits, this child will receive up to 50% of your benefit amount as a dependent in addition to the benefits you collect.

If this child is younger than 16, your spouse can qualify for additional benefits as a caregiver. (The total amount you and your family can receive in a year based on your work record alone, and not your spouse's, is generally capped at 150% to 180% of your benefit amount. So if both your spouse and your child take dependent benefits based on your earnings record, each will receive less than the full 50% to which he would otherwise be entitled.)

All of those additional checks often make it worthwhile to start Social Security benefits as soon as possible.

You need your benefits to pay your bills and/or to afford the retirement you want. The decision to begin collecting early may allow you to do things that you wouldn't otherwise be able to afford.

Social Security After a Spouse Dies

Nancy Dunnan, a New York City–based financial and travel adviser and author or coauthor of 25 books, including *How to Invest $50–$5,000* (HarperCollins).

If your spouse dies, you might be able to collect more Social Security than you had been collecting. But first, you must report your spouse's death to the Social Security Administration (call 800-772-1213 or visit *www. ssa.gov*).

As the surviving spouse, you can continue to receive your own Social Security benefits. Or, you could receive 100% of your deceased spouse's benefits, whichever is greater. In other words, if you earned less over your lifetime than your spouse, you are entitled to receive his/her benefits.

The full 100% benefit from your deceased spouse's account starts at your full retirement age, which ranges from 65 for those born in 1937 or earlier to age 67 for those born in 1960 or later.

A reduced widow's benefit can be claimed starting at age 60. (If you are disabled, then you need to be only 50 years old.) The same benefit also applies to widowers and surviving divorced spouses.

In order to determine the exact monetary amount of your widow's benefits, the Social Security Administration asks that you make an appointment and visit your local office. (It does not give out the amounts on its Web site.) You can locate that office on the agency's Web site or by looking in the blue (government) pages of your phone book.

Common Social Security Errors

Robert M. Freedman, Esq., of counsel, Mazur, Carp & Rubin, PC, a law firm that concentrates on trusts and estates, New York City. He is a certified elderlaw attorney.

Be sure to avoid these four common mistakes that could contribute to reduced Social Security benefits...

•**Earnings record errors.** Social Security benefits are based on your 35 highest-earning years—but errors can occur in your earnings record. If your earnings aren't recorded or are underreported, your future benefits may be reduced.

What to do: Check your annual personal "Social Security Statement" every year. It contains a complete record of your year-by-year earnings. If you find a mistake, call your local Social Security Administration (SSA) office to report it.

Note: You have three years, three months and 15 days from the close of the taxable year in which the error occurred to make the correction. (Under certain circumstances, earlier years can be corrected.)

•**Wrong address.** If you're employed and the address for you in the SSA's records doesn't match that on your W-2 form and tax return (which report your Social Security tax payments and earnings), an error may occur in crediting your tax payments and earnings. A tip-off that this problem exists is failure to receive your annual Social Security Statement.

What to do: The SSA obtains its address records from the IRS, so file IRS Form 8822, Change of Address (800-829-3676, *www.irs.gov*). Whenever you move in the future, head off possible complications by filing Form 8822 with the IRS.

•**Wrong name.** If your name in the SSA's records doesn't match that shown on your W-2 and tax return, your taxes and earnings may be miscredited.

If you change your name, get Form SS-5, Application for a Social Security Card, from your local SSA office (or call 800-772-1213 or visit *www.ssa.gov*).

•**Miscalculation of benefits.** Even if your earnings record is completely correct, there's a chance that the SSA will make a mistake in calculating your benefits.

You can check the correct size of your benefits yourself by using calculators provided at the SSA Web site. Enter "benefits calculator" into the search box. Call your local SSA office to report any mistakes and have them double-check the figures.

Sign Up for Social Security in 15 Minutes!

When signing up for Social Security, use the new Web form, which can be completed in about 15 minutes. The previous version took 45 minutes. With the shorter form, applicants are not required to complete every item—only those that apply to their personal situations. Also, many applicants will no longer need to provide the original copy of their birth certificate by mail or in person at a Social Security office. If additional documents are needed, Social Security will contact you. Go to *http://ssa.gov/retireonline* for additional information.

Michael Astrue, commissioner of Social Security in Baltimore.

Be Wary of "Senior Specialists"

Beware of investment salespeople who label themselves "senior specialists" at seminars in hotels and restaurants. These people, who may also label themselves "retirement counselors" and "senior counselors," may have little or no investment training. They may urge attendees to sell off their investments and put their proceeds into other products, including some that have high commissions and early withdrawal penalties. Before giving money to anyone claiming special expertise in investments for seniors, read the SEC article "Check Out Brokers and Investment Advisers," available at *www.sec.gov/investor/brokers.htm*.

Kristi Kaepplein, director, Office of Investor Education and Advocacy, Securities and Exchange Commission, Washington, DC.

Don't Use Your IRA to Buy Foreign Stocks

If you buy foreign stocks or mutual funds through a taxable account, and pay taxes to a foreign government on them, you normally can claim a credit on your US tax return for the foreign taxes paid. But if you buy foreign stocks or funds through an IRA, you can't claim any such credit, even though foreign taxes have been withheld. So be wary of incurring this tax cost of foreign investments in an IRA account.

Seymour Goldberg, Esq., CPA, Goldberg & Goldberg, PC, Jericho, New York.

IRA Distribution Rule More Lenient

When you do not take the required minimum distribution (RMD) from an IRA or a retirement plan after age 70½, you are subject to a penalty of 50% of the distribution that you should have taken. In the past, you had to pay the penalty first and then request a refund. The IRS has revised Form 5329 to allow a filer to seek a waiver and attach an explanation—you pay the penalty only if the IRS denies your request.

Please note: Congress has suspended RMDs for 2009.

Barbara Weltman, Esq., an attorney based in Millwood, New York, and publisher of the free online newsletter, *Big Ideas for Small Business, www.barbaraweltman.com.*

What to Do with Your 401(K) If You Lose Your Job

Rick Meigs, president of 401khelpcenter.com, a non-partisan independent trend and information service covering 401(k)s, Portland, Oregon.

If you lose your job and have less than $5,000 in your 401(k), you probably will be required by the terms of the plan to close your account by rolling your money into a different retirement account or withdrawing it as cash. If you have more than $5,000, you can, by law, opt to stay in your current plan, but I would not advise it. Companies change names, sell off divisions, go bankrupt, merge or simply move away—and you may have a hard time tracking down this 401(k) at a later date.

You might be able to do a direct rollover into a new employer's 401(k) plan if the new plan accepts such rollovers. But what I generally recommend is rolling a 401(k) over to an IRA, which offers you far greater control through more investment options—plus you don't have to pay fees to a 401(k) administrator. There may be no fees for an IRA account at a discount broker, such as Charles Schwab or Fidelity, or a mutual fund company, such as Vanguard.

Lump-Sum Pension Payouts Might Not Be Available

Lump-sum pension payouts might not be available to all holders of defined-benefit plans. The new law requires employers to tell their workers if a defined-benefit plan is fully funded—that is, if it has all the money needed to pay all of its obligations. Fully funded plans may offer retirees either a series of payments or a lump-sum payout, but plans that do not have enough money to pay in full at least 80% of employees are allowed to pay only 50% of a retiree's pension in a lump sum. And plans that do not have enough money to pay at least 60% of employees do not have to make any lump-sum payments at all. Ask your defined-benefit plan's manager for details on the financial health of your company's plan.

Brett Goldstein, pension administrator and president, Pension Department Inc., consultants, Plainview, New York.

Recent Housing Law Benefits Seniors Ages 62 or Older

The Housing and Economic Recovery Act of 2008 raises the maximum amount for a reverse mortgage to $625,500—up from the previous amount of $200,160 to $362,790, depending on where a borrower lived. The new, higher limit applies nationwide rather than by county. Also, reverse mortgages—which do not have to be repaid until a borrower moves permanently, sells or dies—now will cost less.

Most important: Origination fees may not exceed 2% of the initial $200,000 borrowed and 1% of the remaining balance, to a maximum fee of $6,000. This cap is subject to future inflation adjustment.

Kiplinger.com.

Top Four Home-Buying Mistakes Seniors Often Make

Steve McLinden, real estate adviser, Bankrate.com, North Palm Beach, Florida, a provider of interest rate information and personal finance news, articles and commentary.

I f you are over age 50, buying a home, and planning to live in it a long time, do not make these common mistakes...

• **Failing to check community offerings.** Don't move to a community just for its looks, low local taxes or cost of living. See if the community offers entertainment, adult education, sports and recreation opportunities, a senior-friendly community center and quality health facilities.

Idea: Take vacations in the community to learn what it is like before moving there.

• **Buying a home with too many stairs.** Seek a level, single-floor layout in the home you buy.

Also: Look for nonslip flooring and senior-friendly bathrooms. It will be more expensive to remodel a house to add these things later.

• **Overlooking future transportation needs.** Will you be able to get around via public transportation if and when you can't drive or choose not to?

• **Being too far away from family.** In later years, personal contact with siblings, children and grandchildren may be very important to you. Don't move too far away from them.

Medicare Doesn't Cover Everything: Protect Your Retirement Funds

Sunit Patel, CFA, a senior vice president and actuary in the benefits consulting group at Fidelity Investments in Boston. Patel consults with large companies to develop corporate health-care strategies for employees. He is on the American Academy of Actuaries defined-contribution health-care task force, which works with Congress on health-care issues.

M edicare does not pay for *all* of your health-care costs during retirement. The government-administered health insurance plan for people age 65 and over has deductibles, co-payments and exclusions that can add up to significant out-of-pocket costs. And unlike most private sector health plans, Medicare does not offer an annual limit for out-of-pocket expenses. The average 65-year-old couple retiring in the near future will need $225,000 in current savings to cover health-related bills over their lifetimes, assuming average life expectancy (82 for men and 85 for women).

Do not count on your former employer to help you pay these bills. Health-care benefits for retirees, once common, now are rare. The fortunate few who do have retiree health benefits from their employers still must be ready to pay for high retirement health-care expenses because their employers could cancel these benefits with little warning, as General Motors recently announced it is doing for certain retirees over age 65.

WHAT'S MISSING FROM MEDICARE

Medicare does not cover certain health-care expenses at all. This includes over-the-counter medications and hearing aids. *It also does not cover or offers only severely limited coverage for...*

• **Dental care.** Medicare does not cover dentist bills unless the visits are related to a covered procedure, such as reconstruction of the jaw after an accident.

If possible, get expensive dental work done prior to retiring and leaving your employer's dental coverage. Individual dental insurance

209

policies are available, although these can be expensive and provide very limited coverage. Community dental clinics and local dental colleges might offer lower-cost dental services.

• **Custodial care.** The average cost of a private room in a nursing home today is more than $75,000 per year. Medicare is not likely to pay any of this bill. Private long-term-care insurance is available, but it generally is very expensive. Medicaid will cover nursing home bills, but only after you have depleted virtually all of your assets. Veterans Administration long-term-care facilities can be a much more affordable option for veterans of the armed forces. Otherwise, the only option is to pay nursing home bills out-of-pocket.

HOW TO FILL THE GAPS

To reduce the odds that health-care costs will derail your plans...

• **Make saving for retirement health-care expenses a specific financial goal,** and use a separate investment account rather than just lumping this in with your general retirement savings. Keeping health-care savings separate makes it much less likely that you will spend the money on discretionary purchases.

Strive for a retirement health-care savings target of at least $100,000 per retiree (that is, $200,000 for a retiring couple). Curtail plans for retirement travel, a second home or other luxuries if that is what it takes to reach this savings goal.

• **Consider signing up for a Medicare Advantage plan** if one is available in your region. These privately owned health insurance plans typically provide more benefits at a lower cost than otherwise would be available through the traditional Medicare system. These health plans can provide health-care savings of more than 10% for individuals with good or fair health compared with traditional Medicare coverage. The downside is that enrollees in some plans receive health-care services only through the plan's affiliated doctors and medical facilities. Many Medicare Advantage plans are essentially HMOs for those over age 65.

• **Sign up for a Medigap plan.** These are privately offered health plans that fill in some coverage holes in government Medicare coverage. These plans will not reduce the average

retiree's projected health-care expenses, but they will make these expenses more predictable by replacing large deductibles and co-pays with a preset monthly premium.

Medigap plans are particularly helpful for people who have long-term health problems which are likely to lead to large out-of-pocket costs. If you sign up for a Medigap plan within six months of turning 65 or enrolling in Medicare Part B (which covers a portion of nonhospital medical care, such as doctor visits), you cannot be turned down because of preexisting health conditions. The prices charged and coverage offered by these optional plans vary significantly.

For more information: To find out how Medicare-related plans work and to compare them, call 800-MEDICARE or log on to *www.medicare.gov*.

• **Sign up for a Health Savings Account (HSA)** if you qualify. Preretirees who have "high-deductible" health plans—medical insurance with deductibles in 2009 that are more than $1,150 ($2,300 for families)—are eligible, and they can sign up through banks, credit unions, insurance companies and some employers. HSAs function somewhat like IRAs, but funds placed in them are earmarked for health-care expenses. In 2009, participants can contribute up to $3,000 ($5,950 for families) and use this money to pay health-care costs with pretax dollars.

Note: Once an individual enrolls in Medicare, he/she is no longer eligible to contribute to an HSA (but can still make withdrawals).

CHALLENGES OF EARLY RETIREMENT

Early retirees must arrange their own health coverage until they become eligible for Medicare at age 65.

What to do: If possible, get health coverage through your spouse's insurance plan...or remain on your former employer's group health plan through COBRA, a benefits-continuation program that generally lasts up to 18 months. COBRA might not be available from a small company, and there could be complications if you intend to retire to a different state.

COBRA coverage can be expensive (cost depends on the program and your state), but it is likely to be a lot cheaper than an individual health insurance policy offering similar coverage. For a couple ages 63 or 64, an individual policy could easily cost $10,000 to $20,000 per year.* Cheaper plans might be available, but they are likely to have very high deductibles.

Potentially cheaper routes to get private coverage: Alumni groups and senior groups, such as the American Association of Retired Persons.

*Prices subject to change.

Serious Health Danger Related to Falls

Older people fear breaking a hip when they fall, but a more serious consequence is hitting their heads. Brain injuries account for half of all fatalities due to falls among elderly people annually. Aging causes veins and arteries to tear more easily from a blow to the head.

Self-defense: Exercise to improve balance and leg strength, which helps prevent falling. Take care when using medications that may cause dizziness or disorientation.

Marlena Wald, MLS, MPH, epidemiologist, Centers for Disease Control and Prevention, and research director, division of emergency medicine, Emory University, both in Atlanta, and coauthor of a study of 16,000 deaths due to falls in 2005, published in the *Journal of Safety Research*.

Answers to the Legal Health-Care Questions Seniors Most Often Ask

Robert Fleming, Esq., Fleming & Curti, PLC, a practice specializing in elder law, 330 N. Granada Ave., Tucson, Arizona 85701. The coauthor of *Alive and Kicking: Legal Advice for Boomers* (Carolina Academic) and *The Elder Law Answer Book* (Aspen), he is a fellow of both the American College of Trust and Estate Counsel and the National Academy of Elder Law Attorneys.

Retirees and preretirees often ask health-care questions of their attorneys. *What clients most often want to know...*

• **Are there any strategies that can preserve assets and still allow someone to qualify for Medicaid?** A "reverse half-a-loaf" plan is one of a handful of options—and even it will not work in every state (check with a local elder-law attorney before pursuing the idea further).

How this works: You give away assets to someone who you trust to keep half available to you if you need a long nursing home stay.

Recent federal rules say that Medicaid applicants need to reveal any transfers of assets within the prior 60 months. A waiting period for Medicaid eligibility may be enforced, but won't start until the applicant is already in a nursing home and meets all the tests for Medicaid eligibility.

Situation: Jane Smith has no assets except $300,000 in the bank. She resides in an area where nursing home expenses average $6,000 a month. Jane goes into a nursing home and gives away her $300,000 to her daughter Betsy. Under Medicaid rules, Jane has a 50-month waiting period before Medicaid will pay for her care—$300,000 divided by $6,000.

Next step: Betsy pays Jane's $6,000-a-month nursing home bills. Under the Medicaid rules, these payments reduce Jane's waiting period, month by month. That is, after Betsy makes a $6,000 payment, the waiting period is recalculated as though Jane had given away only $294,000.

After 25 months, the waiting period will be pared from 50 months to 25 months. Jane will have been in the nursing home for 25 months—so she will have met this new, recalculated waiting period requirement. Betsy will have spent a total of $150,000 of Jane's gift to her on Jane's care, leaving Betsy with $150,000 of it (half the loaf).

Result: Jane can then qualify for Medicaid, which will cover her ongoing nursing home bills. Betsy can keep the $150,000 that would otherwise have been spent on Jane's nursing home bills.

Caution: This strategy works only if Betsy can be trusted to pay all of Jane's nursing home bills—otherwise Jane might be saddled with high nursing home expenses, no money to pay them and no eligibility for assistance.

In addition, you must work with an attorney experienced in Medicaid planning to prevent making a mistake that would result in the rejection of your Medicaid application.

• **How can I keep from losing my house if I go into a nursing home?** This probably won't be a problem if your spouse stays in the house. Many nursing home stays are financed by Medicaid. To qualify for Medicaid, you must have very little in the way of assets, but you can have up to $500,000 worth of equity in a house (in some states, up to $750,000). If your home equity exceeds these levels, you won't qualify for Medicaid.

After your death, the state can reclaim the money that it paid for your nursing home care from any home equity that's in your estate, but only if you are age 55 or older at your death. However, federal law prohibits this "estate recovery" process if your spouse survives you. A few states have attempted to recover Medicaid expenses after the later death of the spouse who did not receive Medicaid benefits, with mixed results.

Bottom line: If your spouse survives you, the family home will be safe from the cost of long-term care. If you have never been married or are divorced or are a widow or widower, it is still protected until your death at least up to the $500,000 (or $750,000) limit.

How to Make the Most of Unexpected Early Retirement

Nancy K. Schlossberg, EdD, a top specialist in the area of adult transitions, retirement and career development and professor emerita in the department of counseling and personnel services at the College of Education at University of Maryland, College Park. She is past president of the National Career Development Association, copresident of the consulting group TransitionWorks and author of *Revitalizing Retirement: Reshaping Your Identity, Relationships, and Purpose* (American Psychological Association).

Studies indicate that people who choose when to retire are happier than people who retire unexpectedly. Yet for many people, especially in these difficult economic times, retirement is forced upon them—often because of job layoffs or health problems.

Those who retire unexpectedly are forced to take stock of their financial and psychological resources and decide what to do next. *Important steps…*

• **Create a new "card."** Most of us define ourselves by the work we do. When we meet people, we say things such as, "I am a professor" or "I am a cook." Those who retire unexpectedly have lost their previous "tags."

At workshops, I ask people to think about what they would put on a postretirement business card. Some write "grandparent," "world traveler" or "golfer." Those who are beginning second careers might write down things such as "consultant" or "landscaper." How we define ourselves says a lot about the roles we want to assume.

Most people doing this exercise will write two or three "cards" as they transition from who they were to who they are.

• **Follow your pleasures.** Take the time to think about what challenges you and gives you pleasure. Maybe there's a hobby that you would like to pursue more seriously. Maybe you want to travel or spend more time in the garden or take another job that's entirely different from the one you had before.

Example: I talked to an investigative reporter who worked at the *Baltimore Sun*. He always had loved painting and hoped one day to become a serious artist. When he retired, he had all the time in the world to pursue this passion. It paid off when a prestigious gallery agreed to show his work.

It's easier to adjust to an unplanned retirement if you already know what you want to do. But there's nothing wrong with struggling for a few months—or even a few years—until you find the path that's right for you.

• **Form a transition group.** Spend time with people who, like you, have recently retired. None of us see ourselves as clearly as others see us. If you aren't sure what you would like to do next, getting feedback from your peers can be very helpful.

Another approach is to work with a career coach. These people are trained to evaluate our strengths and weaknesses, and they can help us move forward.

• **Keep your connections.** Loneliness and social isolation are among the main risks of retirement, particularly when retirement comes unexpectedly.

It is important to keep up with friends and establish friendship bases, activities and places where you can make new friends. These might include church committees or volunteer organizations. The Internet is a great resource. Web sites such as *www.meetup.com* help people with common interests—everything from building model ships to wine tasting—plan meetings and get-togethers.

• **Structure your days.** You need a framework to make your days enjoyable and meaningful. Some people make lunch plans every day. Others take classes or go to the health club.

Every day, make a list of all the things you would like to do that day. It does not matter if you complete them all, as long as you stay engaged and active. Merely waiting for things to happen almost guarantees that they never will.

Today's Top-Paying Retirement Jobs

Robert Skladany, a chief career counselor and vice president of research and certification, RetirementJobs. com, a job Web site and resource for workers over age 50 based in Waltham, Massachusetts.

Look around your bank, the bookshop, drugstore and doctor's office. Jobs once taken by 25-year-olds now go to older adults. Industries facing labor shortages realize that older candidates are more reliable, experienced and have a strong work ethic—and they are available. That's why you see so many 50-plus bank tellers, customer service representatives, accountants, medical technicians—now even Starbucks baristas.

Some of these "age-friendly" positions pay as much as $70 an hour. Many offer excellent health benefits plus flexible schedules that appeal to retirees seeking to earn extra income, yet still leave time for travel, hobbies, volunteering and visiting grandchildren.

During the next decade, the Bureau of Labor Statistics expects the number of workers over age 55 to grow at five times the rate of the overall workforce. The demand is already here. At RetirementJobs.com, the Web site that I work for, more than 30,000 jobs are listed, with more than 500 employers actively seeking older adults. The Web site also includes advice on résumé-writing, interviewing and online learning opportunities to retrain or update your skills.

As a start, here are some of the fastest-growing industries eager to hire mature workers, with pay rates of about $10 an hour or better.* Salary.com, the online compensation consulting firm, provided the median hourly wages.

STAFFING COMPANIES

You may not think of temp agencies as employers, but companies like Manpower, Robert Half International, Kelly Services and Adecco offer some of the highest paid professional and managerial limited-duration contract work.

Workers with relevant experience and background can expect $30 to $70 an hour for project work in accounting, engineering, human resources, law, information technology (IT) and project management. Clerical and administrative jobs can pay from $9 to $16 an hour for entry-level to skilled administrative positions. Computer skills are a must, but companies often provide training.

HEALTH CARE

With an aging US population, there's a huge need for health-care workers in hospitals, clinics, doctor's offices, laboratories and patients' homes. Many jobs don't require special training, certification or hands-on care of patients. Clerical workers can earn up to $15 an hour. And, higher-level administrators and managers, who supervise staff and plan work, earn from $20 to $25, sometimes more. Jobs involving patient care, such as nursing, as well as

*Rates subject to change.

physical and occupational therapy, pay well but usually require at least an associate's degree and a license. Assistants to physical therapists and occupational therapists can get nearly $20 an hour and dental hygienists around $30 an hour. Nurses are among the most sought-after health workers, earning $20 to $60 or more an hour depending on their specific training and specialization.

There's a big demand now for pharmacists. But if you don't possess a doctor of pharmacy degree and license, consider that chains like CVS provide training for pharmacy aides and technicians and pay about $14 an hour.

Demand is strong for home health-care and personal aides, some positions do not even require a high school diploma, and pay hourly wages up to $11 for personal care and up to $15 for advanced care. (Go to the Web site of large home health agencies in your area and contact them for job listings.)

ACCOUNTING AND TAX PREPARATION

There is a very strong demand for accountants due to increased regulations created in response to the collapse of the energy-trading company Enron. Trained accountants with a bachelor's degree in business can earn $25 to $40 per hour, with temporary, contract or full-time positions available. If you don't have all the educational credentials, but are handy with calculations and details, tax preparation firms like H&R Block provide training and pay $15 to $30 an hour depending on education and experience. You will stay busy from December through April.

INSURANCE, INVESTMENT AND BANKING SERVICES

Financial institutions, such as Fidelity, John Hancock and Vanguard, have discovered that their customers do not want a 20-something telling them how to handle their money. Some office-support positions don't require a college degree. Other positions, such as financial analyst, require a business degree and industry-specific licensing and certification. (Or they need to know that you are working toward those designations.) Entry-level workers at investment companies can expect $12 to $18 an hour, and $15 to $25 for technical or licensed

jobs. Sales commissions often plump up those hourly wages.

SPECIALTY RETAIL

Specialty stores selling sporting goods, cosmetics, office supplies, furniture and electronics (such as Eastern Mountain Sports, Sephora, Staples, IKEA and Best Buy) all have flexible schedules with good benefits, a pleasant environment and wages of $15 to $25 an hour.

Examples: Barnes & Noble prefers to hire retired librarians, teachers and others who have a passion for books. Starbucks just earned our "age-friendly" employer designation because of the company's generous health benefits, even for employees working just 20 hours a week.

GENERAL RETAIL

If selling and customer service are your strengths, check out general merchandisers like Macy's and even grocery chains like Safeway and Trader Joe's. Wages start at $7 to $22 an hour for sales associates and customer service representatives and can range from $10 to $29 an hour at the supervisory/managerial level.

GOVERNMENT

From 2000 to 2007, more than half of senior-level federal executives left their jobs or retired, and many workforce experts predict labor shortages in the federal workforce. State and local governments face a similar challenge. Federal jobs are now scattered all around the country and cover a huge range of professions. Jobs listed recently on our Web site ranged from management analyst to translator to summer playground leader. Pay depends on qualifications and experience, but many openings are expected from entry-level to managerial and professional. Agencies such as the IRS, Peace Corps and US Small Business Administration Office of Disaster Assistance are seeking age 50-plus adults for seasonal, part-time and full-time work.

TRANSPORTATION

Got a good driving record? There are nearly 3,000 openings for drivers posted at RetirementJobs.com—for example, with Schneider National, Inc., the country's largest truckload carrier. Just type in your zip code and the keyword "driver" to see what's available. Drivers are needed for limousines, school buses, medical transport vehicles—even tractor trailers. Training is often provided, although special licenses may be needed. Expect $10 to $15 an hour for small vehicles and $12 to $24 an hour for larger trucks.

Aging Gracefully: Top Model Tells How (Not for Women Only)

Valerie Ramsey, coauthor with her daughter Heather Hummel of *Gracefully: Looking and Being Your Best at Any Age* (McGraw-Hill). Ramsey was the public relations manager for the Pebble Beach Golf Resort, Pebble Beach, California, and is currently a fashion model represented by agencies in San Francisco and New York. Her Web site is *www.valerieramsey.com*.

Looking young is a $60 billion a year industry—that's $1,600 worth of hormone treatments, plastic surgery, skin creams and supplements for every retiree in the US. But you don't need to spend a lot of money to age gracefully—looking and feeling your best.

Here, 68-year-old Valerie Ramsey, one of the most sought-after cover models in the country, reveals her secrets. This grandmother of eight is the "centerpiece" for print ad campaigns for fashion and beauty magazines and has graced the runways at numerous fashion shows. In addition, Ramsey is a motivational speaker and has made regular appearances on the *Today* show, *Fox Business News with Neil Cavuto* and *Extra*. She's never hidden her age or tried to pretend her hair wasn't gray. *Her "grace" is as much about feeling great and staying healthy as it is about maintaining her looks...*

MY STORY

My life has unfolded in a reverse direction. Until my 50s, I was a stay-at-home mom raising six children. Then, my husband and I relocated cross-country to California, where I learned how to use a BlackBerry and a computer and got a job in public relations. Not long afterward, I discovered that I had uterine cancer

as well as a severe case of cardiomyopathy (a weak heart muscle).

I wasn't ready to retire and become an old lady with medical problems. I've always had a sweet tooth and rarely exercised when I was younger. In fact, I was famous in my family for doing "vertical laps" in the pool—bobbing up and down. But in the 1990s, I decided that I had to and would live a healthier lifestyle. I began nutritional and workout regimens and was able to beat the cancer and control my heart problem.

At age 63, a television producer I met liked my look and recommended me to a modeling agency. Out of the blue, this agency booked me to do a runway show in the Fairmont Hotel Grand Ballroom in San Francisco!

Standing backstage surrounded by 18-year-old waiflike models, I felt like Grandma Moses. What was I doing here?

But I also had a revelation—aging gracefully isn't just about looking younger. That's a losing battle with diminishing returns. It's about feeling younger, making the most of the time you have by becoming happier and more content with who you are. It's about choosing behaviors and attitudes that promote robust health. When you feel young inside, it creates a potent energy that bubbles out of you. Everyone notices it, and heads turn when you walk into a room. *My secrets...*

EATING WELL

Many of us fall into the trap of eating the same foods the majority of the time. It is very easy to slip into eating habits you aren't even aware of. *Rules that I follow every day...*

•**I drink an eight-ounce glass of water first thing in the morning,** which helps me to rehydrate and wake up. (I drink a total of at least 64 ounces of water daily to hydrate my body and skin.)

•**At every meal I sit down—and eat slowly.** Not only do I enjoy the food more this way, but I consume less.

•**I eat a big breakfast** (half a grapefruit, one slice of whole-grain toast with butter and two scrambled eggs) or, at the very least, a snack within 45 minutes of waking, a balanced lunch (turkey or chicken with a complex carbohydrate, such as sweet potatoes, and veggies or half a tuna sandwich on whole-grain bread) and a light dinner (salmon, tomatoes and vegetables) by 7 pm. I also snack on fruit, especially apples, and protein drinks made with whey.

• **I never go longer than four hours without eating.** Otherwise, I get too hungry and tend to overeat at the next meal.

• **I always opt for natural carbohydrates,** the ones that come from the ground, such as rice, yams, sweet potatoes and beans…and whole-grain breads and cereals in moderation. And when eating carbohydrates, I add some fat or protein. When you eat a carbohydrate by itself, you get a bloated-belly feeling.

EXERCISE

I think of working out as the secret weapon that provides me with the stamina for everything else I want to do in life. I have a 30- to 45-minute routine every day that my daughter, who's a personal trainer, prepared for me. This includes 30 minutes on a treadmill or elliptical trainer followed by 15 minutes of weights for my shoulders, biceps and upper body.

To find an exercise regimen that works for you: Do something you like enough to stick with. Start daily power-walking, join a class at your gym, play tennis, do Pilates. Or go back to what was fun when you were a kid, such as bicycling and/or swimming.

SLEEP

I try to get at least seven hours of uninterrupted sleep a night. Sleep is how your body repairs itself from the day's activity. Our bodies are a chemistry lab, not a bank account. When you shortchange your sleep patterns, you're not only tired the next day—you've also lost out on critical healing.

COMMUNICATION

I look people in the eyes and smile when I talk with them. When you greet someone, focus on sending them positive energy, and this energy will translate through your own eyes. People will experience you as radiating warmth—and, yes, youth.

ATTITUDE

Think positively all of the time. According to the National Science Foundation, we have more than 65,000 thoughts each day, nearly 95% of which are the same thoughts we had the day before. We have the ability to create and shape our life experiences through our thoughts. This is so essential for older people because it's downright rejuvenating to believe that there is still plenty of time left to create positive experiences in life.

As you go through your daily exercise routine, practice turning every negative or fearful thought you have into a positive one. *See the examples below…*

• **You are taking your car to the shop because you need new tires.** Rather than dwell on how much they will cost, focus on how much easier and safer it will be to drive through snow and rain.

• **You are waiting for your spouse to come home so that you can go to a dinner party.** You think, "I don't want him to be late."

Better: Turn the thought around and think, "I want him to be on time." That small twist can alleviate a lot of tension when your spouse does arrive.

OTHER STRATEGIES

• **Make a list of your best qualities** and stick it on your mirror to read while you brush your teeth.

• **When someone compliments you, thank him** and believe what he said.

• **Try to turn confrontations into positive experiences.**

Example: If a situation erupts during a conversation, you can calm the other person down without speaking a word.

How: Imagine a band of gold light beaming down on the other person's head. Keep the imagined stream of light steady as you listen when the other person speaks (or yells). The person will feel you relax, and that will diffuse his own tension.

COSMETIC PROCEDURES

I favor only minimally invasive, outpatient procedures with board-certified doctors, as this prevents you from spending enormous amounts of money and from winding up with an unnatural, plastic look.

I personally have had treatment on my face to remove skin cancer and sun damage…photorejuvenation, a treatment performed with a cool-tip laser that reduces fine lines and age spots and stimulates production of collagen… and copper bromide laser treatments to repair broken blood vessels and sun damage.

Why This 94-Year-Old Doctor Says, "It's Fun To Be Old!"

Marion P. Downs, DHS, DSc (Hon.), an audiologist and a pioneer in universal hearing screening for newborns and the namesake of two hearing centers at the University of Colorado, where she taught for more than 40 years. She is author of *Shut Up and Live! (You Know How): A 93-Year-Old's Guide to Living to a Ripe Old Age* (Avery/Penguin).

How do some people, as they grow older, continue to lead happy, vigorous, event-filled lives, while others don't? Meet Dr. Marion Downs. *In her 94 years, she has…*

• **Participated in a mini-triathlon** (running, swimming and biking) at age 89.

• **Won Senior Olympics gold medals in tennis.**

• **Achieved mandated hearing tests for more than 90% of US newborns** when she was an audiologist in her 50s.

• **Retired—often.**

Here's what she has to say…

It's fun to be old. I can do almost anything I want to do. Nobody cares! But one thing I know—to continue, I must take care of myself physically and mentally.

My "old age" got off to a great start. The day I turned 51, I stood at the top of a hill wearing ski gear that my kids had left in a closet, scared to barrel down that first slope. I turned to the instructor and said, "I can't do this! It's too steep. What should I do?" He said, "Shut up and ski! You know how." I did? Yes, even though it was my first time, somehow I did. So I went.

Now, whenever life gets strange and I don't know what to do next, I tell myself, "Shut up and live! You know how."

Most of us are living longer than our parents did, with no guidelines to see us through those critical years. "Girls" in their 80s and younger claim I'm their role model and ask for my longevity secrets.

A few years ago, I noticed that youngsters in their 50s and 60s dared to write books about how to live to a ripe old age. Why not me? I know how! So I wrote a book, too.

MY PRIORITIES

My three children, 11 grandchildren and 24 great-grandchildren are 38 of the best reasons to stick around. But only I can take care of myself. And I do.

I believe in taking total responsibility for one's own life. Stop blaming your Grandpa. According to an aging report from Harvard, our genes account for only about 25% to 35% of our longevity and 30% of our physiological changes. My parents died at 72. Not me.

Maintaining a vigorous old age requires a lot of determination.

My number one priority: Daily exercise.

Every morning I stretch for 15 to 20 minutes. Back stretches keep me free of pain from a serious back problem decades before. Neck and shoulder stretches keep my head up and shoulders back. Daily leg stretches prevent the old folks' shuffle, caused by short, weak leg muscles. Striding is better.

At home, I do an hour of strengthening exercises (with weights, stretchy exercise bands, on a large balance ball and with a soccer ball) three times a week and one to two hours of aerobics (mostly running, but I love my three-wheel bicycle, too) four times per week. My trainer, whom I call the Marquis de Sade, protects me from harm but keeps me hopping. I see him periodically for consultations about increasing the number of repetitions of an exercise, trying a new exercise regimen or device and general advice and help.

Exercise is play, too. Tennis has been my game since I retired from full-time work at 68. I prefer it over golf because it involves more activity. I play two hours three times a week in a league with changing partners.

MY SO-CALLED DIET

I'm no dietitian. But I look pretty good for a nonagenarian, and people ask for my nutritional secrets.

What I eat: Foods high in protein and low in carbohydrates. Lots of fruit and as many veggies as I can swallow.

That regimen keeps me lean, clean, healthy and strong.

Another essential food group: Each morning I put a milk chocolate "turtle" on the kitchen counter. I admire it all day and eat it at night.

MY FAVORITE DISEASES

I've had them all, done research and come up with some answers...

●**Osteoarthritis.** This age-related degenerative joint disease is the most common condition of older people. Deal with it, forget it and get on with your life.

Keep your joints moving. Exercise is the best long-term remedy.

Recommended: If you injure yourself at all, ask a sports medicine orthopedist to oversee your exercise program. While the torn rotator cuff in my shoulder was healing, my doctor let me play tennis as long as I didn't raise my arm high while serving.

●**Bursitis.** At one point, hip pain shut down my tennis game. Unacceptable! Acupuncture helped only one side. Cortisone shots worked, but cannot be repeated indefinitely. Vioxx is effective, but was taken off the market four years later because it raised heart attack risk. By then, though, it had let me exercise all my joints and subdue the pain for a long time.

Sleeping on my side with a hard pillow between my knees has kept my hip bursitis away.

Bonus: This position helps to prevent back trouble.

Double bonus: Lying on my left side prevents acid reflux, the surging up of stomach acid that plagued me for years.

●**Lung disease.** Many oldies, including me, pay the price of having smoked in youth. I smoked two packs a day (except during pregnancy and breastfeeding) from ages 18 to 58. At 80, I developed chronic obstructive pulmonary disease (COPD). My breathing is impaired, but I live with it under treatment by a pulmonary specialist. Drugs such as bronchodilators can help. If I weren't a lifelong exercise fiend, I would be on oxygen.

●**Vertigo.** Benign *paroxysmal positional vertigo* (BPPV) is very common in older people. With older age, especially if we have had migraines, the small calcium stones floating inside our ears that help us balance can cut loose and drift into the wrong spaces.

My BPPV started one morning almost 10 years ago when I got up and fell right back. I was taken, in a wheelchair, to a vestibular (inner-ear-regulated balance) expert, who maneuvered my head for 30 seconds and sent the rocks back where they belong. Fortunately, the problem hasn't returned.

●**Hearing loss.** I've worn hearing aids since age 80. People who refuse them despite increasing deafness miss a lot. Those who resist (typically, men) may not only lose contact with the world but also destroy their marital relationship.

First step: Go to an ear specialist to make sure the cause isn't a medical problem.

●**Skin cancer.** Four doctors called my two-inch sore a spider bite. My son-in-law suggested a wound clinic, where a biopsy was done.

Diagnosis: Squamous cell carcinoma, one step short of melanoma.

A terrific specialist removed it.

Tip of the century: Find the right doctor. Persevere until you do. Get second and third opinions...ask everyone you know for recommendations...do thorough research.

●**Alzheimer's disease.** I have not had this one. But both of my husbands did, one older than I and one younger, for a total of 20 years. Was it rough? Oh, yes.

My bridge games, finishing crosswords in pen—who knows if they help my brain stay healthy? I keep active and hope for the best.

MY KIND OF FUN

When I turned 90, I decided to try skydiving. My family tried to stop me. Ha!

Strapped to an instructor, I did a 3,000-foot free fall at 120 miles per hour. The landing was nice. We glided in. I sat down on a sand pile.

For my 95th, next January, I plan on doing it again.

13

Estate Planning Guide

Has the Market Crash Ruined Your Estate Plan? How to Fix It...

If your portfolio took a pounding in 2008, your estate plan probably needs some attention. You might have to make adjustments to limit the impact that the losses have on you and your heirs. *Pay attention to...*

YOUR WILL

Does your will still leave your spouse with sufficient assets to live on comfortably? If the value of your estate has declined precipitously, this could be in doubt. If so, it is probably better to leave more to your spouse and cut back the amount bequeathed to other heirs or charities.

If your will includes specific bequests of assets to beneficiaries, make sure that the assumptions you made about the value of these assets are still valid.

Example: You left your property to your son and your stock portfolio to your daughter. When the will was written, these were roughly equal in value. If your stock portfolio has lost 40% of its value since then, but your home's value is down just 10%, you might need to leave your daughter additional assets to keep the gifts equal.

GIFTS AND LOANS

Did it seem that just a few years ago you had more than enough money to finance your retirement? If so, perhaps you have been taking advantage of the federal government's gift tax exclusion, your right to make annual gifts of up to $13,000 a year to each of your children or grandchildren or other recipients without triggering gift tax. These gifts are a great way to reduce future estate taxation—they remove

Martin Shenkman, attorney and CPA who specializes in trusts and estates in New York City and New Jersey. He is also author of numerous books, including *Estate Planning: Protection for People with a Chronic Disease or Disability* (Demos) and *The Complete Book of Trusts* (Wiley). His Web site, *www.laweasy.com*, provides sample forms and documents.

money from your estate. But if your net worth has declined sharply in the past year, it's time to reevaluate your financial position and make sure that you can still afford such generosity.

If there is any chance that you or your spouse could outlive your now-depleted savings, it might be wise to reduce, suspend or discontinue these gifts. Inform your heirs of this as soon as possible so that they can adjust their own savings and spending plans accordingly.

Hard hit: If this horrible economy has left one of your family members in a particularly difficult financial predicament, consider continuing your annual gifts only to this person. Helping a loved one through tough times may be more important than keeping your gifts to your heirs exactly even. You can balance the gifts out later, after this descendant is back on his/her feet. Or, you can adjust your will to give less to the family member you are now helping out financially.

If you *lend* money to a family member, put the terms of the loan in writing. This can help prevent the IRS from treating the loan as a gift. It can also protect the money if the loan recipient is sued or divorces.

TRUSTS

If you are the *beneficiary* of a trust, ask the trustees how the market correction will affect future distributions. Reevaluate your spending and saving plans accordingly.

If you are the *trustee* of a trust that has lost a significant portion of its value, contact an estate-planning attorney before speaking with the trust's beneficiaries or taking any other actions.

Reason: You could be personally liable for some portion of the losses if you don't comply with the terms of the trust and the *Uniform Prudent Investor Act.*

FOR BUSINESS OWNERS

For those in the process of passing a business to their heirs, this bad economy could actually be a golden opportunity.

What to do: Have the business reappraised. Most businesses are worth substantially less in recessionary economies, at least on paper. That means you might be able to pass your

heirs a larger percentage of the business each year without gift tax being imposed.

In fact, you can give your heirs an even larger percentage of your business each year than the $13,000 gift tax exclusion limit suggests. Because the gifted portion of your business is illiquid and does not give the recipients any control over business decisions, the IRS will allow you to "discount" its value for tax purposes. Larger discounts may be acceptable in tough economic times like these.

Discount calculations can be very complex, so consult an estate-planning attorney or CPA.

INSURANCE

You should think twice before you cancel insurance policies even if you are desperate to trim your costs. Living without health, disability, life, business, homeowner's or automobile insurance is an unacceptable risk that could cost you all of your savings. Consider increasing the size of your policy deductibles and removing nonessential riders to reduce costs instead.

It is reasonable to cancel insurance policies only if the reason you purchased the coverage in the first place no longer applies.

Example: It might be OK to cancel (or to cash out or sell) life insurance or disability coverage if you have retired and no longer depend on this insurance to replace lost income in an emergency.

Even large, well-regarded insurance companies can face problems in this economy. Ask a financial adviser or trustworthy independent insurance agent about the financial health of your insurance providers and your options if these companies are at risk. It might be possible to switch your coverage to a more financially secure company. This could be done tax free through what is known as a Section 1035 Exchange. Consult your tax adviser.

More from Martin Shenkman, JD, CPA...

What's a Springing Power of Attorney?

Durable power of attorney for finances is a written agreement by which you delegate authority to another person to manage your financial affairs in the event of your illness or incapacity. It allows the person you designate to pay your bills, make investments for you or open your safe-deposit box.

The drawback is that you are giving this person the right to handle your finances immediately, which makes many people uncomfortable. Now, a specialized type of durable power—"springing" durable power of attorney—is recognized in more than 20 states. Springing powers do not take effect until a specific event that you stipulate occurs, such as you become physically or mentally incompetent or you are admitted to a nursing home.

Caveats: To avoid confusion, make sure the legal document specifies exactly how the triggering event is determined. It might happen only when your personal physician declares in writing that you can no longer take care of your financial affairs.

Check that your bank and brokerage firms will accept your springing durable power of attorney. Some require you to fill out their own power-of-attorney forms or make your relatives get a court order before gaining control of your money.

Also from Martin Shenkman...

It's Hard to Cut a Spouse Out of Your Will

Most states require that one-third to one-half of a person's assets go to his or her spouse. If you and your spouse agree that your assets should go to someone else—such as a child from an earlier marriage—the spouse must waive his or her rights to the inheritance by signing a waiver and be represented by an attorney. Many prenuptial agreements include these provisions. Consult an estate lawyer for details.

Martin Shenkman on protecting a bequest...

Don't Let an Heir Squander Your Bequest

You might wish to leave a significant bequest to an heir but are afraid that he/she won't be able to manage it and will quickly squander it.

One solution: Instead of leaving a bequest of cash outright, instruct your executor to use the cash to purchase a noncancelable annuity for the heir. The annuity may be for life or an extended period, such as 20 years. This prevents the heir from disposing of all the money at once, guarantees an investment return on the bequest, and avoids the cost and complications of trust arrangements.

Consult your estate-planning adviser.

How to Avoid Costly Mistakes When Naming Beneficiaries

Mary Randolph, JD, an attorney and senior vice president at legal publisher Nolo Press, Berkeley, California, *www.nolo.com*. She is author of numerous publications on estate matters, including *8 Ways to Avoid Probate*, and coauthor of the book-and-software package *Quicken WillMaker Plus 2009* (both from Nolo).

If you have drafted a will, you may think that it dictates who inherits all of your assets and how those beneficiaries will split them. But if you are not careful, the bulk of your assets could end up being distributed in very different ways than you intended.

Example: Beneficiaries you designate for life insurance policies...certain investment accounts, such as 401(k)s and IRAs...and even US savings bonds...take precedence over those you name in your will.

Some of the biggest mistakes...

NAMING THE WRONG BENEFICIARIES

Mistake: **Naming your estate as beneficiary.** If you name your estate as beneficiary of your retirement account or life insurance (or don't designate a beneficiary at all), these assets will be subject to probate, a time-consuming and expensive legal process in which a court oversees the payment of debt and distribution of assets. Creditors will be able to make claims against these assets during the probate process. Also, your heirs will not have the option of allowing the assets in your tax-advantaged retirement plans to continue to grow on a tax-deferred basis. That's because tax laws allow human beneficiaries to withdraw money from inherited IRAs slowly, based on their remaining life spans, while estates do not have this right.

Example: Tom, 71, named his estate as beneficiary of his life insurance policy. The $500,000 payout was tied up in probate for nearly a year, and probate fees added up to $25,000.

What to do: Name a spouse or a child as beneficiary, or name several children as co-beneficiaries.

Mistake: **Naming a trust as beneficiary of a retirement account** when there are significant differences in the ages of the heirs.

Snag: The designated beneficiaries of your tax-advantaged retirement accounts can choose to allow these funds to continue to grow tax-deferred after your death. The beneficiaries are required to make withdrawals based on their own estimated remaining life spans, which can mean many decades of tax benefits for younger beneficiaries. When a tax-advantaged retirement plan's designated beneficiary is a trust, all of the trust's beneficiaries must make their withdrawals based upon the age of the oldest beneficiary.

Example: Martha wanted her three children, ages 38, 40 and 58, to receive her IRA after her death. Had her children been named beneficiaries of this account, the younger two would have obtained the benefits of tax-free growth for decades. Because Martha named a trust as beneficiary and her children as the trust beneficiaries, the two younger children had to take faster withdrawals based on the estimated remaining life span of the oldest sibling.

What to do: Name beneficiaries directly in retirement accounts, and take those designations into account when apportioning other assets to beneficiaries in your will.

OMITTING KEY STEPS

Mistake: **Failing to obtain a spousal waiver for your 401(k) account** if you do not wish the assets to go to your spouse. If you are married, by law your spouse is the beneficiary of your 401(k), even if your will or a prenuptial agreement says otherwise.

Example: Harold, 65, remarried after the passing of his first wife. His new wife, Gwen, 62, had assets of her own and signed a prenuptial agreement stating that Harold's savings should pass to his children from his first marriage. But because Gwen did not also sign a beneficiary waiver for Harold's 401(k), those assets still passed to her.

What to do: Obtain a signed waiver from your spouse.

Mistake: **Ignoring "transfer on death" (TOD) opportunities.** In most US states, it is possible to name a TOD beneficiary for an investment or bank account and, in several states, for a home and/or car. This is comparable to joint ownership except that the TOD beneficiary does not assume any control until the owner dies. Naming TOD beneficiaries can be the wisest way to help your beneficiaries avoid the time and expense of probate. Ask your brokerage house, mutual fund company or bank for the necessary forms.

Example: Sally, a 73-year-old Arizona resident, wanted her home to pass directly to her only son, Kevin, when she died, without the expense of probate. She could have named Kevin co-owner of the home, but that would have put the home at risk if Kevin divorced or was sued. Instead, Sally signed and recorded a new deed that listed Kevin as TOD beneficiary.

What to do: Consider TOD designations if they're available in your home state. For TOD rules in your state, check *www.nolo.com* (click on "Wills & Estate Planning," then on "Living Trusts and Avoiding Probate," and finally on "Avoiding Probate in Your State").

FAILING TO UPDATE

Mistake: **Overlooking the descendants of deceased children** in beneficiary designations for retirement plans, life insurance policies and savings bonds. Parents with several adult children often designate their children as equal beneficiaries. But, unfortunately, this seemingly fair system becomes inequitable if one of the adult children dies before the parents do. In such cases, the children of the deceased child could get nothing.

What to do: Use your will to help balance out distributions.

Example: Leave your surviving children as the only beneficiaries of your life insurance policy. Then name the children of your deceased child as beneficiaries of an appropriate amount in your will, to balance how much they get with how much your living children get. Include an explanation in the will of why this was done so that no child feels unfairly treated. Alternatively, you could deposit money into a bank account naming the grandchildren as beneficiaries "payable on death" of the account holder.

Mistake: Forgetting to update beneficiary designations when you marry, divorce or are widowed. Even those who remember to update their wills when they gain or lose a spouse may forget to update retirement plan and life insurance policy beneficiary designations.

What do: Contact your investment and life insurance companies to ask how to update your beneficiary designations, or ask your estate-planning attorney for assistance. To update the "co-owner" or beneficiary designations on US savings bonds, contact the Federal Reserve Bank at *www.treasurydirect.gov* to obtain the forms necessary to have the bonds reissued.

What Your Will *Won't* Do

Many kinds of property that you leave to your heirs may pass outside of your will.

Examples: Jointly owned property and financial accounts pass to the joint owner. IRAs, 401(k)s and other pension accounts, and life insurance policy proceeds, pass to the beneficiaries you name in the account documents.

Traps: Instructions that you leave in your will regarding such properties will be disregarded …if you neglect to update beneficiary designations for retirement accounts and insurance policies as your circumstances and intentions are altered, they may be distributed contrary to your intentions…if beneficiary designations are lost by the institutions that held them—as

may happen after the passage of many years—assets may pass contrary to your intentions.

Safety: Make sure that your estate plan takes into account assets that aren't governed by your will. Keep all beneficiary designations up-to-date, and keep copies of the designations with your will and other vital papers.

Barbara Weltman, Esq., an attorney based in Millwood, New York, and publisher of the free online newsletter, Big Ideas for Small Business, www.barbaraweltman.com.

Drafting a Will? How To Avoid Fights Over Who Gets What

Wynne A. Whitman, Esq., a partner specializing in trusts and estates with the Morristown, New Jersey, law firm Schenck, Price, Smith & King LLP. She is author of several books on estate planning, including Smart Women Protect Their Assets (FT).

Preparing a will can turn into a battle of wills for too many couples and families. Creating or updating a will forces you to think about money, mortality and extended family—topics that can cause conflict in even the closest of families. *To avoid fighting with your partner over drafting a will…*

•**Do not be critical of family members.** Fights over wills often have more to do with perceived affronts to relatives than with who gets what. If you do not believe that a particular descendant deserves a share of your estate or you disagree with your partner's choice of executor, search for a way to present your position without speaking poorly about the person in question.

Examples: Explain that you wish to give a particular descendant less than an equal share of your estate not because this person does not deserve the money (even if he or she doesn't), but because other descendants need the money more or will put it to better use… explain that you are not disagreeing with your partner's choice of executor or trustee because there is something wrong with this individual (even if there is), but because you think that

223

there is someone else even better equipped to handle the task.

•**Propose compromises.** Fights are particularly likely when one partner feels his voice is not being heard.

Solution: Listen to all your partner's positions, and look for middle ground.

Potential compromises when you cannot agree on how to divide up the estate: Leave a ne'er-do-well descendant a family heirloom of sentimental value, but little financial value …establish a charitable trust that provides for the family as one partner wishes, but later donates whatever remains to charity as the other wishes…agree to give a small percentage of the estate to a partner's children from a former marriage rather than shut these descendants out entirely…include a statement in the will explaining that the descendants who received less are no less loved.

Potential compromises if you and your partner cannot agree on an executor for your will: Name the two candidates for executor as coexecutors rather than selecting one over the other…name a mutual friend or a bank as executor rather than arguing over which family member to select.

•**Discuss potentially difficult issues with your partner before meeting with your lawyer.** Paying an attorney a steep hourly fee to listen to you argue with your partner will only increase everyone's tension level.

Solution: Sit down with your partner before the meeting to hash out who should be executor…who should be responsible for any minor children…and who should receive what from your estate. Even if you cannot bring every issue to a mutually satisfactory conclusion, this premeeting discussion will allow you to clearly and calmly explain any disagreements to your attorney. Perhaps he can then offer acceptable solutions.

•**Agree on a primary goal.** What do you most want your will to accomplish? If you and your partner can agree on this, you are less likely to bicker over details.

Example: If you have minor children, you and your partner probably can agree that the main goal of your will is to ensure that they are brought up properly. If your partner claims that giving someone on your side of the family custody of the children will anger members of his family, remind your partner of the primary goal and explain why living with your family would be best for the children—perhaps your family lives nearby, so your kids would not be uprooted…or perhaps your sister is your kids' favorite aunt.

•**Say the words "for now."** Your will can be amended in the future. Reminding your partner that the decisions made today are not necessarily permanent can help remove some of the emotion.

Example: Your partner believes that a family member with a substance abuse problem will eventually recover and should receive a portion of your estate. To your partner, leaving this family member out of the will is like giving up on him forever.

Solution: Agree that this individual will be added to the will as soon as he overcomes the problem.

Who Needs to Have Your Financial Passwords

Nancy Dunnan, a New York City–based financial and travel adviser and author or coauthor of 25 books, including *How to Invest $50–$5,000* (HarperCollins).

Most people know they should not give out any of their financial passwords. But it is a good idea to let the person who will serve as executor or to whom you gave power of attorney have ahead of time all the passwords needed to manage your affairs. As a backup, make a list of your financial passwords (along with the names of the institutions, contact names and phone numbers) and leave it in a safe-deposit box, telling your executor and whoever has your power of attorney where the key is located. Arrange with the bank for them to have access to the box.

Or, leave the list with your lawyer or in a locked drawer at your home. Let your executor or the person who will have power of attorney know that this is where a copy of the list will be. Let him/her know where to find the key.

This list should also include the answers to common identity questions, such as your mother's maiden name, the town where you were born and any other ID questions that you chose when setting up accounts—for example, the name of your favorite pet.

Preparing Your Spouse to Handle The Finances

Wendy F. Roy, CFP, director of Ernst & Young's Survivor Financial Counseling Service, New York City. She provides financial counseling to widowers and widows.

Y ou may be doing a good job of handling the family finances, paying bills and investing, but what happens if you pass away? Would your spouse understand the financial choices you were making as a couple? Would he/she turn to the right person for financial advice? I have seen many surviving spouses who feel utterly lost and panicked about money matters. That's why it is important to handle the finances together. *Here's how…*

• **Communicate all your concerns to your spouse**—but avoid blaming. Your spouse may have deferred responsibility for all the finances, but you were equally complicit by taking charge all those years. Tell your spouse that you would like to work as a team going forward. Stress that your spouse doesn't need to become an investing wizard or an insurance expert, but that it is important to know enough to keep everything functioning even if you are not there.

• **Put your spouse in charge of organizing the finances.** It's a simple, nontechnical way to get your spouse involved. Have your spouse compile a list, including phone numbers, addresses, Web sites and passwords, of all your accounts at banks and brokerage firms and any other financial institutions. Also have your spouse list insurance policies…financial professionals you use…and the individual to

contact at your job about employee benefits and retirement plans.

Have your spouse make copies *and* maintain records of wills, trusts and deeds to the house in both a bank safe-deposit box and a fireproof box in your home.

• **Divide up all financial chores.** Ask your spouse to relieve you of some of the weekly and monthly paperwork. Do the tasks together at first, then let your spouse take over some. Begin with the most basic tasks that would need to be done if you died. *These include…*

• Paying the bills. Your spouse should have a good idea of your personal cash flow—what's going in and out of accounts each month.

• Maintaining an emergency cash reserve. Your spouse should make sure that there's enough for at least three months' worth of expenses and know what to do in order to replenish the fund if some of the money is used.

• **Make sure your spouse trusts your financial advisers.** Involve your spouse in meetings with your estate attorney, accountant, financial planner, etc. It is important that your spouse establish enough of a relationship with your advisers to be comfortable working with them in your absence.

Many of my clients expect their grown children to help the surviving spouse with all the finances. Children often lack the time and expertise to do an effective job. Also, after you're gone, your kids may have their hands full dealing with all the other changes in your spouse's life beyond finances.

• **Jot down explanatory notes on your financial plans and documents.** Clearly explain your intentions behind decisions and how they were meant to benefit your dependents.

Examples: "I bought this deferred annuity because…" "I stopped adding money to this retirement fund and started contributing to that one because…"

Reason: A major problem for widows and widowers is figuring out why their spouses made certain investments or bought particular policies. A simple explanation gives your spouse and advisers a foundation to work from.

• **Recommend that your spouse wait for a year before making any major financial decisions.** It takes at least one 12-month cycle for a surviving spouse to fully understand the finances and the consequences of financial decisions on long-term planning.

Example: A widow in her early 60s used the proceeds of her husband's life insurance policy for a comprehensive kitchen remodeling project that she had put off while he was alive. She reasoned that it would help assuage her sorrow. Halfway through the project, however, she got hit with the annual property tax bill for her home. She hadn't factored that in.

A Gift to Your Family

Rebecca Shannonhouse, editor, *Bottom Line/Health*, Boardroom Inc., 281 Tresser Blvd., Stamford, Connecticut, 06901.

Most people do not like to think about end-of-life medical care. But the failure to do so can result in patients receiving unwanted—and often prolonged—medical care even when there's no hope of recovery.

If you're like the three out of four Americans who have not stated their wishes in writing, you probably want to change that.

"Consider it a gift to your family," says Nathan A. Kottkamp, an attorney and chair of the National Healthcare Decisions Day (NHDD) initiative, a grassroots effort to promote advance-care planning.

By completing an advance directive, you can give a trusted person power of attorney over your health-care decisions in case you're unable to make them…and specify in a living will exactly what types of care you want—or do not want—to receive. *To prevent mistakes…*

• **Share the documents.** Less than half of severely or terminally ill patients have an advance directive in their medical records. Copies should be given to your doctors…and if you go to the hospital, bring a copy with you.

• **Be specific when preparing a living will.** Avoid terms like "always" or "never." You might write that you "never" want to be put on a ventilator, but if you've been in an accident, you may need help breathing for only a few days.

For more information—including free advance directive forms—go to the NHDD Web site, *www.nationalhealthcaredecisionsday.org*, or call 800-658-8898.

A Difficult, but Necessary Discussion

End-of-life conversations may be difficult, but they make dying easier.

Recent finding: Compared with patients who did not have end-of-life discussions with their doctors, patients who did discuss their wishes about the kind of care they would like to receive were more likely to enter a hospice in time to make their deaths as comfortable as possible. Plus, they were three times as likely to complete do-not-resuscitate requests…and twice as likely to make living wills.

Also: These patients were no more likely to be clinically depressed or to become worried, anxious or frightened when they were asked directly about their impending death.

Study of 323 cancer patients by researchers at Dana-Farber Cancer Institute, Boston, presented at a meeting of the American Society of Clinical Oncology.

Should You Buy a Funeral Plot Now?

Do not buy a grave site in advance. Years ago, when people lived and died in the same community, that made sense. But now you may relocate late in life—requiring your body to be shipped back to the burial site at great expense. Or you may opt for cremation …or remarry late in life and decide to be buried near your new spouse. There are hundreds of thousands of unused graves that people are trying to resell now because individuals bought them while alive but were buried elsewhere.

Joshua Slocum, executive director, Funeral Consumers Alliance, South Burlington, Vermont.

14

Savvy Travel

Find Great Travel Bargains Online in Five Simple Steps

Shopping online for airplane tickets, hotel rooms and rental cars could save you hundreds of dollars on your next vacation. A big challenge is knowing where to find the best deals. Dozens of new travel Web sites appear each year, all of them claiming to offer big savings, but no one has time to try them all. *Here's the smart way to find online travel bargains...*

Step 1: **Go to the source.**

The special bargain prices offered directly by airlines, hotel chains and car rental chains on their company Web sites often are lower than the prices available through third-party travel sites.

Type the name of an airline, hotel chain or car rental company into a search engine to locate its Web site, then look for a tab labeled "Special Fares," "Special Deals," "Special Offers" or something similar. Most of these sites also let you sign up for e-mail notification of future bargain rates, which is a great way to keep posted on travel deals.

Example: On Continental Airlines' Web site, click "Deals & Offers," then click "continental.com Specials" for last-minute bargain fares, or "Special Offers" for ongoing promotional rates. (Continental is particularly likely to provide bargain fares to or from Houston, Cleveland and Newark, New Jersey, where the airline operates hubs.)

Such special deals are most appropriate for travelers who can be flexible about when and where they go, not those who need to reach a specific destination on a specific date.

Sandy Berger, author of *Sandy Berger's Great Age Guide to Online Travel* (Que). She is president of Pinehurst, North Carolina–based Computer Living Corp., a computer consulting company, and has been a guest on hundreds of radio and TV programs. Her Web site, Compu-KISS, provides tutorials and lifestyle technology information for baby boomers and seniors, *www.compu-kiss.com.*

If you do not have time to check every major airline or hotel chain site, at least check the sites of the airlines that have the most flights out of your local airport and the large hotel chains that you like the most.

Note: Try the same kind of search on car rental sites.

Cruise lines also feature attractive last-minute deals on their Web sites in the weeks prior to departure. Before accepting one of these deals, however, consider that unless you live in or near the cruise's city of departure, you will have to buy airline tickets as well. If last-minute airfare to the cruise's departure port (and back from its destination port) is expensive, your last-minute cruise bargain might not be so cheap after all.

Step 2: Try the "big three" Internet travel services.

Expedia.com, Orbitz.com and Travelocity.com are the largest, most comprehensive travel Web sites. (While not one of the top three, Kayak.com, which searches multiple other travel sites, is worth trying, too.) You can use these sites to search for the best rates on a specific travel itinerary or scan their lists of last-minute specials. Though these sites are very similar in many ways, it is worth trying all of them. They frequently turn up different rates and different deals for the same itinerary.

Expedia, Orbitz and Travelocity tend to offer their very best deals less than one week in advance of the travel date—but only if airlines, hotels and rental car companies happen to have excess inventory. When demand is strong, last-minute prices can be extremely high. If you have a specific destination and date of travel in mind, it is best to search these sites two months or more in advance.

During holidays: If you can be flexible, you might be able to snap up last-minute bargains by looking just before the date you hope to leave. Otherwise, shop far in advance.

Consider searching these sites for package deals that bundle airfare, hotel and rental car—or two of the three—together. Expedia, Orbitz and Travelocity sometimes offer very attractive deals to those who buy two or three of these things at once, particularly when they are traveling to a popular vacation destination such as Orlando, Las Vegas or San Francisco. (Also

search for airfare, hotel and rental car individually, to make sure that the package really is a good deal.)

Note: The prices quoted by travel Web sites can change rapidly. If one rate is substantially better than any other rate that you have found, wrap up your rate comparison quickly and take the deal before it disappears.

Step 3: Search bargain-hunter travel site Hotwire.com if you are putting together a last-minute trip.

Hotwire.com works with airlines, hotels, automobile rental agencies and cruise lines to sell remaining inventory in the week or two before the travel date. Markdowns of 50% or more are common.*

Example: The site sometimes offers rental cars for less than $10 per day.

Other helpful bargain-hunter travel sites include Cheapflights.com and LastMinuteTravel.com.

Step 4: Vet your hotel online.

Hotel "bargains" are not truly bargains if the hotel is not a nice place to stay. Unfortunately, it sometimes is difficult to judge the quality of a hotel before you arrive. Ratings found in printed travel guides can be inaccurate or out of date.

Solution: Visit Web sites TripAdvisor.com and VirtualTourist.com to read hotel reviews from other travelers before reserving a room online.

Do not let just one or two extremely positive or negative reviews sway you excessively—these reviews might have been posted by a biased source, such as the hotel's management or a disgruntled ex-employee. Pay most attention to the latest reviews, because older reviews could include out-of-date information.

Step 5: See if Priceline.com can beat the best deal that you have located.

Priceline.com lets users make an offer, then either accepts or rejects their bids.

Once you have located the best price that you can find on airline tickets or a rental car from the Web sites mentioned above, bid perhaps 20% less on Priceline.com. If your bid is

*Prices, rates and offers subject to change.

rejected, accept the best offer that you have found elsewhere.

Helpful: The Web site BidonTravel.com offers more strategies for smart Priceline bidding.

Priceline.com is best used for airline tickets and rental cars, not hotel rooms. The Web site does not tell you which company is accepting your bid until after you have completed the transaction. That usually is not a problem with airline tickets and car rentals—it doesn't make much difference whether Hertz or Avis rents you a car—but it can make a huge difference with hotel rooms. When you bid on a hotel room at Priceline, you gamble that the hotel that accepts your bid is somewhere that you would want to stay—that is not a worthwhile gamble, in my view.

Note: You have limited control over what you get. For example, you can't choose flight times, and while you can choose the size of a rental car, you can't choose the model.

CLOSING THE DEAL

Use a credit card to pay travel Web sites. Credit cards provide a measure of consumer protection that debit cards and other forms of payment do not—if unexpected fees or charges are tacked on to your bill, you can contest them through the card issuer.

Specialized Travel Web Sites

Specialized travel Web sites provide consumer reviews, information sharing and more. Boo.com (*www.boo.com*) has travel reviews from consumers for 2,500 destinations in 170 countries…Vayama (*www.vayama.com*), for booking international air travel, has flight and fare options for 190 countries…hotel Web site Hotelicopter (*www.hotelicopter.com*) combines user reviews, search capabilities and more… Professional Travel Guide (*www.professional travelguide.com*) features hotel and restaurant reviews by professionals, such as journalists and travel-industry members.

Note: The specialized sites may not have as many hotel and/or airline listings as major sites, such as Expedia, Orbitz and Travelocity.

Great Travel-and-Learn Vacations: Pack Your Bag and Open Your Mind

Gregory Hubbs, editor in chief, Transitions Abroad, an Amherst, Massachusetts–based company that provides information about working, living, traveling, volunteering and studying in dozens of countries around the world, *www.transitionsabroad.com*.

Opportunities to travel and learn are growing quickly. *Apart from seeing the sights while you learn, there are other big advantages…*

• **Many travel-and-learn vacations are less expensive than staying at popular resorts** in the same area.

• **A lot of overseas learning programs are in fascinating out-of-the-way spots** that you might not otherwise visit.

• **You're likely to be with others who share your interests** and to have the opportunity to meet local residents.

• **A growing number of programs are designed for people over age 50.**

To find travel-and-learn opportunities, check with universities that specialize in areas of study that interest you. Many universities now have adult study programs in the US and overseas. Two of the most prominent are the University of Wisconsin (608-263-7787, *www.dcs. wisc.edu/lsa/travel*) and a program run jointly by Oxford University in England and the University of California (510-642-3824, *www.unex. berkeley.edu/oxford*).

Still other universities have travel study programs specifically for their graduates, so also check with your own university's alumni association. My Web site, *www.transitionsabroad. com*, lists hundreds of programs throughout the world.

Some of today's most interesting travel-and-learn programs…

ITALIAN LANGUAGE

If you sign up for the two-week "Pane, Vino e Lingua" (Bread, Wine and Language) course from International Partners for Study Abroad, you'll arrive at the Florence airport on Sunday and settle into accommodations with a local family or at a hotel.

Language lessons begin on Monday morning, and in the afternoon, you're taken on an orientation tour of Florence. There are more language lessons on Tuesday, followed up by an afternoon cooking class. Later in the program, language classes precede tastings of Tuscan wines and more cooking lessons. These activities are interspersed with visits to farms, vineyards, restaurants and historic sites. One-week courses are also available.

Price: 990 euros (approximately $1,400)* per person for two-week instruction and tours (585 euros for one week). Accommodations in private homes, including breakfast, are 265 euros for two weeks per person, double occupancy (165 euros for one week). Guesthouse and hotel accommodations are available at higher prices.

Information: International Partners for Study Abroad (602-743-9682, *www.studyabroadinternational.com*).

CHINESE HISTORY

During the two-week tour of Chinese sites along the ancient Silk Road, students learn the fascinating history of the highway that served as a route for trading merchandise as well as for religious, cultural and artistic ideas. Visitors will tour the sites and hear lectures by museum curators, community leaders and local residents who provide insights into the highway that stretched 4,350 miles from China to the Mediterranean.

Price: From $3,049 per person, double occupancy, at hotels along the Silk Road. The price includes most meals but not airfare.

Information: Smithsonian Journeys (877-338-8687, *www.smithsonianjourneys.org*).

*Prices subject to change. At recent exchange rates, one euro was worth $1.39. To find the latest rates for the euro and other currencies, look in the business section of a major newspaper, or visit *www.oanda.com/convert/classic*.

RAIN FORESTS, UP CLOSE

For an on-site chance to learn about tropical rain forests, consider a 10-day tour of Costa Rica. Travelers will visit several rain forests that are home to macaws, hummingbirds, iguanas, sloths and monkeys. Students hear lectures from expert scholars who spend most of the year studying plant and animal life in the rain forests.

Price: From $1,380 per person, including meals and lodging in hotels that are rustic with modern conveniences. Transportation to and from Costa Rica is not included.

Information: Proyecto Campanario (011-506-2258-5778, *www.campanario.org*).

VIRGINIA'S PRESIDENTS

Several of our most influential presidents came from Virginia—including Thomas Jefferson, James Madison and James Monroe. You'll learn about their fascinating lives on a six-day tour that includes visits to each president's home—Jefferson's Monticello, Madison's Montpelier and Monroe's Ash Lawn-Highland.

Based in Charlottesville, Virginia, you'll attend lectures by visiting presidential scholars from the College of William and Mary in Williamsburg, who will speak about the presidents' political careers and personal lives.

Price: From $743 per person, including lodging at the English Inn in Charlottesville. Meals are also included but not transportation to Charlottesville.

Information: Elderhostel (800-454-5768, *www.elderhostel.org*).

GERMAN IN HISTORIC BERLIN

Long a divided city, Berlin is now resuming its status as one of Europe's cultural capitals. The Brandenburg Museum, the unique design of the 2,711 gray stone slabs of the Berlin Holocaust Memorial and other world-class museums are just part of what you'll see when you study German at Languages Abroad, a Canadian company that offers language classes in more than two dozen countries.

The language courses are taught at a private language school in Berlin, with programs available between one and 12 weeks. The basic one-week course consists of 20 classroom hours, and the intensive course includes 30 hours. All teachers are native speakers with degrees in German language and/or literature.

Price: From $840 a week, including accommodations, for the basic course, and from $990, including accommodations, for the intensive course. Tours to historic and cultural sites are also included, but not transportation to and from Berlin.

Information: Languages Abroad (800-219-9924, *www.languagesabroad.com*).

IRISH FIDDLE LESSONS

Whether you have never played a fiddle or are already competent, you can acquire new skills during the week of instruction at Kerry Fiddles, a school in the town of Kenmare in southwest Ireland. Students can participate in weekend workshops with some of the best-known Irish fiddlers, including Kevin Burke, Brendan McGlinchey and Tommy Peoples.

Lessons, which are designed for adults, are in the mornings and afternoons, leaving the evenings free for listening to local musicians or for sightseeing.

Price: 375 euros per person for one week, not including transportation or lodging.

There's a wide range of hotels in the area.

Typical rate: 32 to 50 euros a night per person for a double room at the Shaminir, a nearby bed-and-breakfast (011-353-64-42678, *www.shaminir.com*).

Information: Kerry Fiddles, (011-353-644-2387, *www.kerryfiddles.com*).

How to Complain to The Airlines

Peter Greenberg, known as the "Travel Detective," travel editor for NBC's *Today* show and editor of the travel Web site PeterGreenberg.com. He's author of *The Complete Travel Detective Bible* and *Tough Times, Great Travel* (both from Rodale).

Your flight was delayed...the airline lost your luggage...or you got hit with an undisclosed extra fee.

Complaints about airlines have risen to record levels—most airlines receive hundreds of complaint letters every day.

As a travel writer who flies more than 400,000 air miles a year, I have learned what works and what doesn't when it comes to getting airline complaints resolved.

How to increase your odds...

•**Be your own devil's advocate.** Ask yourself whether your complaint is justified. Did you really arrive at the airport with sufficient time to make your plane and check your bags? Was your plane delayed because of airline incompetence...or weather, over which the airline had no control? Did the airline really fail to disclose important information to you...or did you simply fail to read all the fare rules ahead of time? If you can't honestly say that your complaint is justified, do not waste your time complaining.

•**Deal with the situation quickly.** As soon as a problem occurs, seek out the airline official with the highest seniority at your location.

My never-fail rule: Never take a "no" from someone who is not empowered to give you a "yes." Always ask to speak to the supervisor. When you speak with him/her, calmly explain the nature of your problem and ask for his help in solving it.

•**Write a letter.** If talking with a supervisor fails to get you an immediate solution to your problem, then it's letter-writing time. Send your letter certified mail, return receipt requested, to the chairman of the airline.

Always send a copy to the Consumer Affairs Office, Aviation Consumer Protection Division, C-75, US Department of Transportation, 1200 New Jersey Ave. SE, Washington, DC 20590.

•**Be a good reporter.** Writing a letter that simply expresses your displeasure with the airline or an individual incident isn't enough. It's the details that you include that often can make the difference. Include specific dates, flight numbers and times. It's also important to get the first and last names of the airline representatives with whom you interacted and, if appropriate, the names of any witnesses. Keep the letter short, and stick to the facts.

• **Be nice.** Let the airline know that you intend to fly on its planes again and that you hope things will be better next time. If you're a frequent-flier, be sure to include your account number—it stands to reason that the more you fly a particular airline, the more it will want to keep you happy.

• **Never say the word "never."** Threatening never to fly the airline again sends the message to that airline that it has already lost you as a customer, therefore it has no incentive to be nice to you.

• **Don't send originals.** Send photocopies, but make sure that you send everything that has a bearing on your complaint—boarding passes, ticket receipts, purchase receipts for lost items and, where appropriate, photos.

• **Understand the rules.** For example, if an airline lost your bag, you can't claim damages for lost jewelry, furs and negotiable financial documents (or cash). Each airline has a specific list of excluded items. If the airline lost your bag for more than 24 hours, there's a reasonable expectation (if you're not at your home airport) that you would need to buy some replacement clothes. But purchasing a $2,000 designer suit as "replacement" clothing won't get you a reimbursement check for that amount from the airlines. Keep in mind that airlines have limited liability and compensate for lost items in luggage at their depreciated value, not what it would cost to buy them new.

• **Ask for what you want—but be realistic.** If your plane was delayed, that probably doesn't qualify you for a first-class seat to Hong Kong.

• **Don't be surprised if the airline doesn't send you a check,** but instead it offers you some vouchers for your "inconvenience," usually dollar-value coupons that are good for discounts on a future flight on that airline. Read these vouchers carefully. Many have restrictions and expiration dates.

• **Write again.** If you don't hear back after three weeks, or you get a form letter that doesn't address your complaint, write to the chairman again—and again copy the US Department of Transportation. As before, enclose copies of your tickets, boarding passes and any other written or photographic evidence you have to support your claim.

Last resort: Go to small-claims court. This is a lot easier than it might seem. You do not need to hire a lawyer, and many states have increased the claim limits for filing cases in small-claims court (some states have increased the limit to $10,000 or more). Keep in mind that an airline ticket is a contract for service and that your argument probably will need to center around the airline's failure to live up to that contract.

For Better Airline Service...

Search airlines by quality of service. At Insidetrip.com, you can search for a flight and find out its rating based on the number of stops, legroom, connection time, etc. You can deselect any component of the rating and recalculate the TripQuality score to see which flights offer those factors that are specifically most important to you.

Example: If you don't care how many stops the flight makes, you would deselect "number of stops."

Best Time to Book Airline Flights

The best time to book most airline seats is around midnight eastern time any day of the week. That is when most airlines update availabilities. If you are looking for weekend specials, check airline sites late Thursday night or just after midnight. Most airlines post their weekend specials late on Thursday night.

Assen Vassilev, cofounder and CEO, Lessno.com, a discount flight and hotel Web site.

Hold On to Flight Reservations Longer

You can hold on to your flight reservations longer by working with an agent over the phone instead of booking online. Most online sites will hold a reservation for only 24 hours, but an agent can hold it for three days—then immediately cancel and rebook it, giving you an additional three days to firm up your plans. It also might be easier to get a longer hold if you are buying a ticket in a high-fare class… traveling during off-peak periods…or taking an international flight. However, when booking through an agent over the phone, you may incur an additional charge.

Travel + Leisure, 1120 Avenue of the Americas, New York City 10036, *www.travelandleisure.com.*

Business-Class Bargains

For big discounts on business-class airline tickets, sign up for free e-mails from Flight-Bliss.com. The e-mails give each week's top business- and first-class deals from more than 30 US and international carriers. In the slowest times for business travel—summer, Thanksgiving and Christmas—discounts can be as much as 80%.*

Travel + Leisure, 1120 Avenue of the Americas, New York City 10036, *www.travelandleisure.com.*

*Rates subject to change.

Are Frequent-Flier Miles Safe?

Your frequent-flier miles probably are losing value. Airlines have been suffering financially and therefore have been cutting back on what it costs them to offer frequent-flier programs.

Though every airline's case is different, in general, airlines are reducing the benefits that frequent-flier miles provide, adding fees to the use of miles and having miles expire sooner.

The bottom line: Think of your frequent-flier miles as an investment that has been losing its value and is expected to continue to do so—and use them sooner rather than later. If you won't be ready to take your vacation for some time, visit the sites that will redeem your miles for merchandise, such as LoyaltyMatch. com and Points.com.

Tim Winship, editor-at-large, SmarterTravel.com, specializing in frequent-flier information.

Get Paid *More* for Being Bumped

Airlines must now pay passengers more for being bumped. Fliers will receive up to $400 if they are bumped from a domestic flight and rescheduled to reach their destination between one and two hours of their original arrival time. The $400 amount also applies to international flights if passengers arrive between one and four hours of their originally scheduled time. For shorter delays there is no compensation. Longer delays make passengers eligible for up to $800. And all flights using aircraft with 30 or more seats are now covered —the rules used to apply only to planes with 60 seats or more. The exact amount of each payment is determined by the ticket price as well as the length of the delay.

US Department of Transportation, Washington, DC, *www.dot.gov.*

Flying vs. Driving

Compare the price of gas with the cost of flying by using the free calculator at *www. fuelcostcalculator.com.*

Example: Driving four people from Denver to Nashville in a 2007 Toyota Corolla uses about 62 gallons of gas and recently cost about $130/round-trip...compared with at least $952 for four round-trip air tickets.*

Nancy Dunnan, publisher of *TravelSmart,* New York City, *www.travelsmartnewsletter.com.*

*Prices subject to change.

The Safest Rental Cars Now

The safest rental cars are foreign-made ones. One safe car that many rental firms now offer is the Subaru Legacy. You also may be able to rent a top-rated Volvo S80 or Nissan Versa. Customers who prefer domestic cars can try the widely available and safe Chevrolet Malibu or Ford Taurus. For more information about auto safety ratings, check *www.safercar. gov* and *www.iihs.org.*

SmartMoney, 1755 Broadway, New York City 10019.

Don't Fall for This Car Rental Trap

Never agree to pay to have the rental company refill the gas tank when you return a rental car—always refill it yourself.

Why: Rental companies charge extraordinarily high prices for the gas. AAA found one rental firm near the Philadelphia International Airport charging $13.50 per gallon. The Maryland Attorney General found rental companies commonly charging $8 a gallon and negotiated a settlement with them limiting their charge to $5.85 per gallon, or 140% of the market price—still very high.

ConsumerAffairs.com, a free consumer news publication, Washington, DC.

Don't Be Charged for Damage You Didn't Cause

When you rent a car, look for any dents or other defects in it. If there are any, take digital pictures and have the rental agent note it on the contract before you take the car—that way you will not be charged for damage you didn't cause. Keep the pictures and a copy of the rental agreement in case a claim is filed against you at a later date.

AARP.org.

Hotel Adventures: Sweet Dreams in Weird But Fun Places

Joan Rattner Heilman, an award-winning travel writer based in New York. She is the author of *Unbelievably Good Deals and Great Adventures That You Absolutely Can't Get Unless You're Over 50, 2009–2010 edition* (McGraw-Hill).

Been there, done that? Looking for something different? Try reserving a cave or a tree house. You can reserve accommodations in the strangest places these days, and I am going to tell you about some of the most interesting ones on the continent, many of them surprisingly affordable. All of these unusual hostelries are guaranteed to give you a thrill while you're there and plenty to talk about when you get home.

SURROUNDED BY ICE

The Hôtel de Glace (Ice Hotel) just outside of Quebec City comes and goes. Made entirely of 15,000 tons of snow and 500 tons of ice, it is built every winter and melts in the spring. Meanwhile, from January 4 to April 4, you can sleep on a bed carved from ice in a guest room with a temperature of 23°F to 26°F. You will be toasty enough, however, in your insulated sleeping bag atop a special mattress.

Visit the Ice Café or the Ice Bar for a drink in an ice glass, or even hold your wedding in the Ice Chapel. Warm up in three outdoor hot tubs and a sauna, or escape to the warmth of a "regular" hotel just next door, all part of the Station Touristic Resort that also offers dog sledding, snowmobiling, ice slides, skating and other outdoor activities. Before you're shown to your room, you'll get a 40-minute information session about what you need to know for a frigid night. Restaurants and bathroom facilities are heated.

Cost: $350 to $800 per person, per night, includes breakfast, dinner and cocktails.*

Information: Hôtel de Glace, Quebec City (877-505-0423, *www.icehotel-canada.com*). Day visits and tours are also available.

ABOARD AN OCEAN LINER

The elegant *Queen Mary*, built in the 1930s, sailed back and forth across the Atlantic for 31 years, serving first as a luxury ocean liner, then as a troop transport ship in World War II and, finally, as a royal mail ship. For the last 40 years, she has been permanently docked in Long Beach, California. All of the 314 first-class staterooms on three decks are hotel rooms and suites (including the Royalty Suites, which were once reserved for nobility and heads of state) with their original wood panels, Art Deco style and artwork. The second- and third-class staterooms have been converted into meeting and exhibit space.

Take a few turns around the sundeck, eat in your choice of three restaurants, use the business center and fitness rooms, and take tours of this historic ship. In the evenings, live entertainment in the cabaret will keep you busy. Day visits and tours are also available.

Cost: $139 to $629 (double occupancy) per night, depending on stateroom level.

Information: Queen Mary Hotel in Long Beach, California (800-437-2934, *www.queen mary.com*).

A STRETCH IN PRISON

The former Charles Street Jail, a national historic landmark built back in 1851 in Boston's Beacon Hill neighborhood which is above the Charles River, was recently transformed into a plush 300-room hotel that retains some of its original ambience. Once home to the Boston

*Prices and offers subject to change.

Strangler and other legendary inmates, the jail was considered to be a model of prison architecture in the 19th century. An octagonal central building featuring circular wood "ocular" windows and four radiating wings, its Romanesque granite exterior and central atrium have been retained. So have some of the original catwalks and an old cellblock with iron-bar doors and bluestone flooring that has become the Alibi Bar. There's plenty of prison ambience, but this is still an upscale hotel located in an upscale neighborhood.

Cost: $295 to $1,950 (double occupancy) per night.

Information: The Liberty Hotel, Boston, Massachusetts (866-507-5245, *www.libertyhotel. com*).

IN A CAVE

You can be a cave dweller without having to carry a club or hunt for your food when you book into this luxurious cliff dwelling carved from 65-million-year-old rock. Located in the Four Corners area where New Mexico, Colorado, Arizona and Utah meet, Kokopelli's Cave Bed & Breakfast is 70 feet below the surface, with its entrance in a vertical cliff accessible by a series of trails and paths and a short ladder.

What you will discover is a one-bedroom dwelling that consists of a living room with a couch that sleeps two, a den, plush carpeting, Southwestern-style decor, a full kitchen, a flagstone hot tub, TV, a cascading waterfall shower and a balcony overlooking the Plata River Valley 280 feet below. The refrigerator and cabinets are stocked with basic groceries, but you can shop for more and cook your own meals indoors or out on the gas grill, or take advantage of a variety of restaurants in nearby Farmington, New Mexico. The temperature underground remains at about 65°F to 70°F.

Cost: $260 (double occupancy) per night… $300 per night for three to four guests…$50 for each additional person.

Closed in December, January and February. No children under 12. No pets.

Information: Kokopelli's Cave Bed & Breakfast, Farmington, New Mexico (505-326-2461, *www.bbonline.com/nm/kokopelli*).

UP IN A TREE

If you're not intimidated by heights, and especially if you are accompanied by your kids or grandchildren, consider sleeping in a tree. At the Out'n'About Treehouse Treesort in Cave Junction, Oregon, which is next to the Siskiyou National Forest, you have a choice of 18 different hand-built tree houses scattered around 36 acres of land, with the tallest perched almost 40 feet off the ground.

These houses, some connected by bridges, are reached by ladders, swinging bridges or winding stairs, and have heat, electricity and comfortable beds. Some have running water (with toilets and showers at ground level nearby), while others have full bathrooms or even kitchens.

On the grounds are seven swinging bridges (12 to 90 feet long), 20 flights of stairs, platforms, forts, rope courses, swings, riding horses, swimming pool and more than a mile of zip lines that can carry you flying through the trees at 35 miles an hour. Day visits are also available.

Cost: Depending on the house, rates range from $120 a night for two occupants to $250 per night for four. Additional guests are $20 per night per person. Full breakfasts are included. Two-night minimum on weekdays in the summer months, three nights on weekends.

Information: Out'n'About Treehouse Treesort, Cave Junction, Oregon (541-592-2208, *www.treehouses.com*).

Hotel Bargains Just Ahead

Fewer than 60% of hotel rooms are expected to be filled this year, as business and leisure travelers cut back due to the recession. Because many new rooms will become available—the result of hotel development started in 2005—there will be strong pressure to cut room rates, which have been rising by 7.5% a year for the past five years. Hotels also are likely to reduce

236

staff and eliminate some amenities to keep costs down.

Analysis from PKF Consulting, Atlanta, reported in *USA Today*.

When Renting A House...

Nancy Dunnan, publisher of *TravelSmart,* New York City, *www.travelsmartnewsletter.com*.

Beware of renting a vacation property directly from an owner. Rent-by-owner Web sites may offer great deals on vacation rentals, but they also open the door to scams. For starters, the property may not actually exist. Many Web sites will not guarantee that the advertised properties are real. Some sites recommend that the renter meet with the owner prior to sealing the deal, but that isn't practical for many vacationers. Also, you may not get what you think you are getting. Photos and descriptions in the ads may not represent the true condition of the property. Finally, your identity may be stolen. The renter usually must provide personal information, including credit card and sometimes bank information.

To avoid these and other problems: Use a company that offers protection, such as Rentalo (*http://rentalo.com*), which rents apartments and villas around the world and offers $5,000 payment protection* against rentals that turn out not to be legitimate. Or you may want to use a company that has been around for a while and has a good track record, such as Untours (888-868-6871, *www.untours.com*), which has been in business for 34 years and offers rental packages throughout Europe.

*Offer subject to change.

More from Nancy Dunnan...

Travel Abroad...Even with a Weak Dollar

The dollar has lost a great deal of value compared with many other currencies in recent years.

Example: The dollar has lost about one-third of its value against the euro since 2002.

But don't let the reduced value of the dollar stop you from foreign travel. *How to get more from your dollars abroad...*

• **Check exchange rates.** The dollar performs much better against the currencies of some nations than others.

Recent examples: Guatemala, Hungary, Morocco, Thailand. The list fluctuates continually.

Useful: The Yahoo! Finance Web site (*http://finance.yahoo.com/currency*) provides current exchange rates.

• **Visit nations that use the dollar.** The Bahamas and several other nations in the Caribbean, such as Belize and the Cayman Islands, use the dollar as a currency or peg their own currency to the dollar.

• **Book travel costs in dollars.** Many tour organizations and cruise lines take payment in dollars with payment made in the US on more favorable terms than abroad.

Also: Similar savings often can be obtained by booking a rental car in Europe from the US before you leave home.

• **Travel off-season.** Expenses for the same resorts and destinations can be much cheaper.

• **Travel to Eastern Europe instead of Western Europe.** There's a lot of history in post-Communist Eastern Europe, but costs remain much lower than in the tourist areas and major cities of Western Europe.

• **Visit the countryside instead of cities.** Costs are typically lower in rural and suburban towns of foreign nations than in their big cities. Take day trips to the big cities if you wish.

Wallet-Sized Passports

New wallet-sized passport cards are available for land and sea travelers to Mexico, Canada and the Caribbean. The cards are good for 10 years for adults and five years for children younger than 16. Passport cards cost $45* for adults, $35 for minors and $20 for passport

*Prices subject to change.

holders (versus $100 for an adult passport, $85 for minors and $75 for a renewal). A traditional passport still is required for most international travel, and passport cards may not be used for air travel.

Information: 877-487-2778, *http://travel.state.gov/passport*.

An Affordable Way to Live Abroad

Teaching English abroad can be an affordable way to live overseas for a year or more —but don't expect American-style amenities. China is the biggest market for English teachers. Other major ones are South Korea, Thailand, Taiwan, Vietnam, Indonesia and some Middle Eastern countries. There also are some jobs in Eastern Europe, Russia and former Soviet republics.

Various schools with courses and training for potential overseas English teachers: Boston Language Institute (877-998-3500, *www.teflcertificate.com*)...Oxford Seminars (800-779-1779, *www.oxfordseminars.com*)...TEFL International (866-384-8854, *www.teflintl.com*).

The Wall Street Journal, 200 Liberty St., New York City, *http://online.wsj.com*.

International Emergency Numbers

For emergencies, most of Canada uses 911 ...the European Union uses 112...Australia, 000...Hong Kong, 999...The People's Republic of China, 110...Israel, 100...Japan, 110...Mexico, 060...Switzerland, 117...Thailand, 191. For more emergency numbers, visit *www.sccfd.org/travel.html*.

Santa Clara County Fire Department in Los Gatos, California.

Vaccination Precautions For Travelers

William Schaffner, MD, professor and chair of the department of preventive medicine at Vanderbilt University School of Medicine in Nashville. An internationally recognized expert on vaccines, Dr. Schaffner has published more than 60 professional articles on the subject and is president-elect of the National Foundation for Infectious Diseases, *www.nfid.org*.

Ask your doctor about the following vaccinations at least six weeks, if possible, before leaving the US. This will give your body time to build maximum immunity. *What's currently recommended by the Centers for Disease Control and Prevention (CDC)...*

•**Hepatitis A,** transmitted through food or water. Areas with high or intermediate risk include Greenland...all of Central and South America and Africa...and most countries in Asia and Eastern Europe.

•**Hepatitis B.** Areas with high risk include Africa, much of southeast Asia and the Middle East (excluding Israel). The vaccine is recommended for health-care workers and others who stay in these countries for long periods, as well as for travelers who have intimate relationships with residents of these countries.

•**Meningitis,** transmitted from person to person, especially in crowded conditions. The high-risk "meningitis belt" runs across central Africa, from Mali to Ethiopia.

•**Polio,** transmitted via contact with the feces of an infected person, is most common in areas where sanitation is poor. Risk is highest in Africa, India and Indonesia.

Note: Even if you had a polio vaccination as a child, you should get a booster as an adult if you're traveling to these areas.

•**Rabies,** transmitted through contact with infected animals. Risk is highest in parts of Africa, Asia, and Central and South America.

•**Typhoid,** transmitted through food and water. Areas having the highest risk include all of South Asia...and developing countries elsewhere in Asia, Africa, the Caribbean, and Central and South America.

Certain countries require a certificate of vaccination for such diseases as...

•**Meningitis and polio.** Saudi Arabia requires proof of these vaccinations during the annual pilgrimage to Mecca (due to the large numbers of visitors).

•**Yellow fever,** a mosquito-borne disease predominantly in Central and South America, and sub-Saharan Africa.

For a more detailed summary, go to the CDC Web site, *www.cdc.gov/travel*.

For a Safer, Healthier Vacation...

Tamara Eberlein, editor, *Bottom Line/Women's Health*, Boardroom Inc., 281 Tresser Blvd., Stamford, Connecticut, 06901.

Getting away means sun, fun and relaxation—but an illness or injury can quickly spoil the trip. To avert problems, use foresight when packing. *From my travels, I have learned to bring...*

•**Travel shoes with closed toes and backs.** With sandals, toes can get crushed in a crowd ...and soles suffer when feet slide out of flip-flops and onto hot pavement.

Also smart: Beach shoes to protect against sharp shells and stinging sea critters.

•**Hand sanitizer.** To kill germs, choose a brand that's at least 60% alcohol. If you are flying, the container cannot exceed three ounces.

•**New bottle of sunscreen.** Active ingredients in sunscreen break down in as little as one year. I like SPF 30—it protects well but is not too goopy.

•**Wheeled suitcases.** Don't hurt your back carrying heavy luggage.

•**Night-light.** Stumbling around an unfamiliar hotel room in the pitch-dark can lead to falls.

•**First-aid kit.** Stock it with adhesive bandages, sterile wipes, tweezers, pain relievers, antacids, and antibiotic and anti-itch ointments.

• **Personal medical info card.** Record doctors' names and phone numbers, insurance information, and names and dosages of all the medications that you take.

• **A foreign-language health translation card.** If going abroad, look up the terms for any chronic medical condition you have. It could be very helpful to know that "peanut allergy" in French is *allergie à l'arachide.*

Eat to Beat Jet Lag

When traveling from one time zone to another, eat pasta the night before your flight—the carbohydrates boost your brain's supply of the sleep-inducing neurotransmitter *serotonin.* Skip in-flight meals. Eating is one of the ways your body sets its internal clock, and airlines generally serve meals according to the time zone from which you took off, not the one where you will land. After you land, order a steak or eggs—foods that are rich in protein prompt your brain to produce neurochemicals that increase alertness.

Bradley Connor, MD, president, International Society of Travel Medicine, New York City.

To Reduce In-Flight Motion Sickness...

Eat protein before boarding a plane to prevent in-flight nausea. Motion sickness occurs when the body's motion detectors sense conflicting things—for example, your view of the cabin stays the same while your inner ear detects altitude changes. Having a high-protein meal before a flight can reduce nausea by up to 26%, compared with consuming a high-carbohydrate meal or no food at all.

Robert M. Stern, PhD, professor of psychology, Pennsylvania State University, University Park, and coauthor of a study of motion sickness, reported in *Men's Health.*

Don't Get Seasick on Your Next Cruise

Murray Grossan, MD, otolaryngologist and head and neck surgeon, Tower Ear, Nose and Throat Clinic, Cedars-Sinai Medical Center, Los Angeles.

Motion sickness is a common inner ear disturbance in which motion affects your sense of balance and equilibrium. Symptoms include dizziness, nausea and/or unsteadiness. Ordinarily, your brain senses movement by receiving signals from your inner ear, eyes, muscles and joints. Motion sickness can occur when your brain gets signals that do not match. For example, when you're sitting below deck on a boat, your inner ear detects motion, but your eyes cannot tell you that you're moving.

Helpful strategies: Try sitting on the lower deck of the boat and focusing on the horizon or on a distant stationary object. Do not read or drink alcohol, as both can worsen seasickness. Keep your head still by resting it against a seat back. Also, ask your doctor about trying behind-the-ear *scopolamine* (Transderm-Scop) patches, which help prevent motion sickness. If you do get motion sickness, try Emetrol liquid, an over-the-counter antinausea medication that is excellent for settling the stomach. Take it as often as needed.

For Travelers with Food Allergies...

Travelers with serious allergies to peanuts, shellfish and other foods can order allergy emergency cards in several languages at *www.selectwisely.com.* The cards can be used at restaurants and hotels in other countries to communicate what you are allergic to.

Cost: Starting at $6.50.*

Arthur Frommer's Budget Travel, 530 7th Ave., New York City 10018, *www.frommers.com.*

*Price subject to change.

Better Sleep in a New Time Zone

Trouble sleeping when you travel to a different time zone? Take melatonin one hour before bedtime. The usual dose is one to three milligrams. Melatonin is a naturally occurring hormone that will help adjust your circadian rhythms and sleep cycle to a new time zone.

Also: To help you relax so it is easier to fall asleep, try the herbal extract of passionflower. Take one capsule three times a day for general relaxation.

Melatonin and passionflower are available at health-food stores.

Mark Stengler, ND, a naturopathic physician, director of the La Jolla Whole Health Clinic in La Jolla, California, and adjunct associate clinical professor, National College of Natural Medicine, Portland, Oregon. He is also author of the newsletter Bottom Line/Natural Healing, *available at* www.DrStengler.com.

The Best Reason to Take a Vacation

Middle-aged men who don't take annual vacations are 17% more likely to die from all causes and nearly 35% more likely to die from heart disease than men who do take vacations every year.

Brooks B. Gump, PhD, health psychologist at State University of New York, Oswego, and leader of a nine-year follow-up study comparing mortality in men who did and didn't take vacations, reported in Psychosomatic Medicine.

How to Protect Jewelry When Traveling

To keep jewelry safe while traveling, pack it in your carry-on bag, not your checked luggage. Airlines are not responsible for loss or theft. Use containers that fasten tightly—a purse-sized organizer or plastic bags that zip closed. Never put jewelry in the plastic bins that go through security. Instead, put it in a purse or briefcase and close it. In hotels, lock jewelry in the front-desk safe. If a safe is not available, hide jewelry in a bag, inside another bag, hanging inside a dress or in a suit pocket. Always write down your hiding place. Do not leave valuables visible in your room. Finally, never take anything on a trip that cannot be replaced. Leave antiques and family heirlooms at home.

Susan Eisen, certified gemologist and jewelry appraiser in El Paso, Texas, and author of Crazy About Jewelry! The Expert Guide to Buying, Selling, and Caring for Your Jewelry *(Full Circle International).*

Better Car Travel with Your Pet

Think about how you'll travel with your pet in your vehicle before you depart, planning ahead for safety and convenience. *Ideas…*

•**Keep the pet on a harness attached to the seat belt or in a carrying case.** An animal that jumps around can be a distraction and could also be hurt in an accident or if you have to stop suddenly.

•**Feed animals three or four hours before departing** so that they won't start agitating for food too soon into the trip.

•**Bring plenty of water.** The excitement and stress of a trip can make your pet thirsty.

•**Bring along a litter box for a cat.**

•**Never leave your pet in any vehicle unattended**—you may be away from the vehicle longer than you expect or your pet could even be stolen. It's also dangerous to leave any animal in a poorly ventilated vehicle.

Jeff Feinman, VMD, CVH, a certified veterinary homeopath in Weston, Connecticut, www.homevet.com.

15

Have Some Fun

10 Must-Play Golf Courses Across the USA

Even casual golfers are familiar with such legendary courses as Pebble Beach, Pinehurst and Doral. But marquee course names often involve marquee pricing. There are excellent courses that are off the beaten track or under the radar—and more affordable.

Next time you are planning a golf vacation, consider some of these lesser-known but superb locations...

BANDON DUNES GOLF RESORT
BANDON, OREGON

This resort on the Oregon coast offers three magnificent courses, two of which (Bandon Dunes and Pacific Dunes) are on towering bluffs overlooking the Pacific. The food and lodging are high-quality but not fancy—it's a resort for true golf aficionados. Greens fees are $75 to $220 for hotel guests, depending

on the season.* Lodging ranges from $120 to $270 per night, depending on the season. You may encounter some wind and rain even in summer, which adds to the appeal for some.

What golfers love: No golf carts. This is a walking-only facility.

Information: 888-345-6008, *www.bandon dunesgolf.com*.

CHAMBERS BAY
TACOMA, WASHINGTON

This brand-new course offers visitors the rare opportunity to play a rough-hewn coastal layout, practically teetering into Puget Sound. The course received a boost in prestige when the United States Golfing Association awarded it two important championships—the 2010 US Amateur and the 2015 US Open. Nearby

---

*Rates subject to change. Additional package deals available upon request.

Joel Zuckerman, a noted golf journalist, who is the author of five books, including *Pete Dye Golf Courses* (Abrams), an authorized celebration of legendary golf course designer Pete Dye's remarkable 50-year career. His Web site is *www.vagabondgolfer.com*.

lodging runs the gamut from chic (Hotel Murano) to simple (Holiday Inn Express) for $159 to $170 per night. Midweek greens fees begin at $149 per person…weekend fees start at $169.

What golfers love: A course that the world's best players have yet to play but will soon discover.

Information: 877-295-4657, *www.chambers baygolf.com.*

CIRCLING RAVEN GOLF CLUB
WORLEY, IDAHO

Owned by the Coeur d'Alene Indian Tribe, this beautiful course has been awarded best-in-kind status by the publications *Golf, Golf Digest, Golfweek, Zagat Survey* and *Men's Health.* The layout takes full advantage of its stunning setting, with pine-draped mountains, forested meadows and protected wetlands—the occasional elk or moose may ask to play through. The adjacent Coeur d'Alene Casino and its hotel offer top-notch entertainment, dining and gambling. Accommodations for two, golf included, are less than $270 per night.

What golfers love: Playing in the wild—the course is surrounded by 345,000 acres of wilderness.

Information: 800-523-2464, *www.circling raven.com.*

THE FORT GOLF RESORT
INDIANAPOLIS, INDIANA

Created by the famous golf-course designer Pete Dye, this is one of the best public-access golf courses in the Midwest. It is on the grounds of historic Fort Harrison State Park—named in honor of Benjamin Harrison, our 23rd President and a resident of Indianapolis. The course climbs, dives and dips among thick woodlands and native grasslands. The nearby Harrison House, formerly used as officers quarters, offers seven spacious suites with rates as low as $69 per night. Greens fees start at $66 for the general public and $49.50 for military personnel.

What golfers love: A Pete Dye creation that is much more affordable than his better-known golf courses, such as Harbour Town, Whistling Straits and Kiawah Island's Ocean Course.

Information: 317-543-9597, *www.thefortgolf course.com.*

PINEHILLS GOLF CLUB
PLYMOUTH, MASSACHUSETTS

Less than an hour from Cape Cod, this first-class public-access facility, designed by Rees Jones and golfing legend Jack Nicklaus, features two new 18-hole courses set among 300 acres of stately pines and rolling hills. It offers extensive practice facilities and three top-notch golf schools. A Hilton Garden Inn and a Radisson are within 15 minutes' drive. Greens fees are about $100 midweek…$10 more on weekends and holidays.

What golfers love: To play a course designed by one of the greatest golfers in history.

Information: 866-855-4653, *www.pinehills golf.com.*

PRINCEVILLE RESORT
KAUAI, HAWAII

The beautiful Hawaiian island Kauai is home to Prince Course, *Golf Digest's* number 39 rated course in "America's Top 100 Greatest Courses." The resort offers you 45 holes of golf—the 18-hole Prince and the 27-hole Makai course. The Princeville Hotel overlooks exquisite Hanalei Bay, site of the mythical Bali Hai in the movie *South Pacific.* Rates at the hotel start at $465 per night. Hotel guests may be eligible for discounts on greens fees.

What golfers love: The 13-acre facility features three separate teeing locations that allow for different shots and wind conditions.

Information: 800-826-1105, *www.prince ville.com.*

SADDLE CREEK RESORT
COPPEROPOLIS, CALIFORNIA

The Saddle Creek golf course is considered one of the top 10 in California—no faint praise in a state with iconic venues such as Pebble Beach, Spyglass Hill, Cypress Point and Torrey Pines, among hundreds of others. Located in the historic town of Copperopolis, the course features more than 100 white-sand bunkers, beautiful streams and a dramatic landscape set off by the foothills of the Sierra Nevadas. In summer, bungalow accommodations begin at $125 midweek and $165 on weekends. Greens fees are $69 midweek and $99 on weekends.

What golfers love: The perfectly manicured course with the foothills backdrop.

Information: 800-611-7722, *www.saddle creek.com.*

SUN VALLEY RESORT
SUN VALLEY, IDAHO

Though best-known for skiing, this Idaho icon also offers 18 holes of championship golf on its Trail Creek Course. It unveiled nine holes of its White Clouds Course in the summer of 2009—the other nine will open in the near future. Also set to debut at Sun Valley this year is a beautiful clubhouse, 25-acre practice facility and an 18-hole putting course. Rates start at $350 per night per couple, golf included.

What golfers love: The small, classic putting greens, which require precise approach shots.

Information: 800-786-8259, *www.sunval ley.com.*

THE WATERCOLOR INN & RESORT
SANTA ROSA BEACH, FLORIDA

This golf vacation destination includes two "must-play" private golf courses, Camp Creek and Shark's Tooth, and the innovative short course called Origins built for beginners and families. Guests of the 60-room hotel can enjoy three-day, two-night getaway packages, including one round of golf every day at Camp Creek and Shark's Tooth and one dinner in the gourmet restaurant Fish Out of Water, for $1,320 per person.

What golfers love: A wonderful variety of courses that satisfy the expert as well as the beginner.

Information: 866-426-2656, *www.water colorinn.com.*

THE WINTERGREEN RESORT
WINTERGREEN, VIRGINIA

This beautiful resort spans 11,000 acres on the eastern slopes of the Blue Ridge Mountains, about 90 minutes from Richmond, Virginia, and three hours from the nation's capital. At an elevation of nearly 4,000 feet, Devils Knob is the highest course in the state and routinely 10 degrees cooler than 27-hole Stoney Creek, which features equally spectacular views of the Blue Ridge despite its lower elevation. Greens fees are $65 to $115 for 45 holes, and a one-bedroom condo is $149 to $209 per night.

What golfers love: The juxtaposition of two dramatically different courses in a single spectacular location.

Information: 800-266-2444, *www.winter greenresort.com.*

Smarter Strategies to Shape Up for Golf

Edward Jackowski, PhD, CEO of Exude Inc., a New York City–based motivational company that teaches people how to make proper fitness part of their lives. He is author of several books on fitness, including *Fit to a Tee: The Ultimate Endurance, Strength & Flexibility System for Golfers of Every Ability* (Sterling). His Web site is *www.exude.com.*

Many golfers aren't sure how to get in shape for the game or have misconceptions about how to do it. *Also, men and women tend to have different weaknesses that they need to focus on…*

MEN

Men often believe that adding muscle is the secret to adding distance to their drives. Actually, adding flexibility and range of motion is more beneficial. Men usually lack the flexibility to rotate their bodies through a golf swing, robbing them of the torque that produces long drives. Older men are especially likely to lack flexibility, but this need not be so. With proper stretching, you can have nearly as much flexibility in retirement as you did in your 30s.

Perform three simple stretches before beginning a round of golf or hitting at the driving range…

• **Hamstring stretch.** Lie on the floor with your legs extended in front of you, feet about two feet apart. Stretch toward your toes by bending at the waist. Hold the stretch as far as you can reach for 15 to 30 seconds. Do not "bounce" the stretch to hold on closer to your toes—that could cause a hamstring injury.

• **Shoulder stretch.** Windmill your arms in large, slow arcs around your shoulders. The arcs should be as large and complete as you can manage. Do five to 10 circles in each direction. If you have a bad shoulder, it is safest to focus on each arm individually. Otherwise, it is okay to do both arms at once.

• **Torso stretch.** Sit on the floor with legs extended straight in front of you, then cross your left leg over your right. Slowly turn your upper body to the left as far as you can with your right elbow against your left knee, and hold for several seconds. Then reverse positions, and stretch in the opposite direction. Repeat three times in each direction.

Men who lift weights usually lift the heaviest weights they can in order to build bulky muscles. But bulky muscles add little to any golf game and might even hurt your swing if the muscle makes you less flexible. Instead, use lighter weights but lift them more times, which builds muscle endurance rather than size. Select weights light enough so that you can do 50 reps of a particular exercise. For most men, that will be weights of no more than 10 to 20 pounds.

WOMEN

Women golfers often need more upper-body strength. Push-ups are the best way to correct this. Start by doing push-ups from your knees if you cannot do them from your toes. Don't become frustrated if you can complete only a single push-up the first day. Just do as many push-ups as you can, and try to do more with each passing day, working up to two sets of 15 to 25 push-ups.

Other ways that women can get in shape for golf...

• **Build hand strength.** Women golfers tend to lack hand strength. Your distance and accuracy will suffer if the club moves around at all in your hand during your swing. Use a simple "hand grip" exerciser or squeeze a tennis ball to build hand strength. Do this every other day for five to 10 minutes.

• **Jump rope.** Many female recreational golfers have trouble consistently centering the ball on the club face, resulting in poor accuracy. Jumping rope is one great way to overcome this hand-eye coordination problem. Using a jump rope forces the hands, eyes and body to work together, much as they should during a golf swing.

Three Easy Ways to Improve Your Golf Game

Tee up in the center of your stance—so that you don't have to shift your weight. Your drives will become straighter. Also, shorten up your putter shaft to 32 inches. This relaxes the arms. Finally, use a heavier putter head—450 grams (g) to 500 g instead of 300 g to 350 g—to improve accuracy, especially on long puts.

Robert Anthony Prichard, Somax Performance Institute, Tiburon, California, and author of The Efficient Golfer (Somax Sports).

Don't Hit the Ball So Hard And Other Tips That Will Raise Your Tennis Game

Greg Moran, director of tennis at the Four Seasons Racquet Club in Wilton, Connecticut. A teaching pro for more than 30 years, he is author of Tennis Beyond Big Shots (Mansion Grove House, www.tennisbeyond bigshots.com) and has a new book called Tennis Doubles cowritten with his tennis pro wife, Kelley Moran, and from the same publisher.

Nearly 80% of points in amateur tennis are lost on missed shots, not won on great shots. To win more, stop trying to hit the ball as hard as you can or drop it on the lines. Instead, play patiently and wait for your opponent to make mistakes. *Also...*

SINGLES

• **Rethink your serves.** Most amateurs blast their first serves as hard as they can and frequently miss. Then they float in soft second serves, which their opponents anticipate and return aggressively. Instead, hit both your first and second serves half to two-thirds as hard as you are capable of serving. This will allow you to get most of your first serves into play. As long as you vary the placement—and spin, if you can—of your serve to keep your opponent off balance, you will be in good shape to win most of your service points. If you do miss your first serve, hit your second serve just as hard.

The perfect toss: Bad serves often are the result of bad tosses. Pretend that the ball is a glass of water that you are balancing on the palm of your hand. Lift your hand upward, releasing the glass upward when your arm is fully extended. Begin your swing when the ball pauses at its apex so that you hit it just as it starts to descend.

●**Stop trying to hit winners when you return a first serve.** Instead, try to return first serves safely down the middle of the court, five to seven feet above the net (one to two feet above the net and at the server's feet if the server charges the net after service). The server has the advantage on the first serve. If you try to hit quick winners, you are likely to fail more often than you succeed.

●**Be more aggressive against the second serve.** Move three feet forward, then try to drive your return deep crosscourt.

●**Hit most ground strokes cross-court in singles tennis.** The ball crosses over the net at the net's lowest point, the middle, when you hit crosscourt, reducing the odds that the ball will hit the net. Because hitting crosscourt lets you aim at the long diagonal dimension of the court, it also reduces the odds that you will hit long—and increases the distance that your opponent must run.

●**When in trouble, hit up.** When your opponent has you on the run, lob your return high and deep. Lobbing forces him to retreat to the backcourt and gives you a chance to regroup.

DOUBLES

●**Avoid the one up, one back formation against skilled opposition.** This conventional doubles formation can be reasonably effective against teams of limited abilities, but skilled opponents will exploit the huge gap that it creates between you and your partner. Instead, play both up if you are skilled at volleying and covering lobs…play both back if you are not. Both back is the best way to remain competitive against a doubles team of greater skill.

●**Don't try to "hit 'em where they ain't."** It is very difficult to hit a shot where neither opponent can reach it when two opponents are patrolling the court. *Instead, aim…*

●At your opponents' feet. These shots are very tricky to return.

●Right down the middle of the court. Your opponents will have trouble finding a winning angle on their return, and there might be a crucial moment of confusion as your opponents decide who will return the shot.

●Over your opponents' heads if both opponents are up at the net.

Better Biking

For safer, more comfortable bicycling, adjust the bike's handlebars so your upper body is positioned at a comfortable angle and so your hands are a comfortable width apart. Also, adjust the seat so it is level…your knee is centered over the pedal axle when the pedals are horizontal…and your leg can extend almost fully when the pedals are vertical. Your helmet should be level on your head, not tilted back, with a strap that fits snugly—so the helmet tightens when you open your mouth.

Consumer Reports on Health, 101 Truman Ave., Yonkers, New York 10703, *www.consumerreports.org/health*.

Pond Danger

Warm freshwater lakes, ponds, rivers or natural springs may be inhabited by the deadly amoeba *naegleria fowleri* that enters the body through the nose and travels to the brain. Symptoms of infection, which include headache, stiff neck, body aches, high fever and loss of smell, begin one to 14 days after contact with the organism.

Self-defense: Avoid swimming in natural bodies of water above 80°F…if you choose to swim, wear nose plugs.

If you think you may be infected: See a physician immediately. Certain drugs, such as *miconazole*, *rifampin* and *amphotericin*, may fight the amoeba if administered quickly.

Kevin Sherin, MD, MPH, Orange County Health Department, Florida.

A Landscaper's Money-Saving Tricks For a Beautiful Yard

Kate Anchordoguy, a licensed landscape contractor and designer in Sebastopol, California. She has advised consumers as a Master Gardener through University of California Cooperative Extension Service and is author of *Dig This! Landscaping Without a Backhoe or a Big Budget for Northern California and Beyond* (Sasquatch). Her Web site is *www.landscapekate.com*.

Improvements in your yard and garden don't have to cost a lot. *Tricks for having the yard you want on a budget...*

PLANTS

•**Buy plants in the smallest size available.** If the same variety of plant comes in a five-gallon pot and a one-gallon pot, buy the smaller pot. Mature plants are more expensive —you are exchanging money for growing time. Smaller plants look more sparse at the beginning, but they grow faster than large plants.

•**Negotiate a discount.** Once you have determined which plants you want and how many, consider purchasing them all at the same nursery. You probably can negotiate a good price. The nursery also may be willing to hold your purchases for you until you are ready to plant them.

What to say: "Here is a list of the plants that I need. I would like to buy from you, but I also am shopping around for the best price. If I buy all the plants from you, what price would you be able to offer me?"

•**Shop roots, not top.** Ask to see a nursery's "hospital"—the place where plants that have cosmetic problems are kept. Droopy or scorched plants with healthy roots that form a cohesive ball should do fine once they are planted. You can get these ugly ducklings for next to nothing.

Nursery plants look best in spring and get progressively worse throughout summer and fall when you can find bargains.

•**Move low-performing plants.** A shrub or small tree that is getting too much shade or sun may thrive in a different spot. Dig a hole in the new location. Then dig up the plant, getting as much of the roots as possible. After replant-ing, make sure that the new plant gets plenty of water for the first year or so. In mild winter areas, the winter is the best time to plant. In areas where the ground freezes, fall or spring is better. Summer is never ideal, but if you need to move a plant then, be extra vigilant that it does not dry out.

•**Start lawns from seed, not sod.** A lawn grown from seed doesn't provide the instant gratification of a sod lawn, but the preparation is nearly identical. If you have the patience and are willing to keep dogs and children off the lawn for several months, you can save by using seed (where I live, you can save up to 30 cents a square foot). Your lawn also will be deeper rooted and healthier.

On the other hand, if you already have a lawn and it's not doing well, don't waste time and money tearing it out. Instead, mow the lawn very short. Cover the area with sheets of newspaper, then a layer of topsoil or mulch, and plant on top of it—this works for seed, sod and other plantings.

SUPPLIES

•**Check online.** Scan Craigslist.org for cast-off benches, decorative rocks, ceramics and plants. People sometimes offer these items at no cost just so that they don't have to pay to have them hauled away.

•**Buy local.** You may love the look of Ari-zona flagstone for a garden path, but if you live on the East Coast, you will pay a premium for it because of transportation costs.

Before setting your heart on a feature that you loved in a magazine or on a TV design show, spend a few hours walking around your local landscape supply store. Get a feel for the range of materials available and how much they cost. Keep an open mind. Rock from a nearby quarry may be just as elegant, and far less expensive, than the current fad.

•**Buy in bulk.** Soil, mulch and gravel are cheaper in bulk from landscape stores than bagged from hardware or big-box stores.

•**Measure carefully.** Ordering more materi-al than you need is a waste of money. Ordering too little of what you need incurs extra charges to have the additional materials delivered.

The landscape supply yards use cubic yards for bulk orders of mulch, soil and gravel. To calculate cubic yards, multiply the square footage to be covered by the thickness (in inches) of what you need, then divide that number by 324.

Example: You need to cover up a 1,000-square-foot area with three inches of mulch. Multiply 1,000 by 3, then divide that amount (3,000) by 324. You will need to order 9.25 cubic yards of mulch.

LEARN FROM THE EXPERTS

The more you know, the more you can do for yourself. Call on the expertise of Master Gardeners (volunteers who have received intensive training in horticulture from university extension agents). They offer affordable workshops and advice. To find Master Gardeners in your state, visit *www.ahs.org/master_gardeners*. Also, community colleges and adult-education programs may offer low-cost gardening courses. And, check your newspaper's home-and-garden section for talks and tours.

Got an Idea for a TV Show?

Think up your own reality TV show, and you may be paid for your idea—and have a chance to help make it happen. The new Web site TalpaCreative.com is soliciting reality-show ideas from the public. It is free to join the site, but you must explain why you want to participate—and agree to certain rules and restrictions regarding ownership of your ideas. The site, cofounded by reality-show producer John de Mol, plans to buy the rights to promising concepts and develop them—with help from the originators.

Calling All Book Lovers

Watch your books travel the world. Register favorite books that you own at Book-Crossing.com and write the identifying number on the inside cover of each book. Then leave the books in public places for other book lovers to find. When people find these books and go to the Web site, you can watch as the books travel across the country and around the world.

Get Answers on the Go

If you need some information, such as movie showtimes or fast-food nutritional data, but you're not near a computer, you can call 800-2-ChaCha (800-224-2242) on your cell phone and ask your question. The question is sent to one of ChaCha.com's guides, who locates the information and answers you by text message just a few minutes later. There is no charge for the service, and it works with most major cell phone carriers.

Entertaining for Less at Restaurants

Barbara Pachter, president of Pachter & Associates, a communications training firm in Cherry Hill, New Jersey. She is author of many books, including When the Little Things Count…and They Always Count *(Da Capo).*

Business and personal budgets have been cut to the bone by this recession—but we still may need to take clients out for a meal or treat out-of-town guests to dinner.

Solution: Limit the cost of eating out while still appearing as munificent as ever. *Here is how…*

•**Choose restaurants that seem pricier than they are.** You don't have to bring guests to the most expensive restaurant in town—just avoid eateries that look cheap. When we entertain, the visual impression offered by the dining room can be as important as the quality of the food. The waitstaff must be professionally dressed—no jeans or fast-food–type uniforms…the tables must have tablecloths…the room must seem clean and fresh…and there should not be a TV.

Be ready to explain why you chose this restaurant over better-known alternatives. *Two options…*

247

•Eat at the restaurant before inviting important guests, then provide a personal endorsement. *Example:* "It's one of those great places that only locals know about."

•Cite a glowing review. Search the online archives of your local newspapers...or search the name of the restaurant and town on Google.com to find reviews. *Example:* "The Tribune gave this place a great review. I've been meaning to give it a try."

•**Recommend dishes from the midprice range.** You can't tell your guests what to order, but you can provide a rave review of an entrée that isn't too expensive.

Example: "I always come here for the chicken marsala. It's really the best thing on the menu."

•**Use a little wine research to trim a lot from the bill.** Restaurants usually offer some perfectly nice wines for less than $25 a bottle. Trouble is, selecting one of these less expensive wines could make you appear cheap.

Solution: Review the restaurant's wine list prior to your important dinner, and jot down several of the more affordable offerings. (The wine list might be available on the restaurant's Web site. If not, visit the restaurant in person and ask to see it.) Look these up in a wine guide, such as *Parker's Wine Guide* (Simon & Schuster) or *Hugh Johnson's Pocket Wine Book* (Mitchell Beazley). Note two or three wines of different varieties from the list that earn favorable reviews. At your dinner, use these ratings to validate your inexpensive choice in the eyes of your guests.

Example: "Robert Parker gave this wine 91 points. Let's give it a try."

•**Preorder dinner for large groups.** Ask to speak with the restaurant's manager when you call to make a reservation for a group of 10 or more. The manager might be willing to let you create a special menu for your group. To control your costs, omit the restaurant's priciest dishes from this menu.

The restaurant manager even might be willing to negotiate a special discount...or a fixed "per head" cost for your dinner, particularly if it is on a slow weeknight.

You will have to give the restaurant at least several days' notice to arrange a special menu.

The larger your party, the greater the odds that the manager will agree.

Helpful: Let the manager know if you treat groups to meals frequently. Discounts and other special terms are most likely for customers who bring repeat business.

•**Don't order the specials.** Specials often are priced 10% to 40% higher than menu listings. Many restaurants do not even say how much the specials cost unless customers ask—and you'll seem cheap if you ask.

You can't prevent your guests from ordering the specials...but avoid restaurants likely to feature ultra-pricey lobster, crab or steak entrées.

•**Clip coupons.** Even upscale restaurants sometimes issue coupons during difficult economic times. These coupons might be in regional "entertainment" coupon books...in local newspapers...or sent to those who sign up for the restaurant's mailing list on its Web site.

Do not let your guests see you use a coupon —doing so seems cheap. Excuse yourself from the table to pay the bill. If a coupon must be presented in advance, arrive at the restaurant before your guests and ask the manager to have the discount applied confidentially.

•**Remain sober.** A tipsy host might fail to notice that a guest has taken over the wine ordering and made a budget-busting selection. Besides, the more you drink, the more your guests are likely to drink, driving up your bill.

•**Host a lunch rather than a dinner.** Restaurants often price their lunch entrées as much as 50% lower than dinner entrées...and your guests are likely to drink less at lunch.

•**Avoid paying a big bar tab.** If the group wants to go to a bar after dinner, agree and pay for the first round—then come up with a polite reason why you cannot stay. Otherwise, you'll be expected to pick up the entire tab.

Example: "I'd love to stay longer, but I have an early meeting tomorrow."

Dining Discounts

To save money when dining out, book a reservation in advance online through Dinner-Broker.com or via OpenTable.com. You'll get discounts and points that can be turned in for cash—exact amounts depend on the restaurant and time of reservation. Also, clip coupons from the Sunday newspaper, mailbox coupon packs and free penny-saving publications. Restaurants often offer discounts this way. The *Entertainment Book* (about $15*) offers a wide variety of restaurant discounts—using just one or two discounts pays for the book (888-231-7283 or *www.entertainment.com*). If you like a specific restaurant, sign up for its reward program—you will get special deals by e-mail. Watch for promotions, such as Kids Eat Free or Early-Bird Specials.

Mary Hunt, editor, *Debt-Proof Living*, Box 2076, Paramount, California 90723, *www.debtproofliving.com*.

*Price subject to change.

Restaurant Coupons

Y ou can get $25 in restaurant coupons for just $10.

How: Log on to the Restaurant.com Web site. Enter the zip code or city where you wish to dine. The site will produce a list of restaurants for which you can buy a $25 coupon for $10.* Make your selections and print your coupons from the computer. Use them yourself or make a gift of them to friends.

More than 8,500 restaurants now participate nationwide.

*Offer and rate subject to change.

How Restaurants Lure You into Spending More

Gregg Rapp, a menu "engineering" consultant based in Palm Springs, California. He has helped design menus for places ranging from Taco Bell to the Peninsula Hotel in Hong Kong. His Web site is *www.menutechnologies.net*.

Y ou can save on meals in restaurants by being aware of the following sneaky menu tricks…

MENU LAYOUT

The human eye tends to go first to the upper right-hand corner of a page. So, that's where you can expect to locate the menu's "stars"—restaurant industry lingo for popular entrées with the highest gross profit margins. The upper right-hand corner won't necessarily display the most expensive things on the menu, only the most profitable. That's because highlighting a costly porterhouse steak or lobster might scare customers away.

This doesn't mean that you should avoid these items if they appeal to you, but study the price carefully—there may not be as much value for the dollar as with dishes listed elsewhere.

Commonly overpriced: Filet mignon in a steakhouse…salmon in a seafood restaurant …a margarita at a Mexican restaurant.

Hint: Get better value with Mexican beer.

Slick: Shrewd restaurateurs leave out the dots between an item and its price, making it harder to connect dishes to their prices. If you see this sort of layout, you are being distracted from watching your wallet.

In contrast, a menu that lists its items down a left-hand column on a page and uses a series of dots to guide your eye to their prices practically invites comparison shopping.

Extra slick: The menu at Norma's at the Parker Meridien Hotel in New York City lists a $1,000 lobster frittata with caviar and, right above it, a $28 lobster and asparagus omelette that seems like a bargain in comparison. It is not a deal.

MENU STYLE

A menu's details can make you spend more, too. When a trendy restaurant rounds its prices ($15 instead of $14.95, for instance), it sends a flattering message that you, the customer, don't need to feel as if you're getting a bargain when you dine out. You are getting the same signal when the dollar signs are missing. Even the typeface can put you in a spending mood—if it seems elegant, it can make you feel elegant. That may induce freer spending.

A block of type printed in all capital letters is hard to read, so some restaurants use that for less profitable meals, such as hamburgers or soup and salad, to "downsell" them.

Extra information can divert your attention from how much an entrée costs. When you see calorie counts listed or a long description of how a dish is prepared, make sure that you're not ignoring budgetary caution because an item is touted as healthful or organic.

SELF-DEFENSE

The best way to get good value—ask your server what's good but also what regular customers order. Regulars know where the value is.

How to Give a Memorable Toast

J. Lyman MacInnis, a Toronto-based executive coach and public-speaking expert who has given more than 100 toasts. He is author of *The Elements of Great Public Speaking: How to Be Calm, Confident, and Compelling* (Ten Speed). His Web site is *www.lymanmacinnis.com*.

A good toast can be the highlight of an evening and remembered for years. *How to do it…*

PERSONAL TOASTS

Personal toasts are given at social occasions, such as weddings and retirement parties.

• **Share an anecdote,** preferably a humorous one. Stories are more engaging for listeners than lists of accomplishments or glowing praise. *Select anecdotes that…*

• Convey something meaningful about the individual, perhaps reflecting his/her character or importance. It also should have some relevance to the event at which the toast is given. If this relevance is tenuous, add a sentence at the end that ties things together. *Example:* If your anecdote about the groom has little to do with his new wife, add, "But I know he's found the perfect bride, because she's already heard this story and she's marrying him anyway."

• Are interesting to most of your audience, not just certain insiders. *Example:* Your funny accounting anecdote could be appropriate for the toast at an accountant's retirement party—if only accountants are present. If the accountants' spouses are present, choose another anecdote.

• Feature the person being toasted as the obvious star of the anecdote. If several people in your audience play supporting roles, all the better—this holds listeners' attention.

• Are not embarrassing to the guest of honor. *Exception:* Almost anything goes with bachelor party toasts.

• **Quickly describe your relationship with the person being toasted** at the start of your toast if some in the audience do not know you (assuming that you were not introduced). The audience will be distracted if people are asking one another, "Who's that?"

Example: "For those who don't know me, I'm Larry Peterson, the groom's cousin."

• **Keep the toast to five minutes or shorter.**

• **Do not tell jokes.** Jokes such as those in joke books often fall flat.

• **Never mention the bride or groom's previous romantic partners.**

• **Save the punch line for the end of your story.** If you open with, "Let me tell you the story of the time Hal's pants fell down at the ballpark," you will not get as big a laugh when you reach the big moment in the anecdote.

• **At the end, give a concluding sentence.**

Example: "Let's all raise our glasses to one of the greatest men I know, Bob Smith."

• **Speak toward the audience,** not to the person being toasted. Turn toward the guest of honor only when you deliver the final line.

• **Write your toast out before the event,** and rehearse it.

FORMAL TOASTS

A formal toast is given at a business meeting or a professional conference. It should be short, just a minute or two. If you do not know much about the guest of honor, speak instead about the accomplishment being recognized.

Example: "This is not a routine honor we're presenting to Mr. Williams. XYZ Alliance has been around since 1950, and this is only the third time we have made this award…"

The best way to end a formal toast is to simply repeat your congratulations and, if appropriate, add a wish for continued success.

16

Cars and Drivers

To Keep Your Car Running Smoothly— Six Things You Should *Never* Skimp On

People are understandably worried about the gloomy economy—many are trying to avoid any unnecessary expenses. When it comes to your vehicle, there are some aspects of car maintenance that you might think you can skimp on to save money, but do not. Cutting corners or postponing maintenance actually can end up costing you more money over the long run.

What you should never skimp on...

•**Oil.** Buy the grade of oil that meets the vehicle manufacturer's recommended American Petroleum Institute (API) or Society of Automotive Engineers (SAE) service rating, which is indicated in the owner's manual.

Using lower-grade oil may damage your engine. It also could invalidate your warranty coverage if you have a contested oil-related engine problem and you cannot prove that the vehicle was serviced according to the manufacturer's requirements.

In addition, be sure that the oil filter you use meets the vehicle manufacturer's requirements, as specified by the owner's manual or the dealer.

Helpful: Keep all receipts related to servicing your car, including those for oil and filter changes, so that you can prove your car was serviced according to the manufacturer's specifications.

If you know how to do it, changing the oil and filter yourself is the least expensive approach. But not everyone likes to do that—or wants to deal with the mess of disposing of the old oil and filter.

Eric Peters, a Washington, DC–based automotive columnist and author of *Automotive Atrocities! The Cars We Love to Hate* (MBI). His Web site is *http://ericpeters autos.com.*

Mechanics and independent shops generally are less expensive than having the work done by the car dealer.

Regardless of who does the job, check the dipstick afterward to confirm that the oil level is between the low and high marks. Some places have been known to overfill or underfill the crankcase.

•**Oil changes.** It might seem that stretching out the time between the manufacturer's maximum recommended oil change interval is a good way to economize, but it's not. It can accelerate wear and tear on your engine. I recommend erring on the side of caution—and always trying to change the oil at the prescribed interval. You probably won't hurt the engine if you miss the mileage/date interval by a little bit—for example, up to a month or about 200 to 300 miles—but don't go longer than that.

•**Radiator service.** The key to a well-performing radiator is the quality of coolant, the liquid that runs through it. Old or contaminated coolant can ruin an engine by causing corrosion or rust, especially because many engines today are made of alloy, not cast iron. It also can lead to overheating, which in a modern engine that has aluminum cylinder heads (which warp more easily than cast iron) risks serious damage.

Check the condition of the coolant in your radiator—or have a competent mechanic check it for you—at least every two years regardless of the advertised shelf life of the coolant.

This is easy: When the engine is cold, open up the radiator cap and take a look. (Touching the cap when it is hot is dangerous—taking the cap off the pressurized system can result in a spray of coolant.)

Fresh coolant is bright green or orange-red (if it's the "long-life" type) and translucent, not cloudy. Coolant should never look dirty. If it does, there is a problem with the coolant or something else in the engine—and this should be checked immediately.

Smart: Periodically have a mechanic open the radiator cap when the engine is cold to check on the fill level. Looking at the translucent coolant overflow tank is not as effective. These tanks often are discolored, and the level

is hard to gauge accurately, especially if the car is more than a few years old.

Any loss of coolant is cause for further investigation. Catching the problems both big (a failing head gasket) and small (a minor, pinhole-type leak) can help avert a major, and expensive, breakdown.

•**Wiper blades.** For the sake of visibility and safety, do not skimp on replacing your wiper blades. Blades should be replaced as soon as they no longer clear the glass without causing streaks. Wiper blades typically last about six months but sometimes wear out much sooner if subjected to harsh conditions. Brutal summer sun and rough, ice-encrusted winter windshields are especially hard on wiper blades.

•**Car washes.** It is false economy to not wash your car. Keeping your car clean helps prevent rust and maintains the paint's shine, which aids the resale value at trade-in time. If you have the time to wash your car yourself, you'll save money. But if you don't have time, it's worth paying to have it done for you.

•**Regular unleaded vs. premium gas.** If your car requires premium gas (as indicated in your owner's manual), do not use regular (or even midgrade) gas. You probably won't hurt your car's engine, but your mileage will suffer and you will have lower horsepower output. To accommodate the lower-octane gas, the engine will perform in the midrange—it won't run poorly, nor will it run at its absolute best.

How to save: If your owner's manual merely *recommends* premium gas, you could save money by using regular gas, which typically is at least 20 to 30 cents less per gallon. You might not get all the horsepower your engine is capable of delivering, but this is something you may not miss.

You might suffer a slight mileage drop that could eat away at the savings at the pump, so compare mileage when running on regular and premium gas to see whether using premium is worth it.

More from Eric Peters...

Save on Tires

There is one simple way to save money on car maintenance—tires. When it's time to replace a vehicle's tires, many people just return to the dealer and buy the original brand of tires that came from the factory. That's often expensive—and not necessary.

What you might not know: The prices for high-quality tires vary tremendously. You can potentially save hundreds of dollars by buying the same general type of tire—such as all-season, high-performance, touring, etc.—but a different brand and/or model. Always make sure that your new tires meet the minimum requirements for load (the weight the tire is designed to carry), heat and traction ratings recommended by the vehicle manufacturer.

Prices also can vary by season. High-performance summer tires, for instance, often go on sale in the fall.

In addition, it is sometimes possible to realize tremendous savings by purchasing tires from online retailers, such as The Tire Rack (*www.tirerack.com*), where you also can read reviews of tire models by customers. Be sure to factor in the cost of shipping the tires, as well as the cost of having them mounted and balanced.

Helpful: Have your tires rotated regularly. A good rule of thumb is every 3,000 to 5,000 miles. People often forget that this basic service helps ensure that tires last as long as possible. Many tire shops do it for free if you buy the tires from them or have the tires mounted there.

• **Never sign a blank repair authorization** —always get a signed work order with the specific estimated costs.

• **When you get a second opinion,** do not tell the second mechanic any details of the first opinion.

• **Ask about the warranty on new brake pads**—lengths and terms of these warranties vary widely.

• **When buying tires, ask for their "build date" (it's imprinted in code on the tires)**—tires that look new could have been manufactured years ago.

Note: It isn't safe to drive on tires that are more than six years old.

• **Make sure of the reputation of anyone who works on your catalytic converter or emissions system,** as these are very sensitive and complex.

A Fair Estimate

Get unbiased estimates of car-repair costs at RepairPal.com. Enter information about your car, location and what service you need, and the site will give you an estimate of how much the service will cost. You also can find local shops and read reviews of their services. The site lists more than 270,000 shops.

Self-Defense Against Shoddy Car Repairs

Gary Montesi, owner, Montesi Motors, Inc., North Haven, Connecticut.

To protect yourself from getting substandard auto repairs, follow these six helpful tips...

• **Look for mechanics certified by the National Institute for Automotive Service Excellence,** commonly referred to as ASE (at 888-273-8378 or *www.ase.com*)...or by AAA (*www.aaa.com*).

Stay Away from These Repair Shops

David Solomon, a certified master auto technician and the chairman of MotorWatch, an automotive safety watchdog organization, and editor of *MotorWatch,* Box 123, Butler, Maryland 21023, *www.motorwatch.com*.

There are a variety of clues to alert you to problems with a particular auto repair shop...

• **Ban on checks.** If signs on the wall say, "No Checks, Cash Only" or "$35-a-Day Storage

Fee After 24 Hours," consider taking your business elsewhere. These cash-only and storage charge signs may suggest that the shop has been stung by unhappy customers who have put stop payments on their checks or abandoned their cars.

- **Abandoned cars.** If there are many cars with flat tires and expired tags, they were probably deserted because the repair garage could not fix them or wanted to charge too much. An empty shop also is a bad sign, indicating little business.

- **No cars like yours.** If you see only one particular brand of foreign car or other kinds of cars that are not at all similar to yours, the shop may not have expertise in your type of vehicle.

- **Dirty shop.** Is the shop well-lit and properly ventilated…or is the air foul, with a decade of grease and grime on the floor and piles of junk? The condition of the shop is a good indication of what kind of job it does. On the other hand, if it seems more like an operating room than a garage, look out. The staff may not have anything to do but clean floors all day.

More from David Solomon…

Do You Really Need Premium Gas?

Your car's engine is designed to work on premium if the manual tells you to use it. Premium gas is processed to burn more slowly in high-compression engines, so it provides power without causing knocking or pinging. In an emergency, you can use regular fuel in an engine designed for premium, but your car will get significantly better mileage on premium gas. In fact, despite premium's higher cost, you will get more miles per dollar from premium fuel. Frequent use of regular gas in an engine designed for premium can lead to a buildup of carbon deposits and a permanent drop in power and gas mileage.

Bottom line: Only buy a car designed for premium fuel if you are prepared to put premium gas in it all the time.

Gas-Saving Tips: Myth and Reality

Philip Reed, senior consumer advice editor at Edmunds.com, an automotive information Web site. He is author of *Strategies for Smart Car Buyers* (Edmunds).

Tips for saving gas when driving abound. Do they make a difference? *Edmunds.com put several to the test…*

- **Don't drive aggressively.** True. Constantly hitting the gas to speed up and brakes to slow down really wastes gas. Aggressive drivers who switch to moderate driving behavior can improve their gas mileage by more than 30%.

- **Do not speed.** True. Today's cars get the best mileage at speeds between 35 and 60 miles per hour (mph). Driving at 75 mph or faster may reduce gas mileage by 15% or more from the car's best level.

- **Use cruise control.** True. Keeping the car automatically at a steady speed improves gas mileage by 7%.

Exception: It wastes gas in hilly terrain.

- **Avoid excess idling.** True. Running your engine burns gas, and when the car isn't moving it gets zero miles per gallon. If you will be stopped for more than a minute, turn the engine off (unless, of course, you're in a place where doing so wouldn't be safe). Savings depend on how much you idle.

- **Turn the air conditioner off.** False. While the air conditioner does draw power off the engine, it draws too little to affect gas mileage measurably. Similarly, raising or lowering the windows to affect "drag" has too little effect to be noticed at the gas pump.

- **Adjust tire pressure.** Somewhat true. Inflating tires to the correct pressure is more important for safety and to prevent excessive tire wear, however, there will also be a modest improvement in fuel economy compared with driving underinflated tires or tires at the wrong pressure.

Four Ways to Use Less Gasoline

Here is how to reduce the amount of gas your car consumes…

1. Limit "short hops." Multiple round-trips from your home to local destinations that are near each other (such as to the grocer in the morning, bank in the afternoon, etc.) are the largest gasoline-wasters for many families. Instead, go to all your local destinations on a single trip.

2. Have a soft foot. Every time that you hit the gas or brake pedal hard, you waste energy. Drive at steady speeds, and accelerate and decelerate as smoothly as possible.

3. Maintain your car. Keeping tires properly inflated, having clean oil and gas filters, etc., will increase gas mileage.

4. Move the junk out of your trunk. Every extra pound of weight in your car causes the engine to use more fuel. Remove from your car anything you don't really need there.

Mary Hunt, editor, Debt-Proof Living, *Box 2076, Paramount, California 90723,* www.debtproofliving.com.

Tighten Your Gas Cap

Almost one in five vehicles is driven with a loose gas cap. Each year, 147 million gallons of gas evaporate because of loose, missing or broken gas caps. So, after filling up, twist your gas cap tight until you hear it click.

Lauren Fix, spokesperson, Car Care Council, a nonprofit consumer education organization of 6,200 automobile industry companies, Bethesda, Maryland, www.carcare.org.

Simple Ways to Get a Cleaner Car

To clean the outside of the car windshield, make a paste of baking soda and water.

Remove bird droppings by very gently rubbing waterless hand cleaner, such as Purell, into the spot with an old rag, letting it sit for a few minutes, then rubbing it off. Saturate road tar with linseed oil, let soak for a few minutes, then wipe off with an old rag. Keep used fabric-softener sheets in the car to wipe the dashboard, clean air vents and polish the rearview mirror.

Linda Cobb, cleaning specialist, Phoenix, and author of A Year of Tips, Tricks, and Picks for a Cleaner House and a More Organized Life! *(Pocket). Her Web site is* www.queenofclean.com.

Where to Find the Best Used-Car Bargains Today

Philip Reed, senior consumer advice editor at Edmunds.com, an automotive information Web site. He is author of Strategies for Smart Car Buyers *(Edmunds).*

Used vehicles after just one year on the road typically sell for 20% to 30% less than they did new. They often sell for a small fraction of their original price after eight to 10 years, though many still have plenty of life left in them.

Buying your next car used could save you thousands of dollars—but some used cars are much better bargains than others. *To score a great deal…*

UNDERAPPRECIATED MAKES

A used car's price is driven in part by the reputation of its manufacturer. It's rare to find bargains on used Hondas or Toyotas because these companies' well-deserved reputations for quality ensure strong demand.

You're more likely to find a bargain if you shop for a used Nissan, Mazda or Mitsubishi. All these automakers score nearly as high as Honda and Toyota in reliability rankings, but lack their cachet.

To get an even bigger bargain, buy a used post-2003 Hyundai or post-2006 Kia. These Korean cars have become very reliable in recent years—Hyundai even has beaten Honda in some owner satisfaction surveys—but because of past quality problems, many used-car shoppers don't trust them. That attitude reduces their prices on the secondary market.

Examples: A used 2004 Hyundai Elantra might sell for a little more than $6,000, 57% below the asking price for a new 2009 Elantra...while a comparable 2004 Toyota Camry would still fetch around $11,410, just 40% below the price of a new one.*

Alternate strategy: Because of automaker mergers and joint ventures, virtually the same vehicle occasionally is marketed under different names by multiple carmakers. The version of these "twins" released by the less-respected automaker could be a bargain when it's purchased used.

Examples: The Pontiac Vibe is virtually identical to the Toyota Matrix, but Toyota's superior reputation for quality means that used Vibes sometimes sell for hundreds less, despite a longer warranty...the Ford Fusion is essentially the same as a Mazda 6, but because of Ford's lesser reputation for reliability, used Fusions can be found for as much as $1,000 less. Other virtual twins include the Hyundai Accent and the Kia Rio compact vehicles... the GMC Yukon Denali and the Cadillac Escalade SUVs...the Toyota Camry and the Lexus ES350...and the Hyundai Entourage and Kia Sedona minivans.

BUY BIG

The high fuel costs of 2008 have ravaged the resale values of used large vehicles, though prices did rebound a bit after gas prices fell in late 2008.

Used gas guzzlers are not bargains if you drive a lot—any money you save up front will be spent later at the gas pump—but poor gas mileage won't hurt you financially if you drive only a few thousand miles each year.

Example: If you drive just 3,000 miles a year, the difference in gas bills between a car that gets 15 miles per gallon (mpg) and one that gets 25 mpg is just $160 per year if gas costs $2 per gallon, or $280 if it is $3.50.

There currently are many more used SUVs, full-sized pickups and full-sized sedans on the market than there are buyers for these vehicles,

*Used-car prices are estimated prices for base models with normal mileage and wear on used-car lots.

so make lowball offers until you find a seller desperate enough to accept.

AGE AND MILEAGE SWEET SPOTS

Vehicles tend to depreciate quickly in their first year on the road, then plateau in value somewhat for the following three to four years before dropping precipitously once again. *Two ways to get the best deals...*

• **Buy a used vehicle that's just one to two years old** (a 2008 or 2009 model-year vehicle if you are shopping in 2010). You'll save 20% to 30% on a car that's virtually as good as new. If something is wrong with the car, it should still be under warranty—almost all new cars come with at least a three-year, 36,000-mile warranty.

• **Buy a 1999 vehicle with only slightly more than 100,000 miles on its odometer.** Cars from 1999 tend to be bargains because used-car shoppers are psychologically predisposed to think of vehicles from the previous decade as old. Cars showing just over 100,000 miles on the odometer can be bargains, too, because so many used-car buyers believe that 100,000 miles is all you can expect to get out of a car. Vehicles made during the past two decades are designed to last well over 100,000 miles if well maintained.

Open the car's hood and squeeze the hoses—does the rubber seem brittle? Eyeball the hoses—are there any cracks? When an older car's rubber hoses are in good condition, it's a good sign that the car has been well maintained. Still, it's worth paying a mechanic $100 or so to give a used car that's no longer under warranty a good thorough inspection before buying.

More from Philip Reed...

Secrets to Getting the Best New Car Deals Today: Lots Are Overflowing

You may not have a new car on your shopping list if your finances are reeling from the recession. But if you want a new car and feel that you can afford one, this is actually a terrific time to buy. *Consider...*

• **Auto sales cratered in 2008 to reach the lowest levels in 26 years,** so inventories of many models are high and you can get rebates and discounts totaling as much as $10,000…0% financing…and/or other incentives, including a "buy-one-get-two" offer from a Dodge dealership in Florida (you have to pay list price on the one you buy).

Note: You can check current incentives for specific vehicles at NADAguides.com or the site I work for, Edmunds.com.

• **If you currently own a gas hog that you would love to get rid of** in favor of a more efficient vehicle, the recent steep drop in gas prices may have created a window of opportunity. When gas prices topped $4 per gallon in June 2008, very few used-car shoppers were interested in gas-gulping big cars, sports cars, SUVs or trucks. Now gas is back down—and relative interest in such vehicles has picked up. You may be able to sell or trade your gas gulper for a better price now.

• **Even though prices for new automobiles have fallen, prices for parts and service have not.** So, you won't save as much money keeping the car you have, rather than buying a new one with a warranty, as you might have in the past.

BEST WAYS TO USE THE WEB

Of course, there is no "magic" that makes paying for a new auto as cheap as owning a good used car. *But if you are in the market for a new car, there are ways to make sure that you are getting the best deal…*

Get price quotes from dealers through their Internet sales departments. You can request on-line dealer quotes through an independent automotive information Internet site, such as Kelley Blue Book at *www.kbb.com*, CarsDirect.com and Edmunds.com. You can also glean more information from the Web sites of individual dealerships in your region or through most vehicle manufacturers' sites.

The initial price quotes you get this way are often within a couple hundred dollars of the dealerships' best prices and $1,000 or more below the prices that you might get in person. That's because dealers know that online customers are likely to compare quotes from several dealers.

After you test-drive a vehicle to make sure that it is the one you want, do not visit any dealership until you have in hand a firm price quote on a specific, in-stock vehicle and are ready to buy.

Helpful: When you accept a bid and then visit the dealership to sign the contract, bring along a printout of your Internet quote. Disreputable dealerships occasionally try to alter agreed-upon prices, particularly when buyers have traveled long distances.

KNOW THESE DEALER TRICKS

To get the very best possible price on a new car, online or in person…

• **Shop toward the end of a month,** when dealership employees are worried about meeting their quotas.

• **Check online for manufacturer-to-dealer incentives,** which enable dealers to lower prices further, and other incentives that lower the price. Ask the dealer to clarify whether a quote is a pre-incentive price or includes the incentives.

• **Ask, "What is my out-the-door price?"** Some dealers quote low prices to get shoppers hooked but later tack on added charges. Some of these charges—such as sales tax and registration fees—are legitimate and impossible to avoid. Others, such as document fees, advertising fees, dealer-prep fees and even gas-efficiency surcharges, are just dealer attempts to make more money and are negotiable. Disreputable dealers might also attempt to add high-margin extras to the car that you did not request or discuss, such as window vehicle identification number (or VIN) etching, which does not really deter car thieves.

• **Check ahead.** If you are traveling a long distance to pick up your vehicle, confirm in advance that the person you dealt with will be on hand when you arrive. Otherwise, the salesperson who quoted you an unbelievable price over the Internet could be out the day that you are told to arrive, and the other person who stands in may say that he/she cannot match that price.

257

• **Once a car dealer offers a good price through an Internet bid,** have all details of the agreement, including a specific description of the car and options packages and a copy of the window sticker, sent by fax or e-mail so that you know exactly what you are getting.

FINANCING

To get the best possible loan terms, secure preapproval for independent financing from a bank, credit union or online lender before you agree to buy a vehicle. This provides an alternative if the dealership offers an unattractive rate. And it greatly increases the odds that the dealership will offer an appealing rate. If the dealer is offering a 0% rate, you will need a FICO credit score of at least 700 (out of 850), and possibly 720, plus a 10% down payment in many cases. Determine your credit score in advance at *www.annualcreditreport.com* or at *www.myfico.com,* and if it is too low, consider trying to improve it before you get a car loan.

How Not to Buy a Lemon And What to Do If You Get Stuck with One

Craig Kimmel, an attorney and nationally recognized expert on lemon laws and principal of the law firm of Kimmel & Silverman in Ambler, Pennsylvania. Over the past 13 years, his firm has represented more than 45,000 car owners in lemon law suits, recovering more than $140 million for them. For more information, go to *www.lemonlaw.com.*

The last thing you want to buy is a car with recurring problems that can't be fixed. Fortunately, you do not have to get stuck with a lemon. Laws protecting you against automakers for breach of warranties have gotten tougher. In general, a new vehicle (or certified preowned vehicle or used vehicle still under factory warranty) is deemed a lemon if it has been repaired more than three times for the same defect…or if the flaw substantially impairs the vehicle's safety, value or use…or if it spent 30 days or more in the repair shop within your first year of ownership.

The laws vary from state to state, but often the manufacturer is required to replace the vehicle or buy it back from you. About 100,000 lemons are bought back annually by automakers in the US.

Helpful resources: Find a guide to the lemon laws in your state at *www.nationallemon lawcenter.com.* Or phone your state's attorney general's office (*www.naag.org*).

HOW TO AVOID BUYING A LEMON

For new cars, do the following…

• **Look up reviews of different makes and models at *www.edmunds.com.*** Also, check out *Consumer Reports* (available at the library or through subscription at the Web site *www. consumerreports.org*).

• **Review auto complaint data about the vehicle you're interested in.** It is compiled by the National Highway Traffic Safety Administration (888-327-4236 or *www–odi.nhtsa. dot.gov*). For 2008, the most problematic new models include Toyota FJ Cruiser, Dodge Nitro, Lexus ES and Hyundai Entourage.

For used cars that are still under warranty or certified preowned cars, do the following…

• **Ask the car dealer if there is anything about the vehicle's prior history that could void the warranty**—and get his/her response in writing.

• **Check *www.carfax.com,*** which provides you with a vehicle history report so you can learn if the vehicle was ever in an accident or a flood. Also, your insurance company can run the vehicle identification number (VIN) to see if an accident claim was ever made.

IF YOU'VE ALREADY BOUGHT A LEMON

• **Try to resolve all repair issues with the dealer.** The service manager knows that it is in his best interest to fix your car and retain a satisfied customer. Avoid throwing around the term "lemon" or threatening to sue. Once a customer mentions a lawsuit, dealers tend to be much less cooperative.

• **Maintain a good paper trail.** *Make sure the work order for each of your service visits clearly lists the following…*

• Odometer readings. Lemon law provisions are based on the mileage and age when the problem first occurred and vary by state. *Example:* In New Jersey, you can file a claim on a new car in the first 24 months or 18,000 miles from the date of delivery, whichever comes first.

• Why the car was brought in. The Lemon laws generally do not kick in until you have had the same recurring problem repaired more than three times. If the language on the work orders isn't exactly the same, it could endanger your claim. *Example:* If you bring the car in for a defective starter on one visit, do not let the same problem be referred to as an "engine problem" on a subsequent visit.

Dealer trick: "Forgetting" to give you paperwork for a repair performed for free. Always get an invoice.

• **Ask about Technical Service Bulletins (TSBs).** These are instructions from the manufacturer that alert dealers about defects or repairs in certain models. You can find TSBs for vehicles dating back to 1960 at *www.alldata. com/TSB*. This site charges $26.95 per year* for one vehicle and $16.95 for each additional vehicle.

• **Follow all service protocols.** Most lemon laws do not apply if the problem is deemed to be the result of owner "abuse," including failure to correctly maintain and service your vehicle.

Example: If you change your own oil, make sure you have proof that you did it per the factory time/mileage interval with the correct weight oil and an approved filter, not a generic off-brand. Otherwise, the dealer might claim that not following recommended protocols was responsible for the damage to your vehicle.

• **Call the manufacturer if you're not satisfied with how your dealer is resolving a problem.** The manufacturer's phone number is in the back of the service manual. If the manufacturer's representative cannot help, he likely will recommend arbitration. (In some states, arbitration is mandatory before you can

*Prices subject to change.

sue under a lemon law.) Arbitration is a process in which you present your case to a board which consists of consumer representatives, a new car dealer and an automotive expert.

• **If you decide to sue, consider hiring an attorney.** Automakers tend to play hardball with customers who attempt to represent themselves in lawsuits. Be sure you find an attorney who specializes in lemon laws in the state in which you purchased the car. In most cases, a reputable attorney will not charge you for an initial consultation. Also, in most states, the lemon law includes a fee-shifting provision, which means that if you win your case, the manufacturer must pay all attorney fees and legal costs on top of what you, the consumer, receive.

Helpful resource: You can find an attorney specializing in lemon laws at *www.lemonlaw america.com*.

How to Protect Yourself at The Dealership

Don't let your driver's license out of your sight at the auto dealership. You may be asked to provide your license if you want to take a test drive, and the dealer may ask to take your license to make a copy. Some dealers then use the license information to run a credit check on you…others claim to misplace your license so that they can keep you at the dealership longer and increase their chance of making a sale.

Self-defense: Bring your own copy of your license, and write across the page, "Dealer: Do not use this information to run a credit check on me." The Federal Trade Commission forbids anyone from running unapproved credit checks.

Lynette Padwa, publishing consultant and self-help writer, Los Angeles, and author of *Say the Magic Words* (Penguin).

Are Small Cars Really Cheaper?

A small car doesn't save you as much as you may think. Buying a small car to save on fuel may cost you more in insurance—erasing any fuel savings. Smaller cars, such as a Mini Cooper or a Honda Civic, tend to cost more to insure because there tend to be bigger injury claims when they are involved in accidents. Property-damage insurance usually costs less for small cars because they are less likely to damage other cars—but higher rates for other forms of coverage more than offset any savings. Actual costs vary by insurer and are tied to each particular model of car.

Ask your insurer or insurance agent to point you to cars whose fuel savings make up for any increase in insurance costs. The vehicle model is only one of many factors that affect your premium.

The Wall Street Journal, 200 Liberty St., New York City 10281, *http://online.wsj.com.*

Thinking of a Hybrid?

Marjory Abrams, publisher, *Bottom Line* newsletters, Boardroom Inc., 281 Tresser Blvd., Stamford, Connecticut 06901.

A bout one year ago, my husband and I bought a hybrid car (Ford Escape) and we recently bought our second (Toyota Highlander), mainly for the environmental benefits. We do get decent mileage—about 22 miles per gallon (mpg) in city driving—but not as good as we expected.

Top automotive trainer Bill Peek, who has taught other automotive trainers and technicians for more than 35 years (*www.autodataservices.com*), says that hybrid owners have to adopt a different style of driving to save more on gas. *His driving strategies…*

•**Braking.** Hybrid batteries are charged by braking and by the gasoline engine. Stopping recaptures energy for free and stores it in the battery for later use—one reason why hybrids get their best mileage in stop-and-go traffic. Long, light braking works best.

•**Acceleration.** Avoid jackrabbit starts. They cause the gasoline engine to kick in too soon. Accelerate slowly to stay on battery power as long as possible.

•**Speed.** Hybrids switch over from electric to gasoline at 25 to 40 miles per hour (mph), depending on the model—sooner if you are driving uphill. Try to stay under that threshold in local driving.

•**Trip length.** You won't get good mileage if you drive only short distances. The gasoline engine, the catalytic converter and, in various models, the heater need to warm up before the hybrid system kicks in.

•**Tire pressure.** As with conventional cars, tires create drag. Hybrid cars use stiffer tires which are inflated to a higher pressure than conventional tires, causing only about half the drag. Keep tires inflated to their maximum recommended pressure.

•**Watch the monitor.** Hybrids show whether the car is running on the battery or gasoline. This feedback has definitely changed my local driving habits.

Besides the fuel-saving and environmental benefits, there are other incentives to buying a hybrid…

•**Tax credits.** A federal income tax credit of up to $3,400 is available to the hybrid's original owner. Tax credits begin phasing out when the manufacturer sells 60,000 hybrid vehicles. (both Toyota's and Honda's have already expired and Ford's are being phased out). Chevrolet and Nissan still have credits available. Check on the tax credit status of each automaker at the US Department of Energy Web site, *www.fueleconomy.gov/feg/tax_hybrid.shtml.*

Some states, such as Colorado and Oregon, offer their own tax credits.

•**Sales tax exemptions.** The state I live in, Connecticut, is among those states that exempt high-mileage vehicles and hybrids. (Some Connecticut exemptions have expired.)

•**High-occupancy-vehicle (or HOV) lanes.** Certain highways permit hybrids to travel in

HOV lanes even if they are not carrying passengers. Check with your department of motor vehicles.

•**Parking discounts are offered by various hotels** (for example, the Kimpton chain) and other businesses.

•**Auto insurance discounts.** The main insurers are Travelers and Farmers.

As hybrids become more common, some concerns have now surfaced. In an accident, a hybrid's high-voltage cables, which connect the battery pack to the motor, could become exposed, creating an electrocution hazard to emergency personnel. Experts say that hybrids are no more dangerous than conventional vehicles so long as rescuers follow standard procedures, such as making sure that the ignition has been shut off.

Concerns also have been raised about electromagnetic fields (EMFs). It is unclear whether hybrids expose occupants to greater EMFs than traditional vehicles—or whether any vehicle's EMF contributes to health problems.

Why Diesels Are "Greener" Than Hybrids

Modern diesel engines that run on low-sulfur fuel are very clean…get almost the same mileage as hybrids…and do not leave behind nonrecyclable battery packs, as hybrid cars do.

Also: Diesel engines are more dependable and can be serviced more easily.

C.J. Tolson, editor in chief, *MotorWatch*, Box 123, Butler, Maryland 21023, *www.motorwatch.com.*

Most Dependable Cars

Buick and Jaguar tied for most dependable brand in the 2009 J.D. Power and Associates Vehicle Dependability Study. They were followed by Lexus, Toyota and Mercury. The lowest-ranked brands were Volkswagen and Suzuki. Overall dependability was determined by the level of problems experienced per 100 vehicles.

Vehicle Dependability Study 2009 by J.D. Power and Associates, Westlake Village, California, *www.jdpower.com/autos/articles/2009-vehicle-dependability-study-results.*

Safe-Driving Strategies For Small-Car Owners

William Van Tassel, PhD, manager of driver training operations at AAA's national office in Heathrow, Florida, *www.aaa.com.* He is a member of the Transportation Research Board's Committee on Operative Regulation and Education and a sports car racer for the Sports Car Club of America.

Small cars can be major money savers, trimming gasoline bills by 50% or more compared to full-size sedans and SUVs. However, smaller cars also tend to be riskier than larger vehicles, with fatality rates more than twice as high as those of gas guzzlers. *To make small-car driving as safe as possible…*

•**Select the safest small car.** *When buying a car, look for…*

•Side-impact air bags, as these greatly improve your odds of survival if your small car is hit on the side.

•Electronic stability control. This computerized safety system detects when your vehicle is skidding and helps you get the vehicle under control quickly.

•High scores in crash tests. Crash-test ratings from the National Highway Traffic Safety Administration (NHTSA) are available at *www.safercar.gov.* Ratings from the Insurance Institute for Highway Safety (IIHS) can be found at *www.iihs.org/ratings.*

•Bright color. Select a brightly colored car —red and yellow are particularly visible. Avoid black, silver and gray.

•**Turn on your headlights during the day to increase visibility.** If your car doesn't have daytime running lights (low-beam headlights that turn on when the car does), put on the headlights.

- **Wait a bit before entering intersections when the light turns green,** as a driver in a larger vehicle could be barreling through the other way trying to beat the red light.

- **Avoid driving in packs with larger vehicles.** When possible, drop back or speed up slightly to create a bubble of open space around you. If a vehicle is tailgating you, look for an opportunity to pull aside and let it pass.

- **Think ahead.** Consider in advance what you would do if a vehicle fails to notice you and pulls into your path. Preselect an "emergency escape," an open area into which you could safely maneuver. Wide shoulders usually make the best emergency escapes, so it's usually safest to drive in a lane adjacent to a shoulder.

- **Learn your car's capabilities.** Your small car probably can stop and swerve more quickly than larger vehicles. That maneuverability can help you stay out of collisions if you know what your car is capable of before an emergency occurs. Take your small car to an empty parking lot, and practice hard stops and sharp swerves.

Safer Winter Driving

D rive safely in winter. Tires lose traction in cold weather, even when the road is dry and clear, because low temperatures reduce tire flexibility and grip. Cold weather also reduces air pressure in tires.

Smart: Switch to winter tires that offer enhanced cold-weather grip. Be sure that tires are inflated to pressures specified by the vehicle's manufacturer. Also, be wary of having reduced traction even in good weather—take care to accelerate and steer smoothly rather than abruptly, and leave ample space between you and the vehicles ahead of you.

John Rastetter, director of tire information for Tire Rack, South Bend, Indiana, an independent tire tester, *www.tirerack.com.*

A High-Tech Windshield

A windshield for older drivers uses lasers, infrared sensors and a camera to enhance the view of what is happening on the road. The high-tech windshield is in early stages at General Motors, but some elements of it may show up soon in cars designed for older drivers— so that objects on and near the road will stand out better and be more visible to people with aging eyes.

AARP Bulletin, 601 E St. NW, Washington, DC, on the Web at, *www.aarp.org.*

Bumper Sticker Alert

A study of drivers found that people with cars "personalized" with bumper stickers and ornaments are more likely to act out in anger on the road by flashing lights, tailgating and blocking off other drivers. The more markers there are on a vehicle, the more likely the driver is to exhibit road rage when feeling provoked—such as after being cut off. The specific message made no difference—even if innocuous, such as "baby on board."

Paul Bell, PhD, professor, Colorado State University, Fort Collins.

Tell Teens to Buckle Up!

M ost teenagers do not wear seat belts. In a recent finding, only 38% of teens reported always buckling up both when driving and when riding as passengers. Because seat belts can reduce the risk for fatality in motor vehicle crashes by 50% or more, this is one reason motor vehicle crashes are the leading cause of death for US teens, claiming the lives of almost 5,000 teens every year.

Nathaniel C. Briggs, MD, assistant professor of preventive medicine, Meharry Medical College, Nashville, and leader of a study of more than 12,000 high school students, *American Journal of Preventive Medicine.*

17

Family and Home

Easy Way to Make Quick Cash: The Keys to a Successful Garage Sale

A successful garage sale can convert your excess clutter into cash. An unsuccessful garage sale, on the other hand, could be a frustrating waste of a nice weekend. *How to increase the odds that your sale will go well...*

AVOID THE BIG MISTAKES

The following missteps could doom your garage sale...

• **Picking the wrong weekend.** Don't plan your sale for a holiday weekend. Most potential shoppers will have other plans.

• **Ignoring local regulations about signs and sales.** Confirm with the town offices that it's legal in your area to attach signs to streetlamps and telephone poles.

• **Making signs that are illegible from the road.** Use a thick black marker and large print and arrows to steer drivers toward your sale. Make sure that your address and the sale hours are written big enough to be read from a moving car.

• **Failing to provide obvious prices.** Many shoppers will walk away rather than ask for a price on an item.

• **Selling junk.** No one wants broken, unusable garbage.

• **Overpricing.** Garage sale prices must be low enough that bargain hunters cannot pass them up.

• **Not having enough change.** Get a stack of singles and a roll of quarters before the sale.

ITEMS THAT SELL

Some items sell much better than others at garage sales. *Top sellers typically include...*

• **Decorative items for the home in good condition.**

• **Framed prints.**

Sharon Huxford, a coeditor of *Garage Sale & Flea Market Annual* (Collector Books). Based in Covington, Indiana, she has been writing and editing books on garage sales, antiques and collectibles since 1974.

- **Cookbooks.**
- **Kitchen appliances that work.**
- **Needlework,** such as embroidered or crocheted items.
- **Tools.**
- **Fishing gear.**
- **Houseplants,** including rooted cuttings.

Items in good condition that evoke past decades are always popular, particularly if they date to the 1960s or earlier. These might include vintage decorative items, fashion items or even ordinary household items.

Caution: If your older items are potentially valuable antiques or collectibles, a garage sale is not the best place to sell them. Few garage sale shoppers are willing to spend more than $10 to $20 on any single item, particularly in rural regions. Look up your items in a price guide or see what similar items have fetched on eBay. If something is worth significantly more than $20, you probably would be better off selling it on eBay or through your local antique shop.

Clothing does not sell well at garage sales. Most shoppers will not share your size or taste in clothing, and even those who do are likely to think twice before buying used clothes at a garage sale where they cannot first try them on. If clothing is in good shape and in style, it is likely to bring a better price at a consignment store.

Exception: Children's clothing sells well at most garage sales if it is priced well—parents know that their children will grow into these clothes.

Strategy: Consider combining a bake sale with your garage sale. Baked goods are very popular with most garage sale shoppers hungry from a morning spent driving around.

HOW TO ADVERTISE

Take out classified ads in local newspapers starting at least a few days prior to your sale as well as on sale day. Your ad should include the hours and location of your sale and a few of the categories of merchandise that your sale will feature.

Example: "Garage Sale. Saturday. 8 am–1 pm…789 Smith Lane, Jonesville…collectible glassware, quilts, houseplants, kitchen appliances, women's clothing sizes 8 to 12, more."

Hang flyers advertising your sale on community bulletin boards, such as those often found in the entrances of supermarkets. The morning of your sale, also hang signs along busy roads near your home to attract drive-by customers.

If you live in or near a city, you also can advertise your sale for free on Internet classified ad Web site Craigslist (*www.craigslist.com*).

BEST TIMES

The best time to hold your garage sale is a weekend when there are several other sales advertised in your neighborhood. A concentration of sales encourages garage sale shoppers to come to your part of town and visit them all.

Helpful: One large sale can attract crowds just as well as many small ones. Invite your neighbors to join you in setting up a multifamily or block-wide garage sale.

The majority of garage sale purchases are made within the first three hours that the sale is open, typically on Saturday morning. By Saturday afternoon, most garage sale shoppers are heading for home—they assume that anything worth buying has been bought.

Best: Schedule your sale for Saturday between 8 am and noon or 1 pm, and you still will have most of the weekend to do other things. Or, consider starting your garage sale Friday evening between 5 pm and dusk, then continuing it Saturday morning. You will have far less competition from other garage sales on Friday evening, and you may attract shoppers on their way home from work.

Watch the weather reports during the week, and delay your sale to a future weekend if rain seems likely for sale day.

PRESENTATION

Your merchandise will sell much better if it is placed on tables rather than on the ground. Clothes sell best if they are hung on hangers, not folded or piled.

Place larger items, such as furniture or lawn mowers, out front where they can be seen from the street. Someone driving by might stop if he/she sees something of interest even if he had no intention of visiting your garage sale. Small items will not attract drive-by customers because they are not visible from passing cars.

PRICING

How much you charge for your merchandise depends on the item, its condition, your region and—most important—your goal for the sale. If your main priority is to clean the clutter out of your attic, set your prices so low that any visitor will think, "How can I afford not to buy?"

If your main priority is to make money and you do not mind hauling unsold items back into your house, price merchandise at what you might pay yourself if these were things that you needed or wanted. Garage sale shoppers really like to haggle, so do not price your goods at the lowest amounts that you are willing to take.

Write in prices on small pieces of masking tape and stick them onto the merchandise, or purchase small colored stickers and make up a sign explaining what price each of the colors represents.

If you know something about the condition or history of the item, include this on a sign or tag as well.

Examples: "Works fine" on an appliance… "Only worn once" on an item of clothing…or "circa 1950" on a vintage item.

Do not be too chatty with shoppers unless they seem interested in speaking with you. Some garage sale shoppers do not wish to be slowed down with small talk. Do say, "Good morning," and answer shoppers' questions. If an item seems to be of particular interest to a shopper, provide more information about it. Offer to plug in electric items so that the shopper can see that they work.

Don't Let Items from the Past Clutter the Present: How to Rid Your House of Excess Mementos

Peter Walsh, an organizational consultant who's based in Los Angeles. He is featured on The Learning Channel program *Clean Sweep* and appears regularly on *The Oprah Winfrey Show*. He is author of *It's All Too Much: An Easy Plan for Living a Richer Life with Less Stuff* (Free Press). His Web site is *www.peterwalshdesign.com*.

Some people fill their homes with memories, packing room after room with objects that have some connection to their past but no purpose in the present.

There's nothing wrong with saving a few mementos that recall people we have loved or victories we have achieved. But too much "memory clutter" can interfere with the enjoyment of our lives and our homes.

Examples: Your guest bedroom is so full of boxes of children's clothes that your now-grown children cannot sleep there when they visit…or you don't like your living room furniture but continue to use it because you inherited it from your grandmother.

Here's how to get rid of memory clutter…

POWER OF THE PAST

Objects have power, and those linked to important events and people from our past have more strength than most. Some of us unconsciously fear that if we dispose of these possessions, we also will lose the memories that we associate with them. These could include memories of grown children…deceased relatives…or long-ago accomplishments.

Occasionally, we keep objects from our past not because they are linked to our memories but because they are linked to our dreams. Getting rid of such things can feel like we are surrendering these dreams.

Example: A man in his 50s still has all of his college textbooks and term papers. He studied English in college and hoped to become a novelist but instead ended up in real estate. The college coursework is all he has to connect himself with the world of writing.

Throwing it away would mean confronting the fact that he never will be a writer.

Objects inherited from people important to us often are saved even when these objects are unloved and unused. Heirs feel that they have been entrusted with inherited possessions and that disposing of them would represent a violation of this trust.

Example: A woman kept all of her departed grandmother's possessions in a storage unit for 26 years.

CLEAR YOUR THINKING

Attempts to remove memory clutter from a home often fail. Though home owners might resolve time and again to get rid of all these things, lots of memories and emotions come flooding back as soon as the old boxes are opened. Faced with these strong feelings, they can't follow through.

We must adjust the way we think before attempting to clear away memory clutter. *Rather than focus on the objects themselves, focus on the space that they occupy…*

• **Stand outside the room in your home that is most filled with memory clutter.**

• **Imagine the role that you would like this room to serve in your life.**

• **Think of a few words that best describe what you want from the room.** With a master bedroom, these words might include "peaceful" or "intimate." With a basement, they might include "exercise space" or "workshop."

• **Step into the room,** and remove anything that does not help you achieve this vision.

Example: If the many boxes of mementos in your basement take up the space that you would like to use as a workshop, those boxes must go. If there's heavy furniture you want to get rid of, put a "stickie" on it and arrange for it to be removed from the room later.

• **Repeat this process with each room in your home.**

PICK AND CHOOSE

Think about the person, event or accomplishment that these objects recall, then sort through the clutter in search of the one or two items that best represent this to you. The items that you select should put a smile on your face and make your heart sing. It could be an old chest that your father refinished or your mother's favorite china. If an object rekindles problems from the past, save something else instead.

If you have numerous small items, mount the ones that you have selected in a shadow box—a type of picture frame which is deep enough to hold objects, not just photos. Shadow boxes can be purchased almost anywhere that picture frames are sold. Hang the resulting display on a wall in your home where you will see it every day. If your memory clutter involves mementos from more than one person or event, repeat this process with a new shadow box for each.

Example: One woman's fondest memories of her grandmother were of the time they spent cooking together. From among the many possessions that she inherited, she chose some recipe cards written out in her grandmother's handwriting…and two kitchen tools that she could envision in her grandmother's hands. The woman mounted these objects together in a shadow box and hung it in her kitchen. It makes her smile each time she sees it.

Displaying one or two objects in a prominent place in your home honors and preserves your treasured memories far better than keeping a great number of objects in your basement or attic ever could. This can free you up to get rid of the rest of your memory clutter without feeling that you are throwing away a treasured memory or dishonoring a departed loved one.

GIVING IT AWAY

For the items that you would like to give away, contact relatives and friends who might have fond memories of their own related to your memory clutter. Ask these people if they would like the mementos. It often is psychologically easier to give these things away to others who will value them than it is to dispose of them in some other way.

Examples: Your siblings or grown children might value objects that have been in your family for generations…old friends might want mementos related to the experiences that you shared with them.

When others express an interest in taking some memory clutter, schedule a date when you will drop it off or they'll come to pick it up. Otherwise, you might be forced to hang on to this clutter for months on their behalf.

Offering family-related objects to relatives before disposing of them frees you from any need to feel personally responsible for failing to preserve these mementos for future generations. Your relatives' decisions not to take these items into their own homes are tantamount to a family-wide agreement that they were not worth saving.

If your memory clutter includes antiques, collectibles or other objects that have a monetary value but that you do not like, sell these things and spend the money on something that you will enjoy. Doing this does not dishonor the person or event associated with the original item—it actually preserves the memory. You will be reminded of the person or event whenever you use the new possession. Alternatively, you could spend the money on an experience that you will always remember fondly.

Example: Two brothers sold the furniture they inherited from their mother and spent the proceeds on dinner at a fancy restaurant on the anniversary of her death. They shared stories about their mother all evening. The dinner is a memory that they still treasure.

For Fresher Fruits and Veggies...

To maintain freshness and the taste of fruits and vegetables, trim the bottom ends of asparagus, and store the stalks upright in cool water in the refrigerator. Do the same for broccoli and celery. If you can't eat corn the same day you buy it, wrap the unshucked corn in a wet paper bag, place the bag into a plastic bag and put in the refrigerator. Extend the life of berries by rinsing them off in a bowl with three cups of water and one cup of white vinegar. Drain in a colander, and rinse again with water. Use a salad spinner with three layers of paper towels lining the inside of the spin basket, and spin until berries are completely dry. Store berries in a loosely covered paper towel–lined container.

Cook's Illustrated, 17 Station St., Brookline, Massachusetts 02445, *www.cooksillustrated.com*.

Potato Warning

Cut away any green parts of a potato before cooking or eating it. The green color indicates the presence of *glycoalkaloids*, which can cause gastrointestinal pain, nausea, vomiting, diarrhea, restlessness and mental confusion. Potatoes with widespread areas of green should be thrown out.

Prabhat K. Nema, PhD, assistant professor, department of postharvest management, College of Horticulture, Jawaharlal Nehru Agricultural University, Mandsaur, India, and leader of a study published online in *Journal of the Science of Food and Agriculture*.

Little-Known Uses For Salt

You can remove dirt from greens, such as spinach and arugula, by swirling them in a bowl of salted water. Also, get rid of excess soap bubbles when washing dishes or clothing by hand by sprinkling a pinch of salt into the soapy water. Clean a greasy pan by shaking salt into it before washing—the salt will absorb most of the grease. If your iron gets sticky, sprinkle salt on brown paper and run the hot iron over it to remove the buildup. Finally, prevent frost from forming on the inside of windows by rubbing them with a sponge dipped in salted water.

Woman's Day, 1633 Broadway, New York City 10019, *www.womansday.com*.

Plants Deer Don't Devour

Catriona Tudor Erler, the author of nine gardening books, many of which feature her own photography. Her articles have been published in magazines and newspapers throughout the US and Great Britain. A popular speaker on gardening, she divides up her time between Charlottesville in central Virginia and Smith Mountain Lake in south-central Virginia.

When food is scarce, deer will eat almost any plant, even ones that make them ill. Nevertheless, there are some plants that they are less likely to devour.

Deer avoid some bulbs, including leucojum, iris, daffodils and calla lilies. Other flowers generally safe from deer include agapanthus, calendula, foxglove, lupins, some poppy varieties, California fuchsias, pride of Madeira, hellebore and zinnias. Deer ignore tulip foliage but eat the flowers with relish, leaving the topped stems.

Ferns are considered to be deer resistant, as is boxwood, buddleia, Carolina allspice, Mexican orange, rockrose, jasmine, rosemary, junipers, kerria, oleander, mahonia and lantana. Curiously, deer avoid rhododendrons, but savor their close relative, azaleas. The vines that are considered safe from deer include Carolina jasmine, English ivy, potato vine, Costa Rican nightshade and Cape honeysuckle.

Be aware, though, that no list of plants is completely accurate. Deer's tastes vary from region to region and even from year to year. So a plant that's safe in New England may be a deer magnet in the South...or a plant that deer avoid one year may be their favorite dish the next.

Better Mowing

Mow in different directions each time so that your grass grows straight up. Use a mulching mower so clippings become fertilizer. Sharpen blades after every 10 to 15 hours of mowing. Mow often enough so that you're cutting off less than the top one-third

of the grass blades. Grass should be about 3.5 inches tall to stay healthy in hot weather and prevent weeds.

Zachary J. Reicher, PhD, professor/turfgrass extension specialist, department of agronomy, Purdue University, West Lafayette, Indiana.

Remodeling Permits Are Your Responsibility

Home-remodeling permits are the home owner's responsibility—not the contractor's. Although contractors may promise to file the appropriate paperwork with the city, not all do.

Important: If the correct permits are not obtained, the home owner may have to have work redone when he/she wants to sell the property. Contact your town's building department to find out what permits are required.

Greg McBride, CFA, senior financial analyst, at Bank-Rate.com, North Palm Beach, Florida.

"Test Drive" a House

Some sellers will let you sleep overnight in their home, in the hope that the experience will help seal the deal. The practice isn't common yet, but in today's competitive market, experts say offering potential buyers the option can help sellers gain an edge.

Consensus of home sellers and real estate agents, reported in *The Wall Street Journal*.

Keep Your Marriage Happy

Do new activities together as a couple to keep a marriage happy. Just going out on a date is not enough if you only go to places with which you are already familiar and only do things you have done before. Trying a new restaurant—or going for a whole new experience, such as taking an art class together or visiting an amusement park—can bring new sparks to your relationship. The brain's reward system—the same system that responds when you first fall in love—appears to respond positively to new, exciting experiences.

Arthur Aron, PhD, professor of social psychology, State University of New York at Stony Brook.

Ten Habits of Happy Couples

Mark Goulston, MD, a Los Angeles–based psychologist and consultant, *www.markgoulston.com*. He's also one of the coauthors of *The 6 Secrets of a Lasting Relationship* (Perigee).

Happy couples know that the real relationship begins when the honeymoon is over. *Here are the habits of highly happy couples…*

1. Go to bed at the same time. Remember the beginning of your relationship, when you couldn't wait to go to bed with each other to make love? Happy couples resist the temptation to go to bed at different times even if one partner wakes up later to do things while his/her partner sleeps.

2. Cultivate common interests. Don't minimize the importance of activities you can do together that you both enjoy. If you don't have common interests, develop them. At the same time, make sure to cultivate interests of your own. This will make you more interesting to your mate and prevent you from appearing too dependent.

3. Make trust and forgiveness your default mode. When happy couples have a disagreement or an argument that they can't resolve, they default to trusting and forgiving rather than distrusting and begrudging.

4. Focus on accentuating the positive. If you look for things that your partner does wrong, you always can find something. If you look for what he/she does right, you always can find something, too.

5. Hug each other as soon as you see each other after being apart for the day. Couples who say hello with a hug reaffirm their love for each other.

6. Say "I love you" and "Have a good day" every morning. This is one great way to buy some patience and tolerance as each partner sets out each day to battle traffic jams, long lines and other annoyances.

7. Say "good night" every night, regardless of how you feel. This tells your partner that regardless of how upset you are with him, you still want to be in the relationship. It says that what you and your partner have is bigger than any single upsetting incident.

8. Do a "weather" check-in during the day. Call your partner at home or at work to see how his day is going. This is a great way to adjust expectations so that you're more in sync later in the day. For instance, if your partner is having an awful day, it might be unreasonable to expect him to be enthusiastic about something good that happened to you.

9. Walk hand in hand. Happy couples are pleased to be seen together and frequently are in some kind of affectionate contact—hand in hand or hand on shoulder, for example. They are saying that they belong with each other.

10. Stick with it. Even if these actions don't come naturally, happy couples stick with them until they do become a part of their relationship. It takes 30 days for a change in behavior to become a habit and a minimum of six months for a habit to become a way of life—and love.

Good Marriages Help Women De-stress

After a busier-than-usual day at work, women who come home to a loving spouse have a bigger drop in the stress hormone cortisol than women whose marriages are less

269

happy. Men's cortisol levels drop when they arrive at home regardless of the state of their marriages.

Darby E. Saxbe, CPhil, researcher at the University of California, Los Angeles, and leader of a study of 30 married couples, published in *Health Psychology*.

Revive Your Romance

Judy Kuriansky, PhD, a clinical psychologist and sex therapist on the adjunct faculty of Columbia University Teachers College in New York City. She's the author of five books, including *The Complete Idiot's Guide to a Healthy Relationship* (Alpha). Her online site is *www. sexualtherapy.com/therapists/jkuriansky.htm.*

Everyday life can quash the romance in even the best of relationships. *To restore the magic...*

• **Relive the past.** Try reminiscing with your partner about the beginning of the romance—how you first flirted at a party...that time you filled his briefcase with love letters...how he wrapped you in his coat one chilly night and promised to keep you warm forever. Write all the details as if scripting a movie, then read scenes aloud or even revisit locales to recapture the heady emotions of falling in love.

• **Add spark to the present.** Agree on an activity—a painting course, a book club—you both would enjoy doing together. Hold hands for 10 minutes daily while expressing appreciation ("Thanks for driving Mom to the doctor") or admiration ("I adore your eyes"). Do something overtly romantic each day—dance in the kitchen, kiss in the moonlight—and at bedtime say, "I love you."

• **Make promises for the future.** Create surprises that give anticipatory pleasure. Leave a message on his phone saying, "I have a treat for you waiting at home," and be ready with his favorite DVD or some sexy lingerie. Write an IOU for a backrub or homemade cookies. Establish a weekly "date night" and take turns planning—and dropping hints about—romantic events to come.

How to Affair-Proof Your Marriage

Steven D. Solomon, PhD, a licensed clinical psychologist located in La Jolla, California. He has more than 20 years of experience with couples therapy, *www.the relationshipinstitute.org.* He's also past president of the San Diego Psychological Association and coauthor of *Intimacy After Infidelity: How to Rebuild & Affair-Proof Your Marriage* (New Harbinger).

It seems that every week we learn about another politician, sports star or celebrity caught having an extramarital affair. But public figures are hardly the only ones guilty of infidelity. Surveys show that between 40% and 60% of husbands and between 30% and 50% of wives will be unfaithful at some point during their marriages.

Loneliness is the most common cause for infidelity. Almost everyone who enters into a marriage does so intending to remain faithful to his/her partner, but long-term relationships are difficult. Partners often drift apart. The romance and the excitement of the initial period eventually ends. Many people do not know how to recover the closeness of a relationship once it fades, so they look outside the marriage for the fulfillment that they no longer receive at home.

The secret to a fulfilling and faithful long-term marriage is maintaining "emotional intimacy"—openness, trust, communication and caring between partners. When spouses feel this intimate closeness, they are very unlikely to cheat.

Emotional intimacy is not just one skill—it is a combination of several different abilities...

SELF-INTIMACY

In order to have an emotionally intimate relationship with someone else, you first must understand your own emotions. Men in particular seem to give insufficient attention to their emotions.

What to do: Take one to two minutes a few times a day to ask yourself three questions—What emotion(s) am I feeling right now? What specific situation is causing me to feel these emotions? What, if anything, do I need to do about this situation to take care of myself?

Example: I'm feeling anger...I'm feeling it because that guy cut me off on the highway...The best thing I can do to take care of myself is let the anger go.

Run through these questions two or three times each day for 60 days and you will become much more aware of, and in charge of, your own emotions.

CONFLICT INTIMACY

All couples fight, but the couples with emotionally intimate marriages fight productively. They do not just try to win arguments—they really listen to their partners and come to understand their points of view, even if they do not agree.

What to do: When you are at odds with your spouse, try out an established technique known as Initiator to Inquirer or I to I. One spouse serves as "initiator." This spouse raises a troubling issue and shares his feelings and opinions on the matter. The initiator presents these thoughts as his perspective on the situation, not as the only way to look at it.

Example: The wife, as the initiator, says, "I felt hurt because it seemed to me as if you intentionally were trying to hurt my feelings," rather than "You intentionally hurt my feelings when you said that."

The other spouse's role is "inquirer." He is to repeat back the substance of what the initiator has said to show that he has heard and understood. The inquirer then asks questions that aid in understanding.

The inquirer is not allowed to question the validity of the initiator's feelings. When the desire to do so arises (and it will), the inquirer should silently remind himself that "this is not about me—it is only about my partner's perspective on the situation, and it is important for me to understand this perspective." When the initiator has had her say, the partners can switch roles. Avoid distractions during I to I time, and do not try this when one or both of you are exhausted.

This will not be a comfortable process at first, particularly if lots of negative feelings exist between you and your spouse. If you practice it two or three times each week for about 20 minutes at a time, it could become a very

useful process for working through the marital conflicts that could lead to unhappiness. You and your partner will get good at fighting productively, which will end up bringing you closer.

AFFECTION INTIMACY

Being in love with your partner isn't enough to prevent infidelity. You also must show your love and affection in the ways that your partner requires. Even a well-meaning spouse can run into trouble here if he fails to realize that the type of affection he is providing is not the type that his partner desires. *Types of marital affection include...*

• **Verbal.** How often do you tell your partner that you love him? How often do you express gratitude for the things your partner does for you?

• **Actions.** How often do you do things simply because your partner enjoys having them done? This might include buying a gift or doing some favor or chore for the partner that goes beyond your normal responsibilities.

• **Physical (nonsexual).** How often do you hold hands, hug or kiss your partner? How often do you provide foot massages or back rubs?

• **Sexual.** How often do you have sex with your partner?

What to do: Do not assume that your partner desires the same types of affection that you do or that you know what your partner requires because you have been together for years. Come right out and ask your partner what types of affection he/she would like you to provide more often. Get the specifics. Then communicate your own needs. Do not take it personally if your partner says that you have not shown enough affection. This reflects the partner's personal affection needs, not your own shortcomings.

Example: A man thinks that he shows his wife plenty of affection by buying gifts, holding hands and helping out around the house. His wife feels he is never affectionate, because she wants verbal affection and he never says, "I love you."

If you fail to provide the types and amounts of affection that your partner considers to be appropriate, your spouse may stray. Provide the desired affection, and your spouse is less likely to seek it from others.

More from Dr. Steven Solomon...

To Tell or Not to Tell

My patients who have had or are having extramarital affairs often ask me if they should tell their spouses about the affair. I tell them that if the affair is ongoing and you have no intention of ending it, then you must. Infidelity is a major violation of marital trust, and the very least you owe your partner is the opportunity to deal with the violation as he sees fit, whether that means a divorce, separation, couples therapy or something else.

If your infidelity has ended and you have no intention of repeating it, it might be better to leave the past in the past. Do not confess to unfaithfulness simply because it will feel good to get it off your chest. Telling your spouse could cause more pain and problems than it solves.

The Surprising Reason Couples Fight

Yukio Ishizuka, MD, a psychiatrist in private practice in Rye, New York. He is also author of the eBook *Breakthrough Intimacy: Sad to Happy Through Closeness*, available at *www.lifetrack.com* (click on "What's New and Available from Lifetrack").

When we argue with our partners, we typically attribute the fight to a recent incident. A couple might fight over who forgot to pay the utility bills or why they got lost during a drive.

What couples do not recognize is that the event that seems to trigger a marital fight usually is just an excuse to argue, not the actual root cause. The actual cause of fights between partners in close relationships may be closeness itself.

Research I did with hundreds of married couples has shown that fights are most likely when relationships reach new levels of closeness and intimacy. This increased closeness makes the partners feel more dependent on each other and, therefore, much more vulnerable and threatened.

Example: One couple argues seemingly because a mother-in-law is coming for yet another visit. They do not realize that the real reason they are fighting is that they just had a romantic weekend and felt particularly close to each other, an unfamiliar feeling that left at least one of them feeling more vulnerable.

The good news is that arguments brought on by increasing closeness offer an opportunity for the couple to get even closer.

GETTING PAST FIGHTS

Four key steps to getting closer...

1. Recognition. The initial step is recognizing warning signals, catching yourself in a familiar emotional confrontation with the very person that you care for the most. Recognize negative emotions, such as anxiety, anger and depression, as warning signals that you are facing a challenge.

2. Perspective. Consider why you are facing this challenge, what your options are for solving it and what the consequences are for each of those options. Recognize that closeness is the top priority over all other considerations, such as being right or wrong...or winning or losing an argument.

3. Decision. Should you apologize? Agree to forget the whole thing? The best decision is to take whatever action is necessary to overcome the crisis.

4. Take action. Implement your decision to the best of your ability. Think, feel and act in ways that increase closeness. Sometimes all it takes is to say, "Sorry, I did not mean any of those nasty things I said. I love you." Or simply reach out affectionately as if nothing had happened.

Is Your Marriage Making You Sick?

Theodore Robles, PhD, assistant professor of health psychology in the department of psychology at the University of California, Los Angeles. Dr. Robles' research focuses on the effects of marital conflict on endocrine and immune functioning in healthy adults. He was lead author of "Positive Behaviors During Marital Conflict: Influences on Stress Hormones," *Journal of Social and Personal Relationships* (Vol. 23, No. 2, April 1, 2006).

Researchers have long known that marriage can improve the couple's health. But only recently has scientific proof emerged indicating that serious health consequences can result from a chronically stressful marriage.

Important new findings...

•**Increased risk of heart disease.** Negative interactions in marriage have been convincingly linked by studies at the University of Utah to increases in heart rate and blood pressure, coronary artery fatty deposits (plaques) and decreased elasticity in the arteries—all of which contribute to heart disease.

•**A weakened immunity.** Married couples who were more hostile or angry during a single interaction were found by an Ohio State University study to have decreased function of infection-fighting natural killer cells and, in a later study, slower rates of wound healing.

As a health risk, marital stress is on par with social isolation, high cholesterol, poor diet and lack of exercise, according to these and other findings. For unknown reasons, women seem to be particularly hard hit by marital woes—studies consistently show that wives experience stronger cardiovascular, hormonal and immunological reactions to marital stress.

Good news: While virtually all marriages experience some degree of conflict, research suggests that it's how we *deal with* disagreements—not just whether we have them—that largely determines the effects on our health. For example, University of Utah researchers have shown that a couple's demeanor during disputes—warm, hostile, controlling, submissive—is as good an indicator of underlying heart disease as cholesterol levels.

To minimize the health impact of marital stress...

•**Break the tension.** Ohio State University researchers recently measured blood levels of the stress hormones *cortisol* and *adrenocorticotropic hormone* (ACTH) in 90 newlywed couples before, during and after a 30-minute discussion about sensitive marital problems. When both partners were consistently negative, the wives' cortisol and ACTH levels rose.

However, when one or both partners were supportive and constructive—even during heated discussions—the wives' stress hormones decreased throughout the discussion. (Men's hormone levels were unaffected by both the negative and supportive behaviors.)

What both spouses can do: Agree with your partner on some points...accept responsibility for your shortcomings...and propose compromises.

Research involving women with high blood pressure suggests that more hostile behaviors during marital discussions are associated with elevated blood pressure during the exchanges, and more supportive behaviors are associated with lower blood pressure during talks.

•**Watch your words.** While husbands can appear less physiologically impacted by their wives' hostility, they do react—with increased heart rate and blood pressure—to perceived challenges to their competency or skills.

What both spouses can do: Avoid controlling statements such as "You are never on time...why don't you put on your watch?" or "Why can't you just do what I ask?"

Replace comments such as: "You're spending us into bankruptcy!" with: "I know you love to shop for the grandkids, but we need to stick to a budget."

Helpful: Because we cannot control everything concerning our spouses, look for something to value even in those things you may not readily admire. For example, if you resent your spouse's messiness but value his or her easygoing nature, try viewing these qualities as flip sides of the same coin. You may find you have greater tolerance for—and less need to control—the clutter.

• **Trust your spouse.** In a University of Utah study that involved 300 middle-aged and older couples, the researchers found no correlation between self-reports of anger or antagonism and calcium buildup in their coronary arteries (a risk factor for cardiovascular disease). However, partners whose spouses had rated them high on scales of anger and antagonism were more likely to have significant calcium buildup.

What both spouses can do: Pay attention if your partner says you are being angry, hostile, unreasonable or cold. While you may be unaware of your negativity, your arteries could be paying the price.

• **Speak your mind.** In one University of Michigan study involving 192 older couples, those in which both spouses clammed up to avoid confrontation were much more likely to experience the death of one or both partners over a 17-year period. In fact, among 26 such "dual-suppressor" marriages, 27% suffered the loss of one spouse, and 23% experienced the death of both partners, while among the 166 more communicative couples, a significantly lower 19% experienced one death, and only 6% experienced the death of both partners.

Shocking new finding: In a recent study involving roughly 4,000 married adults from Framingham, Massachusetts, the women who reported regularly stifling themselves during marital disagreements were four times more likely than outspoken wives to die during a 10-year period.

The culprit could be stress. When husbands respond with silence to their spouses' anger, studies show that wives' cortisol levels go up and stay up for the day. Chronically elevated cortisol has been linked to impaired cognitive and immune functioning, heart disease, diabetes and other ills.

What both spouses can do: Communicate openly.

• **Relax.** Studies have shown that the higher a woman's levels of stress hormones before she and her husband engage in a discussion about their relationship, the more likely she and her husband are to be critical, defensive or hostile to one another throughout conflict.

Unfortunately, these negative behaviors only exacerbate the wife's already elevated ACTH and cortisol levels.

What both spouses can do: Make time daily to relax, whether with exercise, meditation, hobbies or spending time with friends. By lowering stress, women, in particular, may be able to keep hostility—and their stress hormones—from escalating during marital conflict.

Why Yogurt Can Cause Hyperactivity in Kids

Hyperactive children should not be given products with food dye. Some FDA-approved additives—such as *allura red*, known as Red No. 40…and *tartrazine*, known as Yellow No. 5—can cause significant increases in hyperactivity in some children under age 10. These colors are added to many foods, including yogurt, so check labels carefully.

William Sears, MD, pediatrician, Sears Family Pediatrics, Capistrano Beach, California, and coauthor of *The Healthiest Kid in the Neighborhood* (Little, Brown).

Peanut Allergies Are Increasing

Peanut allergies doubled between 1997 and 2002 and continue to increase.

Possible reason: In the UK and until recently in the US, doctors recommended that women avoid eating peanuts and all peanut products during pregnancy and while breastfeeding, and that infants not be given products made with peanuts.

Recent finding: In a population comparison study, the researchers found that children who are not exposed to peanuts early on may be 10 times more likely to develop a peanut allergy than children exposed to peanuts at an early age.

Further studies are necessary before public health guidelines can be changed.

George Du Toit, MD, fellow of the American Academy of Allergy, Asthma & Immunology, Milwaukee, and lead author of a study published in *The Journal of Allergy and Clinical Immunology.*

How to Talk to Your Kids About Drugs

How do you warn kids about drugs if you used them yourself? Be honest, and tailor your message to your child, who may want lots of information or only a little. Say immediately that you do not want him or her using drugs, and explain why. Talk about your own drug use directly—for instance, you might say that you tried them because other kids did…or that you made a mistake and ended up doing things you are not proud of. Listen as much as you talk—ask what your child thinks and what his friends think.

Recommendations from the Partnership for a Drug-Free America, *www.drugfree.org.*

Alert! Teens Are Abusing Cough Medicine

Cough medicine is being used by teens to get high. More than three million US teens and young adults have abused over-the-counter (OTC) cough or cold medicines. That is many more than have used *methamphetamines* in this age grouping. The commonly used cough suppressant *dextromethorphan*—found in more than 140 OTC medicines—can cause disorientation, blurred vision, slurred speech and vomiting when taken in large amounts.

Terry Cline, PhD, administrator, Substance Abuse and Mental Health Services Administration, Washington, DC.

Protect Your Kids from Online Dangers

Require your children to tell you all their screen names, e-mail addresses and addresses of their blogs and profiles. Also, check out their sites frequently together, and discuss what you see. Do not let them have computers in their rooms—permit them to use only shared family computers. Create these rules early, before children get heavily involved in social networking.

Caution: Young people may be rejected by colleges or business recruiters based on photos and language that appear in Web profiles and postings.

Megan Moreno, MD, assistant professor of pediatrics at University of Wisconsin-Madison, and leader of a study of 500 18-year-olds, published in *Archives of Pediatrics & Adolescent Medicine.*

Acing the College Application: Don't Let Kids Make These Mistakes…

Michele Hernandez, EdD, a former admissions officer at Dartmouth College and current president of Hernandez College Consulting, a college admissions consulting service in Weybridge, Vermont. She is also a cofounder of Application Boot Camp (*http://applicationbootcamp.com*), a four-day program for seniors to complete their applications. She is the author of *Acing the College Application* (Ballantine). Her Internet site is *www.hernandezcollegeconsulting.com.*

Many students make mistakes on their college applications which cost them the opportunity to attend top schools. *Common errors…*

•**Writing a clichéd essay.** Students seem to think that colleges like essays about "how I overcame a challenge" or "what I learned at a soup kitchen on Thanksgiving."

Students should select unique and interesting topics that they are passionate about.

Some examples: How you developed an interest in plasma physics…or how you taught yourself something interesting. A distinctive essay holds the attention of admissions department readers and tells them something about the applicant.

• **Using "SAT words"** in application essays. Sprinkling $10 words into college essays only makes students look like phonies. I shudder when I see words such as "plethora" or phrases such as "further my studies."

• **Failing to send in official test scores.** Schools will not consider applications unless they receive official SAT I, SAT II, ACT and AP score reports (if applicable) from the testing agencies.

• **Misidentifying the school.** Writing "Dartmouth University" instead of "Dartmouth College" might seem a minor mistake, but to the admissions department, it could suggest that the applicant isn't really interested.

• **Naming a different school in your essay is even worse.** If you use an essay for more than one application, check for any references to other schools.

• **Overlooking the character questions on the common application.** Two yes/no questions are squeezed in after the essay and just before the signature line on the common application. One of these asks whether the applicant has been suspended or expelled, the other whether he/she has been convicted of a crime. Some applicants do accidentally skip over these questions, dooming their chances because colleges assume that the applicants have been in trouble but do not want to talk about it.

• **Leaving a race question unanswered.** Admissions departments tend to assume that these questions would be answered if the answers worked in the applicant's favor and that those who leave them blank are white kids hoping to gain an edge from not answering. Some admissions personnel see this evasion as an attempt to "game the system" and take a dislike to these applicants.

• **Failing to provide a good reason for applying.** It is not sufficient to write that the school is beautiful or highly ranked…or has a low student/teacher ratio. Great explanations show that the student has done a lot of research on the school and has concluded that it is the perfect academic fit. Cite a relatively obscure academic specialty available at the school, or name a specific professor whose research is of particular interest.

Example: "Brown University's Department of Egyptology and Ancient Western Asian Studies is the perfect place for me to pursue my interest in ancient Egyptian history."

• **Waiting until the last minute to request letters of recommendation** from high school teachers. Popular teachers at high school are asked for dozens of recommendation letters each year. Their letters often become hurried and impersonal by the time deadlines near. Beat the rush and ask for recommendation letters at the end of junior year or at the very beginning of senior year. And listen to what teachers tell you. If you sense any hesitance, select a different teacher.

When Your Grown Child Moves Back Home

Nancy Dunnan, a New York City–based financial and travel adviser and author or coauthor of 25 books, including *How to Invest $50–$5,000* (HarperCollins).

In today's economic climate, an increasing number of grown-up children are moving back in with their parents. When this happens, it's important to understand that this is an adult who has been out in the real world, handling his or her own life, running his own household. Returning to yours is probably not his first choice.

Helpful: Think of your adult child more as a roommate than as your child. Set ground rules and discuss them before he moves in. *A checklist of topics to cover…*

• **Heat and electricity.** Your new resident will increase these bills. Determine how much he should contribute.

• **Telephone.** An economical arrangement might be to share cell phones on a family plan or to share the bill for a land line.

- **Groceries.** Divide the increased costs appropriately. Don't forget cleaning supplies.
- **Chores.** You need to agree on shopping, house cleaning, laundry, etc.
- **Rent.** Keep in mind that the fact that your adult child is moving back in with you does not increase your mortgage or rent.
- **Duration.** You might not be able to pin down a specific end date, but it is important to indicate how long, in general, the arrangement should last—until your child secures a new job, for a certain number of months or permanently.

For more ideas, read *How to Live with Adult Children Who Return Home* by Jean Okimoto and Phyllis Stegall (Little Brown).

 # How to Stay Close to Grown Kids When They Push You Away

Jane Isay, author of *Walking on Eggshells: Navigating the Delicate Relationship Between Adult Children and Parents* (Flying Dolphin). She traveled the country, interviewing more than 75 people about how to stay close to grown-up kids. She has been a book editor for more than 40 years and edited the nonfiction classics *Praying for Sheetrock* and *Friday Night Lights*. She lives in New York City (not far from her two grown sons).

Parents often feel marginalized as their children make the transition into adulthood. Grown kids never seem to have time for them. They ask for advice but just as often ignore it. Quarrels and sometimes long silences are almost inevitable—and painful. Both generations find themselves walking on eggshells as they figure out the rules of their changed relationship. *Here is how to successfully make the transition...*

DON'T DEMAND

I call children in their 20s the "gotta go" generation. You phone them to have a nice chat, and they say "gotta go" after about one minute. They rarely visit. Phone calls don't get returned. Parents understandably feel brushed aside—and frustrated.

Children at this age are legally adults, but psychologically they're in an in-between zone. They're learning to be independent and need to push away their parents. At the same time, they crave support and approval from their parents. As they become more confident of themselves and trust that parents will respect their boundaries, things do get better.

A lot of parents make their children feel guilty by saying things such as, "You never call" or "I hardly ever see you." Relationships filled with guilt don't thrive. The more parents demand, the more likely it is that their children will find excuses to keep their distance.

What to do: When things turn tense, stay in touch but without exerting pressure. Send chatty e-mails that don't require a reply. Drop a book or an interesting article in the mail for your child to read. Little gestures help maintain closeness but still allow grown children to set their own agendas.

Humor helps. My youngest son, who now works in politics, is extremely busy. He often does not return my phone messages. Once, when I really needed to talk to him, I left a message that said, "If you don't call back, I'll vote for the opposition." He called back right away.

GIVE RESPECTFUL ADVICE

One of the hardest jobs of parenting is to stand back when a child is having difficulties—failing in college...losing a job...having financial problems...getting a divorce. Our hearts break when a grown child is in trouble. Our instinct as parents is to fix things.

Unfortunately, unsolicited advice can come across as meddling. People rarely change their behavior when they feel lectured to, and often, they withdraw.

Helpful: Wait for your child to ask before giving advice. Even then, make sure that your advice doesn't come across as judgmental. *Instead of saying, "Here's what you should do," say...*

- **"Some people might think that the best thing..."**
- **"Someone I know was in the same situation..."**
- **"Have you thought about..."**

One woman told me that her children often turn to their father for advice because he always says, "Do whatever you think is best." There's no greater gift to a grown child than saying that you trust his/her judgment.

STEP DOWN FROM THE PEDESTAL

We parents spend decades being in charge of our children's lives. Our children see us as symbols of authority and power. Some parents try to maintain the aura of power after their children leave home. That's a mistake. Shedding the parental mystique can lead parents and children into a more realistic and honest relationship—and a closer one.

Share your humanity with your children. Let them know about your hopes, fears and disappointments. Be a real person—not some austere figure to look up to or fear.

Example: A woman I know sought job advice from her successful executive daughter. It worked. The mother got her raise, and the daughter got the satisfaction of assisting her mother.

Some parents do go too far in the other direction, trying too hard to be their children's friends. They share intimate details (such as about their sex lives) that children never want to hear. Be honest—but save sensitive confidences for your closest friends.

ADMIT TO OLD HURTS

All parents have regrets about past behavior relating to their children. People who don't deal with such guilt may find themselves withdrawing from their children, because it's less painful than being in situations that remind them of things they're ashamed of.

If you are feeling guilty about something from the past that involves your now-grown child, put it on the table. Apologize and talk about it. Everyone will feel better afterward. You might even discover that what you feel worst about didn't even bother your child.

Example: One mom I talked to apologized to her grown son for sending him to such a demanding school. He told her that the school was fine—what he really had disliked was camp.

278

NEVER CRITICIZE A SPOUSE

One of the biggest mistakes that parents make is criticizing the spouse or partner of one of their children. There might be disagreements about politics or parenting styles...or there might simply be bad "chemistry."

Share these feelings with your friends perhaps—but not with your children. If you force a grown child to make a choice between you and his partner, you are going to lose. Your child can employ the ultimate weapon—distance. If you criticize the partner or act in a way that's disrespectful to him, your child will pull away. He might do it with regrets, but he will do it anyway.

Also, don't interfere with your children's decisions about raising their own kids (unless you feel they are being truly negligent). Maybe you think your grandkids are getting too many treats or going to bed too late at night. Stay out of it. They will survive.

A Caregiver's Guide to Emotional Well-Being: How to Stay Strong and Positive

Barry J. Jacobs, PsyD, a clinical psychologist and family therapist, and director of behavioral sciences for the Crozer-Keystone Family Medicine residency program in Springfield, Pennsylvania. He is a clinical assistant professor at Temple University and an adjunct faculty member at the University of Pennsylvania School of Nursing, both in Philadelphia. Dr. Jacobs is author of *The Emotional Survival Guide for Caregivers* (Guilford, *www.emotionalsurvivalguide.com*).

When a loved one is seriously ill or disabled and you take on the task of providing his/her care, it's natural to focus your energies on meeting that person's needs. The financial and physical demands you face may quickly become evident, yet the emotional impact often goes unrecognized— even though it may be the most challenging element of all. *Evidence...*

● **In a study in *Archives of Internal Medicine,*** 14% of the end-of-life caregivers reported significant financial strain…18% reported significant physical strain…and 30% reported significant emotional strain.

• **Emotional stress leaves caregivers vulnerable to depression**—sometimes even more vulnerable than the person to whom they provide care.

• **In another study,** caregiving spouses who reported emotional strain were 63% more likely to die within four years of the studied period than caregivers who did not feel strained.

If you are a caregiver, you need to protect yourself as well as your loved one.

Helpful: Knowing what to expect as you move through the various emotional stages of becoming a caregiver…and developing specific strategies for coping.

GETTING OVER THE SHOCK

When a loved one suffers a sudden medical crisis, such as a serious injury, a relative can be thrust into the role of caregiver with zero preparation. He may assume optimistically—and often unrealistically—that life will soon return to normal as the patient recovers.

In other cases, caregiving duties grow gradually as a parent or spouse ages or develops a progressive illness, such as Parkinson's disease or Alzheimer's disease. The caregiver may not be able to admit to himself how much the loved one's condition is deteriorating.

Either way, the caregiver's instinctive reaction to the shock is denial. Initially, this tendency to minimize the impact of the illness can help give the caregiver the strength to do what needs to be done. But persistent denial can compromise a caregiver's ability to make sound decisions.

Example: If your mother can no longer walk without risking a fall, but you cannot recognize the need to insist that she use a walker or wheelchair, it jeopardizes her safety.

Support strategies: It is best to face reality. To see your loved one as he is now rather than as he used to be, keep a log of his symptoms and abilities—writing down other family members' observations as well as your own. Learn enough about his medical condition so that you can understand the treatment options and prognosis. This way, you and his doctors can agree on a medical objective, such as prolonging life or, later, simply making the patient as comfortable as possible.

LIVING WITH NEGATIVE FEELINGS

Many caregivers are heartened to experience positive emotions, such as pride in their ability to help and a deepened sense of devotion. But there are bound to be negative emotions, too, such as resentment and dread. You may feel resentful about being so burdened… then guilty over the resentment…then angry for having been made to feel guilty.

You also may experience many conflicting emotions toward the loved one himself as you struggle with all the changes in the nature of your relationship.

Example: Suppose that, after your husband's stroke, you need to feed and bathe him as you would a child—and this clashes with your longtime image of him as a partner, peer and lover.

Support strategies: Remember that negative feelings about caregiving are normal and predictable—they do not invalidate your love. To overcome resentment and restore mutual respect, it helps to promote a patient's capabilities as much as his comfort—perhaps by being as dedicated to his physical therapy exercises as you are to his personal needs.

Strongly negative feelings also could be a helpful signal, alerting you to a need to adjust your plans. For example, taking care of an ill brother does not necessarily mean that he must live in your home forever, so stay open to all the options.

ACHIEVING BALANCE

Some caregivers worry that they're not doing enough, so they disproportionately expend time and energy on the loved one. This can be detrimental to their other relationships.

Example: If you devote yourself to taking care of an adult child with a progressive illness, you might neglect your spouse, other children, extended family and friends.

Losing ties with other people deprives you of support. The more isolated you become, the more susceptible you may be to depression and other health problems. This risk increases if you come to define yourself solely as a caregiver, losing your sense of personal identity.

Support strategies: Chronic medical conditions unfold over the years, so they should be handled much like a marathon—by pacing yourself. Talk to your doctor or a mental health professional if you show signs of burnout, such as constant fatigue, insomnia, irritability, cynicism or feelings of helplessness. Be committed to staying connected to others. Carving out time to go to dinner with your husband, play bridge with friends or attend a function at your house of worship will help replenish your spirit.

More from Dr. Barry Jacobs...

When You Need Extra Help

Family caregivers can get information, support and/or referrals to professional counselors through these organizations...

- **Family Caregiver Alliance,** 800-445-8106, *www.caregiver.org.*
- **National Alliance for Caregiving,** 301-718-8444, *www.caregiving.org.*
- **National Family Caregivers Association,** 800-896-3650, *www.thefamilycaregiver.org.*
- **The Caregiver Initiative,** 866-466-3458, *www.strengthforcaring.com.*
- **Well Spouse Association,** 800-838-0879, *www.wellspouse.org.*

No More Chewing

To stop a dog from chewing objects, say "drop it" or ask for the object with the "give" command whenever the dog has something inappropriate in its mouth. Keep acceptable chew toys in one place, such as a box, and praise the dog for taking anything from the box. Focus on positive reinforcement—the dog will learn it is better to be praised for chewing an item from the box than to chew items that are not allowed.

Lisa Peterson, director of club communications for the American Kennel Club, New York City.

Dog Training 101

Teaching a dog the "stay" command must be done slowly and progressively. Remain within six inches of a puppy when you start training. Look over the dog's head when practicing—not into its eyes, which can be frightening. Stand tall during training—if you bend down, a puppy will think you want to play. Practice twice a day, varying the amount of time before you say "OK" and release the dog. Resist petting your puppy until you have finished teaching the command.

Sarah Hodgson, trainer of dogs and their people for more than 20 years in Westchester County, New York, and author of nine dog-training books, including *Puppies for Dummies* (Wiley).

When to Get to the Vet... Right Away!

Go to a vet immediately if your dog's abdomen is swollen or very tight...or the animal is retching without vomiting—he/she could have a twisted stomach. A vet visit is also advised if your male cat strains or cries when using the litter box—there could be a urinary blockage.

Other symptoms that require a vet: Your pet's gums are pale, white or blue—this can indicate infection or dehydration. Your pet is in distress—panting, unable to lie down or get comfortable. Your pet eats rat poison or any other known dangerous substance.

Prevention, 33 E. Minor St., Emmaus, Pennsylvania 18098.

18

Life Coach

How to Shutdown Stress …Even in Tough Times

It is no surprise that a new study by the American Psychological Association reports that 80% of Americans are stressed now by the economy, with 60% feeling angry and irritable and 52% having difficulty sleeping at night.

In tough economic times, it's understandable that many people feel financially vulnerable and emotionally stressed. But even in a national crisis, we are never as helpless as we think. Those who develop mental fitness are in a much better position to weather this and other stressful times.

To achieve mental fitness, we need to open our "locks," behaviors or habits that prevent us from finding solutions to problems and keep us from reaching our full potential.

Example: One of my clients coped with his high-anxiety job by eating too much and drinking heavily after work. These negative strategies (his locks) eased his stress momentarily but did nothing to increase his overall resilience and, in fact, undermined his mental fitness.

People who handle stress well use a series of skills, or "keys," to overcome obstacles and unlock their full potential.

The main keys…

DIRECT YOUR ATTENTION

Your brain can focus on one issue at a time (the laser mode), or it can expand its attention to everything around you (glow mode). Both skills are useful. An air-traffic controller, for example, has to keep track of fast-moving and constantly changing situations. He/she needs to be comfortable with the glow mode. But when you're dealing with a specific problem, the laser mode is more efficient.

John Ryder, PhD, psychologist in private practice in New York City, where he is a psychological consultant to executives, athletes and celebrities. He is author of *Positive Directions: Shifting Polarities to Escape Stress and Increase Happiness* (Morgan James).

Many of us have a hard time meeting deadlines not because we have too much to do, but because too many things compete for our attention. We jump around from thought to thought and task to task. We're mentally scattered, which means we excel at nothing—and stress builds. *What to do…*

• **Decide what has to be done first.** The process of prioritizing requires that we rank all tasks along two dimensions—what is most important and what is most urgent. Perhaps there's a project that you have to finish by the end of the day or a meeting later in the week to prepare for. Establish these as your one or two priorities, nothing more. Then selectively ignore everything else. Keep communication flowing when others are involved, and let them know where they are on the waiting list.

• **Create reminders.** Jot down your immediate goal on an index card. Keep this card somewhere in your field of vision. If your attention begins to wander, seeing the card will remind you to stay on target. Some people also find it helpful to set an alarm or cell phone to ring every 15 or 30 minutes as a reminder to focus on the goal.

STAY ALERT

We all get distracted when life is stressful. We forget to pay attention to what's going on around us. That's when we do stupid things, such as forget where we put our car keys or bounce a check because we forgot our bank account balance.

People who handle stress well almost always are observant. They watch what's going on around them in order to acquire information and choose the best course of action.

What to do: Practice observing every day. When you put down your car keys at home, for example, take in the whole environment, not just the spot where you put them. Notice the table you put them on, the lighting in the room and so on. Not only will you find your keys more quickly, you'll sharpen your ability to acquire new information.

KNOW THE OBJECTIVE *YOU*

We all have two visions of ourselves. There's our subjective self-image, which often is colored by self-doubt and insecurity. Then there's the objective self, which usually is closer to reality.

Many experienced people with impressive résumés fall apart when they lose their jobs and have to find new ones. They're paralyzed with self-doubt because all they see is their subjective (inferior) self. This is the equivalent of stage fright. Even though they have done the same type of work a thousand times, an inner voice tells them that they are not good enough.

What to do: Do a reality check. Suppose that you have spent three months looking for work without success. Before doubting yourself, get objective verification. Show your résumé to different people in the field in which you are applying. Ask them what they think about your qualifications.

Perhaps you are not qualified for the jobs you're applying for. More likely, you have just had a run of very bad luck. Trust your objective history of accomplishment.

BOOST WILLPOWER

This is one of the most vital skills during difficult times. Someone with strong willpower, for example, will find it relatively easy to cut back on spending. Most people think that willpower just means resisting temptations. It is much more than that. It's a set of skills that you can use to achieve specific goals.

Example: Suppose that you are in debt and know you need to create a budget and stick to it, but you've never been very good at that. Willpower means knowing your weakness…identifying ways to correct it…and then taking the necessary steps to improve it. These might include taking a personal finance class at a community college or getting a book on that topic from the library.

What to do: Some people naturally have more willpower than others, but everyone can develop more. The trick is to start small. Maybe your goal is to save 10% of your paycheck each month, but the first step is to reduce your credit card debt by paying off 10% more than the minimum payment each month.

REPLACE NEGATIVE PATTERNS

We are all creatures of habit. Any behavior that's repeated a few times can turn into an automatic pattern. These patterns can be positive (such as arriving at work on time) or negative (thinking you're going to fail).

Negative patterns are particularly hard to manage because they're often internalized—we do not always know that we have them. People often possess an inner voice that says things such as, I can't succeed…I'm not smart enough…It's not worth my trouble.

Negative self-talk has real-world effects because it guides our behavior and prevents us from coping well with difficult situations.

What to do: Pay attention to the thoughts that go through your mind. Are they helpful and affirming? Or do they bring on fear and anxiety?

When your thoughts turn negative, create opposite mental patterns. When you think, I'll never get this project done, consciously come up with a positive alternative and say it aloud if you can or to yourself if the situation warrants. Be specific. Rather than something general, such as I can do it, say something such as, I'm glad to be completing this project with pride, on time. Say it three times.

This might sound like a gimmick, but our brains like routines. Focusing your mind on positive outcomes—even if it seems artificial at first—causes the automatic part of the brain to build more positive thought patterns that enable us to achieve more. The key is to constantly monitor yourself. Are you aiming for the center of the target? If not, refocus on the bull's-eye.

A Simple Stress Reducer: Get More Sleep

Going without sleep can causes the brain to overreact to bad experiences.

Recent study: After staying awake for 35 hours, the emotional centers of the brains of research participants were 60% more reactive when they were shown negative images. Researchers speculate that the profound change in brain activity is due to a shutdown of the prefrontal lobe, the region of the brain that keeps emotions under control.

Self-defense: Get seven and a half to eight hours of sleep each night.

Matthew Walker, PhD, neuroscientist, University of California, Berkeley, and leader of a study published in *Current Biology*.

Can You Learn to Be Happy? Yes! Says the Teacher of Harvard's Most Popular Course

Tal Ben-Shahar, PhD, one of Harvard University's most popular lecturers. Over the past 10 years, he has taught personal and organizational excellence, leadership, ethics and self-esteem topics, and his best-selling book, *Happier: Learn the Secrets to Daily Joy and Lasting Fulfillment* (McGraw-Hill), has been translated into more than 20 languages.

Recent scientific studies and scholarly research have arrived at some surprising conclusions about what makes people happy. *Here, Harvard lecturer and best-selling author Tal Ben-Shahar, PhD, answers our questions and tells how you can be happier in your life…*

Each semester, more than 800 students at Harvard register for my life-changing course on positive psychology. My students explore the question "How can we help ourselves and others to become happier?" The students read academic journal articles, test theories, share personal stories and, by the end of the year, emerge with a clearer understanding of what psychology can teach us about leading happier, more fulfilling lives.

•**Is a person just "born happy" or "born unhappy"?** There is a genetic component to happiness. Some people are just born with a happier disposition than others or with personality traits that are very strong predictors of happiness, such as being sociable, active, stable and calm.

However, that doesn't mean how happy we feel is out of our control. Our genes define a range, not a set point. "Grumpy" may not be able to cultivate the same view of life that

"Happy" enjoys. A natural-born whiner may not be able to transform himself/herself into a Pollyanna. But all of us can become significantly happier. Most people fall far short of their happiness potential.

• **Your research suggests that money and success matter little in terms of happiness. Yet wouldn't most people be happier if they won $5 million or a Nobel Prize?** This is a concept that my students and our society in general struggle with. Happiness largely depends on our state of mind, not on our status or the state of our bank account. It depends on what we choose to focus on (the full or the empty part of the glass) and on our interpretation of external events. For example, do we view failure as catastrophic, or do we see it as a learning opportunity?

One of the most common barriers to happiness is the false expectation that one thing—a promotion at work, a prize, a revelation—will bring us eternal bliss. As soon as you achieve your goal, the "what's next" syndrome kicks in, leaving you as unfulfilled as before.

Let me tell you one personal story. When I was 16 years old, I won the Israeli National Squash Championship. I always believed that winning the title would make me happy and alleviate the emptiness I felt so much of the time. Winning the championship was necessary for fulfillment. Fulfillment was necessary for happiness. That was the logic I operated under.

After a night of celebration, I retired to my room to savor that feeling of supreme happiness. But my feelings of emptiness returned. I sat around trying to convince myself that perhaps substituting a newer goal—winning the World Championship—would finally lead me to happiness.

What I came to realize was that an important victory can contribute to our well-being, but at best, it forms a small part of the mosaic of a happy life. The fairy-tale notion of happiness—that something will carry us into the happily ever after—inevitably leads to disappointment. A happy life is rarely shaped by some extraordinary life-changing event. Rather, it is shaped incrementally, experience by experience, moment by moment.

• **So what does make us happy?** We must first accept that this is it! All there is to life is the day-to-day, the ordinary, the details of the mosaic. We are living a happy life when we derive pleasure and meaning while spending time with our loved ones or learning something new. The more our days are filled with these experiences, the happier we become.

The other significant component of happiness is that helping oneself and helping others are inextricably intertwined. The more we help others, the happier we become…and the happier we become, the more inclined we are to help others. Our nature is such that there are few more satisfying acts than sharing with others, than feeling that we contributed to the lives of others.

• **What else can people do to be happy?** There are several things you could start right away…

• Simplify. We are all very busy trying to squeeze more and more activities into less and less time. Quantity influences quality, and we compromise on our happiness by trying to do too much.

• Introduce some rituals into your life that are motivated by deeply held values. Think about what rituals would make you happier. It could be watching two movies a month or going on a date with your spouse every Tuesday. People are resistant to the idea of introducing ritualistic behavior in their lives because they think it will detract from spontaneity. But if you don't ritualize activities you cherish, you often don't get to them.

• Learn to appreciate and savor the wonderful things in life, rather than taking them for granted. One of the best ways to do this is by keeping a daily gratitude journal. Each night, before you go to sleep, write down at least five things that made or make you happy. These can be little or big—from a meal you enjoyed to a meaningful conversation you had with a friend, from a project at work, to God.

• **What if a person is going through a really hard time in his life—for example, he dislikes his job, but there's nothing he can do about it right away. How can that person be happier?** We all must endure periods, sometimes extended ones, in which much of what we do affords us minimal satisfaction. During those times, it's important to see these periods with a broader perspective and find ways to imbue them with meaning.

In a fascinating study of hospital janitors, one group experienced their work as mostly boring and meaningless, but the other group perceived these same duties as engaging and meaningful because they crafted their work in more creative ways. They interacted more with nurses and patients, and they saw their work not merely as removing the garbage and washing dirty linen but contributing to the patients' well-being and the smooth functioning of the hospital.

When changing your perception isn't feasible or effective, I find that one or two happy experiences during an otherwise uninspiring period can transform our general state. These brief but transforming experiences that I call "happiness boosters" provide us with meaning and pleasure.

For example, I recently met a partner in a large consulting firm. Now in his 50s, he no longer enjoys consulting, but at the same time, he doesn't want to leave his profession or give up the lifestyle that he and his family have grown accustomed to. He was able to reduce his workload enough to spend two evenings each week with his family. He also plays tennis twice a week and reads for three hours. He joined the board of his former high school, where he feels he can contribute in a meaningful way to the next generation. In an ideal world, he would be spending all his working hours doing something he's passionate about, but he is still happier than he has been in a long time.

Letting Go of Regret

Judy Kuriansky, PhD, a clinical psychologist and sex therapist on the adjunct faculty of Columbia University Teachers College in New York City. She's the author of five books, including *The Complete Idiot's Guide to a Healthy Relationship* (Alpha). Her online site is *www.sexualtherapy.com/therapists/jkuriansky.htm*.

Frank Sinatra sang, "Regrets, I've had a few…" and most individuals can relate to all of those nagging "shoulda woulda couldas." Minor regrets can be motivating—"I

should not have eaten dessert, but now I am determined to stick to my diet." But serious remorse—"Why didn't I reconcile with Mom before she died?"—unless dealt with, leads to long-lasting emotional anguish. *To make peace with the past…*

• **Admit your mistake to a friend or therapist**—not to dwell on the pain, but to release toxic guilt and persistent shame.

• **Analyze regretted events, looking for a lesson.** "Did my husband actually divorce me without warning, or did I ignore the signs of trouble?"

• **Accept responsibility for your actions**—"If I hadn't been fiddling with the radio while driving, I might not have hit the car that ran the red light." But also accept that you cannot control other people's behavior…and that "the past is what it is."

• **Apologize and make amends**—"I'm sorry I didn't visit you in the hospital. May I bring some meals while you recover at home?"

• **Appreciate what you did rather than bemoan what you missed.** Perhaps you never made it to law school, but as a full-time mom, you raised great kids. Take pride in saying, as Sinatra did, "I've loved, I've laughed and cried…I did it my way."

Boardroom Founder Reveals His Simple Secrets for Success

Martin Edelston, founder and chairman of Boardroom Inc., which is publisher of *Bottom Line/Personal, Bottom Line/Health, Bottom Line/Wealth, Bottom Line/Retirement, Bottom Line Natural Healing, Bottom Line/Women's Health* and numerous books, including *Bottom Line Yearbook 2010*. He is author of *I-Power: The Secrets of Great Business in Bad Times.* Boardroom's Web site is *www.bottomlinesecrets.com*.

When I was founding Boardroom Inc. in the basement of my home more than 35 years ago, I started with just $5,000 and a dream. Today Boardroom is one of the world's largest publishers of consumer newsletters, as well as one of America's largest publishers of hardcover nonfiction books, reaching many millions of readers.

The strategies I have followed over the years have helped my company to be successful in good times and resilient in bad times. They also have enriched my personal life. *In this difficult economy, these specific strategies are more important than ever...*

•**Seek out the top experts, and get their advice.** Learning from the top experts is what Boardroom is based upon—our publications make the world's best advice readily available to readers. I am passionate about getting expert advice because I have done this all my life.

Whenever I need to learn about a subject, I read every book about it that I can find. I learned graphic design, sales skills, even how to be a swimming teacher and a top-notch long-distance runner—all from books.

I also go directly to the experts themselves with my questions, and I have taught my children to do this as well.

Example: When my son, Sam, was trying to decide which colleges to apply to, both he and I wanted him to get the best advice possible. Max Birnbaum, author of a best-selling college guide, had been one of my high school teachers, so I called him and set up a meeting for the three of us.

One of the colleges Max recommended was Haverford College in Haverford, Pennsylvania. Neither my son nor I knew very much about this college, but it had an excellent academic reputation and was small enough to offer students a friendly, personal environment. Sam decided to turn down several bigger, better-known schools to attend Haverford—where he thrived, got a fine education and enjoyed more direct contact with professors than he would have had at a large college.

•**Think big...plan carefully...execute perfectly.** In 1993, after the first World Trade Center bombing, I became concerned about the safety of my employees. A number of experts I consulted believed that New York City was likely to be targeted again. After meeting with my company's executive team, I decided to relocate our offices out of New York City.

We spent two years researching and planning to make sure the move would be successful. A search committee and real estate consultant worked hard to find the optimal location—one that would be an easy commute, either by car or public transportation.

We found the perfect building in Connecticut, very close to the train station and shopping. We hired a relocation specialist to help us manage logistics—not only for the office move but also for employees who might want to move into homes closer to the new site. We designed a package of financial incentives to encourage employees to stay with us through the transition.

Our planning paid off big. On a Friday, we closed the New York office. The movers, transition team and computer people worked all weekend—and on Monday, all the computers in the new Connecticut location were up and running, and employees' boxes were by their new desks. Out of 75 employees, all but two stayed with us.

•**Follow up and follow up again to be sure that it's done right and on time.** We have more meetings than most companies, but all that communication prevents problems. By checking in with each other regularly, we avoid surprises and can make quick adjustments when we need to, saving ourselves time and costly mistakes.

We also have weekly phone meetings with our major vendors. Even when everything is going smoothly, these check-ins permit us to follow up and make sure that nothing is overlooked. We can catch potential problems before they become big issues.

•**Never accept "no"—and make it easy to say "yes."** I make it a point to try to turn "no" into "yes" by being persistent, finding creative ways to get people's attention and asking myself what they would say "yes" to.

Early in my career, I sold advertising space for the phone company. Whenever I thought a company would benefit from a boldface listing in the phone book, I didn't just tell them so. I would bring a mock-up of the proposed ad to the sales call so that the customer could see how it would make his/her business stand out from the others. I sold more listings than all the other salesmen in the office put together.

Many years after founding my company, I wrote to an executive at a major publisher to propose a new marketing venture that I believed could benefit us both. When I received no response to any of my letters, I got a 24-by-36-inch piece of poster board from my art department, wrote by hand a giant-sized letter and had it delivered to the executive by messenger. He replied to that letter, and we began a very successful business relationship.

• **Keep it simple.** There is a tendency to make things way too complicated, adding on bells and whistles without adding efficiency. I don't believe in using a complex system when a simple one will do.

Example: I keep track of my busy schedule using a simple paper calendar that I designed. It consists of one sheet of paper that fits in my shirt pocket. My assistant prints it out for me—one month appears on one side of the paper, the next month on the flip side. I can view my schedule for each month at a glance.

• **Look for constant, incremental improvement.** Over the past 20 years, we have used an employee suggestion system that we call I-Power. All employees, at all levels, are asked to contribute at least two suggestions every week on how to improve their own effectiveness, their departments' effectiveness or the effectiveness of the company as a whole. Every idea—good, bad or indifferent—gets a response and a reward of at least $1. Good ideas are implemented as quickly as possible.

This system of continuous improvement provides dramatic benefits. Productivity and job satisfaction are very high. Employees feel valued. The ideas generated have saved us substantial amounts of money.

Example: Soon after we implemented the I-Power program, an employee suggested that we produce our books slightly smaller so that they would weigh less than four pounds, thus qualifying for a lower postage rate. That one idea saved us hundreds of thousands of dollars a year.

• **Show appreciation.** I am always on the lookout for opportunities to show people how much they matter. This applies to employees, vendors, freelance writers, friends and family.

When I see an article that makes me think of someone I know, I clip it and send it to the person with a note. When we pay writers or vendors, I write personal notes on the payment slips. Sometimes I enclose little gifts. At Boardroom, we celebrate the anniversary of each employee's start date. On my children's birthdays, I not only give them gifts—I also send flowers to my wife.

People contribute so much to our lives. It's important to say thank you.

• **Never compromise integrity.** We stake our reputation on accuracy and integrity. I have excellent editors—and after all of these years, I still personally read every page of every issue of our newsletters.

I have an attitude of healthy skepticism. No matter how well-known a source is, if he/she has nothing substantial to say, we won't run the article. Our readers trust us, and I do everything I can to continue to earn that trust.

How to Achieve Any Goal in Four Simple Steps

Neil Fiore, PhD, psychologist and life coach based in Albany, California. He is author of four books, including *Awaken Your Strongest Self: Break Free of Stress, Inner Conflict, and Self-Sabotage* (McGraw-Hill).

Why do so many individuals fail to achieve their goals? Often the reason isn't their ability, willpower or desire. When the National Institutes of Health examined failed attempts to lose weight, quit smoking or exercise, they found that the most common reason for failure was poor preparation. People didn't make the necessary preparations before attempting big life changes… and they did not mentally prepare themselves for the inevitable setbacks.

Here is my four-step process to overcome these hurdles and accomplish your goals…

STEP 1: DEFINE YOUR GOAL

To achieve a goal, it's important to consider the pros and cons of making a change. It is not enough to tell yourself that you "have to" do something, because then you will feel like a victim and rebel against the process. It is not enough to tell yourself that you "want to" do something, because wanting is only dreaming, not reality. You have to truly "choose" a goal.

Example: Say to yourself, I'm not going on a diet because my doctor told me to. I'm going on a diet because I choose to be healthy.

Sometimes we lack confidence in our ability to achieve a goal because an earlier attempt failed. Do not wait until you feel confident before trying again—you might be waiting forever. We each have a stronger self that can decide that it's worth trying again despite any fears.

Helpful: Imagine that several years have passed and you've done nothing to achieve your goal. How bad would your situation be? How bad would you feel about your life?

By creating a clear mental picture of the future pain you would face if you do not pursue your goal, you can make it easier to face the near-term inconveniences and unpleasantness of taking action.

STEP 2: COMMIT TO CHANGE

Start searching for the best course toward your goal by experimenting with small changes that lead in the right direction. Don't get down on yourself if you have trouble sticking with these changes—at this stage, you're not yet attempting to achieve your big goal. You are simply gathering information about what works for you and what doesn't.

When an attempt doesn't produce the desired result, take a moment to ask yourself what went wrong with the experiment and what you can do to correct it. Do not start actually pursuing your goal until you create a plan that you believe you can see through to its conclusion.

Example: Angela, 29, had trouble with late-night snacking in front of the television. Through trial-and-error experimentation, she found that she had the most success avoiding snacks when she told herself that she was

required to fast for 12 hours in preparation for a doctor's exam the next morning. She used this mental tactic on the nights when she felt particularly tempted to snack.

Once you become more aware of the distractions that could pull you off the path to your goal, you can design a system that makes success more likely. Structure is better than discipline when it comes to clearing the hurdles that keep us from our goals.

Example: Bill, 42, had attempted to quit smoking twice before but failed both times. This time, he began by spending one week just noticing when and why he smoked. He learned that he would automatically reach for a cigarette in the morning to start the day… whenever he felt stressed on the job…when he felt lonely or down…and as a way to unwind at the end of the day.

Instead of struggling with willpower or discipline, as he had done before, this time Bill simply made it more difficult to automatically reach for a cigarette. Even before taking action to quit, he experimented with keeping cigarettes and ashtrays at least 20 feet away from his bedroom and other places where he was more likely to smoke.

This structural change gave him the time to take three deep breaths (about 15 seconds). He discovered that he could calm down without depending on smoking and nicotine. Within a few days, Bill found that most of the time he would rather take a breathing break than get up to find a cigarette.

STEP 3: TAKE ACTION

Accomplishing a goal requires more than just desire—it requires deadlines and a daily plan. Each day, write down the next step you need to take to achieve your goal and the time that day when you're going to work on it. Be clear about when and where you will start and what specifically you will do.

Example: Your goal is to eat more fruits and vegetables. The next step is to stock your kitchen with these foods. The time to do this is 6 pm today, when you stop at the supermarket on the way home from work.

Doing nothing is comfortable—striving for goals takes effort. But the process of working toward a goal becomes easier once we break through inertia and start building momentum. Just as a car must shift through its lower gears before it reaches cruising speed, so we must work our way through the initial discomfort of starting something new before we hit our stride.

Whenever you take a step toward your desired objective, take one moment to envision how wonderful you'll feel when your goal has been achieved. Reward every step along the way by imagining yourself happy, healthy and fulfilled.

STEP 4: BOUNCE BACK FROM SETBACKS

Setbacks are inevitable when we pursue an ambitious goal. To succeed, we must bounce back from all our mistakes and learn how to avoid them in the future.

Understand that a setback does not equal failure. If you successfully cease smoking for 29 days but slipped and smoked a cigarette on day 30, you still managed 29 cigarette-free days. When you get back on track tomorrow, that will be day 30 of your new smoke-free life, even if the 30 days were not consecutive. If you tell yourself you are back to day one, your feelings of frustration and hopelessness will demoralize you.

Self-criticism increases stress and decreases your chances of achieving your goal. Use soothing self-talk when you err.

Example: Tell yourself, I'm not going to make myself feel bad because I slipped up. My commitment is to trying.

Two questions that can help us learn from our setbacks…

• **What were the thoughts that preceded the mistake?** Perhaps you thought, I've had a really hard day. I deserve some ice cream. You need to prepare a better response for the next time these kinds of thoughts come to mind.

Example: Yes, I had a hard day, but I've also made a commitment to my body to eat healthy foods. An apple is a perfectly satisfying snack.

• **What was the situation that led to the lapse?** Perhaps you are more prone to poor decisions when you have been drinking…or when you have had a fight with your spouse…

or when you see others doing what you have resolved to quit.

If you can avoid these situations in the future, you are more likely to remain on course. That might mean having just one beer rather than drinking until your judgment becomes impaired…or making up with your loved one quickly after fights, rather than letting the bad feelings linger…or avoiding locations where other people do the things that you are trying to stop.

Secrets of the Country's Most Successful, And Nicest, Negotiator

Ronald Shapiro, Esq., a principal at the law firm Shapiro Sher Guinot & Sandler, *www.shapirosher.com*, and founder of the Shapiro Negotiations Institute in Baltimore, *http://shapironegotiations.com*. Shapiro is the author of *Dare to Prepare: How to Win Before You Begin* (Three Rivers) and a coauthor of *The Power of Nice: How to Negotiate So Everyone Wins* (Wiley).

You negotiate all of the time, whether it is making decisions with your spouse, haggling over the price of a sales item or booking a hotel and bargaining for a better deal. Many of my clients dislike this process because they think they need to manipulate others to get what they want.

Over the course of my career, I've made successful deals for clients ranging from Fortune 500 companies to police departments facing racial conflicts. I've negotiated more than a billion dollars worth of contracts for professional athletes. But I never burned bridges nor sacrificed my integrity. In fact, being nice helped me achieve more of my goals and build relationships with less stress and greater returns.

MY "WIN/WIN" STRATEGY

It is common to think of negotiation as a onetime, "zero-sum event"—with the goal being I win, you lose. But most "deals" in your professional and personal lives are really daily, monthly or yearly pieces of larger or ongoing deals. If you have an annual family tussle over where and how to spend the holidays, you know what I mean.

Better: Instead of trying to dominate the other person in a negotiation, make the best deal you can for yourself by helping him/her get what he wants. I call this a WIN for you, a win for him.

Example: You go to your local electronics store to purchase a certain DVD player. You don't want to spend more than $150, but the salesman refuses to accept less than $200. At this point, many buyers will walk out, threatening to never shop there again...cave in and spend the extra 50 dollars...or buy a different brand that they don't like as much. Instead, you notice a floor model on display. You offer the salesman $125 for the floor model, but to protect yourself, you ask him to give you the $99, three-year extended warranty for just $25. He agrees.

The result: You walk away with your DVD player at your price without being a pushover. And, the deal is acceptable to the salesman because you helped him get what he wanted, a sale.

BEFORE THE NEGOTIATION

• **Identify what you really want.**

Example: You decide to sell your house and relocate. You spend months in fruitless negotiations with buyers because you refuse to budge from your price, which is the same amount your neighbor down the street sold his house for.

Better: Realize that what you really want is to make enough money to meet your financial goals and buy your next house on your time-table, regardless of whether your sale price is the highest in the neighborhood.

• **Weigh all the alternatives.** If you realize there are several possible solutions that can satisfy you, you'll be less dependent on one kind of outcome. For example, before in the electronics store, what would have happened if the salesman had refused your offer to buy the floor model of the DVD player? If you had considered that possibility beforehand, you could have brought along enough money to offer cash for it—which would let the store

avoid paying a fee for accepting your credit card payment.

• **Know your walk-away number.** Figure out at what point the only satisfying outcome is not to do any deal at all. Face this tough question in advance—otherwise you risk becoming emotionally involved during negotiations and lowering your expectations as the deal progresses.

DURING THE NEGOTIATION

• **Build a relationship**—even if short-term. Look for common ground (for example, "Do you live in the area too?"..."My friend thinks highly of your work"). This builds trust and encourages the other person to believe that you won't ignore his needs.

• **Find out what the other side wants.** The more information you have about the other party's expectations, the easier it is to come up with solutions that make a mutually satisfying deal. *Effective techniques...*

• Ask the other party lots of questions, the same ones you asked yourself beforehand. Ask him about his ideal outcome. What alternatives to his ideal outcome might be acceptable? What's his walk-away number? He may not tell you, but it doesn't hurt to ask.

• Ask the other person to restate what he just said. It is amazing how often the restatement turns out to be different from the original. People tend to explain more each time they state their positions, to give more details, to soften their stances and even offer options to what previously seemed like a hard line.

• **Phrase potentially confrontational questions and statements neutrally.** Ask, "Aren't you charging me more than we agreed?," not "You're ripping me off, aren't you?" Speak hypothetically to soften up your suggestions. Try phrases like "Just suppose..."

MAKING AN OFFER

• **Have the other person speak first.** This works best in price negotiations where you know the other person has a range of prices he may agree to, such as in a salary negotiation.

Reason: If you make the initial offer, you might be setting your sights too low. Even if the offer you get is far less advantageous than you hoped for, you now have a minimum on which to build.

• **Never extend an offer without knowing where you're willing to go next.** If you know where and what you can concede, you'll never feel like you were ripped off. The deals you make will feel satisfying because they fall within the parameters of your plan.

IF NEGOTIATIONS REACH AN IMPASSE OR TURN NEGATIVE

• **Use the "finger-on-the-lips" move.** If I feel that I'm about to blurt out words that I'll regret, I put my finger up to my mouth. To anyone else, it just looks like I am thinking. I follow that action with some deep breaths. Then I switch the tape in my head from an insecure voice to one that is pumping positive mantras such as, "I can handle this. I'm not going to take it personally."

• **Ask, "What would you do if you were on my side of the table?"** Getting the other party to see things through your eyes can help lift him out of an entrenched position.

Hint: If the other party responds, "If I were you, I'd take the deal I'm offering," probe further. Ask, "How do you think that would benefit me?"

• **Change environments.** Sometimes moving to a different location can break negative momentum and create a new atmosphere for the negotiations.

Example: Several years ago, I was negotiating a deal for Cal Ripken, Jr., the soon-to-be Hall of Fame baseball player, with his team, the Baltimore Orioles. The Orioles owner proposed a salary of $20 million over four years—what top shortstops were earning. We wanted a five-year deal worth almost $50 million, on par with the top players regardless of position. The team owner and I were deadlocked at $30 million apart, so I moved the negotiations from my Baltimore offices to my farm in Butler, Maryland. The fresh air and laid-back environment allowed each side to confess its real needs and pave the way for a deal.

Upshot: We arrived at a five-year, $32.5 million deal in which the Orioles agreed to provide post-career compensation guarantees,

which added dollars to the overall contract but did not raise Ripken's pay for active years.

Everybody won. Cal got immediate and post-career security. The Orioles retained their Hall of Famer without having to make him the highest-paid player in baseball.

BEST WAY TO FINISH UP

• **Lay the groundwork to have a continuing relationship.** Compliment the other party, either in person or on the phone, on his negotiating skills that helped lead to a fair deal for both of you. For instance, over the course of my career, I've gone on to represent many ballplayers in negotiation with the Baltimore Orioles, including three other Hall of Famers.

How to Make A Great First Impression

Harry Beckwith and Christine Clifford Beckwith, Minneapolis-based founders of the consulting company Beckwith Partners. Their clients include Fidelity, Merck and IBM. They are authors of the best seller *You, Inc.: The Art of Selling Yourself* (Warner). Their online site is *www.beckwithpartners.com.*

Best ways to make a great impression—whether you are trying to win over a new business contact or impress your future in-laws...

• **Let the joke be on you.** The problem with most jokes is that they are made at someone else's expense, whether it is a blonde joke, a Polish joke or almost any other kind. The one kind of joke that never hurts anyone's feelings is the one aimed at yourself. Pick something small and silly that happened to you recently. This will endear you to others.

• **Be unforgettable.** We knew one marketer with a client who loved baseball. She found an unusual baseball, bought it and sent it to the client. With that one unforgettable gift, she cemented a lasting professional relationship.

• **Don't send a holiday card.** Nearly every company sends its clients and associates cards around the Christmas holidays. With so many holiday cards coming in, yours is just one in the crowd. Instead, send cards throughout the year on truly special occasions—on a client's birthday, his child's graduation or when his favorite team wins a game.

- **Remember people's names.** The easiest way to remember a person's name is through vivid images. You can associate a new person with a famous person.

Example: If you meet a Tom, think of Tom Cruise and imagine the new Tom on a cruise ship.

- **Show respect.** An easy way to show respect is to actively listen. One way to do this is to listen in images. If the person you are listening to is talking about a skiing trip she took, imagine her racing down the mountain. Next, when it's your turn to speak, pause for a second before responding. It shows that you were really listening instead of just waiting for your turn to speak.

How to Get Along with People You Don't Like But Still Need to See

Dale V. Atkins, PhD, psychologist and relationship expert in private practice in New York City and coauthor of *Sanity Savers: Tips for Women to Live a Balanced Life* (HarperCollins). She is author of the online newsletter *Sanity Savers and More.* Dr. Atkins also is a frequent guest on NBC's *Today* and other TV shows. Her Web site is *www.drdaleatkins.com.*

I t is inevitable that at some point we will have to spend time with people we don't like. Maybe you don't like your spouse's best friend or your daughter's boyfriend. *Here are some simple guidelines for getting through these tricky situations…*

YOU DON'T GET ALONG WELL WITH A RELATIVE

This is someone you can't avoid completely but with whom you can spend only so much time before he/she starts to drive you crazy. Perhaps your sister is a slob, and you're very tidy…or you have a parent you love, but who is overly critical.

With these people, it is best to keep activities confined to neutral zones, such as going to a movie or a restaurant. Usually, in these places, conversations will not get too out of hand. With a movie, you'll be able to talk only before and after, though you're still spending time together. Also, these activities have built-in time limits, so you will be spending quality time with someone you love, but you'll also be giving yourself an exit.

Keep in mind that while you may be tempted, it's usually not worth your time to try to redesign someone's personality. This almost always meets with resistance and can lead to fights. Just try to focus on the best aspects of his/her personality.

YOU DON'T LIKE YOUR PARTNER'S FRIEND

When you don't like your partner's friend, it can be difficult for both you and your partner. First, try your best to see things through your partner's eyes, and try to find something you like or can appreciate about his friend. It can be something as simple as appreciating his sense of style or a joke he told once.

Let your partner know that it's OK to do things without you, but try to be there if there's an important event in the friend's life—for example, a wedding or a party for a promotion at work.

Never try to turn your partner against his friend. You don't have to like him as much as your partner does, but you should respect the relationship. Don't be rude or say nasty things about him.

YOUR PARTNER DOESN'T LIKE YOUR FRIEND

Let your partner know that it is OK to not like your friend, but it's not OK to be rude or dismissive to him/her. Ask that the same respect be shown to your friends that you show to your partner's friends.

Cultivate your relationship with your friend without your partner, and do not insist that everyone spend time together. Sometimes it is easier to do this during the week, instead of the weekend, when you may have obligations to your family.

YOU DON'T LIKE YOUR CHILD'S SPOUSE

One of the trickiest situations is when your child marries someone whom you do not like. It can be very hard to hide your feelings, but for the sake of your relationship with your child, it's a good idea. Make every effort to get along with your child's spouse. Do your best to care about him/her and show him respect.

Don't say anything bad about your child's spouse. You do not want to put your child in the middle of a conflict between you and his spouse, and it is not fair to make your child choose between you and the spouse.

If there is a legitimate issue between you and your child's spouse—for example, if she is rude to you in public—it's best to pull her aside at another time and try to work it out.

YOU DON'T AGREE WITH A LOVED ONE'S CHOICES

It is always hard to see someone you love making bad choices. Maybe a child is spending too much time partying at college or a friend is in a damaging relationship.

Talk to him/her in an open way, and share your concerns—but don't pressure and don't be overly judgmental. Discuss with him the consequences of his actions. For example, if your child is partying at school more than studying, there is a real chance that he could flunk out. Remember that he must choose to change—you can't force that on anyone. Tell him that you love him and that you always will, but that you don't agree with his choices.

One way to reduce the stress you feel when seeing a friend or relative in situations you don't agree with is to focus on your own wisdom and be grateful for what you have and who you are.

YOU DON'T LIKE YOUR HOUSEGUEST

Sometimes there's no way to avoid having your castle invaded by people who get under your skin—whether it is your partner's old college roommate or your great-aunt Helen.

Try to carve out a bit of time for yourself. Find something relaxing and recharging that you love to do. Go on a quiet walk by yourself...have a relaxing bath...or meditate.

It may help to put your guests to work if they are staying with you for more than a few days. Having them do some dishes or fold some laundry can help to greatly reduce your own stress level. If you have less stress and less work to do, you might even enjoy your guests.

The Three-Sentence Secret to Resolving Your Differences with Anyone...Yes, Anyone

Lee Raffel, MSW, a practicing psychotherapist for more than 35 years in Port Washington, Wisconsin. She is also author of *I Hate Conflict: Seven Steps to Resolving Differences with Anyone in Your Life* (McGraw-Hill). Raffel is a clinical member of the American Association for Marriage and Family Therapy and a board-certified diplomate in psychotherapy and behavioral medicine.

I am often amazed at the lengths my patients will go to so that they can sweep conflict under the rug—they'll tiptoe around difficult issues and people for years, playing the martyr and hoping that change will occur all by itself.

Examples: Your spouse's family criticizes you, but your spouse says nothing...you find out that a friend has been gossiping about you...you send your grandchildren gifts, but never receive acknowledgment from them.

Many patients suffer emotionally because they're afraid that confrontations will cause more pain and stress and jeopardize their relationships.

Good news: There are ways to defuse tense situations and shape conversations to create satisfying resolutions.

You won't have to sweep conflict under the rug. In fact, you'll likely experience a renewal of energy and more peace from speaking up. *The best strategies...*

ESTABLISH GROUND RULES

To better put aside differences with your spouse or someone close to you, tell him/her that you want to try something new the next time that you have a disagreement—each of you will take turns speaking, saying what you need to in no more than three sentences. Having rules to play by alleviates anxieties during fights.

The three-sentence technique prevents both parties from making long-winded complaints and forces you to focus on what really matters. It also encourages better listening—most listeners tune out after hearing three sentences and start preparing their replies.

Helpful: If you think that the other person isn't paying attention, stop talking. Eventually, he will notice the silence. At that point, say, "I just wanted to wait to speak until I had your full attention."

MAKE COMPROMISES

Think about the compromises that you are willing to make to resolve an issue before you begin discussing it. As soon as an argument begins, most people focus in on their desired outcome, convinced that they are 100% right. They are annoyed and indignant to find out that the other party also feels 100% right.

Example: You and your spouse plan to go on vacation. You want to visit a European city, but your spouse prefers a beach resort in the Caribbean. Every conversation you have deteriorates quickly because you try to convince your spouse to see more cultural places while your spouse says that you need to learn how to relax.

Better: Before you talk the next time, list the specific concessions you might make (for instance, you would go to a European city on the Mediterranean...go to the Bahamas in the winter, but Paris next summer).

AVOID ESCALATION

Certain "loaded" words increase the tension and alienate each side in a disagreement...

• **Starting sentences with the word "you."**

Reason: It's accusatory. "You will not give me a definitive answer"..."You keep attacking me."

Better: Begin sentences with "I." It's less inflammatory and makes the other person more empathetic because you are describing how his behavior is affecting you: "I would really appreciate a firm yes or no"..."I am upset by your repeated verbal attacks."

• **Using the words "always" and "never."**

Reason: They are inaccurate and simplistic absolutes—"You never listen to what I am saying"..."You're always picky." These words sidetrack you from the issue that you're discussing. Inevitably, the other person responds by defending himself and presenting evidence of all the times he did listen or wasn't picky.

• **Saying "I don't know."**

Reason: It's so vague that it leads to misinterpretation.

Example: Someone asks you to volunteer to serve with her on a committee. It is for a good cause, but you really don't want any involvement with this person—nor do you want to offend her. If you say, "I don't know," it could mean "I honestly don't know"..."I don't have enough information"..."I actually do know, but I'm not telling"..."I'm lying, but I don't want you to know." *Instead say:* "I wish I could help you, but I just don't have the time to do it."

KEEP YOUR COOL

If the other person yells, loses control or speaks rudely and inappropriately, this is your cue to stay in control of your behavior. If you retaliate in kind, the bickering will escalate, making resolution very unlikely. *What to do...*

• **Acknowledge his frustration.** Say, "I can see that you are upset." This makes him feel like you are making an effort to understand his point of view.

If the other person continues with an emotional and/or nasty outburst, say, "Stop." If he presses on, then loudly and firmly repeat, the word "Stop."

"Stop" is a good word because it's not particularly offensive, so it does not ramp up the heat in the discussion. In fact, the other person is usually so surprised by this word, he just stops escalating the argument. Next, take a few minutes apart to cool down, or tell the other person that you need to continue the conversation later.

APOLOGIZE EFFECTIVELY

Even if a conflict is ultimately resolved, a hurtful statement made when you argued can trigger bad feelings that lead to more disagreements later.

Solution: Apologizing is one powerful act that can help both parties heal. *But to work, it must be done well…*

• **Be direct and specific about what you did that was hurtful.** Say, "I'm sorry for snapping at you in the car when we got lost."

• **Tell the person how you believe that his actions offended,** and check in with him to see if you've interpreted it correctly. Say: "When you try to help and I raise my voice, you feel anxious and belittled. Is that right?"

• **Explain what you've learned from this experience** and what you will do to address your bad behavior.

Say: "I know I have a sharp tongue when I get frustrated. I need to be more careful and tone it down."

PUT AGREEMENTS IN WRITING

People are more likely to respect the written word, which leads to more long-lasting results. A written agreement can be about how to conduct discussions ("I promise to avoid distractions like getting on the computer or answering the phone when we are having a conflict"). Or it can be about what you've concluded from your discussions ("I will not buy anything from late-night infomercials without checking with you"). Date the document, and have both parties sign it. This is an effective way to ensure that there are no misunderstandings in the future.

AGREE TO DISAGREE

In my practice, I've found that about one-third of all major conflicts are nonnegotiable. Neither partner will change his mind about the issue because each feels it is an integral part of who he is.

Example: An elderly parent who can no longer take care of himself refuses to move into a nursing home. In such cases, it's often best to yield to the person's wishes, but ask him to make a concession to you in some area that's less threatening. For instance, the elderly parent doesn't have to give up his home, but he must accept a day nurse. This is the simplest way to compromise without getting bogged down in useless arguing.

The Right Way To Speak Up When You Feel Wronged

Joseph Grenny, co-chairman of VitalSmarts, a corporate training company based in Provo, Utah, *www.vitalsmarts.com*. He is coauthor of *Crucial Confrontations: Tools for Resolving Broken Promises, Violated Expectations, and Bad Behavior* (McGraw-Hill).

These steps can increase the odds that your confrontations will lead to productive discussion rather than anger…

1. Assume the best. When we imagine nefarious motives behind people's actions, our confrontations are likely to become emotional. Take the self-righteousness and indignity out of your thoughts, and tell yourself it was an honest mistake.

Example: When you assume the best of a line-cutter at the movie theater, you say things like, "I'm sorry, but were you aware that we've been standing here in line?" This presumption of innocence avoids an accusation and starts the conversation on the right foot.

2. Think about how this person is like you. This should make you more understanding, reducing the odds that your confrontation will be taken as an attack.

Example: If someone lies to you, consider occasions when you have been less than 100% forthright before confronting him.

3. Gather the facts. Perhaps there were legitimate reasons why this person did what he did. Do what you can to find out before the confrontation.

4. Ask for "permission" to raise the difficult subject, then present the situation factually and unemotionally. This minimizes the odds that this person will become defensive, improving your chances for a positive outcome.

Example: "I wonder if we could discuss something that has been bothering me."

5. Invite dialogue. Ask, "What's your position on this?" or "How do you feel about what I've just said?" after presenting your case. This turns criticism into conversation.

Don't Lose Your Cool: Better Ways to Defuse Anger

Ronald Potter-Efron, PhD, MSW, clinical psychotherapist, First Things First Counseling and Consulting, Ltd., Eau Claire, Wisconsin.

Most of us have been on the brink of blowing up in anger at one time or another. *Here's how to stay cool before you say or do something you'll regret...*

•**Smile.** You cannot get truly angry when smiling. Relax your jaw, forehead and lip muscles, then grin.

•**Think ahead.** Decide whether the situation making you angry will matter in five minutes, five days or five years.

•**Take charge of your emotions.** Tell yourself that you are choosing not to get angry about something. Or you can choose to express your anger—but telling yourself it is a choice keeps you in control.

•**Become more flexible.** Accept that things will not always go as you wish, accidents happen and people are not perfect.

•**Consider the consequences.** Think about the harm that you may cause if you blow up at a person over something that, in the long run, is not especially important.

Rudeness Is Rampant Today: The Polite Way To Handle It

Pier Forni, PhD, founder and director of Johns Hopkins University's Civility Initiative, a coalition of academic and community participants that assesses civility in contemporary society (*http://krieger.jhu.edu/civility*). Dr. Forni's latest book is *The Civility Solution* (St. Martin's).

In today's fast-paced, youth-oriented culture, ageism often results in rudeness to older people. Here, Dr. Pier Forni, founder of the Civility Initiative at Johns Hopkins University and the author of two books on civility and rudeness, answers questions on how to handle this type of rudeness...

•**Why not just ignore rudeness?** After all, it usually amounts to little more than a few ill-mannered words or a gesture. Rudeness isn't trivial. It can cause stress, weaken self-confidence and harm relationships.

By addressing rudeness head-on, you discourage this kind of behavior while building your self-esteem and reducing stress. The key to addressing rudeness is to do it firmly but politely.

•**What should you do when someone is talking loudly or slowly even though your hearing is perfectly normal?** Sooner or later, most older people encounter this type of behavior, which may be a misguided attempt at being very polite.

You might be tempted just to listen and say nothing about it, but that's usually a mistake. The other person may not realize that he/she is being ill-mannered. So politely inform the person that your hearing is good. But do not get angry or make accusations, which often leads to a stress-inducing argument.

Something like this usually works: "I appreciate your wanting to make sure that I hear everything you say, but I can assure you that my hearing is fine."

•**Assuming that you know nothing about technology, a store clerk speaks to you as though you were a child. How do you set the clerk straight?** If you are technologically astute, mention something to this person that gets this point across. If you're buying a computer, for example, you might tell the clerk that your current machine has a Pentium dual-core processor with a 250-gigabyte hard drive. The clerk will get the message.

On the other hand, if you don't know much about the product you are buying, do some homework before shopping—a strategy that makes sense at any age.

•**A maître d' seats you at an uncomfortable table in the far back of a restaurant. Meanwhile, younger customers are given better tables up front. What is the best way to handle this?** Immediately tell the maître d' that you want another table. If the second table he suggests isn't better, ask to speak with the manager.

Say to the manager something like this: "We're here to enjoy our dinner, but that will be difficult at this table. We do not want to leave, but we'll have to if you can't help us get a better one."

Never be afraid to leave an establishment where you are not treated well. In this case, remember that you're paying the same prices that younger diners at the front tables pay. Sure, you may wind up having to go to another restaurant, but the inconvenience will probably be more tolerable than sitting through a meal at a table that you dislike.

•**According to their stereotype, older people often drive too slowly. So what should you do when you are driving at the speed limit but the driver in back of you honks, flashes his lights or even tailgates?** Driving is one of the few occasions when you shouldn't confront a rude person. Rude drivers are often under stress, and confronting them can lead to an accident.

Instead, depersonalize the incident. Take a relaxing breath and remind yourself that the other driver would likely honk at any car that was driving only the speed limit. In fact, the driver probably hasn't even noticed that you're older. So let him pass, and resist the temptation to curse or make a hand gesture, which risks escalating the incident into violence.

And don't equate honking with rudeness. The other driver may actually have an emergency and need to move around you. More likely, however, he's just having a bad day. (It happens to all of us.)

Incidents like this illustrate an important point: Happiness in life often depends on being satisfied with decisions—not immediately after we make them, but later on when there's time to reflect. It might be immediately satisfying to curse or to make a hand gesture, but on reflection, you'll almost certainly regret stooping to someone else's level or being rude yourself.

•**Today, e-mail from friends can be a major source of rudeness, typically in the form of forwarded messages with coarse jokes, political commentaries, etc. What's the best way of dealing with them?** Don't shy away from asking the sender—either via e-mail or telephone—to stop mailing these messages to you. Politely say that you appreciate the information but that you don't have time to read it. Then, if the sender is a friend, consider making a gracious gesture, such as saying that you would like to get together for lunch or coffee in the near future.

In fact, being considerate and civil can go a long way in preventing many types of rudeness. Most people you deal with will take that attitude as a cue to respond in kind.

For example, when you go to a restaurant, greet the maître d' with a warm smile and say something like: "Tonight is a special occasion for us. We would really like the best table available." You'll almost always get a better table than if you entered the restaurant with a demanding look on your face.

Actually, just smiling can often prevent being slighted. If you're standing at a store counter and others are served first, for instance, tell the clerk, "I've been waiting for some time and just want to make sure that you know I'm here."

Be polite and smile when you speak. Smiling tells the other person that dealing with you will be a pleasant experience...that you want to build rapport, not start an argument.

If you have any doubts about the way others perceive your attitude, ask for an honest opinion from a close friend. All too often, we assume that we're polite and put on a pleasant face when we deal with strangers, but that's not always the case, especially in today's often stressful world. The opinion of a good friend can help you see yourself as others do.

When a Phone Call Is Better Than E-Mail And How to Do It Right

Susan RoAne, a networking expert based in the San Francisco Bay area, *www.susanroane.com.* She is author of several books on networking, including *Face to Face: How to Reclaim the Personal Touch in a Digital World* (Fireside).

E-mail and text-messaging do have their place, but an old-fashioned phone call often is our best communication option. *How to do it right...*

•**Write a one- or two-sentence summary of the reason for your call.** Writing this "note to self" forces you to think through what you want to say and keeps you focused during the phone call.

•**Be prepared to speak to a person or voicemail.** Not being prepared for both possibilities is a common cause of flubbed calls.

If you reach voicemail...succinctly explain the purpose of the call, but speak slowly, particularly when you are providing your phone number. If you want a call back, say so. "I'd appreciate hearing from you" is my choice of words.

If you reach the person and it's not someone you know well, provide your name and a one-sentence explanation of why this person should trust you and speak with you.

Example: "Sally Johnson suggested I call."

•**Ask, "Is this a bad time to talk?"** This question sounds like a polite attempt to consider the other person's schedule, but it also is a simple way to obtain tacit permission to take up this person's time. If their response is "no," then you have permission to proceed with the call now. If the answer is "yes," ask, "When would be a better time?" When he/she

provides a time, he essentially has agreed to speak with you then.

•**Determine whether chattiness or being straight-to-the-point is most appropriate.** The response you receive to the "Is this a bad time to talk?" is a clue. A friendly "Not at all, how can I help?" usually means a little conversation would be welcomed, but a terse "I can spare one minute" suggests that it is probably best to keep it brief.

•**Imagine that you're speaking to a friend** if you're calling someone you don't know well. Act as if the person is already open to talking to you and he's more likely to be so.

Expressing Sympathy: Dos and Don'ts

Phyllis Kosminsky, PhD, clinical social worker specializing in grief, loss and trauma, Center for Hope Family Centers, Darien, Connecticut.

It's often difficult to know just what to do or say when offering your condolences, and you certainly don't want to make the situation worse. *Here are some pointers...*

•**Do say, "I am thinking about you."**

•**Do make a concrete offer to help,** such as by making dinners for three days.

•**Do consider making a donation** in the deceased's name to a charity that you know he or she cared about and letting the family know what you have done.

•**Don't say that the deceased is in a better place**—this may be true for your beliefs but not others'.

•**Don't tell a grieving person that he just needs to stay busy**—you do not know what is best.

•**Do not say that you know what he is going through**—everyone experiences grief differently.

•**Don't force the bereaved to accept a hug** that he may not want.

Better: Approach him with your hands out.

Six-Minute Memory Booster

Napping during the day—for as little as six minutes—brings better performance on memory exercises.

Possible reason: The act of falling asleep might trigger a neurological process that improves memory—even if actual sleep time is minimal.

Olaf Lahl, PhD, researcher, Institute of Experimental Psychology, University of Dusseldorf, Germany.

The Cholesterol/Memory Loss Connection

Memory loss is associated with low levels of "good" (HDL) cholesterol.

Recent study: People whose HDL was below 40 mg/dL at age 55 were 27% more likely to have a memory deficit than people whose HDL was above 60 mg/dL. At age 61, those with low HDL levels were 53% more likely to suffer memory problems.

To boost HDL: Get regular aerobic exercise …maintain a healthy weight…limit intake of saturated fat…don't smoke.

Archana Singh-Manoux, PhD, senior research fellow in epidemiology and public health, University College London, England, and lead author of a study of 3,673 people, published in *Arteriosclerosis, Thrombosis and Vascular Biology*.

Have Someone Remember for You

Your can set up a free account at Rminder (*www.rminder.com*), and the service will call you to remind you about appointments and events, or you can set up reminders for friends or forgetful loved ones. A free account lets you set up to eight reminders a month, and you can send up to 15, 30 or 60 reminders with monthly plans for $3, $5 and $9 a month.*

Dave Boyer, a research editor and resident computer guru at *Bottom Line/Personal*, Boardroom Inc., 281 Tresser Blvd., Stamford, Connecticut 06901.

*Prices subject to change.

Stay Connected to Stem Memory Loss

Social connections might prevent memory loss. A recent study of more than 16,000 people age 50 and older asked participants to take verbal memory tests over six years.

Findings: Those who had the fewest social connections with friends, family and in the community suffered a decline in memory capacity at twice the rate as those with the most.

Conclusion: This is yet another example of how being socially engaged is beneficial for mental health.

Lisa F. Berkman, PhD, department of sociology, human development and health, Harvard School of Public Health, and lead study author.

Web Surfing Builds Brainpower

Did you know that surfing the Web is good for the brain?

Recent study: Researchers measured brain activity in 24 healthy adults (ages 55 to 76) as they either performed searches on the Internet or read books.

Result: Internet searching triggered more extensive brain activity than did reading. Experienced Web surfers showed nearly twice the level of brain function as those unfamiliar with the Internet.

A theory: Internet searching demands the ability to quickly evaluate significant amounts of information.

Gary Small, MD, director, Memory and Aging Research Center, University of California, Los Angeles.

Online Networking For Grown-Ups

Marjory Abrams, publisher, *Bottom Line* newsletters, Boardroom Inc., 281 Tresser Blvd., Stamford, Connecticut 06901.

My teenagers and all their friends love to communicate through Facebook.com. Though Facebook attracts more than 30 million visitors every month—and not just young people—these "social networking" sites simply hold zero appeal for me. I spend enough time on my computer for work.

Then again, I don't want cyber-world innovations to pass me by. I recently talked about these sites with Michael Solomon, PhD, director of the Center for Consumer Research at Saint Joseph's University in Philadelphia. He recently was co-chair of a conference on virtual social identity. Inspired by our conversation, I decided to spend some time on MyBoomerPlace.com, a site that's targeted to people age 40 and up.

I was pleasantly surprised to discover that it does not blitz users with advertisements. Like the other social-networking sites, it does require free registration. Once registered, you can send a message to any member or instant-message other members who are online the same time you are. Messages go through the MyBoomerPlace system, so all personal e-mail addresses stay confidential.

I did not put up a profile, but I did check out some other members' profiles. The profiles give age, city and state of residence and, often, interests—movies, music, etc. Most include a photo.

A friend just moved to North Carolina, so I decided to look for members who live near her. The search turned up roughly a dozen people, and I passed along the new contacts. Members also can search by gender and age.

Internet communities can be an excellent way to find people who have shared interests and concerns. MyBoomerPlace offers close to 200 groups. Topics include chronic pain, barbecues (recipes and equipment), fast cars and hot motorcycles, fishing stories, genealogy and many more. Members with similar interests can post and reply to messages in the forums. Anyone can start a new group at any time.

Among the other social-networking sites for grown-ups…

• **BOOMj.com.** For people born from the mid-1940s to the mid-1960s, this site is similar to MyBoomerPlace, but it includes news stories and more advertisements.

• **Classmates.com.** Find school friends, former colleagues, military buddies and more.

• **LinkedIn.com.** This career-oriented network connects people in different businesses.

• **Multiply.com.** Share photos, music and blogs, as well as restaurant and movie reviews. Schedule events with family and friends.

You can find a specialized online community for almost any interest simply by entering your topic of interest and the words "social network" or "online community" in Google or another search engine.

Online communities can become addictive for some people, Dr. Solomon notes, and they also can play host to deceivers, manipulators and bullies. Don't post details about yourself that could embarrass you or make it easy for a stranger to find or impersonate you. It's difficult to erase information once you put it up.

Which Psychotherapy Is Right for You?

Jonathan Jackson, PhD, a clinical professor of psychology at Adelphi University and director of Adelphi's Center for Psychological Services at the Derner Institute of Advanced Psychological Studies, both in Garden City, New York.

Research has now shown that emotional problems can be just as disabling—and deadly—as physical illnesses. Depression, for example, could worsen a variety of serious health ailments such as heart disease, diabetes, arthritis and asthma.

Latest development: A US law has recently been passed that requires health insurers to provide equal coverage for the treatment of physical and emotional problems beginning in 2010. This change will allow more people to afford psychotherapy.

HOW PSYCHOTHERAPY WORKS

Psychotherapy involves communication between the therapist and the person looking for help, usually in a series of weekly individual sessions ($75 to $200 each,* depending on the part of the country where you live) that typically last 45 to 50 minutes each.

Important: You are most likely to get good results from psychotherapy if you work with a competent therapist who makes you feel understood and accepted. A recommendation by a physician, trusted friend, relative or member of the clergy is often helpful.

In many US states, anyone can call himself or herself a therapist, but only licensed practitioners are sure to have appropriate training and qualifications. Clinical psychologists (who hold an advanced degree, such as a doctor of philosophy, PhD, in psychology or a doctor of psychology, PsyD)…social workers (who have earned a master's degree in social work with an emphasis in clinical approaches)…and psychiatrists (medical doctors who can prescribe medication)—among numerous other practitioners—can all obtain their licenses to practice psychotherapy.

To verify that a therapist is licensed by the professional body that governs his specialty, contact your state's health department.

Most therapists specialize in one particular type of therapy or a combination of therapies.

Best types of therapy include…

COGNITIVE BEHAVIORAL THERAPY (CBT)

Main premise: Psychological problems are tied to irrational beliefs and thoughts—for example, a depressed person thinking that everything in his life is bad. When the irrational beliefs are replaced with more realistic ones, symptoms typically improve.

*Prices subject to change.

What it's good for: Depression, anxiety, obsessive-compulsive disorder, eating disorders and post-traumatic stress disorder.

Typical duration: Six to 20 sessions.

PSYCHODYNAMIC THERAPY

Main premise: Difficulties in the present are rooted in feelings and actions from your earlier life.

What it's good for: Difficulty forming or maintaining relationships and/or interpersonal conflict at work or with friends or family.

Typical duration: Because patterns that are identified in psychodynamic therapy can be subtle and elusive, it may last for six months to two years or more.

INTERPERSONAL THERAPY (IPT)

Main premise: Psychological problems result from difficulties in connecting and communicating with other people.

What it's good for: A person who lacks satisfying relationships or is adjusting to life changes (divorce or job loss, for example).

Typical duration: IPT generally adheres to a timetable, such as 12 to 16 weekly sessions, established at the onset of therapy.

THERAPY SETTINGS

Even though most psychotherapy happens in individual sessions with the patient and a therapist, there are other settings in which the therapies described earlier may be used alone or in combination.

Among the most common…

•**Group therapy.** A grouping of five to 10 people meet and give one another feedback—most often, in the presence of a therapist.

What it's good for: A specific problem that participants share—such as anger, a phobia, panic attacks, social anxiety or grief.

Typical duration: The groups that focus on problems that are shared by its members (such as those described above) are likely to be limited to 12 to 20 sessions. Other groups, which tackle long-standing problems, such as emotional isolation or excessive dependency, can go on indefinitely. Members may stay for several months or years and then be replaced by new members. Sessions generally last 60 to 90 minutes for both types of groups.

Important: Insurance often does not cover group therapy, which typically costs 50% to 75% of the cost of individual therapy.

• **Family therapy.** This approach is based on the belief that a person's emotional difficulties are related to the way his entire family interacts. Generally, all available family members—the more the better—gather to clarify their roles and relationships.

What it's good for: Any issue in which the resources of an entire family can be tapped to address the problems of a member, including an adult child, a grandparent or a divorced spouse. Family therapy also can help families deal better with the serious illness or death of a member.

Typical duration: Twelve to 20 weekly sessions. The cost of family therapy, which is covered by some insurance plans, is determined by the length of the session (typically 90 to 120 minutes each).

• **Couples therapy.** By meeting with both partners at the same time, the therapist can hear each partner's complaints and watch them interact. This allows the therapist to help the couple identify problematic patterns—such as repeated criticism or refusal to change—and make suggestions.

What it's good for: Marital crises (such as infidelity) or frequent fighting, particularly if the same issues come up repeatedly.

Typical duration: Weekly sessions for 20 weeks to a year.

Important: Insurance often does not cover couples therapy. Sessions typically run 60 to 90 minutes with fees set accordingly.

DO YOU NEED MEDICATION?

Medication should be considered when the symptoms, such as depression or anxiety, are severe enough to interfere with your ability to function—particularly if therapy alone hasn't resolved your difficulties. In some cases, medication enhances the effectiveness of psychotherapy—and vice versa. Medication could be prescribed by a psychiatrist, psychiatric nurse or primary care physician.

Don't Let Alcohol Problems Remain Untreated

A lcohol use disorders affect more than 30% of Americans at some point in their lives —but only 24% of alcohol-dependent people receive treatment.

Reason: Many people, including doctors, do not recognize signs of alcohol problems or are unaware of treatment options. The symptoms of alcohol abuse may include legal problems and difficulty meeting responsibilities...while alcohol dependence may entail all these signs plus compulsive drinking and/or withdrawal symptoms (such as tremors and agitation).

Information: Visit the government Internet site at *http://findtreatment.samhsa.gov* or call 800-662-4357.

Bridget F. Grant, PhD, National Institute on Alcohol Abuse and Alcoholism, Washington, DC, and lead researcher on a study of 43,093 people, published in *Archives of General Psychiatry.*

19

Business News

Bulletproof Your Job... And Ride Out the Rough Times at Work

Nearly two million US jobs have been lost in the past year as the country slid deeper into a recession. And, more layoffs are still likely to occur.

In an economy this bad, even doing one's job well is no guarantee of job security. Many skilled, hardworking employees will find themselves out of work. *How to decrease the odds that you will be among them...*

• **Be "low maintenance."** You will be among the first shown the door if your boss considers you a complainer...thinks that you need handholding or special attention...or fields complaints about you from your coworkers. Bosses don't lose sleep about laying off high-maintenance employees such as these—they dream about it. Cutting these people loose can make life easier for them and everyone else in the office.

To avoid the "high maintenance" label, accept without complaint all assignments that come your way...do not ask for special treatment or argue about your rights as an employee...learn to endure your workplace's minor annoyances in silence...and get along well with all of your colleagues.

• **Stay upbeat.** Black humor is common when layoffs loom. Don't join in—others might not have any sense of humor about this economy or the business's current struggles.

Speak with optimism about the company's future—especially when the boss is around. It sends the message that you want to be part of that future.

Stephen Viscusi, founding principal of Bulletproofyourresume.com, a résumé-writing service that creates both traditional and video-streaming résumés in New York City. Viscusi started his career as a headhunter and is author of *Bulletproof Your Job: 4 Simple Strategies to Ride Out the Rough Times and Come Out on Top at Work* (Collins, *www.bulletproofyourjob.com*).

•**Make sure your boss knows you as a human being.** It is easier to fire an employee whom you don't know. Share details of your life with your boss. Your goal is to humanize yourself to make it harder for your boss to fire you.

Also, be sure that your employer is aware of your personal financial responsibilities. Your boss might be less likely to lay you off if he/she knows that the layoff would mean financial catastrophe for you because you have kids…a spouse with a serious health problem…a parent who is financially dependent on you…or some other major financial commitment.

Sparing the job of someone who is especially unable to afford unemployment allows the employer to think of himself as a big-hearted boss who is doing his best to look after his employees during difficult times.

Best: Do not sound desperate or needy when you discuss your financial situation. Just mention it in a conversation with your boss should a natural opportunity arise.

If you are single and debt-free, don't advertise this. Your employer may not feel as guilty about firing you.

•**Make a friend in the human resources (HR) department.** HR employees often know about layoffs months before they occur. If you have an ally in HR, this colleague might be able to warn you about which departments will be hardest hit in time for you to transfer to a safer position. In some layoffs, HR employees even have a say in who stays and who goes.

•**Volunteer to take on tasks that your boss dislikes.** This might mean managing a headache project…training employees who transfer in from other departments…or representing your company at conferences and charity outings. If you don't know which aspects of your boss's job cause him the most displeasure, ask.

If you're in charge of these tasks, your boss won't be able to let you go without worrying that he will have to take on these unloved responsibilities once again. That's powerful motivation to keep you around.

•**Don't let your boss catch you not working.** Employees who are seen as slackers usually are among the first to be let go. Don't take long lunches, and don't get caught shopping online…playing computer games…or making long personal phone calls.

•**Arrive at least five minutes before your boss every morning, and stay five minutes after he leaves.**

•**Add value to the company.** Employers lay people off to save money. If it's clear that you earn or save your company more than you are paid in salary and benefits, there's nothing to be gained by letting you go.

If you are not in a sales position and cannot easily bring more money into your company, search for ways you could help your employer stem costs. Take on additional responsibilities to save the company the cost of hiring an additional employee. Brainstorm creative ways to trim company expenses.

•**Become your employer's specialist on a crucial chore.** Your job is much safer if your boss sees you as the one person in the office who can keep the computer system running… the most important client happy…or the files organized.

•**Watch for warning signs that your specialized role might become obsolete.** Have a plan in place to transition to another vital role if this occurs.

Example: You always have managed one particular client's account, but now the client's struggling in the recession and could go out of business. Start cultivating a relationship with another key client so that you will not be expendable if the first one disappears.

•**Build allies.** Layoffs are rarely distributed evenly across large corporations. One department might lose 30% of its staff, while a more profitable department might lose no one at all.

Give colleagues in your organization's most promising departments reason to like you. If your own department appears particularly vulnerable to layoffs, contact your allies in these safer-seeming divisions and ask them whether a transfer might be possible.

•**Try to negotiate a layoff into a pay cut or a part-time job.** If you are laid off, tell your employer that you would consider a pay cut or a part-time position if one were offered. In this economy, an underpaid job is better than no job at all.

your state requires this, go to *www.workplace fairness.org*.

Check Yourself Out

Check yourself out on the Web when you are job hunting. Human-resources executives routinely check Google, Facebook, YouTube and other Web sites for information on candidates. Knowing in advance what they will find can help you handle the interview better —and head off anything potentially embarrassing or distracting.

Barbara Pachter, president of Pachter & Associates, a communications training firm in Cherry Hill, New Jersey, and author of *When the Little Things Count...and They Always Count* (Da Capo).

 ## Looking for Salary Info?

Find out sensitive salary information at *www. glassdoor.com*. The site currently allows any visitor to find out salary information and read reviews of working conditions at Microsoft, Google, Yahoo and Cisco Systems. To see data on other companies, visitors must reveal their own salaries and feelings about their employers. The site hopes eventually to raise money from advertising by convincing companies that it is a good tool for getting genuine feedback from their workers and competitors' employees.

USA Today, 7950 Jones Branch Dr., McClean, Virginia 22108, *www.usatoday.com*.

Did You Know?...

Unused vacation pay must be included in an employee's final paycheck in 24 states and the District of Columbia. Not all employers know the requirement. To find out whether

Stimulus Tax Breaks for The Unemployed

The first $2,400 in unemployment benefits is excluded from income tax in 2009.

For workers laid off on or after September 1, 2008, and before January 1, 2010, the federal government will pay 65% of COBRA health insurance premiums for nine months. (COBRA is the federal law that allows unemployed workers to extend their employer health insurance.)

Catch: A taxpayer's modified adjusted gross income (MAGI) in the year he or she receives the subsidy can't exceed $125,000 (single), or $250,000 (joint) to be fully tax free.

New opportunity: A provision in the stimulus law allows laid-off workers to switch to more affordable coverage in COBRA, as long as the more affordable plan is also available to workers employed at the company.

Clint Stretch, JD, managing principal, tax policy, at the tax advisory firm Deloitte Tax LLP, Washington, DC, *www.deloitte.com*.

The "10,000-Hour Rule" And Other Secrets to Extraordinary Success

Malcolm Gladwell, a staff writer since 1996 for *The New Yorker*, New York City. He is author of the best-sellers *The Tipping Point: How Little Things Can Make a Big Difference...Blink: The Power of Thinking Without Thinking...*and *Outliers: The Story of Success* (all from Little, Brown). In 2005, *Time* named him one of the country's "100 Most Influential People." His Web site is *www.gladwell.com*.

What are the secrets to success and wealth? Why are certain individuals able to have such amazing careers, earning accolades and millions of dollars? The answer may surprise you.

Best-selling author Malcolm Gladwell, one of the most provocative cultural thinkers today, found that the usual explanations—that extraordinary achievers are much smarter and talented than the rest of us—are insufficient. There are plenty of smart, gifted people who aren't particularly successful. What Gladwell found by talking to Microsoft founder Bill Gates and others is that successful geniuses aren't born...they're created. In other words, their innate qualities are not the only reason they reached the top. The reason is a true mix of several fortunate factors. *Gladwell answers questions on this topic below...*

●**Aren't talent and high IQ vital for great success?** Extensive research shows that they matter only to a point. For instance, once you have an IQ of 130, more points don't seem to translate into any measurable real-world advantage. A scientist with an IQ of 130 is as likely to win a Nobel Prize as one who has an IQ of 180.

●**So what's the crucial factor?** One of the most significant factors is what scientists call the "10,000-hour rule." When we look at any kind of cognitively complex field—for example, playing chess, writing fiction or being a neurosurgeon—we find that you are unlikely to master it unless you have practiced for 10,000 hours. That's 20 hours a week for 10 years. The brain takes that long to assimilate all it needs to know to achieve true mastery.

Take the case of Bill Gates. When Bill was age 13, his father, a wealthy lawyer in Seattle, sent him to a private school that happened to have one of the only computers in the country where students could do real-time programming. At age 15, Gates heard that there was a giant mainframe computer at the nearby University of Washington that was not being used between 2:00 am and 6:00 am. So Gates would get up at 1:30 in the morning, walk a mile, then program for four hours. All told, during the course of seven months in 1971, Gates ran up 1,575 hours of computer time, which averages out to about eight hours a day, seven days a week. By the time Gates dropped out of Harvard after his sophomore year to try his hand at his own computer software company, he had been programming nonstop for seven

consecutive years. Gates was way past 10,000 hours. In fact, there were only a handful of people in the entire world who had as much practice as he had.

●**How young do you have to be when you put in those 10,000 hours? Is there any hope for adults in their 50s or beyond?** The interesting thing is that the age at which you devote 10,000 hours doesn't seem to matter. Sure, the freshness and exuberance and freedom from responsibility that you possess as a youth are helpful. But what is necessary is the application of time and effort. Putting in many years late in life and being successful are real and achievable phenomena. For instance, the artist Cézanne didn't have his first one-man show until age 56. Laura Ingalls Wilder, who wrote the Little House series of children's books, published her first novel at age 65. Colonel Sanders began his Kentucky Fried Chicken franchise in his late 60s.

●**What other factors open the door for great achievements?** The culture we belong to and the legacies passed down by our ancestors often shape the patterns of our achievements in astonishing ways. For instance, I've always been fascinated that so many math geniuses are Asian—disproportionately so. Students from Singapore, South Korea, Taiwan, Hong Kong and Japan score much higher than students in America or Europe on country-by-country–ranked math tests.

Asians aren't born with some calculus or algebra gene that makes them excel, but they do have a different kind of built-in advantage. Children in Asian countries have more persistence than their Western counterparts.

Research has attributed this greater willingness to stick with tough problems to a cultural legacy of hard work that stems from the cultivation of rice. Growing rice demands constant attention. Asian survival depended on working relentlessly and exalting the virtues of patience and dedication. Cultures that believe in working relentlessly don't give their children long summer vacations. The Japanese school year is 243 days long, and the South Korean school year, 220 days. The US school year is, on average, 180 days long.

•**Doesn't luck play a big role?** Luck is too simple a term. Great success typically comes from a steady accumulation of advantages and a confluence of circumstances. For example, timing is important. Extraordinary achievement is possible if you have just the right skills when massive changes in our culture present opportunities. The election of President Obama is a perfect example of this. Another is the inordinate number of multibillionaires in the US today that were all born between 1953 and 1955—people such as Bill Gates, Steve Jobs (CEO of Apple Inc.) and Eric Schmidt (CEO of Google).

Why? Because they were all in their early 20s when the computer revolution hit in 1975. The early 20s is the optimal age to be during the early part of a revolution. If you were still in high school in 1975, you were too young to start a computer company. If you were in the workforce and had a mortgage and a family, you weren't going to quit a good job to take a risk.

•**How can you predict if someone will be a great success?** Studies have shown that intelligence is a bad predictor of how well anyone will do in a highly complex position. The best approach is to let them do the job for a while. In other words, you are better off using your time, money and energy establishing an apprenticeship system and observing which one of multiple candidates does the best than trying to predict who will do well.

Get More Done in a Day: The "Hour of Power" And Other Ways to Boost Productivity

Gary Bencivenga, a renowned direct marketing advertising copywriter based in Garden City, New York. He also is editor of the e-zine *Success Bullets* and author of *12 Life-Changing Quotations*, both available free at his Web site, *www.successbullets.com*.

W e all have the same 24 hours in a day, yet some people accomplish so much more than others. What are their secrets? *Here are the best ways to boost productivity from some of the brightest minds on the subject…*

SMARTER STRATEGIES

•**Apply the 80/20 rule to all that you do.** Roughly 20% of your day-to-day activities are responsible for 80% of your success, income and personal happiness. These are your "big-payoff" activities.

Conversely, 20% of your activities are causing 80% of your wasted time. These are your "low-payoff" activities.

The best way to multiply your productivity is simple—always be looking to free up more time for your big-payoff activities by ruthlessly eliminating the dozens of low-payoff ones that you unwittingly tolerate.

Example: One of the most successful executives I have met keeps a framed sign over his desk and carries an index card in his shirt pocket with the same message—*Is this leading me to my main goal?* He checks that reminder numerous times in a day and saves countless hours each week by staying on track—getting out quickly from time-wasting telephone calls, meetings, gossip, etc., and relentlessly getting back to the big-payoff activities for himself and his company.

•**Harness your "hour of power."** Whatever your highest-payoff activity, rise early and give it the first hour of your day—what I call your "hour of power." This will get your day off to a highly productive start.

The late Earl Nightingale, a management advisor, explained that if you spend this early-morning hour in the study of your chosen field, you'll be a national expert in five years or less.

•**Gain six to eight extra hours of productivity every day.** Your second-most-productive hour is right before you go to sleep. This is a great time to leverage your productivity by arranging for your mighty subconscious mind to solve a problem while you sleep peacefully.

How to do it: Just before going to bed, think about a problem or question that you're working on. Then say to yourself, *Great subconscious mind, I don't want to work on this matter too hard, so please just figure this out for me by the morning while I sleep peacefully.* Then completely forget about the matter and drift off to sleep.

You'll likely find that during your hour of power the next morning, you will be brimming over with ideas that are perfect for your project. Be aware that your morning ideas are slippery fish. If you don't catch them immediately on getting up, they'll swim away forever. Keep a pad and pen at your bedside to capture your ideas.

• **Do not carry a "to-do" list in your head.** You not only will forget things that are on the list, but an inner voice will perpetually nag that you must be dropping balls somewhere. Use a written to-do list to capture everything you must remember—every phone call, task and follow-up action. Review the most urgent and important items daily and all items weekly.

• **Don't multitask.** As Confucius said, "A man who chases two rabbits catches neither." Modern studies show that when you try to accomplish two activities that require focused attention at the same time, both suffer significantly.

• **Slow down.** When focusing on one high-priority item at a time, don't rush through it. You do your best thinking when you are focused and relaxed. As Mae West advised with a wink, "Anything worth doing is worth doing slowly."

• **Get enough sleep.** Research shows that productivity, clarity, alertness, judgment, creativity, memory skills, motivation, relaxation, cheerfulness and lots of other wonderful qualities all thrive with adequate sleep and suffer without it. Also consider an afternoon nap—one of life's most rejuvenating luxuries.

• **Do what you love.** It's much easier to be productive when your work is your play. You will want to give it your full attention and every minute you can—and you easily will brush off countless distractions that seduce others. So in all of your activities and goals, and especially when deciding which to choose as your highest priorities, remember the words of editor and author Christopher Morley, "There is only one success—to be able to spend your life in your own way."

YOUR "NOT-TO-DO" LIST

Your not-to-do list is even more important than your to-do list. You must work every day to minimize or get rid of those 20% of activities that are wasting 80% of your time—by maintaining a not-to-do list. *Helpful...*

• **Never answer e-mail in the morning.** Reserve all your precious morning time for your highest-payoff activities. Also, shut off your e-mail program for most of the day so that you won't be interrupted by each new incoming message. Limit reviewing your e-mail to specific periods, perhaps once around noon and again later in the day. Keep replies short with answers such as, "Thanks"..."Look forward to it"..."Will do"...or "I agree."

• **Don't answer phones just because they ring.** Too often, it is a salesperson, fund-raiser or other pesky soul out to waste your time and ruin your focus. Have an assistant or answering machine screen your calls, or let them go to voice mail. As psychiatrist Edward M. Hallowell, MD, author of *Crazy Busy*, says, "If you don't manage your time, it will be taken from you."

• **Flex your *no* muscle.** Whenever someone asks you to do something that you would rather not do, remember this simple two-part formula—(1) "Thanks for asking" (for having confidence that I could do this, etc.), (2) "I can't, because..." (you've just been given a major new assignment or whatever) "so I wouldn't be able to give it the time that it deserves." If the petitioner persists, don't debate the issue. Just keep robotically repeating your reason for declining, and the person soon will let you be.

Of course, if the person making the request is your boss, remember that he or she is your number-one customer and that it's important to be on the same page about what's important. Sound out whether this new request supersedes your current tasks. In other words, know what is most important at all times, and put your focus there.

Ask two questions of every task: (1) *Does this have to be done?* (2) *If so, does it have to be done by me?*

In all matters, strive to be not just efficient but effective as well. *Efficient* means doing things right, but *effective* means doing the right things, which is far more important.

• **Delegate the kaizen way.** If you're a control freak and can't delegate easily, do it the kaizen way. Kaizen is the Japanese approach of continuous improvement utilizing small, nonthreatening, easy-to-take baby steps. Ask someone to do a small task for you. As soon as you get comfortable with one delegation baby step, take another and so on. It's easier to get 10 people to work for you than for you to do the work of 10.

How to Manage the McDonald's Way: Four Vital Principles For Stunning Success

Paul Facella, president and CEO of Inside Management, Ltd., a management consulting firm based in Lynbrook, New York. He is author, with Adina Genn, of *Everything I Know About Business I Learned at McDonald's: The 7 Leadership Principles That Drive Break Out Success* (McGraw-Hill).

In these difficult economic times, strong leadership seems elusive. But even during times such as these, there are principles that you can adopt to help you become a better leader—whether it's in the office, in your community or at home. There is no better place to learn about these principles than McDonald's, one of the most highly regarded, well-run corporations in the world. Even during this recession, McDonald's stood out as one of the few companies to post gains.

To learn more about the principles that define leadership, we talked with management consultant Paul Facella, who spent the first 34 years of his career at McDonald's, rising from behind-the-counter cashier to regional vice president. There he developed an understanding of the company's culture and the principles of leadership underlying it.

LEAD BY EXAMPLE

At McDonald's, I learned that effective leaders model the behavior that they want to see in others. This started first and foremost with Ray Kroc, McDonald's founder.

I saw humility and graciousness the first minute I met Ray. He was known for visiting with regional employees whenever he came to town. Because I was the highest-ranking staff member in the New York franchise where I worked, it was decided that I would dine with him. I was a director of operations at the time, and so this was quite an honor for me. In the limousine, Ray insisted on taking the small "flip seat," offering me the most comfortable seat because I was his guest.

Having the head of one of the most successful businesses in the world put me at ease made a huge impression on me. I have never forgotten his efforts to make an ordinary employee feel special. I vowed to adopt this mind-set in my own life.

Even today, I always try to remember the impact I have on others. When new members join an organization that I belong to, I go out of my way to interact with and welcome them.

It was not unusual at McDonald's to see leaders, such as Ray himself, show workers what needed to be done. No task was too humble, even for the boss.

During a visit to one New Jersey restaurant, Ray picked up cigarette butts in the parking lot, setting the tone for cleanliness. When executives were out in the field, they always made a point of pitching in. If there was a problem, they would jump behind the counter and help out.

The influence of Ray Kroc and others at McDonald's has always stayed with me. Even though I am a senior member and former officer of my local volunteer fire department, I always try to be the first to pick up a mop or a broom. When junior fire department members see me doing this, they invariably pitch in as well.

FOSTER RELATIONSHIPS

Integrity is valued above all else at McDonald's and permeates the culture of the company. Everyone is treated as a partner. Some even say it is like a surrogate family. There was an unprecedented level of trust between people involved in all aspects of the business. We called it the "three-legged stool." This meant that the relationship between the three interdependent partners—the franchisees, the suppliers and the corporate staff—was understood to be vital to the company's success.

Making the "three-legged stool" work often required taking gutsy steps that might have seemed counterintuitive.

Example: There were times when Ray told suppliers to raise their prices. He figured that for these companies to become long-term partners, they needed to succeed, and they wouldn't if he forced them to accept profits that were too low. This worked. When vendors increased profits, the result was stronger loyalty to McDonald's. Vendors had so much faith in McDonald's that they actually helped bail out the company in 1959, when it was in trouble because of a real estate deal gone bad.

This culture of trust was so strong that important agreements often were made with a handshake rather than a written contract. Many suppliers, now second- and third-generation businesses, haven't had a formal contract with the company for 50 years.

The high level of trust also reaped rewards for the company. Because they felt such loyalty, suppliers, franchisees and employees often suggested some of McDonald's most successful products and concepts.

Example: Herb Peterson, a McDonald's franchise owner, was the creator of the Egg McMuffin in 1973.

RAISE THE BAR

At McDonald's, the company philosophy is "Never be satisfied." We always were looking to break our records, whether it was increasing the number of customers or lowering costs.

To raise the bar as high as it could be, we used metrics, or measurements, to determine whether we had reached our goals. We measured everything from hourly sales to how many bags of potatoes were used each day. We made goals measurable, which especially helped team members know what they were working toward and gave them a real sense of ownership. It also encouraged an environment of friendly competition.

Example: When I was a manager, many cashiers were coming up short each day, so I put up signs showing just how over or under each cash register was. Within 24 hours, every person's total was perfect. No one wanted to be the lowest performer in the store.

PROVIDE RECOGNITION

At McDonald's, recognition is everywhere. The company makes it a way of life, encouraging managers to recognize employees regularly. Ray knew that there is no better way to inspire people. Even our frontline employees were recognized. You might think of a crew job at McDonald's—working the kitchen—as menial, but if you worked hard, you were noticed and got rewarded. For many, that meant being promoted and advancing from crew to operator to the corporate office.

Result: About 42% of the current worldwide leadership at McDonald's started out as crew members.

Whenever possible, employees at McDonald's are recognized in public with fanfare.

Example: To acknowledge a McDonald's staff attorney who had joined a national Hispanic organization, the company president addressed the entire floor of the office to offer congratulations and then gave the attorney an all-expenses-paid week at a corporate retreat. The move also encouraged other employees to join similar organizations.

At McDonald's, recognition always is sincere, meaningful and tailored to the individual—whether it is a bonus check, concert tickets or time off.

When I was an assistant manager, I was out one evening with my future wife at a restaurant that I could barely afford. I saw the owner/operator of the franchise where I worked. We waved to each other. When I was ready to pay the check, I found that he had paid for our dinner. At times such as these, I felt as if I would do anything for the company.

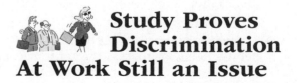

Study Proves Discrimination At Work Still an Issue

W omen MUST work harder than men in the workplace for the same recognition.

Recent study: Statistical analyses show that the gender discrepancy is not due to any differences in job levels, qualifications or family responsibilities.

The results imply that women must work harder and produce superior performance to obtain the same evaluations as men who do the same jobs.

Elizabeth Gorman, PhD, assistant professor of sociology, University of Virginia, Charlottesville, and coauthor of a study analyzing five surveys, published in Gender and Society.

What Your Handshake Says About You

A solid grasp during a handshake conveys confidence, and this is always appropriate. Placing your left hand on top of the handshake is more intimate and should be used only with people you know very well. Offering only your fingers conveys a sense of superiority and should be avoided.

Also: Always stand when shaking hello or good-bye, and make eye contact as you shake.

BusinessWeek, 1221 Avenue of the Americas, New York City 10020, www.businessweek.com.

Better Brainstorming

For better brainstorming sessions, choose someone from outside the department to be the team leader. An insider brings bias and personal relationships that can inhibit the flow of ideas. It's best to be specific with your topic, but general enough to allow room for creativity. Define the subject in terms of the market or consumer needs and habits. Try beginning the session with a word game or improvisation to loosen up the participants. Ask higher-ranking attendees to give their opinions last

so that they don't influence the open outflow of ideas. Emphasize creative problem-solving and discourage negative comments. Be sure to mention past successful innovations in your firm or unit. Finally, record ideas on tape instead of having someone write notes, which discourages participation.

Investor's Business Daily, 12655 Beatrice St., Los Angeles 90099, www.investors.com.

 ## Stuck in a Boring Meeting?

To appear interested during a dull meeting, tilt your head to the right—the gesture tells the speaker you are listening. Also, smile occasionally at the speaker, and keep blinking —people who are bored often stop blinking, giving them a glazed look. Nod in agreement from time to time—being sure you know what has just been said, so you do not nod at the wrong time. If you still feel bored, move your body to a different position to help you stay awake.

Tonya Reiman, body language expert and author of The Power of Body Language *(Pocket).*

E-Mail Etiquette

Avoid the "reply to all" function when answering e-mail—unless a message really needs to go to everyone on the list.

Also: Do not combine multiple subjects and themes in a single e-mail. Reread your message before clicking "send." Do not follow up an e-mail immediately with an instant message or a phone call—give the recipient time to read the message and respond.

Jonathan Spira, CEO and chief analyst, Basex, Inc., an information technology research and advisory firm, New York City.

Pension Protection

Marc Hopkins, Pension Benefit Guaranty Corporation, Washington, DC, *www.pbgc.gov*.

I s your pension threatened by the financial crisis? What happens if your employer goes bankrupt?

If you have a traditional (defined-benefit) pension plan that pays a predetermined benefit for life, that plan is insured by the Pension Benefit Guaranty Corporation (PBGC). If your pension plan is taken over by the PBGC, it will ensure that workers and retirees continue to get a retirement benefit, up to limits set by Congress.

The maximum insurance benefit for participants in pension plans taken over by the PBGC in 2009 is $54,000 per year for those who retire at age 65 (up from $51,750 for 2008). The amount is higher for those who retire later and lower for those who retire earlier or elect survivor benefits.

It's possible for the PBGC to cover a benefit in excess of the guarantee limits. For instance, if it recovers enough funds from the bankruptcy workout of the organization that sponsored the pension plan.

Of retirees who receive their pensions from the PBGC, about 84% get the entire amount promised by their pension plans.

If, instead of a pension, you have a defined-contribution plan—such as a 401(k)—funded by your own contributions, it is not insured by the PBGC. Its balance is held in a trust that protects it from your employer's creditors and bankruptcy, but the amount of the balance, and thus the future benefit it will pay, typically is determined by your own decisions regarding how to invest it.

Consider a Commuter Savings Account

U se pretax dollars to pay for commuting expenses with a Commuter Savings Account. This lowers taxable income—and money left in the account at the end of the year rolls over to the next year. Under IRS rules, employees can put up to $230 per month in pretax dollars into a commuter account for mass-transit passes, including van pools...$230 per month for qualified parking. New in 2009 is a $20-a-month allowance for biking expenses, but you cannot claim the biking benefits in any month in which you use the parking or mass-transit benefits. These accounts are set up by employers at their discretion—if your company does not offer them, ask about having them established.

Barbara Weltman, Esq., an attorney based in Millwood, New York, and publisher of the free online newsletter, *Big Ideas for Small Business*, *www.barbaraweltman.com*.

Why Tough Times Are Good Times to Start a Business: Do It Yourself For Less Than $5,000

Rieva Lesonsky, former editor in chief of *Entrepreneur* and author of *Start Your Own Business* (Entrepreneur). She currently runs SMB Connects, a company that helps major marketers connect with small business owners and entrepreneurs, Irvine, California. She answers small business questions for free at *www.askrieva.com*.

T he weak economy is making jobs harder to find. One option for frustrated job seekers is to stop looking for employment and start working for themselves.

A recession is an excellent time to launch a small business. Larger companies rein in their advertising and expansion plans when the economy slows, making it easier for new companies to get noticed and capture market share.

Newer, small companies also tend to have lower fixed expenses than the older, larger ones, and that allows them to underbid the competition. That's very important during a recession, when customers are particularly price-sensitive.

The trouble is that starting a new business can be risky. Sinking all your savings into a start-up or taking out a small business loan could leave you in a deep financial hole if the business fails.

There's no way to eliminate all the risk from entrepreneurship, but you can greatly reduce your downside if you keep your business's expenses to a minimum. *Here's how to launch a business for less than $5,000...*

THINK SERVICE

The service sector offers the best opportunities for low-cost business start-ups. *Unlike retail or manufacturing businesses, service-sector companies...*

• **Rarely require major up-front outlays of cash for inventory or materials.**

• **Often can be run out of the home,** eliminating the need to rent an office, factory or storefront.

• **Tend to be local,** so there is no need for expensive nationwide marketing campaigns.

Four ways to come up with a low-cost service business idea...

• **Keep lists of the things that frustrate you and the things that you wish you didn't have to do for yourself.** Consider both your personal life and your previous professional career. Perhaps other people would pay you to help them avoid these annoyances.

Example: Two brothers in Irvine, California, were frustrated that it took them much of their lunch hour to get from the local business district to area restaurants for lunch. They started Restaurants on the Run, a service that delivers restaurant food to office workers at their desks. The company has expanded into multiple cities and now does millions of dollars in business each year.

• **Find out which service-oriented businesses (and other low-cost businesses) are thriving in big cities.** Trends tend to begin in big coastal cities, such as New York and Los Angeles, and only later work their way to the rest of the country. Read the business and lifestyle sections of magazines and newspapers from major coastal cities to find out what new business ideas are successful there. Consider whether similar businesses would be successful in your region.

Examples: Frozen yogurt franchises and bakeries specializing in high-end cupcakes are among this year's hot new businesses in large, trendsetting cities. Buying a franchise or opening a bakery would not be cheap, but perhaps you could inexpensively open a street-corner dessert cart selling comparable frozen yogurt treats...or bake premium cupcakes at home and sell them through area stores or restaurants.

• **Target a growing demographic.** Open a business that serves a rapidly expanding demographic, and the odds for success are in your favor. Currently the fastest-growing demographics are seniors and children. (Make sure these national trends apply to your local region before launching your business.)

Examples: Potential service businesses that cater to seniors include transportation services...shopping and grocery delivery services ...adult day-care services...and senior "transitional" services, handling the details involved in moving to a nursing home or assisted-living facility. Service businesses catering to the youth market include day care...transportation services...tutoring...college-preparation classes ...and college-application assistance.

• **Search for service opportunities related to your professional experience.** If your new business is in a field that you already know well, your learning curve will be shorter and your Rolodex will already be full of potential customers and other helpful contacts. Make sure that your new business does not violate any noncompete agreements that you might have signed with former employers.

AVOID UNNECESSARY COSTS

Some start-up expenses that your business can live without...

• **Renting an office.** Work from your home if at all possible. Meet with potential clients and other business contacts in their offices...at the local coffeehouse...or in the lobby of a hotel.

• **Buying office furniture and business equipment.** Try to make do with the furniture, phones and computers you already own. If you must purchase business furniture or equipment, search for used items. One advantage of starting a business during a recession is that other companies are going out of business and selling off their business furniture and equipment at low prices.

• **Expensive marketing efforts, such as direct mail and television ads.** Their high cost makes them too risky for your start-up.

Helpful: Turn your customers into your marketing team. Tell them you'll give them a good discount on their next order if they refer another customer to you and it leads to a sale.

FOUR EXPENSES WORTH PAYING

Not all start-up expenses should be avoided. *Do try to do the following...*

• **Incorporate your business.** An attorney might charge about $2,000 to help you set up a Limited Liability Company (LLC) or corporation, but it's money well spent. If your business is not an LLC or a corporation, your personal assets could be at risk in a lawsuit.

• **Launch a Web site.** A Web site does not need to be elaborate, but it must look professional. This is particularly important if your company doesn't have an office or a long track record. To learn more about how to start a Web site for your business, go to *www.allbusiness.com* and type "Web site" into the search window.

• **Arrange for health insurance.** Obtaining health insurance at a reasonable price can be a major problem for those who are self-employed. Find out if you are eligible for COBRA benefits (in 2009, the federal government may even subsidize some of the premiums) from your last job or if you can get coverage through your spouse's health insurance plan. If you are past your 50th birthday, you should be eligible for health insurance through AARP (888-687-2277, *www.aarp.org*). Or find out if a health insurance plan is offered by a trade association that your business makes you eligible to join.

• **Buy Business Plan Pro.** If you don't have experience writing business plans, this software is the cheapest, easiest way to do so. (Palo Alto Software, $99.95,* 800-229-7526 or *www.bplans.com*.)

• **A business plan is like a road map.** It helps you lay out your route to move from where you are to where you want to be. Good

*Price subject to change.

business-plan software prompts you to think about vital factors such as competition, staffing, pricing and marketing.

Best Franchise Opportunities Now

Businesses that benefit from today's lifestyles and the aging population are the best franchise opportunities currently. Rather than buy a well-known franchise, such as 7-Eleven or Subway restaurants (two popular choices of past years), take advantage of current trends.

Examples: Lawn care, residential cleaning and handyman businesses can market to dual-income couples who want to spend more quality time together rather than doing chores. Travel and home health-care services especially appeal to older consumers.

Among sites for franchise listings, check *www.franchiseopportunities.com* and *www. franchising.com*.

Joel Libava, president of Franchise Selection Specialists Inc., Cleveland, www.franchiseselectionspecialists.com.

Take a Successful Entrepreneur to Lunch

If you're starting a business, one of the best investments you can make is lunch. First, find an entrepreneur in your area who is doing work that you find interesting or different. It does not have to be your exact industry—chances are the advice that you get still will be helpful. Call or e-mail to see if you can buy him/her lunch. If he agrees, ask how he succeeded and what mistakes he made along the way and get his advice on your business plan. Most entrepreneurs love talking about themselves and are happy to help others succeed.

Getrichslowly.org.

Why New Businesses Go Under—Protect Yours

Most new businesses fail simply because they don't find enough customers.

Basics of effective selling: Meet with each potential client to determine how their buying decisions are made, and target your approach to all people who influence the buying decision. Focus on your firm's strengths, and not on the competition—which you cannot control. Listen to each prospect carefully to determine his/her needs and find ways to meet those needs. Figure out why the prospect should buy from you—you must be able to articulate this to him. Anticipate losing the business, and analyze why this could happen—then adjust your approach so that it doesn't.

Martyn Lewis, founder, president and CEO, Market-Partners, sales consultants, Santa Rosa, California, and author of *Sales Wise* (Fenestra).

Stop the Layoffs! Other Ways Businesses Can Save

Andrew J. Sherman, a partner with the law firm Jones Day in Washington, DC, *www.jonesday.com*. He is also a leading expert on the legal and strategic aspects of business growth and founder of Grow Fast Grow Right, an education and training company with operations in the US, Canada and Europe. Sherman is the author of 17 books, including the recent three-part series, *Grow Fast Grow Right, Build Fast Build Right* and *Start Fast Start Right* (all published by Kaplan).

US businesses have cut millions of jobs since the recession began, and the numbers keep mounting. But layoffs hurt the morale and loyalty of remaining employees —plus they can trigger lawsuits from those forced to leave. *Best ways for small businesses to avoid or limit layoffs...*

CUT EMPLOYEE COSTS

Often the best way to cut costs is to change ways employees work and get paid...

•**Cut salaries across the board.** Most employees would be willing to take a pay reduction for as long as a year in exchange for job security.

One caveat: To boost morale, everyone, including the company head, has to feel the pain. Cuts should be at least 15% of salaries, but you might make them larger for higher-paid executives, depending on how big the gap is between lower- and upper-level employees.

•**Ask employees to telecommute.** Many companies have permitted certain employees to work from home as a lifestyle choice, but this can be done to cut office space costs, as well. For the best results, tap only employees whose work is largely computer-based. You may need to supply proper equipment.

Shift employees to a four-day week and/or part-time status. Employees will embrace these moves if they understand that it's a way to keep their jobs. Such steps are especially useful in cases where you need employees only part-time, anyway.

Example: A software company recently switched several programmers to a 30-hour week. The firm also started paying only part of their health insurance benefits.

Alternative: Furlough every employee for one week without pay at different times during the year, as one large corporation recently announced it would do. Because of federal and state rules, you must be certain that the employees do not even check their e-mail or voice mail during the weeks they are off.

•**Freeze hiring.** When employees choose to leave, don't fill their positions. Redistribute their work to those remaining.

Best move: Call a meeting of employees to explain what you're doing and why. Then, get their input on how to rearrange the workload.

CUT NONEMPLOYEE COSTS

Yet another approach to saving money is to address how you run your company...

•**Do a total cost audit.** If you analyze your expenses, you'll probably find all sorts of items that can be eliminated or postponed, such as industry conferences, client and employee entertainment, and new technology purchases. One consumer goods wholesaler saved more than $250,000 just by eliminating such expenses and avoided laying off three employees.

• **Renegotiate with suppliers.** Approach all vendors about reconsidering terms. In the current economy, with many customers unable to pay their bills, they'll probably be willing to comply with a reasonable reduction.

Example: A restaurant chain agreed to a three-year contract with a supplier in exchange for lower prices.

• **"Shack up" with another firm.** Many professional services firms that expanded when business was booming now need to sublease their space. One financial adviser recently left his office and moved in with his accountant, allowing him to retain his eight employees. He's providing financial management services to the accountant in exchange for the space.

Keep the Spirits Up!

To maintain company morale during difficult economic times, owners and company leaders need to spend extra time and effort communicating with employees. Do what you say you will do—strive for reliability, consistency and predictability. Management at all levels should project calm confidence—be honest and direct, but don't scare people by describing a potential but unlikely calamity. Don't become isolated—seek information and differing viewpoints before making any decisions.

Dee Soder, PhD, founder, CEO Perspective Group, an advisory firm that coaches top executives, New York City, *www.ceoperspective.com.*

Recession Smarts

Keep your business thriving during a recession by contacting inactive clients with whom you have lost contact.

Also: Keep tabs on and improve customer satisfaction. Create risk-free introductory offers. Revive programs that worked in the past. Collect testimonials. Make it easy for customers to choose your business—give them reasons to pick your company.

Marcia Yudkin, PhD, creative marketing consultant and author of *33 Keys to Thriving During a Recession,* a free downloadable report. For more information, go to *www.yudkin.com/recess.htm.*

Paying Too Much for Shipping?

Find out if your business is overpaying its shippers by having a shipping audit done. Refund-Retriever (713-401-7906, *www.refund-retriever.com*) and Refund Technology (888-438-7801, *www.refundtechnology1.com*) look through your records to find out about packages that arrived late...third parties using your account without permission...charges for items you did not send...and other errors. Generally, the audit company keeps half of what it recovers, and you get the other half.

Barbara Weltman, Esq., an attorney based in Millwood, New York, and publisher of the free online newsletter, *Big Ideas for Small Business, www.barbaraweltman.com.*

Smart Move for Start-Ups: Section 1244 Stock

If you set up a new corporation, be sure to have your business issue "Section 1244" stock.

Why: Many new businesses fail. And a loss suffered on regular corporate stock is a capital loss that must first be offset against capital gains, with only $3,000 of a net capital loss deductible against ordinary income annually.

However, when a loss is suffered on Section 1244 stock, up to $100,000 ($50,000 for singles) is deductible against ordinary income. Only losses over that amount are subject to the regular capital loss limitations. *The main rules...*

•**Shares can be issued only in exchange for money or property**—not in exchange for services or as a gift or inheritance.

•**Total money and property received by the corporation for the stock cannot exceed $1 million.**

•**Investors must be individuals,** or they need to be partnerships.

•**The shareholder must be the original purchaser of the stock.**

•**More than half of the corporation's gross receipts must be derived from active operations,** not investments, and limitations apply to the amount of "passive income" the corporation may have (from dividends, rents, royalties, etc.).

Tactic: Have the corporation's organizational documents authorize the sale of more Section 1244 shares than it will sell at first. That way, it can sell more shares to new investors it attracts later.

More information: IRS Publication 550, Investment Income and Expenses.

Location Incentives: Valuable Tax Breaks For Businesses

Mark A. Plostock, CPA, CITP, a tax manager at the CPA firm Israeloff Trattner & Co., PC, 1225 Franklin Ave., Garden City, New York 11530. He specializes in state and local tax issues and teaches taxes for the New York Society of Certified Public Accountants.

The US federal government wants companies to operate in economically distressed areas to bring employment and improvement to those places. State and local governments also want to draw businesses to their communities to bring jobs and property improvements to their jurisdictions and, in the long run, to expand their tax bases. To accomplish these goals, governments offer a variety of tax breaks (collectively called "location tax incentives"). *Included...*

•**Abatements**—a reduction of real estate tax for a limited time.

•**Credits**—dollar-for-dollar savings off federal and/or state and local tax liability for rehabilitating real estate, creating jobs, etc.

•**Deductions**—subtractions from income subject to tax for investments in equipment within designated areas.

•**Exemptions**—income items that are not subject to tax.

Here are some breaks you may qualify for—and their tax implications for your business...

FEDERAL TAX BREAKS

•**Employment credits.** A credit of 20% of wages up to $15,000 (for a top credit of $3,000 per qualified employee).

•**An enhanced Section 179 deduction for equipment purchases.** An additional $35,000 limit on annual purchases (on top of the basic deduction limit, which is $250,000 in 2009).

•**Special capital gains rules for sales of assets located within qualified areas.** This means no tax at all on gains on the sale of qualified assets held more than five years (e.g., business property, stock, or a partnership interest within the area).

There are three different types of federal qualified areas—empowerment zones, enterprise communities and renewal communities. There is no clear-cut distinction between areas—the distinctions lie with designation requirements. The areas cover both urban and rural locations. You can find an area's designation by going to the US Department of Housing and Urban Development "RC/EZ/EC address locator" (*www.hud.gov/crlocator*), or calling 800-998-9999 for urban areas...800-645-4712 for rural areas.

However, not all of the special tax breaks apply to each type of designated area. For instance, the enhanced Section 179 deduction for equipment purchases applies to empowerment zones and renewal communities but not to enterprise communities. A full exclusion for capital gains from the sale of certain assets held more than five years applies only to renewal communities.

•**Special zones.** After certain catastrophies and because of other special factors (such as general urban decay), the government created special zones eligible for extra tax incentives. *These include...*

• DC Zone—various parts of the District of Columbia.

• Gulf Opportunity Zone—the areas affected by Hurricanes Katrina, Rita and Wilma.

• Liberty Zone—the area in southern Manhattan devastated on 9/11.

For more information about federal tax incentives for certain areas, see IRS Publication 954, *Tax Incentives for Distressed Communities.*

STATE AND LOCAL INCENTIVES

States and local governments also offer a wide array of tax breaks as inducements for companies to locate in particular areas. Some states have special economic zones similar to the federal empowerment zones and enterprise communities. *Examples...*

• **Georgia Opportunity Zones**—started in 2004 and expanded in 2008. Businesses in these zones qualify for a tax credit for creating new jobs.

• **New York Empire Zones**—there are 85 zones statewide (at least one in every county) and a number of Qualified Empire Zone Enterprises that qualify for enhanced taxation breaks. Applications must first be approved by local officials (city, town, county) and then are forwarded for review by the state Departments of Economic Development and Labor. Breaks include a wage credit for hiring employees within the zone, an investment tax credit for equipment purchased and used in certain types of businesses, including manufacturing and research and development, real property tax credits, a tax reduction credit that can reduce a business's tax liability to zero, and sales tax refunds of a portion of the tax collected.

• **Pennsylvania Keystone Opportunity Zones**—started in 1999, this program has been expanded to include thousands of acres within the state. Qualified businesses can enjoy tax reductions—perhaps even to zero.

More information: Contact your state business development agency, found on your state's Web site.

Impact on federal income taxes: The IRS has concluded that location tax incentives to a business, regardless of the form they take (abatements, credits, deductions, exemptions), are not gross income to C corporations or to owners of pass-through entities.

Note: If your business receives any state or local tax breaks, the C corporation or the owners of the pass-through entity can deduct only amounts that they actually pay, after taking into account any location tax incentives.

HOW TO BECOME ELIGIBLE

If your business is thinking of relocating or expanding into new areas and wants to take advantage of tax breaks to achieve substantial savings, plan ahead...

• **Determine whether your proposed location is within a federally designated area** by using the locator listed on page 317.

• **Talk with local authorities to find out about opportunities in a proposed location.** Depending upon the scale of your presence in an area, localities can move boundaries to accommodate you and ensure that you'll receive the tax breaks you seek.

• **Talk to your state economic development agency.** Find the link through the Economic Development Administration at *www.eda.gov/ Resources/StateLinks.xml.*

• **Work with a knowledgeable tax expert.** Your regular accountant or attorney may not have the expertise to deal with the red tape required to nail down a business's eligibility for state and local tax breaks.

Consider Using a Fiscal Year for Your Small Business

Frederick W. Daily, Esq., a tax attorney based in St. Pete Beach, Florida, and author of several tax books, including Stand Up to the IRS *and* Tax Savvy for Small Business *(both from Nolo.com).*

I ndividuals report their income to the IRS on a calendar year basis, so when starting a new small business, they usually use a calendar year for it, too. But do not overlook the possibility of having the business compute its income using a fiscal year—one that ends on the last day of a month other than December. For a seasonal business, this can provide significant benefits. *Examples…*

• **If the business's busy season is during the holidays at year end,** its managers may then have neither the time nor the information needed to conduct "year-end" tax planning to be in place by December 31.

But if the business's year-end is postponed until perhaps March 31, the managers have more time to both gather their information and take action.

• **There may also be opportunity to offset a company's income with its expenses** (or losses) by choosing a non-calendar fiscal year based on the company's financial particulars.

A regular C corporation—other than a personal service corporation, such as a professional corporation (PC) for lawyers, doctors, etc.—can choose any fiscal year it wishes.

"Pass-through entities"—partnerships and S corporations—must obtain IRS permission to use a fiscal year by showing that they have a seasonal business or some other justification, or by making a Section 444 election. To do so, submit Form 8716, *Election to Have a Tax Year Other Than a Required Tax Year*. (PCs can also make a Section 444 election on this form.)

For more information, see IRS Publication 538, *Accounting Periods and Methods*.

Leasing vs. Buying And the IRS

Even though a business equipment transaction is structured as a lease, the IRS may take the position that you really purchased the asset.

Consequence: Instead of deducting the entire monthly lease payments, you will be required to depreciate the cost of the asset using IRS guidelines. The IRS will generally challenge

a leasing transaction if you are able to purchase the equipment for a nominal fee at the end of the lease.

Strategy: Ask your accountant to help structure the lease to make sure that it will survive an IRS challenge.

Ms. X, Esq., a former agent with the IRS who is still well connected.

More from Ms. X, Esq.…

Don't Be an IRS Target

The most efficient way to achieve a tax-related criminal conviction, the IRS has figured out, is to charge a violation of non-payment of payroll taxes or fraudulent preparation of payroll tax returns. Small-business owners are especially susceptible to being targeted for criminal prosecution, as these businesses often employ workers who are paid off the books, in cash, and other workers who are arbitrarily treated as independent contractors. Restaurants and contractors employ millions of workers for whom payroll taxes are not paid.

Latest development: Large employers are being hit.

Increased Audits For Businesses

The IRS has informally let it be known that it will be using a new electronic matching program to find companies that pay at least five workers $25,000 or more whom they classify as independent contractors where such workers do not perform services for any other businesses. In the IRS's view, these workers are effectively employees and should be treated as such.

Bottom line: Review your worker classification to be sure that you're treating workers properly. For more information, listen to the IRS Tax Talk Today podcast recorded on November 6, 2007, entitled "What's Hot in Employment

Taxes: Independent Contractor or Employee?" at *www.taxtalktoday.tv*.

Sharon Kreider, CPA, EA, 1309 S. Mary Ave., Sunnyvale, California 94807, *www.kreidercpa.com*, and Vern B. Hoven, CPA, EA, MT-Tax, 10912 Moorelands St., Gig Harbor, Washington 98335, *www.boven.com*.

Succession Planning Loopholes

Edward Mendlowitz, CPA, partner in the CPA firm WithumSmith+Brown in New Brunswick, New Jersey, ranked among the top 35 accounting firms in the US by the industry's leading publications, *www.withum.com*. He's the author of many books including, *The Adviser's Guide to Family Business Succession Planning* (American Institute of Certified Public Accountants).

Business owners who carefully plan the transfer of ownership of their companies to family members or longtime employees can trim the tax bill for the transfer. *Consider these tax loopholes...*

Loophole: **Sell your business interest on an installment plan.**

This freezes the value at the current price. The seller reports capital gain on the installment basis, delaying taxation because gain is recognized only when and to the extent that installment payments are received. Interest must be added to these payments. The purchaser's note will be included in the seller's estate and the unpaid balance (the remaining portion of the capital gain, even though not yet received) will be subject to income tax upon death.

Loophole: **Use a "self-canceling" installment note to minimize estate taxes when selling to family members.**

No estate taxes are owed on any unpaid portion of the notes remaining at the time the seller dies because they are canceled at that time. This is one way to reduce your estate and effectively give a tax-free bequest. The gain attributable to the canceled installment note will be subject to income tax to be paid by the estate. The purchaser will not have to make any more

payments. The interest rate on the note needs to be higher than market rates to "pay" for the cancellation feature.

Loophole: **Reduce estate taxes by "selling" shares of a limited liability company (LLC), partnership or S corporation to a "defective" grantor trust on the installment basis.**

Set up an intentionally defective irrevocable trust, also known as a grantor trust, to hold shares of the business. For income tax purposes, the person who sets up the trust—the grantor—is considered the owner of the shares held in trust. The company's income is taxed with the grantor's other income on his/her individual tax return, and is paid to the grantor to reduce the installment note. There is no capital gains or interest income taxation to the seller. This is a good way to transfer ownership to a family member who will continue to operate the business.

Triple benefit: Using a trust takes those shares' ownership out of the grantor's taxable estate and maintains cash flow for the seller who receives the money on the installment note. The seller pays tax on the trust income, creating a tax-free gift from the grantor to the trust beneficiaries.

Loophole: **Give a partial ownership interest as additional compensation to an employee/buyer and a cash bonus to cover the taxes due.**

The business can deduct the total value of the ownership interest and the bonus, saving enough taxes to cover the cash outlay.

Benefit: This passes ownership to relatives with no tax cost. If not doing this with a relative, then you would omit the cash bonus and the employer would get a tax deduction for the value of the shares.

Loophole: **Service businesses can set up a deferred-compensation agreement that becomes effective when the majority owners retire or die.**

This applies to doctors, lawyers and other service businesses. The agreement will provide compensation for the owner or spouse for the time specified in the agreement. Income taxes are owed when payments are received under the agreement and an offsetting deduction can be claimed by the business at that time.

Benefit: This will provide continuing cash flow to retired owners out of the business's cash flow with little or no cash outlay by the successors.

Loophole: **Transfer "phantom ownership" to employees.**

Units that correspond to shares of ownership are assigned to employees, who receive the benefits as if they were actual shares (an amount equal to the dividend and any increase in the value of the shares). Income taxes are not paid until cash, such as from the dividend equivalent, is received by the employees.

Loophole: **Use the applicable federal interest rate (AFR) for deferred-payment terms instead of higher market rates of interest.**

The AFR is the minimum rate that can be charged in a transaction without having the IRS recharacterize the price to include interest paid to the seller taxable at ordinary rates rather than at the tax favored capital gains rates.

Exception: Where the purchase price is allocated to intangibles such as "goodwill," interest does not have to be included in the note payments.

Loophole: **Keep the business's value low by using IRS "fair market value" (or FMV) methods to value the portion transferred.**

The FMV method uses techniques that tend to value the business lower than the market price of the business because…

• **It is based on historical financial data,** not on current or prospective earnings.

• **It ignores such factors as strategic value** (unique features and synergy added to the buyer's business when the business is acquired) to the buyer, and whether the buyer wants to actively work in the business, not hold it solely for investment. (If the buyer intends to work for the business, he is more interested in cash flow than the price paid for the business.)

• **When selling a partial interest,** it allows discounts (to the proportionate value transferred) for lack of control and difficulty in marketing a noncontrolling (partial) interest.

Get Set for Success: Six Costly Career Myths Recent Grads Need to Avoid

Lindsey Pollak, author of *Getting from College to Career: 90 Things to Do Before You Join the Real World* (Collins). Based in New York City, she speaks frequently on college campuses about career issues. For more information, go to *www.gettingfromcollegetocareer.com.*

The tight job market is not the only challenge facing today's college graduates. They also must overcome their own misconceptions of how best to launch their careers. *Six common career myths…*

Myth: My first job will set the stage for the rest of my career. If I don't get my foot in the door of my dream profession from the start, I never will.

Reality: Applying for a job isn't like applying to college—rejections are not the final word. If you don't land your dream job right out of school, you can apply again in the future, as many times as you like.

The secret is to continue to acquire new skills and experience relevant to your dream job. Try to find work in a sector that is related in some way to your dream profession…or work that involves some skill that you will require. Improve your résumé during your free time by volunteering in the sector…freelancing… or taking relevant night classes.

Example: Your dream is to work for a major recording company. If you cannot land this job right out of college, volunteer to manage a local band or assist at a local radio station.

Myth: It is important to get your first job with a big, well-known company.

Reality: Landing a job with a well-known company isn't necessarily any better for your career than working for a smaller firm that is not a household name. Numerous entry-level employees discover that they have a broader range of responsibilities and greater access to upper management at a small company, which helps their careers in the long run.

Myth: Now that I have graduated, I need to start a full-time job immediately.

Reality: Employers no longer frown upon applicants who have a gap between the end of their university years and the beginning of their careers—as long as this time was spent productively.

Freelance for a year…start your own business …volunteer for a year with a nonprofit. Just be ready to explain to potential employers why this experience makes you a better potential employee.

Myth: My first job should be related to my college major.

Reality: Many college grads go into fields completely unrelated to their majors. Just be sure that you have some relevant skills and experience on your résumé. Accept an unpaid internship in the field…or sign up for relevant night classes at a community college.

Myth: I need to establish my career path immediately—jumping from profession to profession will hurt me in the eyes of potential employers.

Reality: The only way to be certain that a profession is right for you is to give it a try. If it's a bad fit, it's better to switch to a different career now, while you're still young, than stick it out and spend the rest of your working life in the wrong field. Employers will not hold an early career change against you as long as you can make a plausible case that the previous experience will somehow benefit you in this new role.

Myth: I should take the highest-paying job I can find.

Reality: Take your most lucrative job offer only if the job is something you really want to do. Your financial responsibilities are likely to be lighter in the years immediately after college than they will be in the future. It is better to accept a lower income now if that is what it takes to build a career you enjoy.

Where the Jobs Are Now: "Hot" Sectors

David DeLong, a doctor in business administration (DBA), and president of David DeLong & Associates, a research and consulting firm that specializes in accelerating knowledge transfer across the generations to decrease the risks for skill shortages, Concord, Massachusetts. He is author of *Lost Knowledge: Confronting the Threat of an Aging Workforce* (Oxford). He is also a research fellow at MIT AgeLab. For more information, go to *www.lostknowledge.com*.

Despite the grim news about unemployment and layoffs, there still are jobs to be found in today's economy. *Employers have positions to fill immediately, even for older workers…*

HOTTEST SECTORS

•**Federal government.** In 2010, almost 60% of all federal government supervisors and nearly half of all nonsupervisory workers will be eligible to retire. That's because the huge baby boomer population is beginning to reach retirement age. While concerns about health-care costs and the economy may keep many from leaving, a significant number will retire. So federal agencies are hiring now, and not only in the nation's capital. Five out of six federal employees work outside Washington, DC, with the next largest concentrations of federal jobs in Atlanta, Baltimore, Chicago, Los Angeles, New York City, Salt Lake City and San Diego.

The federal government is looking for human resources managers, office clerks, accountants, information technology security workers, engineers, scientists and policy analysts, among other types of positions. The Veterans Health Administration needs human resources specialists. People under the age of 31 can apply for jobs as air-traffic controllers for the Federal Aviation Administration, where thousands of controllers are about to retire.

All federal jobs now are listed on one Web site, *www.usajobs.gov*.

•**Health care.** Next to work in government, the best job security is in health care, an expanding industry as the baby boomer population ages. If you can afford to invest some time in training, consider studying for a certificate to work as a medical records specialist or as a pharmacy technician. Community colleges offer two-year associate degrees in both these fields—online courses can be completed in a few months and cost less than $1,500.*

• **Hospitals and nursing homes** need many people to fill a variety of jobs, including positions for information systems and human resources professionals, cleaning people and clerical workers. Rural hospitals tend to be especially shorthanded.

• **Education.** Schools will require approximately 2.8 million new teachers in the next eight years, according to the National Center for Education Statistics. Like federal government workers, today's older teachers who have spent their careers within school systems have good pensions that will allow them to retire. Although budget cuts mean many local school districts won't be able to replace every retiree and some have instituted hiring freezes, they can wait only so long. Eventually, there will be a huge push to find good teachers, particularly in math and science. The experience of older teachers could be a real asset, especially in areas with the greatest demand. There also should be a need for principals, school administrators, education consultants and tutors. If you have technical skills or experience in any trade, look into openings for teachers at vocational schools and community colleges.

GROWING DEMAND

Other potential employers include security service providers, accounting firms, grocery chains and companies that benefit from investments in roads and bridges funded by the economic stimulus package.

• **Security.** Tough times lead to crime. The stimulus package includes money for 100,000 police officers over the next eight years. Even cash-strapped local governments are looking now to fill positions related to public safety. In the private economy, security services for computer systems are expanding and private security guards are in demand.

Besides filling slots vacated by retirees, the federal government has 83,000 new positions in defense and homeland security services to

*Price subject to change.

fill. The Transportation Security Administration needs another 22,000 airport screeners who can be trained quickly.

• **Accounting.** While Wall Street jobs now are scarce, workers with a background in finance still can find jobs. Many regional and community banks, for instance, are doing just fine. And major accounting firms, such as KPMG (*www.us.kpmg.com*), PriceWaterhouseCoopers (*www.pwc.com*) and Ernst & Young (*www.ey.com*), will continue to aggressively hire accountants and administrators and will be searching for a blend of recent graduates and experienced workers. Consulting firms, such as Booz Allen (*www.boozallen.com*) and Accenture (*www.accenture.com*), are hiring thousands of people with information technology skills in specialties such as Java and SAP. There will be more demand for personal financial planners—new baby boomer retirees will need help managing investments and planning for old age.

• **Grocery chains.** People are buying food to cook at home—and grocery chains require cashiers, retail clerks, managers and other professionals for back-office functions. Chains include Wegmans Food Markets (*www.wegmans.com*), a 72-store chain; Publix Super Markets (*www.publix.com*) in Florida and Whole Foods Market (*www.wholefoodsmarket.com*).

• **Going green.** An explosion in green jobs seems on its way, although the credit freeze is slowing things down. If you don't need a job to pay the mortgage next month, consider specialized training to help companies respond to new environmental-safety laws and demands for green products. See *www.greenbiz.com* for information about educational resources on sustainable business practices.

• **Infrastructure.** The $787 billion stimulus plan includes money for roads, bridges and other transportation projects, as well as for energy and education projects. It should create job openings at construction and engineering firms, as well as at companies with new energy projects, including utilities.

Follow your local news to learn how your region will benefit.

HIRING DURING LAYOFFS

Don't write a company off your list just because it's laying off some workers. Companies can be actively hiring even while downsizing. Big corporations require many kinds of specialized skills and operate in many locations —a freeze in one department may not prevent another from staffing up.

WHERE THE JOBS AREN'T

Every sector presents opportunities if your skills, personality and passion give you a competitive advantage in that area. *Still, there are some job categories where the odds definitely are stacked against you today...*

- **Automotive parts assemblers.**
- **Stockbrokers.**
- **Home builders.**
- **Real estate agents.**
- **Manufacturing jobs.**
- **Journalists.**

For Older Job Seekers...

Older workers searching for jobs should register with the temp firms, which care more about experience than age—jobs taken through temp firms often lead to permanent positions. Also, have a practice interview with an employer you do not care very much about before going to one where you really want to work. And, consider having your résumé rewritten or updated professionally to emphasize accomplishments and current skills. Finally, visit job-hunting Web sites to post your résumé and research potential employers.

Art Koff, founder, RetiredBrains.com, online job board for older workers, Chicago.

You Can Get a Raise... Even Now!

To score a raise in this difficult economy, keep track of how much more you are doing since any layoffs...make your accomplishments clear to your boss...show him/her that you care about the company's bottom line by helping to cut costs, for example, even as you ask for more money.

Helpful: Educate yourself about the firm's financial health before you ask for a raise.

When to ask: Right after a major accomplishment—or after you have just gotten significant praise for doing your job well.

Cynthia Shapiro, career and business strategist, Los Angeles.

20

The Best Defense

Tricks to Keep Burglars Away from Your Home— Former Jewel Thief Reveals His Secrets

A man's home might be his castle, but so few houses provide moats and battlements. If a burglar wants to break in, he probably can—and in these tough economic times, a burglar is more likely to do so.

Fortunately, burglars are mostly lazy and fearful. They target the homes that look like they will be the easiest to rob with the lowest risk of capture. Your home does not need to be impregnable—it simply needs to be less appealing to burglars than other homes in your neighborhood.

How to reduce the odds that your home will be targeted—or send the would-be burglar running if it is…

• **Keep your garage door closed as much as possible.** Leaving your garage door open when you go out tells all who pass that there's no car inside and it is likely that no one is at home.

Open garages also provide convenient cover for burglars. They can simply walk or drive into the garage, shut the door behind them, then force open the door connecting the garage to the home without worry that they will be seen.

Regularly leaving your garage door open when you are home and there is a car parked in the garage is a poor strategy, too. A burglar might figure out that your garage door tends to be closed only when no one is home.

Of course, if you have expensive bikes or yard equipment in your open garage, you're

Walter T. Shaw, one of the most notorious jewel thieves of the past half-century. Based in Fort Lauderdale, Florida, he is author of *A License to Steal* (Omega, *www.alicense2steal.com*), an account of his career as a jewel thief and his father's career as a telecommunications inventor.

inviting burglars to walk right in and take off with them.

• **Keep out of the obits.** The newspaper obituary page offers burglars a handy guide to which homes are going to be vacant when. Burglars simply wait until the time and date listed for a funeral or memorial service, then break into the homes of the local residents mentioned among the relatives of the deceased.

If you provide an obituary for a family member to a local paper, either do not list survivors or do not mention when the memorial service will be held. Instead, provide a contact phone number for those who wish to attend.

• **Post a "Beware of Dog" sign.** Dogs bark and bite, which makes them effective burglar deterrents. Even if you do not have a dog, a sign warning that you do could encourage a burglar to target a different home. You also could attach a dog's chain to a stake in your yard to add to the illusion.

If you buy a dog to scare off burglars, favor a small, "yippy" dog over a big one. Most little dogs bark incessantly when strangers approach their homes. Bigger dogs might bark a few times, but unless they are trained as guard dogs, they're less likely to keep it up.

• **Leave a sandbox, tricycle or other outdoor toys in your yard** even if you do not have young kids. Most burglars prefer to stay away from homes that have young children. These homes are less likely to be vacant than others—a stay-at-home parent might be inside during working hours, and families who have young children are less likely to go out at night.

Find a cheap used tricycle or sandbox at a garage sale so that you can leave it outside without worrying that it will be stolen. Leave toys on your lawn even when you go on vacation. Most families take children's toys inside before heading out of town, so leaving them out creates the impression that the home is not vacant.

• **Post a "video surveillance" or "you are being videotaped" sign** on the front gate or elsewhere around your home. Burglars fear being photographed even more than they fear alarm systems. They have time to flee if an alarm sounds, but there might not be much they can do once their image has been recorded on tape.

Hanging up inexpensive, fake video cameras in conspicuous locations throughout your home improves this illusion. These cameras are available in home stores or on Web sites, such as Amazon.com, for $10 to $20 apiece,* sometimes less.

• **Remove thick hedges and privacy fences.** Burglars love to break into homes with doors or windows that are not visible from the road and from neighboring homes. They can take their time breaking into these homes without fear that they will be seen.

If a high hedge or fence around your home provides potential cover for burglars, replace the hedge with plants no higher than knee-height…and replace a high fence with a lower fence, a chain-link fence or a wood fence that has spaces between the slats.

• **Do not let mail or newspapers pile up when you are on vacation.** This makes it easy for burglars to see that the home is unoccupied. Unfortunately, stopping delivery informs newspaper deliverymen and other strangers that you will be away. It is better to ask a trusted neighbor to collect your mail and newspapers for you.

Also, be sure to have someone mow your lawn in the summer or shovel your walk if it snows in the winter.

• **Use lights and radios to make it seem that someone is home.** Homes that are completely dark before bedtime are obvious targets for burglars. Timers, available for several dollars at home stores and hardware stores, are a reasonably effective solution.

Also, leave a radio on and tuned to a talk station when you're away so that anyone who approaches the home will think someone is inside.

• **Install motion-activated floodlights on every side of your home,** not just over the driveway and front door. Bright lights scare away most burglars.

*Prices subject to change.

More from Walter Shaw…

Where to Hide Your Valuables

The master bedroom is the first place that all burglars search. Valuables stored there are likely to be found even if they are well-hidden. The main living area of the home also is likely to be well-searched.

Least likely to be searched are young children's rooms…garages…unfinished basements …and the space above hung ceiling panels.

I would not recommend installing a safe. Home safes consolidate the family's valuables in one place, which makes them easier to steal. If the burglar lacks the know-how to crack your safe, he might take the whole safe with him…or wait for you to return and force you to open the safe, turning a bad situation into a dangerous one.

One potentially effective strategy is to set up your home so that it convinces the burglar that he has found your valuables before he actually has. Hide your most precious possessions in a room unlikely to be targeted, but leave a few less important "valuables" in a location a burglar is likely to search, such as a drawer in the master bedroom. These "valuables" might include a stack of small bills with a $20 bill on top…a few credit cards that are expired or cancelled…a broken, but impressive-looking camera…or some costume jewelry that looks more precious than it is.

For maximum security, rent a bank security deposit box. Banks always are more secure than any location in the home.

If Your Home Is on the Market…

If you take photos of your home for posting online, be sure the pictures do not show off valuables.

Also: Before holding an open house, lock up valuables or store them off the premises. There have been recent reports of well-dressed thieves coming to open houses and stealing jewelry, handbags, clothing, even champagne.

Pamela Liebman, president and CEO, Corcoran Group, real estate agency, New York City.

The Big Money Rip-Offs Facing Seniors Today

Sheryl Garrett, CFP, founder of Garrett Planning Network, an international network of fee-only planners, Shawnee Mission, Kansas, www.garrettplanningnetwork. com. She is author of Just Give Me the Answer$: Expert Advisors Address Your Most Pressing Financial Questions *(Kaplan Business) and* Investing in an Uncertain Economy for Dummies *(Wiley). Garrett was recognized by* Investment Advisor *as one of the 25 most influential people in financial planning.*

Seniors are prime targets for scammers. Many have amassed impressive financial resources, while many others are struggling with the challenges of living on a fixed income. Scammers often jump in to exploit this situation. *Biggest rip-offs targeting seniors…*

MEDICARE POLICIES

Rip-off: **Unscrupulous insurance agents misrepresent Medicare policies.**

Medicare beneficiaries have a bewildering array of health insurance options now. They can choose from dozens of "Part D" prescription drug plans to supplement Medicare, and they can opt out of traditional Medicare and enroll in private Medicare Advantage Plans for their medical and drug coverage. *This is fertile territory for scam artists…*

• **Medicare Advantage.** To reap hefty commissions, some insurance agents push seniors into buying a type of private policy called a Medicare Advantage Plan without explaining the limitations of the plans.

Examples: You may use only doctors and hospitals in the plan's network…you may lose supplemental coverage from a former employer's plan. They've even been known to sign up people without their knowledge.

How: The agent says that he/she needs the senior's Social Security number, and the senior gives it to him. The agent then uses the number to enroll the senior.

• **Part D.** Posing as "Medicare representatives," unscrupulous insurance agents call and ask you about the Part D plan that you have already signed up for. Since you know that you do have Part D, you can be tricked into thinking that it's safe to give personal information to the caller, such as your Social Security number, which the scammer then uses for identity theft.

• **Drug discount cards.** An individual may be offered a plan from a licensed insurance agent that costs less than Medicare Part D, but the agent does not disclose that the plan provides much less coverage than Medicare.

Self-defense: Before buying any Medicare-related plan, card or policy, contact your state insurance department. Ask if the agent is licensed, if the product is legitimate and whether there have been any complaints against the agent or the company. If you have been fraudulently enrolled in a Medicare Advantage Plan, contact State Health Insurance Assistance Programs (SHIP) at *www.shiptalk.org.* (Click on "Find a Counselor.") Also contact your state insurance department and attorney general's office, which can take action against agents for sales abuses.

TODAY'S PONZI SCHEMES

Rip-off: **Investment deals that are really Ponzi schemes.**

In a Ponzi scheme (named for a 1920s con artist), you are offered the opportunity to put money into a sophisticated investment—such as real estate, oil and gas leases—that will pay very high returns. You invest, and soon you're getting statements and the promised returns. But after a while, the statements and the payments stop coming. You can't get your money out because the scammer has disappeared.

In December 2008, Bernard L. Madoff was charged with perpetrating what may be the largest investor fraud ever committed by a single person. His Ponzi scheme bilked an estimated $50 billion from investors worldwide.

There never really was an investment. You were paid with money that later participants "invested" in the scheme.

Self-defense: Be especially suspicious of an investment company that claims to be registered

in one state, physically exists in a second state and sells to investors in a third state. It's likely the company does not exist.

Always check in with your state securities regulator to confirm an investment company's registration. You can find your state's regulator through the North American Securities Administrators Association (202-737-0900, *www. nasaa.org/home/index.cfm*). At its Web site, click on the "Contact Your Regulator" link and the state where the business is supposed to be registered. Or go to the Financial Industry Regulatory Authority Web site (*www.finra.org*) to look up a securities firm or broker. If you think you may be a victim of a Ponzi scheme, contact your state attorney general's office.

HIGH-YIELD INVESTMENTS

Rip-off: **International investment schemes that "offer" extremely high yields in a relatively short period of time.**

The scam artist purports to have access to "bank guarantees" that he can buy at a discount and sell at a premium, producing exceptional returns. To make the schemes more enticing, con artists often refer to the "guarantees" as being issued by the world's "prime banks."

The legal documents associated with such schemes often require victims to enter into nondisclosure agreements, offer returns on investments in "a year and a day" and claim to use forms required by the International Chamber of Commerce (ICC). The ICC has issued a warning that no such investments exist.

Self-defense: Reject any investment that offers unusually high yields by buying and selling anything issued by "prime banks."

FORECLOSURE RESCUES

Rip-off: **Claiming to be able to prevent foreclosures.**

The scammer makes misleading promises that a victim's home will be permanently saved from foreclosure by signing the title over to the scammer. The victim ultimately loses his home, along with the money he paid to the scammer, who walks away with the title and equity in the home.

Because foreclosure filings are public information, scammers target already troubled home owners, repeatedly contacting them by phone or mail. *Self-defense...*

• **Check the credentials,** background and references of anyone who offers to buy your home to save it from foreclosure.

• **Take your time.** Don't sign anything without checking with your lender. Never sign away ownership of your property to settle a default.

• **Have paperwork reviewed by an attorney or a financial professional,** such as an accountant, before you sign anything.

• **Don't let anyone persuade you to cut off communication with your lender.** The lender should be your first contact if you're struggling to make your mortgage payments.

Mortgage Scam Alert

With the launch of the federal mortgage assistance program, people calling themselves "loss-mitigation specialists" are preying on consumers. They charge upfront fees of as much as several thousand dollars, claiming that they can help get modified loans for people who are having trouble paying their mortgages.

Self-defense: Nonprofit agencies approved by the Department of Housing and Urban Development provide free counseling. Go to *www. hud.gov* for a list, or call 800-569-4287.

Henry Sommer, Esq., a Philadelphia attorney and president of the National Association of Consumer Bankruptcy Attorneys, *www.nacba.org.*

Tough Times Are Boom Times for Scammers: Don't Fall for These Cons

Audri Lanford, PhD, cofounder and coeditor of Internet ScamBusters, a Web site that has educated more than 11 million consumers about scams and cons, *www. scambusters.org*. Dr. Lanford is based in Boone, North Carolina.

Rising unemployment rates, a plunging stock market and falling home values have landed many Americans in difficult financial straits. This can make people psychologically predisposed to jump at a potential solution—without stopping to consider whether this solution is truly as appealing as it seems.

Scams designed to take advantage of America's current economic problems...

UNPAID FUEL BILL

Someone claiming to be the representative from your heating-fuel company phones you on one of the coldest days of winter. He or she says that you didn't pay your last bill, so the company has no choice but to turn off your gas (or suspend your oil deliveries) immediately. He would like to be lenient, but company policy requires immediate action.

You protest that you paid your bill, but the representative insists that the payment wasn't received. The only way that you can prevent a disruption in service is to make the payment immediately by supplying your credit or debit card number. The representative warns you that if you do not do this, it could be weeks before the company can send out a technician to restart your service.

The caller is a con man, not a heating-fuel company employee. This is true even if caller ID says that the call is coming from the fuel company. Sophisticated scammers can make caller ID say whatever they want it to. If you supply your credit card number, it will be used to make unauthorized purchases.

The heating companies are heavily regulated by state governments and usually cannot suspend customers' service until they have sent several written warnings.

What to do: Hang up, then phone your heating-fuel provider to confirm that you are paid in full.

TECHNICIANS AT YOUR HOME

Two technicians from your oil, gas or electric company unexpectedly arrive on your doorstep. They say they have reason to believe there is a minor problem with your furnace (or gas line or some other component of your heating or electrical system) that is causing it to burn fuel faster than it should or causing you to be billed for more fuel than you are using.

These technicians really are thieves. If you let them into your house, one will distract you while the other steals from you. Home owners normally are careful about whom they allow into their homes, but anxiety over finances makes the promise of lower heating bills too appealing for many to pass up.

What to do: If utility company technicians visit your home when you have not arranged a service call, ask them to wait outside (keep your door locked) while you phone the company to double-check their story. Do not back down even if they claim that they do not have time to wait. While you're making the call, the scammers most likely will disappear, but if not, call the police.

WORK-AT-HOME

A help-wanted e-mail says that you can earn hundreds of dollars each week from home in your spare time by filling out online surveys …sorting e-mails for a large company…or performing some other simple task.

Work-at-home opportunities are attractive to the millions of Americans who have now lost their jobs and to those in need of extra cash to keep up with the rising cost of living. Unfortunately, almost all work-at-home help-wanted e-mails are scams.

If you respond, scammers may try to…

•**Convince you to buy a list of companies in search of work-at-home employees.** The list is worthless.

•**Sell you a list of online survey companies that pay participants.** Even online surveys that do compensate participants pay so little that it is generally not worth your time or trouble.

•**Ask you to pay an "application fee."** The scammer pockets your fee. There is no job.

•**Get you to reveal your Social Security number or other personal information** so that they can run a background check before hiring you. They steal your identity.

•**Sell your contact information to other con men and Internet scammers,** who will try to take advantage of you.

What to do: Delete work-at-home e-mails. They almost always are scams.

More from Dr. Audri Lanford…

The Trickiest Scams Yet: If You Own a Credit Card Or Debit Card, Watch Out

Credit card crooks are becoming more sophisticated. It often takes the victims longer to spot today's complex credit card scams, giving thieves extra time to make fraudulent purchases.

Five of the latest credit card scams today…

KEYSTROKE LOGGERS

You input your credit card to make a purchase from a reputable Internet retailer. The next time you try to use the card, it is rejected because it has been maxed out.

Many computers are infected with a "keystroke logger," a type of computer spyware that tracks everything typed into the computer and reports it back to a scammer via the Internet. When an online purchase is made, the scammer is able to obtain the victim's credit card number.

Victims often download and install keystroke logger spyware without realizing that they are doing so.

Example: Thousands of high-ranking executives across the country recently received e-mail messages that appeared to be official subpoenas sent by the United States District Court in San Diego. A link embedded in this message offered a copy of the subpoena. When the recipients clicked on the link to view the subpoena, they unknowingly installed the software that secretly recorded their subsequent keystrokes, including credit card numbers, user IDs and passwords.

Self-defense: Purchase and install an up-to-date Internet security program, such as Zone Alarm Internet Security Suite (877-966-5221, *www.zonealarm.com*) or AVG Internet Security (*www.avg.com*).

CELL PHONE CAMERA SCAM

A shopper chats on his/her cell phone near a store's cash register while you pay for your purchase…or he talks on a cell phone outside a restaurant window while, just inside, you use your credit card to pay for a meal.

Though the bystander appears to be deeply engrossed in his conversation, he actually might be using the camera built into his cell phone to snap digital pictures of your name, your credit card number and the expiration date. Some cell phones now contain five-megapixel cameras, with sharp enough resolution to snap a legible picture of a credit card even from several feet away.

Self-defense: Be aware of people around you whenever your credit card is out of your wallet, particularly if someone nearby is holding a cell phone. Conceal your credit card under your hand, or at least turn the card over.

CARD SWITCH

You pay for a restaurant meal with your credit card. When the waiter returns, you sign the receipt and slip the card back into your wallet, same as always. But the next time you use the credit card, it is declined. When you examine the card, you realize that it's not your credit card, but rather a similar-looking card with someone else's name on it.

Unscrupulous restaurant and retail employees occasionally carry a few old credit cards, perhaps ones stolen from previous customers that have been canceled by their owners. When a customer pays with a card that is similar in appearance, the scammer pockets the new card and substitutes the old one. If the victim fails to notice, the thief goes on a shopping spree.

Self-defense: Always double-check that the credit card returned to you really is your card.

SKIMMERS

Some high-tech scammers working in restaurants, gas stations and other establishments have small electronic boxes known as "skimmers" hidden near the cash register. Skimmers steal the information—name, address, telephone number, credit limit, PIN—encoded on credit cards when the cards are swiped through them. Unlike a conventional credit card scanner, a skimmer is not attached to a phone line or cash register and typically is concealed out of customers' view.

Self-defense: Try not to let your card out of your sight. Of course, this isn't always possible, but when it is, pay close attention. That

alone may make a scammer less likely to try anything.

CREDIT CARD FRAUD "ASSISTANCE"

You receive a phone call from someone who identifies himself as a Visa or MasterCard representative. He asks if you authorized a particular purchase (often electronics). You did not. The representative explains that someone has stolen your credit card number and is running up your bill. "Don't worry," the rep says, "I can help you cancel the card and have the fraudulent charges removed from your account."

This caller does not really work for a credit card company, and your card number has not really been stolen—yet. The caller is a con artist who will ask you to "confirm" your credit card number and perhaps the three-digit code on the back of the card while pretending to help you stop a fictitious thief.

Self-defense: Never give out your credit card number or the code on the back of your credit card to anyone who phones you, even if he/she claims that you must act fast to protect your account. Hang up, phone your credit card company's toll-free number and ask a real credit card company rep to check for the fraudulent charge that the caller mentioned, as well as for any other suspicious activity. If there is any sign of trouble, cancel the card.

Also, check your accounts regularly online for any fraudulent charges.

Also from Dr. Audri Lanford...

Credit Card Liability Limits

Fortunately, victims of credit card theft generally are liable for only $50 of the thief's charges (and banks usually waive even this fee for good customers). But victims often have to cancel their cards and update any automatic charge arrangements (such as for Internet service, electronic toll collection, etc.).

That $50 liability limit also applies to ATM and debit cards, though the holders of these cards might be liable for up to $500 if they fail to report the card's disappearance within two business days after they learn of the loss or theft of their card. (Debit and ATM card owners can be held responsible for all losses if they fail to report the theft within 60 days of when a bank statement showing unauthorized charges is mailed.)

Victims also face cash-flow problems and bounced-check charges when thieves clean out their bank accounts.

One more scam from Dr. Audri Lanford...

Don't Pay for a Scammer's Phone Calls

With the "*72" telephone scam, the victim receives a phone call in which he/she is asked to use his own phone to call a number that begins with *72.

Example: The caller might say that a relative has died and advises the call recipient to dial a number beginning with *72 to learn more information.

Trap: The keypad sequence *72 is the code for forwarding all incoming calls to the number entered after *72. The scammer can then call that phone number (a long-distance number, even overseas) by calling your phone—with you paying the bill.

Avoid ID Theft— Don't Make These Mistakes on the Internet

James Christiansen, former senior vice president of information security at Visa International and former chief information security officer at General Motors. He is author of several books on Internet security, including *Internet Survival Guide: Protecting Your Financial Information* (Sheltonix).

High-tech thieves can use the Internet to gather the account numbers and other personal data they need to steal your identity. You could be at risk if you shop, pay bills or access your bank accounts online— or even if you store personal data, such as your Social Security number or credit card numbers, on your own computer.

Here is how to steer clear of the Internet missteps that can lead to identity theft. *These include...*

Mistake: **Sending e-mails that contain confidential information.**

Even if the recipient of your e-mail is reliable enough to be trusted with your sensitive information (Social Security number, driver's license number, credit card number, date of birth, mother's maiden name), others could gain access to your message as well. E-mails do not transfer instantly from our computer to our recipient's computer. They make stops at several points along the way, where they could be read.

Alternately, if a criminal gained access to your computer or the message recipient's computer, he/she could find your e-mail stored in memory.

Self-defense: Convey any sensitive information over your phone, not the Internet. If you must e-mail sensitive information, use the encryption program WinZip E-Mail Companion ($19.95,* *www.winzip.com*).

Mistake: **Providing personal details on social networking Web sites or chat groups.**

The Internet is a great place to converse with people who share your interests, but sharing too much information could put you in danger. A criminal might decide that you make a good target for identity theft—or worse.

Self-defense: Keep all personal details to a minimum when online. Never mention your address, phone number or financial institutions with which you have accounts. Use your nickname. Withhold personal information even in private e-mail exchanges with people you meet through the Internet. These people might not be what they seem.

Mistake: **Downloading free programs from the Internet or clicking on pop-ups.**

When you download a program from the Internet, you can also unknowingly load spyware onto your computer in the process. This spyware could give a scammer access to any information you typed into or saved on your computer. Clicking on a pop-up could create similar problems. (There often is no way to tell the safe pop-ups from the unsafe ones, so the best policy is to skip them all.)

*Prices subject to change.

Self-defense: Download software from the Internet only if you're confident in the integrity of the site providing the program.

Internet security programs can help prevent spyware from reaching your computer and remove it if it does. ZoneAlarm Internet Security Suite is the most reliable and comprehensive ($49.95, 877-966-5221 or *www.zonealarm.com*). However, ZoneAlarm has been experiencing problems with Microsoft's latest operating system, Windows Vista. Another good choice is Microsoft Windows Live OneCare that includes virus control, firewall and automatic backup software ($49.95 per year, *www.onecare.live. com*). Free spyware protection programs are available as well, and can do a reasonable job. The best of these include Ad-Aware Free (*www. lavasoftusa.com*) and Spybot Search & Destroy (*www.safer-networking.org*).

Best: Ask your Internet service provider if access to an Internet security program is included in your monthly fee.

If you have only one spyware program, download another one and run it every few weeks as a backup—no single security program catches every problem.

Mistake: **Assuming e-mail messages are from who they seem to be from.**

Scammers can make e-mail messages appear to have been sent by anyone, including people and businesses you know.

Examples: You receive an e-mail that appears to be from your bank. It asks whether you made a particular transaction and warns that you must respond immediately if you did not. Or, you receive an e-mail that appears to come from the IRS. It says you will be audited if you do not reply to their message quickly, then asks for your Social Security number or other personal information.

Self-defense: Be very suspicious of e-mails claiming to be from financial institutions or the IRS, particularly if these messages ask you to enter passwords, account numbers or Social Security numbers (or steer you to Web sites that ask for any of these things). These messages are likely to be from scammers. Instead, look up the phone number of the company or agency that the e-mail claims to be from (do not trust the phone number that might be included in the e-mail) and call to confirm the validity of the message.

If you receive an e-mail message that seems to be from a friend featuring an Internet link or picture and a simple message such as "you have to see this," it might have been sent by a scammer. If you click the link, it could load spyware onto your computer, and open the door to identity theft. Do not click the link or open the picture until you have contacted your friend and confirmed that he sent the note.

Mistake: **Entering important data or passwords into a public computer.**

The public computers in libraries and coffeehouses are often contaminated with spyware.

Self-defense: Assume that everything you input on these computers is being recorded. Never use a public computer to make online purchases or to do your online banking. Do not even check your e-mail, a scammer could learn your user name and password and gain access to personal information stored in your e-mail files.

Mistake: **Trusting Web sites that have weak security.**

Most Internet companies that accept credit card numbers or other sensitive data work very hard to keep this information secure. Unfortunately, some sites' security measures fall short, increasing the odds that a criminal could be monitoring your transaction and stealing your information.

Self-defense: Do not enter your credit card number or any other important data into a Web site unless its Web address begins "https," not just "http." The "s" indicates an added level of security. A small picture of a closed lock should appear on the Web address line as well.

Note: Never enter confidential information onto a site if you clicked on it from an e-mail, even if it has "https." Always type in a URL.

Mistake: **Picking obvious passwords.**

Scammers have software that can help them guess common passwords. If your password is a date, a name, a word or a repeating or progressive series of letters or numbers, such as "zzzz" or "2468," it could be cracked if a high-tech criminal targets you. If you use the same password for many accounts, this could give the criminal wide access to your personal and financial information.

Self-defense: The most secure passwords are multiple-word phrases. If the site permits, these should include numbers or symbols, such as "my2dogsareyellow" or "Ilikeham$alad."

Select phrases that are memorable to you. Use different ones for each account, and don't write them down near your computer. A program called RoboForm (*www.roboform.com*) provides an encrypted computer "password safe" that can remember up to 10 passwords for you for free. RoboForm Pro, which costs $29.95, can remember more than 10 passwords.

Beware Bank Web Sites

B e wary of using bank Web sites for online banking. More than 75% of the 214 bank sites examined in a study had at least one serious security design flaw, the most common being log-in boxes and places to type your contact information on unsecured Web pages. That leaves customers vulnerable to cyber thieves who want to steal their money or identities.

Self-defense: Make sure that the Web page address begins with "https://", followed by the bank's Web address. The 's' indicates that the connection is secure.

Atul Prakash PhD, professor in the department of computer science and electrical engineering at University of Michigan, Ann Arbor. He surveyed 214 financial Web sites in a study of online security.

ID Theft at the Gas Pump

T hieves are stealing credit card data at fuel pumps. Using hidden cameras and devices called skimmers, thieves pick up credit card information at the pump and use it to create phony credit and debit cards. The devices may be installed outside or inside the pump and are painted to match the pump's colors.

Self-defense: Before filling up at a gas station, look for anything that appears out of the ordinary or suspicious, and report it to the local authorities.

Ed Donovan, spokesman, US Secret Service, whose financial and electronic-crimes units are investigating skimming, Washington, DC.

SSN Safety

K eep your Social Security number's last four digits secret. You're only legally required to give out your Social Security number (SSN) when applying for new financial accounts, to an employer or for governmental purposes. The last four digits combined with your name and address could be used to obtain a wealth of information.

Safety: Ask why a company would need your SSN—if you're not comfortable with the answer, seek another company or means of ID.

Linda Foley, founder, Identity Theft Resource Center, San Diego, *www.idtheftcenter.org.*

Beware of Staged Auto Accidents

Advice from the National Insurance Crime Bureau, *www.nicb.org.*

C ar accidents staged by criminals to collect medical and car insurance benefits could result in much higher premiums for a driver involved in such an accident, says the National Insurance Crime Bureau (NICB). *Self-defense against staged accidents...*

• **Don't tailgate.** Suddenly stopping to get hit from behind—making the accident the tailgater's fault—is the favorite tactic of stagers.

• **Call the police to any accident scene immediately** and get a police report that documents the damage, even if it is very slight.

Why: If a police report says that damage is minor, it will be difficult for those in the other car to make a big insurance claim.

• **Beware of older, larger cars with three or more people in them**—the most common scenario used to stage accidents.

Example: The driver of such a car might motion you to go ahead in heavy traffic, then cut in ahead of you to cause an accident, then deny that he/she motioned you ahead while his passengers back up his story.

• **Keep a disposable camera in your car** so that you can take photos of the vehicles, the full scene and the number of people in each car, if any accident occurs.

• **Record license plate numbers, witness information, the number of people in each vehicle, their names, addresses** and any other significant information.

• **Avoid anyone who suddenly appears on the scene and offers the services of a particular lawyer or doctor**—both of these parties are likely to be part of the scam.

• **If you suspect an accident was staged,** call the police and NICB at 800-835-6422.

Medical Identity Theft

A thief uses your Social Security number or insurance data to get free medical treatment—or to collect insurance money for services that were never performed.

Problem: This can cause incorrect or fictitious information about you to appear in medical databases—leading to incorrect treatment or future refusal of insurance benefits.

Thieves change the address to which claims and statements are sent, so you may not know of their actions for years. In addition, patient privacy laws can make it difficult to find out about phony information—and make doctors reluctant to change errors, for fear of liability.

Self-defense: Every year, get a copy of your medical records from all of your health-care providers and a list of benefits paid in your name by your insurer.

Question any charges you don't recognize—and contact police if you suspect fraud.

James C. Pyles, Esq., principal, Powers, Pyles, Sutter and Verville PC, a law firm specializing in health care, education and government relations, Washington, DC.

Caretaker Scams

Protect an elderly family member from manipulative caretakers. Caretakers employed to tend to the heads of affluent families have been known to manipulate their way into the confidence of their charges—and into receiving significant bequests through their wills.

Safety: Employ a caretaker under a contract drafted by an attorney who specializes in elder or family law, which will eliminate the risk for such an abuse.

Martin Shenkman, attorney and CPA who specializes in trusts and estates in New York City and New Jersey. His Web site, *www.laweasy.com*, provides sample forms and documents.

Injuries in the Home

A fatal injury occurs in the home every 14 minutes. And a disabling injury happens every four seconds.

To protect elderly loved ones: Get rid of unnecessary furniture. Cushion any sharp corners. Install railings and grab bars. Put nonskid tape on the edges of stairs or steps, and install thinner, rather than thicker, carpeting for easier mobility for walkers and wheelchairs. Place nonskid mats on hard floors and in tubs and showers.

StrengthforCaring.com, an online resource community for family caregivers.

Dangerous Lightbulbs

Exposure to a broken compact fluorescent lightbulb (CFL) can be dangerous to young children and pregnant women. CFLs contain small amounts of mercury, which can damage internal organs.

If a CFL breaks: Immediately open up a window in the room, and shut off central air-conditioning and forced-air heating...leave the room for at least 15 minutes. Then carefully place the pieces of glass in a glass jar with a metal lid or in a sealed plastic bag. Use duct tape to pick up smaller glass pieces and powder. Throw away in a trash container outside. Check with your town to find out about any special rules for disposal of hazardous waste.

Information: www.epa.gov/mercury/spills.

United States Environmental Protection Agency, Washington, DC.

Safer Smoke Alarms

New *photoelectronic alarms* are better than the traditional ionization alarms at detecting cooler, slow-smoldering fires.

Another plus: Photoelectronic alarms are less likely to go off by accident—because of cooking smoke, for instance.

Recent study: Nine months after installation, 20% of ionization alarms no longer worked—mostly because home owners had removed the batteries because the alarms were being triggered accidentally—while only 5% of photoelectronic alarms were not working.

Photoelectronic alarms cost $15 to $20.*

UC Berkeley Wellness Letter, www.wellnessletter.com.

*Prices subject to change.

Ward Off a Dog Attack

If you encounter an unleashed dog that indicates signs of aggression, stand still, be quiet and avoid eye contact. Running away may encourage its instinct to chase and attack. When the dog calms down, wait for it to walk away, then back away slowly. If the dog continues to approach, assert verbal dominance by giving commands such as "no," "sit" and "go home." If the dog still advances, try "feeding" him a jacket or other garment. If the dog bites, resist the instinct to pull back—it will cause the dog to bite harder to hold on and worsen any injury. If a bite breaks the skin, cleanse the

wound with soap and water and get medical advice—especially if the dog is a stray.

UC Berkeley Wellness Letter, www.wellnessletter.com.

A New Safety Gadget: The Personal Location Tracker

A personal location tracker uses satellites to keep track of where you are and lets you call 911 or request nonemergency help from family and friends with the touch of a button. It also lets you send your location to Google Maps, so friends and family can use a computer to see where you are. Because it is based on satellite technology, it can be used nearly anywhere—while camping, skiing, etc.

Cost: $170.* Service plans start at $99/year. For details, go to *www.findmespot.com*.

*Prices subject to change.

Hands-Only CPR

Mouth-to-mouth breathing is not necessary to save the life of someone whose heart has suddenly stopped.

Better: Call 911, then use hands-only CPR—rapid, deep presses on the victim's chest—until help arrives. Aim to do 100 chest presses per minute until emergency medical personnel can take over.

This applies to adults who unexpectedly collapse, stop breathing and are unresponsive.

When to start mouth-to-mouth: Do use mouth-to-mouth breathing (30 compressions to two breaths) for children who collapse, since the cause is probably due to breathing problems. Mouth-to-mouth is also needed for adults who suffer from lack of oxygen because of a drug overdose or drowning.

Michael Sayre, MD, emergency medicine professor, Ohio State University, Columbus, and chair of a committee that made CPR recommendations to the American Heart Association.

Index

E-mail
business etiquette for, 311
phone call preferable to, 298
recommended precautions for, 332, 333
rude, 297
worst time to answer, 308
Energy saver, 195
Ephedra, danger of, 70
Epidemics, rise of, 1–3
Erectile dysfunction (ED)
daily drug for, 108
holistic cures for, 108–9
memory loss caused by drugs for, 108
Escherichia coli (E. coli), 5, 6
Estate/inheritance taxes
loopholes for, 320
reducing, 150, 219–20
Section 754 election and, 148
Estate planning, 219–26
end-of-life decisions for, 226
including spouse in, 225–26
post-market crash and, 219–20
springing power of attorney in, 220–21
Estrogen drugs, hypertension risk and, 41–42
Exchange-traded funds (ETFs), short, 168
Exercise
in bed, 74–76
belly fat reduction and, 74
centenarians and, 80
coffee for aches following, 76
diabetes risk reduction and, 97
erectile dysfunction diminished by, 108
getting the most from, 76–77
for seniors, 78, 216, 217
walking for, 77–78
weight loss and, 68
Eyeglasses
depression relieved with, 104
shopping around for, 192
Eyes
circles under, 63
diseases reflected in, 14
glaucoma and, 35
pinkeye remedy for, 62–63

F
Falls
insurance claims for, 144
serious danger of, 211
vitamin D and reduced risk of, 101
Fasting, heart health and, 95
Fat. See Body fat; Dietary fats
Fatigue, aromatherapy for, 53
Federal Deposit Insurance Corporation (FDIC), 126–27, 169
Fertility, cell phones and issues with, 109
Fiber, weight loss and, 69–70
Fibromyalgia, chlorella for, 101–2
Financial advisers
how to hire, 169–71
reasons to fire, 171
Fish
arthritis risk reduced by, 99
healthiest, 95
hostility reduced by, 96
Fish oil, 60, 94, 100
Flaxseeds, 88, 91
Flu
bird (avian), 1
defenses against, 60–62
swine (see Swine flu)
vaccines for, 3, 32, 60
Foot soreness, self-massage for, 56–57
Foreclosure
avoiding, 131
buying property in, 178

eligibility for rescue plan, 130
scams, 328–29
401(k) plans
bigger contributions permitted for, 151
job loss and, 208
spousal waiver for, 222
Franchise opportunities, 314
Fruits
arthritis-fighting, 99
maintaining freshness of, 267
smaller and more nutritious, 92
Funeral plots, advance purchase of, 226

G
Gallstones, 83, 85
Gambling winnings, taxes on, 156
Garage sales, keys to successful, 263–65
Gardens and yards
better mowing of, 268
deer-proof plants for, 268
money-saving tricks for, 246–47
Garlic, 88
Gas, intestinal, 62
Gasoline
money-saving Web sites for, 184
regular vs. premium, 252, 254
for rental cars, 234
saving tips for, 179, 254, 255
Generic drugs, caution on use of, 36
Germs
copper for combatting, 6
defenses against, 60–62
places high in, 4–6
Gifts
low-cost, 193
tax-free, 151, 219–20
Ginger, 88–89, 90, 100
Glaucoma, 35
Glucosamine, 100
Goals, achieving in four steps, 287–89
Gold, investing in, 175–76
Golf
best courses for, 241–43
health benefits of, 77
shaping up for, 243–44
three easy ways to improve, 244
Grapefruit and grapefruit juice
medication interactions with, 39–40, 72
weight loss and, 72
Groceries, saving on, 182, 184–86, 186–87
Gum, sweet tooth satisfied with, 72
Gum disease. See Periodontal disease

H
Hair dye, cancer and, 23
Hands, cancer linked to changes in, 22
Handshakes, 61, 311
Hand washing
importance of, 3, 4, 50, 61
instructions for, 62
Happiness
learned, 283–85
marital, 268–70
Headaches
aromatherapy for, 53–54
chiropractic for, 55
migraine, 58
sinus, 56
tension, 55, 56
Health insurance
getting claims paid by, 137–39
getting dropped from, 139
health questionnaires for, 139
hidden perks in, 139–40
for the self-employed, 314
Health Savings Account (HSA), 210
Hearing loss, 218
Heart attacks
calcium supplements and risk of, 15

delayed care for, in women, 16
emergency kit for, 16
excessive drinking and, 15
hospital response to, 46
kidney stones and, 15
periodontal disease and, 8
pets and recovery from, 82
psoriasis and, 14
respiratory infections and, 14–15
runner's high reduces damage from, 96
statins taken following, 15
Heart disease
air quality and, 10
chocolate and reduced risk of, 94
CT screening for, 14
fasting and reduced risk of, 95
hostility and, 95–96
marital unhappiness and, 273
new way to determine risk of, 14
osteoporosis drug and, 10
periodontal disease and, 8
psoriasis and, 14
wine and reduced risk of, 84–85, 94, 95
Heirs/beneficiaries, 221–23
Helicobacter pylori, 22
Hepatitis, 4, 238
Herbs. See also Spices
grilling foods with, 90–91
with unexpected health benefits, 87–89, 98
Homes
auctioning of, 132, 178
future pricing of, 132
GI Bill loans for, 135
injuries in, 335
owner financing of, 132–33
remodeling permits for, 268
renting out your, 133
renting vacation, 236
retirement and, 200
ridding of clutter, 265–67
selling, faster, 131–33, 133
selling, protecting valuables during, 327
seniors, mistakes when buying, 209
staying in, before buying, 268
tax break for widowed owners of, 157
tax breaks for vacation, 153–55
tax credit for first-time buyers of, 152
tax deductions for owners of, 152
Home equity line of credit (HELOC), 200
Homeowner's insurance
five ways to cut costs of, 146
getting dropped from, 120
increasing deductibles on, 183
and risky claims, 143–44
umbrella coverage, 145
Hormonal imbalance, under-eye circles and, 63
Hormone replacement therapy (HRT), hypertension risk and, 41–42
Hospitals
bacteria in, 50
evaluating, 46–47
medication errors in, 48
requesting decreased charges from, 196
surviving your stay at, 49–50
Hotels
bargains at, 236
online vetting of, 228–29
sneaky new fees from, 181–82
unusual, 234–36
Hot flashes, 42, 110
Human papillomavirus (HPV), test for, 111
Hybrid cars, 152–53, 260–61
Hyperactivity, yogurt as cause of, 274
Hypertension. See also Blood pressure
better screening for, 12
experimental vaccine for, 13
medication for, improper use of, 35

Steroids, cataracts and, 28
Stocks
   allocation adjustments for, 203
   avoiding "cheap," 162
   delayed opening of, 168
   determining right amount of, 167
   donating, for a break in taxes, 148
   emerging-market holdings of, 162
   foreign, through IRAs, 207
   infrastructure, 163–65
   limiting US holdings of, 162
   lump sum distribution of, 147–48
   taking risks with, 203
   in taxable accounts, 202
   and Section 83(b) election, 148
   trading down effect and, 165–66
Stockbrokers, protection from, 171, 172
Stomach cancer
   antibiotics for prevention of, 22
   garlic and risk reduction of, 88
Stomach upset, self-massage for, 56
Stores/shopping
   dollar-store deals and rip-offs, 188–90
   going-out-of-business sales, 190–91
   highly-rated, 192
   investing in stocks of discount, 166–67
   lost receipts and, 193
   avoiding retail therapy at, 193
   sneaky new fee from, 181
Stress
   alcohol intake and, 85
   belly fat and, 74
   periodontal disease and, 9
   reduction methods, 65, 66, 82, 281–83
   sleep and, 283
Stroke
   aspirin resistance and, 17
   detecting, 16–17
   excessive sleep and, 17
   recovery from, 17–19, 96
   respiratory infections and, 14–15
   restless legs syndrome and, 17
   tea and reduced risk of, 96
Sugar
   blocking cravings for, 70–71
   gum to reduce cravings for, 72
   sex drive dampened by, 109
Sun exposure
   cataracts and, 28
   vitamin D and, 86–87
Sunscreen, oral, 22
Surgery
   for colon cancer, less invasive, 116
   evaluation of hospital care during, 47
   hypnosis for pain after, 52
   statins to curb complications of, 52
Swine flu
   protection against, 3
   spread of, 1
Sympathy, expressions of, 298

T
Taste, loss of, 104
Taxes, 147–60
   avoiding overpayment of, 150–51
   bartering and, 180
   bigger breaks available for, 151
   clothing donations, deductions for, 155–56
   on ex-dividends, 174
   and fraudulent return preparation, 159
   on gambling winnings, 156
   hybrid car purchase and, 152–53, 260
   IRS secrets on, 159–60
   license plates, deductions for, 151
   life insurance sale and, 141–42
   loopholes, for financial losses, 148–50
   loopholes, greatest of all time, 147–48
   on overseas accounts, 153
   and physical injury damages, 156–57
   Ponzi scheme losses, deductions for, 172–73
   preparation of returns for, 157–58
   refunds, strategies for quickest, 158–59
   rewards for turning in cheaters, 157
   scams related to, 160
   statute of limitations on, 159–60
   stimulus breaks, 152
   tax-deferred accounts, 202
   on tax-exempt bonds, 174
   on unemployment benefits, 305
   and vacation, 153–55
   widowed home owners, breaks for, 157
Tea
   for appetite suppression, 70
   for arthritis risk reduction, 99
   for blood pressure reduction, 93
   boosting power of green, 93
   garlic, 59
   ginseng, 63
   for Parkinson's reduction, 103
   for skin cancer risk reduction, 93
   for stroke risk reduction, 96
Telecommuting, 315
Telephones
   saving money on, 183
   scam with, 332
Television, 5, 68, 97, 247
Tennis, advice from a pro, 244–45
Tension headache
   chiropractic for, 55
   self-massage for, 56
Tetanus vaccine, 32
Time-shares, secrets to selling, 133
Tinnitus, quieting, 29
Toasts, giving, 250
Tomatoes, cholesterol lowered with, 94
Tongue cancer, 8
Trans fats, breast cancer and, 111
Travel, 227–40
   abroad, teaching while, 237
   abroad, with a weak dollar, 236–37
   insurance plan discounts on, 140
   international emergency numbers, 237
   learning during, 229–31
   online bargains for, 227–29
   online sites, specialized, 229
   protecting jewelry during, 240
   safer, healthier, 238–39
   sleeping in new time zones, 240
   tax deductions for, 154–55
   vaccinations for, 238
   veterans benefits for, 136
Trusts, 220, 222
Tuberculosis, 1, 2
Turmeric, 89–90
Typhoid vaccine, 238

U
Ultrasound, 111, 114
Urinary tract infections, antibiotics for, 38

V
Vacations, health benefits of, 240
Vaccines, 3, 32, 47, 60
   experimental, for hypertension, 13
   for travelers, 238
Vegetables
   arthritis-fighting, 99
   for cataract risk reduction, 104
   maintaining freshness of, 267
Vertigo, 218
Veterans benefits, 135–36
Viral infections, protection against, 3

Vitamins/supplements
   for arthritis relief, 100
   for cholesterol reduction, 94
   at dollar stores, 190
   expiration dates on, 104
   insurance coverage of, 140
Vitamin B-12, 103
Vitamin C
   for arthritis relief, 100
   for bruise reduction, 66
   for cold prevention, 62
   for under-eye circles, 63
   for wrinkle reduction, 64
Vitamin D
   for back pain, 57
   for cold prevention, 60, 61–62
   deficiency risks of, 86–87
   falls reduced by, 101
   healing properties of, 86

W
Walking, 77–78
Water
   bottled, 6–7, 183, 184, 190
   exercise and, 76–77, 78
   before meals, 70
   pond, danger of, 245
   tap, 6–7
Watermelon as an aphrodisiac, 107
Web sites. See Internet
Weddings, spending less on, 193
Weight loss
   aromatherapy for, 54, 72
   eating more slowly for, 71
   fitness trumps, 74
   food logs and, 71
   grapefruit for, 72
   holiday foods and,
   maintaining, 67–68
   natural ways for, 69–71
   peppermint scent and, 72
   portion size warning and, 73
Weight-loss surgery, diabetes "cured" by, 24
Whole grains, 97
Willpower, boosting, 282
Wills
   averting fights over, 223–24
   evaluating, 219
   limitations of, 223
   living, 226
   removing spouse from, 221
Wine
   health benefits of, 83–85
   heart health and, 94, 95
   for liver disease protection, 98
Women
   golfing exercises for, 244
   heart attacks and, 15, 16
   job discrimination against, 310–11
   marriage benefits for, 269–70
   skin cancer risk in, 23
   stress-busters for, 65
   Viagra for, 107
Wounds, rubbing alcohol vs. hydrogen peroxide for cleaning, 66
Wrinkles, reducing, 63–64

X
X-rays, cancer risk and, 20

Y
Yellow fever vaccine, 238
Yogurt. 9, 274

Z
Zinc, 104